# ArchitecTorah

# ArchitecTorah

## Architectural Ideas in Judaism and the Weekly Torah Portion

Joshua Skarf

Urim Publications
Jerusalem • New York

ArchitecTorah
Architectural Ideas in Judaism
and the Weekly Torah Portion



Typeset by Ariel Walden

Printed in Israel

First Edition

ISBN 978-965-524-368-0

Urim Publications
P.O. Box 52287
Jerusalem 9152102
Israel

www.UrimPublications.com

Cover image based on illustration found in Niccola Zabaglia, *Castelli, e ponti di Maestro Niccola Zabaglia: con alcune ingegnose practiche, e con la descrizione del trasporto dell'obelisco Vaticano e di altri del Cavaliere, Domenico Fontana* (1743), from the Collection of Vincent J. Buonanno, *The Theater that was Rome*, Brown Digital Repository, Brown University Library.

Library of Congress Cataloging-in-Publication Data

Names: Skarf, Joshua, author.
Title: ArchitecTorah : architectural ideas in Judaism and the weekly Torah portion / Joshua Skarf.
Other titles: Architect Torah
Description: First. | Jerusalem ; New York : Urim Publications, [2023] | Includes bibliographical references and index. | Summary: "ArchitecTorah is a collection of short essays on the weekly biblical portion that investigate the Torah through the lens of architecture. Each essay briefly introduces a piece of architectural theory, a building, or a section of building code and then reexamines a well-known topic in the Torah to uncover new and insightful interpretations"— Provided by publisher.
Identifiers: LCCN 2022019654 | ISBN 9781602804722 (hardcover)
Subjects: LCSH: Bible. Pentateuch—Criticism, interpretation, etc. | Architecture—Biblical teaching.
Classification: LCC BS1225.6.A68 S53 2022 | DDC 222/.106—dc23/eng/20220718
LC record available at https://lccn.loc.GOV/2022019654

מלך בשר ודם בונה פלטין - אינו בונה אותה מדעת עצמו אלא מדעת אומן. והאומן אינו בונה אותה מדעת עצמו. אלה דיפתראות ופינקסאות יש לו, לדעת היאך הוא עושה חדרים, היאך הוא עושה פשפשין. כך היה הקב״ה מביט בתורה ובורא את העולם. (בראשית רבה א)

A mortal king building a palace does not build it by himself; rather, he relies on a designer. And the designer in turn does not build it by himself; rather, he uses plans to know where to make rooms and where to make openings. So too God would look at the Torah and create the world. (*Bereshit Rabba 1*)

שאל אבנימוס הגרדי את רז״ל, אמר להם הארץ היאך נבראת תחלה? אמרו לו אין אדם בקי בדברים אלו, אלא לך אצל אבא יוסף הבנאי. (שמות רבה יג)

Oenomaus of Gadara asked the Sages: "How was the land created first?" They told him – "most people are not experts in these matters, go ask Aba Yosef the builder." (*Shemot Rabba 13*)

# Contents

## SHEMOT

## VAYIKRA

# Abbreviations

| | | | |
|---|---|---|---|
| ARN | Avot deR. Natan | PdRE | Pirkei deRabi Eliezer |
| b | Bavli (Babylonian Talmud) | PdRK | Pesikta deRav Kahana |
| BamR | Bamidbar Rabba | R | Rabbi |
| BerR | Bereshit Rabba | RutR | Rut Rabba |
| CM | Choshen Mishpat | ShmR | Shemot Rabba |
| DevR | Devarim Rabba | ShSR | Shir Hashirim Rabba |
| EichaR | Eicha Rabba | SZ | Sifri Zuta |
| EsterR | Ester Rabba | t | Tosefta |
| KohR | Kohelet Rabba | TPsY | Targum Pseudo Yonatan |
| m | Mishna | VayR | Vayikra Rabba |
| MdRS | Mechilta deRabi Shimon bar Yochai | y | Yerushalmi (Jerusalem Talmud) |
| MdRY | Mechilta deRabi Yishmael | YBZP | Yad Ben Zvi Press |
| OC | Orach Chaim | YD | Yoreh De'a |

## TRACTATES

| | | | | | |
|---|---|---|---|---|---|
| Ara | Arachin | Kil | Kilayim | San | Sanhedrin |
| Av | Avot | Kin | Kinim | Shab | Shabbat |
| AZ | Avoda Zara | Maas | Maaserot | Shek | Shekalim |
| BB | Baba Batra | Mach | Machshirin | Shev | Shevuot |
| Bech | Bechorot | Mak | Makot | Sheviit | Shevi'it |
| Beit | Bietza | Meg | Megila | Sot | Sota |
| Ber | Berachot | Mei | Me'ila | Suk | Sukka |
| Bik | Bikurim | Men | Menachot | Taan | Taanit |
| BK | Baba Kama | Mid | Midot | Tam | Tamid |
| BM | Baba Metzia | Mik | Mikvaot | Tem | Temura |
| Chag | Chagiga | MK | Mo'ed Katan | Ter | Terumot |
| Chal | Chala | MS | Maaser Sheni | TY | Tevul Yom |
| Chul | Chulin | Naz | Nazir | Toh | Toharot |
| Dem | Demai | Ned | Nedarim | Ukz | Uktzin |
| Eduy | Eduyot | Neg | Nega'im | Yad | Yadayim |
| Eruv | Eruvin | Nid | Nida | Yev | Yevamot |
| Git | Gitin | Ohal | Ohalot | Yom | Yoma |
| Hor | Horayot | Orl | Orla | Zav | Zavim |
| Kel | Kelim | Par | Para | Zev | Zevachim |
| Ker | Keritot | Pea | Pe'ah | | |
| Ket | Ketubot | Pes | Pesachim | | |
| Kid | Kidushin | RH | Rosh Hashana | | |

# Introduction

An architect is never bored walking through a city. There is always something, good or bad, to notice in the built environment. Similarly, everyday life continually presents a Torah scholar with new ways to consider and apply ancient traditions. In a way, we live our lives surrounded by both the Torah and architecture.[1] It is inevitable that the two interact frequently. *ArchitecTorah* examines the many instances where this occurs. This unique approach, studying Torah with a focus on architectural design and theory, engenders new and illuminating perspectives on the familiar biblical verses.

Learning multiple subjects concurrently generates insights, as the material you study in the morning influences how you understand your research in the afternoon. When learning multiple tractates, studying Tanach and Halacha, and exploring secular subjects alongside Torah, the mind naturally makes connections across the different disciplines. For a scholar who is deeply involved in multiple fields, it makes sense to apply any expertise to Torah studies and vice versa. This is one important way in which combining secular and Jewish study enriches our understanding of Judaism.

I have been planning a book on architecture and the weekly Torah portion since I began studying architecture at the University of Michigan. I was intrigued whenever a lecture on architectural theory overlapped with ideas in the Talmud. As I was caught up in the demanding life of an architecture student, barely sleeping but making time for the study of Talmud, I also began to read architectural themes into the Talmudic debates.

After graduating, when I moved to Israel and joined a firm in Jerusalem, I began researching these areas of intersect. I also started systematically marking architectural references in the Mishna, Tosefta, Talmud, Mishna

1. DevR 6:3 makes this point while commenting on the commandment to install a roof guardrail. It states that in life one is constantly accompanied by the commandments and quotes a further architectural example of *mezuzot* on doorposts.

Torah, and midrash, and indexing them by subject. Each week I read the Torah portion with a careful eye for architectural ideas and I compiled a list of topics that I wished to explore. Many of these ideas were eventually developed into the essays in this book.

⊣T⊢

Neither the Torah nor Halacha has much to say about architectural *design*. Studying Torah will not teach you how to design a building properly, be it a house, court, or *beit midrash*. While architecture can be inspired by Jewish concepts or verses from Tanach and rabbinic literature, there are very few things that Halacha demands from a building. The brief list would include making sure the building is not dangerous, that windows preserve the privacy of neighbors and that the building does not cross property lines. The Talmud does include plenty of property law, such as who shares in the expenses of rebuilding a house that collapsed, but it does not say anything about what a building should look like or how it should function. Most architectural references in the Mishna and the Talmud simply reflect the material culture of the time. The Rabbis have a standard definition of a "house" which applies to the halachot of *sukkot, mezuzot,* guardrails, spiritual impurity, selling houses in a walled city, exemption from war, and *eruvin*,[2] but this is simply a minimum requirement for a habitable structure. The only building type that does have several halachot and customs that govern its design is the synagogue.[3] On the whole, while Jewish sources can inspire architecture, they do not dictate architecture. In the debate over a definition of "Jewish architecture," I would argue that buildings inspired by Jewish sources or traditions qualify as Jewish architecture, more so than a building that happens to have a Jewish function.

The point of this book, therefore, is not to explain to architects how to design, or to specify what features a building should contain. Rather, this collection aims to do four things:

(a) Find insights in the weekly Torah portions by reading them from an architectural point of view.
(b) Collect the various parts of the Torah and rabbinic literature which relate to architecture.
(c) Teach people in the Torah world about architectural design and theory.

2. bSuk 3a–b.
3. The *mikva* has halachot that influence its design, but not its overall architecture.

(d) Serve as a resource for scholars writing about ancient architecture who are not familiar with sources in rabbinic literature.

The challenge in writing a book of this nature is finding topics relating to architecture for each Torah portion. Some of the fifty-four weekly portions are rich in architectural themes, such as those in the second half of Shemot, which deal with the *Mishkan*, or the portion of Noach, which contains the other two major building projects described in the Torah. In other parts, the architectural references are sparse. Many of the subjects are not explicitly mentioned in the Torah, but rather appear in rabbinic sources or else relate to a subject that is mentioned in the verse. The essays can be divided into several categories:

(1) Architecture described in the Torah.
(2) Jewish law that involves architecture and is derived from the verses.
(3) Architectural theory connected to the text.
(4) Archaeological discoveries that relate to both architecture and the verses of the Torah portion.

For each of the weekly Torah portions, I have chosen two or more subjects to explore, arranged by chapter and verse, and titled by subject. This organization reflects the goals of the book as serving both those whose starting point is a verse in the Torah and those who begin with an interest in a specific architectural topic. I have drawn on sources from a variety of commentaries on the Torah; rabbinic literature, including the Mishna, Tosefta, Talmud Bavli, Talmud Yerushalmi, Midrash Halacha, and Midrash Aggada; archaeological studies and reports; Roman and Greek literature from antiquity; and books dealing with architectural theory starting with Vitruvius and continuing to the present day. I have used Vitruvius' *Ten Books on Architecture* as my guide in determining which subjects can be considered "architecture" for the purpose of this book. Where relevant, reference is made to (Israeli) building code. All sources are noted in footnotes. In instances where a Torah commentary relates to the main verse under discussion, no chapter or verse number is listed. Sources for illustrations are noted in their captions, and when no credit is listed, the image is my own. While topics occasionally delve into halacha, these essays should never be treated as halachic rulings, which are far beyond my expertise.

Although there has not been much written on this subject, there are several books that touch upon it, though not in the framework of the weekly Torah portion. The closest book to this subject is Daniel Sperber's *The City in Roman Palestine,* which looks at the Jewish sources for certain urban features, such as roads, water supply, and markets. Sperber's other books on Talmudic *realia* also touch on architectural subjects, as in certain chapters of his *Material Culture in Eretz-Israel During the Talmudic Period.* The most thorough study of the subject is Samuel Krauss' *Kadmoniyot Hatalmud,* which collates the rabbinic sources on any number of architectural features. *The Architecture of Ancient Israel: From the Prehistoric to the Persian Periods,* edited by Aharon Kempinski and Ronny Reich, surveys construction during the Biblical period from an archaeological perspective, while the second volume of Yoram Tsafrir's *Eretz Israel from the Destruction of the Second Temple to the Muslim Conquest* does the same for the Roman and Byzantine periods. Synagogues, the Temple, and the *Mishkan* have been addressed by countless books and articles. Other studies have covered specific building types, such as domestic architecture, aqueducts, *mikvaot,* and theaters. These works, many devoting chapters to aspects of architecture in rabbinic sources, have been valuable resources in preparing this collection.

The combination of architecture and Torah is an obscure subject for a book, and I would like to thank my friends, family, colleagues, and teachers who have encouraged me to complete this project. My parents, Barry and Barbara Skarf, and my sisters, Michal, Shayna, and Alissa, have given me a lifetime of love and inspiration. Professors at the University of Michigan and Bezalel Academy inspired more than a few of these essays. It has been a pleasure to work with Tzvi Mauer, Pearl Friedman, and the staff at Urim. I would also like to thank Bar Ilan for allowing me to use an adaptation of an article I authored in the journal *Bekhol Derakhekha Daehu.* Ari Sherizen was an early and enthusiastic reader when the book was still embryonic. Rebecca Wein-David gave valuable feedback and encouragement. I appreciate the advice I received from Joshua Teplitsky, Chanan Gafni, Martin Lockshin, Michael and Jacob Freedman, Fruma Farkas-Aspir, Hillel Abramson, John Loike, Tziporah Levine, and Deena Glickman when preparing my manuscript for publication. Rav Amnon Bazak, Rabbi Dr. Daniel Sperber, and Ellie Levi each generously contributed kind words for the book cover. Thanks to my children, Ezra, Yochai, Rena, and Aharon, who more than once served as the first testing board for a *dvar Torah* around the Shabbat table. Marian Stoltz-Loike fastidiously read the entire manuscript with a knowledgeable eye. Joshua Meyer advised me on the design of the book cover. My wife Gila gave constant support and feedback, patiently helping me smooth out subjects which I found hard to tame. As with all things, she was a trusted partner and advisor in this endeavor. This book would not have reached publication without her enthusiastic support and encouragement.

In looking at the weekly Torah portion from an architectural perspective, this book will touch on many well-worn themes and others that have been neglected, raising unexplored issues on the interface of architecture, Torah, and rabbinic literature. I hope readers will find the combination of subjects to be a fertile source of insight.

## TRANSLITERATION

For transliterations, I have aimed for clarity and simplicity. Words are generally spelled without an "h" at the end and without double letters. There are a small number of exceptions, like *Torah* and *Shabbat*, and words where their omission would change the word into a different English word (as in *tameh*). Apostrophes are added only when similar confusion would exist, (as in *ha'ir* and *be'er*). No special indication is given for prefixes. The Hebrew letters ח and כ are both written as "ch" and צ as "tz." I have used the transliteration of Hebrew names and places ("Yitzchak" instead of Isaac), but common English spellings for names in other languages ("Babel" rather than Bavel). The same applies to Jewish texts ("Bereshit" and not Genesis). When capitalized, "the Rabbis" refer to the Jewish concept of *Chazal*, and "Mishna" (or Halacha/Midrash/Tosefta) refers to the entire corpus, while lowercase "mishna" references a single entry.

# BERESHIT

# The Imperative to Build

וַיְבָרֶךְ אֹתָם אֱלֹקִים וַיֹּאמֶר לָהֶם אֱלֹקִים פְּרוּ וּרְבוּ וּמִלְאוּ אֶת הָאָרֶץ וְכִבְשֻׁהָ וּרְדוּ בִּדְגַת הַיָּם וּבְעוֹף הַשָּׁמַיִם וּבְכָל חַיָּה הָרֹמֶשֶׂת עַל הָאָרֶץ. (בראשית א:כח)

And God blessed them, and God said to them, "Be fruitful and multiply, and replenish the earth, and subdue it, and have dominion over the fish of the sea and the birds of the air and over every living thing that creeps on the earth." (Bereshit 1:28)

After creation, God blessed mankind, telling them to multiply, replenish the earth, and subdue it (*kivshua*). This imperative is traditionally used as a divine mandate for humans to rule the world and use its resources.[1]

Ramban connects this verse with a dictate to build. He writes that God "granted man both strength and governance on earth, to impose his will on the other living creatures, as well as to build, to uproot and to mine copper." By including permission to build, Ramban implies that building is part of man's mission on earth. Why would building be so important?

There are two ways to explain the role that building plays in the human condition. On one level, building is a prerequisite for humans to be able to assert their control over the earth. Humans without fire, or language, or metallurgy, would not be in a position to rule the world. The same is true about the built environment; a minimum level of safety and comfort is needed for humanity to fulfill its role as steward. Therefore, people must build as a *precondition* for fulfilling the other clauses that appear in the verse.[2]

1. Ramban and Sforno.

2. George Hersey writes that the impulse to build is an evolved necessity of the human species, that "we humans have ensured our survival by elaborating our territories into towns and cities, creating the adaptation that is architecture." See George Hersey, *The Monumental Impulse* (MIT Press, 2001), 182.

This viewpoint is emphasized by both Malbim and Ohr Hachayim who each point out that a desolate, unbuilt space is not hospitable to humans. Beyond the edges of civilization there exist many dangers, and only by building can we keep the wilderness at bay and assert our control over the world. R. S.R. Hirsch explains our verse similarly, writing that to conquer the earth means "the mastering, appropriating and transformation of the earth and its products for human purposes," but calls this a preliminary duty.

On the other hand, the act of building is a *fulfillment* of man's mastery of the world. While many species build homes and, in doing so, control nature, none can do so on the scale of the human race. Buildings do far more than provide shelter from rain; they regulate temperature, remove waste, and create a sense of wellbeing. Structures can cross rivers, withstand earthquakes, and change weather patterns. While modern buildings do this on a greater scale than in the past, these functions are not new. They demonstrate the extent to which mankind is dominant. Beyond physical control, architecture can also make a statement about our aspirations and values. Rather than a prerequisite of mankind's sovereignty, building is a *manifestation* of that dominance. From this point of view, people build because building is part of what it means to be human.

What emerges is a dual view of the importance of architecture. On the one hand, architects design the built environment to help mankind function. There is great joy in helping a family build a home, in helping a business construct a headquarters, in designing a hospital or a university which will help mankind thrive. This is one of the great motivations that attracts people to the field.

On the other hand, architecture is a demonstration of human mastery over nature. Architects shape the world. They contend with gravity, leave a mark, take resources and shuffle them so that raw materials are shaped into foundations, walls, and roofs. The desire to make an artistic statement on such a large scale is also a part of what motivates architects.

Together, the two sides of architecture can serve as a metaphor for the human condition. The human race struggles to survive and to be comfortable, but also has a deep drive to change the world. Both are aspects of our biblical mandate to conquer the world.

# The Primitive Hut: Architectual Justification

וַיִּטַּע ה׳ אֱלֹקִים גַּן בְּעֵדֶן מִקֶּדֶם וַיָּשֶׂם שָׁם אֶת הָאָדָם אֲשֶׁר יָצָר. (בראשית ב:ח)

And the Lord God planted a garden eastward in Eden and there He put the man whom he had formed. (*Bereshit* 2:8)

THE Torah states that God prepared the Garden of Eden for man but makes no mention of Adam and Chava's abode therein. Although this matter may seem trifling – after all, the couple only remained in paradise for a couple of days and did not have clothing – the nature of Adam's house in Eden has been the subject of fierce debate among architectural theorists.

Before discussing the history of this debate, we can point to two verses that might hint as to where Adam and Chava would instinctively have taken refuge. The first comes when they decided to clothe themselves:

> And the eyes of both of them were opened, and they knew that they were naked; and they sewed fig leaves together and made themselves loincloths.[1]

The second hint is in the next verse:

> And they heard the voice of the Lord God walking in the garden toward the cool of the day, and the man and his wife hid themselves from the presence of the Lord God amongst the trees of the garden.[2]

In Eden, Adam and Chava used trees both for clothing and for hiding. Although the discussion about their first house can have no real answer,

1. Bereshit 3:7.
2. Bereshit 3:8.

there is a definite inclination toward some manner of tree shelter.[3]

The conjectured tree shelter recalls a drawing, *The Primitive Hut*, by Marc-Antoine Laugier, an eighteenth-century French philosopher.[4] It shows a building in the wilderness constructed from living trees. Trunks serve as pillars and branches as the roof. The stripped-down structure depicts Laugier's notion of how a house or temple should be designed, complete with columns and pediment. With this drawing, Laugier was trying to demonstrate the ancient roots of this architecture style, dating back, he believed, to the origin of humans. By claiming that ancient people built this way and that this so-called "primitive hut" is harmonious with nature, Laugier hoped to demonstrate that this style was the most authentic way to design a building.

The primary concern of architectural theorists, going back to Vitruvius, has been to justify design choices. Some architects attempt to prove the correctness of their buildings by relying on logical analysis. Others look to nature as a justification and try to show how buildings and ornaments mimic the natural world. Related to this second category are theorists who justify their architecture by hearkening back to the dawn of time and claiming that ancient humans, guided by some innate or divine knowledge, built in the same style.[5] Architects sometimes try to connect their designs with the primitive hut to justify their design decisions.

These arguments are traced by architectural historian Joseph Rykwert in his book *On Adam's House in Paradise*. Rykwert gives numerous examples, all attempting to identify existing architectural styles with the primitive hut. Le Corbusier, the father of Modern architecture, believed that design should begin without preconceived notions about how buildings should look and spoke of primitive man as someone who had this clarity. As the first builder, Adam's architecture was uncontaminated by

---

3. Inferring this from the text is tenuous, but extrapolating information from the story of creation falls in line with similar attempts found in bRH 11a, where R. Yehoshua and R. Eliezer debate the month during which the world was created. They even derive halachot based on their readings of the verses.

While midrashim do not concern themselves with Adam and Chava's house, some state that God made thirteen wedding canopies for Adam in Eden, decorated with gold and jewels, which would have been the earliest architecture in history. See PdRK 4:4, 26:3 and parallels. bBB 75a states that in the future God will create seven canopies for every righteous person. BerR 15:7 describes how the fig tree "opened its doors" to Adam even after his sin.

4. The drawing and argument appear in his *Essay on Architecture*, reissued in 1755.

5. Filarete hypothesized that architecture began when Adam steepled his hands to protect himself from rain. See his *Treatise on Architecture* 1.4.5. This imagery appears in a discussion about bed hangings in a *sukka*. See ySuk 1:4 (52b).

1. Primitive Hut. (Charles Eisen, from Laugier's *Essay on Architecture*, Wikimedia)

preconceived notions of how a building ought to appear. The very first house, Le Corbusier believed, must have been based solely on the rationale of its builder, and would therefore have been logical and untainted by historical conventions.[6] In the same period as Le Corbusier, Adolf Loos, another early Modern architecture theorist, believed that primitive man (the equivalent, he believed, of the simple peasant of his day) was in touch with some basic wisdom simply due to his detachment from civilization.[7] Laugier's primitive man was at ease with nature and built a "correct" house because it was based on nature. Others, such as James Hall, sought to demonstrate the natural underpinnings of the various architectural orders.[8] These theorists used nature and their own logical contortions to justify their architecture.

Some architectural theorists looked to the first house because they believed that the craft of building had been taught to humankind by God.

---

6. Joseph Rykwert, *On Adam's House in Paradise* (MIT Press, 1981), 15.
7. Ibid, 27–28.
8. Ibid, 82–90. He claimed that Gothic cathedrals were meant to represent a forest with a leafy canopy of trees.

This could have been through two paths: by way of Adam, who would then have passed the knowledge on to his descendants,[9] or via the divinely mandated architecture of the Temple.[10] The idea that Adam's house represents an ideal architecture was quite widespread and continued to come in and out of fashion for centuries.

Jewish thought tends not to look to Eden as a source of architectural inspiration, or for that matter, as a general source of knowledge. Though there are some midrashic suggestions that wisdom was transmitted to mankind via Adam, including how to make fire,[11] Jewish thought predominately favors the giving of the Torah as the source of divine wisdom. Perhaps this is why Jewish architecture – if such a thing exists – tends to find inspiration in the architecture of the *Mishkan* or the Temple more than in the primitive hut.[12]

While mentioning the midrash about the origin of fire at the end of the first Shabbat, there is also a theory that architecture could only exist once fire was invented. Vitruvius places the discovery of fire at the origin of construction.[13] Both construction and combustion take existing, raw materials and use them to provide warmth and protection. Rayner Banham illustrated this dichotomy with a parable about a primitive tribe that must set up camp and has at its disposal some fallen branches, which can be used either for fire or for shelters.[14] Luis Fernández-Galiano uses this to emphasize the central role of the hearth in architecture and points out that "In all beginnings or origins, in myths and rituals . . . construction and fire

9. MdRS Beshalach 16:32 quotes an opinion that Adam's clothes are included in the group of the mystical objects made at dusk between the sixth and seventh day of Creation. By analogy, we can imagine architectural theorists might claim that Adam's house was created in this period as well, and some, like John Wood the Elder, do indeed claim that the architectural orders were taught to man by God, and then disseminated to the Greeks and others. See Rykwert, *On Adam's House,* 130.

10. Juan Bautista Villalpando was the strongest champion of the view that all architecture was derived from the Jerusalem Temple.

11. yBer 8:5 (12b) and bPes 54a tell of how God taught Adam to make fire following the first Shabbat. The latter also mentions that God taught animal husbandry, vis a vis the creation of the first mule.

12. This despite the prohibition against copying the design of the Temple and its vessels found in bRH 24a, bAZ 43a, and bMen 28b. One prominent example of architecture inspired by the Temple was the unbuilt design of Louis Kahn for the Churva Synagogue in Jerusalem's Old City.

13. Vitruvius, *Ten Books on Architecture,* I.1.1.

14. Reyner Banham, *The Architecture of the Well-Tempered Environment* (Architectural Press, 1969), 19.

are intermingled and intertwined.[15] By this understanding, there would be no point in looking for the first house prior to the gift of fire.

Even if it is less common today to look to Eden as justification for architectural design, the same underlying logic continues to be in use. Architects construct narratives about their buildings and their design process, intended to show that their design follows some logic and is therefore justified. This is true when architecture enlists something in the Bible or rabbinic literature to explain a building's design,[16] and when decisions are made based on physical conditions on-site. While the logic can be judged in each instance, this search for inspiration is no different than looking backward to Adam and Chava's house in Eden as justification for design decisions.

15. As understood by Luis Fernandez-Galiano in *Fire and Memory: On Architecture and Energy* (MIT Press, 2000), 8–9. See, for example, Aeschylus, *Prometheus Bound,* 450–453, which states that prior to the theft of fire, mankind "had no knowledge of well-built houses warmed in the sun, nor the working of timber, but lived like crawling ants in the ground in deep, sunless caverns."

16. Two examples from personal experience: One former teacher of mine designed a synagogue around the midrash (bMeg 29a) that the synagogues and houses of study in Babylon will be relocated to Israel in the future. In another project, I worked in an office which designed a courthouse using Tehilim 85:12 as inspiration.

# The Four Rivers of Eden And Paradise Gardens

וְנָהָר יֹצֵא מֵעֵדֶן לְהַשְׁקוֹת אֶת הַגָּן וּמִשָּׁם יִפָּרֵד וְהָיָה לְאַרְבָּעָה רָאשִׁים.
(בראשית ב:י)

And a river went out of Eden to water the garden, and from thence it was parted and became four streams. (Bereshit 2:10)

THE Torah provides a brief geographic sketch of Eden, mentioning that four rivers flowed out from the garden. This description has generated some debate about the location of Eden[1] but the four rivers are also ascribed symbolic meaning. What is the significance of the four rivers?

The description of the rivers includes three components: a single river, its division into four, and the general abundance of water flowing out from Eden. Most commentators connect the number four with the four cardinal directions and explain that this symbolizes that the rivers reach all parts of the world.[2] The Netziv sees the rivers as symbolic of four types of people, each with a different way of connecting to God.

Malbim also focuses on the number four but emphasizes the significance of rivers to civilization. He writes that God created the rivers in preparation for when mankind would be scattered around the world. The rivers would flow out of Eden and sustain four great civilizations, each with unique traits. However, the branching of one river into four implies a reduction. In Eden there was only one river, for all good was concentrated there. Outside of Eden, humankind is divided into different groups, each

1. Jean Delumeau, *History of Paradise: The Garden of Eden in Myth & Tradition* (University of Illinois Press, 1995), 39–70 traces the debate over the location of Eden and the identity of the rivers in Christian thought. In bBech 55a–b, Rav identifies the Euphrates as the main river, which splits into four via subterranean channels.

2. Ancient scholars sometimes claimed that the Nile flowed across much of Africa, passing underground. See Herodotus, *Histories*, 2.28–34 and Vitruvius, *Ten Books on Architecture*, VIII.2.6–7.

with some good but none with the full connection to God that existed in Eden.

The description of these four rivers has served as inspiration for paradise gardens, primarily in the Muslim world. Gardens were an important part of the landscape in Persia, providing a respite from the harsh climate. With the rise of Islam, these gardens adopted the imagery of paradise that appears in Bereshit and the Quran. The classic Persian garden is known as *chahar bagh*, literally "four gardens." It is usually rectangular and divided into four parts by crossing water channels, all built within a walled enclosure.[3] Although inspired by the Bible and Quran, the motif of four water channels radiating from a central spring came from contemporary irrigation techniques.[4] *Chahar bagh* gardens remained popular for centuries, with the most famous example found in Mughal India as part of the Taj Mahal complex.[5]

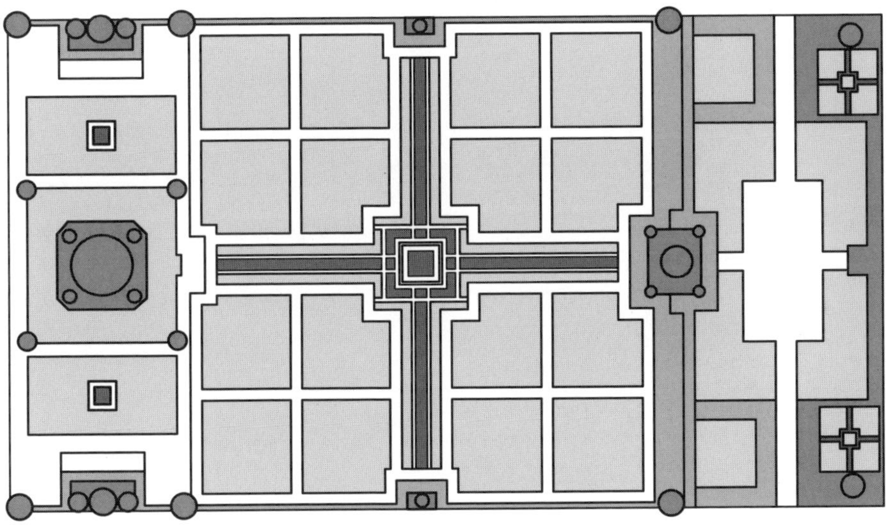

2. Plan of the Taj Mahal complex.

3. John Brookes, *Gardens of Paradise: The History and Design of the Great Islamic Gardens* (Meredith Press, 1987), 19.

4. Jonas Lehrman, *Earthly Paradise: Garden and Courtyard in Islam* (Thames and Hudson, 1978), 32, 37, and 187. In the Quran, Sura 55 describes four gardens adjacent to one another.

5. The motif of the four rivers also appears in mosaics of several church buildings from the Byzantine period in the Holy Land. In these, rather than showing a map of the rivers, the four are depicted as anthropomorphic characters. See Rachel Hachlili, *Ancient Mosaic Pavements: Themes, Issues and Trends* (Brill, 2008), 180 and 242.

While the verse in Bereshit was certainly an influence on both the Quran and the *chahar bagh* style, the two are not identical. The *chahar bagh* depicts a state of paradise lush with water, where the rivers all serve the garden. The Torah's description, however, is of a divided river. As per Malbim's interpretation, this indicates a more tenuous connection with God after the expulsion from Eden, emphasizing humankind's fallen status.[6] We are no longer living in paradise and not all the goodness flows to each land. While we rely upon God for our survival and comfort, it is far more difficult to maintain a robust and direct connection with God after the expulsion from Paradise.

6. Some see the vision of Yechezkel, in which a river will flow out of the Temple, as a correction to this reduced connection. See bSan 100a on the verse in Yechezkel 47:12. See also Daphne Baratz, "A Golden Vine/Garden in the Temple" in *Josephus and the Rabbis,* ed. Tal Ilan and Vered Noam (YBZP, 2017), 346 (Hebrew).

# Beautifully Designed Synagogues

וְהֶבֶל הֵבִיא גַם הוּא מִבְּכֹרוֹת צֹאנוֹ וּמֵחֶלְבֵהֶן וַיִּשַׁע ה׳ אֶל הֶבֶל וְאֶל מִנְחָתוֹ.
(בראשית ד:ד)

And Hevel, he also brought of the firstlings of his flock and of the fat thereof. And the Lord had respect to Hevel and to his offering. (Bereshit 4:4)

Both Kayin and Hevel offered sacrifices to God, but only Hevel's offering was accepted. Rambam learns from this verse the importance of selecting the best produce or animals for ritual offerings. Beyond sacrifices, Rambam expands this lesson to include items used to perform mitzvot. He writes that if you clothe or feed a pauper you should give from your finest. Likewise, if you build a synagogue it should be "more pleasant than your private house."[1] This same language appears in the Shulchan Aruch.[2]

The idea of giving your finest is similar to the concept of *hidur mitzva* – performing a commandment with beautiful items – which is found in the Talmud.[3] The examples of *hidur mitzva* in the Talmud are building a beautiful *sukka,* buying a beautiful *lulav,* having beautiful *tzitzit* and a beautiful *shofar,* writing a beautiful Torah with a beautiful quill and ink, and covering it with a beautiful mantel. However, unlike Rambam's halachic ruling above, which includes synagogues, the discussion of *hidur mitzva* makes no mention of permanent architecture.

Looking at both Rambam's list and the examples of *hidur mitzva,* the main difference seems to be ownership. *Hidur mitzva* is preparing superlative objects *for yourself* – a *shofar, tzitzit, lulav,* and even a Torah are objects that you own and use. These objects beautify the mitzva, but also benefit the owner. In contrast, the examples cited by Rambam are

1. Hilchot Isurei Mizbeach 7:11.
2. YD 248:8.
3. bShab 133b.

donations of items that, once given, do not belong to the devotee. This makes Rambam's contrast between a house of prayer and a private house an especially fitting example.

While it may seem strange to think of a building, even one for public use, as a donation similar to clothing or food, religious structures were sometimes depicted in exactly this way. A well-known motif in Medieval church mosaics was to show the patron of the church presenting it – in miniature – as a gift. Some of the earliest physical models of architecture are thought to have been votive offerings of a similar nature.[4] Passages in the Talmud also describe the pride which donors of edifices felt. R. Chama bar Chanina expresses pride in his family's role in financing synagogues in Lod.[5] R. Abun felt similar pride for the gates of a synagogue in Tiveria.[6] It was not uncommon to think of buildings as commodities to be donated.

The halachic ruling about donating a synagogue does not clarify what it means to be "more pleasant than your private house." This criterion implies a relative scale – the materials and design need not be of the highest quality, but rather they must be favorable compared to your own dwelling. There are many ways to improve the quality of a building, even without considering its ornamentation.[7] This starts with the level of craftsmanship and can include layout (is there a grand entrance?), area (will it feel crowded?), and height. The level of finish materials, such as paving stones, door handles, and the like, is also easy to distinguish.

This understanding of what increases the quality of a building can help us make sense of the juxtaposition of Shlomo's palace and the Temple found in Melachim I. Shlomo's palace took longer to construct and was larger than the Temple.[8] However, most commentators do not see this as

---

4. Matthew Mindrup, *The Architectural Model* (MIT press, 2019), 13. Later, Mindrup explains that models were used in a similar way in triumphal marches, to demonstrate conquest. This recalls the depiction of the *menora* on the Arch of Titus. See Mindrup, 18.

5. yShek 5:7 (49b).

6. Ibid. It should be noted that in both cases a colleague questions their pride and asks if the funds could not have been better spent on supporting scholars. See also Steven Fine, *Art and Judaism in the Greco-Roman World* (Cambridge University Press, 2005), 65–66, where the author identifies this theme in *Ben Sira*. In addition, see Serafina Cuomo, *Technology and Culture in Greek and Roman Antiquity* (Cambridge University Press, 2007), 162, which discusses the emphasis on dignitaries' financial involvement in construction projects in the early Roman Empire, and how this was replaced by the suggestion of hands-on involvement as the role of architect gained prestige in the later years of the Empire.

7. Modern architecture, for example, eschews ornament, yet one would not have trouble imagining two Modern buildings in which one is noticeably more deluxe.

8. Melachim I 6–7.

3. Emperor Justinian I presenting a model of Hagia Sophia. (Mosaic above the southwest entrance of Hagia Sophia, Istanbul, Wikimedia)

criticism of Shlomo.[9] While part of the reason might be because of the palace's different function,[10] size is only one metric by which buildings can be measured. Other factors, such as materials and location, are important. Presumably, no corners were cut in the construction of the Temple.

The lesson from the gifts of Kayin and Hevel is that one should strive to maintain a comparatively high standard when keeping mitzvot or making donations. This does not always mean bigger or fancier, but one should find some metric in which the donated item is superlative.

---

9. See Rashi and Metzudat David on Melachim I 7:1, bSan 104b, and BamR 14:1. Josephus gives another explanation, writing that Shlomo felt much less urgency to build his palace, so he did not press for it to be completed quickly and did not make efforts to gather all the materials ahead of time. See *Antiquities* 8.130–132.

10. See Abarbanel on this verse.

# Homelessness

וְעַתָּה אָרוּר אָתָּה מִן הָאֲדָמָה אֲשֶׁר פָּצְתָה אֶת פִּיהָ לָקַחַת אֶת דְּמֵי אָחִיךָ מִיָּדֶךָ. כִּי תַעֲבֹד אֶת הָאֲדָמָה לֹא תֹסֵף תֵּת כֹּחָהּ לָךְ נָע וָנָד תִּהְיֶה בָאָרֶץ. וַיֹּאמֶר קַיִן אֶל ה׳ גָּדוֹל עֲוֺנִי מִנְּשֹׂא. הֵן גֵּרַשְׁתָּ אֹתִי הַיּוֹם מֵעַל פְּנֵי הָאֲדָמָה וּמִפָּנֶיךָ אֶסָּתֵר וְהָיִיתִי נָע וָנָד בָּאָרֶץ וְהָיָה כָל מֹצְאִי יַהַרְגֵנִי. (בראשית ד:יא-יד)

And now cursed are you from the ground, which has opened her mouth to receive your brother's blood from your hand. When you till the ground it shall not henceforth yield to you her strength, a fugitive and a wanderer shall you be on the earth. And Kayin said to the Lord, "my punishment is greater than I can bear. Behold, you have driven me out this day from the face of the land, and from your face I shall be hidden, and I shall be a fugitive and a wanderer in the earth, and it will come to pass that whoever finds me will slay me." (Bereshit 4:11–14)

THE curse of Kayin, a punishment for killing his brother Hevel, was that (a) the earth would not cooperate with him and (b) Kayin would henceforth be "a fugitive and a wanderer" – *na venad*. What was the meaning of the second part of this curse, and why did it seem so terrible to Kayin?

One can read the *na venad* clause as a continuation of the first part of the curse, which deals with agricultural activity. Radak writes that agriculture was Kayin's livelihood and was, therefore, a fitting target for a curse.[1] He explains that Kayin saw that his crops were failing and convinced himself that relocation was the solution. However, no matter how many times he

1. Similar to how Adam, the breadwinner, was cursed with: "in the sweat of your face shall you eat bread" (Bereshit 3:19) and Chava, the mother, was cursed that, "in sorrow you shall bring forth children" (Bereshit 3:16). For Kayin's connection to agriculture, see Bereshit 4:2.

moved, the situation remained the same. Kayin found no rest and was never able to establish a proper home.

Rashi explains the curse more simply, without involving agriculture: Kayin was repeatedly banished by his neighbors.[2] One midrash records that the earth physically shook wherever Kayin went so that no one wanted to live near him.[3] Whatever the mechanism that prevented Kayin from staying in one place, the prospect of forever wandering was enough to cause him to exclaim "My punishment is greater than I can bear."

While most commentators are satisfied with defining *na venad* as perpetual wandering, the Netziv takes it one step further. He writes that part of the curse was that Kayin would never be able to have a home. Without a physical domicile Kayin would be exposed to all sorts of dangers. The curse is focused less on wandering and more on missing the benefits that a fixed house provides: safety, security, and a social network. Kayin is denied any sense of stability and deprived of a normative human experience. This was what made his punishment unbearable.[4]

While Kayin's curse was a special situation, it is not so different from the plight of homeless people. Having a permanent home brings with it many benefits that are fundamental to the human experience. Community, agriculture (in agrarian societies), equity, security, and stability are some of the benefits. Governments try to reduce homelessness in part because it is inhumane and destabilizing to society for people to be without homes, but also because having a home can be the first step in escaping poverty. Many housing projects, however, fail to create the conditions needed to reduce poverty. Often when large housing projects fail it is because the homes they create do not engender community, security, and the other benefits that normally come with having a permanent dwelling.

Kayin recognized how fundamental having a house is to the human experience. He realized the deep and terrible impact of being condemned to a life of perpetual wandering, without a permanent home, and that is why he recoiled from his curse.

---

2. See also ShmR 31:17.

3. Tanchuma, Bereshit 9 *Miketz Shanim*. This idea is quoted by R. Yaakov Slonik in his *Nachalat Yaakov* commentary on this verse.

4. On a larger scale, the Jewish exile similarly deprived our nation of a normative national experience, lacking a permanent homeland.

# The Origin of Cities

וַיֵּדַע קַיִן אֶת אִשְׁתּוֹ וַתַּהַר וַתֵּלֶד אֶת חֲנוֹךְ וַיְהִי בֹּנֶה עִיר וַיִּקְרָא שֵׁם הָעִיר כְּשֵׁם בְּנוֹ חֲנוֹךְ. (בראשית ד:יז)

> And Kayin knew his wife and she conceived and bore Chanoch, and he built a city and called the name of the city after the name of his son, Chanoch. (Bereshit 4:17)

THIS verse marks the first time that cities are mentioned in the Torah. Historians once believed that cities developed in a single civilization and then spread to others, the so-called diffusion theory. Most contemporary historians now believe that cities came into existence independently in different locations, supported by the right conditions and circumstances.[1] This second theory fits the tone of our verse. While the adjacent verses mention the origins of various crafts and identify someone as the "father" of musical instruments or animal husbandry, here no such honorific is given. We are told that Kayin built a city, but not that cities were his invention. The concept of a city is taken as a normal occurrence, not a revolutionary idea.

There are many theories about what triggered the development of urbanism – markets, surpluses,[2] religious shrines, the need for defense, and more.[3] As a corollary, historians also debate the chicken-or-egg question of

1. Spiro Kostof, *The City Shaped: Urban Patterns and Meanings Through History* (Thames and Hudson, 1999), 29–30.

2. The narrative of Yosef in Egypt describes a situation in which surplus leads to a strong, centralized state. As per Bereshit 47:19, in exchange for food, Yosef collects the people's money, livestock, land, and finally themselves as slaves. With the history of cities, some argue that a surplus of food brings more people to the city, who in turn require more food, until a centralized authority is needed to maintain the system. Surplus also allows a class of artisans to form and helps trade develop.

3. Some consider the founding of the city by Kayin is an act of rebellion. See Kostof, *The City Shaped*, 34–6.

whether these factors caused the rise of cities, or whether cities triggered these developments. For example, improved agriculture could have led to a surplus of food, which allowed specialized crafts to develop and cities to form. Alternatively, perhaps the organization of cities was what led to improved agriculture. There are no definitive answers to these questions.

While some have suggested that the involvement of cursed Kayin hints at a disapproval of urban life,[4] most Jewish commentators take a decidedly positive view of cities. R. S.R. Hirsch sees the founding of a city as the proper response to Kayin's curse. Kayin could no longer rely on the land for his livelihood, so he had to rely on his own ingenuity. A city was the only setting in which it would be possible to live off his talents, where "all the slumbering capabilities of men are awakened." This explanation focuses on cities as places that enable skilled craft and specialization. The Netziv, assuming that urbanism is a superior way of life, explains that Kayin realized that humans were meant to progress from a nomadic to an urban lifestyle to better serve God. Malbim likewise views the city positively, explaining that this was Kayin's way of atoning for his sin of murder. While manslaughter causes people to live in fear and stay apart, a city joins people together and promotes laws, philosophy, and comradery. R. Yitzchak Karo focuses on cities as places of trade: to build a city, one must import materials from all sorts of distant locations. This, he writes, allowed Kayin to embrace the wandering component of God's curse, while at the same time building a future for his progeny.

The commentators do not attempt to explain the conditions that led to the founding of this city. Instead, they focus on the special qualities that a city possesses: exchange of ideas, safety, stability, trade, and the specialization of labor.[5] These qualities were what drove Kayin to establish a city. Each commentator highlights what he considers to be the defining attributes of a city – trade, exchange of ideas, specialized crafts, or defense – and sees Kayin's decision to build a city as a logical response to his curse.

---

4. Frank S. Frick, *The City in Ancient Israel* (Scholars Press, 1977), 206–7.

5. These are not the only special conditions of a city. Kostof lists nine conditions, including density, boundaries, written records, and monuments.

# Music, War, and Architecture

וְשֵׁם אָחִיו יוּבָל הוּא הָיָה אֲבִי כָּל תֹּפֵשׂ כִּנּוֹר וְעוּגָב. וְצִלָּה גַם הִוא יָלְדָה אֶת תּוּבַל קַיִן לֹטֵשׁ כָּל חֹרֵשׁ נְחֹשֶׁת וּבַרְזֶל וַאֲחוֹת תּוּבַל קַיִן נַעֲמָה. (בראשית ד:כא-כב)

And his brother's name was Yuval, he was the father of all such as handle the lyre and pipe. And Tzila, she also bore Tuval-Kayin, the forger of every cutting instrument of brass and iron, and the sister of Tuval-Kayin was Naama. (Bereshit 4:21–22)

As part of the genealogy that appears in Bereshit, we are told about Yuval and Tuval-Kayin, each responsible for originating a craft. Yuval was the first musician, while Tuval-Kayin was the first to forge metal tools, which according to Rashi refers to weapons.

In the modern world, we think of the invention of metallurgy and musical instruments as long processes and not singular inventions. Why are we told about the role of these two figures? Malbim explains that this story was included in the Torah as a way of contravening the different mythologies that were circulating at the time, which tended to elevate the creators of music or tools into gods.[1] The Torah upends these myths by attributing their creation to humans, and to children of the damned Kayin, no less.

We can find another answer to this problem by looking at how metalcraft and music are treated in Vitruvius' *Ten Books on Architecture*. Vitruvius explains that an architect:

> should know music in order to have a grasp of canonical and mathematical relations, and besides that, to calibrate *ballistae*, catapults, and [the small catapults called] scorpions.[2]

1. For example, see Pliny the Elder, *Natural History*, 7.57.
2. Vitruvius, *Ten Books on Architecture*, I.1.8. The strings of such war machines had to be carefully "tuned" to ensure an accurate release. See also X.12.2 for the same point. Vitruvius (II.1) also gives a brief origin story for architecture, which involves mankind

That is, Vitruvius felt that music is directly connected to both design and warfare, just as Yuval and Tuval-Kayin appear together in our verses. This is not the only place we see these subjects together. David was both a warrior and a musician, master of the harp and the sling. Similarly, Leviim were called upon to serve in the Temple both as guards and as musicians.

Instead of viewing these verses as an attempt to debunk mythology, perhaps they are reinforcing the relationship between music and metalcraft, which is to say, art and war. Often inventions can be applied both to cultural advancement and to new weaponry. In the distant past, architects were called upon to mediate both uses. They were masters of a set of skills that could be applied in either realm.[3] One of the main items on Vitruvius' resume was his knowledge of "the repair of all the other sorts of war machines"[4] and a considerable portion of his tenth book deals with this subject. Despite the vastly different applications, the two sets of skills are in fact related. Juxtaposing Yuval's invention of musical instruments and Tuval-Kayin's creation of metallurgy stresses this connection and the double-edged sword that technology represents.

harnessing fire and developing speech.

3. In BerR 23:21, "lyre and pipe" (*kinor ve-ugav*) are explained as *adrablin vekarbelin,* which Jastrow translates as "organists and flute players." A textual variant reads *ardichalin*, "architects," but this makes little sense in the context, despite my explanation above. See also Simon and Mordechai Bondi, *Or Esther* (Dessau, 1812), 67.

4. Vitruvius, Ten Books on Architecture, Preface.

# Building the Ark as an Architectural Statement

עֲשֵׂה לְךָ תֵּבַת עֲצֵי גֹפֶר קִנִּים תַּעֲשֶׂה אֶת הַתֵּבָה וְכָפַרְתָּ אֹתָהּ מִבַּיִת וּמִחוּץ בַּכֹּפֶר. (בראשית ו:יד)

Make you an ark of gofer wood. With rooms shall you make the ark and shall pitch it within and without with pitch. (Bereshit 6:14)

ALTHOUGH God could have saved Noach miraculously, He instead commanded Noach to manually build an ark. According to midrash, this massive task took one hundred and twenty years. Rashi explains that God wanted Noach to build the ark over a long period of time so that the sinners of his generation would see him toiling and inquire about his work.[1] Noach could then respond that God was unhappy with their actions and tell them to repent.

This mode of sending a message differs radically from the method of divine warning used in later centuries when prophets were dispatched to warn both the Israelites and other nations.[2] Whereas prophets warned people directly, Noach took a more passive approach. Why was it appropriate for Noach to be passive?

---

1. BerR 30:6 and Tanchuma Noach 5 say that Noach began work on the ark by planting cedar trees, knowing that it would take decades for them to reach maturity. When people would inquire about the purpose of the trees, Noach would warn them about the flood and ask them to repent. For another instance of this type of advanced planning, see my commentary on Bereshit 46:1.

One hundred and twenty is also the reduced lifespan of man as per Bereshit 6:3, which Sforno points out in his commentary on that verse. This raises the idea that a limited lifespan also limits the ambitions that one man can have for his lifetime. While building projects can potentially span several generations, as with medieval churches, a shorter lifespan limits any individual's building projects to what can be accomplished in that time. Noach, who lived longer than this, was able to complete the ark and do so in a way that made a statement to his neighbors. In later generations, such a process would be impossible.

2. Both Yona and Yirmiyahu were sent to warn other nations.

Rabbi Aharon Leib Shteinman explains in his commentary, *Ayelet Hashachar,* that Noach was famous in his generation and *could* have warned his fellow man to repent before the flood. However, words would not have influenced his contemporaries. Rather, they needed to be shown through actions that they were in mortal danger. The tangible act of shipbuilding was a more potent message than any call for repentance Noach could have issued. Though Noach was not confronting his neighbors directly, neither was he being passive.

There are times when a physical edifice is a far more powerful message than any amount of oral direction, when the act of building demonstrates that you are serious about your message. We find an example of this principle in the books of Ezra and Nechemia. When they first returned to Judea, the Jews in Israel were floundering. It was only when Ezra returned and acted decisively, both by calling for repentance and by physically beginning the rebuilding of the Temple, that progress began. Later, Nechemia did the same with the walls of Jerusalem. In modern Zionism, this resolve was shown by the Tower and Stockade settlers of the 1930s, who built new settlements overnight and established facts on the ground, shaping the borders of the future State of Israel.

More abstractly, building projects are often used to send a strong message about the future of a company or municipality. Cities looking to rejuvenate their downtown area might construct a sports stadium or a theater. Crime-ridden cities can erect a new police station. Companies build new headquarters. A Jewish community might build a synagogue, yeshiva, or *mikva* in a city to attract new members. Some monuments also broadcast the aspirations of a polity, such as the Statue of Liberty. Buildings can thus make a statement in both a practical and symbolic manner.

A building can be a powerful message that is readily understood and widely discernable. This is why it was a potent – if ultimately unsuccessful – way for Noach to warn his fellow man.

NOACH

# Design Briefs

עֲשֵׂה לְךָ תֵּבַת עֲצֵי גֹפֶר קִנִּים תַּעֲשֶׂה אֶת הַתֵּבָה וְכָפַרְתָּ אֹתָהּ מִבַּיִת וּמִחוּץ
בַּכֹּפֶר. וְזֶה אֲשֶׁר תַּעֲשֶׂה אֹתָהּ שְׁלֹשׁ מֵאוֹת אַמָּה אֹרֶךְ הַתֵּבָה חֲמִשִּׁים אַמָּה
רָחְבָּהּ וּשְׁלֹשִׁים אַמָּה קוֹמָתָהּ. צֹהַר תַּעֲשֶׂה לַתֵּבָה וְאֶל אַמָּה תְּכַלֶּנָּה מִלְמַעְלָה
וּפֶתַח הַתֵּבָה בְּצִדָּהּ תָּשִׂים תַּחְתִּיִּם שְׁנִיִּם וּשְׁלִשִׁים תַּעֲשֶׂהָ. (בראשית ו:יד–טז)

Make yourself an ark of gofer wood. Make it an ark with rooms and cover it inside and out with pitch. And this is how you shall make it: the length of the ark shall be three hundred cubits, its width fifty cubits, and its height thirty cubits. A light (*tzohar*) shall you make for the ark and finish it within a cubit of the top. A door to the ark shall you set in its side; make it with a bottom, second, and third deck. (Bereshit 6:14–16)

THE ark is one of the great building projects described in the Torah, along with the *Mishkan* and the Tower of Babel. The above verses give a sparse description of the ark, a skeleton of what we today would call a design brief, and that in classical Greece was known as *syngraphai*.[1] A design brief is a document given to the designer at the start of a project, which states the project's requirements. From these three verses, the Talmud and commentators extrapolate the design requirements of the ark, adding insight into each clause to help flesh out the description:

A. Materials: the ark had to be constructed of wood. As with most building materials in a project, *gofer* wood was presumably chosen for either its physical properties or some unknown symbolic reason.[2]

B. Waterproofing: the ark had to be watertight to be seaworthy.

1. J.J. Coulton, *Ancient Greek Architects at Work* (Cornell University Press, 1982), 54 and 58. In the ancient world this was the most important part of the design set, more than any technical drawings that may have been used in that period.

2. Ibn Ezra writes that it is the most buoyant wood. Rashi suggests a symbolic quality of *gofer* wood, as does Malbim.

Commentators point out that pitch is an appropriate choice for waterproofing wood and is suitable for the ship's function of housing people and animals.[3] Radak interprets the verses as mandating a sloped roof, to allow rainwater to flow off the ark rapidly.[4]

C. Required spaces: the ark had different functions, which were separated vertically into three floors. According to the Talmud, the top floor was inhabited by people, the middle floor was used for animals, and the bottom floor for waste.[5] Disease and odor were apparently not of sufficient concern to require the disposal of biological refuse.

D. The floors were to be further partitioned into rooms. The design brief is surprisingly vague, as the Torah does not specify what functions took place in these cells, nor how many cells were needed. Rashi writes that individual cells were required for each animal. Ibn Ezra mentions the needs of the different families on the floor above. Malbim explains that each family was able to regulate the climate of its individual cell. Despite this concern for keeping animals and families separate, no mention is made of food storage,[6] dining facilities, nor spaces for exercise by people and animals.

E. Size: the overall dimensions of the ark had to be large enough to hold all the required functions. In a typical design project, this is calculated by figuring out how much area is allowed by law and how much space is needed for each function. These two figures are compared to make sure they are compatible, and a final size is determined. In our case, legal requirements for space are not a concern, although presumably the size of the ship is limited by material constraints (i.e. the size of available trees).

Ibn Ezra also mentions that the height of the ark was limited to one tenth its width so that the ark would not be top-heavy and flip over.[7]

F. Lighting: the interior had to be a functional space for people to live, day and night, for an extended period. Therefore, enough light had to be provided for them to go about their business. R. Yohanan writes that rather than a window, the *tzohar* mentioned in the verses were jewels that emitted light.[8] It seems that R. Yohanan recognized that the sun would not

---

3. A different waterproofing solution was used for Moshe's basket, because of its more delicate function – holding a baby. See Rashi on Shemot 2:3.

4. See Kli Yakar for a symbolic reason for sloped roofs.

5. bSan 108b. I find this ecological consciousness fascinating; the Talmud felt that even in a world being destroyed by a flood, waste could not be tossed overboard but was rather kept until it could be disposed of or recycled in some manner.

6. Despite an explicit command to bring suitable food onboard in Bereshit 6:21.

7. See also BerR 31:6, which makes the same statement.

8. bSan 108b. See also BerR 33:8, and BerR 31:16 for *tzohar* and its various explanations.

have been a practical source of light, for at least three reasons: sunlight was most likely scarce during the flood; sunlight is only sufficient during the day; and open windows would also let rain into the ark. Therefore, in a world without electric lighting, he identified an alternative source of light without these problems. Addressing these same concerns, Radak writes that there were wax candles on board and Chizkuni gives one interpretation of *tzohar* as oil for lamps.

G. Egress: There must be a route for entering and exiting the ark. In a building, we would want there to be multiple exits in case of emergency, but in the unique case of the ark, there really could be no emergency exit into the floodwater. Several commentators explain that the *tzohar* was the window Noach used to release the raven and dove, in which case it served as a secondary exit.

H. Sealed Door: Once everyone was aboard the ark, the door had to be sealed and made watertight. The Torah states that "the Lord shut him in"[9] and some explain that this was accomplished with a strong wind.[10] Sealing a door is usually accomplished nowadays with flexible gaskets around the edge of the opening.

I. Steering: Ibn Ezra explains that the connotation of the word "ark" rather than "ship" meant that the vessel could not be controlled by any internal forces (such as oars). The function of the ark was not to get from point A to point B, but rather to survive the flood.[11]

J. Timeframe: The ark had to be completed before the rain started, but the construction process was drawn out to facilitate repentance.[12]

These verses give us a good picture of "practical" considerations related to the ark. The way that the various commentators flesh out these three verses show that they also relate to them as a type of design brief for the ark, explaining the project parameters in a more detailed manner.

---

See also yPes 1:1 (27b) for a source about precious gems emitting light so that Noach could know when it was time to feed each animal. bMeg 12a mentions a glowing stone that Achashverosh used. Pliny the Elder mentions a similar stone in *Natural History* 37.56, which "is pale by day, but of a fiery lustre by night." See also the Bologna Stone, a persistent luminescent material discovered in 1603.

9. Bereshit 7:16.

10. Chizkuni and Bechor Shor.

11. A similar distinction was made with early aerostats, or lighter-than-air aircrafts. These were classified either as balloons, which could not be steered, or dirigibles, which could. The word "dirigible" means directable.

12. See my commentary to Bereshit 6:14.

NOACH

# Graphic Standards And Technical Drawings

וַיְהִי כָל הָאָרֶץ שָׂפָה אֶחָת וּדְבָרִים אֲחָדִים. (בראשית יא:א)

And the whole earth was of one language, and of one speech. (Bereshit 11:1)

ONE of the major themes of the Tower of Babel story is communication between people. The story begins with a statement that "the whole earth was of one language" and ends with God "confounding the language of all the earth." The shared language plays a critical role in the tale, as it seems to be what facilitates the project and what ultimately dooms it.

A midrash colorfully relates that one worker would ask for an axe and another worker, misunderstanding, would bring a trowel, leading to frustration, anger, and bloodshed.[1] While miscommunications on a construction site could easily turn deadly, this midrash is almost cartoonish and keeps us from thinking more seriously about the importance of a shared language or vocabulary when it comes to building.

The main way that architects communicate with the people who execute their designs (i.e., the construction workers) is through technical drawings. Architects and draftsmen learn how to create a set of technical drawings that gives precise instructions. The goal is for the directions to be exact and without any vagaries. These drawings include plans, sections, elevations, enlargements, and details, all referencing one another in a way that can be easily navigated to find all the relevant information.

Technical drawings use a number of conventions that help convey the intentions of the designer. For example, a draftsman will use different line weights (thickness of lines) and line types (dashed, dotted, etc.) which help others understand if something is above, below, hidden, or intersected in the drawing. There is also a system of symbols and hatch patterns that

1. Or possibly tongs and shovels, depending on the translation. See BerR 38:7.

are recognizable to experienced workers and help them understand and navigate the drawings. In short, there is a whole language that architects use to communicate with the construction crew. If they fail to provide clear instructions, the best scenario will be an incessant stream of questions from the construction site. In the worst scenario, the builders will build whatever they understand from the drawings, often resulting in something different from the architect's intentions.

For a particular set of plans, an architect can set out a list of different symbols, hatch types, and lines to be used in that project. However, there are also several institutions, both national (as in the American Institute of Architects *Architectural Graphic Standards* book) and international, that have published standard guidelines for architectural drawings.[2] Although there are many ways to mark elements on plans, the shared language of technical drawings helps architects provide effective instructions and avoid miscommunications.

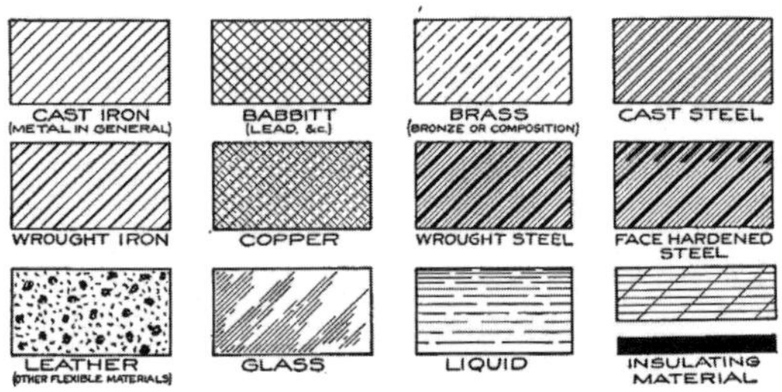


4. Hatch Patterns. (Thomas E. French, A Manual of Engineering Drawing for Students and Draftsmen, 175 (McGraw Hill Book Company, 1911))

A construction site is a very appropriate setting for a story about universal communication. Construction itself is a universal human experience and one of the most powerful tools that humans possess. The people in our story are trying to control their environment and use architecture, building technology, and language to accomplish this goal. Ultimately, even though the architecture and technology appear to be sound, the project fails because of a failure to communicate. Even in a monolingual environment, precise communication between the architects and the builders is a challenge. Two people speaking the same language can easily

2. A given office often has its own standards, though there were attempts at standardization in the early twentieth century. See George Barnett Johnston, *Drafting Culture* (MIT Press, 2008), 40, 142.

misunderstand one another. Adding a layer of foreign language increases the difficulty.

All this may make it seem like the linguistic issues faced in the Tower of Babel story were not so different from a typical building site. However, there is a difference, which makes the midrash more poignant. An architect-worker relationship is asymmetrical, with the architect giving orders. The assumption is that the architect will have a different and fuller understanding of the design and must find a way to communicate it to the workers. In contrast, the midrash describes a breakdown in communication between the workers themselves. This could not have been anticipated and therefore led to chaos on site.[3] While every architect must keep in mind the challenges of communicating the design to the workers on-site, with the Tower of Babel it was the communication between the workers that scuttled the project.

3. This emphasis on miscommunication between the workers also helps to call out the collective nature of the story, as a group of like-minded citizens banding together rather than a building project imposed by the local rules.

NOACH

# Brickmaking And Building Technology

וַיֹּאמְרוּ אִישׁ אֶל רֵעֵהוּ הָבָה נִלְבְּנָה לְבֵנִים וְנִשְׂרְפָה לִשְׂרֵפָה וַתְּהִי לָהֶם הַלְּבֵנָה
לְאָבֶן וְהַחֵמָר הָיָה לָהֶם לַחֹמֶר. (בראשית יא:ג)

And they said to one another, Come, let us make bricks, and burn them thoroughly. And they had brick for stone, and bitumen had they for mortar. (Bereshit 11:3)

In the preamble to the story of the Tower of Babel, we are told that the people made bricks and mortar. This, as explained by the commentators, represented a change in the existing building technology, with the new kiln-fired bricks as the basic masonry unit. According to Rashi and Radak, the innovation was out of necessity: there was not enough stone available in Babylon.[1] It was part of the regular development of technology, whereby necessity breeds innovation. The kiln-fired stone replaced sun-dried mud bricks, contributing a stronger, more stable, and more permanent wall. This allowed taller structures to be built.[2] Hence the technological innovation led to the construction of a tower.

The Torah seems to be striking a conservative tone regarding new

1. Historically, stone was not available in Babylon. In Israel, where stone is abundant, no kiln-fired bricks have been found before the Early Roman period (Ronny Reich, "Building Materials and Architectural Elements in Ancient Israel" in *The Architecture of Ancient Israel* (Israel Exploration Society, 1992), 7. Bricks were highly characteristic of Mesopotamian monumental buildings. See Victor Hurowitz, *I Have Built You an Exalted House* (Sheffield Academic Press, 1992), 104.

2. Mud bricks were used first, and then improved upon when techniques to bake the bricks were discovered. See Edward Allen, *Fundamentals of Building Construction, Third Ed.* (Wiley, 2000), 246. Therefore, when the Torah uses the term "stone" in our verse, it does not literally mean stone, but "masonry unit." Vitruvius (*Ten Books on Architecture,* I.5.8) specifically mentions the use of burnt brick in Babylon. Both Pliny the Elder (*Natural History,* 35.169–173) and Vitruvius (II.8.17) record that in Rome, buildings made of mud bricks could only be one story tall. Buildings made with kiln-fired bricks could be taller.

technology. While there is nothing morally wrong with kiln-fired bricks, these bricks are presented as part of this ill-fated building program. It is fair to ask why the Torah emphasizes their role in the story.

The Netziv connects the brick kilns with the midrash about Nimrod attempting to execute Avram by having him tossed into a furnace.[3] He writes that Nimrod's furnace was the same kiln used to prepare the bricks. The point seems to be that while new technology can be used for positive purposes, it can also be used for evil. To reference a Biblical example, metallurgy can be used to make agricultural equipment, or it can be used to make military gear.[4]

Another perspective of the role of kiln-fired bricks in this story can be gained by looking at the nineteenth and twentieth centuries when iron, steel, and glass revolutionized architecture. At first, iron was used in bridges by pioneering engineers who experimented with beams of different shapes and depths. Iron struts were then adapted for use in large public spaces, like markets, railway stations, and libraries, often together with newly available sheet glass. The lessons from these buildings were applied by Gustave Eiffel in the design of his eponymous tower in Paris.[5] At that time the cost of land in city centers was rising. Architects utilized steel frames to enable the construction of tall buildings without bulky masonry walls that took up valuable ground-floor retail space. In the hands of architects like Louis Sullivan, and together with the introduction of safe elevators, this led to the development of skyscrapers, which quickly became a mainstay in cities around the world.[6]

While this is how modern architectural history played out, we can take a step back and ask whether the introduction of skyscrapers was inevitable. Did the new technology plus land prices inescapably create tall buildings, or could cities have developed differently? While Le Corbusier argued in 1930 in favor of cities dominated by towers,[7] there were certainly competing visions for how cities should be designed. Frank Lloyd Wright's 1928 Broadacre City plan called for cities to be dispersed and decentralized

---

3. BerR 38:28.

4. As per the imagery of beating swords into plowshares and vice versa, in Yishayahu 2:4, Yoel 3:10, and Micha 4:3.

5. Kenneth Frampton, *Modern Architecture: A Critical History* (Thames and Hudson, 1992), 29–36.

6. Ibid, 51–56.

7. In his Ville Radieuse plan, he proposed a city comprised only of towers, which were lifted off the ground on pillars. This allowed for uninterrupted open space below. This model was highly influential and pushed urban planners to design blocks of skyscrapers to reduce congestion in cities and provide more amenities for the residents.

with small houses. Ebenezer Howard described a system of sprawling Garden Cities in 1898 that thrived without tall buildings. Various "linear city" schemes, such as that of Nikolay Milyutin in the USSR, envisioned cities without skyscrapers. After seeing the effect of skyscrapers on cities, Jane Jacobs argued that tall buildings surrounded by open space destroyed the city fabric and promoted crime.[8] While cities with towers became the norm, there was a vibrant debate about whether tall buildings were beneficial.

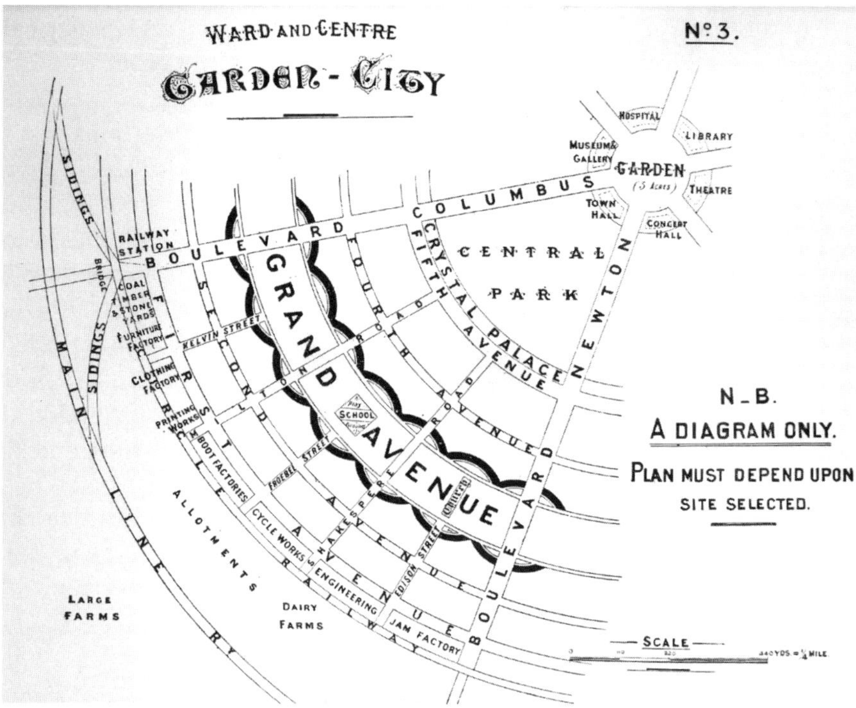


5. Diagram of a Garden City.
(Ebenezer Howard, *Garden Cities of To-morrow*, Wikimedia)

Looking back at our text, we can detect a similar debate beneath the surface. The Torah tells us, "And they said, let us build us a city and tower." While the other side of this discussion is not recorded, presumably opponents of the plan were arguing against centralization and in favor of "scattering abroad upon the face of the whole earth." The tower project is

8. In her book *The Death and Life of Great American Cities* (Random House, 1961).

presented as a decision, not something that happened inevitably. It can even be viewed as a dispute about urban living.[9]

The role of kiln-fired bricks is central to the story because it is the trigger for this debate. The new building material opens fresh possibilities for designers, triggering the discussion about the proper use of bricks and leading to the construction of the tower by ambitious citizens. The story thus speaks to us about wise design and innovative technology which can lead to unintended consequences and accountability, themes that are central to the human condition.

9. Would life be improved by building vertically, or would this destroy the community they sought to preserve? One could also read the story as a debate over urban versus agrarian society, as Frank S. Frick does in his *The City in Ancient Israel* (Scholars Press, 1977), 205.

NOACH

# Skyscrapers as Civic Icons

וַיֹּאמְרוּ הָבָה נִבְנֶה לָּנוּ עִיר וּמִגְדָּל וְרֹאשׁוֹ בַשָּׁמַיִם וְנַעֲשֶׂה לָּנוּ שֵׁם פֶּן נָפוּץ עַל פְּנֵי כָל הָאָרֶץ. (בראשית יא:ד)

And they said, "Come, let us build us a city and a tower, with its top in heaven, and let us make us a name, lest we be scattered abroad upon the face of the whole earth." (Bereshit 11:4)

THE story of the Tower of Babel is one of the most explicit discussions of architecture in the Torah, telling of the construction of a city and a tower.[1] Although some Jewish texts provide more elaborate motivation for the building project,[2] the Torah records that the people built the city and town to "make us a name, lest we be scattered." Most commentators use this as their starting point when explaining the impetus for the tower. In addition to helping us understand the text, their explanations demonstrate how the commentators thought about tall buildings in general. Many of the reasons they give are still used today to justify the construction of tall buildings.

Ibn Ezra writes that the people of Babel wanted the tower as a civic

1. In pre-Industrial society, it would have been hard to envision buildings the height of modern skyscrapers or to describe what a tall building feels like in a way that could be comprehended. In BerR 38:4, R. Huna quotes R. Idi as saying that one who climbed to the top of the ruins would be so high above the palm trees that the trees would appear tiny. To compound this, R. Chiya bar Aba relates that one third of the tower was burned, one third sunk and only one third remained standing.

2. These include: (a) revenge against God by building a tower too high for another flood to destroy (Josephus, *Antiquities*, 1.4); (b) to ascend into heaven (Hayovlim 10:19–20); (c) to challenge the division of heaven for God and earth for man (BerR 38:1); (d) to help prop the earth up (ibid); (e) to place a statue up above, holding a sword (*Targum Yerushalmi* 11:4 and BerR 38:1). bSan 109a states that the Babylonians themselves were divided: a third wanted to dwell in Heaven, a third wanted to use it for idol worship, and a third wanted open war with God.

symbol, a source of pride, and a landmark.[3] There are many cities today that are associated with specific buildings, often tall ones: the Gateway Arch in St. Louis, the Golden Gate Bridge in San Francisco, and the Eiffel Tower in Paris, to name a few. In Medieval Europe, there were similar examples of civic pride in architecture, such as the Dome over the Florence Cathedral. If we look even further back in history, there are additional examples of architecture appearing as civic icons. In 1859, T.L. Donaldson published a collection of architecture appearing on Greek and Roman coins, appropriately called *Architectura Numismatica.* It includes examples of temples, tombs, columns, arches, bridges, theaters, stadia, city gates, walls, and amphitheaters appearing on ancient coinage from around the Roman world.[4] These structures were chosen because they were symbols of each city. Similarly, the people of Babylon may have been motivated to build a tall structure to serve as an iconic landmark.

No. 33

TEMPLE ON MOVNT GERIZIM

No. 79

AMPHITHEATRE OF VESPASIAN ROME

6. Coins from the Roman Empire showing city landmarks. (*Architectura Numismaticai*, 33 and 79)

Ibn Ezra lists pride as an additional reason for the construction of the tower. Even today, pride remains one of the major factors driving the construction of skyscrapers. The history of competition over the world's tallest building bears this out, as in the construction of the Chrysler Building and

3. In twelfth century Córdoba, where Ibn Ezra lived, the tallest building was the *sawma'a* of the Great Mosque, reaching a height of forty-seven meters. It was built as a statement in the rivalry between the Umayyad state and the Fatimids. See Jonathan M. Bloom, *Architecture of the Islamic West* (Yale University Press, 2020), 61–63.

4. There is one example from Mount Gerizim, where a Samaritan Temple stood, dating to the second century. In modern times, we occasionally find monuments used in sports logos to represent a team's city.

the Empire State Building, or the one-upmanship for the tallest building in Asia.

Radak explains the motivation differently. The main characteristic of a tower is its height, and Radak writes that the tower was for the dual purposes of keeping watch from inside the city and providing a landmark for orientation from outside the city, a sort of terrestrial lighthouse. It is true that tall buildings help with orientation in narrow, medieval streets. Still, this does seem to have an aspect of after-the-fact justification.[5] This is akin to building a skyscraper and adding a zeppelin moor (as with the Empire State Building)[6] or a radio antenna (as with the Eiffel Tower) on top as a way of justifying the design decision.

Sforno explains that the tower was intended to be a pilgrimage destination. The Babylonians wanted to build a fabulous, tall place of worship, to attract visitors. They hoped this site would be so important to the people of the world that whoever controlled it would have tremendous leverage over everyone else. This again is a familiar idea; many of the most important Medieval building projects were built as pilgrimage sites, designed to bring wealth and prestige to the municipality. Saudi Arabia's control of Mecca continues to give it a commanding role in the Islamic world. Today, cities use architecture for a similar purpose, to help bring in tourists. This is famously known as the "Balboa Effect" after Frank Gehry's Guggenheim Museum in Balboa, Spain. This museum was such a revelation that the city immediately became a tourist destination, attracting money and fame. After noting the museum's positive effect on Balboa, many other cities have sought to build similar architectural attractions.

Building a monument seems like a reasonable endeavor, whether as a source of pride and civic identity for the residents or as an attraction for foreigners. It is difficult to find something inherently wrong with the concept of tall buildings, even ones that aspire to reach heaven. Why was it viewed unfavorably by God?

As with most skyscrapers, the question is partially about the motivation, but also about the ramifications. A skyscraper today might disrupt traffic, change the weather, cast shadows on adjacent buildings, stimulate commerce, provide housing, create slums, drive up (or down) prices, etc. In the case of the Tower of Babel, the motivations may have been justifiable, or at least understandable, but most commentators explain that the net

5. Chizkuni, perhaps thinking along the same lines, concludes that the tower was built for defensive purposes.

6. Christopher Gray, "Not Just a Perch for King Kong" in the New York Times Sept 23, 2010, http://www.nytimes.com/2010/09/26/realestate/26scapes.html.

result was a failure to fulfill God's plan for mankind to repopulate the earth. The people instead wished to stay clustered together and this was unacceptable.

If we read the text carefully, there does not seem to be anything negative about the tower itself. God comes down to see the tower and city, notes that the people are united and share a common language and that they had begun to build this presumably impressive tower. God finishes by saying that man seems to have unlimited potential, saying "now nothing will be withheld from them." The problem here does not seem to be a mastery of technology or any interpersonal transgressions. Rather, it is a disappointment with their choice of a tower and city, as an unworthy goal for their unlimited potential. Of all the ways they could have chosen to expend their resources, this choice was underwhelming.

Architects, planners, and developers must view this as an open-ended question. What is a worthy cause? To what end do we build, and what projects are worthy and helpful to mankind? Which structures advance the general good and allow humanity to fulfill God's will? These are big questions, but tall buildings require lofty answers.

LECH LECHA

# Domestic Architecture In Mesopotamia

וַיֹּאמֶר ה' אֶל אַבְרָם לֶךְ לְךָ מֵאַרְצְךָ וּמִמּוֹלַדְתְּךָ וּמִבֵּית אָבִיךָ אֶל הָאָרֶץ אֲשֶׁר אַרְאֶךָּ. (בראשית יב:א)

Now the Lord said to Avram, "Get you out of your country and from your kindred and from your father's house, to the land that I will show you." (Bereshit 12:1)

THE first time in the Torah that God communicated with Avram was to command him to leave his father's house and journey to an unknown land. Ramban and Radak explain the nature of this challenge, saying that it is hard to leave your family and the place where you were born. This verse, they explain, comes to praise Avram for taking this difficult step.

Despite these supposed difficulties, a few verses later we learn that when Avram carried out this commandment he did not, in fact, leave everything behind. Avram took his wife, nephew, his material possessions, and his associates with him on his journey to Canaan.[1] Various commentators make it clear that Avram had not been comfortable in the culture of his homeland, and while much in Canaan was uncertain, he had many reasons to feel secure in his new home. If so, we can again ask: what was Avram leaving behind that made his emigration such a challenge?

One answer can be found in the phrase "your father's house." While this expression appears often in the Torah,[2] in this context it may emphasize what Avram was leaving. In Mesopotamia, successive generations often inhabited the same house. The house was usually the only property privately owned by a citizen, so people did their best to strengthen their connection

1. Bereshit 12:5–7.

2. It is used in several stories about women: Rivka (Bereshit 24:23), Tamar (Bereshit 38:11), Rachav (Yehoshua 2:18) and Delila (Shoftim 14:15), as well as in several other narratives.

with their domicile. One way to do so was by burying relatives in tombs directly underneath the house.[3] The words "your father's house" alludes to the generational connection Avram had to his homeland, which would be absent in Canaan.[4] The house itself symbolized the stability and deep roots that Avram was abandoning, both geographically and perhaps also ideologically in his departure from mainstream religion.

The attachment to house and homeland was considered a strong and even sacred connection. Later, in Greek and Roman times, founders of a new city would bury clods of earth from their old hometown together, "where their hearth had been; that is where their fathers lived and were buried." Religiously, it was forbidden to leave the place where your ancestors rested, and thus a piece of land had to be taken to any new abode.[5]

The importance of a permanent physical home is again stressed when Avram returned from his temporary refuge in Egypt, where he had gone to escape a famine. On his way back to Canaan,

> He went on his journeys from the Negev even to Bet-El, to the place where his tent had been at the beginning, between Bet-El and Ai, to the place of the altar which he had made there at the first.[6]

The Torah notes that Avram returned to the exact location where he had previously lived. In the Talmud, Rav uses this verse as a proof that a person should always lodge in the same place when visiting a city.[7] This verse speaks to the human need for a home base, a familiar location, and familiar structures. Avram found himself in a land where he had no connections and no physical structure to mark his territory or call his own, a stark contrast with the land of his "father's house."

Even though Avram was living a mostly nomadic life in Canaan, one of the first things he did was to build an altar, and he continued to build altars wherever he went. When he traveled from his new homeland for

---

3. Karen Radner, "Death and Burial Practices in Ancient Mesopotamia" in *Encyclopedia of Society and Culture in the Ancient World* (Facts of File, 2007), 315. See also mOhal 18:7 and Rashi bPes 9a *mi lo tanan*. This was also true in ancient Canaan. See Gavriel Barkay, "Burial Caves and Burial Practices in Judah in the Iron Age" in *Graves and Burial Practices in Israel in the Ancient Period*, ed. Itamar Singer (Hebrew), 102 ff.14.

4. BerR 39:1 addresses this challenge by stating that it is better to dwell in the wilderness of Israel than to stay in a palace elsewhere.

5. Joseph Rykwert, *The Idea of a Town* (MIT Press, 1995), 124, who bases this on Fustel de Coulanges, *La Cité Antique*, 154.

6. Bereshit 13:3–4.

7. bAra 16b. The idea is repeated by Rashi in his commentary on this verse.

the first time, he returned to one of these structures. This was one way that Avram marked Canaan as his home, erecting permanent structures. This practice emphasizes the significance of a tangible, built structure in making a place feel like home.

Although Avram was not traveling to Canaan alone, he was leaving deep roots symbolized by his familial house. Once in Canaan, he began establishing roots, building altars, and establishing a home base for future generations.

LECH LECHA

# Prayer in a Set Location

וַיֵּלֶךְ לְמַסָּעָיו מִנֶּגֶב וְעַד בֵּית אֵל עַד הַמָּקוֹם אֲשֶׁר הָיָה שָׁם אָהֳלוֹ בַּתְּחִלָּה בֵּין בֵּית אֵל וּבֵין הָעָי. אֶל מְקוֹם הַמִּזְבֵּחַ אֲשֶׁר עָשָׂה שָׁם בָּרִאשֹׁנָה וַיִּקְרָא שָׁם אַבְרָם בְּשֵׁם ה׳. (בראשית יג:ג-ד)

And he went on his journeys from the Negev even to Bet-El, to the place where his tent had been at the beginning, between Bet-El and Ai, to the place of the altar which he had made there at the first, and Avram called there on the name of the Lord. (Bereshit 13:3–4)

WHEN Avram departed from Egypt, he returned to his former location where he had previously built an altar, "to the place where his tent had been at the beginning." This verse is used in the Talmud to teach that one should have a set place of worship. R. Chelbo connects the practice of having a set place for prayer with Avram, saying that whoever does so is one of Avram's students.[1] The practice is codified as law by Rambam.[2]

Commentators differ as to why it is important to pray in a set place. According to the Netziv, it is best to perform acts of devotion in an established place of worship.[3] This implies that a special aura exists around a place of prayer, which can persist even after worship has ceased in that location.[4] Radak gives a non-mystical reason, writing that "a person's heart is more settled in a place which he frequents."[5] This indicates that it is a

1. bBer 6b and using Bereshit 19:27 as a source. This discussion is found in yBer 4:4 (8b) as well.

2. Hilchot Tefila 5:6.

3. He also quotes bChul 91b, which tells a story about a miracle that allows Yaakov to pray in a location where his forefathers had done so.

4. There are also examples of holiness that is temporary and does not persist. bTaan 21b lists two examples: Mount Sinai and the *Mishkan* in the desert.

5. This idea is also supported by a ruling in the Talmud that you cannot force someone to move houses during a holiday, even if the living situation is improved, as people

matter of comfort and regularity, rather than stemming from metaphysical reasons.

What does a set place of worship entail? The Rosh writes that one should have a specific place to pray within a synagogue. R. Yona Gerondi disagrees, writing that the whole synagogue constitutes one place of prayer, so it should not matter whether someone prays in one corner or the other.[6] In the Shulchan Aruch, R. Yosef Karo rules that a person should have both a set synagogue and a set location to pray within that synagogue.[7]

One could consider the disagreement over set places within a synagogue as an extension of the opinions expressed by the Netziv and Radak. If we are concerned about the aura around a location, then the exact spot within the synagogue should not matter greatly. Instead, the imbued holiness permeating the entire synagogue is paramount. If, however, we are concerned with the devotee's habits and peace of mind, then the specific seat does make a difference.

One possible ramification of this debate would be a synagogue renovation. A renovation does not change the geographical location of the synagogue. However, it does change the interior of the space and as such, it may influence the comfort level and familiarity of the worshipers. In such a situation, new locations of prayer would need to be found. For architects renovating an existing place of worship, sensitivity to the comfort level of the worshippers is therefore needed; perhaps it is even desirable to minimize disorientation by limiting the changes to the interior space.

As another practical ramification, one could ask what would happen if an existing synagogue were to be moved, either all-at-once or taken apart brick by brick and reassembled elsewhere.[8] Such a situation might arise in a community evacuated by the Israeli government, or transported from Europe after the Holocaust, or even in the Messianic Age if exilic synagogues were to be reconstituted in Israel. Several synagogues from around the world have been reconstructed at the Israel Museum in Jerusalem, and the interior of some Italian synagogues have been reconstituted in Israeli communities. There are also examples where the design of one synagogue

---

prefer their own house. See yMK 2:4 (81b).

6. In his commentary on R. Alfasi, Berachot 3b, which may have actually been written by his students.

7. Shulchan Aruch OC 91:19.

8. For an example, the B'nai Abraham synagogue of Brenham, Texas, relocated to Austin in 2014. See Samuel D. Gruber, "Lone Star (of David) Story in *Tablet*, 24 Dec 2014, https://www.tabletmag.com/jewish-life-and-religion/187754/lone-star-of-david-story, retrieved online on 29 Nov 2019. The article mentions several additional examples, including Beth Israel in Charlottesville, Virginia and Adas Israel in Washington, DC.

is copied in another location, as has occurred with 770 Eastern Parkway, the Chabad headquarter. In such a situation, a reconstruction that is identical to the original would make sense if we are concerned primarily with familiarity to worshipers. If the holiness of the location is the main factor, then this is largely irrelevant.

Avram's return to his previous location highlights the importance of having a set place of prayer. This can be viewed as an issue of familiarity and comfort, or one of an accrued metaphysical presence. How we understand this issue may impact whether "a set place" refers to a synagogue in general or a specific location within a synagogue.

LECH LECHA

# Population Density and Urban Planning

וְלֹא נָשָׂא אֹתָם הָאָרֶץ לָשֶׁבֶת יַחְדָּו כִּי הָיָה רְכוּשָׁם רָב וְלֹא יָכְלוּ לָשֶׁבֶת יַחְדָּו.
(בראשית יג:ו)

And the land was not able to bear them that they might dwell together, for their substance was great so that they could not dwell together. (Bereshit 13:6)

THOUGH Avram and Lot originally lived alongside one another, the Torah states that they were compelled to part company "for their substance was great so that they could not dwell together."

While some commentators view this as an excuse for Avram to distance himself from Lot for ideological reasons, most see it as a case of scarce resources. Both Avram and Lot raised large flocks of livestock and grazing land was limited.[1] If Avram and Lot had wished to remain neighbors, their shepherds would have had to range farther from home, an inconvenience that was apparently untenable.

Availability of resources is a basic component of city planning. A city street is typically designed with a certain population density in mind – so many houses with *x* number of occupants. With this calculation in mind, planners can make all sorts of estimates for the number of parking spots needed, how much electrical infrastructure to build, how much sewage capacity to install underground, how many kindergartens to construct, the number of parks to erect, etc. This is one reason why it is necessary to limit the height and size of buildings through zoning. If apartment buildings were zoned to be four stories high but are built with ten floors, there will not be adequate resources available for the residents. If each building adds even one new apartment or subdivides existing apartments, it may disrupt municipal services.

Some cities tackle this problem head-on by linking building rights to

1. As per Rashi and Sforno.

municipal improvements. In this scheme, if a developer requests additional building rights for his property – for example, the right to build ten stories instead of four – the city may opt to grant these rights, but only on the condition that the developer funds the improvement of existing infrastructure. The city may ask for additional parks, wider roads, or greater capacity in the sewage system. In this way, the city can ensure that appropriate resources are available for the real-life population density.

Successful cities, however, do more than just ensure that enough resources are available for their citizens; they also include shared spaces that bring neighbors together. Doing so increases the level of trust and sense of community, but it also enables spaces to be consolidated and used communally. If residents have access to a neighborhood pool, for example, there is less impetus to waste resources building private ones. If safe and well-kept parks are in place, large private lawns become less important. Shared spaces have the additional benefit of helping neighbors get to know one another and thus strengthen the community.

R. S.R. Hirsch writes that this component – the shared resources – was what made Avram and Lot unable to remain in close proximity of one another. If the shepherds had been able to let their sheep graze together, there would have been enough space. Malbim explains that they could not live together because of a lack of trust and an unwillingness to share. The need to separate the flocks reinforced the lack of trust, forming a feedback loop that eventually forced Avram and Lot to separate.

This verse gives us a glimpse of two of the most important components of urban planning. We see the importance of managing resources and ensuring that enough infrastructure is available for the populations. We also see the importance of having shared spaces that promote interaction and trust. Without them, it is difficult for neighbors to dwell together, as Avram and Lot discovered.

# Porches and New Urbanism

וַיֵּרָא אֵלָיו ה׳ בְּאֵלֹנֵי מַמְרֵא וְהוּא יֹשֵׁב פֶּתַח הָאֹהֶל כְּחֹם הַיּוֹם וַיִּשָּׂא עֵינָיו וַיַּרְא וְהִנֵּה שְׁלֹשָׁה אֲנָשִׁים נִצָּבִים עָלָיו וַיַּרְא וַיָּרָץ לִקְרָאתָם מִפֶּתַח הָאֹהֶל וַיִּשְׁתַּחוּ אָרְצָה. (בראשית יח:א-ב)

And the Lord appeared to him by the terebinths of Mamre, as he sat in the tent door in the heat of the day. And he lifted up his eyes and looked and, lo, three men stood by him, and when he saw them he ran to meet them from the tent door and bowed down to the earth. (Bereshit 18:1–2)

Avraham is described as sitting in the opening of his tent following his circumcision. Rashi explains that Avraham situated himself so that he would be in the perfect position to extend an invitation to travelers. Malbim emphasizes that the entrance to his tent was filled with activity, rather than a quiet place for recuperation. Avraham was happy to be in the middle of the action, even in his convalescence.

This incident is followed by three additional scenes that take place in a doorway. The first comes when the visitors tell Avraham that he and Sara will have a son and Sara responds with laughter.[1] Sara's reaction, the most dramatic part of this story, occurs in the tent's opening.

As the narrative continues, the messengers arrive in Sedom. Avraham's nephew Lot greets them at the city gate and invites them into his house.[2] Rashi explains that Lot had been appointed the judge of Sedom and was therefore positioned at the entrance to the city. R. S.R. Hirsch writes that Lot was taking a great personal risk by acting hospitably in such a public location. It seems that Lot was trying to influence his fellow citizens for the better.

A few verses later, Lot is confronted by the townsmen of Sedom for

1. Bereshit 18:10–12.
2. Bereshit 19:1–2.

welcoming the visitors. When the angry citizens surround his house, he is forced to go outside and confront them, closing the door behind him.[3] Lot's closed door contrasts with Avraham's open tent in Mamre and paints an unwelcoming portrait of Sedom. This closed door sets the tone for the type of city Sedom has become. Instead of being welcoming, Sedom is closed, cold, and cruel.

The repeated motif of the doorway as a place of action is no coincidence. The doorway is a small but significant component of domestic architecture that can set the tone for how neighbors interact. The design of doors in suburbia has been a focus of criticism. Suburban houses are commonly built with a deemphasized pedestrian entryway. Often, the face of a house is its garage, as residents drive in and drive out, rarely encountering one another. This arrangement is contrasted with older and denser neighborhoods where houses are more tightly grouped, and porches are a dominant design feature.

In the late 1980s, an architectural movement called New Urbanism coalesced around the goal of creating more personable neighborhoods with places for citizens to interact. New Urbanism pushed for local parks and porches to replace dominant front yards. It called for pedestrian-scale entrances in place of garage doors bordering the street. New Urbanism pointed to the doorway as one of the prime places of activity and interaction. Doors were to set the tone for how neighbors interact with one another.

We see this same emphasis on doors as places of interaction in these Torah verses. Avraham encouraged activity in the entrance to his house and warmly welcomed weary guests. Lot, on the other hand, was forced to defend his door, to keep it shut, and to prevent neighbors from storming the house.

We cannot say whether people interact with each other because of how their houses and neighborhoods are designed; or if, alternatively, they design their built environment to reflect how they wish to interact. However, architecture does have the ability to influence behavior on some level. Avraham's door was geared toward outreach, while Lot's house needed to be a barrier. With Avraham and Lot, the different ways their doorways were used and described make their values abundantly clear.

3. Bereshit 19:4–7.

# The Kitchen "Work Triangle"

וַיְמַהֵר אַבְרָהָם הָאֹהֱלָה אֶל שָׂרָה וַיֹּאמֶר מַהֲרִי שְׁלֹשׁ סְאִים קֶמַח סֹלֶת לוּשִׁי וַעֲשִׂי עֻגוֹת. וְאֶל הַבָּקָר רָץ אַבְרָהָם וַיִּקַּח בֶּן בָּקָר רַךְ וָטוֹב וַיִּתֵּן אֶל הַנַּעַר וַיְמַהֵר לַעֲשׂוֹת אֹתוֹ. וַיִּקַּח חֶמְאָה וְחָלָב וּבֶן הַבָּקָר אֲשֶׁר עָשָׂה וַיִּתֵּן לִפְנֵיהֶם וְהוּא עֹמֵד עֲלֵיהֶם תַּחַת הָעֵץ וַיֹּאכֵלוּ. (בראשית יח:ו-ח)

And Avraham hastened into the tent to Sara and said "'Make ready quickly three measures of fine meal, knead it and make cakes." And Avraham ran to the herd and fetched a calf tender and good, and gave it to the servant, and he hastened to prepare it. And he took butter and milk and the calf which he had dressed and set it before them, and he stood by them under the tree and they did eat. (Bereshit 18:6–8)

Avraham went to great lengths to welcome his guests. The Torah describes his food preparations using the word "hurry" three times and "run" once, emphasizing the urgency with which Avraham fulfilled the commandment of welcoming guests.[1]

Although commentators make note of Avraham's alacrity, they fail to highlight the several stations that Avraham visited to prepare this four-part meal. Avraham began by going to the tent where grinding, kneading, and baking took place so that his guests would have cakes. He continued to his herd to select a source of meat. The cattle also yielded milk and, somewhere nearby, butter was churned. No mention is made of a water source, which we can assume was also needed for food preparation.

To a medieval or even early twentieth-century commentator this would hardly be worthy of attention, as the same reality of food preparation existed for them. Workstations for food preparation could not be located close to each other. Livestock, hearth, and water were found in separate locations. For people living with modern kitchens, however, it should

1. Radak on Bereshit 18:7.

serve as an inspiration and perhaps even as a source of chastisement when considering the (literally) great lengths our ancestors went to prepare food for guests.

By way of comparison, kitchen designers have long been taught about the "work triangle" formed by the sink, refrigerator, and oven/stovetop. When designing a kitchen, the *overall* distance between these three stations is, by rule of thumb, not supposed to exceed seven meters. Conventional wisdom states that any greater distance will be inefficient and tiring for the cook. Kitchens are arranged to minimize the distance needed during food preparation.

This helps explain why the Torah uses the language of hurrying and running in describing Avraham's hasty meal preparations. While running would be unnecessary in an efficiently designed kitchen, Avraham clearly could increase his efficiency by hurrying from station to station.

Reflecting on modern kitchen designs and amenities in comparison to those of the past serves to emphasize the hospitality of Avraham. It should also help us appreciate our current lifestyle and perhaps encourage people to perform the mitzva of welcoming guests.

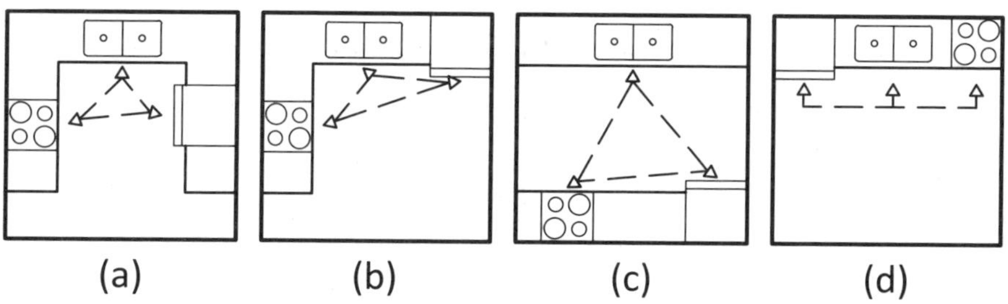


7. Kitchen Layouts: (a) U-shape (b) L-shape (c) parallel (d) straight. (Based on *Neufert Architects' Data*)

# Door Details and Swing Direction

וַיֵּצֵא אֲלֵהֶם לוֹט הַפֶּתְחָה וְהַדֶּלֶת סָגַר אַחֲרָיו. (בראשית יט:ו)

And Lot went out to them at the door and shut the door after him. (Bereshit 19:6)

THE narrative of Lot's confrontation with the people of Sedom centers on his front door. Lot exited and closed the door behind. The mob then tried to break down the door. Lot was pulled back through the doorway to safety and the door was once again closed.[1]

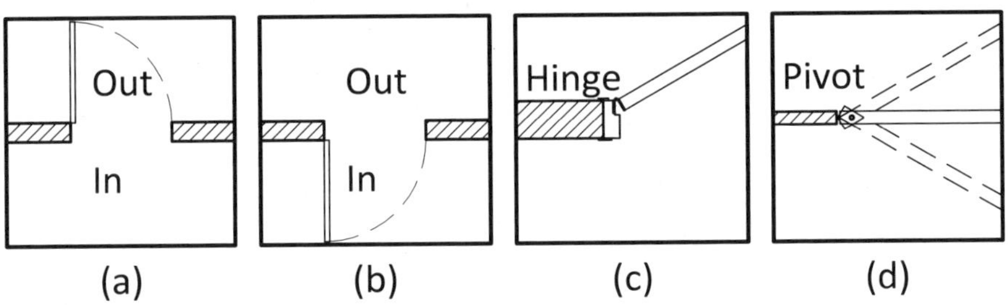


8. Door Openings: (a) outward (b) inward (c) hinge detail (d) pivot detail.

Hinges or pivot doors (as opposed to sliding doors) can open either inward or outward.[2] Legal requirements often exist for the swing direction. For example, doors in hospital bathrooms must swing outward, so that if a patient collapses inside, their body will not impede the door from

1. Bereshit 19:9–10.

2. bShab 6a and 9a teach that the direction in which a door swings alters the jurisdiction of the threshold, whether it is counted as public or private space. R. Moshe Isserles on YD 286:2 describes how the direction of the door swing can affect the hanging of a *mezuza*. BerR 66:5 explains the scene of Bereshit 27:30, with the disguised Yaakov leaving while Esav arrives, with an *istropomata*, a type of double hinged door, whereby the brothers just miss seeing one another.

being opened.[3] Doors that are part of an escape route must swing in the exit direction since in an emergency it is easier to push a door outward than to pull it inward. These doors often require panic hardware, which opens when pushed rather than by the turning of a knob or handle. Panic hardware ensures that the door will open in the event of a crush, when the first person to reach the door may not have time or space to operate a normal door handle.[4]

Residential doors do not usually need to take these concerns into account, as private residences do not have masses of people inside. Instead, their front doors mostly open inward.[5] There are several reasons why this makes sense, some of which are highlighted by the story of Lot. An inward swing makes it easier to admit a guest, who after knocking might get hit by an outward swinging door. When seeking to prevent an intrusion, an inward-swinging door is easier to close while pushing intruders out. If the door were to open outward, then intruders could prevent the door from closing by sticking an arm or leg into the path of the door. An inward swinging door allows one to push the door closed and in doing so, push potential intruders out.

Inward swinging doors are also more secure due to the location of their hinges. While most doors described in the Mishna used a pivot, which could allow doors to swing in either direction depending on the jamb detail, nowadays it is more common to find doors with hinges, that open only in one direction. These usually have the knuckles in the room into which the door swings. If a door swings outward, its hinges will be on the outside of the house, where they are less secure and easier to tamper with. For hinges to be located on the more secure inside, the door should open inward.

An outward-swinging door is also in danger of being blocked from the outside. Vandals or pranksters can pile heavy objects in front of the door,

---

3. This is sometimes circumvented by having a door that normally swings inward but has a special latch that allows the door to be opened outward from the outside. A similar mechanism exists on airplane restrooms.

4. In 1856, a fire in the great synagogue of Lublin resulted in several deaths because the exit doors opened inward. Afterward, Polish authorities surveyed all synagogues in Poland to ensure they were safe. See David Biale, *Hasidism: A New History* (Princeton University Press, 2017), 448.

5. In some hurricane zones, building code requires that doors open outward, because the air pressure caused by hurricanes pushes doors inward. An outward swinging door cannot be blown inward without the door or frame physically being destroyed. Another advantage to outward-swinging doors is that they do not require leaving interior space clear of furniture. This is why one often finds side-doors off of kitchens, living rooms or other furniture-heavy rooms with outward-swinging doors.

trapping those inside. This is also a factor in climates with a lot of snow, which could pile up in front of a door and block it from opening.

In the Torah's story, Lot was outside his house. To rescue him from the mob, his guests had to open the door, pull him in, and then quickly close the door. If the door swung outward, it would have been hard to open with a mob on the doorstep, and getting it closed again would have been difficult. With an inward swinging door, this maneuver would have been simpler to achieve, as closing the door would have simultaneously pushed the mob out.

# Salt as a Building Material

וַתַּבֵּט אִשְׁתּוֹ מֵאַחֲרָיו וַתְּהִי נְצִיב מֶלַח. (בראשית יט:כו)

But his wife looked back from behind him, and she became a pillar of salt. (Bereshit 19:26)

At Avraham's behest, Lot and his family were removed from Sedom before the city's destruction. They were warned not to look back at the devastation,[1] but Lot's wife did not heed the warning and became a pillar of salt.[2] Why was this punishment appropriate?[3]

One midrash explains that Lot's wife had committed a sin with salt. When the three messengers arrived at her house, she went to the neighbors to borrow salt. This was her way of letting the townspeople know that Lot had broken their code and accepted guests into his home. Therefore, Lot's wife was punished with salt.[4]

The transformation of Lot's wife may be seen as a reaction to the natural phenomena in the region. Salt pillars are common in that area, so it is easier to claim that Lot's wife turned to salt as opposed to some other substance.[5]

---

1. Bereshit 19:17.

2. This is not the only instance of execution by salt in history. Al–Mansur, Caliph from 754–775, had a rebel named Abdullah imprisoned in a house built with salt foundations which was then inundated with water. The house collapsed, crushing the prisoner. See Tabari, *The Early 'Abbasi Empire: The Reign of Abu Jafar al-Mansur,* A.D. *754–775* (Cambridge University Press, 2010), 330.

3. Some commentaries consider the salt metamorphosis to be the fate of all the residents of Sedom, and not just Lot's wife. Ibn Ezra writes that she was turned to salt by the brimstone that rained down on the city. R. S.R. Hirsch writes that when she turned around the plague which turned all of Sedom to salt caught up to her.

4. BerR 51:5 (Vilna ed.) in the name of R. Yitzhak. Rashi also quotes this story. TPsY includes it in the translation of this verse.

5. The apocryphal book *The Wisdom of Solomon* alludes to the existence of a specific pillar of salt identified as the remains of Lot's wife. (10.7). Josephus is explicit, saying "I

The history of structures made of salt may suggest an alternative answer. Beyond its culinary uses, salt has a long history as a building material. This can be seen, among other ancient texts, in two passages in the Talmud. The Talmud describes how a block of salt was used to repair the altar.[6] In another case, Rav and Shmuel, third-century Babylonian *amora'im*, argue about whether salt walls may be used as part of an *eruv*.[7] The Talmud suggests that this depends on the type of salt, differentiating between sea salt and mined salt.[8] It concludes, however, that it relates to the structural soundness of the walls.

Several other ancient writers make note of towns built of salt – Pliny the Elder and Strabo both mention Gerra, with its "houses built of square blocks of salt."[9] Herodotus speaks of a Libyan community with houses built of salt.[10] Ibn Battuta, the fourteenth century traveler who chronicled many Arabic communities, visited the salt-mining town of Taghaza in 1352 and described its salt buildings that were roofed with camel skins. Salt is still occasionally used in construction, usually in areas directly connected to salt mining. Bolivia's Salar de Uyuni salt flats boast a hotel made entirely of salt, the Palacio de Sal. Salt mines sometimes contain carved-out religious spaces, to help reassure the miners in their difficult and dangerous work. The Wieliczka Salt Mine in Krakow, in use for over 700 years, has several chapels carved out of salt. It is a UNESCO world heritage site. In Punjab, the Khewra Salt Mine contains a small mosque made of salt bricks. Claude-Nicolas Ledoux designed the columns at the entry to his Royal Saltworks to look like salt crystals. The city name "Salzburg" literally means "salt fortress."

One thing in common with almost all these structures is that they combine tremendous wealth with abject poverty. Until about one hundred years ago, salt was an important but costly commodity. Governments tried to control the supply of salt, which could dependably generate funds.[11] However, salt was often available only in desolate locations or in dangerous

have seen it, and it remains at this day." (*Antiquities*, 1.203) A *beraita* includes it in a list of sites where one must praise God. (bBer 54a).

6. ySuk 4:6 (54d), bSuk 48b.

7. bBB 20b. Rashi explains that Rav felt that salt walls could deteriorate.

8. Jastrow, *Dictionary of the Talmud*, 99. Literally, salt from Sedom or *Istrakonit* salt.

9. Pliny the Elder, *Natural History* 6.32 and Strabo, *Geography*, 16.3. In the previous chapter, Strabo gives a brief history of the Jewish people.

10. Herodotus, *Histories* 4.185. He was a fifth century BCE Greek Historian.

11. The word "salary" also comes from the Latin "salarium" meaning salt-money. yBM 4:2 (9c) mentions a salt merchant reneging on a deal, implying that this was an important transaction.

mines. The people working to extract the salt lived in miserable conditions. They were forced to build their structures from salt because no other suitable building materials were available. While essentially living amidst wealth, their lifestyle was pitiful and wretched.

This symbolism is appropriate for the people of Sedom. Although they lived in an area rich with natural resources, they created for themselves an untenable way of life. When God overturned the valley, he was making the appearance of Sedom match its soul. By looking over her shoulder as she fled, Lot's wife was expressing solidarity with the people of Sedom and thus deserved their fate. The salt pillar symbolizes both wealth and desolation, the very crux of the morality tale of Sedom.

# Cave Dwellings

וַיַּעַל לוֹט מִצּוֹעַר וַיֵּשֶׁב בָּהָר וּשְׁתֵּי בְנֹתָיו עִמּוֹ כִּי יָרֵא לָשֶׁבֶת בְּצוֹעַר וַיֵּשֶׁב בַּמְּעָרָה הוּא וּשְׁתֵּי בְנֹתָיו. (בראשית יט:ל)

And Lot went up out of Tzo'ar and dwelled in the mountain, and his two daughters with him, for he feared to dwell in Tzo'ar, and he dwelt in the cave, he and his two daughters. (Bereshit 19:30)

FOLLOWING the destruction of Sedom, Lot fled his temporary refuge in Tzo'ar and headed for the hills, taking shelter in a cave. Caves were one of mankind's earliest dwellings and have frequently been used as shelters during times of desperation. The Daat Mikre commentary points out that Lot's cave is referred to as "the cave" rather than "a cave" and explains that this cave was stocked with food and wine, either for an emergency or because it was being used for storage.[1]

Although caves have been inhabited throughout history, in most cases they do not qualify as architecture.[2] Rather, they occupy a middle ground between natural feature and domicile. This distinction is relevant to a discussion about Shabbat boundaries, *techumei Shabbat*. The Mishna discusses a case when this boundary – 2000 cubits around a city or habitation – partially overlaps with a neighboring city.[3] Normally one can traverse a city in its entirety without the city's footprint counting against

---

1. See also Sifri Devarim 43 and Rashi on verse 19:33. Other examples of caves as hiding places include bShab 60a, R. Shimon bar Yochai in bShab 33b, yPes 1:1 (27b) which deals with maintaining diurnal rhythms while living underground, and yChag 2:2 (77d) which describes a cave sheltering a coven of witches.

2. The Talmud also points to a cave dweller as lacking basic needs such as light. See yMak 2:5 (31d) and Pnei Moshe *beyoshev beveit afel hi matnita*. A *beraita* in bMen 84b distinguishes between the roof of a cave dwellings and the roof of a house regarding plants that require the taking of first fruits.

3. mEruv 5:9. See also tEruv 3:13, in which there is no disagreement and also no distinction between inhabited and uninhabited caves.

the overall distance of 2000 cubits which one is permitted to walk outside a city on Shabbat. However, there is a disagreement in the case of a partial overlap, where the 2000-cubit boundary falls in the middle of a second settlement. In the debate, R. Akiva attempts to prove his point by invoking a case where residency is established in a cave that is over 2000 cubits long.[4] The sages dispute his assumption and explain that the status of a cave depends on whether it is inhabited. If a cave is inhabited, then the Sages rule that it should be treated the same as a city, with the person being allowed to walk its entire length and an additional 2000 cubits beyond.[5]

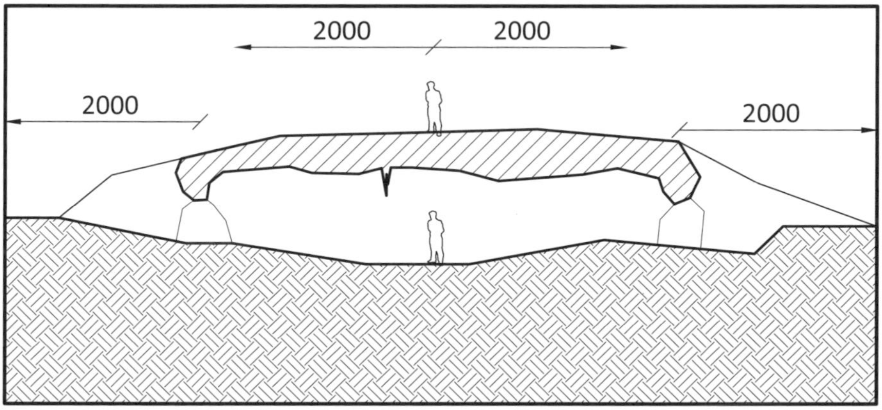


9. Discrepancy in *techumei Shabbat* from inside and outside a cave.

In his commentary on this mishna, Rambam explains that the main factor is not habitation, but whether any walls or other man-made features exist in the cave.[6] If they do, the cave is treated as a city and does not count against one's 2000 cubits. Rambam continues with this point and writes that the same is true for an abandoned or ruined city – if its walls

4. Residency is established either by being present in the cave at the start of Shabbat or by placing an *eruv techumim* – a food portion – there before the start of Shabbat.

5. The Hebrew phrase used is *yesh ba diyurin*. The Mishna also notes that this creates a strange situation in which someone inside the cave is permitted to travel farther than a person standing on top of the cave. See also tEruv 4:10, yEruv 5:8, and yEruv 5:1, in which R. Shimon bar Yochai states he can walk from Tyre and Sidon to Tiveria and Tzipori via caves.

6. This is in line with bEruv 62b and Rashi there. For another example of the special circumstances of living in a cave, and whether it can be dedicated to the Temple, see bMei 20a and Rashi, *amar reish lakish*.

are still standing, it retains the status of a city for the purpose of *techumei Shabbat*.[7]

The point Rambam is making hinges on the in-between status of a cave as both a shelter and a natural phenomenon. In Rambam's opinion, a cave alone cannot be thought of as a structure. However, even minor man-made construction within a cave is enough to render it a house, at least for the purpose of *techumei Shabbat*.

While some commentaries emphasize that Lot's cave had been previously inhabited, the discussion about caves and an *eruv techumim* may call this into question. Lot was told that his city was going to be destroyed, along with all the cities in the region. The reason Lot fled to the mountains and found a cave was presumably because he wanted to get as far away as possible from any inhabited area. Since a cave that has been inhabited and contains man-made walls can, on some level, be considered a settlement, one can imagine that Lot, in his fear from the destruction he witnessed, would not take any chances and would seek out the most desolate and uninhabited cave he could find, without any walls, storage spaces or amenities whatsoever. This understanding may help us gain a proper picture of the pitiful and desperate state of Lot and his daughters and help us understand their subsequent behavior during what they deemed to be the end of the world.

---

7. Perhaps Rambam felt compelled to explain the Mishna in this manner because a cave with an *eruv techumim* in it is, by halachic definition, inhabited. It would therefore make little sense for the point to hinge on whether the cave was inhabited. The Yerushalmi also writes explicitly that the Mishna means that the cave is *fit* for habitation.

# Halachic Parameters of Cemetery Design

שְׁמָעֵנוּ אֲדֹנִי נְשִׂיא אֱלֹקִים אַתָּה בְּתוֹכֵנוּ בְּמִבְחַר קְבָרֵינוּ קְבֹר אֶת מֵתֶךָ אִישׁ
מִמֶּנּוּ אֶת קִבְרוֹ לֹא יִכְלֶה מִמְּךָ מִקְּבֹר מֵתֶךָ. (בראשית כג:ו)

Hear us, my lord, you are a mighty prince among us, in the choice of our tombs bury your dead, none of us shall withhold from you his tomb, but that you may bury your dead. (Bereshit 23:6)

PREPARING for the burial of his wife Sara, Avraham became the first person to create a Jewish cemetery. The Hittites were happy to accommodate Avraham within one of their tombs, but Avraham insisted on having a special place set aside for his family.

The Tosefta records that non-Jews may be buried with Jews due to *darkei shalom*, preserving the peace. Rashi, however, explains that while one should tend to the dead of non-Jews, Jews must have a separate burial ground.[1] Rambam and the Shulchan Aruch both rule accordingly.[2]

In ancient times, Jewish burial took place in different types of venues.[3] While in the earliest periods bodies were left to decompose and then bones were gathered and reinterred, in the Roman period burial took place in excavated caves[4] or mausolea. These practices were primarily for the aristocracy; lower classes were buried in the ground, often on private property.[5] After the Second Temple period, cemeteries became

1. tGit 3:14, quoted in bGit 61a, and Rashi in the Talmud, *im metei yisrael*. For requiring burial of any sort see bSan 46b.
2. Rambam Hilchot Avel 14:12. See Radbaz there. Shulchan Aruch YD 367:1.
3. See survey by Joseph Patrick in "Graves and Burial Practices in Talmudic Sources" in *Graves and Burial Practices in Israel in the Ancient Period* (YBZP, 1994), 190–211 (Hebrew).
4. The dimensions of burial caves are discussed in mBB 6:8 and bBB 100b–101b in one of the most detailed descriptions of dimensions given in the Talmud. See my commentary on Bereshit 49:29. While the Talmud presents an idealized burial cave, many of the excavated sites follow similar patterns, adapted to fit site conditions.
5. This is a why "lost graves" are an issue in rabbinic literature.

more common and we start finding halachically-defined cemeteries in the archaeological record.

Many of the issues that shape cemeteries are universal, applying to Jew and non-Jew alike. Guides to cemetery design, such as J.C. Loudon's *On the Laying Out, Planting and Managing of Cemeteries* from 1843, raise the issues of sanitation, drainage, soil composition, paths through the cemetery, protection of the graves, maintenance, plantings, and upkeep. Space requirements, determined by the size of a human body, dictate how many lots can fit into a given property.

Most of these issues come up in halachic sources as well. The Mishna writes that graves must be at least fifty cubits away from a city, perhaps for sanitary reasons.[6] The cemetery should ideally be fenced.[7] Graves should be laid out in neat rows[8] and oriented in a single direction.[9] In other halachic sources, we find that the graves themselves should be separated by a minimum of one cubit or a partition. The overriding concern is that the burials must be honorable.[10]

The Mishna and Talmud discuss how to distinguish an organized Jewish graveyard from random burials, and in doing so they reveal standard burial practices. If three graves are spaced at regular intervals and the bodies are laid out "in the normal manner" then the area is considered a graveyard.[11] The Talmud further clarifies that the bodies cannot appear to have been killed or fallen haphazardly.[12] The Jerusalem Talmud is more specific, saying that the legs must be straight and the hands placed on the chest.[13]

While halachic sources do not spend much time discussing the landscaping of cemeteries, there are some relevant passages about trees and plants. Cemeteries are not to be used for the grazing of animals nor for the passage of aqueducts, two things you might find in a normal field.[14] Trees

6. mBB 2:9 and Rashi on bBB 25a. Records from the 1800s describe the smell of churchyard cemeteries as overpowering.

7. This helps keep kohanim from accidentally entering, it prevents issues with performing mitzvot in front of the dead, it protects the graves, and it helps create a sacred space. For guarding graves, see bBB 58a.

8. Ramban, *Torat Adam, kevura* – see the final line in the passage.

9. Responsa of R. David Oppenheim printed at the end of *Chavot Yair* by R. Yair Bacharach. (p.135b in the Jerusalem, 1987 reprint of the Lemberg, 1896 edition.)

10. The Religious Authority in Israel requires that graves be spaced a minimum of 50 cm apart, with 80 cm between rows, and that graves be a depth of 120 cm. ("Refresher on Rules of Managing a Cemetery," 20 Nov 2006) (Hebrew).

11. mNaz 9:3.

12. bNaz 65a.

13. yNaz 9:3 (57d). The body should be lying on its back, face up.

14. Shulchan Aruch YD 368:1.

can be planted and their fruit gathered, as long as they are not growing directly on graves.[15] However, while the emphasis is on being respectful to the dead, there is no direct impulse to make the cemeteries idyllic or even well-groomed. In fact, there is a concern with deriving enjoyment from a cemetery. This is a far cry from the trend that began in the nineteenth century to make cemeteries into parks for the enjoyment of all.

*The* issue when it comes to cemeteries is limitations on space. Graveyards eventually fill up, at which point the cemetery cannot generate new income and risks abandonment and disrepair. Otherwise, the cemetery operators must turn to the alternatives of shoehorning in new graves and reusing existing graves.[16] Some non-Jewish cemeteries would routinely add layers of earth, causing the ground level of the cemetery to rise over the years.[17] Halacha does allow this practice, provided that at least six handbreadths of dirt be left above the old grave.[18] However, Jews generally tried to avoid it. Loudon, who argued vociferously against the reuse of graves, even lauded Jewish cemeteries for being the only ones that do not follow this practice.[19] However, this was partially due to the nature of Jewish communities as minorities whose cemeteries were under less demographic pressure. In modern Israel, metropolitan cemeteries have resorted to all sorts of mechanisms to fit the dead into existing cemeteries, including architectural flights of fancy and wall burials.

The laws that pertain to Jewish cemeteries are very similar to the issues facing cemeteries at large. This only serves to emphasize the significance of requiring separate Jewish cemeteries. There is nothing about a Jewish cemetery, per se, that sets it apart, other than the fact that the people buried there are all Jewish. It is a very powerful statement to make, that even in death Jews identify with their tribe and beliefs, one last declaration of belonging. This is the same statement that Avraham made when he set a precedent and insisted upon a separate burial site for his family.

---

15. Ibid 368:2. See also Yechiel Yaakov Weinberg, *Seridei Eish* 3.102, which rules that one may plant trees around the perimeter of an abandoned cemetery to keep it from becoming forgotten but questions the underlying logic of doing so.

16. This reality is evident in yKil 5:2 (29d), which states that sometimes a graveyard begins with wide spaces between graves and later chooses to space them more tightly, but that the opposite never occurs.

17. Norman Cantor, *After We Die* (Georgetown University Press, 2010), 93.

18. Shulchan Aruch YD 362:3–4. Other than respect for the dead, it was important to leave enough earth between corpses to absorb the gases that were released by the decomposing body.

19. Loudon, *On Laying Out Cemeteries*, 2.

10. Burial complex in the Yarkon Cemetery, Tel Aviv.
(Photo by Michael Yacobson, Wikimedia)

# Building on a Historic Site

וַיִּתֶּן לִי אֶת מְעָרַת הַמַּכְפֵּלָה אֲשֶׁר לוֹ אֲשֶׁר בִּקְצֵה שָׂדֵהוּ בְּכֶסֶף מָלֵא יִתְּנֶנָּה לִּי בְּתוֹכְכֶם לַאֲחֻזַּת קָבֶר. (בראשית כג:ט)

That he may give me the cave of Machpela which he has, which is in the end of his field, for the full price let him give it to me in the midst of you for a possession of a burying place. (Bereshit 23:9)

After the death of Sara, Avraham wished to buy a family burial plot. He had a specific property in mind and negotiated with Efron the Hittite to purchase the field, trees, and the Cave of Machpela. Why was Avraham so driven to bury Sara in this specific spot?

The history of any geographical location often begins with understanding its name. Rav and Shmuel argue in the Talmud about the meaning of *machpela*, which they understand to mean "double." Either the cave had two stories, or else it had an outer and an inner chamber. The Talmud then adds a third, supplementary explanation: that couples were buried there in pairs.[1] According to legend, it was the burial place of Adam and Chava, and later three additional couples were to be buried there.

Ramban starts by recognizing that the original meaning of place names is often forgotten as language and population change.[2] He writes that the whole region was known as Machpela, but like so many places whose origins are shrouded in mystery, no one knew the meaning behind the name. Quoting R. Abahu, Ramban explains that the name is a reference to Adam's burial place, as God had folded up Adam's body and buried it in the cave.[3] The Hittites must not have known this, for if they had, the historic site would not have been for sale at any price.[4]

1. bEruv 53a. Rashi quotes this explanation.
2. See my commentary on Bamidbar 32:38.
3. BerR 58:17.
4. Isaac Aboab of Castile (d.1493) in his supercommentary on Ramban contrasts the

How is it that Avraham was privy to the history and significance of the site? The Zohar records a legend that Avraham found the cave while chasing after a ram.[5] When he first saw the cave, he sensed it was a holy place. He investigated and found the outline of Adam and the overturned earth of two graves. Avraham then understood that this was the gravesite of Adam and Chava and decided that he wished to be buried there as well.[6] Abarbanel makes do without a narrative and explains that Avraham simply received divine knowledge of the cave's significance.

According to Abarbanel, Avraham did not seek this burial site because of any innate holiness or special connection with God. Rather, Avraham chose the cave for its historic symbolism. The original forbearers of mankind were buried in that spot and he wanted the originators of the chosen nation to be buried in the cave as well. This would show that he was starting something new and unique and that his offspring were going to have a special status, just like Adam and Chava.

This type of symbolism can be found in architecture as well. We sometimes find a new edifice erected on the ruins of an old, significant structure. The message in this situation is usually one of continuation or replacement.[7] In Jewish history, the most obvious example is the Temple Mount. In Midrash, the location of the Temple Mount had earlier historic significance as the site of the Binding of Isaac and the creation of the world. After the Temple was destroyed, the Romans, Christians, and Muslims all built new places of worship on the site. The Christians and Muslims wished to demonstrate how their faith had superseded Judaism. This type of symbolism can appear in non-religious settings as well. Recently, Israel opened a consulate on Karolinenplatz in Munich, across from the location of the

---

way that Avraham and the Hittites refer to this area as proof of this ignorance. The Hitttites called it "the field in Machpela" while Avraham called it "the cave of Machpela."

5. The allegory of making a discovery after following an animal appears in many stories, such as Shaul searching for his lost donkeys (Shmuel I 9:3), a legend about Aba Shaul chasing a deer and discovering the grave of Og (bNid 24b), the legend of King Edmund, in which a wolf leads people to his severed head, a legend about the discovery of Singapore, Alice and the white rabbit in *Alice's Adventures in Wonderland,* and Shai Agnon's *Maase Ha'ez.*

6. Zohar Chaye Sara 127a. Joseph Rykwert discusses how in ancient times, significant places, such as the site of a new town, had to be revealed by some divine agency. See Joseph Rykwert, *The Idea of a Town* (MIT Press, 1995), 90.

7. This is not always the case. Often the site of a former edifice or Temple is simply a convenient, well-located parcel of land on which to build a new structure. Many of the ancient temples in Rome were converted into churches only long after they were abandoned, and not as a deliberate expression of supercession. See Feyo L. Schuddeboom, "The Conversion of Temples in Rome" in *Journal of Late Antiquity* 10:1 (2017), 166–186.

Brown House, the former Nazi headquarters. This was depicted by the Foreign Ministry as a triumph over the Nazis.[8] Situating a new structure on or near the site of a previous one can thus be a potent symbolic gesture.

For Avraham, the significance of being buried adjacent to Adam and Chava was paramount. It symbolized that he too was a forefather. He specifically sought out the Cave of Machpela to make this point.

8. https://www.ynetnews.com/articles/0,7340,L-4724274,00.html

# Color as a Symbol and Stimulant

וַיֵּצֵא הָרִאשׁוֹן אַדְמוֹנִי כֻּלּוֹ כְּאַדֶּרֶת שֵׂעָר וַיִּקְרְאוּ שְׁמוֹ עֵשָׂו. (בראשית כה:כה)

And the first came forth red, all over like a hairy mantle, and they called his name Esav. (Bereshit 25:25)

The Torah states that Esav was an especially red and hairy baby.[1] While Esav's hairiness is important for us to understand the subsequent narrative, as it is central to the story of Yaakov's deception of his father, why was it necessary to mention that Esav was red?[2]

Most commentators agree that Esav's redness was not merely a physical description; rather, it symbolized an inherent quality in Esav. R. Aba bar Kahana explains that the color red foreshadowed that Esav would cause great bloodshed.[3] He recalls that another biblical figure – David – is described as having the same redness[4] and that in both cases, red symbolizes bloodshed. Kli Yakar connects Esav's redness with his nature as a sly and tricky hunter. Malbim is even more explicit, writing that his redness indicates "anger and jealousy and all the bad traits that are rooted in redness." Other commentators connect red with positive traits of virility and health which Esav possessed.[5]

Although the commentators do not agree on what precisely the color means, they agree that colors can be symbolic and evocative. Red (*adom*) relates on the most basic level to blood (*dam*), or to man (*adam*) and his strength. Red is also used in the Yom Kippur service when a scarlet string changes to white to show the purification of sins. Likewise, a string of blue

1. There is some contention regarding the translation of *admoni* as red. Onkelos, TPsY, BerR, and other commentators give this translation, but Chizkuni disagrees.
2. Siftei Chachamim asks this, adding that Esav's hairiness is important in terms of understanding his name.
3. BerR 63:25, echoed by Rashi in his commentary.
4. Shmuel I 16:12.
5. See Radak and S.R. Hirsch.

in *tzitzit* symbolizes the sea, the sky, and the majesty of God.[6] Purple is used in Megilat Esther to connote royalty,[7] and so on.

Colors hold a strong set of subconscious and emotional attachments. In interior design, colors can be used to subtly alter the mood of a room. Studies have shown, for example, that painting kitchens with certain colors can suppress or stimulate the appetite. Warm earth tones can make a building feel homier, while whites give a sense of sterile coldness. Red is known to stimulate metabolism and appetite, while blue has the opposite effect and suppresses appetite.[8]

Recognizing that red is an appetite stimulant, we can appreciate that Esav's redness is not merely tangential information, but rather foreshadows an upcoming story. This physical quality helps us understand that Esav had a voracious appetite, which was displayed when he returned from the field famished and demanded food from Yaakov.[9] This is reinforced by the red color of the food itself.[10] Just as Esav's hairiness at birth sets up the story about Yaakov's deception of his father, so too Esav's ruddiness at birth portends his inexhaustible appetite and the sale of his first-born rights.

6. bMen 43b.
7. Ester 8:15.
8. Birren, Faber. "Color and Human Appetite" in *Food Technology*, 17 (May, 1963) 45–7.
9. Bereshit 25:29.
10. Bereshit 23:30.

# Texture in Architecture

וַיֹּאמֶר יַעֲקֹב אֶל רִבְקָה אִמּוֹ הֵן עֵשָׂו אָחִי אִישׁ שָׂעִר וְאָנֹכִי אִישׁ חָלָק.
אוּלַי יְמֻשֵּׁנִי אָבִי וְהָיִיתִי בְעֵינָיו כִּמְתַעְתֵּעַ וְהֵבֵאתִי עָלַי קְלָלָה וְלֹא בְרָכָה.
(בראשית כז:יא-יב)

And Yaakov said to Rivka his mother: Behold Esav my brother is a hairy man and I am a smooth man. My father perhaps will feel me and I shall seem to him a deceiver and I shall bring a curse upon me and not a blessing. (Bereshit 27:11–12)

YAAKOV'S main concern with impersonating his brother Esav was that his skin's texture was an obvious giveaway. While Esav was a hairy man, Yaakov's skin was smooth. Yaakov knew that if their father Yitzchak touched him, he would be able to tell the difference, regardless of his poor sight.

An object's texture contains two components: *visual texture* is how its surface appears, based on how the colors and light play on it. *Tactile texture* is how the object physically feels.[1] Since Yitzchak was nearly blind, Yaakov did not have to worry about visual texture. He was only worried about a scenario in which Yitzchak touched his smooth body.

Texture is often used in architecture to attract the eye and create points of interest. Besides creating visual appeal and playing with light, it can also emphasize physical qualities of the building. Sometimes, differences in material can be used as a subtle way of transitioning from one space to another. One who moves from a hard floor to a carpet recognizes that they have crossed into a different area of a building. Imagine going from boardwalk to sand and then to water and you may experience tingles on your feet visualizing the sensation. The textures in a building also affect the sound, with hard and smooth surfaces adding reverberation and echo.[2]

1. Francis D.K. Ching, *A Visual Dictionary of Architecture* (Wiley, 2011), "Design."
2. BerR 65:11 explains Esav's hairiness symbolically, in that he was not easily cleansed

With all the potential cues that texture can provide, it is most potent when two juxtaposed textures are drastically different. If a rough texture appears next to a smooth one, the contrast is obvious and most likely deliberate. Contrasts in texture are highly visible, so they can be used to convey messages about the building. A sharp distinction in materials is an architectural statement, and the viewers should ask themselves what the designer is trying to say with contrasting materials. The contrast in texture indicates a deeper contrast between the different parts of the building.

11. *Fallingwater* by Frank Lloyd Wright. Textures heighten the contrast between horizontal and vertical planes, and the contrast between natural and man-made objects. (Photo by Ariel Irwin)

Yaakov and Esav were a case of contrasting textures. Malbim explains that one could not help but notice their differences. While the twins' voices might have been similar, there was no mistaking their hairiness. Esav was far hairier than the average man and Yaakov was exceedingly smooth. Yaakov was right to fear that his father would notice, because no one could have missed the contrast and because texture is such a noticeable quality, perceptible both visually, tactilely, and perhaps even audially.

While texture is one of the ways in which Esav and Yaakov differed, the Torah makes it clear that there were many contrasts between the two. Color, personality, and temperament are also mentioned. While texture is

from sin, while Yaakov, who was smooth, could easily clear away his sins on Yom Kippur.

so outwardly obvious, Yaakov seems to have been overly worried about it and failed to consider the many other, more intrinsic differences between himself and Esav. Yaakov ultimately *succeeded* in tricking his father by dressing up in hairy garments. It was how Yaakov *spoke* that nearly betrayed him.

While the difference in hairiness was outwardly obvious, it was not the essence of the distinction between Yaakov and Esav. There was a more fundamental, core difference between them. Like many siblings, Yaakov himself must have had a hard time seeing this, or else he would have spent less time worrying about his smooth skin and more time questioning how a person of his character could hope to deceive his father.

# Form and Function

וַיַּחֲלֹם וְהִנֵּה סֻלָּם מֻצָּב אַרְצָה וְרֹאשׁוֹ מַגִּיעַ הַשָּׁמָיְמָה וְהִנֵּה מַלְאֲכֵי אֱלֹקִים
עֹלִים וְיֹרְדִים בּוֹ. (בראשית כח:יב)

And he dreamed and behold a ladder set up on the earth and the top of it reached to heaven, and behold the angels of God ascending and descending on it. (Bereshit 28:12)

Yaakov's dream, in which he sees angels climbing up and down a ladder that reaches heaven, is explained several different ways in various midrashic texts.[1] One interpretation understands the vision of ladder and angels as God showing Yaakov the future Temple in Jerusalem.

This explanation appears in two separate Midrashim: Sifri Bamidbar and Bereshit Rabba.[2] Each midrash breaks down the verse into several elements and explains how each element relates to an aspect of the Temple:

<table>
<tr><th></th><th>Ladder</th><th>Set on the Ground</th><th>Reaching Heaven</th><th>Angels</th></tr>
<tr><td>Sifri</td><td colspan="2">Temple</td><td>Burnt Offerings</td><td>Priests</td></tr>
<tr><td>BerR</td><td>Ramp</td><td>Altar</td><td>Burnt Offerings</td><td>Priests</td></tr>
</table>

The two midrashim have essentially the same message, that Yaakov's dream is a metaphor for the Temple. However, as the above table shows, there is a difference in their emphases. The Sifri writes that Yaakov saw the Temple – the building itself – in addition to the offerings and priests. Bereshit Rabba, on the other hand, makes no mention of the Temple building and instead emphasizes only those aspects that relate to offerings – the

1. Interpretations include (1) it is a metaphor for receiving the Torah at Mount Sinai; (2) it shows the angels preparing to accompany Yaakov beyond the borders of Israel; (3) it symbolized the different exiles to which Bnei Yisrael would be subjected.

2. Sifri Bamidbar 119 and BerR 68:12.

ramp for ascending to the top of the altar, the altar itself, the offerings, and priests.

This minor difference reflects two ways to understand a building's importance. What is the reason for having a Temple? There were certainly periods, before the Temple was built and again during the return to Zion before the Second Temple Period, when an altar was all that was used to bring offerings on the Temple Mount. From one perspective, the Temple could simply be a structure that shelters the altar. From this vantage, the size, shape, and design of the Temple are inconsequential, and there is no need for the building to be included in Yaakov's vision.

On the other hand, the Temple was much more than a shed for the altar. As with all great architecture, it stood for many things – unity of the people, connection with God, power and wealth of the nation, and cultural independence. It recalled the tribes' joint history at Sinai[3] and demonstrated to other nations that God dwelled in Israel.[4] Sefer Hachinuch explains that the building created an atmosphere of awe and reverence which helped individuals reflect on their relationship with God.[5] The Temple stood for all these things and, as such, the building itself held great significance. It could therefore be given equal billing alongside the offerings in Yaakov's vision.

At various points in history, the prophets pointed out that the offerings themselves were less important than the intentions and good deeds of the people. They did not consider the offerings inconsequential but rather believed that offerings also required proper intention. We could add a third tier to our comparison showing not just the Temple and the offerings, but also the intentions of the worshipers. In this equation, we would write:

Temple < Burnt Offerings < Intentions and Deeds

The Temple itself, without burnt offerings, would be akin to having burnt offerings without the proper intentions. However, intentions alone are not enough; burnt offerings are also needed. Burnt offerings are not ideal on their own; they must take place within the Temple, which magnifies their importance and serves many other roles as well.

This same debate takes place in architectural design. Is a building primarily the sum of its function, or can it stand on its own as well, as a piece of sculpture or art? The authors of the influential Post-Modern

3. Sforno on Shemot 25:8.
4. Daat Mikre commentary on Shemot 25:8.
5. Sefer Hachinuch 95.

architectural treatise, *Learning from Las Vegas,* contrasted these two approaches, terming them Decorated Sheds and Ducks (after a building in New York shaped like a duck). In the first, the building is designed around its function and then given superficial ornament to make it presentable. In the second, the building's program is forced into a symbolic shape, which is given primary importance.[6] Perhaps the architecture of the Temple is inconsequential, merely a shelter for the activities that take place within. In such a case, a vision of the burnt offerings is the most precise way to convey to Yaakov the concept of the Temple. However, if the Temple building itself serves a greater, symbolic purpose, beyond the offerings, then it is logical for Yaakov's dream to contain a vision of the Temple as well.

12. The Shrine of the Book, Jerusalem. The roof is designed to mimic the lids of containers that held the Dead Sea Scrolls, thus it would be considered a "duck." (Architects Armand Phillip Bartos, Frederick John Kiesler, and Gezer Heller. Photo by Avishai Teicher)

6. Robert Venturi, Denise Scott Brown and Steven Izenour, *Learning from Las Vegas* (MIT Press, 1993).

In another interpretation of *enayim,* R. Aba states that Tamar turned to a place where many people looked for help.[11] While tetrapyla were mostly used as monumental road markers, the motif of a many-doored building is sometimes invoked to symbolize openness and accessibility. In addition to Avraham, two other people are described in rabbinic literature as having tents open in four directions: Iyov[12] and R. Chana bar Chanilai.[13] In both cases, this anecdote demonstrates their welcoming nature and generosity. In the twenty-first century, the Frank Gehry design for Jerusalem's Museum of Tolerance called for a great hall with "entry doors all along its 360-degree circumference" to symbolize that the museum was open to all.[14] 2018 Pritzker Prize winner Balkrishna Doshi designed the Centre for Environmental Planning and Technology in Ahmedabad without any doors, to encourage open access to education.[15] A structure with many symbolic openings would have been appropriate for someone desperate for help, and again makes the tetrapylon a fitting setting for picturing Tamar's encounter with Yehuda.

11. BerR 85:7.
12. ARN A 7.
13. bBer 58b.
14. Samuel G. Freedman, "Frank Gehry's Mideast Peace Plan" in New York Times, 1 Aug. 2004.
15. This design recalls the story of Hillel on the roof of the *beit midrash* in bYom 35b.

VAYETZE

# Egyptian and Syrian Ladders

וַיַּחֲלֹם וְהִנֵּה סֻלָּם מֻצָּב אַרְצָה וְרֹאשׁוֹ מַגִּיעַ הַשָּׁמָיְמָה וְהִנֵּה מַלְאֲכֵי אֱלֹקִים
עֹלִים וְיֹרְדִים בּוֹ. (בראשית כח:יב)

> And he dreamed and behold a ladder set up on the earth and the top of it reached to heaven, and behold the angels of God were ascending and descending on it. (Bereshit 28:12)

THE central object in Yaakov's dream is the ladder that reaches from earth to heaven. This verse is the only occurrence of the word *sulam* in the Torah, which led some Biblical scholars to suggest that it referred to a ziggurat or other symbolic path connecting heaven and earth.[1] Still, the word is almost always understood to mean "ladder" and it is treated as such in the various traditional commentaries.

There are different types of ladders, each with distinct implications in the context of Yaakov's dream. The two styles of ladders that are most often contrasted are rigid and rope ladders. Rope ladders are more portable and flexible, making them well-suited for curved surfaces, but they are also more difficult to climb. Rigid ladders are supported from below, while rope ladders are hung from above. The wording of our verse implies a ladder fixed to the ground and reaching upward, indicating a rigid ladder.

Another distinguishing feature is a ladder's incline. Some ladders are vertical, or nearly so, and these must be fixed in place lest they topple backward. Other ladders are placed at an angle, which makes them more stable and easier to climb.[2] Modern building codes make this distinction

1. Yitzchak Peleg, "What Do Jacob's Ladder, the Tower of Babel, and the Babylonian Ziggurat Have in Common?" in *Bethsaida in Archaeology, History and Ancient Culture*, ed. J. Harrold Ellens (Cambridge Scholars, 2014), 332. A ziggurat is a tall, stepped temple with a shrine at the top and long stairways connecting each level.

2. The angle of incline is a central component of a discussion in bEruv 78a about a wall between two courtyards with ladders on either side.

and sometimes call for a protective cage around a vertical ladder to prevent falls. Bereshit Rabba makes a point of explaining that the ladder in Yaakov's dream was angled, with its feet in Be'er Sheva and its top reaching above Beit El.[3]

Several rabbinic sources distinguish between "Egyptian" ladders and "Syrian" ladders.[4] While the texts make clear that Syrian ladders are more substantial and permanent, no one is quite certain what distinguishes these two types. These styles existed in the broader context of Egyptian and Syrian construction methods: the Mishna also distinguishes between Syrian and Egyptian windows (Syrian windows are again larger and more substantial)[5] and courtyards.[6] Israel, set between the two larger cultural powers of Egypt and Syria was influenced by these two material cultures and labeled their building types accordingly.

While we mostly think of ladders as having thin rungs that can be used at any angle, step ladders have steps (rather than rungs) that are at a fixed angle, which make them much more stair-like and blurs the distinction between ladder and staircase.[7] A similar distinction may exist in a comparison between attic and dovecote ladders mentioned in the Talmud, where the latter is designed to allow tasks to be performed while perched halfway up.[8] The Talmud also distinguishes between open-tread stairs and solid ones, and these were the two categories of wooden stairs noted in archaeological surveys of Pompeii and Herculaneum.[9] Notched logs served as a primitive form of these devices.[10] Stepladders from this period were far heavier, less mobile, and easier to climb. Perhaps they are the Syrian ladders that appear in our sources.[11]

---

3. BerR 69:17. See also Ramban on Bereshit 28:17 and Rabeinu Bachya on our verse. Joshua Schwartz suggests that this was done to deemphasize Beit El as a potential cultic site. See his "Jubilees, Bethel and The Temple of Jacob" in *Hebrew Union College Annual* 56 (1985), 82.

4. tBM 11:14, yEruv 7:1 (24b), and yEruv 9:1 (25c).

5. mBB 3:6.

6. mMaas 3:5 mentions a "Syrian courtyard" though without mention of a corresponding "Egyptian" courtyard. In this mishna, the Syrian courtyard is larger than a regular one, such that one who brings fruit into it is obligated to tithe it.

7. See Rashi on bEruv 77b, *sheshlivotav porchot.*

8. yBeit 1:4 (60c).

9. Jean-Pierre Adams, *Roman Building: Materials and Techniques* (Routledge, 1994), 410.

10. John Fitchen, *Building Construction Before Mechanization* (MIT Press, 1992), 127.

11. This interpretation seems to be supported by bEruv 77b, and Tosafot *im* there. Elsewhere, Tosafot (bBeit 9b *mai*) distinguish between types of ladders based on their mobility.

Each of these two types of ladders – rung ladders and step ladders – has different implications for our understanding of Yaakov's dream. Yaakov's dream is commonly depicted with a rung ladder rising at an incline. This type of ladder tends to be easier to ascend than to descend and is more portable. Seeing this type of ladder may have been encouraging to Yaakov as he fled Canaan, a reminder that he could take his connection to God with him on his journey.

13. Step ladder made from a notched tree trunk, typical of the Dogon people.

On the other hand, the context of our verse implies a non-portable, site-specific (only in Beit El) apparatus that was anchored above and below, a description that more aptly fits a heavy step ladder. Rather than encourage Yaakov to be at ease in Charan, such a vision would underscore the importance of this specific location and its central role in Yaakov's family's connection to God. This point is reinforced when Yaakov is promised by God that He "will bring you back into this land."[12] The immobile state of the ladder in his vision would thus emphasize the urgency of returning to Canaan.

12. Bereshit 28:15. Yaakov also makes his return to Israel the final clause in his covenant, in Bereshit 28:21.

# Baetyls, Sacred Stones, and Pillars

וְהָאֶבֶן הַזֹּאת אֲשֶׁר שַׂמְתִּי מַצֵּבָה יִהְיֶה בֵּית אֱלֹקִים וְכֹל אֲשֶׁר תִּתֶּן לִי עַשֵּׂר אֲעַשְּׂרֶנּוּ לָךְ. (בראשית כח:כב)

And this stone, which I have set for a pillar, shall be God's house, and of all that you shall give me, I will surely give a tithe to you. (Bereshit 28:22)

THE story of Yaakov's stay in Beit El focuses on the stone pillar he erected.[1] Yaakov picked out a stone to place beneath his head before going to sleep.[2] During the night he had a vision and when he awoke, Yaakov marked his covenant with God by setting up the stone as a pillar and pouring oil on it.[3] He finished his ceremony by declaring that the stone will be God's house and promising a tithe.

Radak explains that one of the purposes of setting up this pillar was to show that Yaakov and his children were the rightful owners of the Land of Israel. Yaakov can build as he sees fit, without needing to get permission from anyone.[4] This point, he writes, is further emphasized by Yaakov naming the place, another imprint of his ownership.[5]

One of the curious aspects of this story is that Yaakov chose to set up a

1. Bereshit 28:11.

2. While it may seem strange to use stones as a pillow, archaeologists have found ancient Egyptian headrests made of stone, ivory and wood, though these were used mainly for the deceased. Burial caves in ancient Israel do often have raised stone headrests. See Gavriel Barkay, "Burial Caves and Burial Practices in Judah in the Iron Age" in *Graves and Burial Practices in Israel in the Ancient Period* ed. Itamar Singer (YBZP, 1994), 117 (Hebrew).

3. Bereshit 28:18.

4. In most places the owner still must get building permits. This requirement is akin to the decrees of Yehoshua upon entering Israel, giving up some personal liberty in exchange for the collective good. See bBK 80b.

5. See Bereshit 26:18 for another example of this phenomenon. There too, almost all the commentaries explain that the significance is to establish ownership.

pillar rather than build an altar, as was done by his father and grandfather in similar instances. Ramban writes that once Bnei Yisrael inherited the land, pillars would be banned as idol worship.[6] He also explains that while an altar is made from many stones, a pillar is monolithic.[7] R. S.R. Hirsch adds that while a pillar is a natural stone, an altar is man-made. He explains that a pillar represents Creation and things we get *from* God, while an altar shows man's involvement and therefore symbolizes offerings *to* Him.

In ancient times, certain special stones were venerated. Often these sacred stones were meteorites, and several Roman coins depict a stone inside a temple. Pliny the Elder refers to these stones as baetyls.[8] Samuel Bochart, a seventeenth-century Biblical scholar, connected this name with the story of Yaakov in Beit El. Later scholars mostly followed his lead, equating the pillar set up by Yaakov with the baetyls and sacred stones known from other religions.

14. Roman coin circa 253 CE in Emesa, showing temple with El Gabal stone. (Classical Numismatic Group)

Augustine Pagolu reconsidered the nature of baetyls and the different biblical stories. He rejected the comparison between the stone in our story and baetyls. Instead, Pagolu argued that the three types – baetyls, sacred stones, and pillars – were not synonymous. Baetyls were generally meteorites with supposed magical qualities. Sacred stones were large stones placed by people as a monument, such as the Kaaba at Mecca and the Linga of Shiva, that were inhabited by deities. The term pillar (*matzeva*) describes several different types of markers: legal stones, marking boundaries, such

6. As per Devarim 16:22. Not all agree that pillars are forbidden. See Ibn Ezra on Bereshit 28:18.

7. See R. Yochanan's opinion in yAZ 4:4 (44a).

8. Pliny the Elder, *Natural History,* 37.51.

as the one set up by Yaakov and Lavan;[9] memorial stones, such as the funerary monument on Rachel's grave;[10] commemorative stones, marking victories;[11] and cultic stones, marking a sacred space. Pagolu identified the pillar in our verse as a cultic stone, marking the location of Beit El as a holy place.[12]

Pagolu's analysis fits with the context of our verse. Yaakov set up the pillar to mark his discovery of Beit El and his covenant. It was a monolithic stone that, according to the midrash, had miraculous qualities, and historic significance as a relic of Yaakov's dream.[13] However, there is nothing in the verses to imply that the stone was anything out of the ordinary. On the contrary, we are told that the stones that Yaakov gathered were "of the place," certainly not meteorites. The stone itself is not imbued with divinity. In the classical sense, despite the similarity of name, the stone of Beit El is not a baetyl.

This analysis also helps us understand why Yaakov did not set up an altar. In other locations, where there was a significant personal event with subjective importance, it was fitting for our forefathers to mark the spot with an altar. In Beit El, where the place held objective and intrinsic importance, rather than subjective importance to Yaakov alone, it was fitting to mark the location with a pillar. No human intervention was necessary to make the spot holy. Yaakov was merely marking Beit El as a sacred location.

---

9. Bereshit 31:46.

10. Bereshit 35:20. After the giving of the Torah, Moshe sets up twelve pillars, matching the number of tribes of Israel. (Shemot 24:4). Rashbam writes there that these were to show that all the tribes agreed to the covenant. R. S.R. Hirsch goes further, explaining that since the twelve tribes were all present, there was no need to represent them symbolically. Rather, these pillars demonstrated that all future Israelites from all the tribes were present at Sinai. "To the tribes of Israel who were present he added symbolically all the future ones in the twelve memorial stones."

11. See Shmuel I 7:12 and 15:12.

12. Pagolu, Augustine. *The Religion of the Patriarchs* (A&C Black, 1998) ch. 4, 135–170.

13. See also bAZ 53b, which distinguishes between a *bimus* and an altar. The former is said to be a single stone, while the latter is comprised of many stones.

VAYETZE

# Safeguarding Shared Resources

וַיַּרְא וְהִנֵּה בְאֵר בַּשָּׂדֶה וְהִנֵּה שָׁם שְׁלֹשָׁה עֶדְרֵי צֹאן רֹבְצִים עָלֶיהָ כִּי מִן הַבְּאֵר הַהִוא יַשְׁקוּ הָעֲדָרִים וְהָאֶבֶן גְּדֹלָה עַל פִּי הַבְּאֵר. וְנֶאֶסְפוּ שָׁמָּה כָל הָעֲדָרִים וְגָלֲלוּ אֶת הָאֶבֶן מֵעַל פִּי הַבְּאֵר וְהִשְׁקוּ אֶת הַצֹּאן וְהֵשִׁיבוּ אֶת הָאֶבֶן עַל פִּי הַבְּאֵר לִמְקֹמָהּ. (בראשית כט:ב-ג)

And he looked and behold a well was in the field and there were three flocks of sheep lying there by it, for out of that well they watered the flocks, and a great stone was upon the well's mouth. And thither were all the flocks gathered and they rolled the stone from the well's mouth and watered the sheep and put the stone back upon the well's mouth in its place. (Bereshit 29:2–3)

YAAKOV arrived at the well in Charan that served as the area's main source of water. He found that the residents had devised a way to protect access to this scarce resource: a large rock had been placed over the well. Only once all the flocks were present could the stone be removed and the flocks watered. Once everyone was finished, the stone could be replaced.[1]

When Rachel arrived, Yaakov unilaterally removed the stone, upending this arrangement. He did not consult with the other shepherds who were waiting, nor did he understand the restrictions in place.[2] Yaakov focused on the perceived injustice of waiting for all the shepherds to arrive but did not appreciate that the stone protected everyone's water rights.

This point is sharpened by the nature of the arrangement. Yaakov was able to move the stone by himself and many commentaries explain that this demonstrated Yaakov's strength.[3] However, even if Yaakov was stronger

1. As per Radak.

2. See Daat Mikre. Compare this with the similar situation in Shemot 2:17, in which the Torah portrays Moshe as righting an injustice.

3. Rashi, Rashbam, and Chizkuni. This despite the previous contrast drawn between

than most men – even if he was the strongest man in the world – is it reasonable to believe that he was two or three times as strong as the average man? The verses tell us that three flocks were waiting to be watered. If Yaakov himself could move the stone, then certainly the combined forces of three shepherds would have been enough to move it. The reason they were waiting to water their flocks was not that they lacked the ability to move the stone; rather, it was because this was a mutually agreed-upon norm designed to provide fair access to all and to prevent any one family from depleting the water resources. No mention is made of Yaakov replacing the stone afterward.

The management of water resources is a major concern for any settlement with a limited supply. Vitruvius describes how Roman cities ensured that no individual could deplete the water supply at the expense of the public at large. Aqueducts would terminate in a reservoir (*castellum*) that was divided into three channels, feeding public pools and fountains, public baths, and private homes. The first, which constituted the drinking supply, was placed in the middle and the pipes were arranged "so that there will never be a shortage of public water, for private citizens will not be inclined to divert public supplies."[4] If the water supply began to run short, the channel that fed private homes was the first to cut off, ensuring that water would continue to reach the public. This system is mentioned in rabbinic literature as well.[5]

Today it is common for public policy to try and ensure that everyone has access to drinking water. When droughts occur, citizens are often banned from watering lawns or washing cars. In Israel, the cost of water rises above a certain level of usage, to help limit egregious consumption. Some might consider this a violation of private rights, but ultimately there is a need to ensure water access for all.

These systems of guaranteed access are quite different from the regulations that are mentioned in the Talmud and Halacha. The Talmud rules that people upriver have no obligation to consumers downriver.[6] One mishna rules that whoever is nearest to an aqueduct has the first right to use the water out of *darkei shalom,* "to preserve the peace."[7] The Talmud quotes an argument between Rav and Shmuel over who gets to use the

---

Yaakov and Esav, in which Yaakov is not portrayed as being particularly strong.

4. Vitruvius, *Ten Books* VIII.6.1–2. Private usage helped fund the system.

5. tMik 4:6. The textual variations are discussed by Daniel Sperber in *Material Culture in Eretz-Israel during the Talmudic Period* (YBZP, 1993), 29–32.

6. bBM 108a. A *beraita* gives the same ruling for springs. The opposite is true for drainage: people downstream need not help repair the drainage system upstream.

7. mGit 5:8.

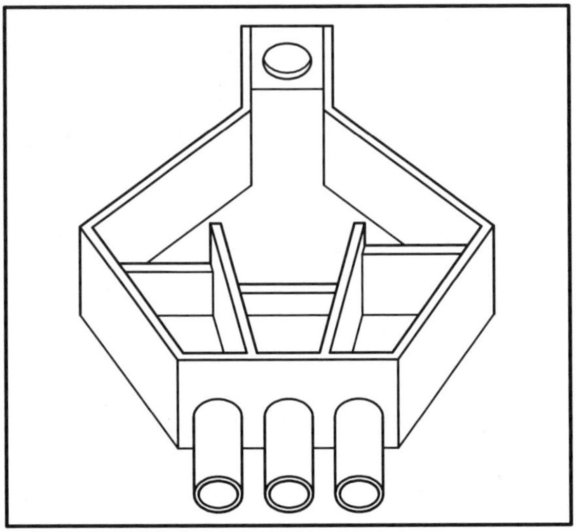

15. *Castellum* from Pompeii, containing three chambers, each with a different height for water cut off.

water first, those downstream or upstream, and ultimately rules that whoever can seize the water is entitled to it.[8] These rulings seem to be in the spirit of Yaakov's actions, preferring a simple "first come, first served" approach. Still, the implication of the phrase *darkei shalom* in the Mishna is that the problem seemed too complex to solve in a logistically plausible manner, but that if such a solution were possible, it would be preferable.

In the story of the well, the "way of peace" was to use a stone to ensure a supply for everyone. While Yaakov may have displayed his strength and temporarily helped his cousin, he also displayed a lack of understanding of local customs. In this way, the story foreshadows his future troubles, when he tries to ignore local customs and marry Rachel instead of Leah.[9]

8. bGit 60b. See also Rambam Hilchot Shechenim 3:9–10 and Shulchan Aruch CM 170:2.

9. See Bereshit 29:26, in which Lavan lectures Yaakov about marriage customs.

VAYISHLACH

# Defensive Cities

וַיִּירָא יַעֲקֹב מְאֹד וַיֵּצֶר לוֹ וַיַּחַץ אֶת הָעָם אֲשֶׁר אִתּוֹ וְאֶת הַצֹּאן וְאֶת הַבָּקָר וְהַגְּמַלִּים לִשְׁנֵי מַחֲנוֹת. וַיֹּאמֶר אִם יָבוֹא עֵשָׂו אֶל הַמַּחֲנֶה הָאַחַת וְהִכָּהוּ וְהָיָה הַמַּחֲנֶה הַנִּשְׁאָר לִפְלֵיטָה. (בראשית לב:ח-ט)

Then Yaakov was greatly afraid and he was distressed, and he divided the people that were with him, and the flocks and the herds and the camels, into two camps. And he said: If Esav comes to the one camp and smites it, then the camp which is left shall escape. (Bereshit 32:8–9)

During Yaakov's journey with his family back to his father's home, he discovered that his brother Esav was coming to meet him with four hundred men. Yaakov feared for his family and split his camp in two. Rashi explains that Yaakov did three things in preparation – he sent presents, prayed, and prepared for war. This division of his camp counted as the war preparations, with Yaakov assuming a defensive position.

How would splitting into two groups help Yaakov's family? The verse describes Yaakov's thinking: if one group were attacked, the other could still escape. This gambit aimed to sacrifice a portion of the family to save the rest. Ibn Ezra postulates that if Esav attacked one camp, the other camp would stand a better chance: either Esav's fury would be sated, or perhaps God would intervene and save the others. Sforno gives an additional possibility: while the first camp was being looted, the others would be able to take advantage of the distraction and escape. One of the lessons Bereshit Rabba learns from this is not to put all your eggs in one basket.[1]

Ramban takes the same lesson of Bereshit Rabba in a different direction, explaining it regarding national defense. He writes that the Jews were

1. Lit. "A man should not put all his money in one corner." See BerR 76:8–9. This idea can also be found in bBM 107a, which counsels diversifying assets into grain, olives, and vineyards.

destined to be living under the rule of Esav for many years. This biblical story was a hint that in times when one kingdom of Esav would persecute its Jews, another kingdom would welcome them. This pattern repeated many times throughout history. It hints at the idea of a widespread diaspora as a defensive tactic: by spreading out across many countries, the Jews would have a greater chance of overall survival.

Rabeinu Bachya expands on Ramban's idea. He too explains that in the future, Jews would find themselves in a similar situation. They could learn how best to respond to challenges from Yaakov's response of prayer, presents, and fighting. However, Rabeinu Bachya is careful to caution against the third approach: "It is forbidden to respond with war, as it says 'I had you swear, daughters of Jerusalem ...' that we swore not to wage war against the nations.[2] Although the best response would be all three methods, he writes that Jews have sworn an oath not to fight against the nations, so war is no longer a viable option, except perhaps to assume a defensive position.

Just as Yaakov set up his camp based on defensive concerns, historically cities were planned with defense in mind. Large walls protected the city's inhabitants and elaborate schemes were drawn up to create "the ideal defensive city." One example was the sixteen-sided, star-shaped city called Sforzinda, theorized by Filarete for the Duke of Milan in 1461–2. Another defensive city, Palmanova, was built in Italy. Many similar examples have been devised.[3]

In modern Israel, architecture continues to reflect this mindset. War conditions have changed drastically since the Renaissance, but this merely changes the nature of defensive architecture. Any building erected in Israel must include a shelter, complete with air filtration, to protect the inhabitants from attacks and allow them to survive rockets or chemical warfare. These requirements came out of the trauma suffered by Israel during the Gulf War in the early 1990s and serve as a proactive defensive measure against possible attacks. One could also point to the repeated attempts by the State of Israel to disperse its population throughout the country, rather than keeping it concentrated mainly on the Coastal Plain, akin to Yaakov's splitting his family in two.[4] In these ways, the defensive tactics adopted by Yaakov continue to find expression in Israeli architecture and urban planning.

2. bKet 111a. The verse quoted is from Shir Hashirim 2:7.
3. Spiro Kostof, *The City Shaped* (Thames and Hudson, 1999), 161, 186–192.
4. See my commentary on Devarim 7:22.

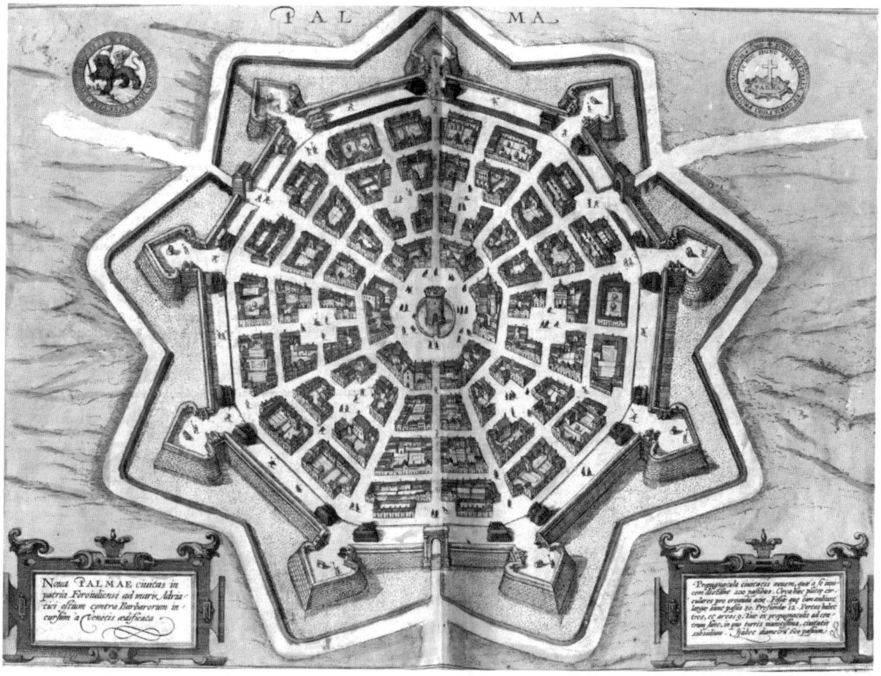


16. Palmanova. (Georg Braun and Franz Hogenberg, *Civitas Orbis Terrarum V*, 1598)

VAYISHLACH

# Rhythm and Intervals

וַיִּתֵּן בְּיַד עֲבָדָיו עֵדֶר עֵדֶר לְבַדּוֹ וַיֹּאמֶר אֶל עֲבָדָיו עִבְרוּ לְפָנַי וְרֶוַח תָּשִׂימוּ בֵּין עֵדֶר וּבֵין עֵדֶר. (בראשית לב:יז)

> And he delivered them into the hand of his servants, every drove by itself; and said to his servants: Pass over before me and put a space between drove and drove. (Bereshit 32:17)

YAAKOV sent several flocks of animals to Esav in an attempt to appease his brother and prevent the slaughter of his family. Yaakov instructed his servants to space themselves out, arriving one drove at a time.

While some commentaries see the spacing of the flocks as a practical concern – Yaakov did not want the various species to mix and become unruly – Rashi explains that this was a design decision. He writes that Yaakov wanted to "please the eye" of Esav and to make the gift seem larger. R. Yaakov Slonik expands on this statement: Yaakov recognized that he was sending animals of different shapes and sizes. If they were not properly spaced, the flocks would appear disorganized and ungainly. He made sure to space them in a way that would make the spectacle attractive and impressive to Esav.[1]

The principles that are expressed in these commentaries are discussed by Vitruvius in his chapter on architectural terms and the basics of design. Vitruvius explains ordering (*ordinatio*) and design (*dispositio*), by which he means the modular layout of the building according to a grid, so that the major elements of a building are arranged symmetrically, with divisions and subdivisions that are spaced evenly.[2] This type of organization is one of the main tools at an architect's disposal.

1. See his commentary, *Nachalat Yaakov*, on this verse.
2. Vitruvius, *Ten Books on Architecture* I.2.2–3 and commentary by Thomas Howe, who ties these terms to the Ecole des Beaux-Arts concept of *parti*. Vitruvius uses the

Alexander Tzonis and Liane Lefaivre examined the primacy of rhythm in Classical architecture, writing that "Repetition, or periodic alternation of compositional units, makes the work stand out in relation to the amorphous random spaces that characterize the surrounding world."[3] Tzonis and Lefaivre focus on the emergence of stressed and unstressed elements, using the columns and intercolumnar space in a portico as an example. The rhythm shapes and controls the space, imposing an order on the environs. Placing columns with regular and even intervals between them allows for an appealing visual image to emerge. Yaakov sought to do something similar with the way he spaced out his gifts, creating order and rhythm that would impress and delight his brother.

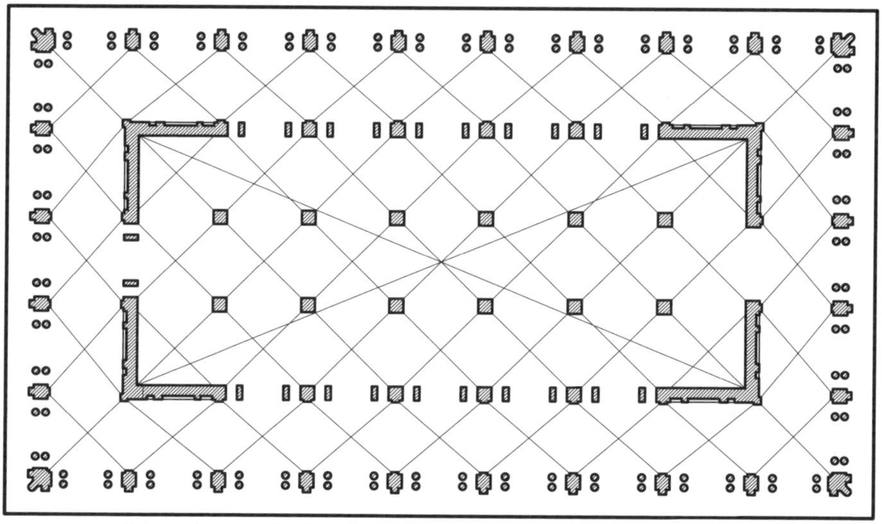

17. Intercolumnar rhythm. (Based on diagram in Palladio's *Four Books of Architecture*, III.42, 1570)

Later in life, Yaakov demonstrates a similar concern with organization. A midrash describing how Yaakov arrayed his sons around his deathbed uses the Greek word *taxis* to describe their deliberate arrangement.[4] This same term is used by Vitruvius to describe how architects must carefully organize a building's individual components while considering how

concept of intervals to connect architecture and music, as spacing influences both optics (in architecture) and rhythm (in music). See *Ten Books on Architecture* I.1.15–16.

3. Alexander Tzonis and Liane Lefaivre, *Classical Architecture: The Poetics of Order* (MIT Press, 1986), 118.

4. Tanchuma (Buber) Bamidbar 12, BamR 2:7.

together they form an overall picture.[5] Just as Yaakov took care in arranging his sons around his deathbed, we can infer that he took similar care in the proportions, rhythm, and symmetry of his gifts to Esav.

Rashi famously explains that Yaakov took three steps to defend his family: he sent presents, prayed, and prepared for battle.[6] While Rashi sees Yaakov's instructions to space out the gifts as a way of enhancing them, there may have been an additional motive. By creating a pattern in space and time, Yaakov was imposing his order on the surrounding area. This could have helped intimidate and deter his brother, like the marching of a well-trained battalion.

Yaakov strategically planned out his presents and deployed every tactic he could think of to maximize his chance of success, including controlling the appearance of his gifts. The effort made the gifts more appealing and helped Yaakov project his power.

---

5. Vitruvius, *Ten Books on Architecture* I.2.1–2. See also Tzonis and Lefaivre, 9–28.
6. Bereshit 32:8.

# Bridges and Fords

וַיָּקָם בַּלַּיְלָה הוּא וַיִּקַּח אֶת שְׁתֵּי נָשָׁיו וְאֶת שְׁתֵּי שִׁפְחֹתָיו וְאֶת אַחַד עָשָׂר יְלָדָיו
וַיַּעֲבֹר אֵת מַעֲבַר יַבֹּק. (בראשית לב:כג)

And he rose up that night and took his two wives and his two handmaids and his eleven sons and passed over the ford of the Yabok. (Bereshit 32:23)

IN preparation for Esav's arrival, Yaakov transferred his family across the ford of the Yabok River.

Not all rivers have a proper bridge. The Talmud relates a story about R. Zeira, who traveled to Israel and could not find a crossing. When no bridge is available, people resort to other methods, such as ferries, stepping stones, and planks, or simply fording the river. One halachic passage in the Talmud describes a makeshift bridge with a guide rope.[1] Even when bridges are present, they are not necessarily safe. Reish Lakish believed that men are judged when they cross bridges, implying that he viewed this activity as perilous.[2] Other stories in rabbinic literature relate that bridges were narrow and rickety, further emphasizing the perception of danger.

Although we know of bridges in the Middle East dating to at least the seventh century BCE[3], it was the Romans who began building bridges systematically.[4] The Romans built at least one bridge over the Yabok.[5] This Roman involvement with infrastructure is reflected in the debate between R. Yehuda, R. Yosi, and R. Shimon bar Yochai about the contributions of the Romans to society. R Yehuda praised their bridge building, while R.

1. bBeit 7b and Rashi *mitzra*.
2. bShab 32a.
3. Colin o'Connor, *Roman Bridges* (Cambridge University Press, 1994), 1.
4. Though judging by the story of R. Zeira, even their bridge building program was not comprehensive.
5. The Yabok is usually identified as the Zarwa River, a large tributary of the Jordan.

Shimon bar Yochai argued that the bridges were built for toll collection, not altruism.[6] While one could argue about the true motivation for Roman bridge building, it is generally accepted that they did improve the infrastructure in the area.

Despite the river's significant role in this story, it is not obvious why Yaakov crossed the river, nor why he did so at night. The story comes amid Yaakov's preparations for meeting Esav. Perhaps the river crossing was part of Yaakov's defensive strategy. However, the verse clearly says that Yaakov transferred *all* his wives and children, while previously he had planned on splitting his camp in two. Furthermore, Yaakov was able to carry his children across the river in darkness, so presumably this river was no great obstacle. When Esav arrives, there is no mention of the river – he approaches Yaakov and embraces him without interruption. Therefore, it seems that the river did not pose an obstacle to Esav's approach. Esav may even have been on the Canaanite side of the Yabok.

To properly appreciate the encounter, it is important to consider that river crossings are natural bottlenecks and places of relatively heavy traffic. Travelers must funnel toward them.[7] Crossings also serve as control points, where governments can collect tolls or regulate movement. The ford of the Yabok was potentially a place where Esav could have blocked Yaakov from reentering Canaan. Yaakov had taken an oath in Beit El that he would return to his homeland.[8] He may have been in a hurry to cross the river back into Canaan so that when he encountered Esav, it would be without any unfulfilled obligations.[9] This also sheds light on the wrestling match that later occurs, perhaps a last-ditch effort to delay Yaakov's return to Canaan.

Bridges and fords serve as chokepoints for travelers. Yaakov recognized that to ensure his successful return to his homeland he needed to cross the river before Esav arrived, prompting his nighttime crossing of the Yabok. This maneuver did not relate to his previous plan to split his camp in two to take up a defensive position. Rather, it was to ensure that all his oaths were fulfilled before his encounter with Esav.

---

6. bShab 33b. See my commentary on Bereshit 33:18 for additional discussions of this story. See also bAZ 2b for a different version of the same debate.

7. O'Connor, *Roman Bridges*, 2.

8. Bereshit 28:21 and 31:13.

9. BerR 76:7 and DevR 1:15 relate that Yaakov was concerned about his encounter with Esav due to his brother's scrupulous performance of "honor thy father." Similarly, he may have been concerned about his own overall merits in light of his absence from Canaan.

# The Defining Characteristics of Cities

וַיָּבֹא יַעֲקֹב שָׁלֵם עִיר שְׁכֶם אֲשֶׁר בְּאֶרֶץ כְּנַעַן בְּבֹאוֹ מִפַּדַּן אֲרָם וַיִּחַן אֶת פְּנֵי הָעִיר. (בראשית לג:יח)

And Yaakov came in peace to the city of Shechem, which is in the land of Canaan, when he came from Padan Aram, and encamped before the city. (Bereshit 33:18)

WHEN Yaakov and his family arrived at Shechem, they set up camp outside the city. Some commentaries state that Yaakov preferred to keep his distance. However, one rabbinic tradition explains that Yaakov was trying to improve the city by providing new amenities, doing so out of gratitude to the people of Shechem for their hospitality. The Talmud has three suggestions for what Yaakov may have introduced: coinage, markets, or bathhouses.[1] Another opinion states that he set up stores, which helped lower prices.[2]

This interpretation of our verse appears in the Talmud as part of the narrative of R. Shimon bar Yochai emerging from isolation in a cave. As he approached Tiveria, R. Shimon bar Yochai decided that he would make improvements to Tiveria, emulating the actions of Yaakov. In this context, the discussion of civic improvement is particularly relevant, as R. Shimon had been forced to hide following a debate about the improvements wrought by the Romans – streets, bridges, and bathhouses – in which R. Shimon took a negative stance.[3] By reporting that R. Shimon chose to make similar

1. bShab 33b.

2. ySheviit 9:1 (38d), BerR 79:14, PdRK 11:16, and KohR 8. See also Michal Bar-Asher Siegal, *Early Christian Monastic Literature and the Babylonian Talmud* (Cambridge University Press, 2013), 133–148, note 49.

3. This is according to the Talmud Bavli version of the story. See also parallel discussion of this issue in bAZ 2b.

contributions to Tiveria, the Talmud seems to be acknowledging the value of these items and questioning only the motivation of the Romans.

The description of Yaakov's relationship with the city of Shechem – at least before the abduction of Dina – is a classic example of what makes a city dynamic. Yaakov arrived at the city and set up camp, presumably for the benefits he would get from being nearby. In turn, he strengthened the city by introducing new improvements. Both parties benefited from the interaction.

Many of the important characteristics of a city can be seen in this story. The city of Shechem had physical borders, which Yaakov did not enter. The city had a social hierarchy, led by Shechem and Chamor, who were able to impose a rather drastic decision upon the populace. The area in which Yaakov camped – *pnei ha'ir* – was akin to the hinterlands, which provide cities with food and resources, and in return received protection and services. Yaakov was presumably drawn to the city to be a part of these hinterlands and reap the corresponding benefits.[4] He in turn strengthened the city, whether with markets, the ability to exchange goods for labor, or public works.[5] Yaakov was not just benefiting from the city, he was participating in the exchange of ideas and enabling its existence *as* a city.[6] Cities draw people into them, and those people make contributions that strengthen the city. This symbiosis is what makes cities dynamic and significant.[7]

This may also explain why Shechem would indulge his son's lusty whim

4. Yaakov's outrage at the danger Shimon and Levi caused to the family after their massacre may hint at this motivation. While Yaakov moved near to the city for protection and benefits, the outcome was drastically different.

5. The Talmud rules that it is forbidden to live in a city without a doctor, bathhouse, court, and perhaps locally grown food. See yKid 4:12 (66b).

6. The city criteria presented here are based on Spiro Kostof, *The City Shaped* (Thames and Hudson, 1999), 37–41. Discussing the requirements of a city of refuge, the Tosefta gives its own list of requirements for a city, including water supply, markets, and significant population. See bMak 10a, yMak 2:6 (31d) and tMak 3:8, which leaves out markets. See also my commentary on Bereshit 4:17, relating to why Kayin responded to his curse by founding a city.

7. It should be noted that the second half of this story, with the abduction of Dina, takes a decidedly gloomier view of cities, one of moral turpitude, corruption, and mass murder. Another view of the city can be found in bBM 107a, explaining the verse Devarim 28:3, "Blessed shall you be in the city and blessed shall you be in the field." The blessing of the city is being close to amenities, such as the synagogue and the toilet, while the blessing of the field is being near your source of income. This is reminiscent of the argument made by Ebenezer Howard in *Garden Cities of Tomorrow* (Swan Sonnenschein & Co., 1898), which imagines cities that are large enough to have major public works, but small enough to be pastoral.

and willingly go along with the plan to undergo circumcision. Shechem presented the plan to his populace as a way to get rich: "Shall not their cattle and their substance and all their beasts be ours?"[8] While this can be read as simple greed, it can also be seen more nobly, as recognition that to become a great city they must be open to accepting new groups into the populace. If, as the midrash explains, Yaakov did introduce new amenities to the city, it is easier to understand why the people of Shechem were willing to bring the Israelites into their community, even at the cost of adopting their cultural norm of circumcision.

---

8. Bereshit 34:23.

# Avraham's Tent As a Tetrapylon

וַתָּסַר בִּגְדֵי אַלְמְנוּתָהּ מֵעָלֶיהָ וַתְּכַס בַּצָּעִיף וַתִּתְעַלָּף וַתֵּשֶׁב בְּפֶתַח עֵינַיִם אֲשֶׁר עַל דֶּרֶךְ תִּמְנָתָה כִּי רָאֲתָה כִּי גָדַל שֵׁלָה וְהִוא לֹא נִתְּנָה לוֹ לְאִשָּׁה.
(בראשית לח:יד)

And she put off the garments of her widowhood and covered herself with her veil and wrapped herself and sat in the entrance of Enayim, which is by the way to Timna, for she saw that Shela was grown up and she was not given to him as a wife. (Bereshit 38:14)

TAMAR situated herself "in the entrance of *Enayim*." Commentators struggle with interpreting this term. *Enayim* seems to refer to a known geographic location, on the way to Timna,[1] but this location is not mentioned elsewhere in Tanach.[2] Instead, many commentators look to the literal definition of the word *enayim* – "eyes" and posit that it means a highly visible place. Some suggest a crossroad,[3] and in the retelling of this story in Sefer Hayovlim, Tamar sat at "the gate on the road to Timna."[4] Rashbam, building on this tradition, writes that *enayim* was "the gateway of a crossroad."

Elsewhere, R. Alexandri explains that Tamar sat in the opening of Avraham's house, which was "a place in the public eye."[5] In two midrashim, Avraham's house is described as having four doorways. One midrash tells that Avraham opened a free inn with entrances in four directions so that no one would be embarrassed to be seen entering.[6] In another, R. Abahu

1. As per Ibn Ezra and R. Chanin on bSot 10a.
2. R. Ami's opinion, BerR 85:7.
3. Rashi, Sforno, Radak, and Saadia Gaon.
4. Sefer Hayovlim 41:9.
5. bSot 10a and Rashi *metzapot liroto.*
6. Midrash Tehilim 110:2, quoted in Rabeinu Bachya on Bereshit 22:1.

explains that Avraham's tent was open in all directions. He uses the Greek loanword, *pilon,* meaning "gate," to describe this setup.[7]

Taking these descriptions together, it seems that the Rabbis, seeking an appropriate, contemporary setting for the story of Tamar, pictured a Roman monument called a tetrapylon. A tetrapylon is a grand, four-way gate situated at a crossroad. Archaeologists suspect that there was one in Jerusalem[8] and there are remains of two tetrapyla in Gerasa, Jordan. A tetrapylon in Caesarea is mentioned several times in rabbinic literature as a prominent landmark.[9] While there is not much ancient literature describing activities that took place alongside tetrapyla, it is a fitting place for the Rabbis to depict the disguised Tamar taking shelter as she waited for Yehuda.[10]

18. North Tetrapylon in Gerasa. (Photo by Jean Housen, Wikimedia)

7. BerR 48:9.

8. Yoram Tsafrir, *Eretz Israel from the Destruction of the Second Temple to the Muslim Conquest, II* (YBZP, 1984), 61,66 (Hebrew).

9. For example, tOhal 18:13. See also Daniel Sperber, *The City in Roman Palestine* (Oxford University Press, 1998), 125 note 32. While some were composed of four adjoining arches, others consisted of four pillars. This may be the distinction mentioned in yKil 4:2 (29b) and may explain why R. Aba bar Mamel says in ySuk 1:1 (52a) that one may not carry under a tetrapylon.

10. An alternative version, quoted by R. Eliyahu Mizrachi and explained by Yafe Toar and Nachalat Yaakov, states that *enayim* was Avraham's burial cave. Midrash Mishlei 9:18 connects the tetrapylon in Caesarea with R. Akiva's burial cave, and indeed tetrapyla were associated with burial monuments. See also Joseph Patrich, *Studies in the Archaeology and History of Caesarea Maritima* (Brill, 2011), 51–55.

VAYESHEV

# Egress

וַתִּתְפְּשֵׂהוּ בְּבִגְדוֹ לֵאמֹר שִׁכְבָה עִמִּי וַיַּעֲזֹב בִּגְדוֹ בְּיָדָהּ וַיָּנָס וַיֵּצֵא הַחוּצָה.
(בראשית לט:יב)

And she caught him by his garment saying: Lie with me, and he left his garment in her hand and fled and went outside. (Bereshit 39:12)

YOSEF managed to withstand the advances of Potifar's wife only by escaping from her house. The Torah seems to repeat itself, stating both that Yosef fled and that he went outside. Sforno explains this repetition by saying that once Yosef fled the room, he was able to leave the house in a more dignified and unharried manner.

Another way of understanding this repetition is by looking at the issue of egress in building code. While nothing in the text describes the design of Potifar's house, Yosef would have benefited from a house with well-designed exits, or egress. In the retelling of this story in Sefer Hayovlim, Potifar's wife had locked the gate of the house. Yosef was forced to break the lock to escape, highlighting the importance of unimpeded egress from a building.[1] Egress can be a life-or-death issue, allowing safe escape from a building on fire. Modern building codes generally require a safe corridor clear of obstacles and with fire-resistant walls, wide enough to accommodate the occupants in the building. No room can be beyond a certain distance from an exit. Dead-end passages are forbidden, to avoid waylaying people fleeing a building.[2] In public buildings, two or more exits are usually required, spread across the building, with sufficiently wide doors and panic hardware that will open when pushed, so that no one will get crushed while fumbling to open a door. These measures help ensure that in the case of a

1. Sefer Hayovlim 39:9–10.

2. R. Nachman demonstrates sharing wisdom with a parable about a large palace that has so many doorways that people cannot find their way out. A wise man comes and hangs up exit signs, allowing everyone to successfully find their way outside (ShSR 1:8).

fire or other emergency, the people in the building have a good chance of escaping. Designing a building that adheres to these codes has the triple merit of avoiding stumbling blocks, distancing people from danger, and following the law of the land.

A comparable situation that exists in halacha is the case of someone who becomes ritually impure while inside the Temple. In such a scenario, the person must exit the Temple expediently. The Rabbis discuss what it means to exit expediently – must one take the most direct route, or must one flee as quickly as possible?[3] Is every extra second in the Temple considered problematic, or must one avoid taking any unnecessary steps in the Temple while impure? We might consider a similar question in fire safety: are we concerned with having direct exits from a building, or exits that can be reached quickly? On the one hand, the goal is to get people out of a building as quickly as possible. On the other hand, the farther one must walk, the greater the chance that one will encounter the blazing fire blocking their safe passage. Therefore, fire safety design accounts for both proximity of exits and ensuring that the passages are wide enough to allow occupants to flee quickly.

Rabbinic literature describes at least two examples of crowds in a space without good egress, both with tragic endings. In one case, defenders of a city rushed into a building to retrieve their weapons, causing a crush of people, and leading to mass casualties.[4] In the second case, Jews were hiding in a cave during a time of persecution. The crowd panicked and ran to escape, again leading to a great loss of life.[5] In both cases, the Rabbis recognized the need to enact legislation to protect individuals in similar situations, but the resulting laws only narrowly addressed the problems.[6] They did not tackle the overarching and fundamental need for safe egress from all structures.[7]

3. bShev 17a.

4. tEruv 3:6 and quoted in yEruv 4:3 (21d) and in bEruv 45a in a modified form, saying "they knocked into one another and killed one another to a greater extent than the enemy."

5. bShab 60a. In an alternative reading, they were in a synagogue.

6. Allowing people to keep their weapons at home and forbidding the type of shoe that made the footprint which set off the panic. However, these enactments can perhaps be seen as historical reminders of the need for safe egress. Another example appears in mYom 2:1 – an injury was sustained when a kohen broke his leg falling off the altar ramp. Rather than install a railing, a safer method for choosing a priest to perform that rite was instituted. R. Yisrael Lifschitz writes in his Tiferet Yisrael commentary at the end of Kodshim that the altar ramp did have a railing.

7. For some medieval laws addressing fire safety, see Lewis Mumford, *The City in History* (Mariner Books, 1968), 283. However, most of the concern for fire safety in the

Returning to the story of Yosef, we can understand what seems like a repetition in the verse. When the Torah says that Yosef fled and went outside, we can appreciate that this is no trivial matter. In the event of danger, it is human instinct to flee and try to escape. However, Yosef was lucky in that he fled in the right direction. Rather than running blindly and remaining trapped, he was able to navigate the building and make it safely outside.

---

ancient world and beyond seems to be with ensuring that fire does not spread, rather than helping those trapped.

In two other halachic situations, the Rabbis establish a minimal opening size for different purposes. An opening of 4 × 4 cubits is the minimum viable passage for combining two *eruvin*, as per mEruv 7:1 and yAZ 4:12 (44b). A similar ruling exists with openings for the spread of impurity, as per mOhal 3:6. While neither case is exactly analogous to safe egress, they do demonstrate the concept of a minimum size for a viable passage.

# Prisons

וַיִּקַּח אֲדֹנֵי יוֹסֵף אֹתוֹ וַיִּתְּנֵהוּ אֶל בֵּית הַסֹּהַר מְקוֹם אֲשֶׁר אֲסִירֵי הַמֶּלֶךְ אֲסוּרִים
וַיְהִי שָׁם בְּבֵית הַסֹּהַר. (בראשית לט:כ)

And Yosef's master took him and put him into the prison, the place where the king's prisoners were bound, and he was there in the prison. (Bereshit 39:20)

YOSEF was imprisoned as a punishment for his alleged crime. The Torah specifies that the prison was "the place where the king's prisoners were bound" and commentators differ as to why this clarification is needed. While some believe that it was because the term *beit hasohar* was foreign and required an in-text explanation,[1] others write that it distinguishes this prison – which held prisoners of the crown – from the common prison.[2]

Instead of these two explanations, perhaps the text is emphasizing the abnormal nature of Yosef's incarceration. To explain this, we can compare this stint in jail with Yosef's previous imprisonment, when Reuven convinced his brothers not to kill Yosef and to instead cast him into a pit.[3] The two cases are connected by the use of the term "pit," which appears twice to describe Yosef's release from the Egyptian prison.[4] However, Yosef's two imprisonments had very different purposes. The purported goal of the brothers was to passively execute Yosef, leaving him alone in a desert. The Torah informs us that Reuven planned to save him, but the other brothers agreed with the plan to leave Yosef for dead.[5]

1. Ibn Ezra.
2. Ramban, who adds that this is to explain how Yosef ends up in a cell with two royal servants.
3. Bereshit 37:22.
4. Bereshit 40:15 and 41:14.
5. See Rashbam and Ramban, Bereshit 37:22.

In contrast, Yosef's imprisonment in Egypt was not an execution. In ancient times, prisons were usually holding cells, used temporarily while judgment was being rendered. This is what happened to the Chief of the Butlers and the Chief of the Bakers, who were placed in Yosef's cell to await their fates. This was also true of other instances in the Torah, such as the Wood-Gatherer in the desert[6] and Yosef's brothers in Egypt.[7] However, Yosef's internment seems to have been an anomaly. Yosef anticipated a quick resolution, but the incarceration dragged on. He stuck around longer than most prisoners and eventually was made a manager of the prison because the prison was not designed for long-term incarceration. Perhaps this is why a midrashic explanation for Yosef's unique circumstances was needed. According to midrash, the angel Gavriel appeared before the king and defended Yosef, proving he was innocent. However, so as not to embarrass Potifar and publicize that his wife had tried to seduce Yosef, Yosef was jailed long-term, a highly unusual occurrence.[8]

The goal of imprisonment has implications for how a prison is designed. When Yosef's brothers wanted him dead, the only requirement was that there be no escape possible. A pit served this purpose well. A holding cell, however, has additional requirements: the prisoners must be secured, but also kept in good shape for the short-term. When prisons are intended for long-term incarceration, they take on a different set of design needs.

The modern idea and design of prisons stem from reforms that began in the seventeenth and eighteenth centuries to do away with corporal punishment. Previously, rulers tried to deter crime by threats of torture and humiliation, like whipping and stockades, or gruesome executions. Prison, as in our story, was a short-term solution. However, with reform, it was adapted as a more humane deterrent and one that could instead rehabilitate criminals.[9] This era of reform produced the most famous architectural design for a prison. The Panopticon, a radial prison with a central guard tower, aimed to allow a small number of unseen guards to supervise many prisoners.[10] As a product of an era that believed in the power of design to alleviate the ills of society, prisons required a different form to match their new purpose. While no prisons were ever built exactly according to the

---

6. Bamidbar 15:34. In this case the Torah is explicit about his imprisonment to await judgment. See also bSan 78b.

7. Bereshit 42:17.

8. TPsY Bereshit 47:22 and quoted by Chizkuni on our verse.

9. The Romans also used incarceration in a similar manner, as we know from the treatment of martyrs. However, the method fell out of use in the Middle Ages.

10. It could also be used for other institutions that require supervision, such as hospitals, schools, asylums, and factories.

Panopticon blueprints,[11] the spirit of this design is still very much alive in modern prisons, which continue to be used for long-term incarceration, even if most of the ideals for humane reformation have been jettisoned.

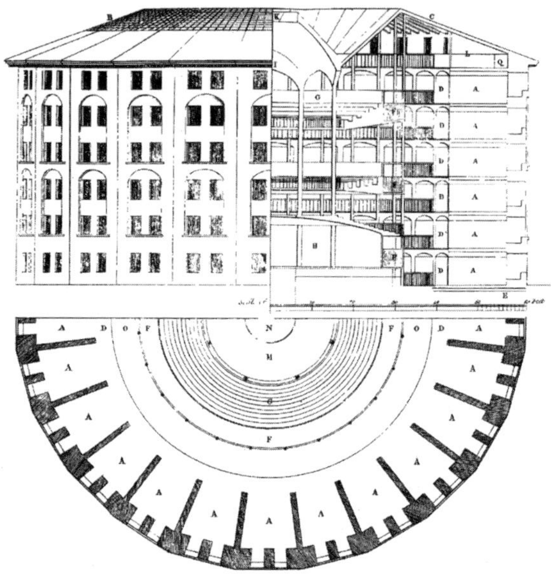

19. Jeremy Bentham's Panopticon in plan and section. (Willey Reveley, *The Works of Jeremy Bentham* IV, 172, 1843, Wikimedia)

When we think about Yosef's imprisonment, it is misleading to consider it in terms of the modern prison, where imprisonment is the punishment itself. Prison in ancient times could be a torture and execution device, as the brothers intended it, or it could be a holding cell, as in Egypt. The Torah tells us that the prison was a place for prisoners to be held, to help set up our expectation that Yosef will soon be judged and either released or punished. Yosef likely had no expectation to be held long-term in Egypt, which helps us understand the strange nature of his protracted incarceration.

11. There have, however, been many prisons inspired by the design. One such prison is the Koepelgevangenis in Arnhem, Netherlands, which means "domed prison." This recalls the Rabbinic practice of locking people in "domes" as a way of passively executing them. (see mSan 9:3, tSan 12:8, and bSan 81b) While it is not clear why domes are specified, perhaps this is related to underground cellars that were common in Israel and were often bell-shaped. Perhaps some such spaces were used for these prison cells, with the prisoners being lowered from above. This is suggested by R. Alexander Kohut in the *Aruch HaShalem* IV.290.

# Moisture Control

וְיִקְבְּצוּ אֶת כָּל אֹכֶל הַשָּׁנִים הַטֹּבֹת הַבָּאֹת הָאֵלֶּה וְיִצְבְּרוּ בָר תַּחַת יַד פַּרְעֹה אֹכֶל בֶּעָרִים וְשָׁמָרוּ. וְהָיָה הָאֹכֶל לְפִקָּדוֹן לָאָרֶץ לְשֶׁבַע שְׁנֵי הָרָעָב אֲשֶׁר תִּהְיֶיןָ בְּאֶרֶץ מִצְרָיִם וְלֹא תִכָּרֵת הָאָרֶץ בָּרָעָב. (בראשית מא:לה-לו)

And let them gather all the food of these good years that come and lay up grain under the hand of Pharaoh for food in the cities, and let them keep it. And the food shall be for a store to the land against the seven years of famine which shall be in the land of Egypt, that the land perish not through the famine. (Bereshit 41:35–36)

After interpreting Pharaoh's dream, Yosef suggested that the Egyptians gather surplus food during the predicted seven years of plenty, for use during the lean years. Pharaoh selected Yosef to oversee this operation.

The commentators identify Yosef's main difficulty as preventing the stored grain from decaying in the climate of Egypt.[1] Ibn Ezra explains that it was necessary to store the grain together with desiccant, which draws moisture out of the air. R. Nechemia lists a type of dirt that helps preserve the grain.[2] Ramban also mentions desiccant, naming one such substance, *chomtin*.[3] He seems more concerned with drying the grain, rather than drawing the moisture out of the atmosphere. Historically, removing moisture from grain has been the tactic of choice, as each type of grain has an optimum moisture content for long-term storage. However, if the grain is not dried, it can still be stored in an air-tight silo or with acid as a mold

1. Egypt's dry climate is actually good for preserving grain. The greater threat seems to be infestation. See Dr. H.Z. Levinson, "Storage and Insect Species of Stored Grain and Tombs in Ancient Egypt." In *Journal of Applied Entomology* 100:321–339 (Jan 1985).
2. BerR 90:48.
3. Mentioned in bShab 31a, possibly from the Greek word for sand. He adds that mercury can be used to kill worms.

inhibitor.[4] Elsewhere, the Talmud assumes some grain will always be lost during storage and discusses how much grain is considered "normal" loss.[5]

In addition to drying out the grain, it was necessary to make sure that the granaries were impervious to moisture. Granaries, along with other storage facilities such as archives, are especially sensitive to water damage. Ancient technical manuals describe important details in designing granaries. Some were designed with thick walls and divided into chambers, in part to help prevent dampness from intruding.[6] Vitruvius wrote that granaries should be elevated and not face north or northwest.[7] Marcus Terentius Varro, a Roman scholar who lived in the first century BCE, wrote about the necessary ventilation and interior finishes. He emphasized the chemical treatment needed to prevent infestation and to preserve the quality of the grain.[8] Pliny the Elder also mentioned the various treatments of grain that were used in his day.[9]

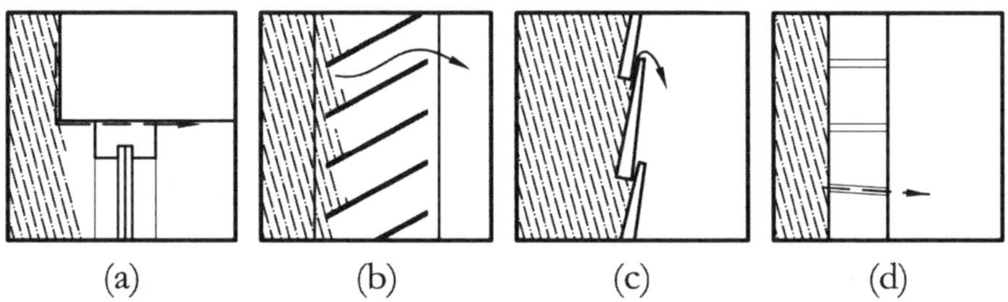


20. Water penetration of the building envelope via (a) surface tension (b) air currents (c) capillary suction (d) gravity. (Based on a diagram by Christine Beall, "Water Penetration in Building Envelopes" in *Interface*, Oct. 2000, 29)

Even in buildings that are less sensitive than granaries, architects must take care to design the exterior in a way that prevents water from entering buildings. Defenses usually include a waterproof membrane along the

4. Donald Brooker, *Drying and Storage of Grains and Oilseeds* (Springers Science and Business Media, 1992). Today most grain is dried with heat, though attempts have been made to dry grain with desiccants. See S.L. Sturton et al, "Drying of Cereal Grains with the Desiccant Bentonite" in *Canadian Agricultural Engineering* (23:101–103, 1981).

5. mBM 3:7. yBM 3:5 (9b) implies that the primary reason for loss is mice, as does Rashi on bBM 40a *im hayta mida meruba.*

6. As with the Tabularium in Rome. See James C. Anderson Jr., *Roman Architecture and Society* (Johns Hopkins University Press, 2002), 262.

7. Vitruvius, *Ten Books on Architecture,* VI.6.4.

8. Varro, *On Agriculture* 1.57. He mentions that farmers treat their grain with amurca.

9. Pliny the Elder, *Natural History,* 18:73. He writes "There is a certain earth found at Olynthus, and at Cerinthus, in Euboea, which prevents grain from spoiling."

perimeter of the building. Nonetheless, the assumption with most exterior walls is that water will manage to penetrate the envelope. Water can seep through walls in several ways: it can be driven in by wind or gravity, it can be drawn in through capillary action, it can condense on the interior, it can enter due to surface tension (if there is no drip for shedding rainwater) and it can be pulled in by a difference in air pressure.[10] Good design must limit water penetration, but also includes a way of removing water that *does* penetrate the building's defenses. This is usually accomplished by drainage built into the walls, but desiccant is sometimes used. Building joints are treated with both external flashing, to keep water out from the onset, and internal flashing, to remove water that does penetrate the walls. Masonry walls are equipped with weep holes – small openings that allow water to escape. Drains are also important on the outside of buildings so that groundwater does not build up around the foundations.

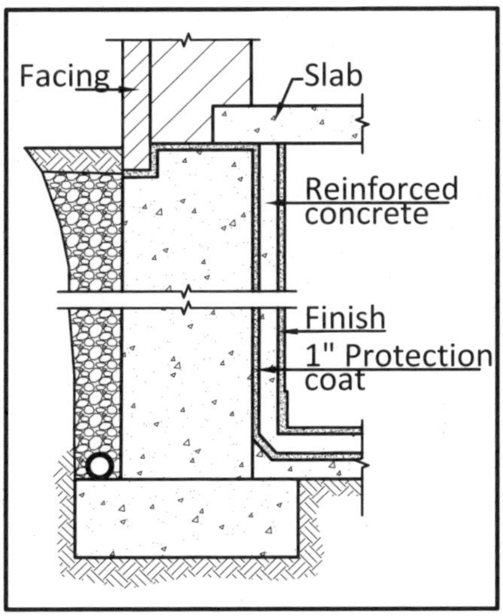


21. Exterior waterproofing detail.
(Based on *Architectural Graphic Standards*, Third Edition, 53)

Double-glazed windows have a similar problem, as water can penetrate between the two panes of glass and condense, reducing visibility. With glass, it is not practical to introduce a hole at the base of the window, so instead a desiccant, often zeolite spheroids, is placed at the perimeter between the two panes of glass to absorb any water that does get in.

10. Christine Beall, "Water Penetration in Building Envelopes" in *Interface* (Oct. 2000) 29–36.

To keep buildings dry and prevent mold, it is both important to keep moisture out and to remove moisture that does penetrate the façade. Although we can assume that early Egyptian techniques were vastly different from our own, Yosef's solution for storing grain would have had to deal with these same difficulties.[11] Keeping the grain dry was a matter of life-and-death for the Egyptians. The fact that Pharoah trusted Yosef to oversee the effort demonstrated the monarch's absolute trust in him.

11. Perhaps ironically, Yosef would eventually be mummified, which usually entailed packing the body cavity with desiccant. See Sehdev Shama, *Five Great Civilizations of Ancient World* (Educreation Publications, 2017), 34.

MIKETZ

# Pharaoh's Throne

אַתָּה תִּהְיֶה עַל בֵּיתִי וְעַל פִּיךָ יִשַּׁק כָּל עַמִּי רַק הַכִּסֵּא אֶגְדַּל מִמֶּךָּ.
(בראשית מא:מ)

You shall be over my house and according to your word shall all my people be ruled, only in the throne will I be greater than you. (Bereshit 41:40)

PHARAOH appointed Yosef to a new position, telling him that "only in the throne will I be greater than you." In this phrase, the word "throne" represents Pharaoh's position as king. While today it is more common to use the term "crown" as a stand-in for the king, the effect here is the same.[1] This type of reference is called a metonym.[2]

The Maharal elaborates on this point, asking rhetorically "what is the greatness of a chair?"[3] Yet despite his dismissal of the idea, furniture size does often reflect the level of importance in a bureaucracy. Office plans usually call for larger offices and larger desks for managers. This extends to chair size as well. Pharaoh's throne was almost certainly bigger than Yosef's chair. The reason it is a good metaphor is precisely because we understand that Pharaoh's chair is the largest. The Talmud makes this point as well when it states that the word "chair" denotes a king.[4]

Rabbinic literature refers to several types of seats. Most chairs at the time would have been stools, but sometimes there are references to a *cathedra*. While in the Roman world this term usually denoted a chair with a back and no arm rests, Jewish sources use it to mean a chair with

1. See Rashi and R. Eliyahu Mizrachi's supercommentary.
2. Another example is calling the president of the United States "the White House." The title Pharaoh is also a metonym, as the word means "great house."
3. In his Gur Aryeh commentary on this verse.
4. bSan 20b, quoting Divrei Hayamim I 29:23.

both. It was considered a seat of honor.[5] For example, members of the Sanhedrin were said to sit on seventy *cathedrae*,[6] and the famous synagogue in Alexandria had seventy *cathedrae* as well.[7] These chairs were larger and more impressive than standard ones, bestowing honor on their occupants.

Similar to the throne of Pharoah, Shlomo's throne is mentioned (twice) in Tanach[8] and described elaborately in various midrashim. These texts mention ornate carvings of animals and historical figures, lavish materials, and mechanization that assisted Shlomo to climb the stairs, crown him, and deliver a Torah into his hands.[9] Not only does Tanach describe a grandiose throne, but it also specifies that the throne was greater than any other throne in the world. Here the chair is being used not only to reinforce Shlomo's role as monarch but also to demonstrate his greatness over all other kings.

A large chair can be used to broadcasts authority. By mentioning chair size, Pharaoh was signifying to Yosef that he was going to be more than a trusted advisor. While we might expect Pharaoh to keep his foreign consultant out of the public eye, this tells us that Yosef's role would not be hidden. Rather, his importance would be broadcast to all, and he would enjoy all the normal trappings of leadership.

---

5. Karen Kirshenbaum, *Furniture of the Home in the Mishnah* (YBZP, 2013), 87–8 (Hebrew). In Greek, a chair with arm rests and a back was called a throne.

6. RutR 2:2.

7. Kirshenbaum, *Furniture of the Home*, 94–5.

8. Melachim I 10:18, Divrei Hayamim II 9:17.

9. VayR 20:1 tells that if someone other than Shlomo tried to sit on his throne, the mechanized lions would harm them. In terms of technological feasibility, Hero, a first-century Alexandrian engineer, describes automated songbirds, door-openers, and trumpeting in *Pneumatics* 1.15–17, 38.

# Lumber for the Mishkan

וַיִּסַּע יִשְׂרָאֵל וְכָל אֲשֶׁר לוֹ וַיָּבֹא בְּאֵרָה שָּׁבַע וַיִּזְבַּח זְבָחִים לֵאלֹקֵי אָבִיו יִצְחָק.
(בראשית מו:א)

And Yisrael took his journey with all that he had and came to Be'er Sheva and offered sacrifices to the God of his father Yitzchak. (Bereshit 46:1)

ON his way to Egypt to reunite with Yosef, Yaakov stopped in Be'er Sheva to offer sacrifices. Some commentators focus on the mention of Yitzchak, who was explicitly forbidden from leaving Israel for Egypt,[1] and conclude that Yaakov was praying for permission to go into exile.[2] However, according to a midrash, Yaakov had a different mission to complete on the way to Egypt. In this alternative explanation, Yaakov went to Be'er Sheva to harvest cedar trees that had been planted by his grandfather Avraham.[3] The trees were to be used in the future for the central bolts of the *Mishkan*,[4] which required exceptionally long, thirty-two-cubit poles.[5] To ensure that such poles would be available when it was time to build the *Mishkan*, Avraham planted the trees decades earlier.

1. Bereshit 26:2.
2. See Ramban, Radak, and Sforno.
3. BerR 94:4, ShSR 1:55. See also yTaan 1:6 (64c) and Korban HaEida *a'ayn d'shitin* there. R. Levi adds that the trees were planted in Migdal Tzvai, and the people of that village left the trees in perpetuity since they were consecrated. These trees are alluded to in Bereshit 21:33. Victor Hurowitz emphasizes the ceremonial act of harvesting lumber in Mesopotamian building projects. See his *I Have Built You an Exalted House* (Sheffield Academic Press, 1992), 212-214.
4. As required in Shemot 26:28.
5. Other than this midrash, the central pole is usually listed as thirty cubits long. In *Beraita Demalechet Hamishkan* 1, R. Yosi gives a length of thirty-one cubits. See also bShab 98b and Tosafot there, *tana*.

22. Mishkan wall panels.
(Based on drawing by the Temple Institute)

Yaakov harvested them and brought them to Egypt, where they were kept for the duration of the enslavement.[6]

One can understand why the poles of thirty-two cubits (~48 feet or 14.6 meters) required some advanced planning. For reference, the longest standard length of lumber in the United States is twenty-four feet. Still, cedar trees can easily grow to more than fifty feet, with most species boasting an average height of over one hundred feet. Most cedars are also relatively fast-growing, with a growth rate of up to two feet per year. While poles of the required length could thus be attained, it would still require some forethought, specifically if they were needed in the middle of a desert. This is why the midrash felt it necessary to explain how Bnei Yisrael obtained such lengthy poles during the construction of the *Mishkan*.[7]

While having access to long pieces of lumber was necessary for fashioning the poles, we can also gain insight into the details of the *Mishkan*

6. A separate midrash tells that Yaakov and his sons planted cedars in preparation for the future *Mishkan* and its wall panels. This is described as a way of giving his sons strength that their stay in Egypt would not last forever. See Midrash Tanchuma Teruma 9:14.

7. An anecdote about the difficulty finding lumber is told regarding the church of St. Denis, in which the abbot felt his successful search was miraculous. See Erwin Panofsky, *Abbot Suger on the Abbey Church of St-Denis and Its Treasures* (Princeton University Press, 1979), 97.

by considering how a tree is processed into lumber. Making rectangular sections of wood is straightforward, as you only need to cut along planes. However, obtaining a round section of wood for the poles requires a lathe, on which the wood is turned and shaved down to size.[8] While a rectangular section of consistent dimensions can be achieved without specialized equipment, it would be very difficult to obtain a round section of wood, thirty-plus cubits in length, with a consistent diameter.

The central pole in the *Mishkan* was designed to key together the separate wall panels that made up the *Mishkan*. The pole had to be inserted through a horizontal cavity in the middle of the wall panels that were coated in gold[9] and thus the poles needed to be perfectly smooth and straight. Despite the difficulty in manufacturing a round pole with a consistent radius, most illustrations show the central beam with a round section. Instead, it would make more sense if the pole had a rectangular section. This would have been easier to produce and would have done a better job of securing the walls of the *Mishkan*, as the rectilinear section would also help prevent the wall panels from rotating.

---

8. For the use of small lathes during the Second Temple period to produce large stone vessels, see Uzi Leibner, "Arts and Crafts, Manufacture and Production" in *The Oxford Handbook of Jewish Daily Life in Roman Palestine*, ed. Catherine Hezser (Oxford University Press, 2010), 237.

9. *Beraita Demalechet Hamishkan*, 1.

# Shifting Populations

וְאֶת הָעָם הֶעֱבִיר אֹתוֹ לֶעָרִים מִקְצֵה גְבוּל מִצְרַיִם וְעַד קָצֵהוּ. (בראשית מז:כא)

And as for the people, he removed them to the cities, from one end of the borders of Egypt even to the other end. (Bereshit 47:21)

The people of Egypt, deprived of food, were forced to give up their livestock and then their land to Pharaoh, becoming his servants. Following Yosef's mass purchase of the people's land in exchange for grain, Yosef forcibly relocated the population. What was his reason for doing so?

One explanation is that moving the people was a way for Yosef to emphasize Pharaoh's new ownership of the land. Once relocated, the people no longer had a strong claim to ancestral territory. Yosef wanted to ensure that no one would be able to claim a connection to the land and try to take it back.[1] In this explanation, his motivation was to protect Pharaoh's interests.

Another possibility is that Yosef was looking out for his own family. Yosef wanted his brothers to settle in a separate and secluded district, Goshen. To do so, he first had to clear out the people who were living there. Yosef had to move the existing population so that his family could benefit.[2]

A third interpretation is that the famine and land repossession caused a general upheaval in Egyptian society that ushered in a period of urbanization. The Egyptian farmers no longer had their own land to work and as a result, they needed to find a new source of income. Yosef helped facilitate this by moving the people from the country to cities.[3] This is a pattern that

1. Rashi, Radak, Rashbam, and Chizkuni. This tactic was later used by the Babylonians after their conquest of the Kingdom of Yehuda.

2. HaEmek Davar. bChul 60b states that Yosef wanted to prevent the family from being referred to as "exiles."

3. As per Malbim.

occurs in times of famine. Something similar may have happened in the Land of Israel in the third century.[4]

While community upheaval and migration are not uncommon, one of the important factors in successfully navigating such a displacement is preserving community bonds that help provide mutual support. R. S.R. Hirsch noted that although Egyptians were uprooted, Yosef made sure to move whole communities and resettle them together, to minimize the turmoil.[5] Yosef arranged:

> That the residents who had always lived together remained together and found themselves still together with their friends but only in a fresh environment. So that the old social and communal conditions remained the same and there was no complete upheaval by the change.

One of the main sources of grief during the period of urban redevelopment in the United States was that cities went to pains to break apart poor, often black, communities. Urban highways were routed through these neighborhoods, dividing them. While this may have been done to encourage movement from "bad" neighborhoods, one of the side effects was to destroy the community bonds among the populace who relied most on such community support.[6] The breakup of communities made it much harder for people to recover from relocation. Israel saw similar problems during the Disengagement when communities in Gush Katif were dismantled and the populace was not resettled by community.

While the Torah describes vast relocations, R. Hirsch felt that Yosef tried to minimize the upheaval and inherent difficulties for uprooted communities, giving the Egyptians a chance to succeed in their new locales.

4. See Daniel Sperber, *Roman Palestine 200–400: The Land* (Bar Ilan Press, 1978).

5. Communities have halachic standing, as evident in the laws of testifying about *gitin*. See yNed 1:2. (37a).

6. Jane Jacobs criticized this type of "slum clearance" in *The Death and Life of Great American Cities* (Random House, 1961).

# Secondary Burial And Family Burial Chambers

וַיְצַו אוֹתָם וַיֹּאמֶר אֲלֵהֶם אֲנִי נֶאֱסָף אֶל עַמִּי קִבְרוּ אֹתִי אֶל אֲבֹתָי אֶל הַמְּעָרָה אֲשֶׁר בִּשְׂדֵה עֶפְרוֹן הַחִתִּי. (בראשית מט:כט)

And he charged them and said to them, I am to be gathered to my people, bury me with my fathers in the cave that is in the field of Efron the Hittite. (Bereshit 49:29)

As Yaakov's death approached, he commanded his sons to bury him in the family burial plot in the Cave of Machpela. Both in this verse and when Yaakov's life ended, the Torah uses the expression "gathered to his people."[1] This phrase is commonly used in Tanach as a euphemism for death. It is understood by some to focus on the gathering of the souls of the righteous – after a lifetime of serving God, Yaakov's soul was returned to God.[2]

In light of Iron Age burial practices, archaeologists have explained this verse as more than a sanitized euphemism. While later ages focused on the sanctity of the individual, in the Iron Age[3] family was the focus of identity. As such, burial was preferably in a family plot. Interment happened in two stages. First, bodies were laid out in the family burial chamber on elevated platforms. This stage was the "gathering." Several bodies could be on a platform at once. Once the flesh decomposed, the bones were collected and reinterred in an on-site pit or repository.[4]

During the Second Temple Period, burial customs shifted, with a greater emphasis on the individual. Burial caves were designed with separate niches around the perimeter of a chamber. A single body at a time was

1. Bereshit 50:1.
2. See Rashi and Malbim.
3. The Iron Age began roughly two hundred years before the First Temple Period.
4. G. Barkay, "Burial Caves and Burial Practices in Judah in the Iron Age" in *Graves and Burial Practices in Israel*, ed. Itamar Singer (YBZP, 1994), 106–113 (Hebrew).

placed in a niche, which was sized to accommodate a laid-out cadaver. Once the body decomposed the bones were collected and buried in a pit or a burial box.[5] The use of burial niches is reflected in a mishna that describes the design standards for these caves.[6]

Most burial caves were dug out of the soft rock that is typical of the Judean Hills. The chambers were most often rectilinear, showing signs that they were excavated according to a preconceived plan. In the time of the Forefathers and the First Temple Period, most were simple and had only an entrance and one chamber, with three platforms along the walls, excepting the wall with the entrance. For larger complexes, an entrance courtyard could have several chambers leading from it. During the Second Temple Period, the chambers grew larger and had many niches. The Talmud discusses how niches in separate chambers need to be excavated precisely to make sure that one niche did not intersect with another, something that would certainly have required advanced planning.[7]

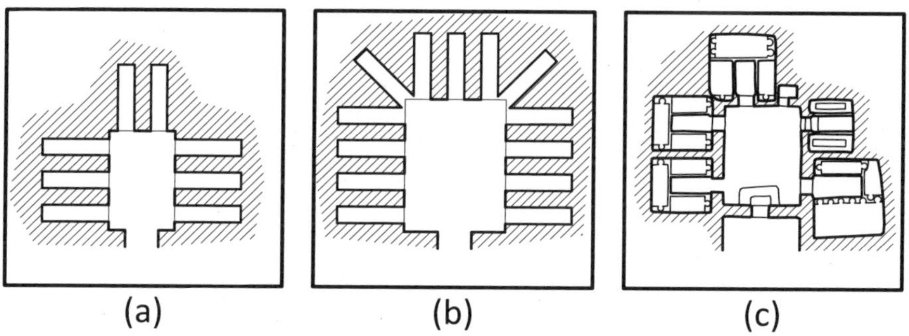


23. First and Second Temple burial cave plans: (a and b) Second Temple-era according to two opinions in mBB 6:8 (c) First Temple-era burial cave in Ketef Hinom, Jerusalem.

Yaakov lived at a time when the family concept of burial was dominant. His request to be buried with his fathers and gathered to his people reflects this notion. His unease with burial in Egypt was heightened by the fear

5. Joseph Patrich, "*Graves and Burial Practices* in Talmudic Sources" in *Graves and Burial Practices,* 196–197 (Hebrew), especially note 42. Patrich explains that this matched both the rabbinic sources and the archaeological remains.

6. mBB 6:8, tBB 6:22–23, bBB 100b–101b. A niche was four cubits long, one cubit wide and seven handbreadths high.

7. R. Ashi's solution was to have niches at different depths so that one could pass beneath the other. According to the archaeological records, this only happened occasionally. R. Huna ben R. Yehoshua's answer to this planning difficulty – to excavate niches at an angle – does not appear in the archaeological record. R. Shisha suggests that the corner niches were truncated and used for infants.

that his children were destined to be buried in Egypt as well. He may have also been concerned with the different attitude in Egypt toward corpse decomposition. By insisting on burial in the family plot, he wished to set an example for his family and strengthen their connection with the family burial plot, in hope that they too would one day return to Canaan.[8]

8. In Bereshit 50:5, when Yosef is convincing Pharaoh to allow him to bury Yaakov in Canaan, he tells Pharaoh "My father made me swear, saying, Lo, I die; in my grave which I have dug for myself in the land of Canaan there shall you bury me." Instead of explaining the pull of a familial burial chamber, he appeals to Pharaoh's concept of monumental graves, explaining that Yaakov had prepared a grave for himself in Canaan. Knowing the manpower expended in Egypt to prepare graves for the monarchs, Pharaoh may have assumed a similar undertaking by Yaakov and agreed to not let this effort go to waste. In the time of the Maccabim we find Jewish rulers who do build monumental graves (in the shape of pyramids), as per Maccabim I 13:28–29.

# Yosef's Grave

וַיַּשְׁבַּע יוֹסֵף אֶת בְּנֵי יִשְׂרָאֵל לֵאמֹר פָּקֹד יִפְקֹד אֱלֹקִים אֶתְכֶם וְהַעֲלִתֶם אֶת עַצְמֹתַי מִזֶּה. וַיָּמָת יוֹסֵף בֶּן מֵאָה וָעֶשֶׂר שָׁנִים וַיַּחַנְטוּ אֹתוֹ וַיִּישֶׂם בָּאָרוֹן בְּמִצְרָיִם (בראשית נ:כה-כו)

And Yosef took an oath of Bnei Yisrael saying, "God will surely remember you and you shall carry up my bones from here." And Yosef died, being one hundred and ten years old, and they embalmed him and he was put in a coffin in Egypt. (Bereshit 50:25–26)

JUST before his death, Yosef reassured Bnei Yisrael that they would one day be redeemed from Egypt and return to their ancestral homeland. Yosef then made Bnei Yisrael promise that, when the time came, they would bring his body with them rather than leave it in Egypt. In the meantime, Yosef's body was embalmed and put in a coffin. During the Exodus, Moshe fulfilled this oath by locating and removing the bones of Yosef.[1]

The story of Moshe's search for Yosef's grave is told in a midrash that appears in several sources.[2] In most versions, Moshe found Yosef's grave by asking Asher's daughter Serach, the last of the seventy people who came to Egypt, for the relevant information. There are two different traditions for the location of his coffin. In the first, Yosef's coffin was placed in the Nile River by the Egyptians so that the waters would be blessed by his presence. Moshe retrieved the body by demanding of Yosef that his coffin float to the top of the water.[3] According to the second tradition Yosef was

1. Shemot 13:19.

2. tSot 4:7, bSot 13a, ShmR 20:19, MdRY Beshalach (vayehi), Petichta, MdRS Beshalach 13:19, and PdRK 11:12, plus versions in Tanchuma, Yalkut Shimoni, and Midrash Hagadol.

3. This tradition is the only one mentioned in TPsY on Shemot 13:19.

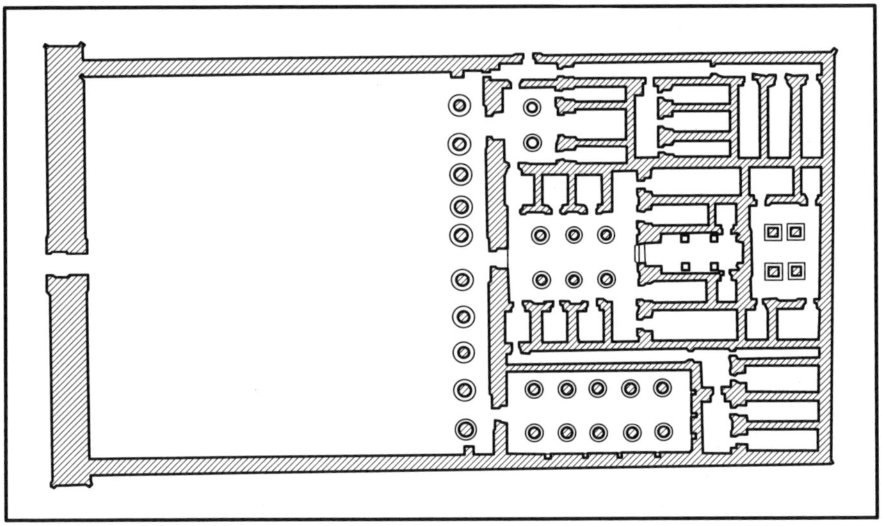

24. Mortuary temple of Seti I in the Theban Necropolis. (Based on drawing by Arthur Weigall, *A Guide to the Antiquities of Upper Egypt*)

interred in a royal burial complex. Here too Moshe demanded that Yosef's body identify itself, whereupon the coffin rattled.[4]

From the context of this midrash, we can understand the nature of this royal burial complex. It must have contained many other coffins, making the identification difficult. We are also told that it was a *royal* chamber. However, the exact term used to describe this facility is difficult to understand. The different versions of the midrash, and variations within each specific version, include the terms *kaveritan, paltorin, kapitolin, kipolsin,* and more. These words are interpreted as cupola, capital, palace, cavern, or labyrinth.[5] Jastrow also explains a variant, *kipolsin,* as referring to Diospolis, the Greek name for the city of Thebes. Thebes is the home of the Temples of Luxor and Karnak, as well as a large necropolis with royal funeral complexes. Whatever the exact nature of the chamber, according

4. Historically, there are Egyptian examples of people having two tombs, a real one and a cenotaph, set up in a different location. These were often concentrated in districts, as with the necropolis of Abydos. See Aly Abdalla, "The Cenotaph of the Sekwaskhet Family from Saqqara" in *The Journal of Egyptian Archaeology* 78 (1992), 111.

5. Herodotus, *The Histories* 2:148 describes an Egyptian labyrinth. A common motif in mythology is a hero's navigation of a maze, especially in relation to the underworld. John Layard codifies a number of traits that are found in these types of stories: they relate to death and rebirth, there is a cave, the presiding person is a woman (in our case, Serach), and the person entering the maze is a man. See John Layard, *Stone Men of Malekua Vao,* (Chatto & Windus, 1942), 652.

to this version of the midrash, Yosef was interred in an important complex with many other bodies.

The description in this midrash fits with much of what we know about Egyptian burial practices. Archaeologists have uncovered burial pits cut into rocky ground and covered by structures of brick. These stone structures eventually were replaced by pyramids, which were also constructed with internal chambers. Later, when pyramids were no longer used for burials, the concept of a mortuary temple for burials remained popular and these temples were sometimes cut into cliffs, as in Deir el-Bahri, opposite the city of Luxor. The interiors were subdivided into small chambers to be used for burial.

In some versions of the midrash, there is a description of creatures that guard the tomb. Pesikta deRav Kahana mentions ceramic dogs and Shemot Rabba describes golden dogs that barked to alert the Egyptians that tomb raiders were present. The creatures sound like the various sphinx sculptures that guard the entrance to some temple complexes.

25. Rams head sphinxes at Karnak in Thebes. (Photo by Daniel Daniel Csörföly, Wikimedia)

The two versions of Yosef's burial place both treat him as an important figure, but in different ways. In the first case, Yosef was given a special burial spot and was identified as an exceptional, holy man, capable of providing a singular boost to the most significant element of Egyptian civilization, the Nile. This sets Yosef apart and makes him a unique figure, but still an outsider. In the second treatment, Yosef was one of many important aristocrats tied to Egyptian royalty. He was buried as a full member of the Egyptian ruling class, no longer an outsider. Both versions of the midrash show the reverence given to Yosef by the Egyptians but point to different understandings of his place in Egyptian history.

# SHEMOT

## SHEMOT

# Groundbreaking and Cornerstone Ceremonies

וַיָּשִׂימוּ עָלָיו שָׂרֵי מִסִּים לְמַעַן עַנֹּתוֹ בְּסִבְלֹתָם וַיִּבֶן עָרֵי מִסְכְּנוֹת לְפַרְעֹה אֶת
פִּתֹם וְאֶת רַעַמְסֵס. (שמות א:יא)

Therefore they did set over them taskmasters to afflict them with their burden. And they built for Pharaoh store-cities, Pitom and Raamses. (Shemot 1:11)

ALTHOUGH the Torah explains Egypt's motivation for enslaving Bnei Yisrael, it glosses over how the enslavement came about, saying only that taskmasters were appointed. The verse uses several pronouns, leaving it unclear who was behind this process.

Two midrashim try to fill in the missing information, explaining how the Israelites were tricked into becoming slaves. One midrash uses the words of our verse, "they did set over *him*" – in the singular form – to claim that Pharaoh was personally involved. According to this midrash, Pharaoh wore a brick around his neck to demonstrate that he was helping make bricks.[1] Bnei Yisrael could not complain about their burden, as even Pharaoh was taking part in the effort.

According to a second midrash, Pharaoh volunteered for the work himself. When Bnei Yisrael saw Pharaoh's example, they followed suit and enthusiastically went to work making bricks. Pharaoh's taskmasters then checked the Israelites' daily output of bricks and demanded a similar quota on subsequent days, establishing the conditions for their enslavement.[2]

A similar story is told about Roman emperor Vespasian by historian Cassius Dio.[3] Upon arriving in Rome as emperor, Vespasian wished to

1. bSot 11a, ShmR 1:10.

2. ShmR 1:11 and 5:18, BamR 15:20.

3. This story, mentioned in the same chapter that records the destruction of Jerusalem, refers to Josephus Flavius by name and deals with Vespasian becoming emperor, a narrative addressed in rabbinic literature as well. For a similar story of a local

construct a temple on the Capitoline hill. The history relates that "he was the first to carry out a load of soil, thereby evidently bidding all the other leading citizens to do likewise, in order that the rest of the populace might have no excuse for shirking this service."[4] In a tactic similar to the midrash's description of Pharaoh, Vespasian set a personal example in the hopes that his subjects would follow suit and provide free labor.

While the midrash describes an act of subterfuge, it is normal for building owners to make a show of being involved in the construction process. This is done either to demonstrate their direct involvement, as a photo opportunity, or as a way of reminding everyone that they are the driving force behind the construction project. Many projects have a ground-breaking ceremony, in which the owners excavate the first spade of soil from the building site. Similar rites are sometimes held for the laying of cornerstones or keystones.[5] The end of a construction project can also be marked by symbolic acts, like the topping out of a building or a ribbon-cutting ceremony. In Judaism, the act of hanging a *mezuza* on the main doorway sometimes takes on similar pomp. In each of these acts, the building owner or a high-ranking official gets involved in the project, even if they are far removed from the actual construction work. We tend not to think of this as a way to motivate better performance from workers, but these acts are sometimes done to elicit goodwill or solicit funds from donors or municipalities.

The ceremonies held nowadays are intended to highlight the importance of a dignitary to a specific building project. With the enslavement of Bnei Yisrael, our verse identifies only a vague "they" and the secondary

---

leader, Dionysius, joining in construction work to hasten its completion, see Diodorus Siculus, *Library*, 14.18.

4. Cassius Dio, *Roman History*, 65.10.2.

5. In ancient times, cornerstones sometimes had an additional connotation. As part of a ritual to ensure a strong foundation for the building, sacrifices were deposited beneath the corners or walls of a building. In Egypt, both ritual objects and animal bones have been found beneath the walls of public buildings. In Canaanite architecture, cornerstone and foundation sacrifices were more drastic, with human bodies, especially of children, sometimes found in the foundations. See James Hastings, John A. Selbie, and Louis H. Gray, *Encyclopaedia of Religion and Ethics*, Vol. IV (Scribner, 1951), 120, "Corners."

Midrashim describe a similar phenomenon of human sacrifice for Bnei Yisrael. MdRS 3:7 explains that after the Israelite babies were drowned, their bodies were entombed in the walls of buildings. See also bSan 101b and Rashi *nitmachmech bavinyan* there. Elsewhere, bSan 111a relates that even in the time of R. Elazar ben R. Yosi, the Egyptians still claimed to know where Israelite children had been enclosed in buildings. Another midrash emphasizes the human toll of slavery, writing that the bodies of almost all who left Egypt were maimed from work accidents during their slavery. See BamR 7:1.

taskmasters. By introducing Pharaoh as the main figure in this process and explaining how he was involved, the midrashim are emphasizing that he was the primary force behind the enslavement of Bnei Yisrael. By focusing on Pharaoh's direct involvement, these stories indicate that the Egyptian ruler bears the responsibility for all that follows.

# Mixed-Use Neighborhoods

וַיְהִי כִּי יָרְאוּ הַמְיַלְּדֹת אֶת הָאֱלֹקִים וַיַּעַשׂ לָהֶם בָּתִּים. (שמות א:כא)

And it came to pass because the midwives feared God that he made them houses. (Shemot 1:21)

PHARAOH decreed that the Jewish midwives were to murder all newborn Jewish boys, but Shifra and Puah resisted this order. The Torah states that because the midwives feared God, "*he* made them houses."

There are two points in this verse which are unclear. We do not know to whom the pronoun "he" refers, nor are we told the nature of these houses. Some commentaries, including Rav and Shmuel in the Talmud, explain that God rewarded the midwives with metaphorical houses, in the form of dynastic lines of priests and kings.[1] Others explain that it was Pharaoh who made houses as a reaction to the midwives' civil disobedience. In one interpretation, the midwives were placed under house arrest, confined to their houses so they could be forced to commit infanticide.[2] Another opinion, however, states that Pharaoh built new houses in the Israelite neighborhoods and settled Egyptians among them. These Egyptians were then able to spy on the Israelite families and report when new babies were born, as the Jewish mothers were unable to muffle the cries of their newborn babies.[3]

When Bnei Yisrael first settled in Egypt, Yosef arranged for them to live in Goshen.[4] This may have been because Goshen had suitable grazing land for their flocks or because Yosef wanted them to have a separate enclave to avoid the influence of Egyptian culture. Before the Exodus, much is

1. Rashi, Chizkuni's first opinion, Rabeinu Bachya's third opinion, and bSot 11b.
2. Malbim, Chizkuni's second opinion, and Rabeinu Bachya's second opinion.
3. Midrash Lekach Tov on this verse and Rabeinu Bachya's first opinion.
4. Bereshit 46:28.

made of the passing over of Israelite houses during the plague of the first-borns,[5] implying that Bnei Yisrael were living in a mixed neighborhood. The midrash that Pharaoh moved Egyptians into the Israelite enclave tells us how the Israelites went from being isolated in Goshen to living among Egyptians.

Later generations of Jews and non-Jews alike have debated the value of living in ghettos versus living among society at large. Gideon Bohak addressed this topic in a study of ancient Jewish communities in Egypt, concluding that while there were many Jews who felt confident that Jews could maintain a separate ethnic identity while living within foreign cultures, those most successful at doing so lived in all-Jewish enclaves.[6] Still, while separation can help preserve the independence of the community, it is also usually the case that separate is not equal. In most cases, ghettos were imposed on Jews and limited their rights, though the dissolution of ghettos was sometimes opposed by the Jewish religious establishment.

Just as Jews have debated whether it is best to live separately or to be part of society at large, zoning laws have similarly swung between completely separating residential, commercial, and industrial uses, and allowing mixed-use. At first, zoning was introduced by municipalities to protect residential areas from the noise and pollution of commercial and industrial zones. This, however, resulted in urban sprawl. Suburbs were not walkable – any shopping required a trip by bus or car to a shopping center and commutes to work grew in length. Residential areas were empty during the day, while industrial zones were deserted at night, which made both more prone to crime.

More recent trends in zoning allow, and even prefer, mixed-use neighborhoods, in which houses are near shops and other amenities, instead of rigidly distant from places of work. This also keeps neighborhoods from being deserted during part of the day and gives neighbors more opportunity for interaction at local shops.

In the context of this midrash, the existence of a separate Jewish neighborhood is seen as an arrangement that enabled the Israelites to resist Pharaoh's decree. The integration of the Jewish enclave, on the other hand, limited Jewish freedom and gave more control to Pharaoh.

5. Shemot 12:13, 12:23.

6. Gideon Bohak, "Ethnic Continuity in the Jewish Diaspora in Antiquity" in *Jews in the Hellenistic and Roman Cities,* ed John R. Bartlett (Routledge, 2002), 175–192.

# Fire Ratings

וַיֵּרָא מַלְאַךְ ה׳ אֵלָיו בְּלַבַּת אֵשׁ מִתּוֹךְ הַסְּנֶה וַיַּרְא וְהִנֵּה הַסְּנֶה בֹּעֵר בָּאֵשׁ
וְהַסְּנֶה אֵינֶנּוּ אֻכָּל. (שמות ג:ב)

And the angel of the Lord appeared to him in a flame of fire out of the midst of a bush, and he looked and behold the bush burned with fire, and the bush was not consumed. (Shemot 3:2)

MOSHE was amazed to see a bush ablaze, yet not consumed by the fire. Some commentators interpret this vision as a metaphor for Bnei Yisrael in exile or during the plagues, as the Israelites would not be consumed by the encroaching dangers.[1]

The burning bush is normally treated as a completely miraculous occurrence – the bush was on fire, yet the fire did not consume it at all. A fire requires fuel to burn, yet the burning bush did not use any fuel. However, another possible interpretation is that the bush did not burn as expected, in the typical manner. One would expect the highly flammable desert bramble to be quickly consumed by flame. Perhaps this bush burned more slowly than expected and Moshe was amazed that it was not consumed *immediately*.[2]

Materials that do not burn immediately, and instead take a specified amount of time to be consumed, are said to be fire resistant. Such materials are *rated* based on how long it takes for them to burn. For fire safety in buildings, architects are often required to use fire-resistant materials to divide the building into fire zones. This keeps any potential fire from spreading and ensures that there will be safe corridors for fleeing occupants to

1. Sforno and Chizkuni. ShmR 2:5 also explains the burning bush as reassurance that Bnei Yisrael would not be destroyed in Egypt.

2. The Targum Yerushalmi, for example, elaborates that the bush acted as if it were damp.

leave the building.[3] For example, a safety consultant might require a door that can safely withstand a blaze for two hours. A wall or floor must be able to remain intact for a specified period during a fire so that occupants of a building have a reasonable amount of time to flee via protected corridors before those routes are engulfed in flames. We rely on materials to be able to stand without being consumed, at least not right away.[4]

If the burning bush acted similarly – burning slowly and withstanding the flames temporarily – then this changes its symbolism significantly. If a miraculous bush that is not consumed *at all* symbolizes the Israelite's safety from the plagues in Egypt, then a bush that is merely resistant to the flames would imply that there is some limit to the amount of time Bnei Yisrael can be expected to stay in Egypt, or in exile, and still remain safe. While they can expect protection for a certain duration, this is not unlimited, and the Israelites best make plans to leave before it is too late. This interpretation supports the theory that God redeemed Bnei Yisrael earlier than initially expected.

From this perspective, the burning bush was not a guarantee of protection for Bnei Yisrael. Rather, it was an urgent call to action; time was limited, and Moshe did not have the luxury of rejecting this mission. Moshe had to act or risk having Bnei Yisrael consumed.

---

3. mBB 2:2 mentions a similar rule, regarding the thickness of attic floors above ovens. See also bRH 4a for an example of fireproofing. In ancient Rome, similar laws were imposed to manage the spread of fire. See Tacitus, *Annals* 15.43, Strabo, *Geography* 5.3, and Gellius, *Attic Nights* 15.1.4–6.

4. bShab 26a and yShab 2:1 (4d) prohibit the use of certain fuels for Shabbat candles based on the danger that some fuels pose to the building walls (as per Rashi, *shehu af* and Korban Haeida, *uman de'amar ein madlikin.*

# Brickmaking in Egypt

לֹא תֹאסִפוּן לָתֵת תֶּבֶן לָעָם לִלְבֹּן הַלְּבֵנִים כִּתְמוֹל שִׁלְשֹׁם הֵם יֵלְכוּ וְקֹשְׁשׁוּ לָהֶם
תֶּבֶן. וְאֶת מַתְכֹּנֶת הַלְּבֵנִים אֲשֶׁר הֵם עֹשִׂים תְּמוֹל שִׁלְשֹׁם תָּשִׂימוּ עֲלֵיהֶם לֹא תִגְרְעוּ
מִמֶּנּוּ כִּי נִרְפִּים הֵם עַל כֵּן הֵם צֹעֲקִים לֵאמֹר נֵלְכָה נִזְבְּחָה לֵאלֹקֵינוּ. (שמות ה:ז-ח)

You shall no more give the people straw to make brick, as heretofore, let them go and gather straw for themselves. And the quantity of the bricks, which they did make heretofore, you shall lay upon them, do not reduce it, for they are idle, therefore they cry, saying: Let us go and sacrifice to our God. (Shemot 5:7–8)

In response to Moshe's demands that Bnei Yisrael be allowed a furlough, Pharaoh made Bnei Yisrael's labor more challenging. Initially, Bnei Yisrael had been required to produce a daily quota of bricks. The same quota still applied, but the taskmasters ceased to provide one of the main ingredients, straw. To make the bricks, the slaves would have to spend a portion of their day gathering straw.

Mud bricks were commonly used in Egypt during this period. They were made using mud from the Nile, which had a high clay content.[1] However, without additional binding material, the bricks would develop cracks. Therefore, it was necessary to add straw or some other organic material.[2]

When Pharaoh halted the supply of straw, he specified that the same *matkonet* of bricks must continue to be produced. The commentators universally interpret this to mean quantity, so that despite the new task of gathering straw, the same number of bricks still needed to be produced. However, the root of this word implies "content" and in modern Hebrew, a similar word, *matkon*, has come to mean "recipe." Although this is a modern usage, such a meaning would make sense here as well: Bnei Yisrael

1. Ronny Reich, "Building Materials and Architectural Elements in Ancient Israel" in *The Architecture of Ancient Israel* (Israel Exploration Society, 1992), 5.
2. See Rashi, Ibn Ezra (long version), and Rashbam.

were instructed that they must continue to use the same recipe and could not circumvent the lack of straw by simply making the bricks without straw. Pharaoh's removal of the straw supply would have almost begged such a response, with Bnei Yisrael continuing to make mud bricks without the binding ingredient of straw. It was important for Pharaoh to specify that bricks without straw would not be tolerated.

The issue of quality control must have been significant because mud bricks were generally not used until years after they were first cast. Pliny the Elder writes that mud bricks "are not approved for use in buildings unless they are two years old"[3] and Vitruvius gives similar instructions.[4] This amount of time was required for the bricks to cure and reach their full strength. It would have been hard to hold a specific slave responsible for a series of cracked bricks if the bricks themselves were only discovered to be faulty months or years later. Nonetheless, no commentators suggest this reading of Pharaoh's statement.

Although it is clear from these verses that Bnei Yisrael were occupied with brickmaking, the Torah previously states that they were tasked with building the cities of Pitom and Ramses. Such a project contained many components and brickmaking was only one of the many tasks required. Pliny the Elder tells us that "the best time for molding [mud bricks] is the spring, since in midsummer they become full of cracks."[5] Vitruvius mentions this as well, although he states that autumn was also an acceptable time for making bricks. Bnei Yisrael were presumably occupied with brickmaking because this was the right time of year for it.

This recommendation for springtime brickmaking has several ramifications for our reading of this story. First, the punishment that Pharaoh gave Bnei Yisrael was not endless; at most it could have lasted a number of months until brickmaking season ended. Secondly, we understand the brickwork in the scope of the general project of Pitom and Ramses. Thirdly, it corroborates R. Akiva's claim that the plagues took place over twelve months, starting in the spring and culminating with the Exodus, also in springtime.[6] Finally, we can wonder whether the brickmaking was mentioned specifically as a way of helping us understand that this was part of the lead-up to a springtime liberation. Today we have certain tasks that are closely associated with the spring (i.e. spring cleaning.) Perhaps brickmaking was equally associated with springtime and helped set the scene for Pesach, the spring festival.

---

3. Pliny the Elder, *Natural History*, 35:49.
4. Vitruvius, *Ten Books on Architecture*, II.3.2.
5. Pliny the Elder, ibid.
6. mEduy 2:10.

# Egyptian Temples and the Plagues

וַאֲנִי אַקְשֶׁה אֶת לֵב פַּרְעֹה וְהִרְבֵּיתִי אֶת אֹתֹתַי וְאֶת מוֹפְתַי בְּאֶרֶץ מִצְרָיִם. וְלֹא
יִשְׁמַע אֲלֵכֶם פַּרְעֹה וְנָתַתִּי אֶת יָדִי בְּמִצְרָיִם וְהוֹצֵאתִי אֶת צִבְאֹתַי אֶת עַמִּי בְנֵי
יִשְׂרָאֵל מֵאֶרֶץ מִצְרַיִם בִּשְׁפָטִים גְּדֹלִים. וְיָדְעוּ מִצְרַיִם כִּי אֲנִי ה׳ בִּנְטֹתִי אֶת יָדִי
עַל מִצְרָיִם וְהוֹצֵאתִי אֶת בְּנֵי יִשְׂרָאֵל מִתּוֹכָם. (שמות ז:ג-ה)

And I will harden Pharaoh's heart and multiply My signs and My wonders in the land of Egypt. But Pharaoh shall not hearken to you, and I will lay My hand upon Egypt and bring forth my armies, my people Bnei Yisrael, out of the land of Egypt by great judgments. And the Egyptians shall know that I am the Lord when I stretch forth my hand upon Egypt and bring out Bnei Yisrael from among them. (Shemot 7:3–5)

PRIOR to the ten plagues, Moshe was given a preview of how the negotiations with Pharaoh would proceed. Moshe would speak to Pharaoh and ask for the release of Bnei Yisrael. Pharaoh would refuse and God would respond with signs and wonders, along with great judgment. Egypt would then recognize God, and Bnei Yisrael would be freed.

This preview sets out the goals of the plagues. While freeing Bnei Yisrael was certainly a part, having the Egyptians "know that I am the Lord" was the primary goal. The plagues accomplished this by showing God's complete control over nature, while at the same time fulfilling the secondary goals of judging the Egyptians and freeing the Israelites.

Though the plagues demonstrated God's omnipotence, none of them confronted the Egyptian pantheon directly. The impressive Egyptian temple complexes would have been obvious targets. This happened when the Ark of the Covenant was captured by the Philistines and God toppled their idols.[1] Why is no punishment directed at the Egyptian temples?

1. Shmuel I 5:3–4. ShmR 15:15 describes how God did destroy the Egyptian idols. bBer 58b states that following the destruction of the Temple it is the houses of the righteous

This question is indirectly addressed in the Talmud during a discussion about idol worship. R. Gamliel was asked why God does not take an active role in destroying idol worship. He responded with a story about a prince who raised a dog and called it by his father's name. R. Gamliel explained that the king would be angry with his son, rather than the dog.[2]

Destroying pagan temples does not uproot idol worship, however dramatic the act. Idols are just metal and stone; it is the people who ascribe importance to the idols. To get at the root of the problem, the people must recognize God. The plagues were therefore directed at the Egyptians rather than their temples.[3]

The dog in R. Gamliel's story is just a dog; there is nothing intrinsically wrong with it. The prince chooses to call the dog by his father's name, but there is nothing wrong with the dog itself. The dog's name is a human construct, given meaning only by the use prescribed by the prince. Similarly, a piece of architecture, even a pagan temple, is not intrinsically a problem, unless it is adorned with idols and sculptures. The building is just a building that is given meaning by its human occupants. There is nothing wrong with the form of the building in and of itself, and it may even constitute great architecture despite its pagan use. Architectural historian Andrew Ballantyne addresses this line of thought, writing that "it is not possible to say that the fabric of the building is of itself ethical or unethical because in the plane of ethics it does nothing – it is an instrument which might or might not be useful, and which could be used to good or bad ends."[4] Halacha sets limits on entering or reusing existent pagan temples, but this is because of the function that took place within the building, not the building itself. It is the human intention that defines the building.[5]

This is one of the debates that Renaissance architects had about appropriating the forms of pagan temples for new uses. While today we associate Classical architecture with banks or government buildings, there was a

---

which are destroyed, and bPes 49a states that the same is a punishment for scholarly men who eat too much.

2. bAZ 54b.

3. The slaughter of the lambs by Bnei Yisrael may also have symbolized the physical defeat of Egyptian gods. See Shemot 12:12.

4. Andrew Ballantyne, "The Nest and the Pillar of Fire" in *What is Architecture?* ed. Andrew Ballantyne (Routledge, 2002), 25.

5. We see this in mAZ 3:7, which discusses whether houses used for idol worship can be used by Jews. The Mishna distinguishes between houses deliberately built for idol worship, ones that were physically renovated to accommodate idol worship, and ones that had idols superficially added to them after the fact. Even the first, most stringent category is only forbidden (according to Rashi) because the building itself takes on the status of an idol.

time when this style was a controversial choice since such forms were so heavily associated with pagan temples. Starting with Leon Battista Alberti's Tempio Malatestiano, this taboo began to loosen. Alberti's contemporary, Filarete, justified the use of Classical architecture, explaining that it was based on the proportions of the human body and was therefore divinely inspired.[6] Eventually, most architects concluded that there was nothing wrong with using the form of a temple since there is nothing intrinsic about that form itself, only the meaning ascribed to it by people.[7]

With the Egyptian temples, we can similarly answer that targeting them would not have accomplished the goals of the plagues. The buildings were not the problem. Instead, the plagues focused on educating the Egyptians about God's control over the world.

6. Filarete (Antonio di Piero Averlino), *Treatise on Architecture*, I.2v, tr. John R. Spencer. Filarete was a fifteenth century Florentine architect. For Vitruvius' comparisons of the classical orders to the human body, see his *Ten Books on Architecture* III.1.3 and IV.1.6–7. Joseph Rykwert describes the process of justification in the writings of several influential architects, including John Wood and Gian Lorenzo Bernini. See Joseph Rykwert, *The Dancing Column* (MIT Press, 1988), 27–30, as well as the discussion in Rykwert, *On Adam's House in Paradise* (MIT Press, 1981), ch. 5. Herod's Temple, as well as earlier versions, borrowed architectural motifs from surrounding cultures.

7. Building forms take on different associations over their existence. For example, basilicas were originally used as Roman public buildings or courts. This was a secular use and was co-opted for other uses. We thus find that the ancient synagogue in Alexandria (bSuk 51b) and the Chamber of Hewn Stone in Jerusalem (bYom 25a) were each described as a basilica. (For this, see my commentary on Bamidbar 11:16.) With the rise of Christianity, the building type was used as one of the two main styles of churches, and today this is the primary association.

# Houses During the Plagues

וְשָׁרַץ הַיְאֹר צְפַרְדְּעִים וְעָלוּ וּבָאוּ בְּבֵיתֶךָ וּבַחֲדַר מִשְׁכָּבְךָ וְעַל מִטָּתֶךָ וּבְבֵית עֲבָדֶיךָ וּבְעַמֶּךָ וּבְתַנּוּרֶיךָ וּבְמִשְׁאֲרוֹתֶיךָ. וּבְכָה וּבְעַמְּךָ וּבְכָל עֲבָדֶיךָ יַעֲלוּ הַצְפַרְדְּעִים. (שמות ז:כח-כט)

And the river shall swarm with frogs, which shall go and come into your house and into your bedchamber and upon your bed and into the house of your servants and upon your people and into your ovens and into your kneading troughs; and the frogs shall come up both upon you and upon your people and upon all your servants. (Shemot 7:28–29)

THE plague of frogs is introduced with a description of the amphibians invading Egyptians homes. Although frogs were normally found in the river, during the plague frogs would be in the Egyptians' houses, their bedrooms, and on their beds. They would be in the Egyptians' food, in their servants' houses, and according to Rashi, even in their bodies.

Several other plagues also encroached upon the houses of the Egyptians: pestilence,[1] locusts,[2] and the plague of the firstborn.[3] Since the plague of frogs is the first to mention houses, it is possible that it serves as a template for the other three plagues, and that the description of houses, bedrooms, and beds applies to those plagues as well.[4] The Torah only had to describe

1. Shemot 8:17.
2. Shemot 10:6.
3. Shemot 12:30. Another plague, hail, specifically notes that the houses will be the only *safe* places. See Shemot 9:19.
4. The added progression of bedchamber and bed also indicates that the use of the word "house" in this verse is not meant as a metaphor for a household, but rather refers to the physical house. It also establishes a hierarchy of privacy within the Egyptian households, which does not exist in all societies. See my commentary on Shemot 36:6.

once what an invasion of the home meant – thereafter it was sufficient to merely say that the locusts and gnats would be in the houses.

Why is there such an emphasis on the houses of the Egyptians? R. S.R. Hirsch writes that the Egyptians had lorded themselves over their slaves for many years and were now getting their comeuppance. The slaves of Egypt had no place to themselves, were deprived of sleep, and lacked food. R. Hirsch writes that "In all those places [the frogs] promenaded and showed the Egyptians what it meant if one could not quietly enjoy even one's house, one's bed, one's bread, without having to fear at every moment that one would be disturbed by annoying entries."[5]

This focus on the sanctity of a house appears later in the Torah as well, in the prohibition against a debt collector entering a house. The Torah demands that "you shall not go into his house to fetch his pledge,"[6] a prohibition repeated in the Mishna.[7] The author of Sefer Hachinuch and R. Yosef Bechor Shor emphasize that this is to protect the self-worth of the debtor.[8] Malbim stresses that this reduces the strife between the members of the household.[9] As with the violation of the Egyptian houses described during the plagues, here too we see the importance of a house as a safe haven and the psychological damage that can occur if it is violated.

The focus on houses during the plagues sets up a contrast with two additional instances in which houses are mentioned. The first and most obvious is when Bnei Yisrael were commanded to paint their doorposts and remain inside their houses while the plague of the firstborn occurred. The Torah states that God would "not allow the destroyer to come into your houses to smite you."[10] By emphasizing how the various plagues, including the final one, invaded the houses of the Egyptians, we can appreciate the miraculous way in which the plague passed over the Israelite homes. Houses were not safe havens for the Egyptians, so it was even more miraculous that they *did* provide safety for Bnei Yisrael during the plague of the firstborn.

5. R. Hirsch focuses on the sanctity of the house and its importance in maintaining Jewish identity while discussing the blood on the doorpost in Shemot 12:7 and emphasizing that it was God, rather than the blood, which was protecting Bnei Yisrael. This contrasts with Chizkuni, who explains that the blood formed a protective seal around the door opening. Sealing the door helped cut off their connection with the outside, Egyptian culture, providing them with an insular location to grow as a unit of a new nation.

6. Devarim 24:10.

7. mBM 9:13. See also tBM 10:8.

8. Sefer Hachinuch, 594 and Bechor Shor on Devarim 24:10.

9. Malbim on Devarim 24:11.

10. Shemot 12:23.

The second case in which houses are mentioned is in the description of the Pesach holiday. Bnei Yisrael are instructed that "Seven days shall there be no leaven found in your houses."[11] Here, instead of God keeping the plagues out of Israelite houses, Bnei Yisrael are responsible for making sure that leaven is kept out of their houses. This creates a parallel between the two cases as if to emphasize the importance of following this commandment. Just as God sealed the Israelite houses against the destructive forces of the plagues, so too Jews are expected, just as meticulously, to keep their houses sealed against leaven during the Pesach festival.

11. Shemot 12:19.

# Failing Systems

וַיִּצְבְּרוּ אֹתָם חֳמָרִם חֳמָרִם וַתִּבְאַשׁ הָאָרֶץ. (שמות ח:י)

And they gathered them together in heaps and the land stank. (Shemot 8:10)

MOSHE prayed for the plague of frogs to conclude, whereupon the frogs outside of the river expired. This created a new problem for the Egyptians, as the land was covered with frog carcasses. The Egyptians dealt with this by gathering the dead frogs into piles, resulting in a considerable smell, as the frogs began to decompose.

R. S.R. Hirsch writes that the Egyptians were trying to clear the land, coping as best they could with this unpleasant development. However, the heaps that they formed "only furthered the decay and foulness."

Egyptian society had an equilibrium of sorts, whereby certain natural phenomena took place in a predictable manner and a way of life developed which took these cyclical events into account. Life in Egypt ebbed and flowed with the rhythm of the Nile River, as its waters flooded and receded. The Egyptians lived with the normal local phenomena, the same as any culture.

When natural patterns are interrupted, the equilibrium is thrown out of order. In a sense, this is what happened with the plagues, as illustrated by the graphic description at the end of the plague of frogs. The Egyptians did not have a system for coping with the massive amount of biological waste that the dead frogs represented. They attempted to address the crisis by piling up the frogs, but this only made the situation worse.[1] Presumably, if dead frogs accumulated annually, the Egyptians would have developed more successful methods to cope.

1. We are told of a similar reaction to the first plague, when the Egyptians responded by digging for water. (Shemot 7:24) By the third plague, the Egyptians threw up their hands and offered no proactive response.

Natural phenomena pose challenges for designers, who are required by building code to meet certain standards. The building code tries to anticipate what type of storms or other natural occurrences may take place over the life of the building and requires structural strength to withstand such storms. For example, a building code may require that a structure be robust enough to weather an extremely powerful "one-hundred-year storm" that is predicted to take place only once every one hundred years. The Talmud addresses this point in a discussion about fire spread by an uncommonly strong wind, distinguishing between gales that are uncommon but still happen from time to time, and windstorms that are truly rare in their ferocity.[2] Still, despite careful planning, unanticipated events can cause system failures. No committee has the prescience to predict every future disaster.

During the plagues, the Egyptians were struck by unanticipated disasters. In one plague, the Torah even states that this was like nothing that had happened to the Egyptians in generations.[3] They were left to deal with the fallout, ten times over. All that was left was to improvise and try to cope as best they could. This unprecedented streak of "natural" disasters was impossible to contend with and upset the Egyptian worldview of dependable natural cycles.[4]

---

2. yBK 6:4 (5b). See also Maggid Mishna on Rambam Hilchot Nizkei Mamon 14:7.
3. Shemot 10:6.
4. The post-plague fallout may have contributed to the idea that each plague contained multiple plagues, as per the debate in the Hagada, where R. Eliezer states that each plague in Egypt was comprised of four separate plagues, while R. Akiva says each plague was comprised of five.

# Wind Patterns

וַיֵּט מֹשֶׁה אֶת מַטֵּהוּ עַל אֶרֶץ מִצְרַיִם וַה׳ נִהַג רוּחַ קָדִים בָּאָרֶץ כָּל הַיּוֹם הַהוּא וְכָל הַלָּיְלָה הַבֹּקֶר הָיָה וְרוּחַ הַקָּדִים נָשָׂא אֶת הָאַרְבֶּה. (שמות י:יג)

And Moshe stretched forth his rod over the land of Egypt and the Lord brought a *kadim* wind upon the land all that day and all that night, and when it was morning, the *kadim* wind brought the locusts. (Shemot 10:13)

THE plague of locusts began and ended with wind. The locusts arrived on a *kadim* wind and departed when God shifted the wind's direction, sweeping them out to sea.[1] The Torah describes a similar phenomenon during the Splitting of the Sea: Moshe stretched out his hand and God brought a *kadim* wind all night, drying out the sea.[2]

Most commentators explain that the *kadim* wind was an eastern wind.[3] In Hebrew, the term denotes the direction of the sunrise. However, Sforno writes that the locusts came from the south, and scientifically this is accurate – locusts come to Egypt from Sudan, which is south. In an article on the subject, Itzhak Meitlis explains that although in Israel *kadim* denoted east, the Egyptians used the term to orient themselves as per their touchstone, the Nile. Therefore, in Egypt *kadim* meant south. It was from this direction that the locusts came. Likewise, in Egypt the direction of the sea, to whence the locusts eventually departed, is north rather than west.[4]

The different winds have been a subject of interest for thousands of years. Ancient scholars made lists of the prevailing winds, giving each a name and ascribing to it certain characteristics. Homer referred to four

1. Shemot 10:19.
2. Shemot 14:21. In this case, no additional wind was needed to reverse the process, since the water naturally returned to equilibrium once the wind ceased.
3. See, for example, Rashi, Ibn Ezra, Saadia Gaon, and Chizkuni.
4. Itzhak Meitlis, "*Meheichan Hegiyua Haarbeh*?" available online at http://www.hatanakh.com/en/node/28529 (Hebrew).

winds,[5] whereas Aristotle listed eight[6] and other scholars had twelve or even twenty-four winds. Rabbinic literature also attributes certain characteristics to the four mains winds. According to R. Chanan bar Aba, the northern wind is the most beneficial, while the southern wind is the harshest.[7] R. Yehuda learned different characteristics of the winds based on a verse in Devarim.[8] Another source explains that the *kadim* wind brings suffering.[9]

Ancient scholars assigned various names to the winds, but the names did not always refer to winds coming from the same direction. One name could denote different directions depending on the cultural context. For example, the wind *Boreas*, which in Homer and Aristotle refers to the north wind, is listed by Vitruvius as an east-by-northeast wind. This point is supported in the Talmud during a debate about which wind is the most beneficial. The Talmud explains that certain winds are beneficial in Israel, while in Babylonia the same winds are harmful.[10] Therefore, it is not surprising that the *kadim* wind could have different connotations in Israel and in Egypt.

Vitruvius discusses winds in his chapter on city orientation. He explains the importance of mapping prevailing winds when laying out a city. In his opinion, streets ought to be oriented so that they do not run in the same direction as the wind blows.[11] He also recognized that architecture should take prevalent winds into account. For example, he writes that a house's library should be located away from the windy side of the building.[12]

The same lesson that Vitruvius mentions applies today, both when setting out a city grid and when orienting a building on a site.[13] In a city, the

5. Homer, *Odyssey*, 5.295.

6. Aristotle, *Meteorology* II.6.

7. bGit 31b, bBB 25a. Nevertheless, King David used the northern wind as part of an alarm system for waking up during the night, as per bSan 16a, yBer 1:1 (4a), and several additional parallel sources.

8. Devarim 32:2, quoted in bBB 25a. In Sifri Devarim 306, this is quoted in the name of Rabbi Simai. See also Louis Finkelstein's note that the Bavli has a corrupted text: in the original reading there is no contradiction and in Israel a western wind is beneficial.

9. MdRY Beshalach (vayehi) 4.

10. bBB 147a, bYom 21b.

11. Vitruvius, *Ten Books on Architecture*, I.6.8. See also Fra Giocondo's 1511 edition for illustrations of this suggestion, and Spiro Kostof, *The City Shaped* (Thames & Hudson, 1999), 131. Vitruvius also discusses how to locate true north in I.6.6–7, a subject that is discussed in bEruv 56a and yEruv 5:1 (22c).

12. Vitruvius, *Ten Books on Architecture*, VI.4.1.

13. A popular textbook on the subject, Vaughn Bradshaw's *Building Control Systems* second ed. (John Wiley & Sons, 1993), 217 teaches that "The site should be studied to determine which are the prevailing seasonal winds so that the building can be placed to

orientation and width of the streets determine how wind filters through the urban fabric. Tall buildings can affect local wind patterns, causing strong gusts and eddies in the surrounding spaces. Within an individual building, wind can affect the thermal comfort level through passive cooling. While today we commonly find buildings that use mechanical systems (i.e. air conditioning) to manage temperature, this is an expensive and often wasteful practice. When a building is oriented correctly and designed with logical openings, wind can passively ventilate and cool the building. In cold climates, buildings can be sheltered from wind with topography or vegetation to help keep them warm. If seasonal winds come from different directions, one can design a building that takes advantage of summer winds and blocks winter winds. All this is predicated on wind being relatively predictable.

The Torah does not specify whether the wind that brought the locusts was normal or extraordinary. Malbim felt that the Torah's emphasis on God's involvement in bringing the wind implies that this was a supernatural event. This reinforces the general message of the plagues – that God has complete control over all of nature. The Netziv, on the other hand, explained that the *kadim* wind was normal and needed to blow all day and all night to be effective. The purpose of this plague, in his opinion, was to show that plagues did not require a supernatural event.[14] Supporting this perspective, we note that the Torah identifies the wind by its name, implying a regular force at work.

It is significant that the Torah mentions the *kadim* wind in connection with the locusts and then uses similar language shortly thereafter at the Splitting of the Sea. In both cases, the wind seemed to behave according to the laws of nature, but still demonstrated God's control over nature. According to Ramban,[15] the splitting of the sea was done in this manner to trick the Egyptians, who soon discovered – when the wind unexpectedly stopped and the water came rushing back to drown them – that the wind was performing the Will of God.

The *kadim* wind is an example of a named wind. While in Israel it referred to an eastern wind, in Egypt it represented wind from the south. Such winds could normally be counted on to act predictably, so this may indicate that the plague operated within nature. However, others understand that in this case, the wind behaved atypically, reinforcing the supernatural nature of the plague.

---

either take advantage of them or be sheltered from them."

14. He contrasts this with the departure of the locusts, which was via a supernatural wind, alluded to in the verse by the words "very strong."

15. On Shemot 14:21.

BO

# Keeping Time

וַיֹּאמֶר מֹשֶׁה כֹּה אָמַר ה׳ כַּחֲצֹת הַלַּיְלָה אֲנִי יוֹצֵא בְּתוֹךְ מִצְרָיִם. (שמות יא:ד)

And Moshe said, "Thus says the Lord, 'About midnight will I go out into the midst of Egypt.'" (Shemot 11:4)

MOSHE warned Pharaoh that "about midnight" the plague of the firstborn would begin. Commentators wonder why Moshe gave an approximate time when later we find that the plague commenced precisely "at midnight."[1] Moshe is even less specific when informing Bnei Yisrael of the evening's schedule, sufficing to tell them that the plague would happen "this night."[2]

The Talmud explains that while Moshe trusted that God would begin the plague on time, he was skeptical about the precision of Egyptian timekeeping. Moshe worried that the Egyptians, falsely confident in their ability to calculate midnight, would claim that the plague did not begin punctually. This would lead them to question the legitimacy of Moshe's prophecy and the omnipotence of God. To avoid this heresy, Moshe left the timetable vague.[3]

Several commentaries reference specific timekeeping tools in this discussion. The Mechilta mentions a sundial, describing a very thin gnomon used for high precision.[4] Ibn Ezra explains that "large, bronze tools" were needed to detect the exact instant of midday and that at night this task was even more complicated.[5] Another passage in the Talmud describes a

---

1. Shemot 12:29.

2. Shemot 12:12. According to the MdRS 12:29, Moshe did not want Bnei Yisrael to worry that the time had already passed.

3. bBer 4a and Rashi *shema yitu itztagninei paro.* See also Rashi on this Torah verse.

4. MdRS 12:29. A type of sundial is reported in the palace of Achaz in Melachim II 20:11 and Yishayahu 38:8, and a mishna discusses the susceptibility of a sundial to *tumah* in mEduy 3:8.

5. ShmR 12:2 tells that for the plague of hail, Moshe made a mark on the wall and

timepiece as being of exceptional value, something a king would bequeath to his son.[6] The assembly of such instruments required very technical knowledge; when discussing timekeeping, Vitruvius pointed to his ability to construct a sundial and orient its gnomon as an example of his expertise.[7] He also described the construction of water clocks ("clepsydra"),[8] which were expensive and rare. Still, despite the complicated nature of these devices, they were not precision tools.

In a summary of his dissertation, David Zvi Kalman explains that much of rabbinic timekeeping worked on this same assumption, that timekeeping was imprecise. Advanced timepieces were rare and inaccessible, so most halachic times had to rely on dividing the day into quarters. For this reason, many halachic times are given in reference to the third, sixth or ninth hour of the day, which are easier to ascertain without specialized tools. While the Rabbis, living in a Greco-Roman world that utilized a twelve-hour day, embraced that conceptualization of time, it would not have been practical to rely on such a system. Kalman writes that the Rabbis "expressed their low-precision expectations in high-precision language,"[9] acknowledging a twelve-hour day yet largely sufficing with division into four quarters.

This analysis, along with the nature of timekeeping in Late Antiquity, reinforces the explanation of Moshe's language in our verse. Unlike today, it would have been exceedingly difficult to determine the exact time, especially at night. Pharaoh may have had access to some technology, yet even by day it would not have been precise. Therefore, Moshe kept the timing of the plague vague. Bnei Yisrael, who most likely had no tools for measuring time, were told only that it would occur at night.

---

stated that the plague would begin when the sun reached that mark on the following day. This, however, could not be done for a plague beginning at night.

6. yRH 1:3 (57b), using the Greek loanword אורלוגין, horologe.

7. Vitruvius, *Ten Books on Architecture,* I.1.10.

8. ibid, IX.7–8. Water clocks are mentioned in BerR 49:12 as an instrument for timing lawyers' statements.

9. David Zvi Kalman. "Turning Clockwise" in *Ancient Jew Review,* 18 Dec. 2019, online at https://www.ancientjewreview.com/articles/2019/12/13/dissertation-spotlight-becoming-clockwise-jews-and-timekeeping-from-antiquity-to-modernity.

# The Pillar of Fire As Visionary Architecture

וה׳ הֹלֵךְ לִפְנֵיהֶם יוֹמָם בְּעַמּוּד עָנָן לַנְחֹתָם הַדֶּרֶךְ וְלַיְלָה בְּעַמּוּד אֵשׁ לְהָאִיר
לָהֶם לָלֶכֶת יוֹמָם וָלָיְלָה. (שמות יג:כא)

And the Lord went before them by day in a pillar of a cloud to lead them the way, and by night in a pillar of fire, to give them light, that they might go by day and night. (Shemot 13:21)

Bnei Yisrael were guided during the day by a pillar of cloud and at night by a pillar of fire. The primary purpose of these pillars was to lead Bnei Yisrael in the right direction.[1] However, the pillars – especially the pillar of cloud – were ascribed additional protective properties. They helped guard Bnei Yisrael from the pursuing Egyptians.[2] According to a midrash, the pillar of cloud flattened the desert terrain to make the journey easier.[3]

The midrashim about these pillars are dramatic and point to an unspoken question – why was it necessary to have these pillars leading the way? If the only purpose was to lead Bnei Yisrael, it would have been sufficient to have a guide like Moshe shepherding them in the correct direction. The bombastic nature of the pillars must have served a greater role, and the Rabbis are happy to oblige by attributing additional powers to the columns.[4]

1. Rashi on Shemot 14:24.
2. Shemot 14:19.
3. MdRY Beshalach (vayehi – Petichta) and BamR 1:2. The midrash may also be in response to Devarim 29:4, which states that Bnei Yisrael's clothes did not wear out in the desert. This imagery seems to contradict the description of this phenomenon as a column rather than a wall. A column – a tall, thin element – would make an excellent, visible symbol to be seen from afar, but would be less useful as a protection against the Egyptians, or as a means of flattening a wide swath of terrain.

Vitruvius briefly discusses the use of columns as rollers to flatten terrain. See his *Ten Books on Architecture*, X.2.12.

4. One can make a case that a single person could not have led a host the size of Bnei

In an essay by architectural historian Andrew Ballantyne, the author compares a nest with the pillar of fire. A nest, he writes, constitutes domestic, comfortable, stable, and perhaps boring architecture. While most people prefer to be surrounded by buildings of this type, it is not usually the "nests" that are studied in architecture school. Rather, architectural history focuses more on what Ballantyne calls "pillars of fire."

> Whereas the nest is anchored and invites us to stay where we are – to snuggle down into it – the pillar of fire beckons as a destiny and invites us to move. It is a challenge to all that is comfortable, having the character rather of a quest. It is grand and inspiring, and suggests that the art of architecture should take us away from the everyday surroundings that enslave us, guiding us to a better place.[5]

Pillars of fire, Ballantyne explains, are buildings of importance and vision that challenge us and make us question how we live. They demand thought and are "exciting, creative, and heroic." These are the buildings that are taught in school and that leave a mark on society.

Bnei Yisrael had spent centuries following the commands of their taskmasters in Egypt. They had a routine, a lifestyle, which they did not question, and which had become second nature. One of the main challenges for Bnei Yisrael after the Exodus was to alter this mindset. To do so, they could not just follow a human leader; they needed extraordinary symbols, such as the pillars of cloud and fire. Every time Bnei Yisrael looked at the pillars they were reminded about their connection with God and their new lifestyle and aspirations. It was a dramatic way to lead Bnei Yisrael, because breaking their longtime lifestyle required drama.

---

Yisrael effectively and that something visible from afar was necessary. However, this seems to have been the function of the flags described in Bamidbar 1:52.

5. Andrew Ballantyne, "The Nest and the Pillar of Fire" in *What is Architecture?* (Routledge, 2002), 38.

BESHALACH

# Gateways and Obelisks

דַּבֵּר אֶל בְּנֵי יִשְׂרָאֵל וְיָשֻׁבוּ וְיַחֲנוּ לִפְנֵי פִּי הַחִירֹת בֵּין מִגְדֹּל וּבֵין הַיָּם לִפְנֵי בַּעַל צְפֹן נִכְחוֹ תַחֲנוּ עַל הַיָּם. (שמות יד:ב)

Speak to Bnei Yisrael that they turn back and encamp before Pi Hachirot, between Migdol and the sea, before Baal Tzafon; over against it shall you encamp by the sea. (Shemot 14:2)

When Bnei Yisrael were leaving Egypt, God commanded them to camp in Pi Hachirot between Migdol and the sea, opposite Baal Tzafon. The place is identified in three different ways, seemingly to give an exact location. Nonetheless, commentators are puzzled by this location, particularly the expression "Pi Hachirot."

Some commentators note a similarity between the word "Hachirot" and the Hebrew *cherut* (freedom), explaining that this site was a type of border for fleeing slaves.[1] Others explain that this was a narrow corridor, or possibly a dead-end, sandwiched between a fortress and the sea.[2] The Egyptians recognized that Bnei Yisrael had stumbled into this strategically vulnerable location and rushed to trap them.[3]

Among the various interpretations, the Mechilta gives a particularly obscure description of this location:

> What were these *chirot*? They were not slanted, but embanked; and they were not straight, but curved;[4] and they were not round,

1. See Ibn Ezra, Siftei Chachamim, and Chizkuni.
2. Rashi, and especially Malbim and the Daat Mikre commentary.
3. According to Daat Mikre, Baal Tzafon was also referenced to give yet another way of identifying the location. It explains Baal Tzafon as a Canaanite god and references an Ugaritic text as a source. Other commentaries explain it as the last standing Egyptian deity, which the Egyptians hoped would defeat Bnei Yisrael.
4. This is the same language used by mMid 2:5 to describe the curved steps in the Temple.

> but square; and they were not man-made, but heaven-made; and they had eyes to open; they were male and female. These are the words of R. Eliezer.[5]

R. Eliezer seems to be describing a processional area, with tapered, squared objects arranged in arcs on either side. Rashi, perhaps based on this description, writes that Pi Hachirot was the place between two tall, upright boulders. Me'am Loez adds that the stones were shaped like a man and a woman, and perhaps had imprints where their eyes would have been, making them especially humanoid.

26. Modern reconstruction of a New Kingdom model of a temple gateway. (Albert Fehrenbacher, Brooklyn Museum, Charles Edwin Wilbour Fund, 66.228)

5. MdRY Beshalach (vayehi) 1, and later in the Targum Yerushalmi, Midrash Lekach Tov, and Midrash Sechel Tov (all on our verse).

Nehemia Brüll, a nineteenth century Reform scholar, attempted to explain Rabbi Eliezer's opinion. Writing in German, he posited that R. Eliezer was talking about a pair of obelisks, which were commonly found at the entrance to Egyptian temples. He explained that the Egyptian god Horus was often depicted as being androgynous and suggested that Pi Hachirot were obelisks with images of Horus. Brüll specifically mentioned Heliopolis, an Egyptian temple-city, which was known for its entrance containing a pair of obelisks, sphinxes, and two collossi.[6] Some ancient sources describing the site mention an unusual number of obelisks present. The architecture is described by historians and geographers from roughly the same time as R. Eliezer, though there is not a report that precisely matches his description.[7]

Part of R. Eliezer's description is reminiscent of obelisks – tall, tapering, square-shaped pillars. It is unclear, though, what he means by their "eyes" or the male and female description, though perhaps these were separate monuments shaped like people. Although we cannot know if R. Eliezer was referring to Heliopolis or a different place, he does seem to be describing a location that was familiar to him, either from a visit or from existing legends.

6. Brüll, *Jahrbücher für jüdische Geschichte* I, S. 148. (German)
7. See Strabo, *Geography* 17.1, and Josephus *Against Apion*, 2.11.

BESHALACH

# Passage Through Walls of Water

וַיָּבֹאוּ בְנֵי יִשְׂרָאֵל בְּתוֹךְ הַיָּם בַּיַּבָּשָׁה וְהַמַּיִם לָהֶם חוֹמָה מִימִינָם וּמִשְּׂמֹאלָם.
(שמות יד:כב)

And Bnei Yisrael went into the midst of the sea upon the dry ground, and the waters were a wall to them on their right hand and on their left. (Shemot 14:22)

THE splitting sea formed walls of water to the right and left of Bnei Yisrael.[1] Classical commentators learn from this description that the water was unnaturally solid,[2] that the walls protected Bnei Yisrael,[3] or that the path was dredged between the two walls of water.[4]

Chizkuni gives a novel explanation based on a gloss by Tosafot.[5] He writes that Bnei Yisrael were not crossing a body of water that blocked their path. Rather, they entered the water, made a half-arc, and curved back to the coast, exiting on the same shore as they entered. The whole purpose of the splitting sea was not to perform a Dunkirk-style rescue operation, but rather to trap the Egyptians in the water.

Whether Bnei Yisrael crossed the sea or curved back to the same shoreline, the transition through the sea was of great significance. If we think about the passage architecturally, Bnei Yisrael traveled through a long, narrow corridor. This type of built space normally serves as a transition between two more significant rooms. The longer and narrower the passage, the grander and more significant the destination feels upon arrival. Entering the sea, Bnei Yisrael were fleeing slavery and were hounded by the Egyptians. After their journey between the walls of seawater, they

1. See also Shemot 14:29, where this description appears a second time.
2. Ibn Ezra's long commentary.
3. HaEmek Davar.
4. Rabeinu Bachya.
5. bAra 15a *keshem*.

were birthed into a new reality in which they were a free nation and safe from the Egyptians. As such, the passage through the sea represented a transition for Bnei Yisrael, not just from the perspective of the reader but also for Bnei Yisrael themselves, experiencing the constricted passage before bursting forth into freedom.

The Mechilta describes that Moshe's ascent of Mount Sinai was a similar situation. The midrash explains that the words "but Moshe drew near to the thick darkness"[6] indicate that he passed between two walls of thick darkness in order to reach God.[7] This too can be seen as a transition as Moshe readies himself to receive the Torah and is, in a way, reborn.[8]

While the main emphasis of the splitting of the sea is the miraculous nature of the Exodus and the escape from the Egyptians, the passage through the water is a significant, transitory moment in the history of Bnei Yisrael. The crossing of the sea saves Bnei Yisrael from the oncoming Egyptians, but it also acts as a ceremonial passage from slavery to freedom.

6. Shemot 20:18.

7. MdRS, Yitro 20:18.

8. bYom 4b notes the parallel between these two situations. Moshe is depicted as a different person following his experience on Mount Sinai.

# Temple from Heaven

תְּבִאֵמוֹ וְתִטָּעֵמוֹ בְּהַר נַחֲלָתְךָ מָכוֹן לְשִׁבְתְּךָ פָּעַלְתָּ ה׳ מִקְּדָשׁ אֲדֹנָי כּוֹנְנוּ יָדֶיךָ.
(שמות טו:יז)

You bring them in and plant them in the mountain of Your inheritance, The place, O Lord, which You have made for You to dwell in, the sanctuary, O Lord, which Your hands have established. (Shemot 15:17)

As part of the song recited by Bnei Yisrael after the splitting of the sea, the Torah mentions that God's "hands have established" a sanctuary. The Talmud understands this as a reference to a future Temple. Rashi quotes this phrase as proof that the Third Temple will be divinely constructed and appear miraculously.[1] This is one of the main texts supporting the idea that the Third Temple will descend from Heaven, rather than be built by human hands.

Rashi is compelled to make this comment due to a scenario discussed in the Talmud, in which the Temple is built suddenly and unexpectedly. If people are unaware of its renewal, they will not realize that different laws apply for the *Omer* offering, changing when new grain may be eaten. The Talmud suggests that this could only happen if the Temple were built overnight. However, *people* are not allowed to build the Temple at night, so Rashi reasons that it must be that the Temple will appear miraculously.[2]

The concept of a Temple descending from heaven serves as a proxy for philosophical differences between Jews who believe in passively waiting for the Messiah and Jews who approve of taking a more active approach.[3]

1. bSuk 41a – Rashi *ee nami*. See also yTaan 2:2 (65c).
2. ShmR 52:3 relates that both the Tabernacle and the First Temple miraculous assembled themselves. See also PdRK, Vezot Haberacha 5, which states that the rebuilt city of Jerusalem will descend from Heaven.
3. That is, between Zionist and non-Zionist religious Jews in recent generations.

The Heavenly Temple approach has several difficulties. There is a positive commandment to build the Temple and as such, it is preferable for it to be built by people, rather than appear miraculously.[4] Rambam writes that it is one of the tasks which the Messiah must perform.[5] Other midrashim state outright that the Third Temple will be built by people.[6] All these sources seem to contradict the idea that the Temple will descend from heaven.

Rashi quotes the idea of a Temple from heaven in part to provide a scenario in which the Temple suddenly appears. To construct an edifice as monumental as the Temple requires many stages of planning, permits, and construction. Such a project would no doubt be a subject of fascination, widely promoted and consecrated amid much fanfare. A situation in which the people are unaware of the Temple's construction seems unlikely.

There are, however, ways in which such a swift opening could take place. One example would be if the entire building were constructed elsewhere and transported into place. Modular units can be dropped into place, connected to water and electricity, and begin to function almost immediately.[7] For example, in 2020, the Chinese government responded to a disease outbreak by constructing a 1,000-bed hospital in ten days. Nonetheless, such buildings are generally generic shapes and would hardly befit the holy Temple.

Another possibility is that technology will make the quick erection of custom-made buildings a reality. The most plausible solution would be a 3D-printed building, for which experiments are currently being conducted. In theory, this or some other technology could make rapid construction possible. However, even in this case, it seems unlikely that all the finish materials and instruments could be installed overnight.

The most likely explanation is that we are not talking about overnight construction at all. Buildings of this scale take time, no matter the scenario. However, with any building, there is a stark line when the edifice goes from "under construction" to "complete." This is more of a concept than an actual finish line, since most buildings open while there is still work to be done. However, at some point a decision is made, a permit issued, or a ribbon cut, and the building is deemed functional. This process is described for the *Mishkan*, when the building was completed yet Bnei

---

4. Rambam, *Sefer Hamitzvot* positive commandment 20, Sefer Hachinuch 95.

5. Rambam, Hilchot Melachim, 11:1.

6. Rashi on bKet 5a, *af yadi*. The Talmud there uses the very same verse to discuss the work of man, rather than the work of God.

7. Such units could be made of concrete or other robust material, and examples do exist of acclaimed architecture constructed in this manner. See, for example, Moshe Safdie's Habitat 1967, though that project was hardly constructed overnight.

Yisrael waited for its consecration.[8] Similarly, a dedication ceremony was held for Shlomo's Temple and every subsequent time work was done on the Temple. In the time of Ezra, worship commenced even though hardly any building existed.[9] The Temple could be under construction, and – without any work taking place at nighttime – a decision made overnight to open the building. Such a pronouncement would render the Temple open for business and alter its halachic standing.[10] Politicians might even insist the Temple be opened in time for the *Omer* offering. In this case, the Temple would be completed "overnight" without any miracles taking place, altering the status of the *Omer* offering.

---

8. BamR, 13:2.

9. Ezra 3:10–13.

10. This possibility is suggested in bShev 15b. A similar scenario exists for the completion of vessels and their susceptibility to impurity. mKel identifies the moment when various types of vessels are deemed complete. See, for example, mKel 5:1–2.

# Four Cubits And Vitruvian Man

רְאוּ כִּי ה׳ נָתַן לָכֶם הַשַּׁבָּת עַל כֵּן הוּא נֹתֵן לָכֶם בַּיּוֹם הַשִּׁשִּׁי לֶחֶם יוֹמָיִם שְׁבוּ אִישׁ תַּחְתָּיו אַל יֵצֵא אִישׁ מִמְּקֹמוֹ בַּיּוֹם הַשְּׁבִיעִי. (שמות טז:כט)

See that the Lord has given you the Shabbat, therefore he gives you on the sixth day the bread of two days, abide every man in his place, let no man go out of his place on the seventh day. (Shemot 16:29)

BNEI Yisrael were instructed not to collect manna on Shabbat. Rather, they were told to "abide every man in his place." The Rabbis use this expression to define the basic area that a man occupies as four cubits.[1] The Talmud explains that a man's body is three cubits tall. Adding a cubit for extended arms brings the total to four cubits.[2]

Though this explanation of the four-cubit measurement makes sense in the context of transporting goods on Shabbat, there is another source from the time of the Mishna that gives a slightly different explanation. Vitruvius, writing about the proportions of the human body, records that a cubit is one-fourth the height of a man.[3] Put another way, a man is four cubits tall. Vitruvius also writes that "If we measure from the soles of the feet to the crown of the head, and this measurement is compared with that of the outstretched hands, one discovers that this breadth equals the height."[4] Just as the idealized man is four cubits tall, his wingspan is also four cubits wide. These two paragraphs in Vitruvius' book, which include ratios of palms, feet, spans, and more, are the inspiration of Leonardo di Vinci's *Vitruvian Man*.[5]

1. MdRY (vayisa) 5, yEruv 4:1 (21a).
2. bEruv 48a.
3. Vitruvius, *Ten Books on Architecture*, III.1.2.
4. Ibid, III.1.3.
5. During the Covid-19 outbreak in 2020, people were instructed to maintain a

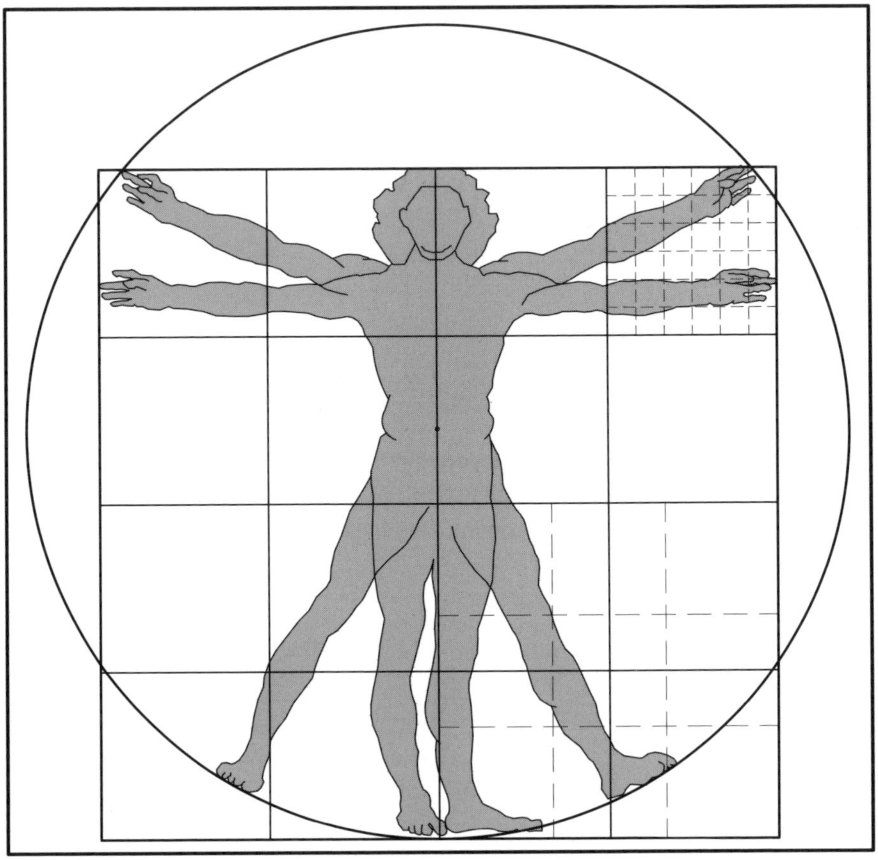

27. Diagram of human proportions with added grids emphasizing cubits, feet, and handbreadths. (Based on Leonardo da Vinci's *Vitruvian Man*, 1490)

What are the differences between the Talmud's measurements of three cubits plus extended hands and those given by Vitruvius, in which man's height is four cubits? One possibility is that the Talmud focuses on the translocation of objects on Shabbat, so it gives a definition that is based on reaching out to grab an object and then stretching to place it as far as possible without moving the body. Vitruvius, on the other hand, is focused on the beautiful symmetry of the body and therefore points to the similar proportions between wingspan and height.

distance of two meters – roughly four cubits – from one another to ensure that airborne droplets could not travel between people. One common guideline for checking this distance was for both people to extend their arms and make sure they could not reach one another.

Another possibility is that the two measurements are based on different systems of proportion. Whereas Vitruvius was relying on the Greek system set forth by the sculptor Polykleitos,[6] perhaps the Rabbis were familiar with the ancient Egyptian system, in which height was given as eighteen fists.[7] At six fists per cubit, this yields a three-cubit height from head to foot.

While it may be surprising that different proportional systems could exist, or even that someone could claim such a thing as universal proportions, this misunderstands the purpose of these measurements. When artists, sculptors, and architects listed these types of sizes, they were not claiming that *all* people have these exact proportions. Rather, these were rules of thumb to help produce depictions of people that appeared realistic. It can be difficult to create figures that look right. Getting the proportion of the head to the body, or the correct length of the arms is crucial to achieving this goal. The building proportions which Vitruvius connects to the human body work in a comparable fashion – they are guidelines so that buildings will look dignified.[8] Similarly, the halachic explanation of four cubits does not mean all men are exactly this size. Rather, the Talmud wanted to give a logical explanation for the area over which a person can exert control. The Talmud uses the standard body size of four cubits to derive a concrete halachic definition for use in a variety of situations, including carrying objects on Shabbat.

---

6. Polykleitos pioneered a canon of proportion. He believed that symmetry and proportion were the two most important components in beauty, and made sculptures to demonstrate these proportions, including his *Doryphoros*, which has survived only as copies. The word canon comes from the Greek word for measuring stick. The Hebrew word קנה, which appears in Yechezkel 40:5, may come from a shared source. See the Daat Mikre commentary there.

7. Smith, W. Stevenson, and Simpson, William Kelly. *The Art and Architecture of Ancient Egypt* (Yale University Press, 1998), 33–34 and figure 53.

8. In the twentieth century, Le Corbusier introduced a system called the Modulor that also supplied a "human scale" to his architecture. He, however, was more interested in measuring the world in the scale of man. This can be compared to bKet 5b, which assigns names to each finger in the hand based on a function it serves in Jewish law. The pinky is called *zeret* for its use in measuring the high priest's breastplate. The ring finger is called *kemitza* for its roles in measuring out a fistful of flour from flour offerings. The middle finger is called *ama* for its roles in measuring the Temple vessels. The pointer is called *etzba* after its use in sprinkling the blood of sacrifices. The thumb is called *bohen* for its use in anointing priests and people afflicted with *tzaraat*. Here the Talmud tries to frame the human body in terms of the various religious measurements.

# Museums and Reliquaries

וַיֹּאמֶר מֹשֶׁה אֶל אַהֲרֹן קַח צִנְצֶנֶת אַחַת וְתֶן שָׁמָּה מְלֹא הָעֹמֶר מָן וְהַנַּח אֹתוֹ
לִפְנֵי ה׳ לְמִשְׁמֶרֶת לְדֹרֹתֵיכֶם. (שמות טז:לג)

And Moshe said to Aharon: "Take a jar and put an omerful of manna in it and lay it up before the Lord, to be kept throughout your generations." (Shemot 16:33)

MOSHE instructed Aharon to place an *omer* of manna in a jar, to be kept indefinitely in the *Mishkan*. The commentators, starting with the Mechilta, speculate that the manna's container was made of clay.[1] Rabeinu Bachya explains the Hebrew word for jar, *tzintzenet*, is related to keeping things cool, *tzonen*. He writes that a clay jar is excellent for keeping its contents at a steady temperature, preserving them.[2] R. S.R. Hirsch points out how the sun's heat was injurious to the manna and that the manna spoiled easily.[3] On the one hand, this emphasizes the importance of keeping the preserved manna cool, while on the other hand, it recalls that the manna was a miraculous substance that could last for two days when needed, so perhaps it is not surprising that a special portion of manna could be preserved in perpetuity.[4]

In addition to the manna, the *Mishkan* reportedly served as a repository for other artifacts from the Exodus period. It held Aharon's flowering staff,[5]

1. MdRS 16:33.
2. This was the tactic originally used to preserve the Dead Sea Scrolls.
3. Shemot 16:20–21.
4. See Ralbag.
5. As per Bamidbar 17:25. Aaron's Rod has served as an architectural design motif, especially in medieval Christian design as a molding with leaves scrolling around a post. It is alternatively depicted with a snake around it, recalling the scene in Shemot 7:10. Since the 1823 edition of Peter Nicholson's *New Practical Builder's Guide,* the term has been included in architectural dictionaries and glossaries. Nicholson added it at some point after 1819, when it was not included in his *Architectural Dictionary.* It is

the anointing oil and the fragments of the two broken tablets, as well as the gifts sent by the Philistines in the time of Shmuel.[6] The Talmud states that exceptionally large grains from the time of Shimon ben Shetach were preserved as well.[7] The Mechilta tells of at least one instance, in the time of Yirmiyahu, when the manna was publicly displayed to demonstrate the miracles that had been performed for Bnei Yisrael.[8]

This method of historical preservation is different than the tactic used for another part of the Exodus story, the matza. Instead of physically preserving a portion of matza, the matza is instead recreated yearly during Pesach. Both tactics attempt to preserve the memory of the Exodus, one via an artifact and the other via reenactment.[9]

While we are told by the Torah that the manna was kept for future generations, it is not certain to what end this was done. Historically, temples sometimes served as repositories for ancient artifacts, a tradition that can be traced as least as far back as the Elamite king Shutruk-Nahhunte in 1160 BCE.[10] These artifacts, however, tended to be items of value or spoils of war. In medieval Europe, many churches were built to hold relics and serve as pilgrimage sites.[11] Some of these relics were said to miraculously remain without decay. The belief was that contact with relics could bring about miracles. However, Judaism does not have a strong tradition of reliquaries. Judaism tends to focus on places or items of historical importance, rather than miraculous objects, though some devotees of visiting the graves of famous rabbis may disagree. The manna was not preserved

---

rarely referenced in architectural works besides dictionaries, but in dictionaries it has a certain prominence due to its alphabetical location. A copy of Aaron's Rod has been adopted as part of the ceremonial objects used by the Masons.

6. tSot 13:1 and tYom 3:7, quoted in bYom 52b, bHor 12a, bKer 5a, and MdRY Beshalach (vayisa) 5. The Mechilta also emphasizes that this is such an important artifact that in the times of the Messiah, Eliyahu will return the jar of manna to its rightful place. See also Hebrews 9:4. ARN A 41 gives a similar list which includes the priestly garments.

7. bTaan 23a and VayR 35:10.

8. Commenting on Yirmiyahu 2:31.

9. With some Japanese buildings, rather than repair an existing structure, the building was dismantled and rebuilt using traditional building techniques every so often, to preserve both the building and the knowledge of its construction methods. See Arthur Drexler, *Architecture of Japan* (Museum of Modern Art, 1955), 35. For more on historical preservation, see my commentary on Vayikra 14:42.

10. Lionel Casson, *Travel in the Ancient World* (Johns Hopkins University Press, 1994), 238.

11. James Steven Curl, "Reliquaries" in *Oxford Dictionary of Architecture and Landscape Architecture*, second edition (Oxford University Press, 2007), 631. Reminiscent of this practice is the Talmud's ruling that even sculptures of a hand or foot are forbidden, "for such objects are worshipped," as per yAZ 3:2 (42c).

to help perform miracles, but rather for historical records, or as a way of strengthening faith.

One proof of this point is the building that held each type of relic. Churches made the reliquaries available to the pilgrims and made the relics a central focus of the architecture. The manna, however, was placed in the *Mishkan,* not to aggrandize the *Mishkan,* but because it was a secure location. The manna was kept out of view, in the Holy of Holies. As such, the jar of manna should be seen not as a relic with the ability to affect miracles, but as a historical artifact that testifies how God cared for Bnei Yisrael in the desert.

# Marking Boundaries

וְהִגְבַּלְתָּ אֶת הָעָם סָבִיב לֵאמֹר הִשָּׁמְרוּ לָכֶם עֲלוֹת בָּהָר וּנְגֹעַ בְּקָצֵהוּ כָּל הַנֹּגֵעַ
בָּהָר מוֹת יוּמָת. (שמות יט:יב)

And you shall set bounds to the people round about, saying: Take heed to yourselves, that you go not up into the mount, or touch the border of it. Whoever touches the mount shall be surely put to death. (Shemot 19:12)

In preparation for the giving of the Torah, Moshe was told to set bounds around Mount Sinai to prevent anyone from scaling the mountain or even touching its edges. The Mechilta records that these boundaries were to be physically marked, ensuring that no person or animal would accidentally wander into forbidden territory.[1] Rashi explains that the boundary markers said "Be warned not to go up from this point. You have been warned."

Among the supercommentaries on Rashi, there is a dispute about what Rashi meant by this statement. Some claim that Rashi believed that the boundary miraculously spoke this warning to all who approached.[2] Most, however, go to lengths to explain that the boundary only acted as a reminder not to advance toward Mount Sinai and that it was Moshe who spoke the warning.[3] The simplest understanding of Rashi is that there were signs posted along the boundary which bore this warning.[4]

There are several cases in which boundary markers are required for

1. MdRS on this verse, which is quoted by Rashi.

2. This appears in R. Yisachar Eilenberg's commentary Tzeida Laderech, though I have not seen the text inside. Many of the other commentaries respond to this statement in disagreement.

3. See especially R. David Pardo's Maskil Ledavid.

4. The major drawback in a sign bearing written instructions is that it cannot be understood by the illiterate or people who do not understand the language. This is why pictograms are often used in signage.

otherwise invisible halachic thresholds. Rashi's commentary is reminiscent of the *soreg* in the Second Temple complex, which marked the 500 × 500 area of the Temple Mount into which non-Jews were prohibited from entering.[5] When the footprint of the Temple complex was expanded, this boundary was marked to show the original, consecrated area and prevent foreigners from accidentally crossing this line. Josephus records that "at equal intervals stood slabs announcing the laws of purification, some in Greek and some in Roman characters. No foreigner was to enter the holy area."[6] Two of these signs have been discovered, bearing text reminiscent of Rashi's words on our verse.

28. Temple warning inscription: "No foreigner is to enter within the balustrade and enclosure around the Sanctuary. Whoever is caught will himself be responsible for [his] consequent death." (Photo by Tamar Hayardeni, Wikimedia)

Other examples existed within the Temple itself. The Mishna describes *roshei psiposim* which marked the boundary between different sections of the Temple.[7] Bartenura explains that these were beams that protruded from the walls, though the Greek word implies that small mosaic stones marked the boundary.[8] Similar markers appeared in the attic of the

5. mMid 2:3.
6. Josephus, *The Jewish War*, 5.193–4. See also *Antiquities*, 15:417.
7. mMid 2:6.
8. Some linguists believe that the word in the Mishna is not a Greek loanword, and that in this case it comes from a Hebrew root for boards. For another example of beams used to subdivide a space, see BerR 50:8, in which Lot's wife demands that Lot's guests remain in the other half of their house, as marked by the beams.

Temple, demarcating the line between the Holy and the Holy of Holies below.[9] Inside the Temple itself, where only initiated priests had access, the markers were subtler than those adorning the *soreg,* and no written explanation was deemed necessary.

The laws of *eruvin* are filled with similar demarcations, accomplished by visible beams and lintels that create a symbolic enclosure and inform pedestrians that they are transitioning from one halachic space to another.[10] In the case of the 2000-cubit Shabbat boundary, the line marking the edge of the boundary is assumed to be imprecise, so there is some leeway if someone accidentally wanders beyond it.[11] There is some blurriness in the case of Mount Sinai as well: R. Eliyahu Mizrachi notes that mountains do not usually have a clear, cliff-like edge, but rather gradually increase in steepness. It would have been hard to mark the exact edge of Mount Sinai, so instead the boundary was placed a safe distance away.

There is a wide range of options for marking spaces in architecture, including changes of material, differences of heights, gateways, signs, lighting, and physical barriers. In some cases, only a subtle reminder is needed, while in others we make absolutely certain to have a robust barrier. Train stations, for example, mark the edge of the platform with paving that is both a different color and which has raised bumps.

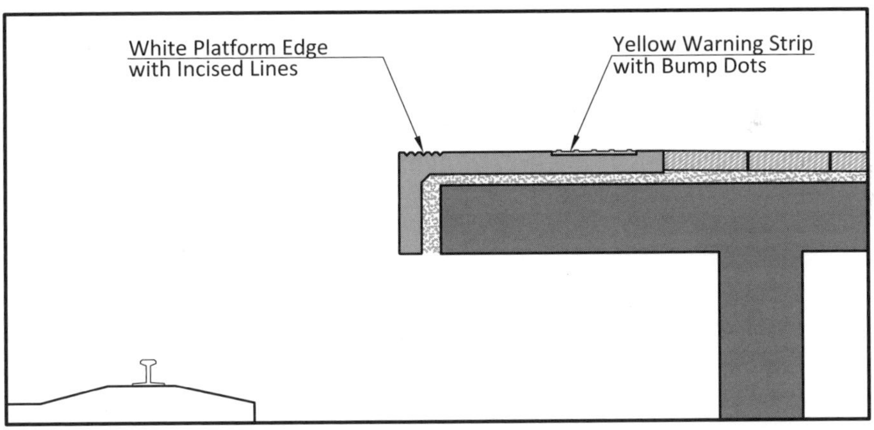


29. Railway platform edge. (Based on standard detail by Israel Railways)

9. mMid 4:5.

10. mEruv 1:1–4.

11. mEruv 4:11. R. Eliezer gives two cubits of leeway, while R. Shimon allows for up to fifteen cubits. In 2011, a rock with an ancient inscription reading "Shabbat" was found east of Timrat, which may have been a marker of the Shabbat boundary. See Mordechai Aviam, "The Shabbat Boundary at Timrat" in *Eretz Magazine* (Aug.–Sep. 2011), 53–55.

In the case of the boundary around Mount Sinai, it was necessary to have an obvious, physical barrier to prevent people from accidentally crossing into forbidden territory. This was a one-time event, so the people would have been unfamiliar with the setup. No subtle demarcations would have sufficed. Rashi's explanation about the boundary markers reflects this and emphasizes the need for a clear and self-explanatory border to prevent any acts of trespassing.

YITRO

# Idols and Architecture

לֹא תַעֲשֶׂה לְךָ פֶסֶל וְכָל תְּמוּנָה אֲשֶׁר בַּשָּׁמַיִם מִמַּעַל וַאֲשֶׁר בָּאָרֶץ מִתַּחַת וַאֲשֶׁר בַּמַּיִם מִתַּחַת לָאָרֶץ. (שמות כ:ד)

You shall not make for yourself any carved idol nor any manner of likeness of anything that is in heaven above or that is in the earth beneath or that is in the water under the earth. (Shemot 20:4)

THE Torah prohibits the making of any idols, and then specifically forbids bowing down or serving them. These prohibitions have been the subject of halachic debates about the status of sculptures that are *not* the object of worship.[1] Sforno writes that making idols is forbidden, even if they are not intended for worship. Rambam records the same position, adding that one may not make idols for non-Jews. Even sculptures that are purely aesthetic are outlawed.[2] However, Ramban argues this point and explains that only idols made for worship are forbidden.[3]

Jews in the Greek and Roman world had to make use of urban spaces that were filled with carved figures. Rabbinic literature relates several cases in which Jews were permitted to interact with idols. The most famous concerns R. Gamliel in the bathhouse of Aphrodite, where he ruled that it is permitted to use the bathhouse despite the presence of an idol.[4] Another

1. See Yaron Eliav, "Viewing the Sculptural Environment: Shaping the Second Commandment" in *The Talmud Yerushalmi and Graeco-Roman Culture* Vol. III. ed. Peter Shäfer (Mor Siebeck, 1998), 421 for an argument about making the distinction thusly, rather than as between religious/non-religious or decorative/non-decorative sculptures. If decoration is done for religious purposes, even if it is not an idol, it can also be prohibited, as in stores decorated for pagan holidays. See bAZ 13a and yAZ 1:4.

2. Rambam, Hilchot Avoda Zara 3:9–10 and *Sefer Hamitzvot*, negative commandment 2.

3. See his commentary on Rambam's *Sefer Hamitzvot*, negative commandment 5.

4. mAZ 3:4. R. Gamliel explains that "I did not enter into her space, but rather she

mishna classifies which idols are forbidden, ruling that only idols holding certain symbolic objects are prohibited.[5] One can take a drink from a waterspout in a fountain that is shaped like a human face, provided one does not appear to be kissing the face.[6] R. Yochanan advised his student to simply avert their eyes when passing an idol.[7] Presumably, these were only some of the ways that Jews coped with living in cities awash with sculptures.[8]

There is a nuanced division between different types of idols found in architecture. The Mishna rules that a house built for idol worship may not be used[9] and that one may not assist in building a structure intended for idol worship.[10] However, the Mishna allows a Jew to help an idol worshiper construct a building for secular use, even if there will be idols in it. He must only refrain from building a niche that will house the idol itself.[11]

While the above statement in the Mishna takes one type of sculpture into account, architecture employs sculpture in two different ways. In some situations, an idol is used as a focal point. A figure placed in an apse or at the center of a rotunda stands alone and serves as a dominant feature, framed by the architecture. This is the situation described in the mishna above, where one cannot build the niche housing an idol. But there are also buildings that integrate sculpture into the walls and use them as a means of telling stories. These are usually found in temples or other places of worship – the frieze, metopes, and pediments of a Greek temple, or scenes of the final judgment in the portals of Romanesque and Gothic cathedrals.

---

entered into mine. We do not say that the bathhouse is a decoration for Aphrodite, but rather we say that Aphrodite is a decoration for the bathhouse."

5. mAZ 3:1.

6. tAZ 6:6.

7. yMK 3:7 (83c).

8. See Steven Fine, *Art & Judaism in the Greco-Roman World* (Cambridge University Press, 2005), 111, who frames the issue in this manner.

9. mAZ 3:7.

10. mAZ 3:6, which states that if a house shares a wall with a pagan temple and the shared wall collapses, it cannot be rebuilt unless the wall is set back from the property line so that it is not shared with the temple.

11. mAZ 1:7. This mishna relates to a bathhouse. R. Moshe Feinstein writes on this subject in *Igrot Moshe* YD I, 68. He explains that Rashi, Rambam, Beit Yosef, and R. Nissim of Gerona all felt that you could even build a building used for idol worship so long as you do not build the dome with the idol, but R. David Halevi Segal and the Vilna Gaon believed that this was only true for buildings not devoted to idol worship, as per the analysis above. R. Feinstein therefore rules that one should be strict and not physically build places of pagan worship but adds unequivocally that a draftsman or architect may prepare blueprints for such a structure. He also adds that there is no problem with either building or designing a Conservative or Reform temple.

Similar elements can be found in triumphal arches, columns, and some secular neo-classical buildings. These types of sculptures are called reliefs and can themselves be categorized based on how much they project from the plane of the wall. High relief is sculpture that is almost detached from the wall; middle relief protrudes about halfway, and low-relief projects less than half of its three-dimensional form.[12]

30. Lintel above the central portal of the Chartres Cathedral. (Photo by Allan T. Kohl)

The Second Commandment is most associated with free-standing statues. Relief sculptures, however, were what inundated Roman cities with carved images.[13] Jewish law tends to be more lenient with this type of sculpture – Rambam concludes that high reliefs of a human face and astronomical figures are forbidden, whereas all other subjects can be depicted

12. "Relief" in *Oxford Dictionary of Architecture and Landscaped Architecture* by James Stevens Curl, (Oxford University Press, 2007), 631. Tosafot (bYom 54a *keruvim*) makes a similar point in arguing that only three-dimensional objects are problematic. (While images in prayer books are potentially distracting, they do not qualify as idol worship.) This argument was the reason that Ephraim ben Isaac of Regensburg ruled that the stained-glass windows in the Cologne synagogue which depicted animals did not violate the laws against idol worship. bAZ 43b, which discusses signet rings, alludes to the topic of sculpture in relief.

13. Eliav, "Viewing the Sculptural Environment," 414. The face-shaped water spout mentioned above is one example of a relief sculpture.

in relief.[14] Perhaps this leniency relates to the above distinction about how the two types of sculpture are typically used. Freestanding idols tend to be used as focal points and are therefore more problematic. Reliefs are typically used to tell a story and create ambiance, rather than serving as the objects of worship. They are therefore treated more leniently.

14. Rambam Hilchot Avoda Zara 3:10–11. Astronomical figures are treated in the strictest manner and cannot even be depicted in low relief. See also Shulchan Aruch YD 141:4–6.

# Tripartite Division in Buildings

וְיוֹם הַשְּׁבִיעִי שַׁבָּת לַה' אֱלֹקֶיךָ לֹא תַעֲשֶׂה כָל מְלָאכָה אַתָּה וּבִנְךָ וּבִתֶּךָ עַבְדְּךָ וַאֲמָתְךָ וּבְהֶמְתֶּךָ וְגֵרְךָ אֲשֶׁר בִּשְׁעָרֶיךָ. (שמות כ:י)

But the seventh day is a Shabbat to the Lord your God, you shall not do any manner of work, you nor your son, nor your daughter, your manservant, nor your maidservant, nor your cattle, nor your stranger that is within your gates. (Shemot 20:10)

BUILDING is one of the thirty-nine categories of activities that are prohibited on Shabbat.[1] The Mishna defines building as "building any amount," but also explores issues of permanence, sturdiness, and fastenings. The Mishna's discussion of this category mostly focuses on stone construction,[2] specifically mentioning chiseling, hammering, chopping, and drilling.[3]

One case in the Talmud discusses two people building a wall, where one applies the mortar while the other lays the stones. Mortar binds the small stones into one cohesive unit, strengthening the building. The Talmud's discussion implies that in some cases mortar is the vital component, while in others, mortar is less critical. The Rabbis clarify that there are three parts of a masonry wall, each with its own mortar needs:

(1) The foundation requires laying stone and backfilling the hole with earth,[4] but does not require mortar.

1. mShab 7:2.

2. This despite the statement in the Yerushalmi that the relevant building activity in the *Mishkan* was the connecting of the wooden wall panels and the metal support sockets. See yShab 12:1 (13c).

3. mShab 12:1. In yShab 7:2 (10d) the Talmud states that the fact that we learn the prohibition of building on Shabbat from the *Mishkan* shows that even temporary buildings are considered buildings.

4. Vitruvius also emphasizes the importance of the backfill for the foundation walls.

(2) The middle portion requires stone and mortar.
(3) The top row can be placed without mortar.[5]

The Talmud's division of a building into three layers is consistent with Greek and Roman architecture. Classical temple façades were vertically divided into three parts: the pedestal or stylobate as the foundation, the column in the middle, and the entablature at the top. However, little is written to explain the reason for this tripartite division. The discussion in the Talmud provides one possibility for its origin: the structural needs of each of the three parts are different. The bottom section must be solid and level, with an emphasis on its contact with the ground. The middle section forms the body of the building and must therefore be structurally strong. The top caps the building and relies on its bulk and gravity to stay in place.

Although the Talmud considers the tripartite division solely as a structural issue, classical architecture has an additional layer of aesthetic considerations on top of any structural reasons. This is evident in the tendency of classical architecture to subdivide each section into further and further divisions of three. Alexander Tzonis and Liane Lefaivre wrote that "As a general rule, tripartition continues to be applied in the same hierarchical manner down to the most basic architectural particle, to the slenderest ripple of matter."[6] For example, the entablature is divided into the cornice, frieze, and architrave, while the column contains the capital, shaft, and base.[7] The reason for the division and re-division into three is because a three-part division is visually far more dynamic, flexible, and appealing than a two-part division.

In the late nineteenth century, when skyscrapers were first being built, architects sought a way to deal with the elongated façades of the buildings. One of the influential architects in Chicago, Louis Sullivan,[8] looked to the tripartite division of columns for inspiration:

> Certain critics, and very thoughtful ones, have advanced the theory that the true prototype of the tall office building is the classical column, consisting of base, shaft and capital, – the molded base of the column typical of the lower stories of our building, the plain or

See *Ten Books on Architecture* III.4.2.

5. bShab 102b and tShab 11:1.

6. Tzonis, Alexander and Lefaivre, Liane, *Classical Architecture: The Poetics of Order* (MIT Press, 1986), 43.

7. Vitruvius, III.5.2–5. The tripartite division of columns is highlighted in VayR 25:8 and BamR 10:1.

8. See my commentary on Shemot 26:33 for more on Sullivan and the skyscraper.

31. The five orders. (Claude Perrault, *A Treatise of the Five Orders of Columns in Architecture*, 1708, plate 1)

> fluted shaft suggesting the monotonous, uninterrupted series of office-tiers, and the capital the completing power and luxuriance of the attic.[9]

This became the most common scheme for the design of tall buildings. The bottom floors appeared like a base, with rougher masonry. The top floors formed a cap, protruding on all sides and providing a flourish. The middle

9. Sullivan, Louis H. "The Tall Office Building Artistically Considered" in *Lippincott's Magazine*, March 1896.

floors, making up the bulk of the building, created a pattern by repeating one floor after another. In addition to the pleasing aesthetic pattern, the division also tapped into the inherent structural dependability associated with the tripartite division. This helped reassured the populace that tall buildings were structurally safe.

The Talmud's description of three-part division in buildings is consistent with the way classical architecture categorized the parts of a building. However, while the Rabbis focused primarily on structural reasons, architects were more concerned with the tripartite division from an aesthetic point of view.

32. Prudential building by Dankmar Adler and Louis Sullivan. (Jack E. Boucher, Library of Congress, Prints & Photographs Division, NY, 15-Buf, 6–2)

YITRO

# Replicas of the Temple

לֹא תַעֲשׂוּן אִתִּי אֱלֹהֵי כֶסֶף וֵאלֹהֵי זָהָב לֹא תַעֲשׂוּ לָכֶם. (שמות כ:כ)

You shall not make with Me gods of silver or gods of gold, you shall not make unto you. (Shemot 20:20)

BNEI Yisrael are forbidden to make gods of silver or gold. The Rabbis debate the limits of this prohibition, including whether astronomical models can be made to aid testimony about the new moon. As part of this discussion, the Talmud quotes a *beraita* that forbids the construction of buildings shaped like the Temple, passages shaped like the *Heichal,* or courtyards shaped like the Temple courtyard.[1] Sefer Hachinuch explains that this law is to preserve the awe and reverence of the Temple.[2]

Making a copy of the Temple was not merely a theoretical issue; two satellite temples were established in Egypt. The first was in Elephantine in the fifth century BCE. The second, the Temple of Onias, is described in the Talmud[3] and by Josephus, who quotes a letter from Onias IV requesting permission from Ptolemy to build a temple "after the pattern of that in Jerusalem, and of the same dimensions."[4] However, later Josephus reports that "Onias constructed a fortress and built his Sanctuary – not like that in Jerusalem but resembling a tower – built of large blocks of stone and rising to a height of sixty cubits."[5] Onias may have altered his plans to comply with the ruling of the sages against duplicating the design of the Temple.[6]

1. bAZ 43a and bRH 24a.
2. Sefer Hachinuch 221.
3. bMen 109a–110a
4. Josephus, *Antiquities*, 13.3.67.
5. Josephus, *The Jewish War*, 7.
6. Zoref, Ephraim. "*Mikdash Chonio*" in *Mahanayim* 105, 1966. This issue is connected to the debate about whether the Temple retains its holiness even after its destruction, as discussed in bMeg 10a and bZev 107b. Onias, as one of the priests who were protesting the usurpation of the office of high priest by the Maccabim, may

As the most prominent architecture in Tanach and the most significant building in ancient Israel, it is not surprising that the Temple has served as inspiration for subsequent buildings. Jewish architecture in Late Antiquity adopted some of the design motifs of the Temple, with the well-to-do using similar décor in their residences and burial chambers.[7] Halacha even suggests that some aspects of the Temple be mimicked in everyday architecture.[8]

Architects sometimes allude to well-known buildings in their designs. This can be playful, an homage, or an indication of the spirit of the building. Sometimes, designers copy previous structures accurately. This was common with Neo-Classicism, where ancient Greek or Roman designs were copied for new edifices. The main waiting room in McKim, Mead, and White's Penn Station was inspired by the Roman Baths of Caracalla.[9] The Arc De Triomphe in Paris was inspired by the Arch of Titus in Rome. The Jerusalem Temple also served as an influence for subsequent architecture. The Sistine Chapel uses dimensions of the First Temple. A synagogue in Worms had two columns, mimicking the two in Shlomo's Temple.[10] The twisted, "Solomonic" columns that were in the original St. Peter's Basilica were supposedly taken from the Temple. These columns inspired other twisted columns that mimicked the Temple's design. More recently, the Temple of Solomon in São Paulo, Brazil is a scaled-up copy of the Temple.

There is some debate as to the extent to which copying the Temple is forbidden. The Shulchan Aruch explains that only a building with the *dimensions* of the Temple violates this precept.[11] R. Shabtai ben Meir HaKohen comments that even a slight deviation from the dimensions is enough to make the design permissible.[12] This limits the scope of the prohibition considerably. Although buildings are sometimes inspired by the architecture of the Temple or copy small aspects of it, they rarely duplicate

have felt that the Temple in Jerusalem had lost its sanctity. See Rachel Elior, *The Three Temples* (Littman Library of Jewish Civilization, 2004), 195.

7. Orit Peleg-Barkat concludes a study of the Temple's design motifs by stating that "There is little doubt that the decorators ... were inspired by what they saw at the entrance to the Temple Mount." See Orit Peleg-Barkat, "Interpreting the Uninterpreted" in *Jewish Art in Its Late Antique Context* ed. Uzi Leibner and Catherine Hezser, (Mohr Siebeck, 2016), 38.

8. tMeg 3:22 states that entrances to synagogues must be from the east, similar to the Temple's entrance. mBB 6:4 states that we learn proper proportions of height-to-width for a house from the proportions of the Temple.

9. They also inspired Chicago Union Station and the Basilica of Maxentius.

10. Carol Herselle Krinsky, *Synagogues of Europe* (MIT Press, 1985), 9.

11. YD 141:8.

12. In his Siftei Kohen (Shach) commentary on YD 141:8.

its dimensions entirely. According to this opinion, the prohibition would hardly ever be relevant to architectural design.[13]

R. Yosef Babad raises an additional, significant limitation on this prohibition in his Minchat Chinuch. He notes that the *Mishkan* and each version of the Temple had different dimensions.[14] He concludes that this prohibition is only relevant when the Temple is standing and, even then, merely outlaws the replication of the current Temple's dimensions.[15] Only when the Temple is standing does a copy lessen the awe for the holy edifice.

This halachic debate is related to what it meant to copy a building in pre-modern times. Before the advent of photography, it was difficult to produce an accurate depiction of a building. Although sketches and drawings could be made, most records of architecture were written descriptions, a type of writing known as ekphrasis. The only way to be certain what a building looked like was to visit it in person. Even then, it was nearly impossible to record all the relevant details and dimensions, to allow for an accurate reproduction. Drawn plans or built models rarely existed. As such, "copies" of buildings were not accurate duplicates. In a study of medieval buildings that were billed as replications of the Church of the Holy Sepulcher, Richard Krautheimer showed that most imitations chose a few important dimensions or features but did not resemble the original.[16] A survey of Temple-influenced architecture would yield similar results. This may well be why the Talmud first writes that one cannot copy the Temple and then follows with a clarification that one cannot copy the entrance or the courtyard shape, since these elements could practically have been copied.

Besides these complications, architects seeking to copy the Temple met with the additional difficulty that the building no longer existed. No visual copies remained, so only written descriptions – and in later periods,

---

13. The Holy Land Experience, a biblical theme park, does strive for a precise copy. It demonstrates how disrespectful it can be to make a copy of the Temple, integrating Christian iconography and proselytizing Jews. See Joan R. Branham, "The Temple That Won't Quit" in *Harvard Divinity Bulletin* 36:3 (Autumn, 2008), 20–31.

14. For restrictions on changing the design of the Temple, see bChul 83b, referencing Divrei Hayamim I 28:19.

15. Minchat Chinuch 254:6. He also notes that we do not know how the Third Temple will look – "there are many things that are obfuscated [in the description of the Third Temple in Yechezkel] and when the Messiah comes and God enlightens us, then we will derive from the verses the design of the Temple." Beit Efraim disagrees, prohibiting a house with the dimensions of any of the historic Temples.

16. Richard Krautheimer, "Introduction to an 'Iconography of Medieval Architecture'" in *Journal of the Warburg and Courtauld Institutes* V (1942)1–33. See analysis in Mario Carpo, *Architecture in the Age of Printing* (MIT Press, 2001), 34–41.

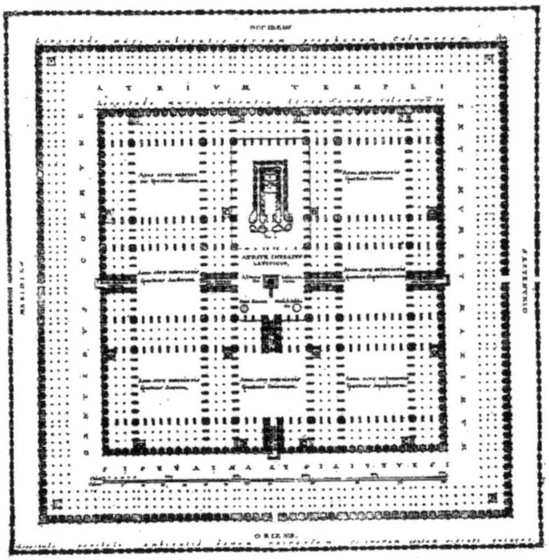

33. Villalpando's Temple plan, with grid that influenced synagogue and church design in the following centuries. (Villapando, *Commentary on Yechezkel*, 1596–1604, Wikimedia)

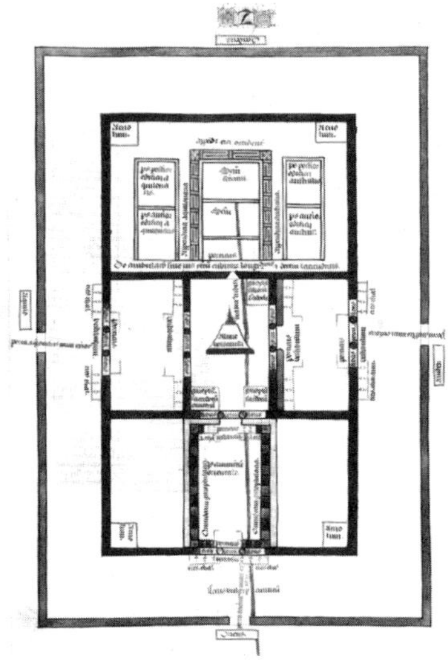

34. Temple plan. (Nicholas of Lyra, *Commentary on Yechezkel*, circa 1500, WIkimedia)

archaeological remains – could be used as the basis for construction. Early architects would have used sketches by Rashi, Rambam, Richard of St. Victor, or Nicholas of Lyra. In the seventeenth century, a model created by Juan Bautista Villalpando influenced the architecture of "nine-bay" synagogues, churches, and monasteries in Poland.[17] Villalpando was followed by many other designers, such as Benito Arias Montano, Yehuda Leon, and Claude Perrault, who illustrated the Latin edition of the Mishna Torah.[18] Louis Kahn's unbuilt design for the Churva synagogue was based on a different recreation of the Temple and looked nothing at all like Villalpando's work.[19] Today, the most popular depictions of the Temple are the ones prepared by Leen Ritmeyer and the Second Temple model by Michael Avi Yonah, which while certainly more accurate than previous offerings, are still based on much conjecture.[20] If a modern architect were to design a

17. Kravtsov, Sergey R. "Juan Bautista Villalpando and Sacred Architecture in the Seventeenth Century" in *Journal of the Society of Architectural Historians,* 64:3, 312–339. See also Joseph Rykwert, *On Adam's House in Paradise* (MIT Press, 1981), 121–140.

18. Perrault's brother, Charles, recorded early versions of many famous fairy tales, and influenced the Grimm brothers.

19. Kahn used James Fergusson's drawings of the Temple for inspiration. See Kent Larson, *Louis I Kahn, Unbuilt Masterworks* (Monacelli Press, 2000), 135.

20. Ehud Netzer, like Vallalpando before him, considered his reconstructions to be

building based on the Temple today, he or she would probably start with these renderings in mind. In each case, the architect is not copying the actual Temple, but rather an imprecise reconstruction of the Temple.

Architects seeking to recreate the Temple's design would have had difficulty even if the Temple were still standing. After its destruction, architects could only copy later interpretations, as they had no way to know exactly how the real Temples looked. This limited the extent to which a building could truly replicate the Temple and supports the opinion of the Minchat Chinuch that one is only prohibited from copying an *existing* Temple. Architects looking for inspiration from the Temple are not duplicating what really existed, but rather what *may have been*. People who view their designs are not comparing them to an existing building, but rather to a memory. As such, these duplicates seem removed from any prohibition against copying the Temple, and we can understand why some rabbis ruled leniently on this issue.

superior to his predecessors because he considered both Josephus and tractate Midot. See Ehud Netzer, *The Architecture of Herod the Great Builder* (Baker Academic, 2008), 142 note 16. In Vallalpando's case, he argued for the superiority of his recreations as he used the original Hebrew sources as well as Vitruvius.

# Unhewn Stones

> וְאִם מִזְבַּח אֲבָנִים תַּעֲשֶׂה לִּי לֹא תִבְנֶה אֶתְהֶן גָּזִית כִּי חַרְבְּךָ הֵנַפְתָּ עָלֶיהָ וַתְּחַלְלֶהָ. (שמות כ:כב)
>
> And if you make Me an altar of stone, you shall not build it of hewn stone, for if you lift up your tool upon it, you have profaned it. (Shemot 20:22)

THE Torah sets guidelines on the dressing of stones for the altar. The verse commands "You shall not build it of hewn stone" and in Devarim, the Torah states "you shall lift up no iron tool upon them."[1] The Mechilta explains that iron is used for weapons and is thus not suitable for the altar.[2] This explanation, quoted by Rashi, is widely accepted.

Commentators debate which of these two verses is the primary prohibition – using hewn stones or using iron tools. Some argue that the use of hewn stones is the main restriction, either out of fear that stone carvers will engrave figures on the stones[3] or to avoid complications when disposing of stone chips.[4] Others state that it is the iron that is problematic, either as tools for chiseling stone or as a building material anywhere in the Temple.[5] Some explain that only in the Temple courtyard was it forbidden to chisel stones, but stones could be dressed outside the Temple and brought to the site.[6]

---

1. Devarim 27:5.
2. As the altar is made to lengthen people's life by atoning for their sins. MdRY, Yitro (BaChodesh) 11. See parallel in tBK 7:6.
3. Rashbam, Rambam *Moreh Nevuchim* 3:45.
4. Ibn Ezra writes that the stone chips may be consecrated. See yShek 4:1 (48a).
5. Ramban and Rabeinu Bachya. However, see bMen 107a, which states that iron was used for the anti-bird spikes on the roof of the Temple, and mPes 5:9, which mentions iron hooks in the Temple.
6. See Rashi, *amar Abayei* on bTam 26b. Normally, stones are roughly cut at the

Addressing the obvious difficulty, the Tosefta recounts how stones were cut without the use of iron. Shlomo is said to have used the *shamir*, which was able to eat through any material.[7] Aristotle quotes a similar legend, writing that "in Cyprus they say mice eat iron."[8] Cutting stone without iron is not impossible. A source describing preliminary work done for the Temple during the reign of Julian states that silver tools were used.[9] In the time of the Mishna, stone could be split using wooden staves, though this still requires holes or trenches to be cut in the stone. Pliny the Elder describes how cutting marble is "actually done by sand, as the saw presses the sand on a very narrow line and brings about the cutting by its very passage back and forth."[10] Nowadays, modern diamond-bit saws use a similar principle, cutting with the abrasion of diamond bits, rather than the metal discs in which they are set. Stone can also be cut with water jets or lasers, which would potentially provide a solution for any future Temple projects.

Returning to the parameters of the prohibition, despite widespread acceptance that iron cannot be used due to its role in weaponry, this statement seems arbitrary. Any material can be used for positive or negative ends, and iron is no exception. The multiple uses of iron, for good and bad, are masterfully utilized in Yishayahu's prophecy about beating swords into plowshares;[11] iron is clearly well-suited for both uses.[12] Even stone can be weaponized, as with Roman *ballistae*. Indeed, while several tannaitic sources quote the idea of iron shortening lives, Malbim implies that it is a moral lesson inserted by R. Yochanan ben Zakkai.

It is possible that the Torah was not seeking to ban iron tools but rather wished to emphasize the symbolism of the altar's material. When the

---

quarry and finished on site. If stonework were completed away from the Temple Mount, all stones would need to be finely cut before arriving on site. It is unclear how precision cuts would be made or how the fine finishes would be protected during transportation. See Orit Peleg-Barkat, *The Temple Mount Excavations, Vol. V* (Institute of Archaeology, Hebrew University, 2017), 16, Victor Hurowitz, *I Have Built You an Exalted House* (Sheffield Academic Press, 1992), 217, and John Fitchen, *Building Construction Before Mechanization* (MIT Press, 1992), 155.

7. tSot 15:1. Lieberman finds support for the *shamir* as a type of grass or plant. See his *Tosefta Ki-fshutah* VIII, 757, lines 2–4.

8. Aristotle, *On Marvelous Things Heard*, 25–26 (832a).

9. John of Damascus, *The Ordeal of Artemius*, 68.

10. Pliny the Elder, *Natural History* 36.51–53.

11. Yishayahu 2:4.

12. In the Iliad, iron is used only for tools, and weapons are always made of bronze. At that time, iron metallurgy was not advanced enough to be trusted for weapons. See Andrew Lang, "Bronze and Iron in Homer" in *Revue Archéologique* (June 1906), 280. By the time of Yishayahu, iron was used for both tools and weapons.

Torah requires an altar of unhewn stones, unshaped by iron tools, it hearkens back to the early altars of the forefathers which were built of whole stones. This connection to the ancient forefathers and their simple altars is crucial. While bringing sacrifices on an altar seems close to a pagan style of worship, there is an emphasis on avoiding decorative altars and their pagan connotations, and instead following the ways of the forefathers. This is in line with Rashbam's explanation, which stresses that the altar stones are to be unaltered and natural.[13] According to this interpretation, the mention of iron in Devarim has more to do with the normal way in which stone is cut and less to do with an actual prohibition against iron tools.[14]

13. See also Sforno and Daat Mikre. Ibn Ezra, however, attacks this interpretation, claiming that the Temple was full of *keruvim* and that other adornments appeared throughout the Temple and its vessels.

14. The Talmud (bZev 44a) quotes a *beraita* which gives a different method of constructing the altar that involves neither stones cut without iron nor fieldstones, but rather a casting method. The *beraita* states that a mixture of stone fragments, plaster, pitch, and lead was poured into formwork and hardened into the altar.

# The Altar Ramp and Accessibility

וְלֹא תַעֲלֶה בְמַעֲלֹת עַל מִזְבְּחִי אֲשֶׁר לֹא תִגָּלֶה עֶרְוָתְךָ עָלָיו. (שמות כ:כג)

Neither shall you go up by steps to My altar, that your nakedness be not uncovered on it. (Shemot 20:23)

THE Torah states that one is not to ascend the altar in the *Mishkan* by way of stairs, explaining that climbing stairs would risk exposing the kohanim as they extend their legs to take steps.[1] The altar nonetheless required some means of ascent and to this end, a ramp was installed.[2]

Although this explanation fits with the Torah's statement about exposing nakedness, the commentators seem somewhat unconvinced as to the need for a ramp, as well as the ramp's utility in solving the Torah's stated concern. The Mechilta points out that the kohanim all wore britches. Even if their clothing opened due to long strides, nothing would have been exposed. Having a ramp would not prevent kohanim from taking long strides. If anything, stairs force people to take measured strides while ramps allow for greater variance. This is why some commentators feel the need to clarify that kohanim had to take small steps, toe to heel, when they walked.[3] Steps up to the altar could have been made sufficiently shallow so as not to require long strides. Although almost all steps in the Temple were designed with risers and treads that were not ergonomic,[4] different dimensions could have been used for the altar.

1. Rashi.
2. MdRY Yitro, (Bachodesh) 11.
3. Chizkuni and yBer 1:1 (2c). See also bZev 63a and yEruv 7:2 (24b), which give the normative slope for a ramp as 33% and for the altar ramp as slightly less steep. See also mShek 4:2 for additional ramps in the Temple and parallel in PdRK, 4:7. Israeli code, by contrast, does not usually allow a ramp greater than 12.5% even under the most lenient of circumstances.
4. mMid 2:3 notes that the steps were a half cubit high and a half cubit wide. See my

We generally associate ramps with greater accessibility. Wheelchairs and strollers can negotiate ramps more easily than stairs. Slopes do not require lifting your legs to the same extent as steps. However, ramps are not always easier to climb. While they are better for a wheeled device, ramps with an incline greater than five percent are considered *less* accessible than stairs for pedestrians. This is why the Israeli accessibility code requires both ramps *and* stairs when inclines are greater than five percent.[5] It is likely that the altar ramp was more difficult than stairs for the kohanim to ascend.[6]

Instead of thinking about the ease or length of strides, the major benefit of having a ramp leading to the altar is the elimination of potential obstacles. While an incline does not make climbing easier and could still cause stumbling, it provides a smooth surface without impediments.[7] This is a significant concern for people carrying large items with limited visibility. Having a continuous surface instead of stairs reduces the chance that a kohen might trip and fall, something that would both risk injuring the kohen and be dishonorable to the Temple service. From the point of view of accessibility, this is the major benefit of having a ramp rather than stairs leading up to the altar.

---

commentary on Devarim 22:14.

5. See Teken Yisrael 1918 part 3.1, 2.5.2.ב.

6. mEruv 10:14 states that salt was sprinkled on the ramp to prevent slipping. bMen 21b also mentions salt on the ramp, but for salting the sacrifices. See also Rashbam's comments on this verse. See, however, John Templer, *The Staircase: Studies of Hazards, Falls and Safer Design* (MIT Press, 1994), 34 and 43, which argues that any ramp with a pitch of less than 20% uses less energy than stairs.

7. Rashi emphasizes the smoothness of the surface. See also Templer, *Staircase*, 44, for a major benefit of ramps being their ability to limit accidents.

# The Evolving Role of Architect

וְכִי יִפְתַּח אִישׁ בּוֹר אוֹ כִּי יִכְרֶה אִישׁ בֹּר וְלֹא יְכַסֶּנּוּ וְנָפַל שָׁמָּה שּׁוֹר אוֹ חֲמוֹר.
בַּעַל הַבּוֹר יְשַׁלֵּם כֶּסֶף יָשִׁיב לִבְעָלָיו וְהַמֵּת יִהְיֶה לּוֹ. (שמות כא:לג-לד)

And if a man shall open a pit, or if a man shall dig a pit, and not cover it, and an ox or a donkey fall into it, the owner of the pit shall make it good, he shall give money to the owner of them, and the dead beast shall be his. (Shemot 21:33–34)

ONE category of property damage described in the Torah is damage caused by a dangerous obstacle. The classic case involves an animal which falls into a pit located in a public space. In this situation, the digger is liable for the damages. Any immobile obstacle is halachically classified as a "pit."[1]

The Talmud addresses a variety of scenarios where damage is caused by a pit. One mishna states that during a building project, one may use adjacent public property for storing building materials. However, any materials stored in the public domain fall under the same rules as a pit: if they cause damage, there is liability.[2] The Talmud discusses who exactly would be liable and rules that whoever has most recently been entrusted with the materials is responsible. Therefore, in the case of stones for construction,

> If the stonecutter gives it to the chiseler, the chiseler is liable. If the chiseler gives it to the donkey-driver, the donkey-driver is liable. If the donkey-driver gives it to the porter, the porter is liable. If

1. mBK 1:1.
2. mBM 10:5. mBB 3:8 states that any cavity beneath a public road must be robustly covered, so that wagons laden with stones may pass over it. If a house has a beam that protrudes into public space, this too counts as a pit, though Rambam explains that if the beams are higher than a man riding a camel, then they do not constitute a danger. See Rambam Hilchot Nizkei Mamon 13:24.

> the porter gives it to the builder, the builder is liable. If the builder gives it to the *adrichal,*[3] the *adrichal* is liable. And if he puts the stone in place on the course of stones, and it then causes damage, they are all responsible to pay.[4]

The Talmud describes the entire stone construction process. A stone-cutter roughly cuts the stones in a quarry and gives them to a chiseler to finish properly. A donkey-driver then transports the stones to the construction site, where a porter brings them up to the part of the building under construction. The builder puts the stones in place. He, in turn, is supervised by the *adrichal,* who carries out the construction work. Once on the building site, the *adrichal* is responsible for any damage inflicted.

In modern Hebrew, *adrichal* means architect. However, the role of *adrichal* has shifted over the centuries. The word is originally Akkadian for "temple-servant." Jastrow translates "*ardichal*" as artist, artisan, architect, and key-stone setter. He bases this translation on Robert Payne Smith's nineteenth-century Syriac dictionary.[5]

In Jewish sources, the term is used in Targum Yonatan on Shmuel II 5:11, which describes King David's partnership with Hiram, the king of Tyre. Hiram sent David cedar wood, carpenters, and masons to help with the construction of the royal palace. The word "masons" is translated as *adrichalin.* A similar translation occurs in Tehilim when David writes that "The stone which the builders rejected has become the chief cornerstone."[6] Here too the Targum translates "builders" as *ardichalia.* In one midrash, the word *ardichal* is used as someone who builds a palace.[7] R. Assi mentions a type of wall which he calls "an *adarchal*'s wall"[8] – a temporary screen used to provide shade for builders working in the sun. Rashi explains that an *adrichal* was the "father of all artisans" and was responsible for making sure that the stones were aligned correctly.

---

3. The word is sometimes spelled *adrichal* and sometimes *ardichal,* with the latter being the more authentic spelling.

4. bBM 118b. See also yBM 10:5.

5. Smith, Robert Payne. *Thesaurus Syriacus,* 27, translates it as a stone-mason, builder, or master-builder.

6. Tehilim 118:22. R. David Altschuler explains in Metzudat David that David felt he had been rejected, like a stone deemed unfit for use in a wall. In the end he had the final say, as he was picked as the best stone, to be used in the corner of the building and thus visible from two sides. While a stone in the corner is indeed visible from two sides, a stone *capping* a corner would be visible from *three* sides.

7. BerR 8:26. R. Yissachar Ber Berman explains in his Matanot Kehuna commentary that this term refers to the chief builder, carpenter, and mason.

8. bEruv 26a.

35. Upper corner stone with three exposed surfaces.

Besides the word *ardichal,* the terms *architekton* and *architektus* also appear in rabbinic literature, the former in Greek and the latter in Latin.[9] Just as *ardichal* used to refer to a job that was part foreman, part craftsman, and part builder, the term *architekton* had a similar meaning. The Greek word is comprised of *arkhi,* meaning chief,[10] and *tekton,*[11] meaning builder. The architect was the master builder in charge of a building site. Both *adrichal* and *architect* are used in modern Hebrew, with some debate as to which term is preferable.

The use of these terms in the various rabbinic texts corresponds with what we know about the historic role of architect. Architects oversaw all aspects of a project, including site supervision, engineering, heating, delivery of materials, etc. This is the role to which our sources are referencing. However, starting in the fifteenth century in Italy, the architect's role began to change from one focused on the construction of buildings to one concerned with the conceptual design of buildings. This shift can be seen in a treatise on architecture published by Leon Battista Alberti in the fifteenth century, *De Re Aedificatoria,* which, unlike the Roman work on architecture by Vitruvius, is more about the theory of how buildings *should* be built, and not how they *are* built. Alberti saw the architect as a master artist.[12] His job was to learn from previous architecture and

9. Two parallel stories that appear in BerR 24:1 (*architektus*) and BamR 9:1 (*archikiton*), alternate between the Latin and Greek. See also yBer 9:1 (13a) and Sefer Chareidim there.

10. "Arch" as chief is still in use in English, such as an archenemy, or the Greek term *archisynagogos,* referred to in Rabbinic literature as the Rosh Knesset, or head of the synagogue.

11. In the New Testament book of Mark (6:3) describes Jesus as "This is the *tekton,* the son of Mary..." which is often translated as carpenter but is at times translated as builder.

12. Spiro Kostof. *A History of Architecture* (Oxford University Press, 1995), 408.

expand upon it, a point of view which was common in arts and science during the Renaissance. This was a revolutionary shift for the architect, one that changed the job from master-builder toward the modern role of architect as designer. By the start of the nineteenth century, an architect's role began to diminish with the rise of specialty skills, as architects ceded the structural design to engineers.[13] This process has continued, with new fields usurping the various historic roles of the architect, until today an architect is still the head of the design team, but not nearly as involved in all aspects of the project as his counterpart from Late Antiquity.

The *ardichal* and architect described in rabbinic literature refer to the original role of an architect as a foreman and master-builder. The passage in the Talmud captures the role perfectly, by describing the *ardichal* as the last and final authority on a construction site, the one ultimately responsible for all that transpires on the building site.

13. See Kenneth Frampton, *Modern Architecture* (Thames and Hudson, 1992), 30.

# Bribes and Kickbacks

וְשֹׁחַד לֹא תִקָּח כִּי הַשֹּׁחַד יְעַוֵּר פִּקְחִים וִיסַלֵּף דִּבְרֵי צַדִּיקִים. (שמות כג:ח)

And you shall take no bribe, for a bribe blinds the wise and perverts the words of the righteous. (Shemot 23:8)

THE Torah prohibits bribes and uses a repetitive phrase to make this point: a bribe both "blinds the wise" and "perverts the words of the righteous." The prohibition is repeated later in the Torah.[1] The Mechilta learns from this repetition that a bribe is prohibited even if the one who accepted it has no intention of changing his behavior.[2]

The Rabbis set an extremely low bar for bribery. Almost any type of benefit that a judge accepts qualifies as a bribe. The Talmud delves into this subject, listing many scenarios in which someone is disqualified as a judge after receiving a minor benefit from one of the parties. These include if he has borrowed something, received help crossing a bridge, had an animal shooed away from him, received a delivery ahead of time, or been offered a present *even if it was not accepted.*[3] The Rabbis recognized the insidious nature of bribes and wanted to make it clear that judges must be extraordinarily careful not to have *any* attachments to the litigants.

Sadly, the construction business is rampant with forms of bribery, both overt and less obvious in nature. This begins with blatant, textbook bribes in which money is offered in exchange for selecting a firm – an architect, a contractor, or most commonly, a supplier. There are also cases of bribes offered to planning committees for extra benefits or speedy approval of plans.[4]

1. Devarim 16:19.
2. MdRY, Mishpatim, (Kesafa) 20. bKet 105a contains a similar message.
3. bKet 105b.
4. Ehud Olmert, former mayor of Jerusalem and Prime Minister of Israel, was convicted of taking bribes for the approval of the Holyland apartment complex.

Kickbacks are also widespread, in which the architect or contractor in charge of selecting a supplier is given a percentage of the overall sale in exchange for choosing a specific business. A typical scenario is when an architect must choose where to buy the doors or lights or plumbing fixtures for a project. The architect picks Company X in exchange for a percentage of the total sale. While this is sometimes seen as the price of doing business, it most certainly harms the client in several ways. First, it inflates the cost of the project, as the supplier must raise prices to cover the kickback. Second, the client assumes that the architect is his or her representative, with only the client's best interest in mind. When the architect accepts a kickback from the supplier, it means he will feel pressure to look out for the good of the supplier as well. If, for example, the product that is delivered is somehow deficient, the architect may be more inclined to overlook this deficiency rather than demand that the supplier replace the goods at their own expense. The architect may even select a supplier who offers a worse price to the client but gives a larger kickback, or supplies a lesser product for a similar price.

These types of bribes can also take more hidden forms. A professional or consultant[5] may treat an architect to lunch, or a construction company might provide a trip to factories in foreign countries at their cost, essentially treating an architect or contractor to a vacation. Though the architect may have no intention of changing his behavior, there may be a lingering influence in the future.

Architects, like many other professionals, must be extremely aware of bribery and take special precautions not to violate these laws. Although this may pose a difficulty in a market that is rife with side deals, this does not excuse the violation of a Torah law.

---

5. Architects work with many professionals as part of the design team: engineers, plumbers, heating and cooling professionals, landscape architects, safety, and accessibility consultants, etc. Someone is always responsible for picking the design team, and this person is susceptible to making choices based on these types of low-scale bribes.

# Heavenly Jerusalem, Earthly Jerusalem

הִנֵּה אָנֹכִי שֹׁלֵחַ מַלְאָךְ לְפָנֶיךָ לִשְׁמָרְךָ בַּדָּרֶךְ וְלַהֲבִיאֲךָ אֶל הַמָּקוֹם אֲשֶׁר הֲכִנֹתִי. (שמות כג:כ)

Behold I send an angel before you, to keep you by the way and to bring you to the place which I have prepared. (Shemot 23:20)

Bnei Yisrael were being led to "the place which I have prepared," an allusion to the Temple in Jerusalem.[1] Midrash Tanchuma concludes from this phrase that God prepared a heavenly Temple, parallel to the earthly Temple.[2] Midrash also describes a heavenly city of Jerusalem corresponding to the earthly Jerusalem.[3]

What does it mean that there is a heavenly Temple and a heavenly Jerusalem parallel to the earthly ones? One possibility is that the physical location of Jerusalem was preordained as a holy spot, an idea termed "sacred geography."[4] Some traditions likewise refer to Jerusalem as the navel of the world.[5] From this perspective, the Temple's location is connected

1. Based on similar word usage in Shemot 15:17.

2. Tanchuma Mishpatim 18 and Rashi on this verse. A similar allusion can be found in BerR 69:17 on Bereshit 28:17, in which the gate to the heavenly Temple is opposite Beit El. bBM 59a contains another reference to the gates of heaven. yBer 4:5 (8c) discusses whether travelers who cannot face Jerusalem during prayer should "direct their heart" toward the heavenly Temple or the earthly one. BamR 12 states that God commanded the angels to create a heavenly *Mishkan* to offer up the souls of the righteous.

3. Tanchuma Pekudei 1. Other midrashim state that there is a heavenly and earthly divine throne. See Ramban on our verse and MdRY, Beshalach (shira) 10.

4. Rachel Elior "From Priestly (and Early Christian) Mount Zion to Rabbinic Temple Mount" in *Where Heaven and Earth Meet: Jerusalem's Sacred Esplanade* ed. Oleg Grabar and Benjamin Kedar (University of Texas Press, 2010), 310.

5. Sefer Hayovlim 8:19, from the Greek *omphalos*. See also Tanchuma Kedoshim 10, and analysis in Philip S. Alexander, "Jerusalem as the *Omphalos* of the World" in *Jerusalem: Its Sanctity and Centrality to Judaism, Christianity and Islam*, ed. Lee Levine (Continuum, 1998), 104–119. mYom 5:2 locates the *even hashetiya* (foundation

to a pre-existing celestial sanctuary. By building the Temple, Bnei Yisrael gained access to this unique nexus.

A second possibility is that the heavenly Temple is a response to the construction of the earthly Temple. In this interpretation, the earthly Temple was constructed first, and only afterward did God build the heavenly Temple to demonstrate His devotion to the Jewish people. This is the approach taken in Midrash Tanchuma, which states that "Out of His great love for the lower [Jerusalem], He made another above."[6] From this perspective, it was the earthly Temple that established the holiness of the site.

These two viewpoints are reflected in the debate about the persistence of the Temple Mount's holiness. The Talmud records a dispute between R. Eliezer and R. Yehoshua as to whether the holiness of the Temple remains even when there is no Temple present.[7] If the Temple aligns with a preexisting heavenly Temple, the site on earth has significance regardless of the building's physical existence. However, if the earthly Temple is what gives holiness to the spot, the Temple's destruction might cause the holiness to dissipate in the absence of the earthly Temple.

In an article about Jerusalem in rabbinic literature during the time of the Mishna and Talmud, Isaiah Gafni lists several possible reasons for the adoption of the heavenly Temple imagery. It may have developed out of various prophetic visions.[8] Alternatively, it may be the influence of Babylonian culture, which held that everything on Earth had heavenly parallels. It could have been in response to Christian doctrine that the heavenly Jerusalem had replaced the defunct earthly Jerusalem of Judaism.[9] The heavenly Temple could also have been a way of reassuring Bnei Yisrael after the destruction of the earthly Temple that there still existed an indestructible Temple in heaven.

In a world without a standing Temple, the theological belief that the earthly Temple preceded the heavenly Temple is both reassuring and

---

stone) in the Holy of Holies, and bYom 54b explains that the world was created from this point. Islamic traditions hold that the rock inside the Dome of the Rock was the source of the four rivers of Paradise, where God stood to create the earth, where Adam was created, the stone formed in Beit El, and several other biblical events. See Andreas Kaplony, "635/638–1099: The Mosque of Jerusalem" in *Where Heaven and Earth Meet,* 109.

6. Tanchuma Pekudei 1. See also bTaan 5a.

7. bMeg 10a, as well as Rambam Beit Habechira 6:15–16 and the Ravad there.

8. For example, Yishayahu 6:1–6, "I saw the Lord sitting upon a throne, high and lifted up, and his train filled the temple. . . ."

9. Isaiah Gafni, "*Yerushalayim besafrut chazal*" in *Sefer Yerushalayim – Hatekufa Haromit Vehabizantit*" ed. Yoram Tzafrir and Shmuel Safrai (YBZP, 1999), 47–50 (Hebrew).

troubling. On the one hand, it confirms a special bond between God and Bnei Yisrael, by reinforcing God's commitment to the Jewish people. On the other hand, it means that without a Temple, part of that link is diminished. Similarly, accepting that the heavenly Temple came first can be both positive and negative: the heavenly Temple continues to exist and is open to prayers, but the site of the Temple is occupied by a non-Jewish place of worship. There remains a sense that the special relationship between God and the Jewish people persists, yet the destruction of the earthly Temple has left a void that cannot easily be bridged.

TERUMA

# The Visual Torah

כְּכֹל אֲשֶׁר אֲנִי מַרְאֶה אוֹתְךָ אֵת תַּבְנִית הַמִּשְׁכָּן וְאֵת תַּבְנִית כָּל כֵּלָיו וְכֵן תַּעֲשׂוּ. (שמות כה:ט)

According to all that I show you, the pattern of the *Mishkan* and the pattern of all its vessels, even so shall you make it. (Shemot 25:9)

THE second half of the book of Shemot details the crafting of the *Mishkan* and its vessels. The verbal descriptions found in these chapters are rich and thorough, yet still, leave a great deal to interpretation. It is exceedingly difficult to communicate designs verbally, which is why architects make use of technical drawings, models, and three-dimensional projections[1] to communicate their design intentions.[2]

Moshe was told to fabricate the *Mishkan* "according to all that I show you." A midrash states that Moshe was shown a model of the *Mishkan* made of red, green, black, and white fire and told to replicate it on earth using corporeal materials.[3] Similar wording is used when describing the design of the *menora*[4] and there too we find midrashim that Moshe was shown a model. One source relates that Moshe had to be shown the model four times.[5] In a *beraita*, R. Yosi bar Yehuda states that Moshe also was shown a fiery model of the ark of the covenant and the showbread table.[6]

1. Such as isometric, axonometric, and perspective drawings.

2. This was apparently true in the Roman world as well. See Jefferson Lawrence Daniel Pierce, *The Organization of Roman Building During the Late Republic and Early Empire*, Ph.D thesis, (Cambridge University, 1974), 100–101. Additionally, he explains that Vitruvius included drawings in his book and writes that architects had to provide plans, elevations, and perspective drawings.

3. PdRK 1.3 and BamR 12:8. Rabeinu Bachya seems to understand that Moshe was shown the heavenly Temple, made of heavenly materials and told to copy it on earth using earthly materials.

4. Shemot 25:40.

5. SZ Bamidbar 8:4.

6. bMen 29a. This *beraita* also states that Moshe did not see a model of the whole

Moshe needed to see these models because he could not understand the verbal instructions alone. A midrash explicitly states that "three things were difficult for Moshe until the Holy One, blessed be He, showed him with His finger: the *menora*, the new moon, and *sheratzim* ... some add the laws of *shechita*."[7] In other places, midrashim relate that Moshe was shown all the kosher animal species,[8] which coin should be used for the half-shekel[9] and the size of a *revi'it* unit of measurement.[10]

These midrashim underscore the vital role of visual communication. Some things are much easier to demonstrate with drawings and models. Although a verbal description of the *menora* could be helpful, and although authors can use ekphrasis[11] to try and capture a design in words, to truly understand the design, a diagram is necessary. This is the same reason why drawings form the main portion of an architectural design package.

Besides this insight, these midrashim do something far more revolutionary. In addition to the Written Torah and the Oral Torah, they describe a third, Visual Torah, given at Sinai. The transmission of a Visual Torah poses difficulties no less complex than that of the Oral Torah. Visual images can be both easier and more difficult to express. With the *menora*, for example, Moshe received a vision that was transmitted to Bezalel. The artisans were then tasked with recreating this vision. Once the *menora* was realized, it was available for all to see and could theoretically be copied freely. Crafting the *menora* had the same function as writing down the Oral Torah. The *menora*, the *Mishkan*, the half-shekel, kosher animals, etc. were all put into immediate use and became part of the life of Bnei Yisrael, so transmitting this Visual Torah was natural and easy, in the same way that religious Jews today grow up knowing how a *lulav* and *tefilin* look.

The trouble comes when the tradition is lost and must be reconstituted.[12] The seventy-year period between the First and Second Temples was *almost* enough for the ritual objects to pass from living memory (though perhaps some of the vessels were still in existence in Babylon or Persia, just as they would later be displayed in Rome after the destruction of the

---

*Mishkan*. ShmR 40:2 states that Moshe saw all the vessels.

7. bMen 29a. Each item has a verse which implies that it was shown to Moshe. The new moon model is mentioned in MdRY, Bo (Pischa) 1.

8. bChul 42a, SZ Devarim 14:4, Sifra Shemini parsha 2 and VayR 13:4.

9. Based on Shemot 30:13, as per yShek 1:4 (46b).

10. bMen 88a.

11. Defined in the *Oxford English Dictionary* as "The use of detailed description of a work of visual art as a literary device."

12. For loss of tradition and the possibility of recovering it, see bTem 16a regarding Moshe, Yehoshua, and Otniel ben Kenaz.

Second Temple). Luckily, there were elders alive who could remember the Temple and reconstruct its appearance from memory.[13] However, once an object disappears and is lost from living memory, its design cannot be recreated with any confidence. We can do our best to understand what the *menora* looked like, and thankfully there is at least one ancient depiction on the Arch of Titus that has survived; we can pour over the sources in Midot and Josephus pertaining to the Temple's appearance, but ultimately the revelation is lost.

13. Ezra 3:12.

# Competing Cubits and the Dimensions of the Ark

וְעָשׂוּ אֲרוֹן עֲצֵי שִׁטִּים אַמָּתַיִם וָחֵצִי אָרְכּוֹ וְאַמָּה וָחֵצִי רָחְבּוֹ וְאַמָּה וָחֵצִי קֹמָתוֹ.
(שמות כה:י)

And they shall make an ark of shittim wood, two cubits and a half shall be its length, and a cubit and a half its breadth, and a cubit and half its height. (Shemot 25:10)

THE Torah lists the basic dimensions of each of the Temple vessels. When listing the dimensions of the ark – 2.5 × 1.5 × 1.5 cubits – the Torah adds that "in the ark, you shall put the Testimony that I shall give you,"[1] referring to the two tablets. This links the dimensions of the ark with the size of the two tablets, which were each said to be 6 × 6 × 3 handbreadths.

In one of the most architectural passages in the Talmud, R. Meir and R. Yehuda discuss the size of the ark and the arrangement of the tablets within. This argument revolves around the number of handbreadths that make up a cubit. R. Meir's cubit was six handbreadths in length, while R. Yehuda's cubit was only five handbreadths long. According to R. Meir, there was enough room for the ark to have slightly thicker walls and still hold a Torah scroll inside. R. Yehuda's five-handbreadth cubit meant that the ark was smaller and had to suffice with walls of a minimal thickness. It had no room for a Torah inside and barely squeezed in the two tablets.[2]

While R. Meir and R. Yehuda disagreed about the makeup of the cubit used to dimension the ark, they both recognized that multiple definitions of the cubit existed. R. Yehuda thought that the six-handbreadth cubit was only used to measure buildings, while R. Meir thought it was also used to measure most of the Temple vessels.[3] An adjacent mishna records that

1. Shemot 25:21.
2. bBB 14a and yShek 6:1 (49d). The latter adds that the broken tablets were also in the ark and ascribes the main debate to R. Yochanan and Reish Lakish.
3. mKel 17:10.

there were two cubit measuring rods in the Temple, both bigger than the cubit used in the time of Moshe. One Temple cubit added a finger-width to Moshe's cubit, while the other added two. According to the Mishna, artisans doing work for the Temple would receive the raw materials according to the smaller cubit, and charge a fee according to the larger one, to ensure that they did not accidentally overcharge the Temple treasury for their work.[4]

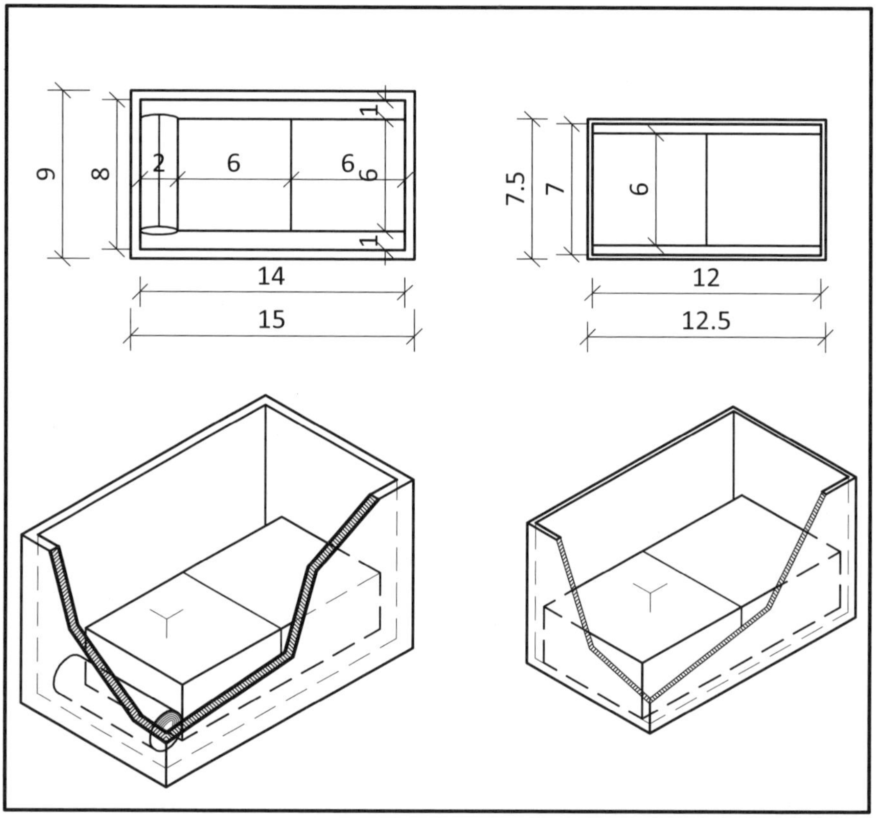


36. Ark dimensions given in handbreadths.

Although it might seem surprising to have competing measurements with the same name, this was common in the Near East. Herodotus recorded the size of the city of Babylon in "royal cubits," which he explained were three finger-widths longer than the standard cubit.[5] Egypt had a royal

4. mKel 17:9. This seems to ignore the precept in Vayikra 19:35–36 to have just measurements.

5. Herodotus, *The Histories* 1.178.

cubit of seven handbreadths and a common cubit of six. Two passages in Yechezkel imply that a cubit alternately measured five or six handbreadths,[6] and a verse in Divrei Hayamim II hints at an "old" cubit and a "new" cubit.[7]

Although these dual systems were common, they were still odd. It makes little sense to have two units of measurement with the same name, yet the Mishna is one of the only places that bothers to provide any justification for the practice. In contrast to the Mishna's justification of two different cubits, Antoine Pierre Hirsch argues that such a setup would never be instituted on purpose, and must occur when two separate systems, each for a different purpose or from a different geographic area, are thrust together. In the case of the Egyptian cubits, the subject of his thesis, Hirsch suggests that the larger cubit came from an agricultural system that harvested barley, while the smaller unit was used for measuring emmer, a type of wheat.[8] In other scenarios, interaction with foreign nations could lead to the adoption of alternate units.

With the measurements in the Temple, the Mishna explains why two cubits existed concurrently. However, the fact that this discussion concerns sacred objects may suggest another reason. Israel was under constant influence from surrounding cultures, including foreign systems of measurement. Still, even if new standards were introduced by powerful neighbors, when it came to determining the size of sacred architecture or vessels, we might expect to encounter insistence that the old units be used. It is one thing to measure agricultural yield in a foreign unit of measurement; it is something else to use those same units for the Temple. A similar phenomenon took place when the *Ashurit* script was adopted for the Hebrew language. Some groups continued to write God's name in the old script, and others wrote their entire Torah scrolls in paleo-Hebrew. The ark, perhaps more than any object, might have been impacted by this phenomenon, resulting in an argument over how to correctly interpret its cubit dimensions.

---

6. Yechezkel 40:5, 43:13.
7. Divrei Hayamim II 3:3.
8. Antoine Pierre Hirsch, *Ancient Egyptian Cubits – Origin and Evolution.* Thesis, University of Toronto, 2013, 3. Barley is one-third heavier than emmer. The difference in volume between wheat and barley is the basis of the ruling found in mBM 6:5.

# Revealed and Concealed Spaces

בְּטַבְּעֹת הָאָרֹן יִהְיוּ הַבַּדִּים לֹא יָסֻרוּ מִמֶּנּוּ. (שמות כה:טו)

The poles shall be in the rings of the ark, they shall not be taken from it. (Shemot 25:15)

THE vessels of the *Mishkan* were designed to be carried. They each had rings affixed to their sides, which could be fitted with poles for transportation.[1] While all the poles were removable when not in use, the Torah instructs that the poles of the ark "shall not be taken from it."

There are several opinions as to why the poles of the ark always remained in place. One possibility is that the ark needed to be ready to move on short notice. The ark was sometimes carried into war, and if a battle was imminent, no time could be spared to reinsert the poles. Such a rush could also cause the ark to be treated without the proper decorum.[2] The poles needed to remain attached to the ark so that it would be battle-ready.

In contrast to this opinion, Meir Simcha of Dvinsk[3] writes that the ark did not truly require any help to be transported – it miraculously provided its own locomotion and could even carry the attending priests.[4] Therefore, as opposed to the other Temple vessel poles, the ones on the ark were not for a functional purpose. Rather, they were part of the integral form of the ark. As such, they could not be removed.[5]

Chizkuni points out a practical difference between the ark and the other vessels. The altar, *menora*, table, etc. rested in parts of the *Mishkan* which were filled with activity. If the poles were left in place, they would

---

1. Ark – see 25:12–15. Table – see 25:26–28. Altar – see 27:6–7. Incense altar – see 30:4–5. The *menora* is an exception.

2. Sefer HaChinuch, 97. For the dangers of treating the ark disrespectfully, see Shmuel II 6.

3. In his Meshech Chochma commentary.

4. bSot 35a.

5. This reason is mentioned in Sefer Hachinuch as well.

have posed serious obstacles to the priests as they went about their daily routine. The ark, in contrast, was kept in the Holy of Holies, where no one ventured, except one person on one day per year. The poles of the ark were not in the way and therefore did not need to be removed. From this perspective, it is preferable for all vessels to have the poles in place, but practical considerations preclude this option for all but the ark.

Another possibility arises from an analysis of a verse in Melachim I describing the poles in the First Temple. The verse explains that the "ends of the poles were seen from the holy place, even before the sanctuary, but they could not be seen outside."[6] The Talmud resolves this apparent contradiction by explaining that the poles poked the curtain at the entrance to the Holy of Holies, leaving an impression that would be visible from outside the curtain.[7] This suggestion implies that although only the high priest was allowed to see the actual ark, it was important for its presence to be perceptible to others as well. Some impression of the ark had to be visible outside the Holy of Holies, even if only faintly.[8] With this in mind, it was important for the poles to remain in the ark permanently, as they projected the ark's existence through the curtain.

Every building contains some hidden elements which are suppressed by the architect. Ductwork and electrical cables, mudrooms and storage units might all be tucked away and kept out of view. Some architects choose to disguise secondary spaces or conceal activities. The architect must mediate the balance between exposing and concealing. In the case of the Holy of Holies, while there was a clear separation of that space, it was important for a trace of the inner holiness to be revealed to those outside the curtain.[9] The protrusion of the poles from the Holy of Holies can thus be seen as a way of subtly revealing the contents of this otherwise concealed chamber.

---

6. Melachim I 8:8.

7. tYom 2:15, yShek 6:1 (49c) and especially bYom 54a, bMen 98a–b, and Beraita Demalechet Ha*mishkan* 7. This despite the larger dimensions of the Holy of Holies in the First Temple (twenty cubits) as compared to the *Mishkan* (ten cubits). To explain how the poles were visible despite the larger room size, some say it was a miracle (see Tosefot on bMen 98b *dochkin*) while others explain that the poles were pulled out partway, so that they jutted forward as far as possible (Radak on Melachim I 8:8, Malbim on our verse, and partially based on the discussion in bYom 72a.)

8. bMen 29a similarly describes how the table was lifted and shown to pilgrims.

9. For an additional example of this balance, see my commentary to Vayikra 10:4–5.

# Fabric Partitions And the Origins of Architecture

וְאֶת הַמִּשְׁכָּן תַּעֲשֶׂה עֶשֶׂר יְרִיעֹת שֵׁשׁ מָשְׁזָר וּתְכֵלֶת וְאַרְגָּמָן וְתֹלַעַת שָׁנִי כְּרֻבִים
מַעֲשֵׂה חֹשֵׁב תַּעֲשֶׂה אֹתָם. (שמות כו:א)

Moreover, you shall make the *Mishkan* with ten curtains of fine twined linen, and blue and purple and scarlet, with *keruvim* the work of the skillful workman shall you make them. (Shemot 26:1)

THE *Mishkan* was constructed with a framework of interconnected wall panels blanketed with textile coverings. The first covering, described in the verse above, was made of linen.[1] The Torah lists a second layer of goat hair, "to be a covering over the *Mishkan*,"[2] a third rams' skin covering and a fourth *tachash* skin covering.[3]

Rashi clarifies the purpose of these textile coverings, explaining that they served both as the roof and as exterior cladding for the solid walls of the *Mishkan*. R. Moshe Met of Przemyśl, explaining Rashi's words, writes that the covering is the *main part* of the *Mishkan*, and is therefore referred to as "the *Mishkan*."[4] This interpretation appears in the Talmud as well.[5]

The importance ascribed to the textiles is somewhat surprising. A roof is one of the main elements in architecture, but in the case of the *Mishkan*, one could argue that the wall panels were the more significant elements in establishing the sacred enclosure. In addition, at least some of the textiles ran down the walls, indicating that they did more than just roof the building. Given the solid and substantial nature of the *Mishkan's* walls, why would there be such an emphasis on the textile coverings?

1. Also described in Shemot 36:8.
2. Shemot 26:7 and 36:14.
3. Shemot 26:14 and 36:19. Whether there were three or four layers is a point of dispute in bShab 28a.
4. See his *Be'er Heitev* commentary on Rashi, printed in his *Ho'il Moshe*.
5. bShab 27b–28a.

R. S.R. Hirsch begins to address this point with the etymology of the word "curtains." He writes that the root of this word "does not mean curtain in general, but quite specifically tent-cloth, material used to surround and enclose a space." Hirsch was active in a time and place where there was a lively discussion about the role of textile in architectural history. Gottfried Semper, an influential German architect, professor, and historian, published a series of essays in the decades proceeding the publication of R. Hirsch's Torah commentary which argued that textiles were the most significant and original component of architecture.[6] Semper identified four main architectural elements: the hearth, roof, enclosure, and mound, and connected each with a type of craft.[7] Enclosures were associated with textiles. He wrote:

> Hanging carpets remained the true walls, the visible boundaries of space. The often solid walls behind them were necessary for reasons that had nothing to do with the creation of space; they were needed for security, for supporting a load, for their permanence, and so on. Wherever the need for these secondary functions did not arise, the carpets remained the original means of separating space. Even where building solid walls became necessary, the latter were only the inner, invisible structure hidden behind the true and legitimate representatives of the wall, the colorful woven carpets.[8]

Beyond identifying textile partitions as the most significant, original architectural element, Semper also wrote that the decorated forms of textiles were crucial to delineating specific realms of occupation. A house's textiles marked it as a place for a family, "the decorative weave produces the very idea of a family that might occupy it."[9] The textiles were important in symbolically dividing space for a particular use.[10]

The textiles of the *Mishkan* do more than simply enclose space. They

---

6. Semper grew up in Altona, where R. Hirsch's grandfather lived, so Semper's ideas were likely in circulation in the intellectual spaces that Hirsch inhabited.

7. Semper built a Primitive Hut for the Great Exhibition of 1851 in London, showing these four elements. For Primitive Huts, see my commentary on Bereshit 2:8.

8. Gottfried Semper, "The Four Elements of Architecture," in Harry Francis Mallgrave and Wolfgang Herrmann, *The Four Elements of Architecture and Other Writings* (Cambridge University Press, 1989), 102–104.

9. Mark Wigley, *White Walls, Designer Dresses* (MIT Press, 1996), 11.

10. Semper, *Style in the Technical and Tectonic Arts*, tr. Harry Francis Mallgrave and Michael Robinson (Getty Publications, 2004), 248. See Semper on our verses, ibid, 292.

act as a visual sign of this holy space, letting people know what type of activity takes place within.[11] They mark the *Mishkan* as a place of worship and interaction with God. This may be the reason they are given such importance and referred to as the essence of the *Mishkan*.[12]

11. This symbolic role is highlighted by R. Yose's opinion in yYom 4:6 (42a) that once the *Mishkan's* curtain is taken down, the space is no longer divided into different sacred camps. Similarly, bTaan 21b states that as soon as the curtain was dismantled, the *Mishkan* was no longer considered sacred ground.

12. Once we define the role of textiles in this manner, we can point to another ring of textiles that served a similar role in the desert camp. Each of the twelve tribes has a flag with its tribal symbols and colors. (Bamidbar 1:52 and 2:2) Just as the textiles around the *Mishkan* marked it as a special place, the flags in the desert served a similar purpose, marking the space for the use of that specific tribe.

TERUMA

# Assembling Parts

וַהֲקֵמֹתָ אֶת הַמִּשְׁכָּן כְּמִשְׁפָּטוֹ אֲשֶׁר הָרְאֵיתָ בָּהָר. (שמות כו:ל)

And you shall assemble the *Mishkan* according to its fashion which has been shown you in the mount. (Shemot 26:30)

THE Torah concludes the section dealing with the wall panels of the *Mishkan* by stating that the *Mishkan* should be set up "according to its fashion." The Talmud questions the meaning of this phrase and explains that the order of the panels must remain constant. Panels that were initially installed in the northern wall of the *Mishkan* must always be placed there, and the same goes for the southern wall.[1]

This statement is found as part of the Mishna's treatment of the prohibition against writing on Shabbat. The Mishna states that writing is defined as "writing two letters," and Rabbi Yosi explains that this is because letters were used to mark the configuration of the wall panels.[2] To keep track of the correct sequence of wall panels, letters were written on the left and right edge of each panel. Each letter would then be aligned with the panel containing the corresponding letter, like a game of dominos. The panel with א marked on its right edge would be placed next to the panel marked with an א on its left edge. Since two letters were needed to mark each pair, the Mishna rules that two letters are considered the minimum needed for the writing to be substantive.[3]

---

1. yShab 12:3(13c), yHor 3:5 (48c), and EsterR 4:4. In the passage, this statement is used as a way to placate a family that wishes to gain precedence over another prominent family in the community. They are told that once an order is set, it cannot be upended.

2. mShab 12:3. This is explicitly explained in bShab 103b. Shabbat prohibitions are learned from the various labors done during the construction of the *Mishkan*.

3. Masons preparing stones for the Temple in the time of Herod relied on similar marks, especially for column drums. These marks were made in the quarry and helped workers on site assemble the pieces in the correct order. The letters were sometimes Hebrew and occasionally Latin, but were most often Greek. See Orit Peleg-Barkat, *The*

The Talmud's ruling that each wall panels must remain in the same location can be viewed in two ways. On the one hand, it can be explained on a metaphysical level. Each spot in the *Mishkan* had its own level of holiness and its own function. As such, a panel that starts off in the Holy of Holies should not be "downgraded" to a spot by the entrance. R. David Fränkel[4] and R. Eliyahu David Rabinowitz-Teomim explain it this way in their commentaries.[5]

However, it is also possible to view the required static arrangement of the wall panels as a practical consideration. While in theory all wall panels were identical, hand-crafted, pre-industrial objects were in practice never identical. When dealing with wood panels that must be aligned in order to fit correctly, it would have been very important to maintain the same sequence. Panel A would fit perfectly with panel B, but not with panel C. Over time, certain panels might have become worn and would only fit properly in a specific configuration. Therefore, each panel had to be labeled and arranged as originally manufactured. This is one of the main differences between hand-made products and machine-made production. Identical components are what makes assembly-line production possible, but in ancient times (in the desert!) such a high level of manufacturing would have been impossible. This could be another practical reason why it was necessary to keep the panels in order.

---

*Temple Mount Excavations in Jerusalem, Vol. V* (Institute of Archaeology, Hebrew University, 2017), 38. See yShab 12:3 (13c) for writing letters from different languages.

4. In his *Korban HaEida* commentary on yShab 12:3 (13c). He points out that the table was located in the north, while the *menora* was located in the south.

5. R. Eliyahu David Rabinowitz-Teomim's commentary, the Aderet, is printed in the back of the Vilna edition as *Tov Yerushalayim*.

# Structural Stability and Wall Thickness

וְנָתַתָּה אֶת הַפָּרֹכֶת תַּחַת הַקְּרָסִים וְהֵבֵאתָ שָׁמָּה מִבֵּית לַפָּרֹכֶת אֵת אֲרוֹן
הָעֵדוּת וְהִבְדִּילָה הַפָּרֹכֶת לָכֶם בֵּין הַקֹּדֶשׁ וּבֵין קֹדֶשׁ הַקֳּדָשִׁים. (שמות כו:לג)

And you shall hang up the curtain under the clasps, and shall bring in there within the curtain the ark of the Testimony, and the curtain shall divide for you between the holy place and the Holy of Holies. (Shemot 26:33)

THE Torah describes the layout of the *Mishkan* and explains that the outer and inner sanctuaries were separated with a curtain. The high priest would enter the Holy of Holies on only one day a year.[1] This part of the Yom Kippur service is described in the Mishna, including an account of how the high priest would ambulate through the opening and enter the Holy of Holies.[2]

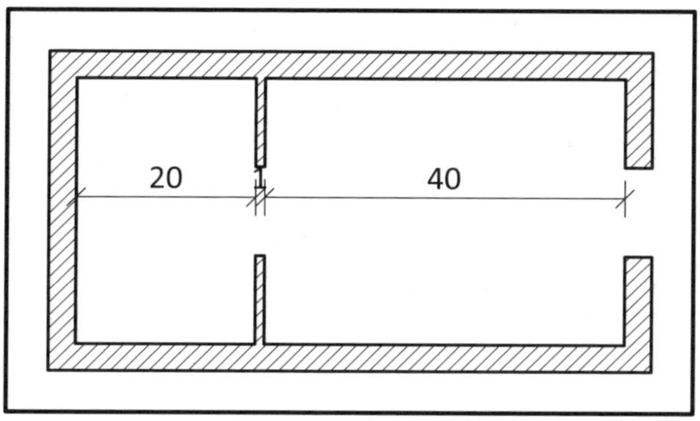


37. Dimensions of the Sanctuary of the First Temple.

1. Vayikra 15:12.
2. mYom 5:1. MdRS (Yitro 20:18) describes a similar approach by Moshe at Mount Sinai, between layers of fog.

The partition in the *Mishkan* was a curtain, but when Shlomo built the First Temple he used a solid wall with doors.[3] The length of Shlomo's Temple is described as sixty cubits, divided into twenty for the Holy of Holies, and forty for the outer sanctuary. However, the wall between the two rooms is not mentioned in the measurements. According to Rambam, the wall was included in the overall sixty, either as part of the inner twenty, or part of the outer section.[4] Others understood that the wall was not part of either chamber and that the dimensions listed do not include the width of the walls.[5]

The First Temple was thirty cubits high.[6] However, when Herod renovated the Second Temple,[7] he increased the height to one-hundred cubits, divided into two stories that were each forty-cubit-high.[8] This created a structural problem for the masonry wall between the Holy and the Holy of Holies. Masonry partitions cannot be built to great heights without increasing their thickness. One-cubit in width was not structurally sufficient for a wall of this height, and Herod was not permitted to make the dividing wall thicker.[9] Due to the uncertainty about the categorization of this interstitial space – whether it belonged to the Holy or the Holy of Holies – the one-cubit-wide strip was instead marked by two curtains, rendering it no man's land between the two sections of the Temple. The ambiguous space became known as the *teraksin* cubit, possibly from Greek words meaning outside and inside.[10]

In a discussion about the thickness of party walls built out of various materials,[11] the Talmud raises the case of the *teraksin* cubit as an example

3. Melachim I 6:31. Divrei Hayamim II 3:14 and 4:22 seem to say that there were both doors and a curtain.

4. See Rambam, Hilchot Beit Habechira 4:2.

5. bYom 52a.

6. This is according to most opinions and in accordance with Melachim I 6:2. However, Ibn Ezra writes that the height of the wall in the First Temple was only twenty cubits, as there was a ten-cubits-high loft built above. He quotes Divrei Hayamim II 3:9 as proof.

7. The original Second Temple, as built at the time of Ezra and Nechemia, was apparently shorter. See Josephus, *Antiquities* 15:385.

8. mMid 4:6 gives the height as one-hundred cubits, separated into two floors of forty cubits plus parapet, floor, and ceiling thickness. Josephus, in *The Jewish War*, (5:212) corroborates this height. Tosafot Yeshanim on Yoma 52a writes that while expanding the x–y dimensions was not allowed, it was acceptable to make the structure higher, as per Chagai 2:9, "The glory of this latter house shall be greater than that of the former."

9. bBB 3a.

10. This is the interpretation quoted in yYom 5:1 (42b) in the name of R. Yona. See also mMid 4:7, bYom 51b–52a, and yKil 8:4 (31c).

11. See a similar comment by Vitruvius in *Ten Books on Architecture* II.8.

of a tall, relatively thin wall. The Talmud reviews the history of the wall and the difference in height between the First and Second Temples but then asks why the architects of the Second Temple did not build a thirty-cubit wall and use a curtain for the remaining space up to the ceiling. It answers that a wall that is anchored both at the top and bottom will be more stable than a wall that is not held in place at the top.[12] In the First Temple, where the wall reached the roof, it could stand thirty cubits. In the Second Temple, where it did not, a thirty-cubit wall would not be stable.[13]

This difficulty with the thickness of masonry walls played a large role in the development of metal-framed skyscrapers at the end of the nineteenth century. When Chicago was destroyed by fire in 1871, architects and developers who were rebuilding the city were confronted with the problem of limited land resources and a desire to maximize square footage. The natural solution, particularly after the invention of safe passenger elevators, was to increase height. However, masonry construction meant that with additional height came a need for thicker walls, which reduced the amount of retail space on the lower levels. The Monadnock building, one of the last masonry skyscrapers, was 150 meters tall but had walls that were 1.8 meters thick. Philadelphia City Hall, currently the tallest masonry building, is 167 meters tall and has walls that are 6.7 meters thick! Innovative architects, led by Dankmar Adler[14] and Louis Sullivan, started using steel members, previously employed in bridges, to build a much thinner frame that could support tall buildings.[15]

While Adler and Sullivan turned to steel, Herod had no choice but to employ a non-structural curtain. One would assume that in a future Temple, the problem of the *teraksin* cubit could be easily solved by introducing a different material that can easily reach one hundred cubits in height without needing more than one cubit width. Metal (other than iron) was certainly used in the construction of the *Mishkan*, so presumably there would be no restriction on a wall supported by a metal frame. A reinforced concrete wall would be possible. One could also consider an opaque glass curtain wall.

The Torah, Mishna, and Talmud describe the evolution of the partition

---

12. Fixing a wall or column at the top steadies it against buckling, as per the Euler equation. It would also be less susceptible to lateral loads such as wind or earthquakes. A column fixed only at the bottom will buckle under one-fourth the weight.

13. bBB 3a–b. The Talmud rejects using a wall up to a certain height with a curtain above on aesthetic grounds.

14. Adler's father was a rabbi in Detroit and later in Chicago. One of his congregants in Detroit was architect Albert Kahn.

15. Louis Sullivan, *The Autobiography of an Idea,* Press of the AIA, 1924, 311–320.

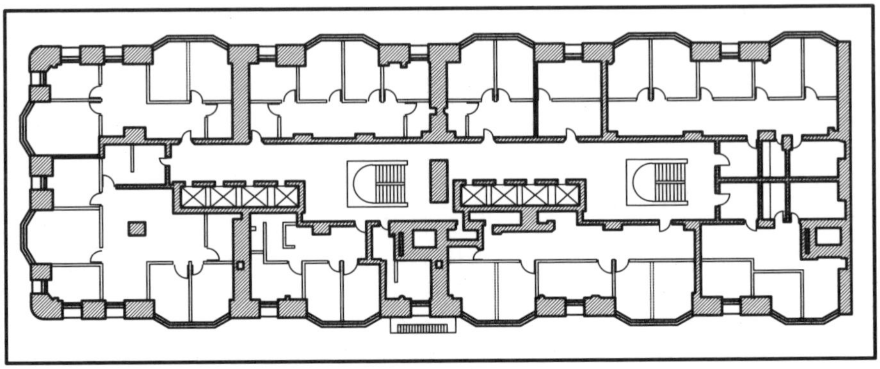

38. North corridor of the Monadnock Building, showing its thick masonry walls.

in the Sanctuary. It began as a single curtain in the *Mishkan*. When Shlomo built a permanent Temple, he used a solid wall thirty cubits high and one cubit wide to separate the Holy from the Holy of Holies. In Herod's renovated Second Temple, which was one-hundred cubits high, a wall could not be used due to structural concerns. Instead, curtains were installed. However, because the designers were unsure if the one-cubit-wide space occupied by the wall counted as part of the Holy or as part of the Holy of Holies, they required two curtains – one on each edge of the one-cubit-wide section. As the architecture changed, the architects of the building were required to develop solutions based on the existing limitations of building materials and their physical properties. Future designers would certainly be called upon to do the same in the Third Temple.

# Pomegranates, Bells, And Temple Ornament

וְעָשִׂיתָ עַל שׁוּלָיו רִמֹּנֵי תְּכֵלֶת וְאַרְגָּמָן וְתוֹלַעַת שָׁנִי עַל שׁוּלָיו סָבִיב וּפַעֲמֹנֵי זָהָב בְּתוֹכָם סָבִיב. פַּעֲמֹן זָהָב וְרִמּוֹן פַּעֲמֹן זָהָב וְרִמּוֹן עַל שׁוּלֵי הַמְּעִיל סָבִיב. (שמות כח:לג-לד)

And upon the hem of it, you shall make pomegranates of blue, purple, and scarlet, round about its hem, and bells of gold between them round about. A golden bell and a pomegranate, a golden bell and a pomegranate, upon the hem of the robe round about. (Shemot 28:33–34)

After several chapters detailing the structure and vessels of the *Mishkan*, the Torah describes the clothes of the priests and the high priest, which are made "for splendor and beauty."[1] Ramban lists several ways in which the clothes fill this role: the clothes bring honor to Aharon and his sons, as they mimic the garments of royalty. The clothes also bring honor to God, who is being served by the priests; they honor Bnei Yisrael, who visit the Temple as pilgrims; and they bring honor to the Temple itself.

The verse states that the hem of the high priest's robe was decorated with bells and pomegranates.[2] There is a disagreement as to whether the bells were *between* the pomegranates or *inside* the pomegranates,[3] but either way, they were meant to decorate the hem of the robe.[4] The pomegranates themselves were made from the threads of the robe, shaped like

1. Shemot 28:2.
2. Though mostly decorative, the bells do ring, which both fill the air with noise and let people know when the priest is moving, as stated in Shemot 28:35.
3. Ramban is the main proponent of the latter theory, perhaps based on the wording in Shemot 39:25, *betoch harimonim* which can either be translated as "between the pomegranate" or "*within* the pomegranates."
4. bShab 58b explains that bells, even without clappers inside, were used as decoration for clothing.

pomegranates "that have not opened up their mouths."[5] In 2011, archaeologists discovered a small, round, golden bell from the first century in a drainage channel adjacent to the Temple Mount, which is reminiscent of this adornment.

39. Golden bell discovered in a drainage channel near the site of the Temple.

Although we have limited information about the architectural ornaments of the Temple,[6] the decoration along the hem of the high priest's robe may help fill in this gap. There are many theories as to the origins of the patterns on classical friezes. Architectural historians claim that these patterns either mimic earlier wooden structures,[7] copy body parts of sacrificial offerings,[8] or symbolize the human body. One possibility, based on the meaning of the word "frieze" in Latin, is that the frieze mimics the hem of a garment.[9] Both Doric and Ionic frieze patterns contain two alternating elements. It would have been fitting for the Temple's frieze

5. bZev 88b. Pomegranates go through various stages before maturing. At first they look like bulbs or small pears. The rounded end then opens, creating the crown shape, and a flower emerges. Once the flower falls off the fruit swells in size and reaches maturity. Rashi writes that the stage being described is when the fruit is reaching maturity, though it sounds more likely to be the first stage, before the crown opens and when the fruit is bulb-like.

6. Josephus describes some ornamentation and small remnants of architectural decoration have been recovered from Herod's Temple complex, which contain capitals with egg and dart patterns, as well as friezes decorated with rosettes and acanthus leaves. See Orit Peleg-Barkat, *The Temple Mount Excavations in Jerusalem, Vol. V* (Institute of Archaeology, Hebrew University of Jerusalem, 2017), 42, 57 and 64. mMid 1:3 describes the decoration above a gate. The reasons for this decoration are discussed in bMen 98a.

7. Vitruvius, *Ten Books on Architecture* IV.2.2.

8. George Hersey, *The Lost Meaning of Classical Architecture* (MIT Press, 1988), 30–31.

9. Joseph Rykwert, *The Dancing Column* (MIT Press, 1988), 182. Other architectural features are also influenced by fashion. See Witold Rybczynski, *The Look of Architecture* (Oxford University Press, 2001), 21–26.

to depict alternating pomegranates and bell shapes, matching the high priest's hem.[10]

40. Ionic frieze from the Erechtheion, Athens. (Wikimedia)

The bells and tassels on the hem of the high priest's robe help us understand how architectural decoration could be influenced by fashion. Even if this pattern was not used in the Temple frieze, the description of the hem of the high priest's clothes is still an example of the type of fashion elements that friezes may once have mimicked.

10. Melachim I 7:18 states that Shlomo's Temple was decorated with pomegranates. See my commentary on Devarim 26:2 for an additional inspiration for architectural ornamentation in the Temple.

# Embossing and Engraving

וְעָשִׂיתָ צִּיץ זָהָב טָהוֹר וּפִתַּחְתָּ עָלָיו פִּתּוּחֵי חֹתָם קֹדֶשׁ לַה׳. (שמות כח:לו)

And you shall make a plate of pure gold and engrave upon it, like the engravings of a signet, Holy to the Lord. (Shemot 28:36)

THERE are several parts of the priestly garments that require lettering. The high priest's head plate – the *tzitz* – must be engraved with the words "Holy to the Lord," as per this verse. The *shoham* stones must be engraved with the names of Bnei Yisrael, "with the work of an engraver in stone, like the engravings of a signet."[1] Likewise, the twelve stones on the high priest's breastplate are to be inscribed with the names of the twelve tribes, "like the engravings of a signet."[2] Rashi explains that the letters had to be carved on the stones just as signet rings are designed to make seals on letters.[3]

Coins and signets can be either embossed, with the letters or figures protruding, or engraved, with the elements inscribed and set below the surface. Generally speaking, in the former the field around the symbol is removed, leaving only the desired shape. In the latter, the letter or symbol is cut into the surface.

Halacha demands that certain ritual objects, such as a divorce contract or *tefilin*, be created through an act of writing. The Talmud identifies the incision of letters as an act of writing – one actively traces the shape of the letter. However, embossed letters are created negatively, by carving away the material around the letters, and this action is not considered a "normal" way of writing.[4]

The Talmud explains that the letters on the headplate were embossed,

1. Shemot 28:9–11.
2. Shemot 28:21.
3. Shemot 28:11.
4. bGit 20a–b.

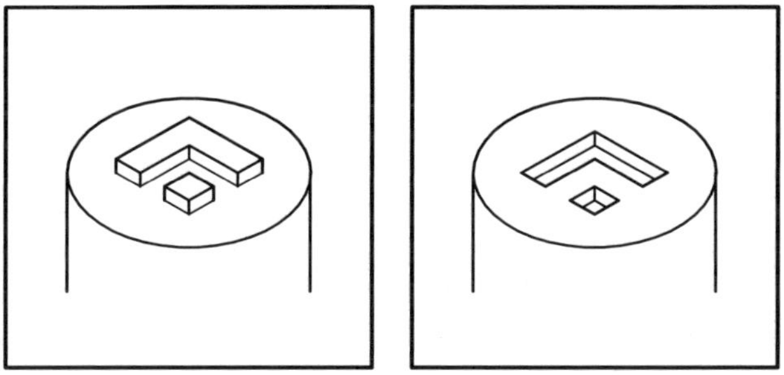

(a) (b)

41. Signets: (a) embossed (*chek tochot*) (b) engraved (*chek yerechot*).

rather than incised. However, because the headplate was a thin sheet of gold, the embossment was made by gently pushing out the letters from the reverse side. In this way, the embossment was created by tracing the letters and was thus also considered an act of writing.[5]

This technique of metalwork, where thin metal is shaped by hammering from the reverse side, is known as repoussé. The opposite technique, where the hammering is done from the front, is called chasing. One of the hallmarks of these techniques is that, unlike chiseling, none of the material is lost. Rather, the metal foil stretches with the pressure. This is useful for the priestly garments, as removing material is problematic because it creates detritus which is nonetheless sacred. One of the criteria for incising the letters on the twelves stones is that no material be lost.[6] With the gold of the *tzitz,* repoussé fulfills both the requirement of writing and the need to conserve all the original material.

5. This is crucial because in Shemot 39:30 the Torah uses the word "write" in reference to the headplate, so the words must be created by an act of writing.

6. bSot 48b, regarding the use of the *shamir* in incising the twelve stones of the breastplate, and the requirement that no material be lost as per Shemot 28:20.

# The Temple *Muchni*

וְעָשִׂיתָ כִּיּוֹר נְחֹשֶׁת וְכַנּוֹ נְחֹשֶׁת לְרָחְצָה וְנָתַתָּ אֹתוֹ בֵּין אֹהֶל מוֹעֵד וּבֵין הַמִּזְבֵּחַ
וְנָתַתָּ שָׁמָּה מָיִם. (שמות ל:יח)

You shall also make a laver of brass and its base of brass for washing, and you shall put it between the Tent of Meeting and the altar, and you shall put water in it. (Shemot 30:18)

THE laver was used to wash the hands and feet of the priests in the *Mishkan*. It is also mentioned in the context of the First Temple. However, the passages in Tanach do not contain logistical details regarding the day-to-day operations of the vessel.[1] Only in the Mishna do we find more information, specifically concerning the *muchni*, a later innovation used together with the laver.

A mishna listing important donations to the Temple[2] states that "Ben Ketin made twelve spigots for the laver, which previously had only two. He also made a *muchni* for the laver, so that its water would not be left out overnight and become unusable."[3] Since water placed in one of the Temple's vessels, including the laver, was considered sanctified, and any sanctified water left out overnight was rendered unusable, it was important to prevent this from happening.[4] We are not told, however, how the *muchni* circumvented this problem. Instead, the Mishna offers only two clues: etymologically, the word comes from the Greek *mechane*, meaning

* A version of this essay originally appeared as "Ancient Water-Raising Devices and the Temple *Muchni*" in *Bekhol Derakhekha Daehu 26* (Apr. 2012), 7–20.

1. Melachim I 7:38 and Divrei Hayamim II 4:6. See also Shemot 40:30–32.

2. The list includes gold vessels for the Yom Kippur service, a mirrored fixture that reflected sunlight, and doors imported from Alexandria. The following mishna censures a number of people for hoarding technology.

3. mYom 3:10.

4. bYom 49b–50a

a machine,[5] and the context of this mishna tells us that the *muchni* was a significant donation and related to the supply of water. Two additional mishnayot tell us that the *muchni* was made of wood, was very noisy,[6] and that only once the *muchni* did its work could the laver be used.[7]

The lack of a precise description for the *muchni* is noted in the Talmud. Abaye explains that it was a wheel and uses the somewhat ambiguous word *mashkaa* – which can mean either "lower" or "fill" – to explain that the *muchni's* function was either to lower or to fill the laver.[8] These two possible meanings influenced the two traditional descriptions of the *muchni* that are found in rabbinic literature: a pulley system used to lower the entire laver into a cistern every evening,[9] or a secondary basin containing unsanctified water, built adjoining the laver. However, the debate on the subject is largely academic since it has no practical ramifications, and Rambam even gives both descriptions in different locations.[10]

Although these two explanations relate to the wording of the Talmud, they do not align with the clues from the content and context of the three mishnayot. The pulley, though classified as a machine, was already common in the time of the Mishna and does not fit with the other wondrous gifts listed.[11] Lowering the laver and raising it in the morning would have been arduous work for the priests and thus seems far from an ideal solution. If we say that the *muchni* was used for lowering the laver at night, why would the Mishna only describe the noise of the *muchni* in the morning? If the *muchni* is a reservoir, how can this be classified as a machine? An explanation is needed that fits all these criteria.

Rather than a pulley or a reservoir, the *muchni* was likely a water-raising

---

5. H.G. Liddel and R. Scott, *A Greek-English Lexicon*, (Oxford University Press, 1843), presented online at http://www.perseus.tufts.edu. See also the Aruch. In antiquity, "machine" had a more specific meaning than today. Vitruvius notes that "A machine is a continuous piece of joinery that has outstanding capacities for moving loads. It is moved systematically by the revolutions of circles." (*Ten Books on Architecture* X.1.1.)

6. mTam 3:8.

7. mTam 1:4.

8. bYom 37a. He, like Vitruvius, links the term *muchni* to radial movement. See also Rashi on bShab 44b, *muchni shela*.

9. Rashi on bYom 37a, *muchni*, and Bartenura, Ritva, and Tosfot Yom Tov on mYom 3:10.

10. In Hilchot Bi'at Hamikdash 5:14 he writes that the laver was lowered into water and raised or refilled the next morning. In his Commentary on the Mishna, Yoma 3, and in Hilchot Beit Habechira 3:18, he explains that it was a vessel around the laver that would feed water into the laver as needed. The Kesef Mishna suggests that Rambam felt no need to isolate the "correct" answer from among the two options.

11. See K.D. White, *Greek and Roman Technology* (Cornell University Press, 1984), 14.

device. A sophisticated, expensive device providing fresh water to the laver and increasing its flow would fit the contexts of our mishnayot perfectly. The Greek *mechane* was frequently used in reference to several types of water-lifting devices.[12] Five types of water-raising devices were in use at the time: the water-screw, water drum, bucket wheel, bucket chain, and force pump, all described in detail by Vitruvius and all showing up in the archaeological and written record of the time, including in rabbinic literature. Hero describes a water wheel traditionally used at the entrance to Egyptian temples[13] and one papyrus refers to a mechanism supplying water to a synagogue.[14] Such a device was regarded as a considerable gift, and we even find an inscription in the Negev recording a similar donation.[15] Water wheels were often operated using a wooden gear system, which created a great amount of noise[16] and were also referred to as *mechane*.[17]

We can speculate that the laver developed in stages. The first laver had only two spigots and was likely smaller in size. It perhaps was lowered and raised into a cistern nightly. At some point, ben Ketin renovated the laver so that it had twelve spigots. The enlarged laver could no longer be practically raised and lowered or easily refilled, so the *muchni* was installed. This allowed simple and practical refilling of the laver on a daily basis. The *muchni* thus provided a solution to a pressing need in the Temple using the advanced technology of the day – a radial water-raising device connected to a wooden gear-train.

As a technical solution used in the Temple, the *muchni* offers proof that the Temple was not averse to adopting new solutions to existing problems. When confronted with a technical problem – keeping an ample supply of water on hand without leaving it overnight – ben Ketin utilized a machine that solved the problem elegantly. Several other examples can be found in rabbinic literature, with both high and low-tech solutions presented for various technical difficulties in the Temple. For example, the greater height of the Second Temple led to a problem with the stability of the wall between the Holy and Holy of Holies. To solve this problem, the wall was

---

12. J. Landels, *Engineering in the Ancient World* (University of California Press, 2000), 59 and John Peter Oleson, *Greek and Roman Mechanical Water-Lifting Devices* (University of Toronto Press, 1984), 127.

13. Hero, *Pneumatics* 1:32.

14. Oleson, *Greek and Roman Mechanical Water-Lifting Devices*, 153.

15. *Revue Biblique* 70 (1963): 255–57, as quoted by Oleson, 95.

16. Vitruvius mentions such a gear train alongside his description of the water raising devices (X.5). See also Oleson, 375.

17. Oleson, *Greek and Roman Mechanical Water-Lifting Devices*, 377–80.

replaced with two curtains.[18] The Mishna tells of spikes on the roof of the Temple to prevent birds from soiling it.[19] A passage in the Talmud relates how artisans unsuccessfully tinkered with musical instruments in the Temple to correct deficiencies.[20] Each of these problems was addressed with the existing technology of the day and innovative solutions were permitted. Presumably, any future Temple would allow for similar uses of technology.

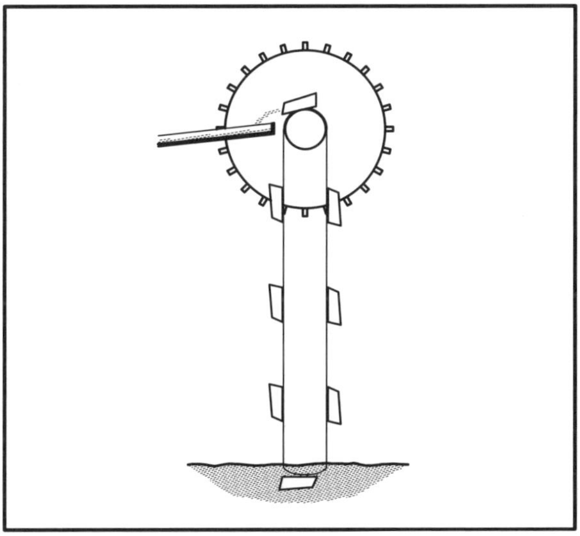

42. Schematic diagram of bucket-chain water raising device. (Based on Landels, *Engineering in the Ancient World*, 71)

18. See my commentary of Shemot 26:33.
19. mMid 4:6 and Josephus, *The Jewish War*, 5.224.
20. bAra 10b.

# Military Camps and Urban Planning

וַיַּעֲמֹד מֹשֶׁה בְּשַׁעַר הַמַּחֲנֶה וַיֹּאמֶר מִי לַה׳ אֵלָי וַיֵּאָסְפוּ אֵלָיו כָּל בְּנֵי לֵוִי.
וַיֹּאמֶר לָהֶם כֹּה אָמַר ה׳ אֱלֹקֵי יִשְׂרָאֵל שִׂימוּ אִישׁ חַרְבּוֹ עַל יְרֵכוֹ עִבְרוּ וָשׁוּבוּ
מִשַּׁעַר לָשַׁעַר בַּמַּחֲנֶה וְהִרְגוּ אִישׁ אֶת אָחִיו וְאִישׁ אֶת רֵעֵהוּ וְאִישׁ אֶת קְרֹבוֹ.
(שמות לב:כו-כז)

Then Moshe stood in the gate of the camp and said: "Who is on the Lord's side, let him come to me." And all the sons of Levi gathered themselves together to him. And he said to them: "Thus says the Lord God of Yisrael, 'Put every man his sword upon his thigh and go to and fro from gate to gate throughout the camp and slay every man his brother and every man his companion and every man his neighbor.'" (Shemot 32:26–27)

Moshe descended from Mount Sinai and discovered that Bnei Yisrael were worshipping the golden calf. After hearing Aharon's account of the events he quickly moved to re-establish order and respect for the Law.[1] The Torah describes how Moshe "stood in the gate of the camp" and called people to his side, with the goal of marching "from gate to gate throughout the camp" and slaying the sinners.

Malbim explains that when the Torah refers to gates, it is talking about the location of the Sanhedrin. According to this interpretation, Moshe went to the Sanhedrin of each tribe to try and convict the sinners. This, he hoped, would embolden the courts to put them to death.[2]

Other commentators explain the gates more literally. Ibn Ezra writes that most semi-permanent camps have gates around the perimeter. Rabeinu Bachya explains that Moshe wished to counteract the desecration of God's name caused by the golden calf, and therefore chose to slay the sinners in public. One midrash explains that the sin took place in public

1. As per R. S.R. Hirsch.
2. This explanation also appears in TPsY.

and therefore had to be rectified in public.[3] Jewish law even uses the expression "gate to gate," taken from this verse, to denote a public space.[4]

What does "gate to gate" have to do with public space, and why is it important to note that this indicates a semi-permanent settlement? To answer this, it helps to consider the design of Roman *castra* or military camps. Each *castrum* was laid out with two main crossroads, which stretched from gate to gate. The roads were known as the cardo (north-south) and decumanus (east-west).[5] The establishment of gates, therefore, implied an organized settlement with a planned layout. The point where these two boulevards met was the main public spaces in the camp or town.[6] Josephus describes this style of military encampment, writing that "Four gates are constructed, one in each length of wall ... the camp is divided up by streets accurately marked out; in the middle are erected the officers' huts and in the middle of these the commander's headquarters, which resembles a shrine."[7]

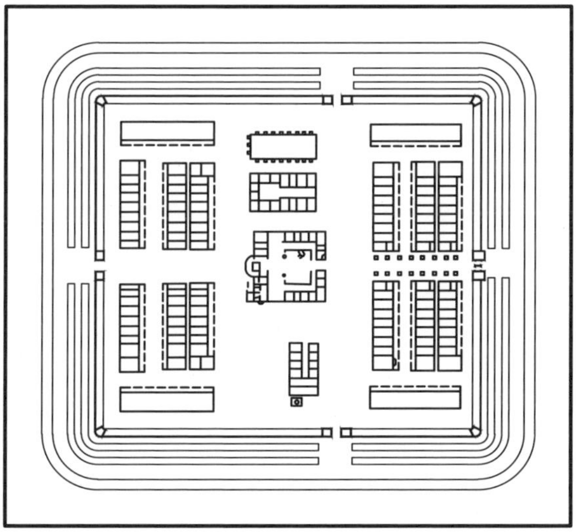

43. Plan of *castra* of Slăveni, Olt County, Romania.
(Based on Cristian M. Vladescu, *Fortificatiile Romane din Dacia Inferior*, 1986, 83)

3. VayR 4:1.

4. Shulchan Aruch OC 345:7.

5. See yBB 5:1 (15a), which states that when building a new city, one should start with four roads leading in the four cardinal directions.

6. Spiro Kostof, *The City Shaped* (Thames and Hudson, 1999), 108, 142 and 165. Kostof also mentions similar military encampments depicted in the throne room of Assurbanipal's palace at Nimrud, from the Assyrian empire.

7. Josephus, *The Jewish War* 3.81.

New Roman towns were built with a similar plan, and existing towns were sometimes redesigned to fit this pattern. When Jerusalem was transformed into Aelia Capitolina, the same process took place, with a partial decumanus and two cardines serving as the main thoroughfares. This is famously depicted in the Madaba mosaic. At the central junction, a temple to Venus was constructed, where today sits the Church of the Holy Sepulcher.

Marching from gate to gate hints at two goals. On the one hand, there is a desire to cross the camp in its entirety, making a show of bringing all sinners to justice. But it also highlights the crossroad at the center of the camp, the most public place, which would later be the location of the *Mishkan*. It was in this spot that Moshe wished to rectify the sin of the golden calf and sanctify God's name in public.

# Isolation in the Desert

וּמֹשֶׁה יִקַּח אֶת הָאֹהֶל וְנָטָה לוֹ מִחוּץ לַמַּחֲנֶה הַרְחֵק מִן הַמַּחֲנֶה וְקָרָא לוֹ אֹהֶל
מוֹעֵד וְהָיָה כׇּל מְבַקֵּשׁ ה׳ יֵצֵא אֶל אֹהֶל מוֹעֵד אֲשֶׁר מִחוּץ לַמַּחֲנֶה. (שמות לג:ז)

Now Moshe used to take the Tent and to pitch it outside the camp, afar off from the camp, and he called it the Tent of Meeting. And it came to pass, that everyone who sought the Lord went out to the Tent of Meeting, which was outside the camp. (Shemot 33:7)

After the sin of the golden calf, Moshe moved his tent from inside the camp of Israel to a place outside the camp. It is unclear whether he was commanded to do so or if this was his own initiative. Either way, this arrangement was not ideal; it would have been preferable for Moshe to remain in the camp. However, the sins of Bnei Yisrael forced him to retreat to an isolated location. This was the fallout of God's statement that "I will not go up in the midst of you, for you are a stiff-necked people, lest I consume you on the way."[1]

Most commentators explain that Moshe was forced to move outside the camp so that he could maintain his relationship with God. Rashbam states that God would not speak with Moshe so long as he remained among Bnei Yisrael. While Rashi writes that the Tent of Meeting was only a temporary location for Moshe to speak with God while the *Mishkan* was under construction,[2] Ramban disagrees, arguing that it was the permanent communication hub, necessary following the sin of the golden calf.[3] Moshe realized that as long as Bnei Yisrael were tainted by the sin of the golden calf he would not be able to communicate with God while dwelling among the nation. He did not wish to abide outside the camp but needed to do so to continue communicating with God.

1. Shemot 33:3.
2. Rashi, Shemot 33:11.
3. See also Malbim, noting that Aharon's prophecy ceased after the golden calf.

R. Yaakov ben Asher has a different perspective on the matter.[4] He learns from our verse that anyone who wishes to learn Torah should *voluntarily* exile himself. He thus sees exile as a positive thing, a way to gain clarity and to focus on learning.

Although Judaism does not have an organized concept of monasticism, Moshe was acting in line with the later practice of eremitism. Hermit monks would remove themselves from society and live in isolation.[5] This was done both to avoid the taint of society and to focus on learning and piety. The word hermit even comes from the Greek for desert-dweller. People would seek out the hermitage where they lived to ask questions and receive guidance, be it a cave, the forest, or on top of a pillar.[6]

Moshe may have been doing something similar when he moved his tent out of the midst of Bnei Yisrael, seeking separation for spiritual growth. This would explain his decision to separate from his wife.[7] However, Moshe's "hermitage" was unique in that his tent remained the main location where Bnei Yisrael could communicate with God. It was not designed to cut off communication with the outside world, but rather to put some distance between Moshe and Bnei Yisrael. The whole nation saw Moshe enter the tent and they saw God's Presence join Moshe there. Moshe did not require a dramatic setting, like a cave or a pillar, to demonstrate his monastic bona fides. Simply moving his tent was enough for him to gain the separation he needed. The location of the Tent of Meeting allowed Moshe to maintain his relationship with God and preserved the link between Bnei Yisrael and God following the sin of the golden calf.

---

4. In his commentary, *Baal Haturim.*

5. In contrast to Cenobitic monks who live in communities of monks according to rigid rules.

6. In Late Antiquity, the practice of dwelling on top of a pillar was sometimes compared to the isolated meditation that Moshe did on Mount Sinai. See Derek Krueger, "The Old Testament in Monasticism" in *The Old Testament in Byzantium* ed. Paul Magdalino and Robert Nelson (Dumbarton Oaks, 2010), 207. Later, Krueger quotes the work of Maximos the Confessor, who specifically relates Moshe's asceticism to this verse. See ibid, 215.

7. As per Bamidbar 12:1–2 and Sifri Bamidbar 99.

VAYAKHEL

# Public and Private Space

וַיְצַו מֹשֶׁה וַיַּעֲבִירוּ קוֹל בַּמַּחֲנֶה לֵאמֹר אִישׁ וְאִשָּׁה אַל יַעֲשׂוּ עוֹד מְלָאכָה לִתְרוּמַת הַקֹּדֶשׁ וַיִּכָּלֵא הָעָם מֵהָבִיא. (שמות לו:ו)

And Moshe commanded and they caused it to be proclaimed throughout the camp saying: "Let neither man nor woman make any more work for the offering of the sanctuary. So the people were restrained from bringing." (Shemot 36:6)

WHEN enough construction materials were amassed for the *Mishkan*, Moshe told Bnei Yisrael to stop bringing donations. The Talmud learns from this verse that it is forbidden to transfer objects from public domain to private domain and vice versa on Shabbat.[1]

In the laws of Shabbat, we find a complex understanding of the distinction between public and private space. Originally, the private domain seems to have consisted of a person's private dwelling. Early texts which pre-date the Mishna prohibit carrying things out of one's tent, house, or *sukka*, a narrow definition of the private domain.[2] The Rabbis significantly expanded the private domain,[3] adding two additional in-between cate-

1. bShab 96b and yShab 1:1 (2b). The Talmud explains that Moshe was in the Levite Camp, which was public domain, whereas the people were bringing goods from their private homes. Elsewhere (bShab 49b) the Talmud also learns this prohibition from the loading and unloading of wall panels on wagons. See Tosafot on bShab 96b *hotzaa*.

2. Shemot 16:29, Yirmiyahu 17:22, and Nechemia 13:15–21. External sources include Sefer Hayovlim 2:29 and 50:8, John 4:10, Damascus Document 11:7–9 and 4Q251, as quoted by Lutz Doering, "New Aspects of Qumran Sabbath Law From Cave 3 Fragments" in *Legal Texts and Legal Issues: Proceedings of the Second Meeting of the International Organization for Qumran Studies* (Brill, 1997), 257.

3. Charlotte Fonrobert sees the concept of private domain itself as an innovation, as it expands upon the more basic understanding found in the earlier Jewish sources. She writes "The abstraction from these concretely named spaces to the רשות היחיד [private domain] is a rabbinic neologism in the 'halachic marketplace.'" See Fonrobert, Charlotte

gories: the first included "the sea, a valley, a *carmelit,* a colonnade, and a threshold,"[4] while the second consisted of "a public courtyard or open alleys."[5] These four domains can be understood as a *tetralemma*:[6] while the private domain must be enclosed and closed to the public, the public domain is unenclosed and open to the public. This creates two "grey" scenarios: a place that is enclosed but open to the public (a public courtyard), and a place that is unenclosed but closed to the public (a *carmelit*).[7]

| | **Unenclosed** | **Enclosed** |
|---|---|---|
| **Open to the public** | Public Domain | Public Courtyard |
| **Closed to the public** | *Carmelit* | Private Domain |

A shared courtyard qualifies as a gray area, so it is only rabbinically prohibited to transfer objects between a house and the courtyard. However, courtyards played a crucial role in domestic life in Late Antiquity, with most daily activities taking place outside when weather permitted.[8] The Rabbis instituted the *eruv chatzerot* to render courtyards private and thus allow the transfer of objects between them and fully private areas, like a house, on Shabbat. An *eruv* is created by completely enclosing the space and symbolically placing some collective food, taken from each household, in one of the houses sharing the courtyard.[9] These two acts ensure that the gray area is enclosed and symbolically one household, thus rendering it

E. "From Separatism to Urbanism: The Dead Sea Scrolls and the Origins of Rabbinic 'Eruv." *Dead Sea Discoveries* 11,1 (2004) 50.

4. tShab 1:4.

5. tShab 1:5.

6. In a *tetralemma,* we give two ingredients, A and B, and build a framework of A and B, A but not B, B but not A, and neither A nor B. *Tetralemma* is a Greek term, referring to a piece of Aristotelian logic.

7. Gad Ben-Ami Zarfati, "*Arba Rishuyot Hashabbat*" in *Sidra 16* 105–109 (Bar Ilan Press, 2000). Zarfati notes that in bShab 6a, the term *makom patur* – a space smaller than four handbreadths squared – is substituted for a public courtyard, breaking the *tetralemma.* This occurs only in the Babylonian text, while yShab 1:1 (2d) maintains the Tosefta's *tetralemma* intact.

8. Hirschfeld, Yizhar. *The Palestinian Dwelling in the Roman-Byzantine Period* (Israel Exploration Society, 1995), 272. Stefano Bianca points out in his *Urban Form in the Arab World* that "the residential alley was outside with respect to the house, but inside with respect to the residential quarter. See Bianca, *Urban Form in the Arab World* (Thames & Husdon, 2000), 79–80.

9. mEruv 3:1–2.

a private domain. An *eruv* works not only with courtyards but in all gray areas.[10]

In contrast to early understandings which defined private space rigidly,[11] this demonstrates that rabbinic law does not have a stark definition of private space, at least for the laws of Shabbat. Instead, there is some gray area between pure public and private space.

The societal conception of public and private space is different depending on the culture. Greek culture traditionally had a sharp separation between private and public space.[12] Public space was the main place where people functioned and gained acclaim.[13] The private home was intended as a self-contained unit, something reflected in the architectural design, which was turned inward.[14] Roman culture, on the other hand, viewed public and private as a continuum, so the two only existed inasmuch as they defined one another. The Roman home was considered to be a mini-version of the public, the owner's personal forum.[15] The home was used for entertainment, business, and social interaction, functions that were not private in nature. This understanding is reflected in a midrash about Moshe's hope for entering Israel, where he is compared to a prince who is forbidden from entering the palace, but nonetheless proceeds from the gate to the courtyard to the main living space (*triclinium*) and is only stopped at the bed chamber (*koiton*).[16] Vitruvius dealt briefly with the separation between public and private, describing how some areas of the house itself, like vestibules and peristyles, were considered public.[17] In the Roman world, public and private were intertwined and could not be cleanly separated.[18]

---

10. The Mishna specifically mentions wells and orchards. See mEruv 2:1 and 2:3.

11. Other Second Temple sects seem to reject the concept of the *eruv*. See mEruv 6:2, and possible evidence in the Damascus Document 11:4–5 as discussed in Eyal Regev, Emdat Hatzedukim Veha'isim Beyachas La'eruv Chazal (Ktav Et La'iyun Vemechkar 6, 2000), 185-203 (Hebrew).

12. Town planner Hippodamus divided his cities into public, private, and sacred areas. See Aristotle, *Politics* II.8 and VII.10.

13. Jean-Pierre Vernant, *Mythe et pensee chez les Grecs* (Paris: 1965) 154 as quoted in J.B. Jackson, *Discovering the Vernacular Landscape* (Yale University Press, 1986), 19.

14. Spiro Kostof, *A History of Architecture* (Oxford University Press, 1995), 138

15. Shelley Hales, Shelley. *The Roman House and Social Identity* (Cambridge University Press, 2003), 1.

16. Sifri Bamidbar 134, referring to Bamidbar 27:12. In bBer 16b, R. Eliezer retreats into the more private sections of his house to avoid visitors. He goes from his house to the upstairs to the hallway to the *triclinium*, and he remarks on how his guests are violating societal norms. See ySan 11:6 (30c) for another example of this point.

17. Vitruvius, VI.5.1.

18. Hales, 4–6.

Change in the conception of public and private domain that took place in the laws of carrying on Shabbat may have been influenced by the significant difference in how public and private were viewed in the Greek and Roman world. While the Greeks drew a clear line between the two, the Romans felt that there was more of a spectrum, just as the Rabbis blended the concepts of public and private for Shabbat by creating the two types of in-between space.[19]

Besides Shabbat, halacha distinguishes between public and private domain in property law and ritual purity. With property law, damage caused in a public space is evaluated differently than damage caused in a private domain. For example, if an animal enters someone else's property and eats his produce, the animal's owner is liable to pay the full value of the damage inflicted. However, if this occurs in the public domain, the owner is only liable to repay a reduced amount.[20] The same distinction between public and private exists in other cases of damage, such as a case where an ox harms someone.[21] With regard to damage that takes place in the public domain, the Mishna mentions several scenarios, including "two people who are walking and injure one another." In this case, the Mishna rules that neither person is liable, with the parallel law in the Tosefta explaining that "each one has the right to walk there."[22] In these cases, the distinction seems to revolve around a question of access rather than an objective definition of public and private domain. A space in which one person has precedence over the other – where one has more of a right to be there than the other – is considered his space.[23] It has less to do with the collective views of public and private space.

Ritual purity is another area of rabbinic law in which there is a distinction between public and private space. If someone is unsure if they have become spiritually impure (*tameh*), the law is affected by where the incident occurred. If the possible contraction of impurity happened in the public domain, the Talmud rules that the person remains pure (*tahor*).

---

19. Doering, *Legal Texts*, 261–2.

20. mBK 2:2.

21. mBK 2:5.

22. tBK 2:11 and mBK 3. yBK 2:5 (3a) brings an additional case in which a man brings a chair into the public forum and it is broken by a passing donkey, ruling that the donkey's owner is not liable. See Daniel Sperber, *The City in Roman Palestine* (Oxford University Press, 1998), 9–10 for more examples.

23. See tBK 1:9, which lists four possible scenarios based on which of the two parties has a right to be present. The third scenario, where both have a right to be present, includes "a shared courtyard or a valley." While a valley is a classic "public" space, the shared courtyard is not, and is rather simply a place where both have an equal right to be present.

However, if it happened in the private domain, the person is considered *tameh*.[24] The Tosefta wonders why the question of domain should impact the halachic ruling, and R. Shimon ben Gamliel answers that "it is possible to ask an individual, but impossible to ask the masses."[25] In other words, in a private space, one is expected to have a certain level of control; in a case of doubt, we can therefore hold to a stricter standard. In public, where one cannot regulate the people passing by, it is reasonable to be lenient. According to this analysis, a person's private space, as pertaining to ritual purity, would be defined as space over which he has control, whereas public space is space which he cannot regulate.

The definition of public space for *tumah* seems to come close to our modern Western understanding of private and public space. Most people today feel that private space is space that belongs to them – which they control – while public space is beyond the control of an individual, space that is not private. Private space is seen as the more important of the two. It is sharply different from the Greek concept of public and private, in which the opposite was true – public space was the more important of the two and the private sphere was defined as space that was not public. Today, we tend to value public space as a place of interaction. Designing lively places of interaction is one of the main goals of urban planning, as vibrant public spaces have become less and less common.

The difference between how public and private spaces are defined for ritual purity and Shabbat is noted in the Mishna and Talmud, which list places that are considered private for Shabbat but public for the laws of purity. They include "a valley during the summer,"[26] a basilica,[27] a colonnade,[28] city parks, and public baths.[29] These are all areas that today would easily be classified as public.

From this analysis of public and private space in halacha, it is clear that the definition of public and private space is somewhat fluid. It can change based on society, as seen in the distinction between Greek and Roman

24. bSot 28a–b.

25. tToh 6:17. Additional answers are given from the laws of *sota* and the paschal sacrifice.

26. mToh 6:7.

27. mToh 6:8. See also tToh 7:5, which states that if the basilica is open to the public during the day and locked at night, it is considered public domain during the day and private domain at night. If one can view all the exits from the basilica, it is considered private domain for ritual purity as well, since there is some control over who enters and exits.

28. mToh 6:10.

29. tToh 7:5.

conceptions of the two. It can also be seen differently within a single culture, as with the three areas of Jewish law. For Shabbat, private space is defined as an enclosed space that is closed to the public. In property law, it is a place in which one has priority over others. In the laws of ritual purity, private space is where you can exert a certain level of control.

# Bill of Quantities

וְהַמְּלָאכָה הָיְתָה דַיָּם לְכָל הַמְּלָאכָה לַעֲשׂוֹת אֹתָהּ וְהוֹתֵר. (שמות לו:ז)

The material they had was sufficient for all the work to be done, with some to spare. (Shemot 36:7)

THE Torah describes the construction of the *Mishkan* several times.[1] Whereas previous descriptions provided the *instructions* for building the *Mishkan*, here the Torah narrates the *Mishkan's* actual construction. Before beginning, however, the Torah informs us that all the building materials necessary for the construction of the *Mishkan* had been gathered.

For the *Mishkan*, as with most projects, construction could not commence until building plans were prepared.[2] Part of this design stage is understanding what materials are needed to complete construction. The architect or a quantity surveyor reviews the plans and calculates how much stone, glass, metal, etc. is needed. The all-encompassing list is presented as a bill of quantities.[3]

Although nowadays we live in a society in which materials are readily available for order, in pre-industrial times this was not the case.[4] Rather

1. Ramban counts five times, as per his commentary on Shemot 36:8.

2. Although in ancient times many projects had no actual, drawn plans, there was still a general concept of how the building would be constructed, which needed to be formulated prior to the start of construction.

3. The B.O.Q. also includes estimated costs of the materials, as well as the labor needed for completing the work.

4. Even today there are cases when it is important to assemble materials ahead of time. For example, during a renovation of an existing train station, the station had to be temporarily closed to complete the work. To ensure that there would be no delays and that the station would be closed for a minimal amount of time, the client requested that all materials be amassed in advance. In another case, a school being constructed during the year of mayoral elections in Israel, the contractor was told to order paving stones well in advance, as it is known that during election years there is a rush to repave public

than order building parts as needed, it was usually necessary to amass all the required materials *before* starting the construction. For example, in a book describing pre-industrial house construction in Palestine, Tawfiq Canaan wrote that "the peasant must prepare his material before building. This may take him several months."[5] Yizhar Hirschfeld's survey yielded similar information: "The first step in the construction process was initiated by the household members who began to gather stones, lime, and other building materials, often a prolonged process."[6] To be able to proceed with construction, it was first necessary to gather the materials.

This construction process also sheds light on the Jewish laws concerning demolishing a synagogue. R. Chisda rules that one may not demolish an existing synagogue until a new one has been constructed. One reason given is that we fear that even with the best of intentions, something might arise that prevents a new synagogue from being built.[7] Josephus describes a similar concern when Herod wished to renovate the Temple. He relates that Herod "told them he would not pull down their temple till all things were gotten ready for building it up entirely again."[8] In both these cases, we see the importance of gathering the materials before starting construction.

Ramban writes that the purpose of emphasizing how the people brought donations for the building fund was to praise Bnei Yisrael for their generosity.[9] However, this verse is also a logical and necessary statement about the progress of the building project. Without the accumulation of all the material, work could not proceed to the construction stage.

---

spaces so as to create a positive impression among the electorate.

5. Tawfiq Canaan, *The Palestinian Arab House: Its Architecture and Folklore* (Syrian Orphanage Press, 1933), 12.

6. Yizhar Hirschfeld, *The Palestinian Dwelling in the Roman-Byzantine Period* (Israel Exploration Society, 1995), 118.

7. bBB 3b. Rambam quotes this reason only. See Rambam Hilchot Tefila 11:12. The Kesef Mishna states that even if the bricks (i.e. the building materials,) have already been amassed, we still worry that a need will arise to ransom a captive and the bricks will be sold to raise money, leaving the community without a synagogue. The passage in the Talmud relates that Josephus was told by his Roman patrons not to continue with the construction, giving credence to the fears of the Jews that the work would not be completed. This presents yet another reason why projects might not be completed: political intervention.

8. Josephus, *Antiquities*, 15:388–389.

9. Ramban, Shemot 36:5.

# Corner Design Problems

וּשְׁנֵי קְרָשִׁים עָשָׂה לִמְקֻצְעֹת הַמִּשְׁכָּן בַּיַּרְכָתָיִם. וְהָיוּ תוֹאֲמִם מִלְּמַטָּה וְיַחְדָּו
יִהְיוּ תַמִּים אֶל רֹאשׁוֹ אֶל הַטַּבַּעַת הָאֶחָת כֵּן עָשָׂה לִשְׁנֵיהֶם לִשְׁנֵי הַמִּקְצֹעֹת.
(שמות לו:כח-כט)

And he made two panels for the corners of the *Mishkan* on the two sides. And they were double at the bottom, but terminated as one at the top into one ring; thus he did to both of them in the two corners. (Shemot 36:28–29)

THE Torah twice describes the arrangement of wall panels that formed the outside walls of the *Mishkan*.[1] Each wall panel was one-and-a-half cubits wide and one cubit deep, with a height of ten cubits. The northern and southern walls each contained twenty panels, while the western wall was six boards long. However, in addition to the six panels, there were also two special corner panels that overlapped with the north and south walls. The Torah states that the panels were connected with rings.

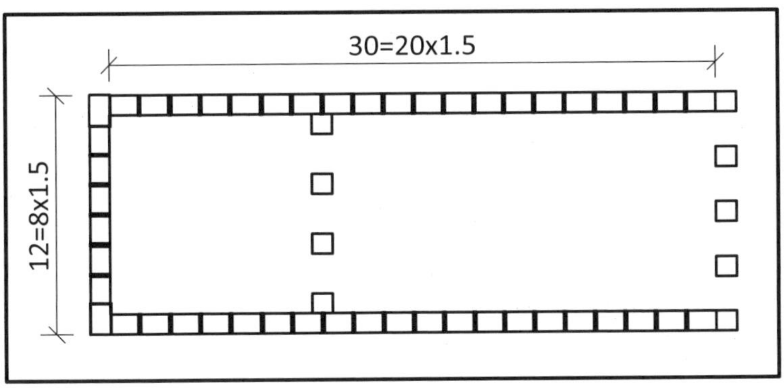


44. Plan of *Mishkan*, with dimensions in cubits.

1. See also Shemot 26:23–24, which has nearly the exact same wording.

While the *Mishkan* is generally depicted with rings connecting every pair of adjacent wall panels,[2] some commentators understood that only the corner boards were thus fastened, to give the walls extra rigidity.[3] It is unclear how the rings in the corners were arranged. Even if each pair of panels in the *Mishkan* was connected by rings, the corner connection would be unique, which explains why the Torah mentions them separately.[4]

Another area of dispute regarding corner designs concerns the shape of the wall panels. While R. Nechemia believed that the boards were the same thickness at the bottom and the top, R. Yehuda explained that they tapered to a minimal thickness at the top, resulting in a wedge shape.[5] The Talmud questions how the corner detail would work according to R. Yehuda, concluding that the corner pieces needed to be specially made in a trapezoidal shape so that they could fit together smoothly.[6] Here too, it makes sense for the Torah to single out the corner panels.

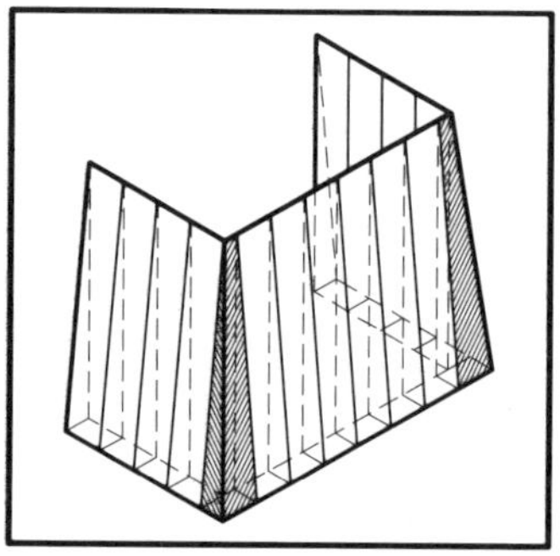

45. Isometric of corner panels according to R. Yehuda.

Designing the corners of repetitive patterns can be tricky. This was famously an issue with the triglyphs and metopes of Doric temples, the so-called Doric Angle Contradiction. While the Doric order calls for

2. Following the opinion of Rashi.

3. Ramban, for example, writes on Shemot 26:24 that this is the simple understanding of the verse.

4. R. Eliyahu Mizrachi, explaining Rashi on Shemot 26:24, adds that also the base sockets were different for the corner panels.

5. mMid 4:4 describes tapered walls in the Second Temple, but there is far more reason for tall masonry walls to be designed in this manner. Remains of the stone barrier at the top of the Second Temple have a similar detail, rounded at the top.

6. bShab 98b. The opinion of R. Yehuda is also slightly unclear, as we do not know if the cross-section of the wall was a right triangle or an isosceles triangle. It would have been easier to fashion the corner if it were a right triangle.

triglyphs to be centered on the columns, a triglyph also conventionally abuts the corner. However, this would locate the triglyph off-center and leave a larger metope than normal. Vitruvius describes several solutions to this problem, but none is completely satisfactory.[7] Ionic façades also have a complicated corner detail, as ionic capitals appear different from the front and side. Here too a special corner capital was needed, with volutes[8] that were carved on two adjacent sides or a single volute projecting at a forty-five-degree angle.[9]

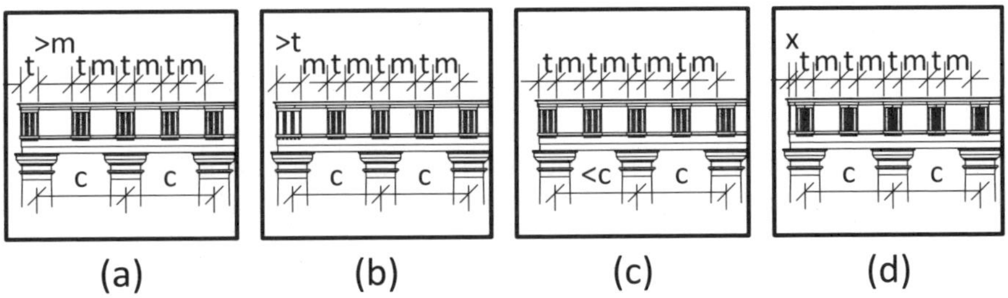


46. Four possible treatments of the Doric angle contradiction, showing measurements of metopes (m), triglyphs (t), and spacing of columns (c).

Heart-shaped columns are another corner innovation that can be found in Israel. These were initially conceived in Asia Minor in the fourth century BCE to help manage the added weight that falls on the corner pillar.[10] Even much simpler corner patterns, such as those in brick walls, require additional planning to preserve the pattern as cleanly as possible.

Architects are generally concerned with these details because they are highly visible. The front façade of a temple and the corner of a building are visible to everyone. Architects, therefore, obsess over getting these details just right. However, when it comes to the corner detail for the *Mishkan*, there is less at stake visually. The external side of the wall was never visible, as it was covered by multiple layers of fabric. The internal side of the wall could only be seen from inside the Holy of Holies, once a year by one person. This was not part of the first impression – or any impression – that the *Mishkan* made as it was rarely seen. Rather, the emphasis here seemed to

7. Vitruvius, *Ten Books on Architecture*, IV.3.2, and Joseph Rykwert, *The Dancing Column* (MIT Press, 1988), 220.

8. A volute is a spiral projection, especially associated with Ionic and Corinthian columns. See also the images accompanying my commentary on Bamidbar 19:14.

9. Rykwert, *Dancing Column*, 246.

10. Antonio Dell'Acqua, "The Use of the Heart-Shaped Pillar in the Ancient Architecture: Examples and Circulation" in *SOMA 2012*, II, 1139–40.

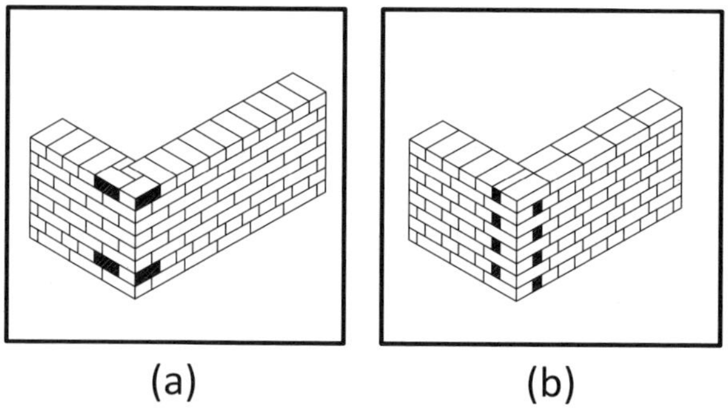

47. Brick corner arrangements showing specially-cut bricks needed to preserve the pattern. Short ends of bricks are indicated by the hatch pattern. (a) common bond (b) English bond.

be on the *Mishkan* being well-crafted and thoughtfully designed, befitting the importance of this central edifice. A thoughtful solution demonstrates that the architect invested time and effort into making sure all details were meticulously designed.

# Dedication Ceremonies

וְלָקַחְתָּ אֶת שֶׁמֶן הַמִּשְׁחָה וּמָשַׁחְתָּ אֶת הַמִּשְׁכָּן וְאֶת כָּל אֲשֶׁר בּוֹ וְקִדַּשְׁתָּ אֹתוֹ
וְאֶת כָּל כֵּלָיו וְהָיָה קֹדֶשׁ. (שמות מ:ט)

And you shall take the anointing oil and anoint the *Mishkan* and all that is in it and shall hallow it and all the vessels, and it shall be holy. (Shemot 40:9)

As one of the final steps in consecrating the *Mishkan*, Moshe was instructed to set up the *Mishkan* and to anoint the building, the vessels, and the priests. Although the verses go on to describe how Moshe set up the *Mishkan* and inaugurated the various vessels, they do not mention him anointing anything. Ramban notes this discrepancy in his commentary but explains that the *Mishkan* and vessels were surely anointed before they were used.[1] The anointing itself is described elsewhere in the Torah.[2]

In the conclusion of this narrative, the Torah describes how the "Glory of the Lord filled the *Mishkan*."[3] Chizkuni writes that after the *Mishkan* was initially filled, the Cloud of Glory withdrew from the whole building and rested on the ark alone. The purpose of filling the whole *Mishkan* was to sanctify it.

The three sections of the final chapter of Shemot thus describe three separate ways in which the completed *Mishkan* was sanctified and dedicated. The first was when Moshe anointed the building and all its vessels. The second was when Moshe inaugurated the vessels by using them for the first time: putting the tablets in the ark, putting the bread on the table, the lamps in the *menora*, bringing sacrifices on the altars, and filling the laver

1. Ramban on Shemot 40:17–18.
2. Vayikra 8:10 and Bamidbar 7:1. See also Shemot 30:26.
3. Shemot 40:34.

with water. The third was when the Glory of the Lord filled the Temple before settling on the ark.[4]

When a building is completed, it is common to have a ceremony marking its completion. However, there is usually more than one occasion that can be seen as marking the true inauguration.[5] One can note the completion of the structure, the day people move in, or the day it starts to function as planned. The three sanctifications of the *Mishkan* mark these occasions. Anointing the *Mishkan* marks the completion of the manufacturing or construction work. The use of the vessels represents the functioning of the building. And the entrance of the Glory shows the occupation of the building. For the momentous completion of the *Mishkan*, it makes sense that all aspects of the inauguration would be marked and noted.

4. SZ Bamidbar 7:1 states that the *Mishkan* was dedicated in three ways, but its list contains assembling, dismantling and anointing.

5. See my commentary on Shemot 15:17.

PEKUDEI

# Creating Courtyards

וַיָּקֶם אֶת הֶחָצֵר סָבִיב לַמִּשְׁכָּן וְלַמִּזְבֵּחַ וַיִּתֵּן אֶת מָסַךְ שַׁעַר הֶחָצֵר וַיְכַל מֹשֶׁה אֶת הַמְּלָאכָה. (שמות מ:לג)

> And he erected the court round about the *Mishkan* and the altar and set up the screen of the court gate. And Moshe finished the work. (Shemot 40:33)

THE design of the *Mishkan* included a courtyard surrounding the main sanctuary, containing the bronze altar and the laver. The courtyard was demarcated with textile hangings around its perimeter, strung between pillars, and anchored with guy lines.[1] It measured one hundred by fifty cubits[2] and was open to the sky.[3]

The courtyard marked the edge of the innermost "camp" in the desert, the most privileged ring of holiness. R. S.R. Hirsch explains that the word "courtyard" indicates a space that was restricted and that served the Temple.[4] He also writes that the courtyard "forms the point of transition out of the ordinary life of the people and into the Sanctuary."[5] Besides housing one of the main altars, the courtyard served as a transitional space. A courtyard can also enhance a building's dignity, disencumbering it from surrounding buildings and increasing its visibility.[6]

Public squares were often associated with religious architecture, though they were used for public functions as well, such as instruction, proclamations, or even storing official weights and measures.[7] The *Mishkan*

---

1. For a discussion about the pillar and hangings, see Beraita Demalechet Hamishkan 5 and Daniel Sperber, *Nautica Talmudica* (Brill, 1985), 1.4.1.
2. See Shemot 2:18.
3. This point is mentioned by Josephus. See *Antiquities* 3.112.
4. See Hirsch's commentary on Shemot 27:9.
5. Hirsch on Shemot 35:17.
6. Spiro Kostof, *The City Assembled* (Thames and Hudson, 1999), 139–140.
7. Kostof, *City Assembled*, 127.

courtyard was also used for mass gatherings, as during the dedication of the Temple.[8] This point is largely ignored, as the *Mishkan* is often considered as a stand-alone structure, even though it was situated at the center of a teeming encampment of people which may not have contained any other open areas. In reality the courtyard was likely one of the few open spaces in the encampment. Still, the courtyard was restricted and could not be used at all times or by all people.

In ancient cities, public spaces were often created in the left-over, interstitial areas within the urban fabric. As such, they could be shaped erratically. Some geometric plazas were the imprint of buildings that once existed on the site, such as Rome's Piazza Navona, where the Circus of Domitian once stood, of the elliptical Piazza del Anfiteatro in Lucca, where there was formerly an amphitheater. In cities with strong central planning, like Rome or Washington, public spaces were deliberately planned. In other case, public spaces were formed due to the arrangement of the street grid, whether orthogonal or triangular, as in New York's Times Square.

The courtyard of the *Mishkan* was shaped orthogonally. This would have been easy to achieve, as the perimeter of the courtyard could be shaped when Bnei Yisrael set up camp. In a city, it is harder to both plan and preserve the shape of a courtyard that is bound by the walls of surrounding structures.

In addition to telling us how a city was shaped – whether by a preordained plan, road patterns, or independent building programs, the shape of a piazza can help us understand its intended use. The *Mishkan's* courtyard was rectangular, but it is the placement of the *Mishkan* within the courtyard which is most informative. Were the sanctuary located in the center of the courtyard, this would indicate a closed and stable arrangement, focusing on the sanctuary as the center of activity. However, Rashi and Rashbam both write that the sanctuary, which was thirty by ten cubits, was set back fifty cubits from the entrance, leaving a square fifty by fifty cubits in front and twenty cubits free on each side.[9] The main free space was thus shaped like a square, and the overall courtyard was what Paul Zucker dubbed a "dominated square," a processional space in which the congregation is expected to interact with the building.[10] Zucker

8. See VayR 10:9, which describes how this open space miraculously expanded for all of Bnei Yisrael to fit. See also my commentary on Vayikra 8:3. For the *Mishkan* as a place where historical artifacts were stored, see my commentary on Shemot 16:33.

9. Rashi and Rashbam on Shemot 27:18.

10. Paul Zucker, *Town and Square* (Columbia University Press, 1959), 8–17. The Women's Courtyard of the Second Temple is also described as square in shape, though the various storage rooms created a cruciform plan.

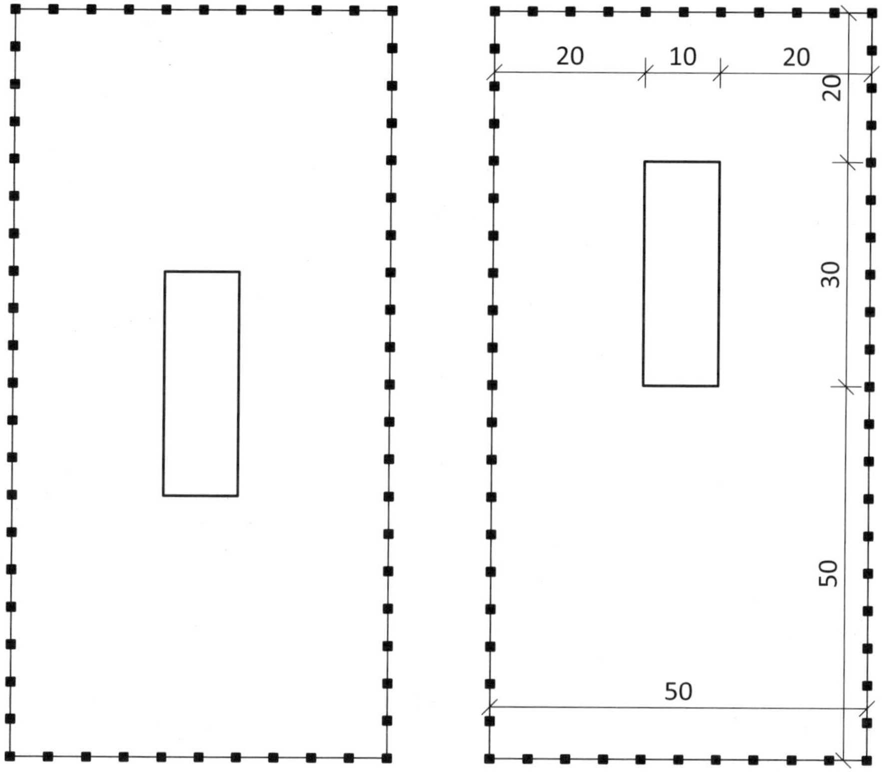


48. *Mishkan* courtyard. The right image shows the position of the sanctuary with the courtyard. The left image shows the sanctuary centered in the courtyard, changing how the courtyard and the building interact.

explained the difference between the two arrangements, writing that a dominated square directs people toward the building and creates motion, while a closed square is more stagnant.[11] Instead of simply surrounding the structure with open space, this configuration sets the stage for precession, compelling interaction with the *Mishkan*. The placement of the *Mishkan* within the courtyard serves to include Bnei Yisrael in the picture, rather than putting the focus solely on the building. Having the sanctuary off-centered makes room for the people in the courtyard, but focuses the activities in the courtyard toward the sanctuary.

11. Zucker, *Town and Square*, 11.

# VAYIKRA

VAYIKRA

# Blood on the Altar

וְשָׁחַט אֶת בֶּן הַבָּקָר לִפְנֵי ה׳ וְהִקְרִיבוּ בְּנֵי אַהֲרֹן הַכֹּהֲנִים אֶת הַדָּם וְזָרְקוּ אֶת הַדָּם עַל הַמִּזְבֵּחַ סָבִיב אֲשֶׁר פֶּתַח אֹהֶל מוֹעֵד. (ויקרא א:ה)

And he shall slaughter the bull before the Lord; and Aharon's sons, the priests, shall present the blood and sprinkle the blood round about against the altar that is at the door of the Tent of Meeting. (Vayikra 1:5)

SEVERAL verses in Vayikra instruct the priests to sprinkle blood from sacrificial animals on the four sides of the altar.[1] Blood was to be sprinkled on both the upper and lower walls of the altar.[2] The repeated sprinkling of blood left a visible mark, so over a short period of time, a pattern of blood splatter would appear on the altar.

While the Torah does not describe the maintenance of the altar, the Mishna records two opinions on the matter. The first states that the altar was cleaned or whitewashed twice a year, for Pesach and Sukkot. The second opinion argues that the bloodied walls were wiped clean every week. While these two cleaning regiments could both apply in conjunction,[3] it is also possible that they conflict with regard to (a) the frequency of cleaning (biannually or weekly), (b) the method for cleaning (whitewash or wiping), and (c) the tool for cleaning (wooden trowel or cloth.) Either way, we see that there is some consideration about cleaning the blood from the altar walls.[4]

1. See Sifra 5:9, quoted by Rashi, for discussion about the mechanics of sprinkling the blood on four sides.

2. To aid the priests, mMid 3:1 explains that a line was drawn at the halfway point of the altar. See also bZev 53a, which learns this from Shemot 27:5. To ensure a margin of error for the priests' aim, the line was given a generous thickness, as per bBech 17b. For another example of imprecise boundaries, see mEruv 4:11.

3. As per Bartenura.

4. This is different than the blood which was poured out at the base of the altar

While architects like to think of their buildings as finished products which are most perfect before they are inhabited and begin to degrade, an important component of design is an awareness of how the object will be used and what processes it will undergo over time. On one level, this means selecting an appropriately durable material or taking maintenance into account.[5] On a more complex level, there are instances where an architect considers the processes that will occur once construction is complete. Most obvious is vegetation, where landscaping will only begin to fill in as years pass, but other processes take place too. Sometimes chemical reactions alter a building with age, as in the greening of a copper roof. Other times a façade is designed in anticipation of how weathering will eventually darken some areas and leave others bleached.[6] Most subtle, however, are the marks left by inhabitants over the course of years, which build up and reveal how the building is used. These could be a worn footpath, or the dirtying of walls, or the smoothing of stones.

In our mishna, it may be that we have two different understandings of how the altar is considered over time. If the altar is indeed cleaned weekly, and certainly if it is whitewashed rather than wiped clean, this would imply that the altar was meant to remain pristine in appearance. While the sprinkling of blood is a necessary component of an offering, it is not meant to leave a permanent mark on the altar. There are some examples in the Temple that imply a desire for sterility which supports this notion. The Mishna, for example, contains a midrash about miracles in the Temple, which states that the meat of the sacrifices did not putrefy, that no flies were present, and that the smoke rose in a straight pillar, unaffected by wind.[7] Additionally, we find a description of how the blood was cleansed from the floor of the Temple before Pesach.[8] In this scenario, it is preferable to remove traces of the blood from the walls of the altar.

On the other hand, if the altar is to be cleaned only biannually, then we can understand that the sprinkling of blood goes beyond a requirement and becomes part of the aesthetic of the Temple, with the blood meant to build up over time. In support of this view, we can point to at least three

and drained to the Kidron valley in mMid 3:2 and mYom 5:6. However, there too the Mishna considers the maintenance of the drainage system, describing a pit that had to be cleaned once every seventy years. See mMid 3:3, tSuk 3:15, and ySuk 4:6 (54d).

5. For example, considering how the outside surface of windows will be washed.

6. Mohsen Mostafavi and David Leatherbarrow, *On Weathering: The Life of Buildings in Time* (MIT Press, 1993), 39.

7. mAv 5:5.

8. tPes 4:12 describes that the priests would flood the Temple courtyard by plugging the drainage of the aqueduct, "until it was as clean as milk."

49. Water stain on the L.A. Mayer Residence, Jerusalem. (Architect: Alexander Friedman)

other instances in the Temple in which this type of process was celebrated. In one case, the drains that were used for libation offerings were noticeably stained.[9] In addition, the heap of ash on the altar was left in place during holidays, since it was considered to be decorative.[10] Finally, the Talmud states that the Temple's drains would be plugged to flood the floor with blood, as having the priests wade up to their knees in blood was considered visually pleasing.[11] In these cases, the built-up traces of past offerings form a kind of decoration, indicating that the Temple is well-used by devotees.[12]

---

9. mSuk 4:9. Another dramatic weathering process that affected the external appearance of the Temple might be implied by the discussion in bSuk 51b about the staggered stone courses in Herod's Temple.

10. mTam 2:2. Besides these examples, yYom 5:4 (42d) and bYom 57a record that R. Elazar ben R. Yosi went to Rome and saw blood splattered on the curtain, implying a persistent mark of blood left in place.

11. tPes 4:12, bPes 65a, and bZev 35a.

12. Sefer Hachasidim 1533 records a similar ruling regarding the blood of martyrs. "A house in which people were martyred and blood sprayed on the walls or stones: the

The gradual buildup of blood on the altar can be seen as either a reminder of sin (in the case of sin offerings) or as a positive trace of devotion. In the former, it is sensible to frequently clean away the blood stain. In the latter, there is a desire to celebrate its function by leaving clear evidence of its usage. The overall traces compound over time and, like a stone being worn away, leave a lasting and positive impact.[13]

owner should not plaster over the bloodstains . . . as long as the blood is visible, God will take revenge, but if the blood is concealed, there will be no urgency to take revenge."

13. For a similar analysis of weathering, see Motafavi and Leatherbarrow, *On Weathering,* 42 who write that "While it may be possible to see all weathering as deterioration, the production of distracting marks that dirty original surfaces, this recognition of the play of shadows and the inevitability of marking suggests an alternative interpretation, one of weathering as a process that can productively modify a building over time." See also page 68, where the authors write that "When this formative process is allowed to continue uninterrupted the surface of the original can be covered so completely that it disappears altogether under a patina, a time-bound "growth of skin" that covers the new surface with an accumulation that represents the tension between a work of art and the conditions of its location."

# Blood Drainage on the Temple Mount

וְנָתַן הַכֹּהֵן מִן הַדָּם עַל קַרְנוֹת מִזְבַּח קְטֹרֶת הַסַּמִּים לִפְנֵי ה׳ אֲשֶׁר בְּאֹהֶל מוֹעֵד
וְאֵת כָּל דַּם הַפָּר יִשְׁפֹּךְ אֶל יְסוֹד מִזְבַּח הָעֹלָה אֲשֶׁר פֶּתַח אֹהֶל מוֹעֵד. (ויקרא ד:ז)

And the priest shall put some of the blood upon the horns of the altar of sweet incense before the Lord, which is in the Tent of Meeting and shall pour all the blood of the bullock at the bottom of the altar of the burnt offering, which is at the door of the Tent of Meeting. (Vayikra 4:7)

Once the blood of a sacrifice has been used for its ritual purpose, the Torah instructs the priest to dispose of the leftover blood by pouring it out at the base of the altar.[1] The Mishna explains that there were two drainage holes in the southwest corner of the altar's base, through which the blood would flow down to a channel and then out to the Kidron Valley.[2]

A second mishna explains that once the blood flowed away from the Temple and into the Kidron Valley, it was sold as fertilizer. Since the blood came from sacrifices, some rabbis considered it to be consecrated. Using the blood as fertilizer would then constitute a violation of *me'ila* – making use of consecrated objects – at least on the level of a rabbinic prohibition.[3] Due to the dispute about *me'ila,* the farmers who purchased the Kidron Valley fertilizer may have relied on the lenient opinion that allowed the use of leftover blood from sacrifices. However, it is also possible that they were doing so out of ignorance, as the Mishna seems to imply.

1. This commandment is repeated in verses Vayikra 4:18 and 4:25.
2. mMid 3:2 and mYom 5:6.
3. The relevance of the laws of *me'ila* to blood is debated in bYom 59a. The text in tYom 3:2 contains this information as well, including the dispute regarding blood and *me'ila.* Rambam rules in Hilchot Me'ila 2:11 that using the blood taken from the Kidron Valley does constitute *me'ila.* The Talmud states that the prohibition is only rabbinic, though Tosafot (bYom 59b *hu*) quote at least one opinion that understood it was a Torah prohibition.

Pipes, by their design, are meant to be out of sight and to deliver substances from one point to another without any thought. When we open our taps and water pours out, there is no immediate reason to consider the water's source. Heat, electricity, light, gas, water, waste, and fresh air are all pumped through our modern buildings behind sealed walls and we tend not to think much about them unless the systems fail.[4] The same is true of any substance that instantly appears, and it was probably true of the blood-infused fertilizer that was being sold in the Kidron, giving credence to the ignorance of those purchasing fertilizer.

The nebulous nature of hidden conduits is evident in the laws of Shabbat. While it is forbidden on Shabbat to transfer objects from a private to a public space, and vice versa, the Mishna discusses whether one can pour out liquid in a private space, knowing that it will drain into public space.[5] The question also arises regarding water on Pesach, and whether to be concerned that the water came from a source containing traces of leaven. The halacha seems to be uninterested in the unseen origin of the liquid, dealing instead with what is readily apparent.

The extra level of concern in our case may have to do with the difference between blood and water. While it is normal for water to emerge from the ground without any apparent source, and we today have learned to expect similar dispensation of air, gas, and electricity, the same is not true of blood.[6] The blood in the Kidron Valley may have arrived via hidden conduits, but it is hard to imagine any situation in which blood could simply appear and be taken for granted. In the case described in the Mishna, there could be no confusion regarding the blood's origin in the Temple. Therefore, only if the laws of *me'ila* do not apply to sacrificial blood which has completed its ritual function could it be permissible to use the blood as fertilizer.

---

4. Witold Rybczynski describes the development of modern building systems in *Home: A Short History of an Idea* (Penguin Books, 1987), ch. 7.

5. See mEruv 8:9 and tEruv 6:18. There is also a discussion of the opposite case, whether one can take water out from a water channel that passes through your private space. See mEruv 8:7 and tEruv 6:18. In both cases, the primary concern of the Rabbis is that the channel itself is a *carmelit*, rather than the fact that the water is actually being transported great distances and quite likely entering or leaving the *techum Shabbat*. Compare this with yBer 6:1 (10a), where the Talmud discusses making a blessing before drinking flowing water and rules that it is fine even though the water in front of you when you make the blessing is not the same water you are drinking. mBeit 5:1 also permits the use of runoff from a roof on Shabbat. See also Shulchan Aruch OC 402.

6. yAZ 3:1 (42a) and bSan 109a record two instances in which drains were said to run with blood after the death of a sage. However, see bPes 22a, which draws a connection in this context between blood and water, taken from Devarim 12:16.

# *Me'ila* and the Value of Architecture

נֶפֶשׁ כִּי תִמְעֹל מַעַל וְחָטְאָה בִּשְׁגָגָה מִקָּדְשֵׁי ה׳ וְהֵבִיא אֶת אֲשָׁמוֹ לַה׳ אַיִל
תָּמִים מִן הַצֹּאן בְּעֶרְכְּךָ כֶּסֶף שְׁקָלִים בְּשֶׁקֶל הַקֹּדֶשׁ לְאָשָׁם. (ויקרא ה:טו)

If anyone commits a trespass and sins through ignorance in the holy things of the Lord, then he shall bring for his guilt to the Lord a ram without blemish out of the flock, according to your valuation in silver by shekels, after the shekel of the sanctuary, for a guilt offering. (Vayikra 5:15)

THE Torah prohibits the private use of consecrated objects, a transgression known as *me'ila*. The Mishna explains that to transgress *me'ila* one must get a minimum amount of utility from the consecrated item. With less durable objects, one must also cause depreciation to violate this prohibition.[1]

After establishing the requirement of utility, the Mishna presents an example: if one takes building materials – a stone or a beam – from the Temple, it does not count as *me'ila*. Even using the stone or beam in the construction of your home does not count as *me'ila*, according to the Mishna, until you benefit by actually living in the house.[2]

This ruling is questioned by the Talmud,[3] since using a beam to build a house seems to provide plenty of utility. Why shouldn't this alone qualify as *me'ila*?[4] Rav[5] answers that the Mishna is talking about a case where the

---

1. mMei 5:1. R. Akiva disagrees with the Rabbis and does not require devaluation in any case. The Mishna mentions several metal objects as examples of durable goods, while textiles and axes are considered objects that experience wear-and-tear.
2. mMei 5:4.
3. bMei 20a.
4. The Talmud protests, "Once you have changed [the stone or beam] you have committed *me'ila*!" A variant recorded in Shita Mekubetzet switches the wording to "Once you have built ..."
5. In bBK 20b this opinion is quoted in the name of Shmuel.

object is not permanently affixed, but rather leans against a skylight.[6] The stone or beam provides some use – by blocking the sun or the rain[7] – but is not part of the building. Were the stone built into the house, this alone would certainly qualify as *me'ila*. If, however, it is unattached, then no benefit occurs until one lives in the building.

The difficulty with this explanation is that it does not seem to fit with the wording of the Mishna. The Mishna says that "If one *builds it into his house*, he has not trespassed until he lives under it [and benefits] the value of a small coin." The Mishna explicitly states that the stone or beam is built-in, yet rules that this is not *me'ila* because there has been no benefit.

Instead, we can explain the ruling of the Mishna, and even the opinion of Rav, in a way that more precisely aligns with its wording. To do so, we must consider what makes good architecture. Vitruvius famously explained that all architecture should contain three aspects: *firmitas* (soundness), *utilitas* (utility), and *venustas* (attractiveness).[8] The building should be structurally sound, function well, and possess beauty. These are the three areas in which there is value in a building.

The stone or beam mentioned in the Mishna cannot be a structural component of the building. If it were – that is, if without that beam or stone the building would collapse – then no one could deny that the stone or beam provides benefit to the owner, and thus its use would constitute *me'ila*, even without residency.[9] Therefore, we can eliminate structural soundness from the equation.

The Mishna only seems interested in the second criterion, utility, and disregards the third, attractiveness. In the view of the Mishna, the primary value of a building comes from its function. A school must serve its students, a factory must be used for output, and a house derives its benefit from serving as a shelter. Therefore, when one uses a stone or beam, the Mishna only considers the value derived from being sheltered by it.

The Talmud seems to believe that there is also value in the appearance of the building and its attractiveness. Its assumption is that value can be added by making the building more outwardly (or inwardly) attractive. Therefore, the Talmud is surprised by the Mishna's ruling and asks why *me'ila* only occurs upon occupancy. Rav then finds a situation in which the stone is not visible from the street, or even from the interior, i.e. when it

---

6. bMei 20a.
7. As per Rashi.
8. Vitruvius, *Ten Books on Architecture,* I.3.2.
9. This fits with the wording of this mishna, which implies an *existing* house to which the stone or beam is *added.*

is leaned on the skylight. Since that situation does not affect the appearance of the building but does contribute to its function, it would indeed describe a situation in which the stone does not provide benefit until one shelters within the building. However, according to the Talmud, a visible and attractive addition to the building would presumably provide enough utility to create *me'ila* even without providing shelter.

The importance of *venustas* is precisely what differentiates between a regular building and Architecture. This distinction was highlighted by architectural historian Nikolaus Pevsner when he wrote that:

> "A bicycle shed is a building; Lincoln Cathedral is a piece of architecture. Nearly everything that encloses space on a scale sufficient for a human being to move in is a building; the term architecture applies only to buildings designed with a view to aesthetic appeal."[10]

The Mishna's opinion is understandable: if we are talking about a building that does not aspire to be Architecture, then its function is by far the most significant component. In such a case, utility is only derived by taking up residence within the house. But if we are thinking about a building with greater aspirations, that qualifies as Architecture in the way Pevsner intended, then a stone added to a building can provide very real benefit, as the Talmud assumes.[11]

10. Nikolaus Pevsner, *An Outline of European Architecture* (Penguin Press: 1943), xix.

11. There is some further evidence that the case we are dealing with involves using the stone or beam for aesthetic or symbolic reasons rather than as part of the soundness or utility of the building. Ritva (bBM 99b *natal even*) writes that the case in this mishna must be one in which the stone has already been incorporated into the Temple and was then removed or fell out. He reasons that, as per bMei 14b, stones that are prepared for use in the Temple are not consecrated until they are added to the structure, as otherwise the workers preparing the stones would risk debasing a sanctified object if they chiseled off too much or made some other mistake. Therefore, the only case in which a stone would be consecrated is if it had already taken its place in the Temple, or possibly if someone had consecrated the stone before donating it to the Temple. The re-use of building materials from ornate buildings (spolia) has historically been a common practice, especially for symbolic reasons. (For reference to this practice, perhaps, see tMeg 2:16, tMak 5:8, and yMeg 3:1 (73d). This lends credence to my argument about the potential aesthetic benefit a stone from the Temple would give to a dwelling, regardless of whether it has been occupied by the owner.

# Stolen Central Beams

וְהָיָה כִּי יֶחֱטָא וְאָשֵׁם וְהֵשִׁיב אֶת הַגְּזֵלָה אֲשֶׁר גָּזָל אוֹ אֶת הָעֹשֶׁק אֲשֶׁר עָשָׁק
אוֹ אֶת הַפִּקָּדוֹן אֲשֶׁר הָפְקַד אִתּוֹ אוֹ אֶת הָאֲבֵדָה אֲשֶׁר מָצָא. (ויקרא ה:כג)

Then it shall be, if he has sinned and is guilty, that he shall restore that which he took by robbery, or the thing which he has gotten deceitfully, or that which was delivered to him to keep, or the lost thing which he found. (Vayikra 5:23)

THE Talmud learns from the words "that which he took by robbery" that a thief who wants to repent must return the object he stole in the same condition as it was taken, provided the object still exists.[1] However, the Mishna mentions an exception to this general rule: if someone stole a beam (*marish*) and used it to construct a large building, he may leave the beam in place and instead compensate the victim monetarily for the loss. The logic behind this ruling is that destroying a large building to return a beam would be beyond consideration. Such a demand would keep people from repenting.[2]

Although it seems odd that such an emphasis be placed on one beam, it helps to understand that the *marish* was not just one of many beams; rather, it was the central beam of the ceiling. In the period of the Mishna, the average size of a house was increasing.[3] In order to facilitate wider

1. bBK 66a, yBK 9:1 (6d), Rambam Hilchot Gezela Ve'aveda 1:5.

2. mGit 5:5. The Talmud (bGit 55a) explains that this was a dispute between Beit Shammai and Beit Hillel, with the former saying that the whole building must be torn down. In bTaan 16a Shmuel likewise rules that the building must be destroyed.

3. The Mishna itself mentions that this is a beam used in a large structure, a *bira*. Around the third century CE, as wood became much less common in the region, wooden roofs declined in popularity and instead stone roofs supported by stone arches became more common. See Yizhar Hirschfeld, *The Palestinian Dwelling* (Israel Exploration Society, 1995), 243. See also BerR 4:1, which may reflect this later situation in claiming that roofs are built from stone, wood and dirt.

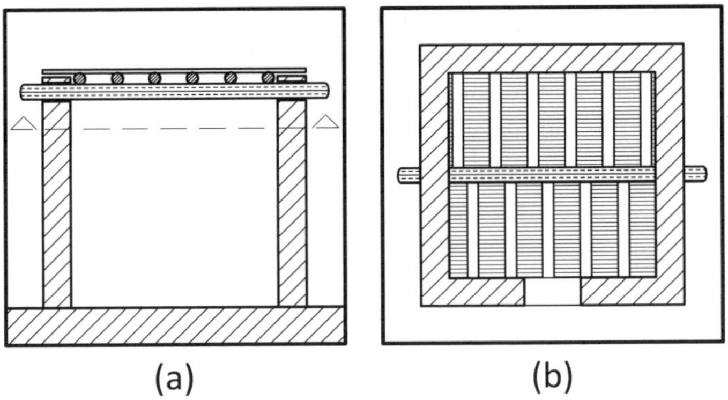

50. *Marish:* (a) section (b) reverse ceiling plan.

rooms, an especially long and thick beam would be used as the central support. This was the *marish*. Such beams were, by their nature, hard to obtain.[4] With the *marish* in place, shorter, more widely available beams could then stretch from the wall to this central beam. If the central beam were removed, the entire ceiling would collapse. This is reflected in a midrash that compares the central beam in a *triclinium* to Avraham, who, rather than being created first, was placed in the middle of the generations, so that he could support those that preceded and succeeded him.[5] In this construction technique, the central beam itself remained unaltered and identifiable as a separate component of the ceiling.[6] It could, therefore, be removed and returned, but only at the cost of destroying the ceiling entirely.

Recognizing this building style helps us understand the specific reference to a "large building" in our mishna. One might be tempted to understand this as a value judgment – only a large building is worth saving,

4. The scarcity of suitable beams is evident in bTaan 25a, which tells of a man who builds a house and fails to procure beams of an adequate length. At a loss, the man approaches Chanina ben Dosa, who miraculously intervenes and causes the beam to grow in length. The house was subsequently known as "the house that was roofed by R. Chanina ben Dosa's prayers." Another midrash tells that Haman had difficulty securing a fifty-cubit beam to build gallows for Mordechai, and considered cannibalizing the beam of his house before his son Parshandata provided him with a beam from Noah's ark. See Midrash Aba Gurion 5. The central importance of beams is emphasized in R. Avin's statement in yEruv 5:1 (22c) that as long as a house's beams remain in place, the house is considered intact.

5. BerR 14:6.

6. Yizhar Hirschfeld, *The Palestinian Dwelling in the Roman-Byzantine Period* (Israel Exploration Society, 1995), 124 and 238. See also Samuel Krauss, *Kadmoniyot Hatalmud*, Vol. 1, Pt 2 (Moriah, 1913), 298 (Hebrew).

and a smaller structure can be dismantled without causing great harm to its thieving but repentant owner. Instead, with knowledge of the building technique, we understand that the stipulation of a large building is simply coming to describe the real-life situation in which a beam like this would be used. Ultimately, all buildings – large or small – should have this leniency applied.

# Wood for the Altar

וְהָאֵשׁ עַל הַמִּזְבֵּחַ תּוּקַד בּוֹ לֹא תִכְבֶּה וּבִעֵר עָלֶיהָ הַכֹּהֵן עֵצִים בַּבֹּקֶר בַּבֹּקֶר
וְעָרַךְ עָלֶיהָ הָעֹלָה וְהִקְטִיר עָלֶיהָ חֶלְבֵי הַשְּׁלָמִים. (ויקרא ו:ה)

And the fire upon the altar shall be kept burning in it, it shall not go out, and the priest shall kindle wood on it every morning and he shall lay the burnt offering in order upon it and shall burn on it the fat of the peace offerings. (Vayikra 6:5)

ONE of the daily duties of the priests in the Temple was to arrange wood on the altar.[1] According to the Mishna, all types of wood could be used except olivewood and grapevines. Fig, walnut, and *shemen* wood were the preferred species.[2] R. Eliezer added carob, palm, sycamore, nettle, and oak to the list.[3]

Why should some species of wood be prohibited? R. Papa explains that olivewood and vines are gnarly and cannot be properly cured; consequently, they would cause too much smoke. R. Acha bar Yaakov gives a second reason: harvesting olivewood and grapevines harms the agricultural productivity of the land. The Talmud is compelled to add that according to this reason, the species of palm and fig in question must be species that do not bear fruit. Alternatively, perhaps olives and grapes were considered the two main crops in Israel, more important than fig and date production.[4]

1. See also Vayikra 1:7, "And the sons of Aharon the priest shall put fire upon the altar and lay the wood in order upon the fire."

2. mTam 2:3. bRH 23a lists *shemen* as one of ten types of cedar in the context of fire beacons for the new moon. BerR 15:1 mentions twenty-four types of cedar, and states that they were only created for use in the Temple.

3. Sifra 8:4 and bTam 29a. See also Sefer Hayovlim 21:12 for another list of permissible wood for the altar. bPes 82a states that reeds and palm branches cannot be used for the altar. Rashi *(kani vecharyuta)* explains that this is because they burn too quickly.

4. A similar explanation can be found in the Lechem Mishna on Rambam Hilchot Isurei Mizbeach 7:3. See also mKil 6:5, in which R. Meir singles out olive and fig trees,

R. Acha bar Yaakov's emphasis on cultivated trees is reflected in other texts from the time of the Mishna. Columella (d. 70 CE), who wrote about agriculture in the Roman world, explained that,

> We also think it proper, as Virgil did, to distinguish plants of trees into two kinds: one of which grows up of its own accord, the other proceeds from human industry and care. That kind, which does not come for human assistance, is more proper for timber; this, upon which labor is bestowed, is fit for fruit.[5]

As with the Mishna, Columella separates the cultivated trees which produce fruit from trees that grow on their own. He is mostly concerned with the use of lumber in furniture, but nevertheless we see a greater willingness to cut down uncultivated species.

R. Papa's opinion, which pointed out the physical characteristics of olivewood and grapevines, is also easy to understand. Wood species each have their own characteristics.[6] Vitruvius wrote about the different woods in terms of their chemical composition (air, fire, water, and earth.)[7] With firewood, most modern literature on the subject sounds very similar to the opinion in the Mishna: almost anything can be burned, especially if cured for the appropriate amount of time, but some species are preferable. The United States Forest Products Laboratory rates firewood species based on heat produced, ease of burning, ease of splitting, amount of smoke, sparks, weight, and aroma.[8] These criteria would have been relevant in ancient times the same as they apply today. The Mishna implies that infestation was also an important component.[9] Availability is another factor, and the Mishna's list contains only species that are native to Judea. In fact, the species mentioned in our mishna are almost identical to a list of the earliest and most widely cultivated species in this region.[10]

---

along with vines, as the most significant agricultural trees.

5. Columella, *On Trees*, I.1.

6. mPes 6:1 insists on pomegranate wood for the roasting spit of the Paschal lamb.

7. Vitruvius, II.9.

8. http://mb-soft.com/juca/print/firewood.html.

9. mMid 2:2 says that the priests inspected the wood for worms. Today lumber is graded for defects, and excessive amounts of infestation can harm the wood and lower the rating of the lumber.

10. As per Daniel Zohary and Maria Hopf, *The Domestication of Plants in the Old World* (Oxford University Press, 2000), 143: "Plant remains retrieved from archaeological excavations indicate that the olive, grape, vine, fig, date palm, pomegranate and sycamore fig were the first fruit trees cultivated in the Old World." The authors explain that these trees were easy to propagate through cuttings without having to resort "to

⊣ † ⊢

The Mishna relates that while anyone could donate wood, several families were given preference for making these donations.[11] Each family had a set date to deliver wood to the Temple. The wood was then stored in a special chamber in the Women's Courtyard.[12] While we might expect the donation dates to be spread throughout the year, in fact two-thirds of the dates fall within the thirty days between Tamuz 20 and Av 20, corresponding to the end of summer.[13] This seems curious but likely has to do with the normative time for harvesting firewood.[14] Vitruvius writes that wood should be cut between the start of autumn and the end of winter.[15] This leaves about six months – usually the minimum period needed – for the wood to cure in time for the main donation period to begin. By the months of Tamuz and Av, the wood would be ready for use. From this calculation, we can understand that the donated wood was likely pre-cured, and did not need to undergo further drying in the Temple's wood storage chamber.[16] This aligns with what we know about the architecture of the wood storage area, which lacked ventilation[17] and had no apparent heat source. Such a conclusion is also logical, as we would expect donations to the Temple to be finished products.[18]

⊣ † ⊢

There are other examples in rabbinic literature in which an emphasis is placed on the difference between wood species. We find one fine example in a ruling about a rented house that collapses. The owner is responsible for rebuilding the house as it was, so that cedar beams may not be replaced with sycamore beams and vice versa.[19] This ruling, which is found in the

---

more sophisticated techniques of vegetative propagation such as grafting."

11. mTaan 4:1.

12. mMid 2:2.

13. The other three dates fall out one per season: the first of Nissan, the twentieth of Elul (since the first of Tishrei is a holiday) and the first of Tevet.

14. This is explained in bTaan 31a and yTaan 4:7 (69c).

15. Vitruvius II.9.2.

16. For the difference between smoke produced by burning wet or dry wood, see EichaR 1:10.

17. By most accounts it was roofed and had solid walls.

18. Raba and R. Yosef describe the fifteenth of Av as the final day for harvesting wood for the altar. See bBB 121b, based on Megilat Taanit. In Eicha Rabba, an opinion states that this is a good time to harvest wood. See EichaR Petichta 33.

19. tBM 8:32. Sycamore was much cheaper than cedar, as per Melachim I 10:27.

Tosefta, does not appear in a series of similar laws that are recorded in the Mishna: a small house cannot be replaced with a big house, one without windows cannot be replaced with a house that has many, and vice versa.[20] With beams, one would be hard-pressed to provide a cogent reason why sycamore would be preferable to cedar. Sycamore was an all-purpose building material that was widely used – the Greek philosopher and arborist, Theophrastus, wrote that sycamore "is useful for many purposes"[21] and Pliny the Elder used similar language in his treatise.[22] But cedar was known for its quality and longevity, a deluxe building material. In the cases given in the Mishna, there is an argument to be made for why someone would prefer a small house or a house with fewer windows, but it is hard to think of a good reason to prefer sycamore beams over cedar. Perhaps the reason why the cedar/sycamore beams case does not appear in the Mishna is due to this difficulty. It is likely that the comparison between sycamore and cedar has less to do with actual material characteristics and more with Biblical verse that contrasts the two. A description of King Shlomo's building program says, "And the king made silver to be in Jerusalem as stones, and he made cedars to be as the sycamore trees that are in the lowlands, for abundance."[23] Similarly, Yishayahu derides people who claim that "The bricks are fallen, but we will build with hewn stones; the sycamores are cut down, but cedars we put in their place."[24] These two verses both make clear the preferable nature of cedar over sycamore construction and link the two as a paradigm that is referenced in the Tosefta.

The specifics given in the Mishna about wood for the altar highlight several lessons about wood. Wood has different characteristics that make some species preferable to others.[25] The information in the Mishna also

20. mBM 8:9. However, it does appear in the Talmud. Additionally, mBB 5:6 presents a similar ruling but with olivewood and sycamore, two types of wood that are more equivalent.

21. Theophrastus, *Enquiry into Plants,* IV:2,1,2.

22. Pliny the Elder, *Natural History,* 13:14. Pliny likely copied his entry from Theophrastus. It also contains some dubious scientific information about the properties of sycamore wood. See also Samuel Krauss, *Kadmoniyot Hatalmud,* II (Moriah, 1913), 258–9 (Hebrew).

23. Melachim I 10:27.

24. Yishayahu 9:9.

25. Discussing Vayikra 23:40, which says "the fruit of the *hadar* tree," the Talmud Bavli explains that this refers to a tree whose wood and fruit have the same flavor. (bSuk 35a) However, the Talmud Yerushalmi instead explains "a tree whose fruit is *hadar* and whose wood is *hadar*." (ySuk 3:5 (53d)). Gisela Richter, in her study of Greek and Roman furniture, writes that "the most prized [wood] was the citron, and goes on to quote Pliny, Cicero, Petronius, and Martial as proof. This, then suggests an alternative

fits with what we know about how different species of wood were used in ancient times. We can learn from the dates of donation that the wood was probably pre-cured before it was brought to the Temple. Finally, we can note other laws with similar preferences and understand the contrast between sycamore and cedar that appears in several places.

understanding to the Bavli – the wood itself was superlative, much like the fruit. See Gisela M.A. Richter, *The Furniture of the Greeks, Etruscans and Romans* (Phaidon Press, 1966), 122.

TZAV

# Standing Room Only In the Temple

וְאֵת כָּל הָעֵדָה הַקְהֵל אֶל פֶּתַח אֹהֶל מוֹעֵד. (ויקרא ח:ג)

And gather all the congregation together at the door of the Tent of Meeting. (Vayikra 8:3)

In anticipation of the inauguration of Aharon and his family as priests, Moshe was instructed to gather all Bnei Yisrael at the entrance to the *Mishkan*. In Vayikra Rabba, R. Elazar reflects on the impossibility of fitting 600,000 people into such a small location. He explains that this is one of several occasions when a small space miraculously held more than its physical capacity. He then lists several other examples from the Torah.[1]

A similar passage in Midrash Tanchuma gives a second list that focuses on crowds at major events.[2] In this midrash, Moshe is told not to worry about fitting all Bnei Yisrael into the entrance to the *Mishkan*, for at the End of Days all the people that have *ever* existed will be able to fit into Jerusalem. Likewise, he is reminded that the space at Mount Sinai miraculously expanded to hold all the Israelites plus all the angels and chariots that descended from heaven.[3]

Among the several examples of this phenomenon, the most well-known instance appears in a list of ten recurring miracles in the Temple.[4] According to the Mishna, when Bnei Yisrael would gather in the Temple courtyard on festivals, they would pack the space standing up. Nonetheless, when the time came to prostrate themselves on the ground, there was miraculously enough space to do so. Vayikra Rabba mentions this as well, with the added

1. VayR 10:9 and BerR 5:9.

2. Tanchuma Tzav 12.

3. See, however, tPes 4:15, which describes a Pesach when there was not enough room for all the Jews on the Temple Mount.

4. mAv 5:5. See also bYom 21a and ARN A, 35 *asara nisim* which takes things one step further and says that no matter how many Jews there are, they will *always* be able to fit together into the courtyard.

information that when prostrated, there would be at least a cubit of space between each person, so that no one would overhear the private prayers of their neighbors.

Even without the stipulation that there were gaps between people, the disparity between standing and prostrating density can be easily demonstrated. Estimates for the density of a standing crowd are readily available, as any public space or event must be planned with this type of occupancy in mind. Most studies give the upper threshold for a standing crowd of spectators as between four and five people per square meter.[5] However, this density is still not the stomach-to-back, pressed-up-against-one-another situation that is described in the various midrashim.

With a density upward of five people per square meter, bodies are tightly packed and not free to move on their own. This is the threshold where crowds become dangerous and crushing is a real threat. If the crowd in the Temple were packed as tightly as described, any attempt to genuflect would almost certainly have resulted in mass casualties. When crowds are packed in this tightly, people can no longer control their own motion due to the pressure exerted on them by their neighbors. If one person stumbles and a sudden gap appears in the crowd, his neighbors find themselves unsupported on one side and tumble into this gap, colliding and opening up other gaps. The crowd surges and cannot control its movement, resulting in pile-ups and death due to asphyxiation. With even greater densities, people are unable to properly inflate their lungs and can likewise suffocate even without falling. It is safe to assume that the authorities would not let the Temple get packed to this extent, so four to five people per square meter is a reasonable upper limit.

Figures for prostrated worshipers are harder to come by. Based on my own estimates, it would be possible to achieve a density of about two people per square meter. In the image below, each square represents 50 × 50 cm, and each person takes up two squares. This figure would indicate that under non-miraculous circumstances, worship requiring prostration would limit the number of participants to half that possible if only standing was required. A tightly packed, but still safe, crowd of four people per square meter would require more than double the area to be able to genuflect, and this is without examining the different possible ways of prostrating[6] – the given estimate is one of the most compact options. In any case, we can understand why the midrashim refer to this as a miracle.

---

5. A good online resource for visualizing different crowd densities is the work of Dr. Keith Still, http://www.gkstill.com/index.html.

6. See bShev 16b.

One interesting, though perhaps overly practical, question we could pose is whether safety requirements for the Temple would be designed to accommodate the miraculous or non-miraculous occupancy. Under normal circumstances, safety engineers estimate the occupancy of a space and design egress accordingly. A space designed to hold *x* number of people must contain *y* number of exits, and each exit must be a specific width. Would a safety consultant for the Temple be able to design the exits based on the non-miraculous occupancy and trust that if a miracle were to take place to allow for greater occupancy, then this miracle would apply to exit widths as well, or would a greater number of exits need to be designed from the onset? Similar questions could be asked about air-conditioning and ventilation, toilet facilities, parking spots, and all other building features that are correlated to the occupancy. Presumably, since "we do not rely on miracles," designers would have to assume the highest number for occupancy.[7]

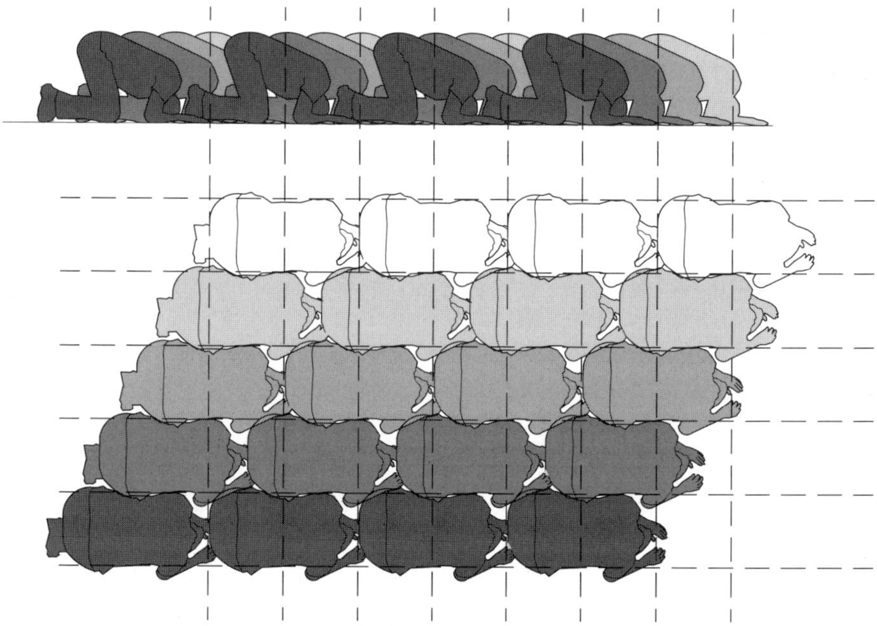

51. Diagram of prostrating worshipers.

7. "We do not rely on miracles" is a principle that is specifically applied to Temple-related situations, as in yShek 6:3 (50a) and yYom 1:4 (39a), and to issues of physical danger, as in bShab 32a and bTaan 20b.

# Servant and Served Spaces

וַיִּקְרָא מֹשֶׁה אֶל מִישָׁאֵל וְאֶל אֶלְצָפָן בְּנֵי עֻזִּיאֵל דֹּד אַהֲרֹן וַיֹּאמֶר אֲלֵהֶם קִרְבוּ
שְׂאוּ אֶת אֲחֵיכֶם מֵאֵת פְּנֵי הַקֹּדֶשׁ אֶל מִחוּץ לַמַּחֲנֶה. וַיִּקְרְבוּ וַיִּשָּׂאֻם בְּכֻתֳּנֹתָם
אֶל מִחוּץ לַמַּחֲנֶה כַּאֲשֶׁר דִּבֶּר מֹשֶׁה. (ויקרא י:ד-ה)

And Moshe called Mishael and Elzafan the sons of Uziel the uncle of Aharon and said to them: "Draw near, carry your brethren from before the sanctuary out of the camp." So they drew near and carried them in their tunics out of the camp, as Moshe had said. (Vayikra 10:4–5)

FOLLOWING the death of Aharon's two eldest sons, Moshe instructed two Leviim to retrieve the dead bodies from the *Mishkan*. The Midrash records a debate between R. Eliezer and R. Akiva over whether the bodies were lying inside the *Mishkan*, or if they were in an outer space where the Leviim were permitted to enter. Even R. Akiva, who concluded that the corpses were inside, claims that the Leviim did not actually enter the *Mishkan* but rather dragged the bodies out with a pole.[1]

Under normal conditions, only kohanim were allowed into the *Mishkan*. This is why both R. Eliezer and R. Akiva explain that the two Leviim, Mishael and Elzafan, did not enter the *Mishkan*. However, if no other options are available, the Tosefta and Talmud make it clear that Leviim or even Israelites are allowed into the forbidden part of the Temple. This was true not just for removing impure items but also for maintenance.[2]

Concerning maintenance, the Mishna provides more information.

1. Sifra, Mechilta demiluim 35, and quoted by Ramban in his commentary on these verses. See also bZev 105a, *bekolsi*, for another example of extracting impure objects with a crook.

2. tKel BK 1:11 and bEruv 105a. The Tosefta is also quoted in bPes 86a. Josephus writes in *Antiquities* 15.390 that for his renovations to the Temple, Herod taught some kohanim "the arts of stone cutters, and others of carpenters."

Above the Holy of Holies, there was a service space that had openings in the floor. Workers could descend through these openings and perform maintenance work, even in the Holy of Holies.[3] The Mishna states that the workers were lowered in boxes which would limit their field of vision so that only the portion of the chamber that needed fixing could be viewed. However, here too the Tosefta is explicit in saying that if this apparatus were not available, the workers could use the normal entrance.

The spaces of the *Mishkan*, and later the Temple, were designed to create areas of limited, privileged access for ritual activities. Nonetheless, it was necessary to plan for maintenance and service of all the spaces, even the most restricted. In this regard, the Temple was the same as any building, which requires access for maintenance, usually hidden away from the occupants of the space so as not to impinge on the architectural experience. The situation in the Temple was more complicated due to its high level of sanctity. In a normal building, we want the people *inside* to remain oblivious to the services which exist outside, while in the Temple we must prevent the people *outside* from intruding on the sanctity within. Normally, there is no problem with a worker entering the main space to provide service, via service openings in the walls, floor, and ceiling. In the case of the Temple, a separate service level was necessary, so that maintenance could be provided from without.

The architect who most famously dealt with distinguishing servant and served spaces was Louis Kahn, who made this a mainstay of his designs.[4] His buildings grouped service components separately in a way that preserved and emphasized the geometric purity or ideal form of his main spaces. Kahn tended to think of this as an almost religious decision, preserving the sanctity of his spaces, concentrating on the experience *inside* the space. Kahn understood that removing the service functions from the main space would give that main space a feeling of sanctity and importance. He wanted inhabitants to feel as if they were experiencing a privileged space.

In the Temple, the design process arrived at a similar solution in reverse; the Temple was *actually* a religious, restricted, privileged space, and service hatches were required to accommodate this reality. The architecture of the Temple did not need to isolate the main spaces in order to make one feel its gravitas; the sanctity of the space was a given. It needed a functional design solution for workers, not one that enhanced the experience of the kohanim.

3. mMid 4:5.
4. Louis Kahn, "Order in Architecture," *Perspecta* IV (1957).

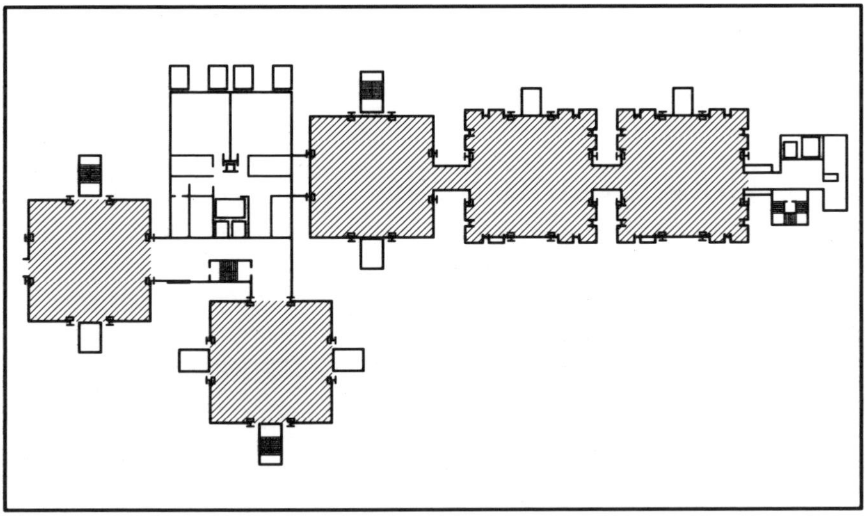

52. Plan of the Richards Medical Research Laboratories by Louis Kahn, showing "served" and "service" spaces.

# *Mikvaot* and Building Typology

אַךְ מַעְיָן וּבוֹר מִקְוֵה מַיִם יִהְיֶה טָהוֹר וְנֹגֵעַ בְּנִבְלָתָם יִטְמָא. (ויקרא יא:לו)

Nevertheless, a spring, or a cistern, a gathering of water, shall be *tahor*, but he who touches their carcass shall be *tameh*. (Vayikra 11:36)

WHILE discussing the laws of impurity, the Torah uses three terms referencing bodies of water: *maayan*, *bor*, and *mikva mayim*. The Talmud learns from this verse that a spiritually impure – *tameh* – vessel, submerged in one of these bodies of water, reverts to its pure status.[1]

Saadia Gaon explains that each of the three terms in this verse has different properties. A *maayan*, or spring, is flowing water that has emerged from the earth. A *bor*, or cistern, is flowing water that is set inside the earth, recessed in the surface. A *mikva*, he writes, is water that has been gathered, presumably into a depression in the earth. These are three different arrangements of what we refer to today as ritual baths, or *mikvaot*.[2] However, while our *mikvaot* today tend to be man-made, these three terms relate to natural bodies of water.

During Late Antiquity, a specific style of *mikva* emerged which can be easily recognized in the archaeological record. Ronny Reich, in his survey of *mikvaot* from this period, notes that the presence of *mikvaot* in settlements allows us to distinguish between the similar domestic architecture of Jewish and non-Jewish settlements.[3] He lists the main design elements

1. bPes 16a and quoted by Rashi on our verse.
2. mMik 1 categorizes *mikvaot* into six groups, although both the *maayan* and *bor* of R. Saadia Gaon's explanation seem to fall into the highest category of the Mishna, *mayim chayim*. This explanation seems to follow Sifra Shemini, parsha 9.
3. Ronny Reich, *Miqvaot Tahara Betekufat Habayit Hasheni ubetekufot Hamishna Vehatalmud* (YBZP, 2013), 12 (Hebrew).

of a *mikva* in this period – a man-made, plastered depression that is either set within or attached to the ground and has relatively wide steps leading down.[4] He also surveys the various mechanisms allowed in rabbinic literature for maintaining the required forty *se'ah* of water and how these match the archaeological record. Reich describes the development of these *mikvaot* which appear in the archaeological record around the second century BCE, whereas previously there seem to have only been *mikvaot* in naturally occurring bodies of water.

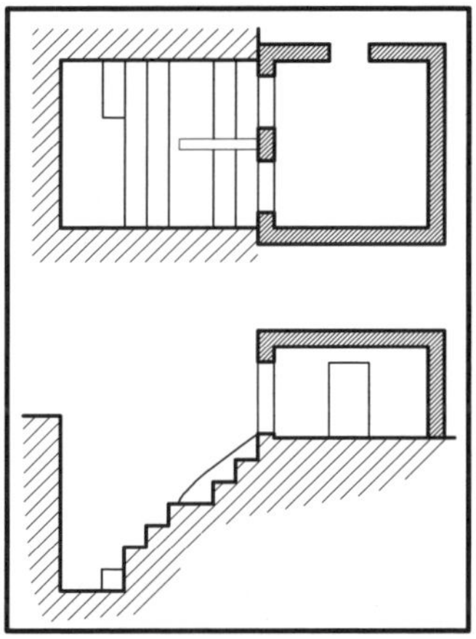

53. Plan and section of a *mikva* with double opening and stair divider. (Based on Reich, *Miqvaot*, fig. 5, 38)

The process which Reich describes, by which *mikvaot* went from natural pools to having some set elements and then eventually a formal set of design features, is a pattern that is common in design. Buildings that fit in with a group of similarly designed structures fulfilling the same design requirements are classed together as a specific building *type*. Greek temples, Roman baths, courthouses, and movie theaters are each a type, in that they have set characteristics and stylistic elements that are recognizable and repeatable. Someone designing a movie theater does not need to start from scratch, because that type of building has already been thought out and a standard exists that fits its purpose. Once a type is honed and established, it can be widely copied and spread. This was described by Rafael Moneo in his essay, *On Typology*.[5]

When it became necessary to design man-made *mikvaot*, there was

4. He also explains how to distinguish *mikvaot* from winepresses and water cisterns. Ibid, 46–52.

5. Rafael Moneo, "On Typology," *Oppositions: A Journal for Ideas and Criticism in Architecture*, 13 (Summer 1978): 22–45.

most likely a period in which the basic design elements were still being figured out, starting with a pool of water, continuing with the steps (of a certain width, later with enough space for separate descent and ascent, and with a dividing line between)[6], an area for cleansing in preparation, and including different methods for maintaining the required volume of water. Once the type was set and was judged to be successful, it spread around the country and became the easily-recognized stepped baths that Reich was able to survey. Although it may seem like an obvious point, it is only possible to find this type in the archaeological records after the type coalesced.

Much of Moneo's article deals with the resistance of architects to typology and the implied stability/stagnations they portend. Moneo pushes back against this idea, and comments that types might exist not due to architectural stagnation but rather because,

> The struggle with an identical problem tends to lead to almost identical forms. Or in other words, stability in a society – stability reflected in activities, techniques, images – is mirrored also in architecture.

The fact that *mikvaot* today remain largely within the same type of their ancient brethren, with very similar design elements, speaks volumes about the stability of the relevant corpus of halacha over thousands of years.[7] The function and regulations have remained the same, and so has the architecture. Likewise, it should not surprise us that this type of *mikva* did not always exist, but rather appeared at a certain time and place and then spread extensively.

6. See mShek 8:2 and Rashi on bPes 19b, *bederech acheret,* as well as my commentary on Bamidbar 19:11.

7. *Mikvaot* in Israel, which are mostly funded by the government, are dictated both by halacha and by the building regulations put in place by government agencies, which publish guides for *mikva* construction.

While *mikvaot* have mainly stayed the same, the same cannot be said for the other standard Jewish building type, the synagogue.

# Sections Through the Temple Mount

וּשְׁלֹשִׁים יוֹם וּשְׁלֹשֶׁת יָמִים תֵּשֵׁב בִּדְמֵי טָהֳרָה בְּכָל קֹדֶשׁ לֹא תִגָּע וְאֶל הַמִּקְדָּשׁ לֹא תָבֹא עַד מְלֹאת יְמֵי טָהֳרָהּ. (ויקרא יב:ד)

And she shall then continue in the blood of purifying thirty-three days, she shall touch no hallowed thing nor come into the sanctuary, until the days of her purifying be fulfilled. (Vayikra 12:4)

WHEN a woman gives birth, she becomes ritually impure – *tameh* – for a set number of days. She may not enter the Temple during this time.

As part of the discussion about entering the Temple while *tameh*, the Talmud tries to delineate the contour of the *Azara*, the courtyard surrounding the main Temple building. This discussion has implications beyond *tumah*, as certain offerings must be slaughtered and eaten in the *Azara*. Two *beraitot* rule that these sacrifices cannot be slaughtered or eaten on the roofs of the chambers surrounding the *Azara*, as these spaces were not suitably sanctified.[1]

There are several Temple chambers mentioned in the Mishna, but the assumption is that we are discussing the roofs of six chambers that were built along the north and south walls of the *Azara*.[2] A gatehouse, the *Beit Hamoked*, straddled the boundary and contained four more chambers, two inside the *Azara's* boundary and two beyond.[3] The Mishna is vague about the exact position of these chambers, so the Talmud needs to clarify whether they were considered part of the *Azara* or the less-holy Temple Mount.

Despite the *beraita's* assertion that the roofs were not sanctified, another mishna rules that the roofs could be a part of the *Azara* under certain

1. bShev 17b, bPes 85b–86a, bZev 56a.
2. mMid 5:3–4.
3. mMid 1:5–6.

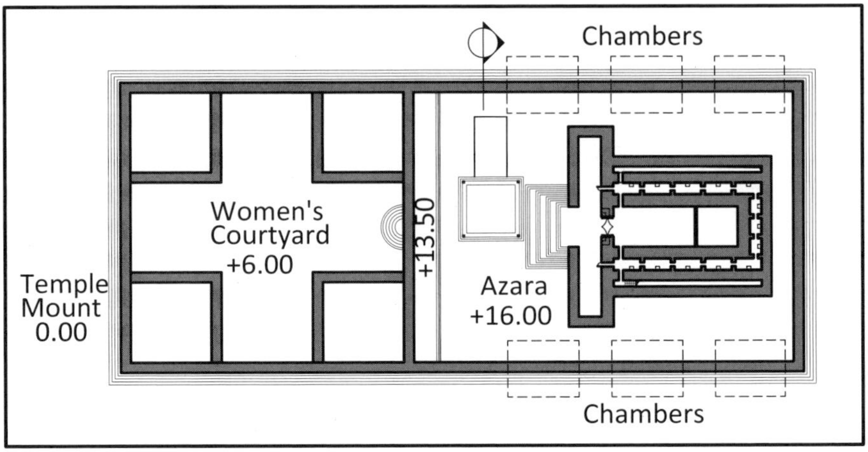


54. Plan of Temple's basic geometry according to Midot, with conjectural location of chambers.

conditions. If a chamber is built within the *Azara*, but its doors open onto the Temple Mount, its interior is considered an extension of the less-holy Temple Mount while its roof counts as part of the *Azara (fig. 55a).*

Conversely, if a chamber is built beyond the *Azara*, but can only be entered from inside the *Azara*, the chamber is considered part of the *Azara* but its roof counts as part of the Temple Mount. *(fig. 55b)*[4] If, like the *Beit Hamoked*, a chamber straddles the boundary and has entrances both from within and without, then the room is split along the border.[5] *(fig. 55c)* To square this contradiction, R. Chisda explains that roofs above the level of the *Azara* were not sanctified, but if the chambers were built below grade, so that their roofs were contiguous parts of the *Azara*, then the roofs would have the sanctity of the *Azara*. *(fig. 55d–55f)*[6] Most renderings of the Temple nonetheless show the chambers built on the level of the *Azara* with elevated roofs.[7]

The Mishna and Tosefta seem to be concerned with the continuity of space. A chamber that can only be entered from outside the *Azara*

4. yBB 4:4 (14c) makes a similar ruling for the sale of houses within courtyards.

5. mMS 3:8. See also tMS 2:13–15, which adds that the second scenario is hypothetical. This is echoed by R. Shimon, who says all the offices were inside the *Azara*.

6. bPes 86a. The Talmud also discusses the roofs of stepped houses in Jerusalem, in which the roof of one dwelling serves as the patio of the next.

7. Other mishnayot describe the roofs of these chambers as private areas, to be used by the high priest or to store equipment, which suggests they were indeed elevated. Tosafot speculate that the roof of the *beit haparva* chamber was on level with the *Azara* and had a private entrance below ground. See bYom 31b *vekulan*.

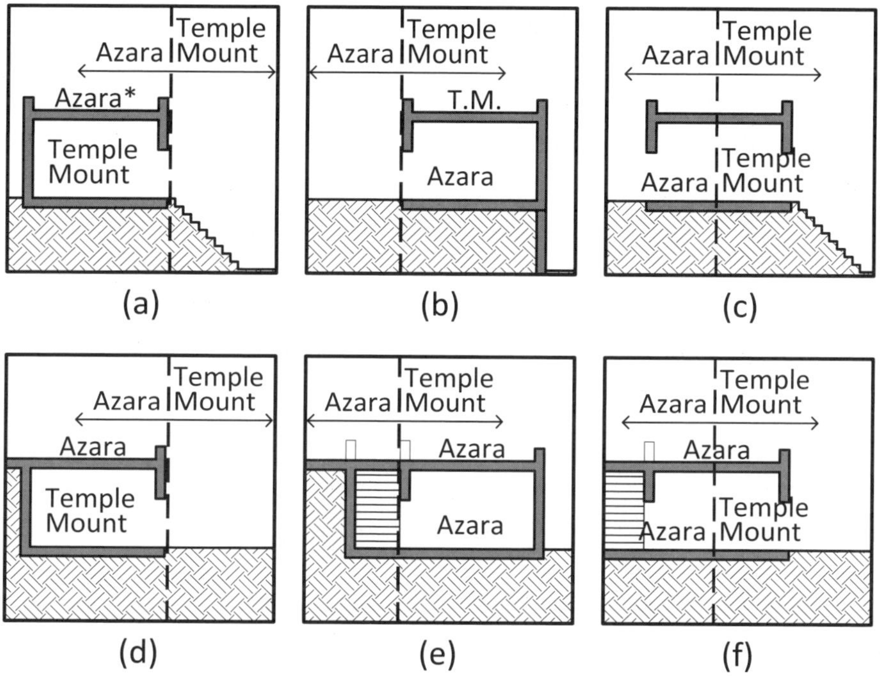


55. (a) Chamber in *Azara* but opening onto the Temple Mount. *According to R. Chisda, the roof is part of the Temple Mount, though this is not the simple interpretation of this mishna. (b) Chamber in Temple Mount territory but opening into the *Azara*. (c) Chamber on the border, openings into both. (d–f) Same as a–c, but with roof at the level of the *Azara*.

"belongs" to the external space, despite its geographic location within the *Azara*. The roof, when above grade, is not a continuous part of either space, and therefore it follows the strict geographic demarcations – if it falls within the *Azara*, it has the higher level of sanctity, and vice versa. There is a practical, if not rigidly geographical, logic to this ruling. In the *Beit Hamoked*, where the boundary bisected the room, the Mishna mentions that a physical marker was installed to interrupt the continuous paving and demarcate that the two halves of the room belonged to different spaces.[8]

One surviving example of a chamber connecting different levels of the Temple is the double gate passageway beneath Herod's royal portico at the southern edge of the Temple Mount. A passage leads beneath the royal portico and then climbs to the level of the Temple Mount. The roof of the passageway served as the floor of the royal portico.[9] While this

8. mMid 1:6.

9. For the arrangement of the royal portico and the double gate passageway, see

part of the Temple complex was outside the *Azara*, its section is akin to the situation described by R. Chisda. The passages between the Temple Mount and the *Azara* may have been similarly arranged.[10] The *Azara* was sixteen cubits higher than the Temple Mount, leaving plenty of height for chambers below grade.

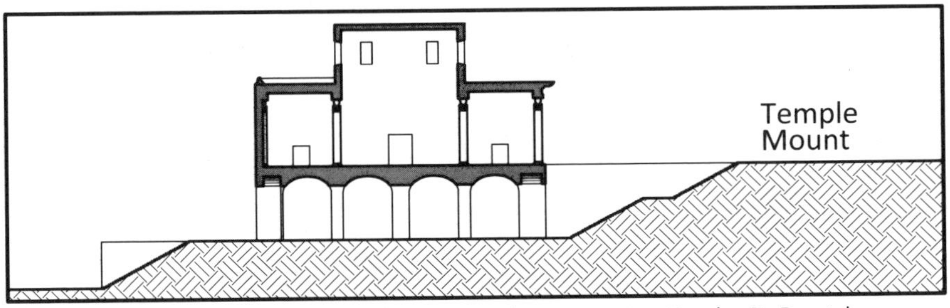


56. Section through Royal Portico. (Based on reconstruction by D. Porotsky and M. Yagod in *The Temple Mount Excavations in Jerusalem*, Vol. V, *1968–1978*, fig. 3.4)

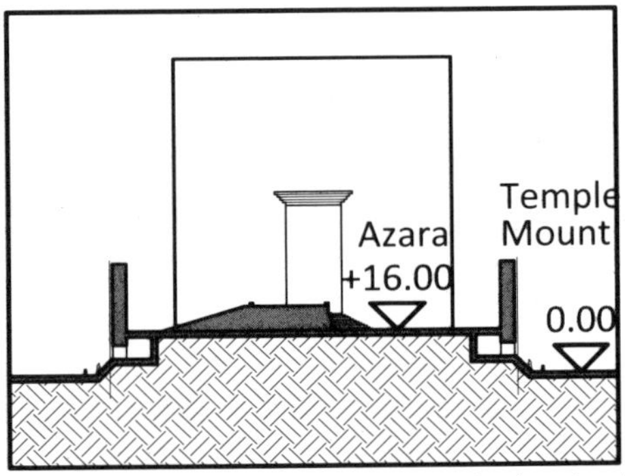


57. Section through Temple, showing sixteen-cubit height difference between the *Azara* and the Temple Mount area for chambers below the *Azara*.

While it is most common to consider two-dimensional boundaries between spaces, the sections through the Temple complex demonstrate that even sacred boundaries can sometimes be circuitous. Understanding the section of the Temple, along with its plan, helps us understand the design,

Orit Peleg-Barkat, *The Temple Mount Excavations in Jerusalem, Vol. V* (Institute of Archaeology, Hebrew University of Jerusalem, 2017), 98–99 and 121–128. Similarly, shops were built against the retaining walls of the Temple Mount, with a staircase leading up to the shops' roofs. See Ronny Reich and Yaakov Billig, "Excavations Near the Temple Mount and Robinson's Arch, 1994–1996" in Qadmoniot 117, 35–6 (Hebrew).

10. mMid 2:6 describes two chambers, used to store instruments, built under the *Azara* but opened into the lower Women's Courtyard.

even if we are unable to conclude definitively how these chambers adjoined the Temple Mount and *Azara.*

Several other *halachot* similarly involve complicated sections. The Mishna considers a tree whose trunk and branches are in different domains for tithing,[11] and a tree that is growing out of a sloped or vertical wall between two gardens.[12] In several locations, the Talmud discusses the distinction between a building and its roof, such as a garden on the roof of an olive press[13] or an *eruv* in a cave versus one above the cave.[14] In another passage, the Talmud rules on the status of openings in the walls of Jerusalem, and whether they are considered inside or outside the city.[15] The Mishna debates a situation in which something *tameh* is located in the mass of a wall.[16] In each of these cases, the law considers these spaces in section rather than in plan and finds in-between space that must be taken into account. In our case as well, the roofs surrounding the Temple constitute grey areas that must be carefully considered and classified.[17]

11. mMS 3:7.
12. mBM 10:6, bBM 118b.
13. mBM 10:4.
14. mEruv 5:9 and my commentary on Bereshit 19:30.
15. mPes 7:12, bPes 85b, yPes 7:12 (35b). See also yShab 1:1 (3a) for the status of ordinary door frames.
16. mOhal 4:1, 6:4.
17. For more on the manipulation of space between walls, see Steven Peterson, "Space and Anti-Space" in *Harvard Architectural Review* I (Spring, 1980).

TAZRIYA

# Shades of White

אָדָם כִּי יִהְיֶה בְעוֹר בְּשָׂרוֹ שְׂאֵת אוֹ סַפַּחַת אוֹ בַהֶרֶת וְהָיָה בְעוֹר בְּשָׂרוֹ לְנֶגַע
צָרָעַת וְהוּבָא אֶל אַהֲרֹן הַכֹּהֵן אוֹ אֶל אַחַד מִבָּנָיו הַכֹּהֲנִים. (ויקרא יג:ב)

When a man shall have in the skin of his flesh a rising, or a scab, or a bright spot, and it is in the skin of his flesh the plague of *tzaraat*, then he shall be brought to Aharon the priest or one of his sons the priests. (Vayikra 13:2)

TZARAAT manifests as white patches on the skin. The Mishna teaches that there are four shades of white that can be considered *tzaraat*: snow-white, fleece-white, plaster-white, and egg skin-white.[1] These different shades range from what is considered the purest white (snow) to an off-white (egg skin).[2]

Why is it necessary for the Mishna to classify these shades of white? One answer is that there is a minimum size requirement for the patch of *tzaraat*, and perhaps not all shades of white can combine to meet this requirement. The Mishna must therefore list the various shades to let us know which types of white can be counted together. However, some opinions hold that all the shades listed *can* be measured together. Instead, Yehoshua ben R. Akiva explains that it is important for the Mishna to list the different shades to let us know that only trained kohanim who know the laws thoroughly and can distinguish between the various colors are qualified to issue rulings about whether a person has contracted *tzaraat*.[3]

In architecture, distinguishing between shades of white is also seen as a

1. mNeg 1:1.
2. bShev 6a also discusses four different shades of red-tinted white, in the guise of milk mixed with various drops of blood. Yishayahu 1:18 juxtaposes two shades of white in a simile about repentance.
3. tNeg 1:1. This opinion is also quoted in bShev 6a and yShev 1:1 (32d). For bloodletters as experts in the shades of red, see bNid 20a.

sign of professionalism. Through the influence of the Modern movement in the twentieth century, white has become synonymous with high architecture. Most paint companies have specific color fan decks just for shades of white, filled with names as creative as the various monikers listed in this mishna: Cotton Ball, Hint of Vanilla, Dove White, and many more.[4] Like the hues in our mishna, these colors are named after naturally occurring shades of white that are not empirically definable colors. Architects, for their part, tend to be proud of having a favorite shade of white. As with the explanation about kohanim being able to distinguish between different shades of white, it is considered a sign of experience and training.

While Modern architecture is closely associated with white plaster, few coherent theories have been put forward for explaining its significance. One theory explains that it is the "abstracting property of the white surface" that is so important to the Modern sensibilities. The white allows people to consider the wall not as a partition, but as a geometric plane.[5]

With *tzaraat*, the whiteness may have a similar function. *Tzaraat* is most often considered a punishment for speaking ill of others. The analysis of different shades of white causes the afflicted person to be scrutinized as an object more than a human, like a piece of clothing or a wall. This reminds them that this type of scrutiny is uncomfortable and degrading, and should not be done to others. By insisting on an analysis of shades of white, the laws of *tzaraat* ensure that a careful, and perhaps demeaning, examination of the subject will take place.[6]

---

4. The examples I listed were taken from the Nirlat collection.

5. Mark Wigley, *White Walls, Designer Dresses: The Fashioning of Modern Architecture* (MIT Press, 1996), 201–202, summarizing the views of Leonardo Benevolo in Storia dell'architettura moderna.

6. There are some other cases in halacha where different shades of a color play a crucial role. According to R. Yehuda in mSuk 3:6, an etrog can be not acceptable depending on its shade of green. As per bSuk 31b, the green color is considered a sign that the etrog is not ripe enough. Another example of color shades in halacha is menstrual blood. See mNid 2:6.

# Light and Depth Perception

וְרָאָה הַכֹּהֵן אֶת הַנֶּגַע בְּעוֹר הַבָּשָׂר וְשֵׂעָר בַּנֶּגַע הָפַךְ לָבָן וּמַרְאֵה הַנֶּגַע עָמֹק
מֵעוֹר בְּשָׂרוֹ נֶגַע צָרַעַת הוּא וְרָאָהוּ הַכֹּהֵן וְטִמֵּא אֹתוֹ. (ויקרא יג:ג)

And the priest shall look upon the plague in the skin of the flesh and if the hair in the plague is turned white and the appearance of the plague is deeper than the skin of his flesh it is the plague of *tzaraat* and the priest shall look on him and pronounce him *tameh*. (Vayikra 13:3)

When a kohen examines a white patch of skin to determine if it is *tzaraat*, one of the cues that he uses is the appearance of depth.[1] According to Rashi, it is the whiteness of the *tzaraat* which creates a perceived depth; he explains that lighter colors appear deeper.[2]

Some commentaries attempt to explain Rashi's statement scientifically. Siftei Chachamim explains that the pupil is the part of the eye that does the actual seeing; since the pupil is black it perceives black objects as closer and white as further away. Ramban, on the other hand, hypothesizes that white reflects too much light into the eye, overwhelming it and causing the eye to limit the amount of light that it takes in. This, Ramban suggests, makes the white seem farther away.

Despite these explanations, Rashi's statement does not seem to comply with what we know about depth perception. Given two equal fields of light and dark, the human eye is just as likely to perceive the light and dark section as the foreground or the background, the figure or the field.[3] If

1. The depth is, according to the Sifra Tazriya Nega'im, parsha 1 perek 2:5, an illusion and not the result of an actual recess in the skin.

2. Rashi draws on bShev 6b / bBB 84a for this pronouncement. See also Rashi on bChul 63a, where he is even more explicit in his statement, as well as yShev 1:1 (32d).

3. The famous optical illusion of the Rubin Vase illustrates this point nicely, in which

anything, since objects closer to a light source appear brighter, we may be inclined to assume that light objects are closer than dark ones.

Within a single object, the varied shading and shadows help us to recognize shapes and can certainly create the illusion of depth. However, light itself does not always indicate depth. In fact, the exact same image turned upside-down can give us opposite readings of depth. The images below are the same image upside-down, but because we innately assume that light comes from above, the left image appears convex while the right image appears concave.[4]

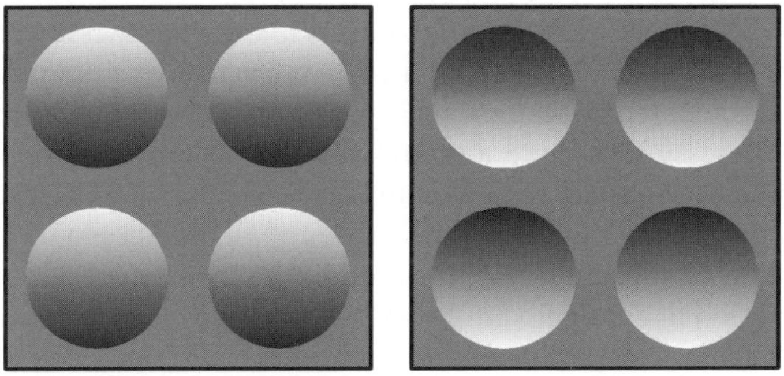

58. Images on left and right are the same, but turned 180 degrees. (Based on *Kalloniatis and Luu, Perception of Depth*)

Several other triggers cause people to perceive depth. Architects and artists use these to depict objects realistically and plan spaces.

- If there are two similar objects and one seems larger, the larger object tends to appear closer.
- Filippo Brunelleschi perfected the method of perspective in the fifteenth century and described how converging "parallel" lines give a sense of depth.
- If one object appears to overlap another, the overlapping item will appear closer.
- Objects closer to the horizon appear further away.

---

the eye is equally likely to see the silhouettes or the vase between them, and neither appears deeper.

4. Michael Kalloniatis, and Charles Luu, *Perception of Depth*, webvision.med.utah .edu/book/part-viii-gabac-receptors/perception-of-depth/.

All these cues allow us to perceive depth, but none of them relies on lightness or darkness.

There is another form of depth perception that does relate to lightness, but it applies only over great distances. An object that is very far away has a greater amount of atmosphere in front of it. That atmosphere has the effect of making the object less defined and hazier, with whites and blues becoming more prominent. This occurs, for example, when looking at mountains in the distance, where more distant peaks seem lighter and less distinct. Perhaps this was what Rashi had in mind, although it would not be relevant when examining *tzaraat* up close.

Rather than translate the word *amok* as "deep," it can instead be understood as a secondary quality of the color. While the lightness of *tzaraat* is white or off-white, *amok* could refer to its saturation or shininess. This is an approach adopted by Malbim, who explains that the Torah distinguishes between a glossy white and a matte white.[5] This explanation bypasses the problem of lightness and its supposed effect on depth perception. Similarly, in a discussion about the shades of menstrual blood, the term *amok* is used to describe a quality of red rather than its depth.[6]

Many different cues help our brain process depth. While lightness can be used to indicate depth in certain conditions, Rashi's statement remains unclear. However, considering what we do know about depth perception, Malbim's explanation that *amok* refers to a different characteristic of color resonates strongly.

5. *Amok* would then be what we today call saturation or intensity.
6. yNid 2:7 (50a) and bNid 19a–20a.

# Shade and Public Spaces

כָּל יְמֵי אֲשֶׁר הַנֶּגַע בּוֹ יִטְמָא טָמֵא הוּא בָּדָד יֵשֵׁב מִחוּץ לַמַּחֲנֶה מוֹשָׁבוֹ.
(ויקרא יג:מו)

All the days wherein the plague is in him he shall be *tameh*, he is unclean, he shall dwell alone, outside the camp shall his dwelling be. (Vayikra 13:46)

SOMEONE stricken with *tzaraat* in the desert had to dwell outside the camp until the affliction passed. Once Bnei Yisrael settled in Israel, the equivalent meant going outside the walls of a city.[1] The Mishna discusses the sanctity of gates and windows in city walls, which carve out interstitial space in the mass of the walls themselves.[2] The Talmud explains that in Jerusalem, these spaces were deliberately left unconsecrated so that people with *tzaraat* who were forced to be outside the city could take shelter in gateways from rain and the harsh Mediterranean sunlight.[3]

This instance is not the only case in which the Rabbis acknowledge the importance of shade in public places. The Tosefta rules that workers who toil in the sun are owed a different wage than those in the shade.[4] The Talmud relates that R. Yochanan ben Zakkai was able to teach in the shade of the Temple walls, without this constituting an inappropriate use of a consecrated object.[5] Although one cannot sit in the shade of an *ashera*

1. mKel 1:7.
2. mPes 7:12.
3. bPes 85b. The opposite was true for the gateways of the *Azara*.
4. tBM 4:11, yBM 6:1 (22d).
5. bPes 26a. Rashi (*veRava amar*) explains that the high walls of the Temple cast a shadow on the wide space beyond, which was good for large classes that could not fit within the *beit midrash*. The context of the Talmud implies that shade might also be in a class of physical properties to which the laws of *me'ila* do not apply, as they are less tangible and do not degrade the consecrated object.

tree,[6] Tosefot explain that this is because the primary purpose of the tree is to provide shade.[7]

The issue of *ashera* trees is particularly interesting because it highlights the fact that opposing forces are sometimes tugging at the issue of shade in cities. On the one hand, shade makes cities more livable and helps moderate the harsh climate. Shade helps prevent heat stroke and skin cancer. Vitruvius mentions the importance of awnings over theaters.[8] In certain places, such as playgrounds and railway platforms, building codes require some amount of shade. On the other hand, sometimes there are reasons that cities resist adding shade in public spaces. According to Jewish law, trees can spread *tumah,* as any overhangs facilitate the spread of impurity via *tumat ohalim.* In our time, cities sometimes claim that shading elements block sight lines, obstruct power lines or create obstacles along the sidewalk. Trees and shading devices must be maintained by the city, creating a permanent expense. At times this becomes a class issue, with shade being more prevalent in higher-class neighborhoods.

With the walls of Jerusalem, we see a priority placed on providing shade, which is seen as an issue of human dignity. There was a purposeful decision to *reduce* the area of holiness in Jerusalem in order to provide shade for those afflicted with *tzaraat,* even though it only benefitted those exiled from the city. The consideration shown by the Rabbis for the thermal comfort of people with *tzaraat* demonstrates the high value ascribed by Jewish law to shade in public spaces.

---

6. mAZ 3:8.

7. bAZ 48b *lo yeshev betzila.* In Yona, the shade provided by the *kikayon* serves an important role in the narrative. See Yona 4:6–8.

8. Vitruvius, *Ten Books on Architecture,* X.Preface.3.

# Tents and *Tzaraat*

וְרָאָה אֶת הַנֶּגַע בַּיּוֹם הַשְּׁבִיעִי כִּי פָשָׂה הַנֶּגַע בַּבֶּגֶד אוֹ בַשְּׁתִי אוֹ בָעֵרֶב אוֹ בָעוֹר
לְכֹל אֲשֶׁר יֵעָשֶׂה הָעוֹר לִמְלָאכָה צָרַעַת מַמְאֶרֶת הַנֶּגַע טָמֵא הוּא. (ויקרא יג:נא)

And he shall look on the plague on the seventh day; if the plague is spread in the garment, or in the warp or in the woof or in a skin, or in any work that is made of skin, the plague is a malignant tzaraat, it is *tameh*. (Vayikra 13:51)

THE Sifra and Tosefta[1] both learn from the expression "or in any work that is made of skin" that tents can be stricken with *tzaraat* of garments.[2] Why is it necessary to deliberately include tents in the set of things that can get *tzaraat* of garments? Malbim writes that one might assume that only things which can be worn can get *tzaarat* of garments. R. Baruch Epstein explains that tents are made from unrefined leather, unsuitable for clothing. However, since the tent can be disassembled and the leather reworked, it still counts as a "normal" leather garment and is thus susceptible to *tzaraat* of garments.[3]

Instead of these approaches, tents may need to be specifically included because, as dwellings, they might otherwise be placed into the "building" category of *tzaraat*. If one were to count tents as structures rather than garments, then they would be ineligible for *tzaraat* since they are not normative buildings made of stone, mortar, and wood.[4] The verse teaches that tents belong in the "garment" category, and as such, they can get *tzaraat*.[5]

Nomadic structures like tents straddle a line between garment and

1. tNeg 5:1 and Sifra Tazriya Nega'im, perek 13:12.
2. *Tzaraat* can affect people, garments, and buildings.
3. In his Torah Temima commentary.
4. See my commentary on Vayikra 14:37.
5. mShab 2:3 outlines a similar distinction for *tumat ohalim*. yShek 4:2 (48a) records a debate about whether the curtain in the Temple counts as part of the building itself, with ramifications about where the funds for it are taken.

house which can be difficult to define.[6] Temporary buildings can be flimsy and fleeting, or they can be quite robust, as was the case with the *Mishkan*. Even with fabric structures, there are some which can last for months or years, like a yurt or domed stadia. Frei Otto won a Pritzker Prize for his innovative use of fabrics in large structures, and Horst Berger designed an airport terminal with a fabric roof. While these are modern structures, in the past tents were normative dwellings and could be quite large. It is not always clear where to draw the line between structure and fabric, between *tzaraat* of buildings and *tzaraat* of garments.

59. Canopy over the National Campus for the Archaeology of Israel by Safdie Architects. (Photo courtesy of Ardon Bar-Hama)

While the Torah establishes these two categories of *tzaraat*, it was the Oral Torah that set the boundaries between them. The main criterion for *tzaraat* of garments is that the material must be cloth or leather.[7] The inclusion of items like curtains, sails, and book covers[8] makes it clear that *tzaraat* of garments is not limited to things that are worn. For building *tzaraat*, the major factor seems to be that it is a "normative" dwelling[9]

6. This tension also appears in a discussion about sleeping beneath a sheet in a *sukka*. The Talmud questions the difference between sleeping beneath a *talit* draped over a bedframe, versus wrapped up in a *talit*. See ySuk 2:1 (52d).

7. Though not all types of fabrics were included. For example, the skin of marine animals is excluded from *tzaraat*.

8. mNeg 11:11.

9. bYom 11b rules that a synagogue can get *tzaraat*, but only if it has an apartment. R. Meir disagrees with this ruling.

with all the basic features – four walls, basic building materials, and built on the land.[10]

Based on the examples in the Mishna, the Rabbis seem to adopt an inclusive definition of cloth, counting things that are not actually worn, but an exclusive definition of dwellings, limiting it to a standard type of house and ruling out certain materials, configurations, and buildings that do not have living spaces. As such, it is logical that tents were included in the cloth category rather than as dwellings.

10. It is possible that tents also fall short of being classified as a building due to their lack of permanence. The laws of Shabbat make such a distinction, as in yShab 7:2 (10d) and 12:1 (13c). A *beraita* on bShab 138a says that only permanent tents violate Torah prohibitions of building on Shabbat. See also Rambam Hilchot Shabbat 10:13. Perhaps a similar distinction is at work in the laws of *tzaraat*.

# Building on Pilotis

כִּי תָבֹאוּ אֶל אֶרֶץ כְּנַעַן אֲשֶׁר אֲנִי נֹתֵן לָכֶם לַאֲחֻזָּה וְנָתַתִּי נֶגַע צָרַעַת בְּבֵית
אֶרֶץ אֲחֻזַּתְכֶם. (ויקרא יד:לד)

When you come into the land of Canaan which I give to you for a possession and I put the plague of *tzaraat* in a house of the land of your possession. (Vayikra 14:34)

For a house to be susceptible to *tzaraat* it must be built on solid ground. This condition is derived from the Torah's stipulation that the house be "a house of the land of your possession." This requirement, which appears in the Mishna, Tosefta, and Sifra,[1] has halachic ramifications. A house on a boat or a house built offshore cannot contract *tzaraat*.[2] Similarly, a house supported by a cantilever is not considered connected to the ground, even if the forces are indirectly transferred to the earth. Furthermore, *tzaraat* may only infect structural walls and not interior partitions.[3]

Despite these requirements, the Rabbis assert that a house need not be built directly on the ground. A house built on stilts *is* susceptible to *tzaraat*. Most houses in ancient Israel were built directly on or in the earth. Foundations of various sorts existed, mainly to support the load-bearing walls, but the ground floor was the *ground*. Today, most buildings are still connected directly to the earth, whether with a basement, crawl space, or a concrete slab on grade that serves as the ground floor.

There are, however, some situations in which it is advantageous to elevate a structure above the ground on poles. This type of foundation can be

1. mNeg 12:1, tNeg 6:4, and Sifra Metzora, parsha 5:4. See also bNed 56a.

2. R. Shimshon of Sens and the Rosh add in their commentaries on the Mishna that a house built on offshore landfill, where new land is made by dumping construction material into the sea, is also not susceptible to *tzaraat*.

3. mNeg 12:4 and Sifra Metzora, parsha 6:11.

useful on sloped terrain, where the building would otherwise need to be cut into the ground. It also has advantages in areas that flood frequently, as the building is elevated above the water. If there is a desire to preserve the existing terrain for environmental or historical reasons, pole foundations allow for a less intrusive intervention. This solution was favored by Modern architects, following the lead of Le Corbusier, who preferred to free up the ground level for circulation and greenery. The use of pole supports, termed pilotis, was one of his five points of architecture.

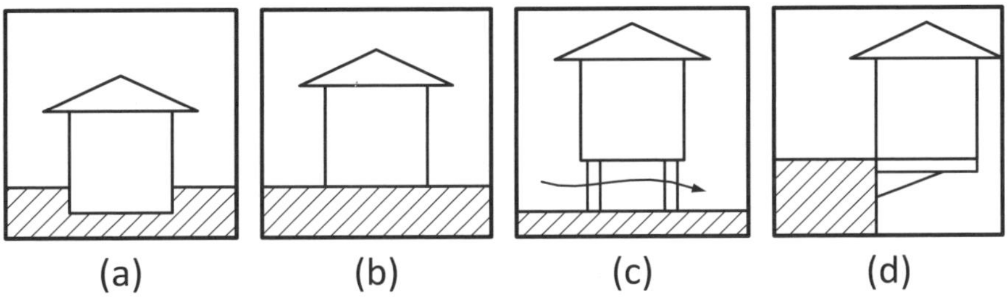


60. House foundations: (a) in the ground (b) upon the ground (c) on pilotis (d) cantilevered.

Although poles disconnect a building from the ground, the Rabbis felt that there was enough of a connection for the building to be considered attached, and thus susceptible to *tzaraat*. The determining factor seems to be vertical support for a building. A building supported by a cantilever – that is, from the side – does not qualify. One suspended from above would be even less connected.[4] However, it is not clear at which angle a building loses this connection. Would a building on pole supports, angled at 30 or 45 degrees, qualify? This question is not addressed by the Rabbis.

61. Engel House by Zeev Rechter, considered the first house in Tel Aviv built on pilotis. Pilotis were a common feature of early Israeli architecture, which was heavily influenced by the Modern movement. (Photo by Itzhak Kalter, Wikimedia)

4. In other cases, the Rabbis bring the example of a house built on a bridge. See

In Modern architecture, where pilotis are used to free up space under the building for circulation, this void remains visually part of the building's volume. The building is extruded upward, creating a new hybrid space beneath for people to inhabit, but the area underneath is still read together with the building. The same cannot be said of a building that cantilevers out. This may be part of the reason why, out of the two, only a house on poles has a strong enough connection with the earth to qualify as "a house of the land of your possession."

---

mEruv 5:1 and tEruv 4:6. Would such a house be able to get *tzaraat*? An arched bridge or a simple slab might, but I presume a suspension bridge would not. Inhabited bridges were common in the Middle Ages and perhaps earlier. Some famous examples include the old London Bridge, Pont Notre Dame, Ponte Vecchio in Florence, and the Bridge House in Ambleside, England.

# Square Houses and Domestic Architecture

וְרָאָה אֶת הַנֶּגַע וְהִנֵּה הַנֶּגַע בְּקִירֹת הַבַּיִת שְׁקַעֲרוּרֹת יְרַקְרַקֹּת אוֹ אֲדַמְדַּמֹּת
וּמַרְאֵיהֶן שָׁפָל מִן הַקִּיר. (ויקרא יד:לז)

And he shall look on the plague and behold if the plague be in the walls of the house with hollow streaks, greenish or reddish, and the appearance thereof be lower than the wall. (Vayikra 14:37)

THE Talmud has a basic definition of a house, which the Rabbis apply to several different commandments, such as whether a house requires a *mezuza*. One of the criteria is derived from the use of the plural "walls" describing the case of *tzaraat* in a house. From the minimum two walls implied by this word in Vayikra 14:37, plus two more when the word is repeated in Vayikra 14:39, the Rabbis learn that a house must have four walls. They also explicitly state that round, triangular, and pentagonal houses cannot get *tzaraat*.[1]

In the case of *tzaraat*, the quadrilateral requirement is seen as a guideline derived from the text, without any obvious reason attached. While a quadrilateral is the most common shape for a house, the prerequisite seems somewhat arbitrary. Perhaps a triangular house does not meet the requirements, but why should a five-walled house not suffice? Many houses, even in ancient times, had side rooms or parts that stuck out, creating houses of six, seven, or more walls.[2] Yet these buildings do not meet the rabbinic standard for a house and are thus not susceptible to *tzaraat*.

1. mNeg 12:1, tNeg 6:3, bNaz 8b, and Sifra Metzora, parsha 6:2. Reference to these shapes is also made in tNaz 1:2. In addition, the Rabbis mention a house shaped like a *digon*, which may refer to a partially open house with only two walls (as per Hai Gaon on mNeg 12:1), or perhaps to a house with one or more curved walls (as per Rashbam on bBB 164b *digon*). Studies of Greek houses from the first 1000–500 BCE show that orthogonal buildings were usually stone, while mud brick and wood buildings generally had rounded walls. See Lisa Nevett, *Domestic Space in Classical Antiquity* (Cambridge University Press, 2010), 24–5.

2. In the Iron Age, the most common houses were the Three-Room and Four-Room

One possible explanation is that this is an arbitrary requirement designed to make it unlikely for a case of structural *tzaraat* to ever occur. Other requirements listed by the Rabbis make the possibility of a real-life case even more remote. This is supported by R. Eliezer ben Shimon, who states that no case of structural *tzaraat* ever took place.[3]

Alternatively, perhaps the Rabbis were not ruling out all buildings with three or five sides. Instead, this requirement may have been specifically aimed at buildings that are *regular* triangles or pentagons. While there are any number of configurations that would yield a six or seven-walled structure, a building designed as a circle or regular polygon (other than a square) would almost certainly be a building with greater aspirations than a simple dwelling.[4] The Pentagon in Washington, or Azrieli Towers (with footprints of a square, triangle, and circle) in Tel Aviv, or the octagonal Dome of the Rock,[5] for example, have their shapes because a regular polygon expresses importance and even gives a mystical quality to the building. These buildings are not the domestic dwellings that are the primary target of *tzaraat,* but rather grand edifices that are excluded from the prohibition.[6] According to this explanation, buildings with a plan in the shape of a regular polygon cannot contract *tzaraat* because they are not normative dwellings.

This same idea is reflected in an additional requirement for houses with *tzaraat.* A second verse mentions three types of building materials:

---

houses, which were often quadrilinear but did often still have protrusions on one or more sides. See Ehud Netzer, "Domestic Architecture in the Iron Age" in *The Architecture of Ancient Israel* (Israel Exploration Society, 1992), 192–4.

3. tNeg 6:1, bSan 71a. This mirrors the rabbinic treatment of a rebellious son and an *ir hanidachat.*

4. For example, Carol Herselle Krinsky describes circular and ovular synagogues of the eighteenth and nineteenth centuries as "Anomalies in the history of synagogue design." See her *Synagogues in Europe* (MIT Press, 1985), 72.

5. One exception to this rule is the octagonal houses that were popular in the United States in the 1850s. However, this was largely due to the influence of one man, Orson Squire Fowler, and the fact that octagonal houses with the same perimeter provide a house with greater area. For an equal perimeter, the area of a regular octagonal is about 1.2 times larger than the area of a square.

R. Yechezkel ben Yehuda Landau wrote a responsa in 1788 on whether synagogues may be built with an octagonal plan. He ruled that there is no concern – synagogue design is not prescribed and can use any shape – but cautions that it is unseemly to pattern synagogues after the buildings of non-Jews. See *Noda Be'Yehuda,* Tanina Orach Chaim 18. Some synagogues had an octagonal *bima,* as in Ansbach, Germany. See Krinsky, *Synagogues of Europe,* 264.

6. bYom 11b and tNeg 6:3 explain that only structures with a living quarter can contract *tzaraat.*

stone, wood, and mud or mortar. The Sifra extrapolates from this list that only a house constructed with each of these materials can be stricken with *tzaraat*.[7] The Mishna takes this a step further and rules that interior wall-cladding other than stone, wood, or mortar disqualifies the house from getting *tzaraat*.[8] This list of materials can either be seen as a way of limiting the likelihood of having a real case of *tzaraat*, or it may simply reflect the building materials that were the most common. Here again, the Talmud seems to indicate that *tzaraat* can only infect a building with typical construction, rather than an exceptional structure.[9]

The archaeological record in Israel from both the time of the Torah and the time of the Mishna shows that wood, stone, and mud or mortar were the basic components of most walls. Wood was important for roofing, doors, and possibly as a stabilizing element between courses of masonry in the walls.[10] This fits with the Mishna, which implies that the main function of the wood, at least concerning *tzaraat*, is to frame openings.[11]

The other two materials mentioned in the verse – stone and *afar* – were closely related. Stone walls were rarely built entirely of stone. Rather, they were built with an outer and inner layer of stone sandwiching a core of dirt and rubble. While it is possible to understand the term *afar* in this verse as referring to the mortar that held the stones together, it may refer to the fill between the inner and outer stones. This fill was the mass of the wall, with the surfaces serving only as a shell.[12] As such, it makes sense that *tzaraat* would affect it as well, since the dirt was not just a secondary element, like mortar. This reading fits well with this mishna, which defines *afar* as the substance placed between the framework.[13] While this could refer to mortar, it more likely describes the fill between two surfaces of stone.[14]

7. Sifra Metzora, perek 5:1, on Vayikra 14:45.

8. mNeg 12:2. tNeg 6:6 also mentions these materials, but only to say that they can get *tzaraat* and can combine to meet the minimum area requirement of two *grisin*. bBM 22a mentions beams, wood, and stone as the main components of a house.

9. BerR 1:1 gives an alternative list of six necessary building materials: water, dirt, wood, stone, reeds, and iron. Yizhar Hirschfeld interprets the list in mNeg 12:2 this way, calling these "the three most common building materials for private houses." See Yizhar Hirschfeld, *The Palestinian Dwelling* (Israel Exploration Society, 1995), 218.

10. Ronny Reich, "Building Materials and Architectural Elements in Ancient Israel" in *The Architecture of Ancient Israel.* Ed. Reich and Kempinksi, 8.

11. mNeg 12:4, tNeg 6:5.

12. Ehud Netzer, "Massive Structures: Processes in Construction and Deterioration" in *The Architecture of Ancient Israel ed.* Ronny Reich and Aharon Kempinski (Israel Exploration Society, 1992), 22–23.

13. mNeg 12:4, tNeg 6:5.

14. Rambam gives this explanation for *afar* in his commentary on the Mishna. There

These three materials can therefore be seen as the fundamental building blocks of houses in ancient Israel, and are used to define the type of structure that is susceptible to *tzaraat,* just as quadrilateral houses may be indicative of normal construction practices.

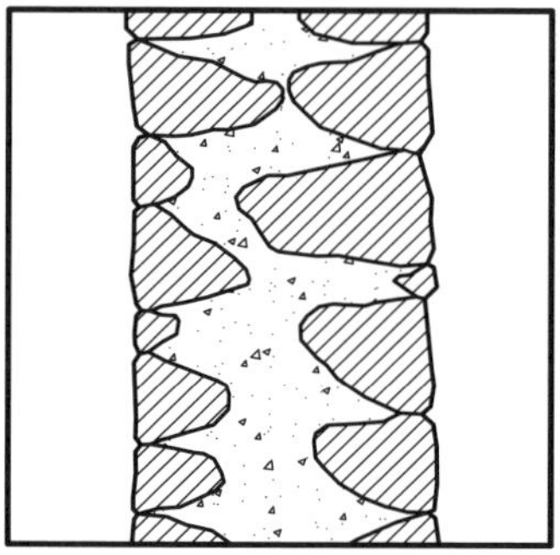

62. Section through wall with stone finish and rubble infill. (Based on Ehud Netzer, "Massive Structures" in *The Architecture of Ancient Israel*, 22 fig. 10)

is a similar awareness of construction methods in a passage in the Talmud concerning neighbors who wish to build a party wall. The Talmud explains that a brick wall takes up only three handbreadths, while a wall of squared stones takes up five, and a rusticated stone wall takes up six handbreadths. See mBB 1:1 and bBB 3a.

# Historical Preservation And the Essence of a Building

וְלָקְחוּ אֲבָנִים אֲחֵרוֹת וְהֵבִיאוּ אֶל תַּחַת הָאֲבָנִים וְעָפָר אַחֵר יִקַּח וְטָח אֶת הַבָּיִת. (ויקרא יד:מב)

And they shall take other stones and put them in the place of those stones, and he shall take other mortar and shall plaster the house. (Vayikra 14:42)

ONCE a kohen inspects a house for *tzaraat*, the house is sealed for a number of days.[1] If the *tzaraat* is still present after this period, the afflicted stones and dirt must be removed from the house and new materials brought to replace them. If the *tzaraat* returns, the whole house must then be dismantled.

During the first part of this treatment, there is a possibility of preserving the house in its original form. Only the minimum number of stones are removed, and they are replaced with similar stones, albeit from outside the original project.[2] The dirt, too, is replaced with as minimal intervention as possible. However, if this treatment does not work, then the whole building is deemed unsalvageable and must be demolished.

When a building requires historical preservation, there is often a question of what can be done to it without destroying its essence or historical authenticity. The architect must decide which interventions are necessary, yet try not to compromise the existing structure by either removing or adding parts. Many preservationists advocate a light touch. Adolphe Napoleon Didron, a nineteenth-century French art historian, set the tone for minimal intervention when he wrote,

1. The number varies depending on how the inspection goes.

2. Sifra Metzora, perek 4:3. Since the word "stones" (plural) is used, a minimum of two must be removed. One must bring stones to replace the afflicted stones that were removed, but the replacements cannot be taken from an existing wall.

> Regarding ancient monuments, it is better to consolidate than to repair, better to repair than to restore, better to restore than to rebuild, better to rebuild that to embellish; and in no case must anything be added and, above all, nothing should be removed.[3]

One can either try to closely match the original materials so that interventions are barely perceivable; or deliberately use different materials so that the new portions cannot possibly be mistaken for part of the earlier, historic building.

Historical preservationists sometimes talk about the Ship of Theseus, referencing a story that is told by Plutarch in *Life of Theseus.* Plutarch asks whether a ship that, over the years, has had every piece replaced, is still fundamentally the same ship. On the one hand, no part of it was present when the ship was first built. On the other hand, the ship has remained in constant use, and its shape, character, and perhaps its essence remain the same. This paradox is one of the lenses through which preservationists evaluate their work, to understand if they are changing the essence of the building, or merely keeping it functional.[4]

In the case of *tzaraat* of a building, a similar situation exists. At first, the owner is required to remove only the bare minimum number of stones and replace them with similar ones. The goal seems to be to keep the house as it is, with minimal intervention. The *tzaraat* causes a disruption, but the house remains the same house.

If *tzaraat* returns a second time, the Torah rules that the entire building must be demolished. Why not replace stones until the building is cured? There are two ways of looking at this, each corresponding to a different view of Theseus' paradox. Does replacing successive rounds of stones result in a fundamentally different house than the original one, or can we keep swapping parts and yet retain the essence of the original house? If the house would remain the same house, then it must be that the second bout of *tzaraat* carries with it an automatic demolition order. At this stage, there is no desire to salvage the building; rather, it must be destroyed. On the other hand, if repeatedly swapping the stones results in a fundamentally

---

3. Adolphe Napoleon Didron, *Bulletin Archaeologique,* 1, (1839): 47. This idea was expressed by the Rabbis in bYev 63a, where people are advised to "plug (a hole) rather than fix, fix rather than build, because building is impoverishing."

4. This same idea is addressed in the laws of impure vessels. How much of an impure vessel can be replaced without rendering it a fundamentally different vessel, and thus removing the impurity? For example, mKel 19:6 discusses this issue regarding a bed that has two slats replaced with new ones. See also mMik 7:2, bYev 82b, and yTer 5:2 (43d) concerning the forty *se'ah* of water in a *mikva.*

different building, then perhaps the Torah is telling us that once the process of evaluating *tzaraat* begins, we are no longer permitted to alter the house, just as one with *tzaraat* of the skin may not have it surgically removed.[5] We can replace stones once, but anything more fundamentally changes the building and is prohibited.

Although there is no change in the outcome – the house is destroyed in either scenario – there is a difference in the way we view the second round of *tzaraat*. In the first view, the destruction of the house is seen as a more severe punishment meted out after the first round of changes has been ineffectual. In the second view, there is theoretically no problem with the continued existence of the house, but technically it is impossible to keep replacing parts and have it remain the same building.

5. bMak 22a. bEruv 24a lists two similar halachic questions regarding filled gaps in an enclosure that cumulatively reach ten cubits, and patched holes in a basket that cumulatively reach the size of a pomegranate.

# Blurred Vision In the Holy of Holies

וַיֹּאמֶר ה׳ אֶל מֹשֶׁה דַּבֵּר אֶל אַהֲרֹן אָחִיךָ וְאַל יָבֹא בְכָל עֵת אֶל הַקֹּדֶשׁ מִבֵּית לַפָּרֹכֶת אֶל פְּנֵי הַכַּפֹּרֶת אֲשֶׁר עַל הָאָרֹן וְלֹא יָמוּת כִּי בֶּעָנָן אֵרָאֶה עַל הַכַּפֹּרֶת.
(ויקרא טז:ב)

And the Lord said to Moshe: "Speak to Aharon your brother, that he come not at all times into the holy place within the curtain before the ark cover, which is upon the ark, that he not die, for I appear in the cloud upon the ark cover." (Vayikra 16:2)

Moshe is told to warn Aharon not to enter the Holy of Holies, "for I appear in the cloud upon the ark cover." While this can be understood as a warning or as instructions for the Yom Kippur service,[1] Rashbam explains that the cloud darkened the room, resulting in a blurred visual experience. The implication is that the cloud of incense was a necessary level of protection for the high priest, one that would save him from the overwhelming experience of the Divine Presence.

Although the circumstances of the Holy of Holies are unique, architects have a variety of ways to manipulate buildings in order to obfuscate the surroundings. The most common example is to use dim lighting to set a mood of mystery or intrigue. Sometimes mirrors are used to alter the visual experience, and windows can be omitted to eliminate external points of reference. In some instances, the architect may even choose to manipulate the walls and floors to create a further sense of uncertainty.[2]

One extreme example of architectural distortion is Diller

1. Both these explanations appear in Rashi's commentary. See bYom 53a for the controversy between the Sadducees and Pharisees. The Talmud also discusses the fluid dynamics of the smoke, quoting a *beraita*: the smoke would rise up to the ceiling, then creep along the ceiling to the walls and flow down the walls, until the room was surrounded and filled.

2. This was supposedly done by Peter Eisenman in his Greater Columbus Convention Center, and again in his Berlin Holocaust Memorial.

Scofidio + Renfro's Blur Building, which created a cloud of mist that obscured vision and increased dependence on other senses. Part of the purpose behind this pavilion was to observe the way people interact in this fog. The original, unrealized vision was to have visitors don "smart" raincoats, which would light up to help visitors find one another and promote new patterns of interaction. Instead of using sight to maintain socially acceptable spacing between one another, the visual impediment would allow people to interact more closely and intimately, especially with strangers who they might otherwise avoid if they were using only visual cues.

63. Blur Building by Diller Scofidio + Renfro. (Photo courtesy of Diller Scofidio + Renfro)

While one might think of the cloud as a way of keeping distance between the high priest and the Divine Presence, the reduced vision may have had the opposite effect. Instead of the cloud obscuring the Holy of Holies and the Divine Presence, it may have engendered a different, non-visual interaction that would otherwise have been impossible. The Talmud alludes to this, explaining that the "light of the ark" would aid the high priest to navigate inside, but that in the Second Temple when there was no ark, he would have to proceed cautiously and blindly.[3] This need not be a literal light, but rather a heightened sense of perception that allowed the high priest to commune with God. Rather than protect the high priest from the Divine Presence, the cloud may have facilitated a more intimate interaction between the high priest and God.

3. yYom 5:3 (42c).

# Contrasting Civilization and Wilderness

וְהַשָּׂעִיר אֲשֶׁר עָלָה עָלָיו הַגּוֹרָל לַעֲזָאזֵל יָעֳמַד חַי לִפְנֵי ה׳ לְכַפֵּר עָלָיו לְשַׁלַּח אֹתוֹ לַעֲזָאזֵל הַמִּדְבָּרָה. (ויקרא טז:י)

But the goat on which the lot fell for Azazel shall be set alive before the Lord to make atonement over him and to send him away for Azazel into the wilderness. (Vayikra 16:10)

As part of the Yom Kippur service in the Temple, the high priest must take two goats for a sin offering. Lots are drawn and one goat is sacrificed in the Temple, while the second is sent off into the desert. The Mishna describes how the second goat would be guided to a cliff in the desert and ceremoniously pushed off the precipice.[1]

R. S.R. Hirsch explains that the two goats are contrasted to show the impact of our choices. The two goats are equal in appearance, height, and value,[2] but one goat remains within the confines of the Temple, serving the Lord and submitting to be sacrificed, while the other is removed from the Temple and banished to the wilderness, where it meets a grizzly death. This choice, R. Hirsch explains, is a lesson for Yom Kippur, to submit to the Divine will.

The juxtaposition between the desert and the city, between civilization and wilderness, is a powerful motif that appears in literature and art again and again. In this pairing, the city is not always the clear winner – Eliyahu escapes to the wilderness and in the process, becomes the prototypical monastic holy man.[3] Hagar is banished to the desert but ends up encountering an angel and finding salvation.[4] Rather, the desert is a foil for

1. mYom 6:6.
2. mYom 6:1.
3. Melachim I 17.
4. Bereshit 21.

civilization – when civilization is corrupt, the desert is a refuge; when civilization is righteous, the desert is seen as a wasteland.[5]

At the end of the Second Temple Period, there were two prominent examples of desert architecture. During his reign, Herod built desert palace-fortresses in Herodium and Masada.[6] These were luxurious dwellings that took advantage of the dramatic landscape and isolation. At the same time, the ascetic community around Qumran built a much sparer, thin-walled architecture.[7] While the structures were quite different, both used the desert as a place beyond the reach of civilization. Those at Qumran sought to escape the corrupt civilization in Jerusalem.[8] Herod, while using architecture to extend the comforts of the city into the desert, saw his fortresses primarily as sanctuaries. Josephus wrote that "it is believed that Herod equipped [Masada] as a refuge for himself, suspecting a double danger" of popular insurrections or invasion by the Egyptian queen, Cleopatra.[9] Ehud Netzer asserted that the same reason existed for building Herodium, though he also mentioned the impressive landscape and the temperate, dry climate.[10] In both Qumran and Masada, high and low architecture, the desert was used as a refuge from civilization.

The symbolism of the goat being sent into the desert also plays on the wilderness as a place beyond the pale. Even when the desert is viewed positively, the choice to leave society and seek out the wilderness is a temporary, desperate decision, with the hopes of rejoining society at a later date. On Yom Kippur, the desert has a decidedly negative connotation and is a place of no return. Though it might seem tempting to flee the city for the desert, it is ultimately better to serve God from within the Temple.

---

5. See my commentary on Shemot 33:7.

6. While the Maccabim used Masada as a fortress, it was Herod who built palaces on the plateau.

7. Magen Broshi, "Daily Life at Qumran" in *The Qumran Scrolls and their World* Vol. I (YBZP, 2009), 25 (Hebrew).

8. Hanan Eshel writes that the site was at a dead end, increasing its isolation. This was due to the higher level of the Dead Sea at the time, preventing passage along the western shore. See Hanan Eshel, "The History of the Discoveries at Qumran" in *The Qumran Scrolls and their World* Vol. I, 13 (Hebrew).

9. Josephus, *The Jewish War*, 7:300.

10. Ehud Netzer, *The Architecture of Herod* (Baker Academic, 2008), 180–1.

# The Influence of Foreign Culture

כְּמַעֲשֵׂה אֶרֶץ מִצְרַיִם אֲשֶׁר יְשַׁבְתֶּם בָּהּ לֹא תַעֲשׂוּ וּכְמַעֲשֵׂה אֶרֶץ כְּנַעַן אֲשֶׁר אֲנִי מֵבִיא אֶתְכֶם שָׁמָּה לֹא תַעֲשׂוּ וּבְחֻקֹּתֵיהֶם לֹא תֵלֵכוּ. (ויקרא יח:ג)

After the practices of the land of Egypt in which you dwelt, shall you not do, and after the practices of the land of Canaan, into which I bring you, shall you not do; neither shall you walk in their statutes. (Vayikra 18:3)

THE Jewish people have always existed as a small culture surrounded by powerful influences. Jewish communities have been guests in the cultural superpowers of Mesopotamia, Europe, and North America. Both ancient and modern Israel were heavily influenced by the dominant cultures of their times. This is especially true in art but can be detected in judicial[1] and religious spheres as well.

From the start, the Torah cautions the Israelites that there is a cultural threat from larger neighbors. On the way out of Egypt and headed toward Canaan, Bnei Yisrael were warned not to follow the ways of these two nations. The Torah does not specify the objectionable practices of the Egyptians and Canaanites, but since this warning is followed by a list of forbidden (incestual) relationships, some commentaries see this as the major concern.[2]

Rashi points to a different aspect of foreign culture. He mentions theaters and stadia, two foreign cultural institutions.[3] These represent centers of non-Jewish popular culture that were frowned upon by the Rabbis. The Talmud contrasts people who visit circuses and theaters with those who frequent synagogues and study halls, showing the perceived competition

1. The Talmud makes such a reference regarding the death penalty. See bSan 52b.
2. See Ramban. Ibn Ezra instead sees the legal system as the problematic aspect of their culture.
3. Rashi draws on the Sifra Acharei Mot, perek 13:8, which also mentions circuses.

between the Jewish and non-Jewish institutions.[4] However, this negative perception has to do with the activities that take place in theaters and stadia rather than the architecture itself. The Talmud even relates that in the future, theaters and circuses will be used for Torah study.[5] Elsewhere we see that the Rabbis prohibited assisting in the construction of a basilica, a place of execution, or a stadium, but allowed collaboration on public bathhouses.[6]

Despite the limited scope of this prohibition, the Sifra raises the possibility of a much wider application of this rule. The Sifra suggests that it might also be forbidden to design buildings or landscapes in the style of Egyptian or Canaanite architecture.[7] However, this approach is ultimately rejected. Instead, the Sifra explains that architectural design is not something to be mandated but rather a matter of artistic judgment.[8]

Jewish building practices are heavily influenced by the surrounding culture. One can see this in the appearance of synagogues or the houses in various Jewish quarters, which tend to follow local styles. We see this in Israel too, where early Zionist architects adopted Modern architecture and Brutalism. Even the two Temples were heavily influenced by the architectural norms of their day, with the First Temple sharing similarities with other Near East temples, and the Second Temple influenced by Greek and Roman styles.[9] The Maccabim used pyramids for some of their mau-

4. yBer 4:2 (7d). See also PdRK 28:1 which explains that on holidays non-Jews pack theaters and circuses, while Jews pack synagogues and study halls. Josephus describes the tumult that was caused when Herod built a theater and amphitheater in Jerusalem. See *Antiquities* 15:268.

5. bMei 6a.

6. mAZ 1:7.

7. Christian architects of the sixteenth and seventeenth centuries had similar concerns with using Greek and Roman "heathen" architecture in their designs. One way to assuage their concerns was by claiming that the Greeks themselves took their cues from the architecture of the Temple in Jerusalem. Connected to this was the idea that all Greek orders of architecture were derived from the human body and were therefore universal. See Joseph Rykwert, *The Dancing Column* (MIT Press, 1988), 27. Orit Peleg-Barkat suggests that the Maccabim were willing to use the Doric order in their architecture because that order "was losing its pagan-temple-related connotation." See Orit Peleg-Barkat, *The Temple Mount Excavations in Jerusalem, Vol. V* (Institute of Archaeology, Hebrew University of Jerusalem, 2017), 6.

8. Sifra Acharei Mot, parsha 9:8. Malbim, I believe, reads this differently and understands that architectural design has a logic and reason, so it is therefore acceptable. Only foreign practices that have no logic are outlawed.

9. Josephus describes the columns used by Herod in the Temple as Corinthian. See *Antiquities* 15:414. Peleg-Barkat does point out that while local artists in the time of Herod adopted classical motifs, "the rather abstract and geometrical character of these motifs, in comparison to their Hellenistic and Roman prototypes, suggests that the

solea. This type of borrowing is acceptable, as the Sifra rules that despite the warning in our verse against adopting foreign culture, one is free to design buildings in any architectural style. Architects are given the full range of creativity, free to borrow or adapt foreign styles without fear of transgressing the clause in this verse.

64. Fragment of Classical decorated ceiling from Temple Mount excavations.

local artists did not simply copy the foreign designs, but, rather, gave them a local interpretation." See *The Temple Mount Excavations, Vol. V*, 8.

# Vomitorea: Theater Architecture and Egress

וְלֹא תָקִיא הָאָרֶץ אֶתְכֶם בְּטַמַּאֲכֶם אֹתָהּ כַּאֲשֶׁר קָאָה אֶת הַגּוֹי אֲשֶׁר לִפְנֵיכֶם.
(ויקרא יח:כח)

Let not the land vomit you out also, when you defile it, as it vomited out the nation that was before you. (Vayikra 18:28)

After outlawing various forbidden sexual relationships, the Torah admonishes Bnei Yisrael to abide by these rules and implies that the acquisition of the Land of Israel is contingent upon them remaining faithful. The previous inhabitants of the land violated these norms and were vomited out.[1] If Bnei Yisrael do not adhere to them, they too will be expelled.

Rashi responds to this verse with a parable. If a prince eats something tainted, it will upset his stomach and he will end up vomiting. The Land of Israel is the same; it cannot stomach sinners and will eject them forcefully. Various supercommentaries on Rashi wonder why he felt the need to explain this descriptive and straightforward passage with a parable. In Be'er Heitev, R. Moshe Met of Przemyśl explains that Rashi found it curious that the Torah would use the verb "vomit" when referencing the land and therefore used a parable to address this concern.

While it may seem strange to find this biological terminology used to describe an inanimate object, similar language appears in the Latin lexicon for theater design. One of the most important problems to solve when designing a large, public building is egress. With a stadium, all those in attendance need to exit the building at once, en masse, once the event concludes. For this reason, large passages are needed to disgorge the attendees back into the outside world. In Latin, this architectural feature is known as a vomitorium. While this terminology came from a period after the Torah, it employs similar imagery, with an inanimate object expelling people.

1. bShab 33a.

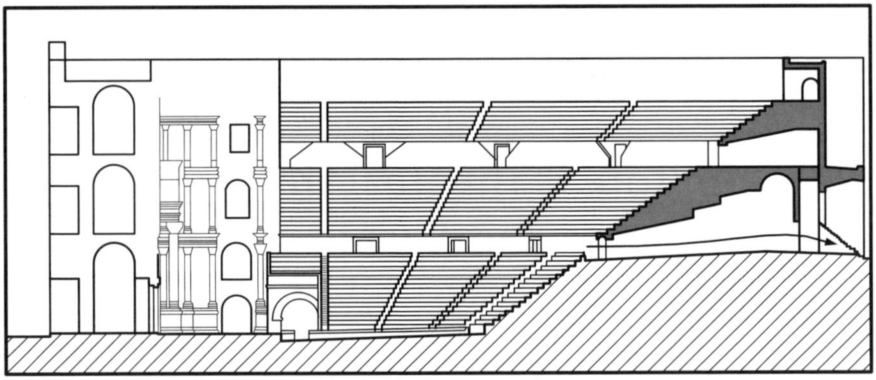

65. Section through Beit Shean theater, showing vomitorium. (Based on Segal, *History and Architecture of the Theaters*, image 60)

If we look carefully at the architectural term, we find that, oddly enough, it has a decidedly positive connotation. In an essay about theaters in rabbinic literature, Esti Dvorjetski points to another midrash which states that when a king and his various servants come to a country, they all enter through the same gate and yet each one manages to find his own place. She explains that this is a description of people entering a theater through a vomitorium.[2] This is reminiscent of a passage in Edward Gibbon's *The History of the Decline and Fall of the Roman Empire*, where the author describes entering the Colosseum:

> Sixty-four vomitories (for by that name the doors were very aptly distinguished) poured forth the immense multitude; and the entrances, passages, and staircases were contrived with such exquisite skill, that each person, whether of the senatorial, the equestrian, or the plebeian order, arrived at his destined place without trouble or confusion.[3]

Here the design of the vomitoria is meant to convey order and planning. Someone designed these passages with the specific task in mind of conveying people to and from their seats as smoothly as possible. The term in this case has a positive connotation. This is a major difference between

2. Esti Dvorjetski, "*Hatiatron Besafrut Chazal*" in Arthur Segal's *The History and Arhitecture of The Theaters in Roman Palestine* (Bialik Institute, 1999), 117–143 (Hebrew), on VayR 18:1. Compare with bShab 152a, which shows no sign of referencing a theater.

3. Gibbons, I.12, 413 (J. M'Gowan 1825).

the terminology used in the stadium design and the intent of our verse; the Torah aims to describe a chaotic, lurching, and painful event and uses the term "vomit" to evoke this feeling. In this way, the term is more poetically used in the Torah, where it makes use of the full meaning and negative connotation of the act of vomiting.

# *Pe'ah* And Affordable Housing

וּבְקֻצְרְכֶם אֶת קְצִיר אַרְצְכֶם לֹא תְכַלֶּה פְּאַת שָׂדְךָ לִקְצֹר וְלֶקֶט קְצִירְךָ לֹא תְלַקֵּט. (ויקרא יט:ט)

> And when you reap the harvest of your land you shall not wholly reap the corner of your field, neither shall you gather the gleaning of your harvest. (Vayikra 19:9)

THE Torah lists several forms of charity that must be given during the harvest season. Among these is *pe'ah*, a commandment to leave "the corner of your field" unreaped. While *tana'im* argue whether it is possible to fulfill this commandment during any part of the harvest – start, middle, or end – they all agree that the basic method is for harvesters to leave crops for the poor at the end of their fields.

Why is the end of the field the preferred location for *pe'ah*? There are six answers given by the Rabbis:[1]

(1) To prevent cheating the poor by waiting until no one is present and then calling specific paupers to the field.
(2) To save the poor from wasting time waiting until the owner declares a portion of the field *pe'ah*. Instead, they can estimate how long the harvest will last and know that *pe'ah* will only be available at the end.
(3) Otherwise, people may not see where the owner has left the field untouched and assume that he did not fulfill the mitzva of *pe'ah*.
(4) To prevent a dishonest landowner from claiming that he left *pe'ah* elsewhere.
(5) To prevent the landowner from leaving the lowest-quality produce as *pe'ah*.
(6) To follow the literal instructions of the verse.[2]

---

1. Even though most of the lists begin by saying "There are *four* reasons."
2. This list follows tPea 1:6, which states that there are four reasons but gives five, or

While one reason on this list (3) aims at protecting the good name of the owner, the majority of reasons focus on protecting the rights of the poor and ensuring that they get a fair deal. This makes sense since *pe'ah* aims to help the destitute and in this case the poor are clearly without power or means to enforce their right to *pe'ah*. The owner of the field is obliged to give this charity, but still has considerable ability to fix the system in a way that increases his benefit (1+5), makes life difficult for the poor (2), or outright cheats the system (4). The list of reasons comes to highlight this fact and encourage a fairhanded approach on the part of the landowners.

There is some vagueness in the question posed by the sages. When they ask about the end of the field, does this mean the physical end, along the perimeter, or does it mean the last part which you harvest? The wording in the Tosefta and Sifra asks why we give *pe'ah* "at the end" while the two Talmuds read "at the end *of his field*." Among the answers, we find indications of both. Answers one and two are talking about a time, while answers three through six refer to the place. Therefore, it seems that both are important factors and both help safeguard the rights of the poor.[3]

The obligation to give *pe'ah* applies only to agricultural goods; one cannot extrapolate from this halacha to other realms and certainly not in the modern day. However, the way in which *pe'ah* calls upon landowners to give a portion of their produce to the poor is reminiscent of modern attempts to create affordable housing within expensive urban areas. Many cities and countries have tried to ensure that housing is available to all without creating poor ghettos. While different approaches have been tried, one current trend is to stipulate that developers must set aside a certain percentage of new units in a project as "affordable" units and in exchange are granted additional building rights. In Israel, this is done by specifying that at least twenty percent of the units must be considered "small apartments."[4] In the United States, incentives are given to create rental units with reduced rates within new properties. In both models, the idea is to set apart a portion of a commodity for the benefit of the poor, similar to *pe'ah*.

As with *pe'ah*, where the sages seemed concerned that landowners

---

perhaps even six. yPea 4:3 (18b) is the only source that explicitly states that there are five reasons. Lists also appear in the Sifra Kedoshim, perek 1:10 and bShab 23a.

3. See also yPea 1:2 (15a), which is explicit in saying one must err toward giving the poor more, and yPea 4:1 (18a), which mandates safe work conditions for the poor while gleaning.

4. *Chok Hatichnun Vehabeniya* 63ב (ב). Note that this does not actually create "affordable housing" but rather ensures a diversity of square footage. In luxury projects, these "small apartments" remain expensive. Currently "small apartments are defined as between 55–80 $m^2$.

would try to bend the regulations in a way that maximized their benefit, real estate developers have, in some cases, tried to find ways to fulfill their obligations without sacrificing profits. In some cities, notably New York City, developers have erected affordable units with separate entrances alongside luxury apartments. Tenants or buyers who pay full price use a posh entrance and have access to various amenities (gyms, pools, storage, courtyards, etc.) while tenants paying reduced rents are given a separate entrance and cannot use all the features of the building. In New York, this practice was decried and soon banned, though elsewhere in the world this technique is still being used. On the one hand, it is certainly distasteful to prevent tenants from using the same entrance as their neighbors, especially when the distinction has a strong correlation with race. On the other hand, it is understandable that developers want to attract expensive clientele by providing exclusive features. The question is to what extent must the rights of the poor be protected.

Reiterating that we cannot apply laws of *pe'ah* to similar modern issues, the various reasons listed by the sages can still be used for guidance. There is concern that the poor will be given low-quality produce, that only people connected to the owners will benefit, and that owners will try to create obstacles – making people wait around endlessly for the *pe'ah* to become available – to encourage the poor to abandon their rights.[5] Although the poor are getting something for free, we are obligated to safeguard their rights. These same concerns exist in the debate about affordable housing: We should develop systems that increase visibility of positive owner actions, ensure that owners do not game the system, and safeguard the rights of the poor.

5. It is also interesting that one obvious answer for why *pe'ah* should be along the perimeter – so that it is easy for the poor to reach it without traipsing through the field and trampling crops – is not mentioned in the list.

# Stumbling Blocks and Accessible Buildings

לֹא תְקַלֵּל חֵרֵשׁ וְלִפְנֵי עִוֵּר לֹא תִתֵּן מִכְשֹׁל וְיָרֵאתָ מֵּאֱלֹקֶיךָ אֲנִי ה'. (ויקרא יט:יד)

You shall not curse the deaf, nor put a stumbling block before the blind, but shall fear your God; I am the Lord. (Vayikra 19:14)

THE Torah describes a relatively narrow situation in our verse – putting a stumbling block before the blind. Rabbinic tradition, however, has greatly expanded the scope of this prohibition by interpreting the expression metaphorically. "The blind" are seen not as people with a visual impairment, but rather people who are unknowledgeable and vulnerable. Bad advice is also considered a "stumbling block."[1] Rashi's commentary on the verse follows this approach.[2]

Several of the supercommentaries on Rashi ask why he forgoes the literal explanation of this verse. Siftei Chachamim answers that putting a stumbling block in front of a blind person is so obviously evil and wrong that it would be unnecessary for the Torah to prohibit such an action. R. Meir Binyamin Menachem Danon writes in his Be'er Basadeh commentary that the literal prohibition is learned from the adjacent verse, "Neither shall you stand idly by the blood of your neighbor."[3] This second verse goes further by demanding the active removal of existing stumbling blocks, not just prohibiting the creation of new ones. This frees our verse to be used for the broader, metaphorical interpretation.

Both Siftei Chachamim and Be'er Basadeh believe that the literal interpretation of our verse is a binding prohibition. However, there still seems to be a distinction between the two: According to Siftei Chachamim, the prohibition applies if you are deliberately trying to cause harm to the blind

1. Sifra Kedoshim, parsha 2:14.

2. One extrapolation of this precept, found in Sefer Hachinuch 240, is that one may not sell weapons (to non-Jews) unless they are for defense.

3. Vayikra 19:16.

person. This is the situation in which everyone can recognize that evil is being done. But according to Be'er Basadeh, no evil intent is required. Even when no harm to the blind is intended, there is an obligation to actively remove the obstacle.

One possible ramification between these two opinions is when determining the halachic obligation toward accessibility for the disabled in buildings. A building without wheelchair ramps or braille exit indicators does not actively intend to harm. Therefore, it seems that according to Siftei Chachamim, this act would not fall under the prohibition of placing a stumbling block. However, according to Be'er Basadeh, obstructing and harming the blind, even unintentionally, is problematic and requires that the situation be rectified.

It is now common practice for countries to have a national accessibility code for building construction. The United States passed the Americans with Disabilities Act (ADA) in 1990, while Israel approved its equivalent in 1998. These codes address issues such as accessible parking spaces, barrier-free design that allows people in wheelchairs to move freely throughout a building, and accessible restrooms. In Israel, the code dictates that there cannot be any low-hanging obstacles, nor objects blocking passages that can harm the blind.[4] Surfaces must be sufficiently smooth, ramps must be installed with reasonable slopes, and handrails must be provided. A flight of stairs must have at least three steps so that it cannot be overlooked and cause someone to trip.[5] Stairs in a single flight cannot deviate more than five millimeters in height or depth, to prevent falls.[6] These are some of the many examples of how stumbling blocks are outlawed by building code.

While Halacha requires that we abide by the rules of the state, the sections of the building code that apply to accessibility have the additional weight of the Torah precept against placing stumbling blocks. There is an obligation to actively eliminate stumbling blocks in architecture and to ensure accessibility to all, not just according to the law but according to halacha as well.

4. Standards Institution of Israel 1918 I 2.9.
5. Ibid, 3.2.2.6.
6. Ibid, 3.2.2.13.

# *Kilayim* in Building Materials

אֶת חֻקֹּתַי תִּשְׁמֹרוּ בְּהֶמְתְּךָ לֹא תַרְבִּיעַ כִּלְאַיִם שָׂדְךָ לֹא תִזְרַע כִּלְאָיִם וּבֶגֶד כִּלְאַיִם שַׁעַטְנֵז לֹא יַעֲלֶה עָלֶיךָ. (ויקרא יט:יט)

You shall keep my statutes. You shall not let your cattle mate with a diverse kind, you shall not sow your field with two kinds of seed, neither shall there come upon you a garment of two kinds of material mingled together. (Vayikra 19:19)

THE Torah describes five different categories of *kilayim* or "mingling" which are forbidden. These five types are detailed in the tractate Kilayim and appear in the following order:

(a) Planting different seeds together or grafting plants;
(b) Planting grains together with grapevines;
(c) Breeding a hybrid of two animal species;
(d) Working (yoking) two species of animals together;
(e) Using linen and wool together in a garment.[1]

Based on the various commentaries, the different prohibitions of *kilayim* exist on a spectrum. Interbreeding animals is the most extreme case, mixing wool and linen is the least egregious example, and mixing plant species comes somewhere in the middle.[2] This corresponds with the autonomy of the groups: interbred animals can subsist on their own, while a linen and wool mixture is a dead and unmoving object that cannot reproduce. Plants are living things with some ability to reproduce on their own but without the autonomy of animals.

1. Some of these are learned from a second verse, Devarim 22:11. The various types are listed in order of their treatment in tractate Kilayim.
2. bSan 56b states that it is forbidden to all non-Jews to interbreed animal species and to graft plants, but permissible to plant seeds together and wear mixed textiles.

Commentators differ as to which of these categories pose an actual problem, and which are just safeguards. Rashbam writes that all species were separate during Creation, and so they should stay.[3] Ramban explains that any attempt to mix two species is a critique of the works of Creation as if to say that God's work was not sufficient. Still, he draws the line differently and explains that mixing linen and wool is only included as a reminder not to mix living species.

The Maharal of Prague, in his Gur Aryeh commentary, rejects the idea of finding fault with Creation. He points out that in various midrashim the Rabbis make a point of saying that Creation is not complete, but rather needs man to perfect it. Maharal only accepts that breeding animals is unnatural and sees it as the main prohibition. R. Eliyahu Mizrachi writes similarly that all the prohibitions of *kilayim* are only instituted to strengthen the prohibition of interbreeding animals. Finally, Rashi writes that these prohibitions are not based on logic but are rather "decrees of The King."

The rules of *kilayim* cover many of the main aspects of agrarian need: clothing, farming, agriculture, and animal husbandry. In this way, they are similar to the laws of *tzaraat,* which affect people, clothing, and buildings. However, in the case of *kilayim,* the Torah stops short of forbidding any form of mixing building materials. There is no prohibition against stone and brick, or concrete and rebar, or any metallic alloys, which are somewhat analogous to the case of linen and wool. The Talmud even rules that stiff cloth, let alone construction materials, cannot be *kilayim.*[4] This supports the opinion that *kilayim* is not logical but rather a "decree of The King."

While there is no halachic rule against *kilayim* in building materials, it is interesting to note that, just as many commentaries point to the infertility of the mule as an example of how interbreeding is unnatural, there are some ways in which building materials cannot naturally be combined. The best example of this is galvanic corrosion. When two metals with different electrode potentials come into contact while exposed to a corrosive liquid, one of the two will begin to rapidly corrode. The contact between copper and iron in the Statue of Liberty caused the iron to corrode so much that renovations were necessary. These types of metals cannot, by their very

3. The Netziv writes that just as interbreeding creates something which deviates from the natural order, so too linen and wool creates a mutant substance. As proof, he claims that linen and wool can interrupt telegraph transmissions. Contrast this with tBer 5:31 and especially BerR 82:12, which state that "fire and *kilayim* were not created during the six days of creation," yet no one claims that fire is unnatural.

4. bBeit 15a and bYom 69a.

nature, be used together without being physically separated by insulation. Another example of the problem of combining different materials is thermal shock. While materials enlarge or shrink depending on their temperature, one material may expand more than another. If two materials with differing coefficients of thermal expansion are used together, the materials can separate or crack, causing structural failure. This can even cause windows in large office buildings to shatter, as occurred in the John Hancock Tower in Boston. Reinforced concrete, combining the compressive strength of concrete and the tensile strength of iron, tends to decay faster due to the combination of materials. These are examples of how there are some natural difficulties with combining different building materials, even if no halachic prohibitions exist.

No one suggests that the combinations of different building materials should be prohibited. If *kilayim* exist on a continuum from most severe to least, minerals would appear at a point beyond linen and wool and are therefore not a halachic concern.

KEDOSHIM

# Tattoos and Modern Architecture

וְשֶׂרֶט לָנֶפֶשׁ לֹא תִתְּנוּ בִּבְשַׂרְכֶם וּכְתֹבֶת קַעֲקַע לֹא תִתְּנוּ בָּכֶם אֲנִי ה׳.
(ויקרא יט:כח)

You shall not make any cuttings in your flesh for the dead, nor imprint any marks upon you, I am the Lord. (Vayikra 19:28)

THE Torah forbids printing "any marks upon you," which is understood as a prohibition against tattoos.[1] There is a dispute in the Mishna about the scope of the prohibition, whether it only applies to tattooing the name of a foreign god, or if all tattoos are forbidden.[2] Explaining the reason for this commandment, Rambam writes that tattoos are a "custom of non-Jews." Just as slaves or cattle were branded to show ownership, people would tattoo themselves to show that they belonged to their god.[3] The Torah, in seeking to eliminate pagan rites, forbade this practice.[4]

1. Rashi on our verse.
2. mMak 3:6. See also tMak 4:15.
3. Rambam Hilchot Avoda Zara 12:11 and Sefer Hachinuch 257. Sforno emphasizes this by stating that Jews only inscribe one symbol on their flesh – circumcision. For more on tattooing as a means of declaring ownership, see Mallory Ditchey, "Body Language: Tattooing and Branding in Ancient Mesopotamia" in *Journal of Ancient Near Eastern History,* III.1 (2017), 1–24. Philo describes this practice in *The Special Laws* 1.58, writing that some "hasten onward to the slavery and service of images made by hands, confessing it in distinct characters ... branding the characters deep on their persons with a burning iron."
4. Mesopotamian literature from the first Millennium BCE shows that tattoos were used for three purposes: marking slaves, punishing runaway slaves, and marking temple servants. See Ditchey, "Body Language," 2. Similarly, John Huehnergard and Harold Liebowitz argue that the original context of this verse was regarding the marking of slaves, while the Talmud applies it to idol worship. See Huehnergard and Liebowitz, "The Biblical Prohibition Against Tattooing" in *Vetus Testamentum* 63 (2013), 59–77. They base this in part on Yishayahu 44:5, but their argument is not convincing. Given the tattooing of temple servants at the time, it is plausible that the verse was referring

In the nineteenth century, tattoos were widely associated with primitive culture. This belief was advanced by Charles Darwin, encouraged by explorers who encountered heavily tattooed Polynesians.[5] Cesare Lombroso, an Italian criminologist, took this one step further and explained that tattoos were the domain of criminals. The impulse to tattoo the body, he felt, was indicative of the same degenerative traits that lead to a life of crime.

In the early twentieth century, architectural theorist Adolf Loos used this understanding – of tattooing as a base impulse – to bolster his position against the use of ornament in architecture.[6] Loos felt that only primitive cultures felt the need to adorn material goods, buildings, and themselves. While decoration was expected of "savages," he argued that the same practices should be an embarrassment to more highly developed civilizations:

> The Papuan covers his skin with tattoos, his boat, his oars, in short everything he can lay his hands on. He is no criminal. The modern person who tattoos himself is either a criminal or a degenerate. There are prisons in which eighty percent of the inmates have tattoos. People with tattoos not in prison are either latent criminals or degenerate aristocrats.[7]

The urge to decorate, Loos claimed, was a degenerate one. Just as criminals tattoo their bodies, so too undeveloped cultures decorate their architecture. Conversely, the more high-cultured a society, the less ornament is preferred in its fashion, design, and architecture. Architecture, when designed with logic and attuned to the building's function, is beautiful without any decoration.

Loos' anti-ornament position became an important tenet of the Modern movement, which taught that buildings should be free of any purely decorative elements. His position was canonized by Le Corbusier and taught in the Bauhaus. Even once the connection between criminal activity and

---

to idol worship, as explained by the Mishna.

5. Charles Darwin, *The Descent of Man.* Darwin specifically mentions that ancient Jews practiced tattooing, though he gives no source for this claim.

6. Loos was influenced by Louis Sullivan's *Ornament in Architecture,* in which Sullivan questioned the need for ornament and suggested a moratorium from using it. Instead, architects were to rely on mass and proportion to make buildings appealing.

7. Adolf Loos, "Ornament and Crime" reprinted in *Ornament and Crime: Selected Essays,* tr. Michael Mitchell (Ariadne Press, 1998), 167. See also Jimena Canales and Andrew Herscher, "Criminal Skins: Tattoos and Modern Architecture in the Work of Adolf Loos" in *Architectural History* 48, 235–256. Immanuel Kant draws a parallel between architecture and tattooing in his *The Critique of Judgement,* 16, while distinguishing between "free beauty" and "dependent beauty."

tattoos was discredited, the arguments set forth by Loos continued to influence the Modern movement.

Loos' view of tattoos as a primitive practice is similar to the language of Rambam, who understood tattooing as a pagan practice. Using tattoos to signify devotion – branding yourself with God's name – is overly literal and lacking sophistication. An advanced religious devotion supersedes any form of branding or tattooing. One shows devotion to God by keeping the mitzvot. This transcends the need for literal ornament upon the body, rendering such inscriptions vulgar and even pagan.

# Rising for the Elderly

מִפְּנֵי שֵׂיבָה תָּקוּם וְהָדַרְתָּ פְּנֵי זָקֵן וְיָרֵאתָ מֵּאֱלֹקֶיךָ אֲנִי ה'. (ויקרא יט:לב)

You shall rise before the aged and honor the face of the old man, and fear your God. I am the Lord. (Vayikra 19:32)

THE Talmud states that the expression, "the old man," which appears in this verse, denotes wisdom and that the commandment to honor the face of the old man only applies to elders who are wise.[1] However, Issi ben Yehuda rules that it applies to all the elderly, no matter their wisdom or righteousness. The Talmud ultimately rules in accordance with Issi ben Yehuda.[2]

Besides rising before the elderly, which appears explicitly in the verse, the Rabbis list other ways in which the elderly must be honored. One should not take their seat, not speak in their presence, and not contradict elders.[3] In this way, "honoring the face of the old man" and standing up before elders are seen as two parts of the same commandment.

Although this is a valid way to read the verse, it is also possible that the two clauses are separate. Standing for an elder is a courtesy that does not necessarily imply honor; it could be a simple kindness out of a realization that it is hard for the elderly to stand. If the elderly are vaccinated first during a pandemic, this is out of the recognition that they are at a higher risk, not as a way of showing them honor. This is how the verse is understood in Israeli society, where it is printed on the inside of buses to remind passengers to offer their seats to the elderly. Rising for the elderly is not necessarily the same as honoring them.

The argument about who must be honored may revolve around these two interpretations. If standing up before an elder is done for purposes

1. bKid 32b–33a. It may also refer to all the wise, regardless of their age.
2. According to R. Yochanan and codified by Ramban in Hilchot Talmud Torah 6:9.
3. Sifra Kedoshim, perek 7:14.

of honoring them, then it is valid to question whether all elders deserve honor or only the wise and righteous ones. However, if the two clauses are separate, then standing up before an elder can be understood as a commandment to offer them a seat, something we do out of kindness. In such a case, the commandment to rise would apply regardless of whether a specific elder deserves honor.

If we read this precept as a form of kindness and recognition of the challenges faced by the elderly, it may also apply when including designated spots for the infirmed or elderly in building plans. Building code demands parking spots for the disabled and resting spots in long hallways for people who cannot walk long distances. Ramps over a certain length must have landings for people to rest. By mandating special spots set aside for the elderly, society as a whole keeps the commandment of standing up before the elderly.

# Honest Measurements

לֹא תַעֲשׂוּ עָוֶל בַּמִּשְׁפָּט בַּמִּדָּה בַּמִּשְׁקָל וּבַמְּשׂוּרָה. מֹאזְנֵי צֶדֶק אַבְנֵי צֶדֶק אֵיפַת צֶדֶק וְהִין צֶדֶק יִהְיֶה לָכֶם אֲנִי ה׳ אֱלֹקֵיכֶם אֲשֶׁר הוֹצֵאתִי אֶתְכֶם מֵאֶרֶץ מִצְרָיִם. (ויקרא יט:לה-לו)

You shall do no unrighteousness in judgment, in measurement, in weight, or in measure. Just balances, just weights, a just *efa* and a just *hin*, shall you have, I am the Lord your God who brought you out of the land of Egypt. (Vayikra 19:35–36)

As part of establishing a just society, the Torah demands the use of honest weights and measures.[1] This is a common-sense matter that is a prerequisite for people to do business without fear of being cheated. R. S.R. Hirsch points out that the requirement is multilayered. On the one hand, people must use weights and measures that are accurate. One should not have a measuring cup that is larger or smaller than its labeled size or a weight that is even fractionally inaccurate.[2] On the other hand, one may not purposely misread measurements by passing off one amount as another. These two obligations apply on a personal level.

In addition to personal responsibility, there is a societal obligation to set up an accurate system of measurements. This means both having consistent standards for weights and measures, as well as having methods for enforcing obedience. In the time of the Talmud, enforcement was done

1. See also Devarim 25:13–16.
2. bBM 61b rules that you should not measure for one in the summer and for another in winter, as the atmospheric conditions will change the physical dimensions of the tape measure.

The law usually gives a range of precision which is acceptable. The Talmud touches on this subject when discussing the precision of measurement required in determining the nearest city to be responsible for a murder, and whether two measurements can ever be considered precisely the same (*tzimtzum*). See bBech 17b.

in part by an *agoranomos,* a market inspector.[3] Today, government and regulation agencies fill this role, enforcing the standards for weights and measures.

The various obligations can be summarized in the following chart:

| | Having Consistent Units of Measurement | Correctly Using these Units of Measurement |
|---|---|---|
| **Personal** | Do not keep inaccurate weights and measures in your house | Do not misread or alter your measurements to mislead clients |
| **Societal** | Establish a uniform system of weights and measures | Have inspectors (*agoranomoi*) and regulation agencies |

Architects have a unique position when it comes to keeping these laws. Architects are called upon to provide accurate measurements for buildings. This takes place at both the permitting and design stages of a project. A request for a building permit includes a summary of the meterage of the building. The overall totals must fall within the allotted zoning rights for the property. Architects and clients have an interest in using all of the building rights, so the building often reaches the maximum allowable meterage. In these situations, there can be pressure to massage the numbers, so they are under the allotted amount. However, misusing measurements runs against the *personal* obligation to give accurate measurements. Various committees exist to check the work of planners and make sure they are not cheating the system. In recent years, there have been efforts made to make the measurement process in Israel more automated and exact. This effort helps fulfill the *societal* obligation to keep measurements accurate.

A second area where this obligation applies is in the depiction of proposed buildings, be they two- or three-dimensional. Architects occasionally show their designs inaccurately, to make them appear more attractive. For example, one might find an apartment plan shown with furniture that is well below standard size, to make the rooms appear more spacious. An architect might render a building within the surrounding city fabric in a way that makes it seem less obtrusive or smaller than reality, to make it more palatable.[4] Both practices violate the prohibition against inaccurate weights and measures, by using a false architectural scale.

3. Sifra Kedoshim, perek 8:8, Sifri Devarim 294, bBB 89a, yBB 5:5 (15b), and bBM 61b. See also Daniel Sperber, *The City in Roman Palestine* (Oxford Press, 1998), ch. 3. Sperber quotes the work of T.H. Dyer that in Pompeii there was a niche which held the official measuring standards.

4. A recent example took place in Jerusalem. See Naama Riba and Nir Hasson,

The Torah and rabbis place a heavy emphasis on accurate weights and measures as a precondition on just society.[5] This emphasizes the important obligation that architects, as trusted professionals, have to provide accurate information for clients and planners. Using professional tools to mislead is akin to using faulty weights, a practice prohibited by the Torah.

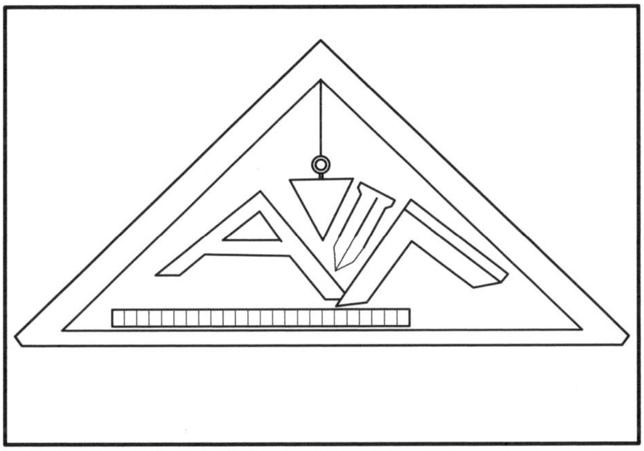

66. Funerary stele of the Aebutii with measuring instruments, housed in the Capitoline Museum.

"Contentious Jerusalem Pyramid Skyscraper Gets Downsized" in Haaretz, Oct. 29, 2015.

5. Ibn Ezra, commenting on the verses in Devarim that emphasize this precept as a bellwether of a righteous society, compares a righteous society to a sturdy building, and corruption to dilapidated structures. See his commentary on Devarim 25:15.

# The Impact of *Tumat Ohalim* On Architecture

וַיֹּאמֶר ה׳ אֶל מֹשֶׁה אֱמֹר אֶל הַכֹּהֲנִים בְּנֵי אַהֲרֹן וְאָמַרְתָּ אֲלֵהֶם לְנֶפֶשׁ לֹא יִטַּמָּא בְּעַמָּיו. (ויקרא כא:א)

And the Lord said to Moshe: "Speak to the priests, the sons of Aharon, and say to them: 'There shall none defile himself for the dead among his people.'" (Vayikra 21:1)

WHILE Bnei Yisrael have many commandments that make them unique, the kohanim have an extra set of rules due to their status as priests.[1] One of these special standards is that kohanim cannot become *tameh met* – spiritually impure due to contact with a dead body – except for immediate relatives.

This law, combined with the halachot of how *tumah* is transmitted, has had an impact on the architecture of buildings in which dead bodies are found, such as cemeteries and hospitals. In Israel, an additional place of concern is the main airport, as dead bodies are frequently flown to Israel for burial. These types of buildings are often designed with features that make it easier for a kohen to enter the space without fear of becoming *tameh*.

The concern with cemeteries is not new. Kohanim are usually given indication where they can safely stand without coming under the same roof as the dead. In many cemeteries, a special room is included for kohanim, where they can remain during eulogies and other burial activities. In terms of landscape design, groundskeepers have to be careful to avoid trees that overhang beyond the walls of the cemetery, so that kohanim passing by do not become *tameh* accidentally.[2]

---

1. Ibn Ezra.
2. The Shulchan Aruch warns kohanim about trees inside cemeteries, though the concern, according to R. Shabtai ben Meir Hakohen in his Siftei Kohen commentary, is that a single branch will overhang both a grave and the kohen. (YD 369:1) The Shulchan

While the Shulchan Aruch does not dwell on the issue of trees, the concern with trees may have become greater with the rise of picturesque garden cemeteries, which became trendy at the start of the nineteenth century. The first example in the United States, Mount Auburn Cemetery, outside of Boston, pioneered the use of English landscapes with winding paths, monuments, and arranged perspectives to make the cemetery seem both peaceful and a place of sanctuary. Before this movement, there were still trees in cemeteries, though frequently these were due to neglect rather than by design. Today, cemeteries take care in designing their landscape, and Jewish cemeteries often consider how the placement of trees will impact visiting kohanim.

An even greater complication for kohanim is the presence of dead bodies and other sources of *tumat met* in a hospital. While such issues were important before the State of Israel, it was easier to be lenient in hospitals in which the majority of patients were non-Jews. With Israel and its Jewish-majority cities, many of these leniencies cannot be relied upon. Instead, sympathetic hospitals have looked for design solutions to alleviate this problem for kohanim, either as patients or as visitors.

The difficulty with *tumat met* in a hospital is two-fold. First, there are actual bodies, body parts, and blood which are sources of *tumah.*[3] These items, however, can be contained by leaving hospital doors closed, keeping severed organs in special closets, and installing two doors in tandem that cannot both be opened simultaneously ("air-locks") at crucial locations like the morgue, where sources of *tumah* are constantly found. Dead bodies can be transferred to sealed gurneys and moved quickly out of the main hospital and to the morgue. In many hospitals, special signs are posted (or turned on electronically) when a dead body is present in the main hospital so that kohanim know not to enter at that precise moment.

A second, more difficult halachic problem exists due to the concept of *sof tumah latzet,* that ultimately the *tumah* will need to exit the building.[4] This concept results in *tumah* spreading along corridors that in the future will be used to remove the dead body. This exists regardless of whether doors are closed because it supposes that in the future the body will be removed, and transmits *tumah* preemptively.[5]

---

Aruch does not express concern with having trees in a cemetery as long as they are not directly over graves, even allowing fruit from fruit trees to be collected and sold. (YD 368:2)

3. For more on how *tumah* spreads through a building, see my commentary on Bamidbar 19:9.

4. See, for example, Rashi *kulam temayim* on bBeit 10a, and the Rama on YD 371:4.

5. yBB 3:10 (14b) quotes the testimony of a builder that a window open to a stoa

In 1984, R. Menachem Mendel Shafran published an article suggesting one solution to the transmission of *tumat met* in hospitals.[6] He proposed that a plenum could be constructed in connecting hallways, below the upper ceiling of the hallway. This plenum, he suggested, would then have the halachic status of an attic, and if a fissure less than one handbreadth wide was cut across the width of the hallway, the *tumah* would go into the plenum and not jump across the gap to spread to the adjacent spaces, nor could the *tumah* reenter the hallway from the plenum, due to the opening being less than a handbreadth.

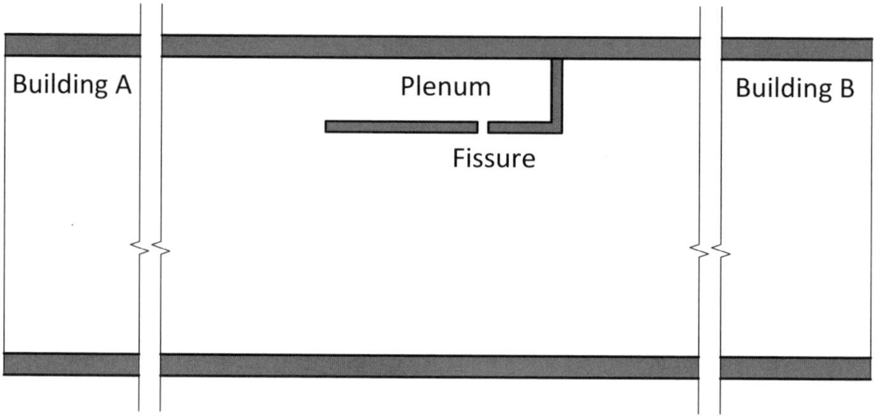


67. *Tumah* plenum for a hospital.

Several objections were raised to this proposal.[7] R. Avraham Shapira, then the Ashkenazi chief rabbi of Israel, considered the plenum insufficient to be considered an attic.[8] R. Eliyahu Bakshi-Doron made this point as

(covered colonnade) only serves to let light enter, and not as a means of ventilation. This changes the status of the window for the transfer of *tumah*. See discussion of this point in Saul Lieberman, "A Few Words on the Book by Julian the Architect of Ascalon *The Laws of Palestine and its Customs*," *Tarbiz* 40 (Tamuz–Elul 5731), 411–413 (Hebrew). Yizhar Hirschfeld sees this as proof that builders were considered experts and could influence halacha with their specialized knowledge. See Hirschfeld, *The Palestinian Dwelling* (Israel Exploration Society, 1995), 228. For a similar discussion regarding the role of tradesmen in city administration, see Plato, *Protagoras*, 319d, and discussion in Serafina Cuomo, *Technology and Culture in Greek and Roman Antiquity* (Cambridge University Press, 2007), 30.

6. Shafran, Menachem Mendel. "*Hatzaa Latikun Baayat Tumat Kohanim Bebatei Cholim*" (Hebrew), *Techumin* 5, (5784) 225–243. This article was based on a design solution performed in Beilinson Hospital, Petach Tikva.

7. These appeared in the following volume of *Techumin*, volume 6 (1985).

8. Both because the real roof of the space is still the main one, and because at least 4 × 4 handbreadths of space, and possibly 10 handbreadths or even as much as 4 × 4

well and stressed that the fissure had to be open to the sky above.[9] R. Shapira raised a second objection, that according to Rambam the walls must contain the same fissure for the flow of *tumah* to be interrupted.[10]

I worked on one hospital in Israel that overcame some of these issues by using a fissure, but instead of leading to a plenum, the fissure was open to the sky above. This has some obvious complications, in that the corridor is then open to the elements, both in terms of letting rain in and in making it harder to have climate control. However, such a design does present a more robust attempt to solve the issue with *sof tumah latzet.* These measures are used to help simplify the problems faced by kohanim in Israeli hospitals.

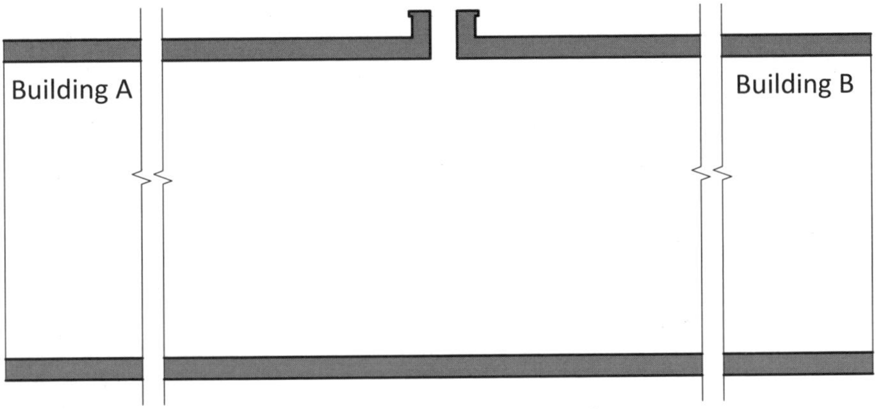


68. *Tumah* opening for a hospital.

Airports are another potentially problematic type of building for *tumah.* With the opening of the new airport terminal at Ben Gurion Airport in 2004, concerns arose regarding bodies flown to Israel for burial. Until that point, passengers deplaned at a distance and were bused to the terminal. Caskets could be removed without spreading *tumah* to the whole airport.[11] However, the new terminal had jetways for docking, creating a continuous connection between the plane and the terminal. To prevent *tumah* from entering the terminal, the airport authority instituted a new

cubits, are required for it to count as a separate, inhabitable space.

9. See his response in *Techumin* 6, 139–148. He also suggests that such a fissure might only count if it was unplanned.

10. R. Shafran contends this point in his response, *Techumin* 6, 149–162. See also Dror Fixler's article in *Technumin 20,* 387.

11. Ilan Shahar, "Fear of Ritual Impurity at Terminal 3" Haaretz, Nov 3, 2004.

protocol, whereby a plane would not be connected to a jetway until all caskets had been removed from the plane. In this case, the solution was not architectural, but rather procedural, though there was some discussion about designing a jetway with a fissure similar to that used in the hospital solution.

The requirement for kohanim to avoid becoming *tameh met* is one of the few halachot that has had a concrete architectural impact on design.[12] While some halachot, such as building a *sukka* or affixing a *mezuza*, are architectural in nature, this is one case where building design can be subtly tweaked to help solve a halachic issue.

12. See Vayikra 23:42 for another example.

# *Sukka* Balconies

בַּסֻּכֹּת תֵּשְׁבוּ שִׁבְעַת יָמִים כָּל הָאֶזְרָח בְּיִשְׂרָאֵל יֵשְׁבוּ בַּסֻּכֹּת. (ויקרא כג:מב)

You shall dwell in booths seven days, all that are citizens in Israel shall dwell in booths. (Vayikra 23:42)

DURING the festival of Sukkot, Bnei Yisrael are commanded to "dwell in booths seven days." The Hebrew term for the booth, *sukka,* which is derived from the term "to cover," implies that the covering of the *sukka* is of primary importance. The canopy of a *sukka* must be beneath open sky, so the *sukka* cannot be inside a house, below a tree, or even below a second *sukka.*[1]

This rule is a rare example of a halacha that has had a tangible effect on architecture in Israel.[2] Due to the requirement for a *sukka* with unobstructed airspace above, apartment buildings in Israel that are marketed to the religious sector are designed so that each apartment has a balcony that has some open sky above.

With any tall building, greater height is met with diminishing return. As a building rises in height, more elevator banks and stairwells are required for both safety and timely movement between floors. The number of elevators required for a ten-story building will not be sufficient for a twenty-story building.[3] This means larger stair cores and elevator banks, and less available floor space. The same type of issue exists for *sukka* balconies; there is only so much perimeter space around the building, and for every apartment to get a *sukka* balcony, that space must be divided between the units. Even with setbacks at the upper levels,[4] more floors

1. Sifra Emor, perek 17:4 and mSuk 1:2.
2. See Vayikra 21:1 for another example.
3. Prior to the advent of steel-framed buildings, extra height also required thicker walls below, again limiting available space.
4. As required by code in many locales.

means less open-aired balcony space per apartment. Up to approximately eight stories, balconies can be arranged in a fairly reasonable manner; above this number, however, the balconies start to be impractical.[5] Units are left either with very small areas open to the sky or without a "*sukka* balcony" at all.

In Israel, the design of balconies has some additional history. Originally, most Israeli apartments were designed with balconies one above the next. However, it became common for people to illegally enclose their balconies with shutters and other flimsy materials to create an extra room in the apartment. The State combated this practice by passing a regulation in 1992 which stated that balconies that had a roof (i.e. the bottom of another balcony) one story above were to be counted as main space, reducing the allowable size of the actual apartment. The intended result, which came to pass, was that architects were forced to stagger the balconies in apartment buildings. This prevented people from illegally enclosing their balconies, but also roughly halved the size of each apartment's balcony. In 2008, this law was annulled, with the promise that illegal enclosures would be more strictly enforced.[6]

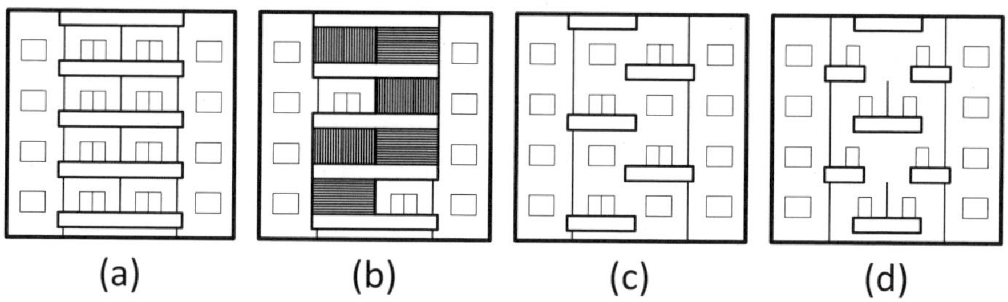


69. Balcony arrangements in Israel: (a) typical pre-1992 balcony design (b) enclosure of balconies to make extra rooms (c,d) examples of staggered balcony design post-1992.

While this history does not have any direct influence on the story of *sukka* balconies, it does present a second way in which regulations forced apartment designers to arrange their balconies in a non-standard manner.

5. "*Kol Bayit Tzarich Mirpeset (Sukka)*" (Hebrew), retrieved 17 Dec 2017 from http://www.kipa.co.il/jew/holidays/sukot/59060.html.

6. *Takanot Hatichnun Vehabeniya (Chishuv Shetachim Veachuzei Beniya Betochniyot Ubeheterim)*, 1992, 4. (8) (Hebrew). There was also a brief period between 2008–2010 in which cantilevered balconies were allowed as service space, specifically to enable the construction of *sukka* balconies.

The result is that the placement of balconies in Israel is one of the most interesting, unconventional, and eclectic features of local architecture, thanks in large part to the desire to build temporary dwellings open to the sky for one week each year.

# *Sukka* of the Leviathan

בַּסֻּכֹּת תֵּשְׁבוּ שִׁבְעַת יָמִים כָּל הָאֶזְרָח בְּיִשְׂרָאֵל יֵשְׁבוּ בַּסֻּכֹּת. (ויקרא כג:מב)

You shall dwell in booths seven days, all that are citizens in Israel shall dwell in booths. (Vayikra 23:42)

On the last day of the festival of Sukkot, there is a custom to take leave of one's *sukka* with a short prayer, that in the coming year you will merit to sit in the "*sukka* of the leviathan."[1]

The leviathan is a creature that is mentioned five times in the Bible. Yishayahu prophesizes that God will slay this beast.[2] Tehilim says that God killed the beast and gave it to people to eat.[3] This may be the reason why the leviathan is connected with the End of Days when according to legend the righteous will feast on its flesh.[4]

In addition to this connection with the End of Days, the leviathan also has a biblical link to Sukkot. Iyov is asked rhetorically whether it would be possible for mere mortals to hunt the leviathan "and fill his skin with hooks," an expression that uses a homonym of the word "sukkot."[5] This prompts R. Yochanan to draw a connection between the leviathan and *sukkot*. He explains that in the future God will make a *sukka* for the righteous out of the skin of the leviathan.[6] Others who are deserving but less worthy

1. Kolbo, 71.
2. Yishayahu 27:1.
3. Tehilim 74:14.
4. bBB 74b. See also Chanoch 6:24, 2 Apocalypse of Baruch 29:4, and 4 Ezra 6:52.
5. Iyov 40:31. The Leviathan is mentioned in Iyov 40:25. See also Iyov 3:8 and Tehilim 104:26 for the other instances in which the leviathan appears in the Bible.
6. While the Talmud, quoting Rabbah in the name of R. Yochanan, generically refers to the righteous, elsewhere R. Levi ties the *sukka* of the leviathan to people who keep the commandment of living in a *sukka*. See PdRK parsha Acheret.

will receive either a belt,[7] necklace, or amulet made of leviathan skin.[8] The remaining skin will be displayed on the walls of Jerusalem.[9]

To appreciate the midrash about the leviathan-skin *sukka*, it is helpful to consider traditional Innuit houses constructed out of whale bones.[10] Whale-bones were used primarily for their architectural utility, as long, strong supports suited for domestic architecture.[11] The houses did not, however, use the *skin* of the sea creatures, which was not durable. The bones were often arranged symbolically, with the jawbones at the entrance to symbolize the mouth of the whale. After a hunting expedition successfully caught a whale, some of the hunters, like the boat owner or harpooner, were entitled to specific parts of the whale.[12] The most successful and powerful hunters could claim the best bones for their construction projects. In this way, the structure of the house broadcasted their success and power.[13]

The leviathan-skin *sukka* may be intended to serve a similar purpose in the End of Days. The midrash explains that the righteous will be ranked and given items accordingly. Just as the whale bones signal power and influence, the leviathan skin will signal one's level of righteousness in the End of Days.

However, bones and skin are not entirely analogous. The whale bones serve a functional purpose, providing structural beams in an environment where alternate options, such as lumber, were scarce. The size of the beast is what makes its bones useful. In contrast, there is no need to seek out the skin of a large sea animal for a *sukka*, as smaller skins can be easily joined to create a larger covering. Any number of wall materials are available. The significance of the leviathan, in this case, must not be its size. Rather, the leviathan is held to be a unique creature, created specially by God for rewarding the righteous. As such, having a *sukka* draped in the skin of the leviathan symbolizes that God is sheltering and looking after the righteous. As whale bones symbolize success in the world of northern hunters, the leviathan skin symbolizes success in the spiritual world and the connection between the righteous and God.

---

7. As per the use of the term on bShab 105a.

8. Otzer Midrashim likewise explains that the feast will be divided based on the level of righteousness, with the most righteous eating from its head.

9. bBB 75a.

10. This is in no way to suggest any connection between the two, as the Rabbis certainly had no knowledge of Innuit construction practices.

11. A. Katherine Patton and James M. Savelle, "The Symbolic Dimensions of Whale Bone Use in Thule Winter Dwellings" in *Inuit Studies* (30:2, 2006), 149.

12. Margaret Lantis, "The Alaskan Whale Cult and its Affinities" in *American Anthropologist New Series* (40:3, Jul. –Sep. 1938), 440.

13. Patton and Savelle, "Symbolic Dimensions," 153.

# *Sukkot* of Clouds

לְמַעַן יֵדְעוּ דֹרֹתֵיכֶם כִּי בַסֻּכּוֹת הוֹשַׁבְתִּי אֶת בְּנֵי יִשְׂרָאֵל בְּהוֹצִיאִי אוֹתָם מֵאֶרֶץ מִצְרָיִם אֲנִי ה׳ אֱלֹקֵיכֶם. (ויקרא כג:מג)

That your generations may know that I made Bnei Yisrael to dwell in booths when I brought them out of the land of Egypt, I am the Lord your God. (Vayikra 23:43)

For seven days during the festival of Sukkot, Bnei Yisrael are commanded to live in booths (*sukkot*) instead of in their regular dwellings. The Torah explains that this is done to remember that Bnei Yisrael dwelled in booths during their forty years journey through the desert. Just as the holiday of Pesach commemorates the historical event of the Exodus, the Sukkot festival is a way to further strengthen the collective memory of this seminal event.

R. Eliezer and R. Akiva argue about the nature of the original *sukkot* in the desert. One understands that Bnei Yisrael lived in nomadic booths while they were in the wilderness, while according to the other, there were no physical booths, but Bnei Yisrael were surrounded and protected by the Cloud of Glory.[1] On the one hand, we can imagine that Bnei Yisrael built portable shelters for themselves while in the wilderness. On the other, the Torah states that the Cloud of Glory protected and cared for Bnei Yisrael, such that their bodies and belongings were sheltered from wear and tear.[2]

Rashbam writes that the simple explanation is that the *sukkot* built on the holiday of Sukkot commemorate actual booths built in the wilderness. He points out that Sukkot is also a harvest festival and explains that the harvest season, when houses are full of crops, is the most important time

1. bSuk 11b, MdRS Bo 12:37, and Sifra Emor, perek 17:11. It is unclear who holds each opinion. In the Talmud it seems R. Akiva believes there were actual booths, while in the Sifra the opposite is true.

2. Devarim 8:4.

to remember your humble, nomadic beginnings. By recalling that in the wilderness there were no crops and no permanent buildings, Bnei Yisrael can better appreciate the land received as an inheritance. According to Malbim, *sukkot* also highlight that this world is temporary, like a *sukka*, and that one shouldn't place too much emphasis on material wealth.

Ramban, on the other hand, explains that "booths" refers to the Cloud of Glory. He quotes verses from Yishayahu which describe God's cloud as "a *sukka* for a shadow in the daytime from the heat and a place of refuge and a cover from storm and rain."[3] This protection from storm and rain, afforded in the wilderness by the Cloud of Glory, is one explanation for why Sukkot is celebrated at the start of the rainy season.

The first mishna of tractate Sukka teaches that a *sukka* built taller than twenty cubits is not kosher.[4] Several reasons are given for this requirement. Among them, Rabba explains that if the walls are too tall, one cannot see the branches which form the roof of the *sukka*. Rava states that anything strong enough to stand twenty cubits high would not be considered a temporary shelter, and a *sukka* – by definition – must be temporary. Malbim suggests that the debate between Rabba and Rava relates to our discussion about what a *sukka* commemorates. Rabba, who requires a visual connection with the roof covering, believes that the *sukka* recalls the Cloud of Glory that provided shelter in the wilderness. Rava, who requires a temporary, nomadic structure, feels that the *sukka* hearkens back to actual dwellings that Bnei Yisrael lived in following the Exodus.

According to both explanations, the *sukka* is a way of using architecture as a historical reference to a previous, simple, and pure, perhaps primitive way of life. The period in which Bnei Yisrael were in the wilderness is viewed as an epoch outside the normal constraints of the world, during which all needs were provided by God. It is also one of the formative eras of the Jewish people. By requiring an annual reconstruction of this earlier, celebrated living condition, the Torah is giving a powerful tool for connecting with history and internalizing a time that included the Exodus, the reception of the Torah, and the inheritance of the Land of Israel.

---

3. Yishayahu 4:6.

4. Other requirements in this mishna include a minimum height of ten handbreadths, at least two walls plus a third wall of at least a handbreadth, and more shade than sunlight.

# Windows in the Temple

מִחוּץ לְפָרֹכֶת הָעֵדֻת בְּאֹהֶל מוֹעֵד יַעֲרֹךְ אֹתוֹ אַהֲרֹן מֵעֶרֶב עַד בֹּקֶר לִפְנֵי ה׳
תָּמִיד חֻקַּת עוֹלָם לְדֹרֹתֵיכֶם. (ויקרא כד:ג)

Outside the curtain of the Testimony, in the Tent of Meeting, shall Aharon order it from evening to morning before the Lord continually, it shall be a statute forever throughout your generations. (Vayikra 24:3)

Bnei Yisrael are commanded to keep an eternal light burning in the Tent of Meeting. This light, the Talmud explains, acts as a testament to the other nations of the world, that the Divine Presence dwells in Israel.[1]

How does the eternal light broadcast such a message to the rest of the world? The Talmud highlights the difficult wording in a verse describing windows in the First Temple. The windows were said to be *shekufim atumim*, "transparent and sealed,"[2] seemingly an oxymoron. The Talmud explains that from one side the windows appeared transparent, while from the other they were sealed.[3] Rashi writes that while many windows are designed with slanted jambs so that they are narrow on the outside and wider internally – thus allowing more light to enter the interior – the windows of the Temple were configured in the opposite way. This allowed the spiritual light of the Temple to shine forth to the outside world.[4] While

1. bMen 86b.
2. Melachim I 6:4.
3. There is a textual variant in the Talmud which makes it unclear if the inside or the outside was sealed, as per the Shita Mekubetzet on bMen 86b (note 4). See also Targum Yonatan on Melachim I 6:4. In PdRK 21:5 and VayR 31:7, the first explanation does not designate which side is transparent and which is sealed.
4. bMen 86b and on the verse in Melachim. Rashi bases his explanation on PdRK 21:5 and VayR 31:7. See the manuscript version of Rashi, which is very descriptive in its explanation. See also the Vulgate, which translates it as *fenestras obliquas.*

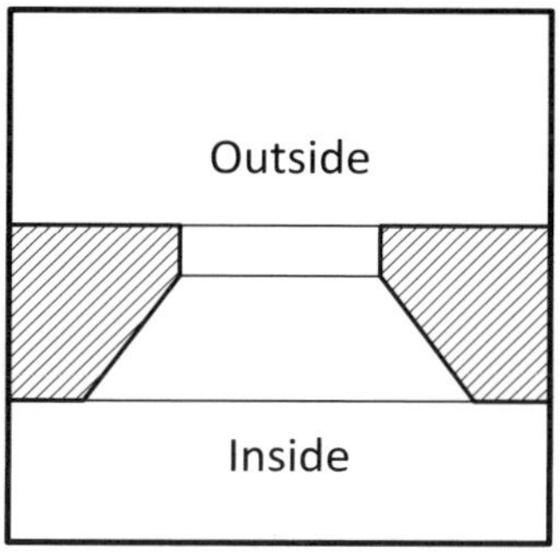


70. Plan of typical splayed window.

a normal house requires sunlight from outside, it is the world that needs the light emitted from the Temple.

The "normal" window design described by Rashi and in midrashim was indeed a common feature of windows, particularly ones found in thick stone walls. Such splayed windows serve the triple function of increasing privacy (by having outwardly narrow openings), increasing daylight, and reducing the amount of rain and dust that entered the building.[5] In Yizhar Hirschfeld's survey of traditional dwellings in Israel, he confirms that this is how many windows were constructed.[6]

Although this design was common, Ralbag believed that engineers had conclusively demonstrated that windows that are wider toward the outside let in more sunlight. Intuitively, Ralbag's position makes sense – a wider outward opening means more sunlight can be caught. The benefit of splayed windows, however, is not simply that they let in more light, but that they combine the extra sunlight which large windows offer with the privacy and shading benefits of small windows.[7] In some cases, double-splayed windows were used to try and gain an even greater advantage.[8] On the whole, splayed windows almost always widen inwardly, as described by Rashi and the Midrash. But as Ralbag explains, the point of this midrash is not to offer engineering advice but to highlight the unique position of the Temple as the source of "light" for the world.

5. See "Window" and "Splay" in James Stevens Curl's *Oxford Dictionary of Architecture and Landscape Architecture* (Oxford University Press, 2007).

6. Hirschfeld, *The Palestinian Dwelling* (Israel Exploration Society, 1995), 258.

7. Lingjiang Huang and Jiafen Wu, "Effects of the Splayed Window Type on Daylighting and Solar Shading" in *Building and Environment* 81 (Nov. 2014): 436 and 443.

8. Guy Points, *An Introduction to Anglo-Saxon Church Architecture & Anglo-Scandinavian Stone Sculpture* (Guy Points, 2015), 51–52.

In addition to the explanation given by Rashi and the Midrash, several other commentators suggest different interpretations for "transparent and sealed" windows. R. David Altschuler explains that the windows were sealed, but were bright like glass.[9] This could either mean that the windows were completely sealed but were polished to appear like glass from the outside or perhaps that they were an ancient type of one-way glass, opaque from the outside but translucent from within. Abarbanel comes to a similar conclusion, suggesting that Shlomo installed either one-way glass which allowed him to see but not be seen, or else opaque, "milky" glass that allowed light to enter the room but concealed the view.[10]

Guy Stiebel, analyzing the word *shekufim,* explains that it refers to the window lintel, as in the Hebrew *mashkof* or the Akkadian *aškuppatu.* He concludes that the verse is describing blind windows – recesses in the walls that appear to be windows but are sealed and thus just for show. This is supported by Yechezkel's description of a future Temple, which simply states "sealed windows" without mentioning the word *shekufim.*[11] Stiebel goes on to connect the description of Shlomo's Temple with Herod's design for the Temple centuries later. He points to the pilasters along the retaining walls of the Temple – raised portions of the wall framing sunken openings. Similar pilasters exist in the Herodian walls of the Cave of Machpela and Elonei Mamrei.[12] The lintels of these depressions are clearly sloped outward. Steibel suggests that Herod designed these pilasters as a reference to the earlier blind windows of Shlomo's Temple, a deliberate architectural homage.[13]

This idea – that one version of the Temple can repurpose elements of a previous version – is both sensible and provides a guide for any future Temple designs. We know that the design of Herod's Temple was different than previous versions and that he employed contemporary styles such as Corinthian columns, stoas, and pilasters. Yet by adapting these elements

9. Metzudat David on Melachim I 6:4.

10. Abarbanel on Melachim I 6:4.

11. Yechezkel 40:16.

12. Shimon Gibson argues that the walls of Elonei Mamrei and the Cave of Machpela are from a later period but were influenced by the Temple design. See Shimon Gibson, "The Pilaster Enclosure Wall of the Temple Mount in Jerusalem" in *New Studies on Jerusalem* 20 (2014), 17–40.

13. Guy Stiebel, "A Light Unto the Nations: Symbolic Architecture of Ritual Buildings" in *Eretz-Israel: Archaeological, Historical and Geographical Studies,* Teddy Kollek volume (2007): 226–228. It is far from certain that this is the reason for the slope – sills are often sloped outward for rain to drain away from the building, and the extreme angle of these slopes could be to prevent birds from landing on the sills.

71. Herodian wall with pilasters at the Cave of Machpela. (Photo by Tova Heller)

to reference the previous designs and, perhaps, existing midrashim, the Temple architecture maintained a through-line with past versions, even concerning ornament. Such adaptation allowed the design to stay current and yet remain connected to tradition.

# Houses in a Walled City

וְאִישׁ כִּי יִמְכֹּר בֵּית מוֹשַׁב עִיר חוֹמָה וְהָיְתָה גְּאֻלָּתוֹ עַד תֹּם שְׁנַת מִמְכָּרוֹ יָמִים תִּהְיֶה גְאֻלָּתוֹ. (ויקרא כה:כט)

And if a man sells a dwelling house in a walled city, then he may redeem it within a whole year after it is sold, for a full year shall he have the right of redemption. (Vayikra 25:29)

During the *Yovel*, or fiftieth year, land that has been sold reverts to its original owner. However, the Torah makes an exception to this rule for houses sold within a walled city. If a house in a walled city is sold, the original owner has only one year to buy it back. After one year the sale becomes final and *Yovel* does not cause ownership to revert to the original owner.

Why should the rules be any different for property within a walled city? Ramban explains that the special rule for walled cities is to encourage homeowners to buy back their houses quickly, out of recognition of how painful it is to be forced to sell one's house. However, this does not explain why a house in a walled city is different from a house elsewhere.

Chizkuni tries to differentiate between houses in a walled city and other houses. He explains that the safeguards of *Yovel* exist primarily to protect agricultural fields, which were the main source of livelihood in the Biblical era. If a family is forced to sell its means of production, it will never be able to regain financial security. *Yovel* allows the family a fresh start. Chizkuni explains that houses in a walled city are fundamentally different because they are not connected to fields. Someone who sells his house in a city is not losing his source of livelihood and therefore only gets one year to buy back the house before losing all rights to it.[1]

While Chizkuni's answer does distinguish between walled cities and

1. In mAra 9:5 there is an argument whether to apply this law to fields within a walled city, or if it applies only to buildings.

rural dwellings, it does not explain why there should be a difference between walled cities and unwalled cities. The existence of walls should not change the well-known differences between urban and rural living.

Instead, the focus should be on the city walls, which symbolize the city's defensive function.[2] Walled cities played an important role in defending the country. For a city and its walls to be well-maintained, it must have a stable and committed populace. Long-term owners can be counted on to maintain their properties at a higher level of upkeep than short-term owners who will lose possession in the near future. If a house in a walled city were sold during the fifty-year cycle, the temporary owners would have a declining incentive to make repairs to their house and contribute to the upkeep of the city. This situation would be untenable for a strategic resource and could potentially threaten the safety of both the city and the country at large. The Torah instead gives one year for an owner to redeem the property before the buyer gains permanent ownership. This way, there is more certainty that homeowners in walled cities will be committed to maintaining their properties and the city's defenses at the necessary level.[3]

---

2. Sifra Behar, parsha 4:1 teaches that only walled cities from the time of Yehoshua bin Nun are included in this rule. However, it should be noted that the cities remembered in the Talmud that belong in this category were all fortified cities that were destroyed during the Great Revolt (66–70 CE). Yisrael Rosenson has pointed out that this is how the Rabbis built the memory of these cities and the Great Revolt into Halacha.

3. In mAra 9:5, R. Yehuda and R. Shimon argue as to whether houses that are physically *part* of the city walls (such as those found in the archaeological record in Gamla) count as houses within a walled city. R. Shimon holds that they do, while R. Yehuda says that only houses within the walls – and not a *part* of the walls – are given special standing. If the goal of this law is to ensure that walled cities remain stout, houses that are part of the wall should certainly be included as per R. Shimon's opinion. See also bAra 32a and yMaas 3:4.

# Stone Paving

לֹא תַעֲשׂוּ לָכֶם אֱלִילִם וּפֶסֶל וּמַצֵּבָה לֹא תָקִימוּ לָכֶם וְאֶבֶן מַשְׂכִּית לֹא תִתְּנוּ בְּאַרְצְכֶם לְהִשְׁתַּחֲוֹת עָלֶיהָ כִּי אֲנִי ה' אֱלֹקֵיכֶם. (ויקרא כו:א)

You shall not make idols for yourselves, neither shall you erect a carved idol or a pillar, nor shall you place any figured stone in your land to bow down upon it, for I am the Lord your God. (Vayikra 26:1)

In a list of several prohibitions relating to idol worship, the Torah forbids installing "any figured stone" for the purpose of bowing upon it. Most commentators explain that the Torah is prohibiting the act of prostrating[1] upon a floor paved with stone. However, rabbinic prohibitions extend this to include prostrating on non-stone floors and kneeling on stone floors even without outstretched arms and legs.[2]

There are three main reasons given by the commentators for this prohibition. The first explains that a common form of idol worship was to bow down on stone floors. The Torah outlawed this behavior to distance people from idol worship.[3] The second possibility is that since the floors of the Temple were paved with stone, the Torah forbade stone floors elsewhere so as not to copy the design of the Temple.[4] This is supported by statements in the Sifra and Talmud that one *is* allowed to prostrate on stone floors in the Temple.[5] A third explanation is that it is only forbidden to prostrate

1. Laying down in worship with outstretched arms and legs.
2. Mishna Berura OC 131:40.
3. Rambam Hilchot Avoda Zara 6:6–7.
4. See Rashi here and my commentary on Shemot 20:20. See also Malbim, who explains these two interpretations, and Gerald J. Blidstein, "Talmudic Prostration and Mosaics" in *Bulletin of the Institute of Jewish Studies* II (1974), 22–3.
5. Sifra Behar, perek 9:5, bMeg 22b, yAZ 4:1 (43d).

on stone floors with graven images. In such a case, someone bowing down would look like he or she is worshiping the images.[6]

The distinction between stone paving and other materials raises questions about what is included in the category of stone paving. Halachic codes clearly distinguish between stone and brick floors, but there are other types of paving whose classification is less obvious. Terrazzo flooring consists of stone chips bonded by cement or resin, so it is *partially* made of stone, though it looks different from natural stone.[7] Porcelain floor tiles are designed to *appear* like stone, although they have little or no stone content. It is questionable whether there is a Torah prohibition against prostrating on either type of floor.

If the prohibition is in place to prevent the copying of the Temple, then perhaps it would make a difference to know the type of paving used in the Temple. In 2016, archaeologists presented various paving stones that were found while sifting through rubble from the Temple Mount. They suggested possible configurations of these precisely cut stones, comparing them to other projects built by Herod.[8] They concluded that the Temple was paved using the *opus sectile* technique, which is done using these types of stones.[9] However, even if this conclusion is correct, that would not necessarily mean that only *opus sectile* pavers are subject to this prohibition. Before Herod's renovations in the first century, there were other types of flooring used in the Temple, as *opus sectile* did not appear in Israel before Herod's time. Based on its normal usage, *opus sectile* was most likely one of several paving styles in Herod's Temple, used only in certain spaces or as an accent.

Ascertaining the specific paving technique used in the Temple may be irrelevant for another reason: it was very uncommon to find any type of paved floors during the Second Temple era. Even some Second Temple-era

---

6. As per Rashbam, and in the Septuagint. In *Art & Judaism in the Greco-Roman World* (Cambridge University Press, 2005), Steven Fine understands this prohibition as being applied by the Rabbis to mosaic floors, based on the passage in bMeg 22b, as did some scholars starting in the Gaonic period.

7. A similar type of mixed flooring is described in tOhal 17:9.

8. Herod used *opus sectile* in other projects around the country, such as Masada and Herodium. See "*Shichzur Harizpot Hatzivoniyot shel Chatzerot Beit Hamikdash Beshalhei Yemei Habayit Hasheni*" by Frankie Snyder, Gabriel Barkay and Zachi Dvira, 2016, retrieved from www.megalim.org.il in 2018, and Frankie Snyder and Assaf Avraham, "The *Opus Sectile* Floor in a Caldarium of the Palatial Fortress at Cypros" in *Hasmonean and Herodian Palaces at Jericho*, V (Israel Exploration Society, 2013), 178.

9. Biblical Archaeology Review, November/December 2016. This may be what Josephus intended when he wrote in *The Jewish War* 5.192–193 that the Temple was paved with many different types of stone.

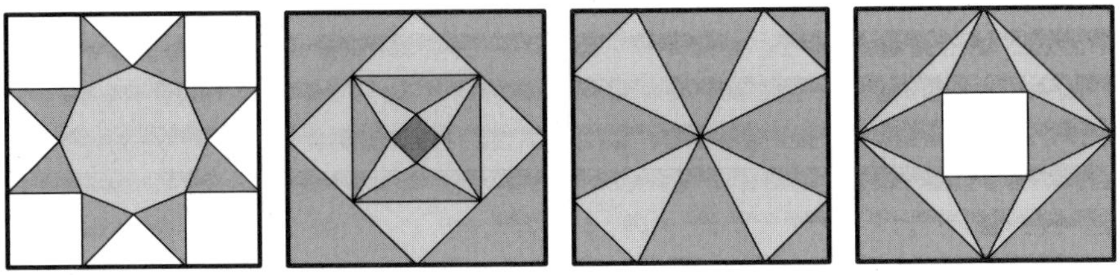

72. Reconstructions of Temple floor patterns from recovered opus sectile tiles found by the Temple Mount Sifting Project. (Based on work by Frankie Snyder)

synagogues in Israel were not paved, but rather had compacted earth floors that were covered with mats.[10] This was certainly the norm for domestic architecture,[11] which is the reason why sweeping floors was not allowed on Shabbat,[12] and why one had to be careful about dragging benches on Shabbat. No matter what style or technique of stone paving existed in each of the Temples, there is a good chance that few other buildings existed with stone paving, and that a strong association existed between stone paving and important buildings such as temples. As such, it makes sense that installing a stone floor would be seen as specifically mimicking the Temple, or as something associated with places of idol worship.

The Torah prohibits prostrating on stone floors. This may relate to known pagan practices. According to some, it applies only to decorative floors with figures. Alternatively, it may be part of the prohibition against mimicking the Temple, as stone paving was relatively rare in antiquity and was used primarily in buildings such as temples.

10. The synagogue in Gamla was unpaved except between its columns. Qiryat Sefer was paved with flagstones, but in Modiin the floor was covered in plaster. In the Byzantine Period, however, it was common to find synagogues with flagstones or mosaic floors. See Levine, *The Ancient Synagogue,* 55,69,70,323, 361. See also Blidstein, "Talmudic Prostration," 21 and 30 note 3.

11. Krauss, *Kadmoniyot Hatalmud* II.2, 340. The Latin *pavimentum* comes from pavio, meaning "beat down" or "tread." See also Yizhar Hirschfeld, *The Palestinian Dwelling in the Roman-Byzantine Period* (Israel Exploration Society, 1995), 270–1.

12. Sweeping a dirt floor levels it and fills in holes. See bShab 95a, which tells that in Mechoza, a rich city with paved floors, one could sweep floors on Shabbat.

# Iron Wall, Iron Dome

וְשָׁבַרְתִּי אֶת גְּאוֹן עֻזְּכֶם וְנָתַתִּי אֶת שְׁמֵיכֶם כַּבַּרְזֶל וְאֶת אַרְצְכֶם כַּנְּחֻשָׁה.
(ויקרא כו:יט)

And I will break the pride of your power, and I will make your skies as iron, and your earth as brass. (Vayikra 26:19)

THE Torah uses a simile comparing the skies to iron.[1] The motif of an iron barrier appears a number of times in rabbinic literature to indicate two properties: an impenetrable defense to keep things out; and an impermeable barrier, holding things in.

As an impenetrable defense, there are several parables concerning kings and fortresses. Avot deR. Natan records a story about a king surrounding his palace with an iron wall to protect against thieves.[2] a similar parable tells of a king who builds an iron wall to separate himself from his servants, as a way of testing their fidelity and willingness to go above and beyond.[3] A legend about the twelve sons of Yaakov in Egypt mentions a tower of iron.[4] The Babylonian Talmud describes the city of Rome as surrounded by mountains, the sea, deep fissures, and an iron wall.[5] The Jerusalem Talmud makes use of this imagery in a domestic setting: "Rabbi Yochanan says: "One who prays in his house – it is as if he has surrounded it with an iron wall."[6] In one midrash, an angel promises to protect Jerusalem from invasion with an iron wall.[7] The concept of an iron wall is also invoked in a legal setting in the Jerusalem Talmud, which quotes Rabbi Elazar's

---

1. In Devarim 28:23, the earth is compared to iron and the skies to brass.
2. ARN B 8, *shaala zo.*
3. Eliyahu Zuta 12 *im tomar, mipnei.*
4. Yalkut Shimoni, Bereshit 133 *vayikan et chelkat.*
5. bMeg 6b. See Samuel Krauss, *Kadmoniyot Hatalmud* (Moriah, 1913), Vol. 1 pt. 1, 51 note 2.
6. yBer 5:1 (8d).
7. EichaR 2:5. Other angels promise to do the same with walls of fire and water.

opinion that even an iron wall is insufficient protection against certain animals."[8] In all these cases, the phrase "iron wall" is used as shorthand for an impenetrable defense.

As an impermeable barrier, we similarly also find several examples of iron walls in rabbinic literature. Here the most common examples relate to prayers. Several parallel passages pertain to the priestly blessings, and state that if people are behind a wall but in front of the priests, "even an iron wall will not stop the blessing" from reaching them.[9] In the Talmud, R. Yehoshua ben Levi is quoted as saying that "even a partition of iron cannot stand between Israel and its Father in Heaven."[10] In contrast, R. Elazar states that ever since the destruction of the Temple, "an iron wall separates Israel and its Father in Heaven."[11] Not all examples deal with prayer. One midrash, marveling at the willpower that keeps a husband and wife separate during her menstruation, asks "What iron wall is there between them? And what iron pillar stands between them?"[12] The Talmud also employs an iron wall in a legal ruling, as a wall that can completely dam the flow of water.[13] A *beraita* rules that "If food and drink are left under a bed, even if it is covered by an iron vessel, a bad spirit comes to rest on it."[14] In these examples, the iron wall symbolizes the most hermetic barrier imaginable, regardless of whether the barrier is actually effective.

Coupled with these two metaphorical characteristics of an iron wall, there are a few instances in rabbinic literature in which an iron wall denotes a wall that can be built taller and more sturdily than a regular (masonry) wall. In Sofrim there is a legend about Abraham constructing a city made entirely of iron for the children of Ketura, "and the sun never shined within, due to its great height . . . ."[15] In the Talmud, Abaye asks whether a *sukka* built of iron is permissible, or if it is considered too permanent to meet the required nomadic nature of the temporary hut.[16] R. Elazar uses an iron pillar as a metaphor for something robust.[17] These three passages

---

8. yBK 4:9 (4c).

9. yBer 5:4 (9d), yGit 5:9 (47b). See also my commentary on Bamidbar 6:23.

10. bSot 38b, bPes 85b.

11. bBer 32b.

12. ShSR 7:7, *bitnech aramt.*

13. bEruv 48a and yBeit 5:6 (63b).

14. bPes 112a.

15. Sofrim 1:1.

16. bSuk 2a.

17. VayR 21:5. Josephus also mentions iron plating as a defense for siege machines, to make them "too heavy to overturn and almost fireproof." (*Jewish War* 3.283 in siege of Jopata, and 7.304 in Masada). This, however, does not refer to architectural elements, nor is it talking about solid iron.

specifically relate to the great strength of iron architecture in a literal manner, complimenting the figurative examples quoted above.

The imagery of iron walls (or pillars) appears often enough in rabbinic literature that it is fair to ask whether the Rabbis drew this language from some other source. The obvious places to look are in earlier Jewish literature and at the surrounding, non-Jewish culture. One example of an iron wall in the Bible can be found in a prophecy of Yechezkel, who is told to set up a model of Jerusalem and place an iron pan as a wall next to the city.[18] Radak writes that an iron wall is used in part because it symbolizes impermeability. The prophet Yirmiyahu similarly invokes an iron pillar, as a way of promising an impenetrable defense.[19] Iron appears in this context in Daniel's interpretation of Nebuchadnezzar's vision.[20] We can assume that the Rabbis were at least partially inspired by these verses.

What about the surrounding Roman and Sassanian cultures? There is little evidence that iron walls were in use at the time. Although iron was occasionally used in ancient Greek architecture as a type of early structural reinforcement, there are no examples of complete architectural elements made of iron.[21] The closest examples are an iron wall from a second century BCE tomb in China[22] and an iron pillar now on display in Delhi was probably made around the fourth century.[23] It seems that iron architectural elements were exceedingly rare in antiquity, and may not have existed at all in the Near East. Although metal elements are sometimes harder to find in the archaeological record due to later reuse of the metal, we would still expect some surviving examples or literary records if such elements did exist.

There is one example in Latin and Greek literature that similarly mentions an iron wall. Plutarch quotes the Greek poet Pindar as saying that fate cannot be stopped, neither by fire nor by an iron wall.[24] We also find two instances in Christian literature: In the New Testament, Peter is said to pass through an iron gate, which guarded the city of Antioch.[25] More

18. Yechezkel 4:3. Of interest is Zechariya 2:9, which speaks of a protective wall of fire, and bBK 60b which uses this verse to draw a parallel between the destructive nature of fire and its defensive properties.

19. Yirmiyahu 1:18. See Yirmiyahu 15:12 for another example of iron as infallible.

20. Daniel 2:40.

21. William Bell Dinsmoor, "Iron in Greek Architecture" in *American Journal of Archaeology*, Vol. 26 No. 2 (Apr.–Jun. 1922):148–158.

22. The Tomb of Duo Wan. Donald Wagner, *Iron and Steel in Ancient China* (Brill, 1993), 337.

23. R. Balasubramaniam, *Story of the Delhi Pillar* (Foundation Books, 2005), 2.

24. Plutarch, *Marcellus*, 29, quoting Pindar (fragment 232).

25. Acts 12.10. Here we are speaking of a gate, rather than a wall or pillar.

relevant is a story in the Alexander Romances, where Alexander is said to have built an iron wall to keep out Gog and Magog. This story also appears in Josephus[26] and the Quran,[27] with the inspiration for these stories most likely coming from fortifications built to defend Persia's frontier. However, here too the examples are meager and do not reflect a broad trend. Rather, it seems that the imagery in rabbinic literature was not influenced by existing architecture or literature in the Roman or Sassanian worlds.

Iron may have been chosen for a supposed mystical property. Several medieval customs held a belief that iron could protect a house: cemeteries were built with iron gates to keep the souls of the dead within; iron horseshoes were affixed above doorways; iron knives were sometimes buried under thresholds to keep out witches;[28] and the Talmud records the use of an all-metal knife for a healing ritual.[29] The Tosefta records several uses of iron that fall under "the ways of the Amorites," i.e. superstition, including throwing iron into a cemetery and placing iron under your head.[30] It could be that iron walls had an aura of providing special protection beyond their material properties.

Despite the possibilities presented above, the most likely reason for emphasizing an iron wall is that iron's physical properties are easily adapted to symbolize strength and infallibility. While iron did not appear much in architectural contexts in antiquity, it was commonly used for tools, nails, weapons, or armor.[31] Iron was a commonplace material, especially for objects that needed to be sturdy. The phrase "iron wall" would have been an easy choice for signifying a sturdy, impenetrable and impermeable barrier. In the same way that we now use the term "iron man," or "iron fist," iron is used as an adjective to connote strength and immovability. We find this use in rabbinic literature, such as in R. Akiva's origin story, where he decided that if water can erode stone, then "the words of Torah, which are hard as iron, can all the more so imprint itself on my heart."[32] R. Sheshet was said

---

26. Josephus, *The Jewish War*, 7.244.

27. Sura al-Kahf, 18:96–7.

28. Rosemary Guiley, *The Encyclopedia of Witches, Witchcraft and Wicca*. "Iron" (Checkmark Books, 2008), 179. A similar custom is mentions by Pliny the Elder.

29. bShab 67a.

30. tShab 6:12–13, 6:19.

31. One notable example appears in Julian *Orations* 2.63b, which describes the Parthian use of elephants with "iron towers full of archers" in war.

32. ARN A, 6 *davar acher*. Note the irony of his mode of death, raked with iron combs, as per bBer 61b, R. Yehuda ben Baba is also executed using iron tools (bSan 14a, bAZ 8b), perhaps indicating that iron was associated with the persecutions of the Romans.

to be a man as hard as iron,[33] and R. Ashi stated that "any scholar who is not hard as iron is not really a scholar."[34] We find the Torah described as possessing the "strength of iron."[35] But the best example is the common idiom for the property that a wife brings to a marriage which does not lose value for her, and is referred to as "iron sheep."[36]

Latin and Greek literature are also replete with these types of references to iron. In the works of Homer, iron appears primarily for tools, while bronze is employed for weapons (as we might expect from an epic set in the bronze age). Nonetheless, at this early stage of iron usage, iron still appears in epithets to indicate "strength, permanence and stubborn endurance."[37] Aeschines refers to "men of iron" who can endure long speeches.[38] In Aeschylus, *Prometheus Bound*, the chorus calls people who ignore Prometheus' plight "iron-hearted."[39] Bdelycleon calls his father "hard as iron."[40] Hesiod describes his generation as a "race of iron, and men never rest from labor and sorrow by day, and from perishing by night; and the gods shall lay sore trouble upon them."[41] Odysseus tells Penelope that "her breast is of iron."[42] Strabo describes an island called Iron Island "because of its ruggedness."[43] Cicero rebukes "iron-hearted men."[44] In short, iron is commonly used as an adjective meaning strong, unmoving, and impenetrable, both in rabbinic literature and in contemporary Latin and Greek literature. It is therefore not at all surprising to find it used similarly concerning architecture.

In modern times iron has been used similarly, and once again we can find iron used in architectural metaphors. The most obvious example is the Iron Curtain imagery of the Cold War, but in twenty-first-century Israel, the nearest and dearest instance is the Iron Dome, Israel's short-range rocket defense system. Designers originally tried the names "Anti-Kassam" and "Golden Dome," but these were rejected in favor of the moniker "Iron

33. bMen 95b.
34. bTaan 4a.
35. BamR 14:4.
36. mYev 7:1, tYev 9:1.
37. Andrew Lang, "Bronze and Iron in Homer" in *Revue Archéologique* (June 1906), 280.
38. Aeschines. *Against Ctesiphon*, 3:166
39. Aeschylus. *Prometheus Bound,* 244. See also his *Seven Against Thebes* 39.
40. Aristophanes, *Wasps,* 875.
41. Hesiod, *Works and Days* 140.
42. Homer, *The Odyssey,* 23.170.
43. Strabo, *Geography*, 10.5
44. Cicero, *Orations, The Fourteen Orations against Marcus Antonius* 8:8.

Dome."[45] Although the selection was made primarily for its non-political nature, the name taps into an existing iconography of iron as an infallible and unbreakable substance; any architectural feature made of iron acquires a mythical aura of strength. Just as the Rabbis spoke of iron walls as absolute barriers, today we use metaphors of iron architectural elements to conjure up a sense of safety and protection. While the Torah originally used iron skies as a punishment, today the iron dome is a blessing.

45. http://www.ynet.co.il/articles/0,7340,L-4207167,00.html.

# Ovens and Courtyards

בְּשִׁבְרִי לָכֶם מַטֵּה לֶחֶם וְאָפוּ עֶשֶׂר נָשִׁים לַחְמְכֶם בְּתַנּוּר אֶחָד וְהֵשִׁיבוּ לַחְמְכֶם בַּמִּשְׁקָל וַאֲכַלְתֶּם וְלֹא תִשְׂבָּעוּ. (ויקרא כו:כו)

When I break your staff of bread, ten women shall bake your bread in one oven, and they shall deliver your bread again by weight, and you shall eat and not be satisfied. (Vayikra 26:26)

As part of a list of consequences for not keeping the commandments, the Torah describes the destitute conditions that will result. The Torah paints a picture of several women sharing an oven and carefully keeping track of every bit of food produced due to the scarcity of resources.

Although this verse depicts great hunger, the focus of the scene is clearly the shared oven. Commentators raise at least three possibilities for what is forcing the women to share one oven. Rashi writes that the women do not have enough wood to heat the oven individually and must pool their wood to cook bread. Rashbam explains the motivation differently: the individual women do not have enough bread to fill an oven on their own. For the bread to cook properly, they must team up to fill the oven.[1] A third possibility alluded to by Ibn Ezra, is that the women cannot afford, or cannot access, the equipment needed to bake. Rather than use a private oven, they have no choice but to use the communal one and share it with their neighbors.

Despite the negative depiction of the shared oven, the imagery used by the Torah recalls a well-known reality of life in the first neighborhoods built beyond the Jerusalem city walls. Nachlaot, Shaarei Chesed, Even Yisrael, and Nachalat Shiva each had a communal oven in a central courtyard that was used by the general population of the neighbor. These ovens

1. The Netziv recalls in HaEmek Davar that R. Shimon ben Elazar bases a halachic ruling on the fact that bread cooks better in a full oven. See bBeit 17a.

are generally remembered fondly, especially as part of nostalgic tours of the areas. In the more distant past, the archaeological record reveals that shared ovens were common: in Hirschfeld's survey of domestic architecture in Palestine, he notes that outdoor ovens were often shared by several households bordering a common courtyard.[2] This is also apparent in several rabbinical sources.[3]

Why is this normative and nostalgic condition depicted so negatively in this Torah verse? The difference between what is described in the Torah and what we see as a societal norm is no doubt the stress caused by lack of food. In a situation where there is enough to go around, there is no latent struggle involved in sharing an oven. However, when coupled with scarcity, the joint use of the oven becomes a fight for survival. For this reason, Rashbam's explanation – about lack of food – seems to me to be the most accurate. The shared oven is not what is causing the stress in this verse; rather it is the careful weighing of bread and the inability to fill stomachs.

2. Yizhar Hirschfeld, *The Palestinian Dwelling in the Roman-Byzantine Period* (Israel Exploration Society, 1995), 140–1.

3. tBM 8:20, mBB 2:1, mBB 3:5, mNed 4:1.

# Ruins Symbolism

וְנָתַתִּי אֶת עָרֵיכֶם חָרְבָּה וַהֲשִׁמּוֹתִי אֶת מִקְדְּשֵׁיכֶם וְלֹא אָרִיחַ בְּרֵיחַ
נִיחֹחֲכֶם. וַהֲשִׁמֹּתִי אֲנִי אֶת הָאָרֶץ וְשָׁמְמוּ עָלֶיהָ אֹיְבֵיכֶם הַיֹּשְׁבִים בָּהּ. וְאֶתְכֶם
אֱזָרֶה בַגּוֹיִם וַהֲרִיקֹתִי אַחֲרֵיכֶם חָרֶב וְהָיְתָה אַרְצְכֶם שְׁמָמָה וְעָרֵיכֶם יִהְיוּ
חָרְבָּה. (ויקרא כו:לא-לג)

And I will make your cities a waste and will bring your sanctuaries to desolation and I will not smell the savor of your sweet odors. And I will bring the land into desolation and your enemies that dwell in it shall be astonished at it. And I will scatter you among the nations and will draw out a sword after you and your land shall be desolate and your cities shall be a waste. (Vayikra 26:31–33)

As part of the covenant at Mount Sinai, the Torah lists the various positive and negative consequences of Bnei Yisrael's observance of the mitzvot. Keeping the mitzvot will result in safety, peace, and plenty. However, failing to keep them will have the opposite results.

Among the many negative consequences listed in the Torah is the destruction of Bnei Yisrael's cities and holy sanctuaries, leaving them as ruins. The Sifra gives two seemingly contradictory interpretations of these verses. On the one hand, it views the desolation of the land as a positive thing – the state of ruin means other people will not move in and supplant Bnei Yisrael, building up a new civilization in place of the old one. On the other hand, the Sifra also sees the waste and desolation of the land negatively – the destruction is total and the ruins indicate that there will be no immediate rebuilding or quick return from exile.[1] How can the same destruction be viewed from such different perspectives?

The symbolism of ruins, employed in these verses, is a motif that appears in several biblical stories, prophecies, and rabbinic literature. While

1. Sifra Bechukotai, perek 6:6 and perek 7:1. For a more positive view, see Sifra Bechukotai perek 6:5.

ruin-symbolism became especially popular in art after the Renaissance, it existed in ancient times as well, a natural outcome of the many ruins that dotted the landscape due to war, migration, and natural disasters. Ruins have come to symbolize several different ideas.

Most commonly we find ruins as a symbol of destruction and punishment. Jewish prophets describe the ruins of proud civilizations, overflowing with wild flora and fauna, as a way of emphasizing the coming judgment.[2] The ruins themselves are cause for shame and embarrassment, and mocked by other nations.[3] In this guise, ruins are an indication of abandonment – not just the people abandoning the site, but they themselves being abandoned by God.[4]

However, ruins can also be a type of monument, a way of remembering the past. We find this in the story of Yericho, where the city is to remain in ruins,[5] and rebellious cities, which are to remain a "heap forever."[6] In some situations, ruins are left as reminders of some injustice – until recently the Churva synagogue in Jerusalem was left as a ruin in part to serve as evidence of the mistreatment of holy sites by the Jordanians after 1948.[7] Ruins can testify to a historic connection, as is done in many archaeological sites in Israel. They can promote contemplation and repentance.[8] Furthermore, as long as ruins exist, there can be hope to rebuild.[9] In such a case the ruins can symbolize the potential for redemption.[10] Ruins can therefore be viewed positively – as a reminder, a connection, and a source of inspiration.

A large component of the Sifra's positive spin on ruins is that they are uncivilized and hard to inhabit. This existence beyond the edge of

---

2. See, among many examples, Yishayahu 17:1, Yirmiyahu 49:33, Yechezkel 26:4–5, 12–14, and 35:4, Micha 1:6–7, and Tzephania 2:14.

3. Yirmiyahu 49:17–18 and 50:14–16, Yechezkel 5:13–15, and Nechemia 2:17.

4. See also yAZ 3:1 (42b), where R. Yochanan rules that one may look at fallen pagan sculptures, as this is symbolic of their downfall.

5. Yehoshua 6:26.

6. Devarim 13:17.

7. For ancient examples, see Livy, *The History of Rome* 21.19.9–10, Isocrates, *Panegyricus* (4) 156, and Lycurgus, *Against Leocrates* 1.81.

8. Such is the ruling in mMeg 3:3, which states that one should not pull out the weeds growing in the ruins of a synagogue, since they add to the anguish (*agmat nefesh).* We find a list of ways in which synagogue ruins, which retain their holiness, must be respected, including no rope-making, hunting, or drying fruits. This implies that these were normative uses for ruins.

9. As described in Yechezkel 36.

10. One theory about the Bar Kochba revolt is that Hadrian's decision to found Aelia Capitolina on the site of Jerusalem, and effectively erase the ruins of the Jewish city, was the final straw that triggered the revolt. See my commentary on Bamidbar 11:16.

civilization is one of the most prevalent characteristics of ruins. Although ruins could exist within the city fabric – the Talmud commonly uses "ruins" as a synonym for open, public space in a city[11] – they were thought to foster the less savory segments of society. We find stories of murder, prostitution, demons, and thieves gathering in ruins.[12] One illustrative passage describes R. Yosi entering ruins to pray and encountering both Eliyahu and a heavenly voice within but learning that we do not enter ruins "due to suspicion [of encounters with prostitutes], due to collapse, and due to harming spirits (*mazikin*).[13] A country in ruins, as the Land of Israel largely remained – was far less likely to attract new settlers and irrevocably displace Bnei Yisrael.

The different perspectives of ruins have a lot to do with one's relationship to them – are they "our" ruins or the ruins of others? How were they formed? What narratives do we tell about them, and what moral lessons do we want to learn from them? This is evident in the different blessings recited upon seeing Jewish and non-Jewish ruins.[14] But nowhere is this disparity clearer than with the ruins of Jerusalem.

The destruction of Jerusalem was generally seen as punishment. The Romans, who wrought the destruction, saw the ruins as a testament to their own strength and the just result of the Jewish revolt. Josephus explains that the city was destroyed but that three towers were left "to show later generations what a proud and mighty city had been humbled by the gallant sons of Rome."[15]

Christians, like the Jews, tend to see the ruins as a symbol of the Jews' failure to keep the commandments. Both groups draw upon the same biblical tradition of ruins in describing Jerusalem, so it is not surprising that they use similar imagery. Eusebius, an early historian of Christianity, describes the site of the Temple as a storehouse and quarry, with stones carted off for reuse.[16] Jerome describes the scene on the Ninth of Av, where the wretched Jews groan over the ruins.[17]

In Jewish sources, we find a third take. Roman general Titus commanded that the city be leveled, but due to divine intervention, the western side – where the three towers mentioned by Josephus stood – was left intact.[18]

---

11. As in bEruv 104a, tBM 2:23, bBK 57a, and bMK 2a.
12. bKet 13a–b and tSan 8:3.
13. bBer 3a.
14. bBer 58b.
15. Josephus, *Jewish War* 7:1.
16. Eusebius, *Proof of the Gospel* 8.9–15 (406b–407b).
17. Jerome, *On Zephaniah* 1.15–16.
18. EichaR 1:32. For historicity of this source, see Meir Ben Shahar, "The Prediction

This was not by Roman plan, but because the Divine Presence remained in that section. The message here is that despite all the destruction, God has not abandoned Bnei Yisrael completely. The same tact is taken in the famous narrative that tells of a group of rabbis ascending to Jerusalem and seeing a fox on the Temple Mount, in the area of the Holy of Holies. There is an acknowledgment of wrongdoing, but also an affirmation that the connection remains and that redemption will one day come.[19]

Ruins are powerful symbols that can indicate several different ideas. They are sorrowful but can also help preserve memory and connection to a site. The perspective is often tied to one's connection to the ruins. Therefore, it is not surprising to find multiple readings, both positive and negative, in the Sifra.

to Vespasian" in *Josephus and the Rabbis* Vol. 2 (YBZP, 2017) 656 note 184. (Hebrew)

19. bMak 24b.

# Appraising Apartments: The Kohen's Role in Sanctifying a House

וְאִישׁ כִּי יַקְדִּשׁ אֶת בֵּיתוֹ קֹדֶשׁ לַה׳ וְהֶעֱרִיכוֹ הַכֹּהֵן בֵּין טוֹב וּבֵין רָע כַּאֲשֶׁר
יַעֲרִיךְ אֹתוֹ הַכֹּהֵן כֵּן יָקוּם. (ויקרא כז:יד)

And when a man shall sanctify his house to be dedicated to the Lord, then the priest shall value it, whether it be good or bad; as the priest shall value it, so shall it stand. (Vayikra 27:14)

THE Torah details several different types of donations that can be made to the Temple. One category mentioned is consecrating one's house, (making it *hekdesh).* The ownership of the house then passes to the Temple, though it can be redeemed by the owner (or someone else). This is done by paying the value of the house plus an additional twenty percent.

As opposed to consecrating a person, where there are set values based on age and gender, redeeming a consecrated house has no set price list prescribed by the Torah. Rather, a kohen is appointed to serve as the appraiser and determine the market value of the house.[1] No details are given as to how the kohen does this work or how he determines a value. The Torah only instructs that his word is the law, regardless of whether the price he determines is good or bad. No appeal process is available.[2]

The need for an appraiser is fairly common in architecture. Law codes typically allow for someone whose property value is harmed by a new development to receive recompense. In such a case, the planning board evaluates whether there is merit in the claim and determines a monetary value for the devaluation of the property.[3] Similarly, when new zoning

1. This is similar to the role a kohen plays in determining *tzaraat*; presumably here, like in that case, he is allowed to consult with experts and simply pronounce the value ritualistically.

2. Rambam rules that there is a set value for a house, and that no evaluation is needed by the kohen. See Rambam Hilchot Erchim Vecharamim 5:3.

3. *Chok Hatichnun Vehabeniya* 198.

laws *increase* a property's value, the owner is required to pay a tax on fifty percent of this increase.[4] A list of appraisers is maintained by the government for this purpose. However, in these situations, the law provides for an appeal process once an initial sum is determined.

Given the high stakes involved, why would the Torah not care about determining an accurate value of the house, going as far as saying that the valuation is final, "good or bad"? Two factors influence this position. First, donations to the Temple tend to err in favor of the Temple. There is concern that someone might accidentally retain money that ought to go to the Temple – a violation of *me'ila* – and so there are built-in safeguards to keep this from happening. There are even different sets of measurement units used for Temple workers to ensure workers don't accidentally overcharge the Temple.[5] It is therefore not surprising that the Torah turns over the appraisal to a kohen and declares that his word is final. Any appeal would only confuse the matter and leave doubts as to whether certain monies are sanctified.

Nonetheless, there is still a certain sense of unfairness. How can someone make a donation without knowing – even roughly – what the value of that donation will be? This leads to the second factor. Why would someone dedicate their house in the first place, when they could just as easily – perhaps *more* easily – give a set value for their donation? The answer is that a house is symbolic in a way that outshines any set number. This is akin to giving a donation that is a factor of eighteen – the number is somewhat arbitrary, but it symbolizes something greater due to its numeric, *gematriya* value. The person who donates the value of their house is no doubt motivated by gratitude and seeks to make a fitting donation that reflects this feeling. The house symbolizes the blessings received from God and is, therefore, a worthy donation. In such a scenario, the donator is not in a mindset to quibble over the precise value of his house; rather, the donor is expressing thanks to the Creator for everything he or she possesses. Here too, any appeals process would detract from the spirit of the donation.

The use of a kohen appraiser in setting a value for a consecrated house makes sense for two reasons: it prevents any doubts about *me'ila,* and it jibes with the mindset of the patron who is making this donation magnanimously.

4. Ibid, 196א, Appendix 3, 2–4.
5. mKel 17:9, bMen 98a. See my commentary on Vayikra 19:35–36.

# BAMIDBAR

# The Levite Camp and Hierarchical Cities

וְהַלְוִיִּם יַחֲנוּ סָבִיב לְמִשְׁכַּן הָעֵדֻת וְלֹא יִהְיֶה קֶצֶף עַל עֲדַת בְּנֵי יִשְׂרָאֵל וְשָׁמְרוּ הַלְוִיִּם אֶת מִשְׁמֶרֶת מִשְׁכַּן הָעֵדוּת. (במדבר א:נג)

But the Leviim shall pitch round about the *Mishkan* of the testimony, that there be no wrath upon the congregation of Bnei Yisrael, and the Leviim shall keep the charge of the *Mishkan* of the testimony. (Bamidbar 1:53)

BNEI Yisrael's camp in the desert was set up in a series of nested squares radiating outward from the *Mishkan* in the center. The Leviim were instructed to camp around the *Mishkan*, with the rest of the tribes arranged in the ring beyond. As the Leviim were charged with taking care of the *Mishkan* and its vessels, it made sense that they were closest to the center. Some commentators learn from this verse that the Leviim were supposed to act as a buffer, restricting access to the *Mishkan*.[1] The Leviim also served as an honor guard, adding to the pomp and reverence of the sacred place.[2]

The concentric plan was not just for the generation in the desert but also for future generations in Jerusalem. The city of Jerusalem was arranged with three corresponding rings: the city at large was comparable to the Israelite camp, the Temple Mount was akin to the Levite camp, and within the *Azara* was the center ring, the Divine camp.[3] The Mishna gives a finer gradation of the rings of holiness, listing ten divisions.[4] A different ten-part

1. Ibn Ezra and Chizkuni. People who were spiritually impure were restricted from entering the inner rings (bPes 67a).

2. Netziv and Ramban. See also SZ Bamidbar 18:4. Kohanim stood guard at three positions on the inside of the complex, while the Leviim guarded twenty-one posts outside, as per Sifri Bamidbar 116 and bTam 26a. For the guard posts, see mTam 1:1 and mMid 1:1. Acts 4:1 and 5:24 mention the captain of the Temple guard.

3. tKel BK 1:12, Sifri Bamidbar 1, Rambam Hilchot Beit Habechira 7:11.

4. mKel 1:6. The ten rings are the Land of Israel < walled cities < Jerusalem < Temple

division is mentioned in reference to the departure of God's presence from Jerusalem following the destruction of the Temple.[5]

While the rings of holiness are two-dimensional, they may have also existed in section. The Talmud discusses whether sacrificial animals can be slaughtered on the roof of the *Heichal*[6] and whether the roofs around the courtyard share its sanctity.[7] Though this type of vertical division is never explicitly described, it does seem that there was three-dimensional consideration, so that instead of rings we can instead picture spheres.

There are many historical examples of cities designed with increasingly restricted zones of access. Examples include Hamadan,[8] Baghdad, Srirangam, and Beijing. This type of urban design is especially common when cities are arranged to accentuate religious or administrative hierarchy. They serve, as architectural historian Spiro Kostof writes, to "engrave a pattern of faith and government." In Jerusalem, God sits at the center, surrounded by the priests and Leviim – an order built in stone, that strengthens this cosmic understanding of how the world is arranged.[9] Anchoring the Temple at the center of this hierarchical diagram helps the arrangement appear permanent and unchanging. The city plan reinforces religious beliefs.

The plan of Jerusalem is interesting in light of the different centers of power in the city. Jerusalem housed both the Temple and the royal residence. Yet, while the Bible focuses on the monarchy as the driving force in ancient Israel, the city's arrangement (as depicted in rabbinic literature) focuses on the Temple. As if to further emphasize the subservience of the monarchy to the Temple, we are told that it was the king who arranged the city this way. Prior to David's and Shlomo's reigns, the central shrine was located away from the capital. When the Temple was established in Jerusalem, it presumably helped the monarchy by reinforcing that city's role as the nexus of power in ancient Israel, but it also firmly established the primacy of the Temple ahead of the king. David and Shlomo's shared

---

Mount < *Cheil* < Women's Courtyard < Israelite Courtyard < Kohanim Courtyard < between the *Ulam* and altar < *Heichal* < Holy of Holies. See also SZ Bamidbar 5:2, which hints that Transjordan has a status higher than other lands. The seven divisions *within* the Temple may reflect a worldview that holds the number seven as especially significant, including seven astronomical spheres and seven heavenly temples. See Rachel Elior, *The Three Temples* (Littman Library of Jewish Civilization, 2004), 77.

5. bRH 31a, EichaR (Petichta 25), ARN A, 34:7.

6. bZev 107b.

7. mMS 3:8, bPes 86a, bShev 17b.

8. Also known as Ecbatana, as described by Herodotus, *Histories* 1:98. It was the capital of the Medes.

9. Spiro Kostof, *The City Shaped* (Thames and Hudson, 1999), 164.

effort to build the Temple is therefore an extremely pious and subservient act, placing their belief in the centrality of Temple worship ahead of their own monarchy.[10]

In addition to the monarchy and Temple, rabbinic literature describes a third center of authority in the city: the Sanhedrin. As opposed to the palace, the Sanhedrin was said to have been located on the Temple Mount, in the Chamber of Hewn Stone.[11] In several locations, the Rabbis note that the Sanhedrin was to be located near the Temple altar.[12] The Rabbis draw a parallel between the ten levels of withdrawal for the Divine Presence and the ten stages of exile for the Sanhedrin.[13] Nonetheless, the Rabbis could not replicate the same architectural demonstration of hierarchy. No separate grand court was ever established on its own, which provided a concrete architectural representation of their authority. The Rabbis recorded these traditions at a time when there was neither a functioning monarchy nor Temple nor even Jewish autonomy, and lacking the ability to physically build an architectural hierarchy, they instead sought to subsume the previous hierarchies and step into the role of central authority. The Sanhedrin is described as a part of the Temple complex, integrated into the well-established order in Jerusalem.

It may be appealing to view the arrangement of the Temple and the Sanhedrin as two separate authorities which must exist in balance, like judicial, legislative, and executive branches of a government. However, this view is contradicted by the story of Yoav, who after being condemned to death by King David, ran to the altar for refuge and was nonetheless executed.[14] In that story, commentators point out that the altar had no authority to overrule Yoav's death penalty. A similar dynamic plays out in the Mishna: in one case, witnesses arrive to testify about the new moon

---

10. Spiro Kostof describes three potential relationships between the "secular" and the religious authority: a) the secular power subsumes the religious, where the head of states is also the chief priest. b) the religious power takes over the secular authority c) the two remain independent and locked in a power struggle in which neither can assert authority over the other. See Kostof, *The City Assembled* (Bulfinch Press, 1992), 82–5.

11. mMid 5:4. In this mishna the Sanhedrin is specifically assigned the function of judging the priests.

12. MdRY Yitro (Bachodesh) 11 on Shemot 21:1, MdRY Mishpatim (Nezikin) 4, commenting on Shemot 21:14, and yMak 2:6 (31d). See also bShab 15a, which connects the relocation of the Sanhedrin with its consequential inability to adjudicate capital cases.

13. bRH 31a–b.

14. Melachim I 2:28. The story of Yoav is explicitly raised alongside the various sources quoted above, making it clear that the altar was in no way meant to balance the authority of the court.

and are accepted by the kohanim, but they are overruled by the court.[15] Another mishna, describing the preparations of the high priest before Yom Kippur, tells that leaders of the rabbinic court deputized the high priest and made him swear to follow their instructions.[16] The view of checks and balances is roundly rejected by R. S.R. Hirsch, who writes that "In Jewry there are not two principles which mutually control and modify each other, like Church and State, Justice and Mercy etc."[17] The judgment of the court is seen as the Divine Will, and the altar, therefore, holds no separate authority that can overrule this judgment.

Instead of seeing the altar and the Sanhedrin as competing authorities, R. Yitzchak Levy argues that the Sanhedrin's authority is derived from the altar and the Temple. The proximity of the altar to the court is the very thing that grants the Sanhedrin the right to judge capital offenses.[18] The altar cannot override the court, but it does symbolize the source of the court's authority.

The arrangement of Bnei Yisrael in the desert, and later in Jerusalem, helped reinforce the central place of God in the Jewish cosmology. The monarchy and rabbinate both existed within this framework, but in a manner that diagrammatically placed them in a subservient position to the Temple.

15. mRH 1:7.

16. mYom 1:5.

17. Commentary on Shemot 21:14.

18. R. Yitzchak Levy, "Placing the Sanhedrin Next to the Altar (ii)", lecture 186, online at https://www.etzion.org.il/en/lecture-186-placing-sanhedrin-next-altar-ii. In contrast, see ShmR 2:4, which states that the Sanhedrin derives its ability to administer capital punishment from Mount Chorev, i.e. the Torah.

# The Pleasure of Good Design

וְלֹא יָבֹאוּ לִרְאוֹת כְּבַלַּע אֶת הַקֹּדֶשׁ וָמֵתוּ. (במדבר ד:כ)

But they shall not go in to see the holy things as they are being covered, lest they die. (Bamidbar 4:20)

THE Leviim were charged with transporting the disassembled *Mishkan* but were forbidden from looking at the unpacked holy vessels. They had to be particularly careful in dealing with the Holy of Holies, making sure not to accidentally catch a glimpse of the sacred space.[1]

The Mishna details some of the methods that were taken to keep the builders from seeing inside the Temple.[2] The workers building the walls of the Temple's inner sanctuary could not work from within the walls, which was holy ground. They instead had to work from the outside. During construction, curtains were hung inside the plane of the walls until they reached eye-level, to keep workers from seeing into the holy space. When building the outer courtyard walls, the builders could stand inside the territory, and therefore curtains were erected *outside* the walls of the courtyard, this time to keep onlookers from peeping.

Once the Temple was completed, the prohibition against seeing inside the holy spaces still created technical difficulties for workers. It was occasionally necessary to make repairs in the Holy of Holies. The Mishna describes service openings in the attic above the Temple. When required, workers were lowered down into the sanctuary through these openings

1. See the previous verse, Bamidbar 4:19.

2. mEduy 8:6. Rambam writes that the construction workers should ideally be kohanim in a spiritually pure state. If none are available, kohanim with physical defects are the next best, followed by Leviim and then Israelites. See tKel BK 1:9 and Rambam Hilchot Beit Habechira 7:23.

in primitive elevators[3] that were enclosed on three sides. Only one side of the lift was open, giving the workers access to make repairs while blocking their view of other parts of the holy space.[4]

The Mishna uses a peculiar phrase, stating that these precautions must be made for the worker "so that his eyes won't be fed from the Holy of Holies."[5] This expression compares the enjoyment one gets from *seeing* with the enjoyment one gets from *eating*. Rashi emphasizes this, writing that the vision of beauty provides "pleasure like food that satiates."[6] This analogy takes one of the basest pleasures people can feel – eating – and compares it with seeing. While sight can be supremely enjoyable, we rarely think of it as providing the same level of physical satisfaction as does eating. Nonetheless, this is the way this mishna chooses to describe the enjoyment provided by a glimpse of the Holy of Holies.

For design professionals, the way this mishna describes the pleasure of seeing the Holy of Holies is empowering. Good design can affect physical reactions and create pleasure for those who experience it. As a farmer might take pride in creating food for his neighbors, designers and architects can similarly revel in making the world a more beautiful, enjoyable place.

3. Similar mechanisms existed in Roman time, as in the Colosseum, where elevators were used to lift animals into the arena. In those cases, capstans were used to help generate the power needed to raise the animals. The Mishna does not relate what mechanism was in place to raise and lower the workers, or how they remained suspended for the duration of their work. It is possible that similar devices were utilized. Another comparable device was used by soldiers to overrun caves of Mount Arbel. See Josephus, *The Jewish War* 1.309 and *Antiquities* 14.420, which says that these chests were suspended from chains.

4. mMid 4:5.

5. This expression is used in a number of other contexts, including sights forbidden due to *erva* (Midrash Shmuel 13:8) and windows with a view (mOhal 13:4), where the expression is "to feast your eyes." The Kli Yakar on Shemot 21:26 implies that this wording comes from Mishlei 27:20, "… and the eyes of man are never satiated."

6. Rashi, bPes 26a, *vayezonu*.

# Tile Openings in the Temple

וְלָקַח הַכֹּהֵן מַיִם קְדֹשִׁים בִּכְלִי חָרֶשׂ וּמִן הֶעָפָר אֲשֶׁר יִהְיֶה בְּקַרְקַע הַמִּשְׁכָּן יִקַּח הַכֹּהֵן וְנָתַן אֶל הַמָּיִם. (במדבר ה:יז)

And the priest shall take holy water in an earthen vessel and of the dust that is on the floor of the *Mishkan* the priest shall take and put it into the water. (Bamidbar 5:17)

ONE of the ingredients in the potion that is used to test a *sota* was "the dust that is on the floor of the *Mishkan*." Only dirt from inside the *Mishkan* was acceptable.[1] However, if dirt was not available inside the *Mishkan,* one could bring dirt in from the outside, scatter it on the ground of the *Mishkan* and then gather it for the *sota* mixture.[2]

The Talmud explains that the same rules which applied in the *Mishkan* were also applicable in the Temple. However, while the *Mishkan* had no paving, the Temple was paved with stone and therefore had no exposed earth from which to gather dirt. To solve this problem, the designers of the Temple were forced to innovate. They included an access hatch in the pavement of the *Heichal,* described in the Mishna: "there was a place, one square cubit, with a marble slab which had a ring affixed to it. [The priest] would lift it up and take dust from underneath."[3] Beneath the tile was earth, which could be gathered as needed for a *sota.*[4]

1. See Ibn Ezra and Chizkuni.

2. bSot 15b–16a. A similar situation exists today in the El Santuario de Chimayo church in New Mexico, where devoted pilgrims go to gather dirt and either rub it on their bodies or eat it. During busy times, the caretakers must truck in dirt from nearby hills daily to replace that which is appropriated by pilgrims.

In a similar discussion, mChal 2:1 asks whether produce grown in dirt imported from outside Israel requires tithing and the rules of *shemita.* In yOrl 2:1 (61a) R. Yoshiya is said to have brought plants from abroad with dirt around their roots to circumvent the laws of *orla.*

3. mSot 2:2, SZ Bamidbar 5:17, and Sifri Bamidbar 10.

4. Precisely cut stone lends itself to seamless access openings. For example, Pausanias

Two other locations in the Temple had similar access panels: the room where the priests slept had a hiding place for the keys to the Temple[5] and next to the altar there was a subterranean opening for cleaning out the altar's drain.[6] The Mishna describes the same detail for each location – a one cubit opening with a ring. However, each situation had different functional requirements. While a square cubit, or about forty-five square centimeters, would be ample size for gathering dirt for a *sota*, it would be an unnecessarily large size for storing a key and would have been a tight squeeze for a person to fit through to clean out the altar drain. While a ring made sense to lift the tile for gathering dirt, the hiding place for the keys was presumably meant to be kept secret, so it is odd to use a stone tile marked with a ring.[7]

While the removable tile for the *sota* ceremony appears in several midrashim, the other two access panels are only mentioned in Midot. The details of the tile – with a ring for lifting and the size of a square cubit – align with the requirements of the *sota* ceremony but make less sense for the other two functions. This suggests that the access hatch detail originally appeared in the context of the *sota* opening and the Mishna later elected to use the same description for the other two access panels. As the general purpose of Midot was to preserve the general features of the Temple rather than to serve as a precise set of building documents, this is not such a radical idea. It was sufficient to note that three places in the Temple required an access panel and to reference a single design solution for each instance.

---

describes two builders, Trophanus and Agamedes, who built a treasury and included a stone that could be removed from the outside, which they used to break into the treasury and steal from it on a regular basis. See Pausanias, *Description of Greece* 9.37.5.

5. mMid 1:9.

6. mMid 3:3.

7. See yShek 6:1 (49c) for paving stones over the hiding spot of the Holy Ark, which had no ring.

NASO

# *Birchat Kohanim* and Solid/Void Theory

דַּבֵּר אֶל אַהֲרֹן וְאֶל בָּנָיו לֵאמֹר כֹּה תְבָרְכוּ אֶת בְּנֵי יִשְׂרָאֵל אָמוֹר לָהֶם. (במדבר ו:כג)

Speak to Aharon and to his sons, saying: "Thus shall you bless Bnei Yisrael: You shall say to them." (Bamidbar 6:23)

Aharon and his sons are instructed to bless Bnei Yisrael. This blessing is known as *birchat kohanim* and is done daily in Israel. While the text of the blessing appears in this Torah portion, the protocol for the blessing is learned from Aharon's blessing during the dedication of the *Mishkan*.[1] The kohanim line up facing the congregation and only those congregants who are in front of the kohanim receive the blessing. Even if people, furniture, or metal partitions are between the kohanim and the congregants, the blessing is still transmitted to those located in front of the kohanim.[2] This is even true if someone is outside the building, so long as they have a good reason not to be inside.[3]

While walls and other obstructions are not relevant in the case of the priestly blessing, they do sometimes play a role in determining who is included in a *minyan* of ten men needed for communal prayers. Tosafot learn in a related discussion in the Talmud that standing behind a metal partition *would* exclude you from the *minyan*.[4]

More interesting, however, is a situation where a full partition does not exist but is merely implied. The Talmud presents a case in which there

1. Vayikra 9:22.
2. bSot 38b, yBer 5:4 (9d). For a discussion about metal partitions, see my commentary on Vayikra 26:19.
3. See Tosafot on bSot 38b. People in the synagogue who do not make the effort to move a few steps and put themselves in front of the kohanim are actively excluding themselves from the blessing. Therefore, they do not receive the blessing. A similar calculus exists for other communal prayers, which are said to include agricultural workers who are unable to attend, provided they are outside of the city. See bRH 35a.
4. bSot 38b–39a, Tosafot *mechitza*, based on bEruv 92b.

are two adjoining rooms, one wider than the other. The wall between the two spaces has been demolished, leaving a "T" shaped space (*fig. 73a*). Someone sitting in the wider space views the edges of the broken wall and still "reads" the spaces as separate (*fig. 73b*). From this perspective, the two wall fragments still seem to be part of the same wall, so the spaces read as two separate rooms. Therefore, if the prayer leader is in the wider room, someone in the smaller room is considered to be in a separate space and is not included in the *minyan*. However, from the perspective of someone in the smaller room, who does not see any walls separating the two spaces, it all appears to be one big room (*fig. 73c*). Therefore, if the prayer leader were in the smaller room, people in the wider space *would* be included in the *minyan*.[5] This is a rare halachic application of architectural solid/void theory, in which walls can imply space without fully enclosing it.[6] A continuous wall need not be present for the space to seem divided.

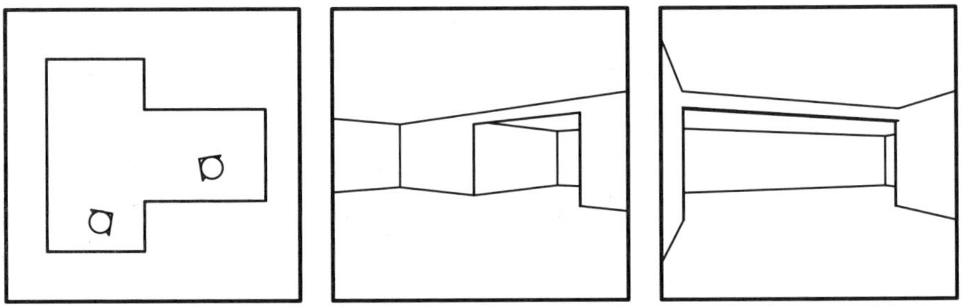

(a) (b) (c)

73. T-shaped room: (a) plan (b) from inside the larger room (c) from inside the smaller room.

With *birchat kohanim,* the issue is one of broadcasting. So long as someone is positioned in front of the kohanim, the blessing is received. Only those who actively exclude themselves by standing in a location that shows contempt for the blessing, do not receive the blessing. However, for forming a *minyan,* it is necessary to be joined together in a single space. Therefore, partitions can divide the group in two, even if the division is only subjectively implied based on one's visual perspective.[7]

5. Shulchan Aruch OC 55:16–17.

6. Other examples include mEruv 9:2, concerning a large and small roof and a large courtyard and small courtyard; mEruv 9:4 concerning a bridge with walls on either side and whether we say that "the edge of the roof descends and closes;" and bEruv 94b, concerning a house with demolished walls from two directions.

7. The Be'ur Halacha in the Mishna Berura quotes a related discussion and similarly rules that there is a distinction between counting as part of a *minyan* (i.e. answering amen) and being included in *birchat kohanim.*

# Tectonic vs. Stereotomic Design And the *Menora*

וְזֶה מַעֲשֵׂה הַמְּנֹרָה מִקְשָׁה זָהָב עַד יְרֵכָהּ עַד פִּרְחָהּ מִקְשָׁה הִוא כַּמַּרְאֶה אֲשֶׁר הֶרְאָה ה' אֶת מֹשֶׁה כֵּן עָשָׂה אֶת הַמְּנֹרָה. (במדבר ח:ד)

And this was the work of the *menora*: beaten work of gold, from its base to its flowers, it was beaten work; according to the pattern which the Lord had shown Moshe, so he made the *menora*. (Bamidbar 8:4)

ONE of the special requirements for the construction of the *menora* was that it had to be "beaten work."[1] Although this was not a unique requirement among the various Temple vessels – the *keruvim* on the ark and the trumpets also had to be of beaten work[2] – it is most strongly associated with the *menora's* design.

The conventional way to construct an intricate candelabrum with various components – bowls, bulbs, and flowers – is to make each element separately and then join them together. However, commentators learn from our verse that the *menora* had to be made from a solid piece of gold and sculpted into the form of the *menora*.[3] Each of the seven branches had to be separated from the block and shaped to fit the description given in the Torah.

Such a requirement is somewhat counterintuitive and makes for a difficult crafting process. According to one midrash, Moshe was not able to figure out how to construct the *menora*. He had to resort to throwing the gold into a furnace, from whence the *menora* emerged miraculously.[4] Few commentators explain why this difficult method of fabrication was required. Malbim writes that these requirements ensured that the *menora*

1. This requirement also appears in Shemot 25:31.
2. Shemot 25:18, Bamidbar 10:2, and Sifri Bamidbar 72.
3. Rashi on this verse and on Shemot 25:31.
4. Tanchuma Behaalotecha 3.

would be the work of a top-notch artist.[5] The Netziv explains that the *menora* represents the Torah, so this mode of construction symbolizes the unity of Torah and warns against creating rifts that will result in two separate paths of Torah.

Although the *menora* is ideally made out of gold, this is not an absolute necessity. The Talmud relates that when the Maccabim captured the Temple, they needed to construct a new *menora* and did so out of iron spears coated in tin. Later, as the monarchs grew wealthier, this *menora* was replaced with silver and then finally one made of gold.[6] There is even a minority opinion that says wood can be used.[7] The Talmud explains that many of the requirements for the *menora* apply only when it is made from gold. When made of gold, the *menora* must weigh a precise amount (a *kikar*), it must have the right number of bowls, bulbs, and flowers and it must be of beaten work. When made of another metal, none of these requirements apply.[8]

Architectural historian Kenneth Frampton wrote an essay in which he distinguished between what he called tectonic and stereotomic construction. Tectonic[9] construction involves building something upon the earth with light-frame construction. Stereotomic[10] construction is building something heavy, *of* the earth. It is more a type of excavation – digging a form out from the earth, carving a shape out of existing material. Frampton wrote, "framework tends towards the aerial and dematerialization of mass, whereas the mass form is telluric, embedding itself deeper in the earth."[11] What this means is that while tectonics deemphasizes the material and the structure, stereotomics is all about the material.[12]

---

5. On Shemot 25:31.

6. bRH 24b. In some Greek temples existing components were replaced with more expensive duplicates. Pausanias describes a temple in which most of the columns were stone but an old oak column remained from the original design. (*Description of Greece* 5.16) See also Joseph Rykwert, *The Dancing Column* (MIT Press, 1988), 204.

7. bMen 28b and Sifri Bamidbar 61. The Talmud rules that the *menora* cannot be made of wood, bone, or glass.

8. Malbim explains that even other metals cannot be constructed piecemeal, but Rambam in Hilchot Beit Habechira 3:4 seems to say that a *menora* that isn't gold can be assembled from components.

9. From the same root as "architect." Tekton in Greek means carpenter or builder.

10. Stereo – solid; tomic – cutting.

11. Kenneth Frampton, *Studies in Tectonic Culture: The Poetics of Construction in Nineteenth and Twentieth Century Architecture*, (MIT Press, 1995) 3–8.

12. The tectonic/stereotomic distinction appears in a number of different halachot: 1) bBB 64a distinguishes between a *bor* and a *dut*, saying that they are both pits, but one is dug out and the other is built up. 2) bSan 47b and bMK 8b distinguish between an excavated and a built grave. 3) bSuk 4a–b distinguishes between a *sukka* whose walls

74. Ad-Deir, Petra, a very literal example of stereotomic architecture. (Photo by Berthold Werner, Wikimedia)

The distinction between tectonic and stereotomic construction helps explain the requirement to craft a golden *menora* from one solid block. The stereotomic construction emphasizes the pure, gold nature of the vessel. However, when the *menora* cannot be made from gold, there is no longer any reason to use stereotomic construction to highlight its physical composition.[13]

are built and one that has been partially excavated. Likewise, mSuk 1:8 disqualifies a *sukka* with stereotomic walls. 4) mOhal 6:6 distinguishes between built and excavated walls in the transmission of impurity. 5) yShab 8:1 distinguishes between built and excavated houses for the purpose of *me'ila*. 6) yAZ 4:4 distinguishes between a built and excavated idol. 7) bChul 16a distinguishes between a built and excavated wall of a house for determining if worshiping the house renders it forbidden for use.

13. One may also consider this requirement as related to Leon Battista Alberti's idea of *concinnitas*, where distinct parts of a unit must be designed together so that their overall composition exists in harmony. See Alberti, *De Re Aedificatoria*, 9:5.

# Building the Temple at Night

וּבְיוֹם הָקִים אֶת הַמִּשְׁכָּן כִּסָּה הֶעָנָן אֶת הַמִּשְׁכָּן לְאֹהֶל הָעֵדֻת וּבָעֶרֶב יִהְיֶה עַל הַמִּשְׁכָּן כְּמַרְאֵה אֵשׁ עַד בֹּקֶר. (במדבר ט:טו)

And on the day that the *Mishkan* was erected, the cloud covered the *Mishkan*, even the tent of the testimony, and at evening there was upon the *Mishkan* as it were the appearance of fire, until morning. (Bamidbar 9:15)

ALTHOUGH the Torah is concerned with the construction of the *Mishkan*, the Talmud learns from this verse that construction work on the Temple in Jerusalem cannot be done at night.[1] In the same discussion, the Talmud rules that work on the Temple does not override the prohibitions of Shabbat.[2]

The underlying assumption behind these discussions is that the Temple is of such vast importance that it should be completed in all haste and without any delays. When a building project is under a tight deadline, the contractors are often asked to keep workers on site for extra hours, including nights and weekends. Even before construction commences, the designers of the building may be asked to do the same, completing the plans in round-the-clock marathons and perhaps even with multiple shifts of workers toiling over the same drawings. We might well assume that building the Temple would occur under similar conditions. This notion is supported by the legend that rain fell only at night during the time of the Temple's construction, "so that the work was not hindered."[3] This was seen as a divine blessing of the building project – the work was so important

1. bShev 15b. For a tangential discussion of this prohibition, see my commentary on Shemot 15:17.

2. bYev 6a, based on Vayikra 19:30.

3. Josephus, *Antiquities* 15.425. See also Sifra Bechukotai perek 1:1, bTaan 23a, and VayR 35:9–10.

that God intervened to prevent any delays. Even so, the work was confined to daytime rather than following a more aggressive schedule.

Herod's renovation of the Temple had an additional difficulty, which in some projects leads to construction work at night and on weekends: it was the renovation of a functioning building. In such a situation, the developers often decide to limit the work to late-night or weekend hours, when the disruption to the existing services is minimal. While Josephus relates some concern about the continuous functioning of the Temple, he does not tell what arrangements were made to continue Temple services during the year-and-a-half of construction. We are only told that Herod prepared all the building materials ahead of time, as an added assurance to the Jews that he would complete the project.[4]

With the practical reasons for wanting to allow construction work at night and on weekends, why does the Talmud rule that such behavior is prohibited? Perhaps it is due to the deficiencies associated with an accelerated schedule. When a project is rushed to meet a deadline, the quality of work inevitably suffers. In a race against the clock, not all the defects that occur are corrected and not all details are completed as indicated. Errors in construction, when caught, are often accepted as part of the reality of an accelerated schedule, as no time exists to halt work and make corrections. This is a reality to which anyone who has worked on such a project can attest. For a project of such importance as the Temple, which demands the highest standards, an accelerated schedule would therefore not be acceptable.[5] The decision not to work on the Temple at night or on Shabbat both preserves the sanctity of Shabbat and helps maintain high standards for the Temple itself.

4. Josephus, *Antiquities,* 15:389–391. But see his *Jewish War* 5.187 as well as John 2:20, which imply a long building process. See also Vered Noam, "The Miracle of the Rainfall in Herod's Day" in *Josephus and the Rabbis,* ed. Tal Ilan and Vered Noam (YBZP, 2017) 411–416 (Hebrew).

5. As per R. Baruch Epstein in Torah Temima on this verse.

# Expanding Jerusalem

וַיֹּאמֶר ה׳ אֶל מֹשֶׁה אֶסְפָה לִּי שִׁבְעִים אִישׁ מִזִּקְנֵי יִשְׂרָאֵל אֲשֶׁר יָדַעְתָּ כִּי הֵם זִקְנֵי הָעָם וְשֹׁטְרָיו וְלָקַחְתָּ אֹתָם אֶל אֹהֶל מוֹעֵד וְהִתְיַצְּבוּ שָׁם עִמָּךְ. (במדבר יא:טז)

And the Lord said to Moshe, "Gather to me seventy men of the elders of Yisrael, who you know to be the elders of the people and officers over them, and bring them to the Tent of Meeting, that they may stand there with you." (Bamidbar 11:16)

THE city of Jerusalem has a special, holy standing, elevated from the rest of Israel. The city corresponds to the Israelite camp in the desert. Certain religious acts can only be done within its sacred boundaries, which are generally defined by its walls.[1]

Since the boundaries of Jerusalem have a sacred status, those boundaries cannot be altered as simply as the contour of a regular city. Rather, one mishna rules that only a high court of seventy-one members, the Sanhedrin, can change the boundaries of Jerusalem.[2] A second mishna mandates an even higher level of formality, demanding a king, a prophet, the *urim vetumim*, two thanksgiving offerings, and song, in addition to the Sanhedrin.[3] The Talmud explains that the offerings are paraded along the new perimeter of the city.[4] The Talmud derives these various requirements from several verses throughout the Bible. The above verse is quoted as the source for requiring the Sanhedrin to be present.[5] The sacred status of Jerusalem requires these extra rites for any expansion to alter the city's spiritual dimensions.

1. See my commentary on Bamidbar 1:53.
2. mSan 1:5.
3. mShev 2:2.
4. For another example of demarcating a boundary by walking, see bBB 100a with regard to a public right-of-way.
5. ySan 1:3 (19b). An abbreviated form of this argument is found in bSan 16b. See also Rambam Hilchot Beit Habechira 6:11–12.

Jerusalem's special religious standing makes it halachically unique in this regard. However, in some other cultures, special rites were also required for marking a city's border. Spiro Kostof describes several ceremonies, including the use of elephants (Antioch), ashes (Baghdad), flags (Gascony), and a variety of sacrifices.[6] Roman tradition called for the path of the city walls to be traced with a bronze plow pulled by a bull and a cow. At points where gates were to be located, the plow would be lifted out of the ground and carried across the opening.[7] Furthermore, Roman sources state that to erase a city, it must likewise be plowed.[8]

If, as per the Roman rite of plowing, a city can only be destroyed by undoing the rites that brought about its founding, then perhaps the logic works in reverse as well. Yericho was destroyed by circling it while blowing the *shofar*. Perhaps this implies that it was originally established with a rite involving *shofar* blowing.

In the years before the outbreak of the Bar Kochba revolt, Hadrian decided to remake the conquered Jerusalem as a Roman colony, Aelia Capitolina. The Roman rites for founding a city were enacted, and a plow yoked to a cow and bull circumscribed the city. A coin depicting this event was cast to celebrate the occasion. This coin, dating from around 130, is seen as proof that the decision to remake Jerusalem as Aelia Capitolina predated the Bar Kochba revolt (132–135), and may have been one of the primary triggers of the uprising. The Jews saw this as a tragedy, a definite step away from the possibility of quickly rebuilding the Temple. The Mishna recalls the plowing of the city as one of the five tragedies that occurred on Tisha B'av.[9]

The expansion of Jerusalem is also tied to prophetic visions of the Messianic era, when Jerusalem will be rebuilt and will become the world's premier city. According to this vision, the city will be enlarged,[10] connect with the Heavenly Jerusalem,[11] and gain many accoutrements such as nymphaea and tetrapyla, important civic features in the ancient

---

6. Spiro Kostof, *The City Assembled*, 11–12. See also Joseph Rykwert, *The Idea of a Town*, 168–9 for the rites of the Mande tribe, and 58 for the founding of Constantinople.

7. Plutarch, *Romulus*, 11, and Cato the Elder, *Origins*, 1.18, quoted in Isidore of Seville's *Etymologies*. Indian tradition had a similar rite.

8. Marus Servius Honoratus, *Commentary on the Aeneid of Vergil*, 4.212. See also Susan Stevens, "A Legend of the Destruction of Carthage" in *Classical Philology* 83,1 (1988) 39–41.

9. mTaan 4:6. This is somewhat ambiguous, as we do not know if the plowing in question was to erase the city or to reconsecrate the city as Aelia Capitolina.

10. PdRK 20:7, Sifri Devarim 1, bPes 50a.

11. bBB 75b.

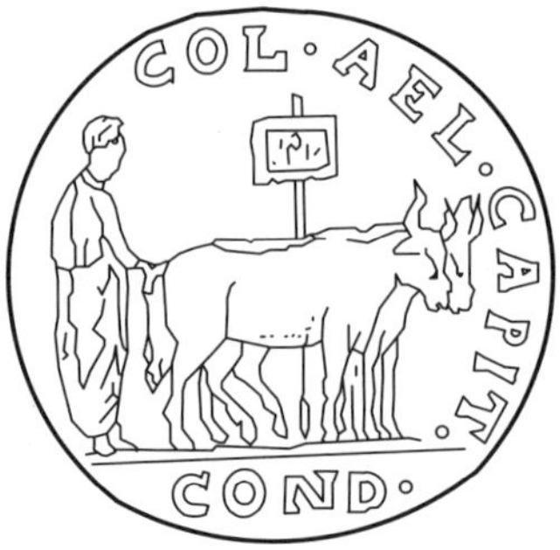


75. Hadrian coin celebrating the founding of Aelia Capitolina, 130 CE.

Roman empire.[12] In modern terms, we would expect messianic Jerusalem to have superlative public buildings, transportation, sanitation, parks, restaurants, etc.

The expansion of a city is normally seen as a straightforward process: as additional buildings are constructed, the city expands. However, even today and even in a normal city, there is still more involved than the physical landscape. The line around a municipality is a legal definition that must be codified and can have ramifications on taxes, services provided, and elections. Within the borders of a city, the municipality might be responsible for paving roads, providing sewage, and collecting garbage, while beyond the border no such services are provided. Following the Six-Day War, Jerusalem was expanding, bringing many new residents into the city and creating a new political entity. Other cities in Israel have also been redefined, such as Modiin and Tel Aviv, which were each expanded to take in neighboring towns. Still, the ceremonial expansion of Jerusalem discussed in rabbinic literature is different, in that it integrates an earthly boundary with a *spiritual* boundary of the city. It is this extra dimension that requires the involvement of ceremonial rites beyond the normal legal and physical measures.

12. bBB 75a, Midrash Tehilim 48:4, as discussed in Daniel Sperber, *The City in Roman Palestine*, 134–5.

# Basilicas and the Chamber of Hewn Stone

וַיֹּאמֶר ה׳ אֶל מֹשֶׁה אֶסְפָה לִּי שִׁבְעִים אִישׁ מִזִּקְנֵי יִשְׂרָאֵל אֲשֶׁר יָדַעְתָּ כִּי הֵם זִקְנֵי
הָעָם וְשֹׁטְרָיו וְלָקַחְתָּ אֹתָם אֶל אֹהֶל מוֹעֵד וְהִתְיַצְּבוּ שָׁם עִמָּךְ. (במדבר יא:טז)

And the Lord said to Moshe, "Gather to me seventy men of the elders of Yisrael, who you know to be the elders of the people and officers over them, and bring them to the Tent of Meeting, that they may stand there with you." (Bamidbar 11:16)

AFTER protesting that he could not bear Bnei Yisrael's complaints alone, Moshe was instructed to gather a group of seventy elders to help him lead the people. The seventy were immediately brought into the Tent of Meeting so that the rest of the nation would recognize their role and give them respect.[1] This, according to the Talmud, was the origin of the Sanhedrin – Bnei Yisrael's high court.[2]

Just as the seventy elders were brought into the Tent of Meeting to boost their stature, the Talmud relates that the Great Sanhedrin had a special edifice in the Temple complex, known as the Chamber of Hewn Stone.[3] This was one of three courts in Jerusalem.[4] It was only partially located in the consecrated area of the Temple[5] and was near the altar.[6] The room

1. See Rashi. See also mSan 11:2, which states that this court was the ultimate arbiter of Jewish law, as per Devarim 17:10.

2. mSan 1:6 and Chizkuni on this verse.

3. The Talmud states that the Sanhedrin sat in this chamber until forty years before the destruction of the Temple, which occurred in 70 CE; it then moved from the Temple into the city of Jerusalem. This was done to show that the court had lost stature and relinquished the right to try capital offenses. See bShab 15a, bSan 41a, and bAZ 8b.

4. bSan 86b.

5. bYom 25a. See my commentary on Vayikra 12:4.

6. MdRY Yitro 11, which supports this by recalling the story of Yoav, found in Melachim I 2:28. Yoav is sentenced to death by the king and flees to the Temple, where he clings to the altar. The Mechilta explains that Yoav desperately wanted to be tried and sentenced by the Sanhedrin, rather than be condemned by the king, since the

was set up so that the judges could sit in a half-circle and see one another during a court case.[7] According to the most impressive description, the Chamber of Hewn Stone was a basilica.[8]

The use of a basilica for this type of building is not surprising. Although nowadays basilicas are associated primarily with churches, they were originally developed as Roman administrative buildings, often overlooking a forum. It was only when the Roman Empire converted to Christianity that the church took over the government's trappings and basilicas became associated with Christian architecture.

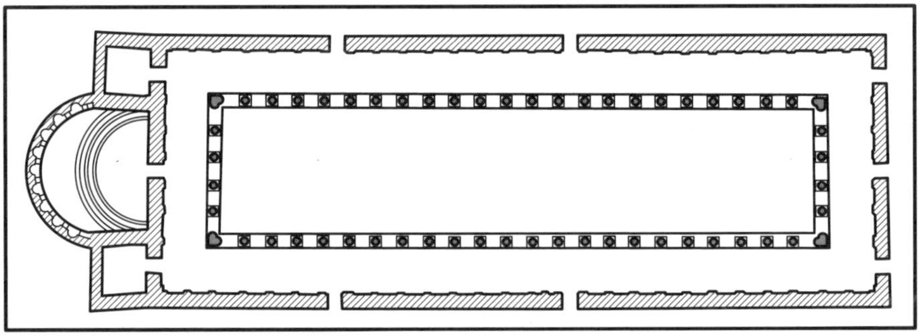

76. Ashkelon Basilic, with apse that contained seating and may have served as a *bouleuterion*. (Based on reconstruction by John Garstang, "Askalon" in *Palestine Exploration Fund Quarterly Statement*, 56, 1924, plate 2)

Basilicas appear in several passages throughout rabbinic literature, always in reference to large public buildings. Jews are forbidden from assisting heathens in building basilicas (along with places of torture, stadia,

property of one executed by the Sanhedrin goes to his next of kin, while the property of one executed by the king goes to the crown.

7. bSan 36b. A precedent for round benches in this type of space has been uncovered in a *bouleuterion* in the Athens agora, made of marble – see Homer A. Thompson, "Building on the West Side of the Agora" in *Hesperia* 6.1 (1937) 157–8. While no dimensions are recorded for the size of the chamber, an attempt could be made to figure out the necessary size based on the number of occupants and seating arrangement which appear in mSan 4:3–4, in the reverse process undertaken by Lily Ross Taylor and Russell T. Scott in "Seating Space in the Roman Senate and the Senatores Pedarii," *Transactions and Proceedings of the American Philological Association* 100 (1969), 529–582.

8. bYom 25a. Vitruvius explains that a basilica's "width must not be less than a third part, nor more than half its length ... The middle vault, between the columns, is one hundred and twenty feet long and sixty feet wide ... The height of the columns, including capitals, is fifty feet, their thickness five feet, and they have pilasters behind them twenty feet high, two feet and a half wide, and one and half thick, supporting beams ..." See *Ten Books on Architecture* V.

and theaters.)[9] In the Talmud, basilicas are classified into three categories: for heathen kings, for bathhouses, and for treasuries.[10] Basilicas were also fit for Jewish spaces: in addition to the Sanhedrin, an elaborate description of a basilica appears in reference to a synagogue in Alexandria, which had a double colonnade.[11] The Talmud recalls that the synagogue was so large that congregants could not hear the service and had to be alerted to answer amen by the waving of scarves.[12] Josephus describes the royal portico on the Temple Mount as a double colonnade in the form of a basilica.[13]

In addition to serving as administrative buildings, basilicas usually had a semi-circular chamber at one end. Orit Peleg-Barkat's reconstruction of the royal portico on the Temple Mount terminates with a semi-circular apse.[14] A similar feature was found in the basilica in Ashkelon. These apses were often used as courts and created an imposing setting for the dispensing of justice. When the Talmud describes the Chamber of Hewn Stone as semi-circular, this is not intended as a unique and revolutionary setting for the Sanhedrin. Rather, the Talmud's description of the chamber depicts it in a normative, contemporary setting. Like many Roman councils, it was in a semi-circular space set within a basilica.

The Talmud describes the Chamber of Hewn Stone as a basilica, a building type commonly used for administrative purposes. Basilicas could also be utilized for Jewish buildings. The court itself sat in a semi-circular space, as was often found in the apse of a basilica. Much like Roman basilicas, it was situated in one of the most important civic areas of the city, at the edge of the Temple Mount. It is a typical setting for an important court of law in a city dominated by Roman architecture.

---

9. mAZ 1:7. Rashi explains that each of these types of structures was used for judging or punishing people. bShab 150a groups basilicas with theaters and circuses.

10. bAZ 16b.

11. bSuk 51b. See also tSuk 4:4 and ySuk 5:1 (55a). It was also said to have seventy-one golden chairs, matching the number of members in the Sanhedrin. ySuk 5:1 relates that Trajan destroyed it in 117 CE and massacred the congregants, making it one of the earliest examples of a synagogue massacre.

12. This same passage in the Talmud also states that one who has not seen the Temple has never seen a beautiful building. Abaye explains that this is referring to the Temple constructed by Herod, which was built with various types of marble and precise masonry construction that rippled like waves.

13. Josephus, *The Jewish War*, 5.190 and *Antiquities* 15.411–415 describe the double colonnade. *Antiquities* 15.393 describes the aisle and naves of the basilica. bBer 33b states that the Temple Mount was a double colonnade, also without referencing the Chamber of Hewn Stone.

14. See Orit Peleg-Barkat, *The Temple Mount Excavations, Vol. V* (Institute of Archaeology, Hebrew University, 2017), 103.

# Reporting on the Canaanite Settlements

וּמָה הָאָרֶץ אֲשֶׁר הוּא יֹשֵׁב בָּהּ הֲטוֹבָה הִוא אִם רָעָה וּמָה הֶעָרִים אֲשֶׁר הוּא יוֹשֵׁב בָּהֵנָּה הַבְּמַחֲנִים אִם בְּמִבְצָרִים. (במדבר יג:יט)

And what is the land in which they dwell, is it good or bad; and what are the cities in which they dwell, are they in camps or in strongholds? (Bamidbar 13:19)

BEFORE sending twelve spies to investigate the Land of Canaan, Moshe gave them special instructions. They were to enter the land from the south and determine whether the inhabitants were strong and numerous, whether the land was fertile, and to report on the nature of the settlements.

Most commentators view this as a fact-finding mission. The spies were supposed to find out the Canaanites' settlement patterns as reconnaissance for the military campaign. Were they nomads?[1] Did they have forts? Battering rams would be required if the natives lived in fortified cities, while if they lived out in the open there would be no need for special equipment.[2]

Commentators dispute the significance of the Canaanite settlement types. The straightforward perspective is that nations living in fortified cities would be more difficult to conquer. However, some commentators claim that fortifications imply insecurity and weakness; strong nations can live in the open, as they do not fear war.[3] Therefore, nations without fortifications would be more intimidating to invading armies.

R. S.R. Hirsch explains this verse in another way. The question, he says, was about the land's influence on the local civilization. Moshe wanted to know how the environment influenced the natives. What "is the value of

1. Ibn Ezra and Saadia Gaon, explaining the word "tents."
2. Rashbam.
3. Sforno and BamR 16:9.

the land as the planting ground of a national development ... whether it would further or hinder the spiritual and moral cultural life of a nation." If the nations have developed an impressive moral and just society, the spies could be confident that the land engenders this type of development. The cities in specific, he adds, can tell a lot about what type of occupations are available – is this land full of nomadic shepherds, or are there cities with marketplaces and artisans? How will this influence the character of Bnei Yisrael? R. Hirsch points out that the nature of a land is reflected by its settlements. Local climate and conditions impact the architecture, which must concern itself with local weather phenomena such as droughts or monsoons.[4] In a sense, the local architectural heritage can be highly informative and even impact the national character. This is the reason it deserved the attention of the spies.

Other commentators explain that rather than asking the spies to consider the military or anthropological implications, Moshe was asking them to be architectural critics.[5] Moshe wanted the spies to report on the beauty of the cities and houses. As Bnei Yisrael were set to take over these existing buildings and cities,[6] it was important to know whether they were wondrous buildings or hovels. It was also important to see how they were constructed. Were the buildings sturdy? Were they built from quality materials? This would inform Bnei Yisrael about the quality of resources that were available in the land. For Bnei Yisrael to get a sense of the true value of the land they would receive, these questions needed to be answered.

These interpretations fall in line with how ancient urban planners thought about city locations. The physical conditions of a city were important considerations both for appraising the value of the city and in judging the strength of the inhabitants.[7] This is highlighted in Bereshit when, after the Tower of Babel, the Torah lists Noach's descendants and highlights that land, as much as language, is what makes them distinct.[8] Hippocrates explains how the physical characteristics of a territory influence disease, but also the populace in general.[9] This same belief appears in

4. For example, bBB 3b describes a town with a winter and summer synagogue. Rashi explains that the winter synagogue was "low with thick walls and few windows to keep out the cold, while the summer synagogue allowed in the wind."

5. Ohr Hachayim and Malbim.

6. See my commentary on Devarim 6:10.

7. This worldview can also be seen in the Talmudic slur against Babylonians: "Stupid Babylonian, because you dwell in a dark land you say things that are dim." See, for example, bBech 25b.

8. Bereshit 10:5, 10:20, and 10:31.

9. Hippocrates, *On Airs, Waters and Places*, 2.

a midrash[10] and is advanced by R. Yehuda Halevi in *Sefer Hakuzari* when his protagonist explains that every land engenders different character traits based on its climate. The Land of Israel, he explains, has qualities that promote connection with God, especially prophecy.[11] Vitruvius mentions the importance of climate, orientation, and sunlight in choosing where to locate a city.[12] He notes the possibility of studying a region's animals, birds, and fish to determine if the site is healthy.[13] He also explains that one must build differently depending on the regions and latitudes of the building site, "according to the distinctive properties of their lands and regions."[14] Cato the Elder advocated a similar method when buying a farm, advising the buyer to "notice the looks of the neighbors. In a good district, they ought to look well."[15] In a sense, this is what the spies were doing, studying the animals and the inhabitants of the land.

One of the first stops on the mission of the spies was the city of Chevron, which the Torah informs us was an ancient city.[16] Rather than connect the trip to Chevron with the Forefathers, it can be understood as a way to answer Moshe's questions. Not only were there large, fortified cities, but these cities were among the most ancient in the world. The walls of the city that the spies would have seen were, according to archaeologists, constructed "entirely of huge, uncut, cyclopean stones, some more than six feet long."[17] These are the walls that the spies would have seen on their mission and would have helped them understand the type of developed civilization existing in Canaan.

When Moshe dispatched the spies to make note of the nature of the settlements, it was about much more than just planning a military campaign. The architecture would help them understand the quality of the land, its resources, and the type of society it engendered.

10. BamR 16:12.

11. *Sefer Hakuzari* 2:9–14. The idea that prophecy only takes place in Israel also appears in midrash, regarding Yona's flight from Israel to avoid receiving prophecy. See MdRY, Bo, (pischa) 1.

12. Vitruvius, *Ten Books on Architecture* I.4.1–6. See also my commentary on Shemot 10:13.

13. Ibid, I.4.7–10.

14. Ibid, VI.1.1–12. Vitruvius predictably writes that Rome is in the ideal location, an "outstanding and balanced region."

15. Cato the Elder, *On Agriculture* 1.

16. Bamidbar 13:22.

17. Jeffrey R. Chadwick, "Discovering Hebron" in *Biblical Archaeology Review*, Sep/Oct 2005.

SHELACH

# Tourist Sites In the Ancient World

וַיַּעֲלוּ בַנֶּגֶב וַיָּבֹא עַד חֶבְרוֹן וְשָׁם אֲחִימַן שֵׁשַׁי וְתַלְמַי יְלִידֵי הָעֲנָק וְחֶבְרוֹן שֶׁבַע
שָׁנִים נִבְנְתָה לִפְנֵי צֹעַן מִצְרָיִם. (במדבר יג:כב)

And they went up into the Negev and came to Chevron where Achiman, Sheshay, and Talmay, the children of Anak, were there. Now Chevron was built seven years before Tzoan in Egypt. (Bamidbar 13:22)

THE twelve spies were dispatched to Canaan with instructions to explore the land and report back. Along the way, one or more of them came to the ancient city of Chevron.[1] According to the Talmud, Calev journeyed there to pray at the gravesite of the patriarchs and matriarchs.[2] Chevron is described as a well-known and important city with a rich history, compared favorably to other royal cities of the region and well-worth a visit.

The Classical world was familiar with the concept of must-see destinations. Writers like Strabo and Pliny the Elder chronicled the important places in the known world, recording the sites for posterity. Before their time, the most impressive sites were famously compiled as the Seven Wonders of the World. The earliest surviving version of this list is in a second century BCE poem by Antipater of Sidon.[3] Additional lists followed,

1. The verse says, "he came," rather than "*they* came." Rashi takes this literally, though some insist that all the spies went to Chevron.

2. bSot 34b.

3. Antipater of Sidon, *Greek Anthology* 9.58 writes: "I have set eyes on the walls of lofty Babylon on which is a road for chariots, and the statue of Zeus by the Alpheus, and the hanging gardens, and the colossus of the Sun, and the huge labour of the high pyramids, and the vast tomb of Mausolus; but when I saw the house of Artemis that mounted to the clouds, those other marvels lost their brilliancy, and I said 'Lo, apart from Olympus, the Sun never looked on aught so grand.'" See also 8.177 in the same collection, by St. Gregory the Theologian.

often with variation and sometimes with more than seven structures. For example, some authors mentioned the house of Cyrus in Ecbatana,[4] the city of Rome[5] and several others. Later Christian authors included the Temple of Solomon and Noach's Ark.[6] Some ancient writers do not have a complete list but mention a specific building as "one of the seven wonders."[7] Vitruvius, for example, refers to two buildings in this manner.[8] In addition to the seven wonders, other ancient travelers provided their itinerary, demonstrating that ancient tourists were most interested in sites with historical or mythological significance.[9] Lionel Casson, a professor of Classics, writes that:

> At Salamis, the visitor was shown the stone where old Telamon sat and watched his sons, Ajax and Teucer, sail off to Troy, near Sparta, the point in the road where Penelope made up her mind to marry Odysseus; . . . at Panopeus in central Greece, remains of the clay from which Prometheus moulded the first humans; and those intrepid enough to make their way into the Caucasus mountains could look up to the cliff where Zeus once had the Titan chained . . .[10]

The Talmud includes its own list of impressive Jewish sites. In one passage there are three "wonders" presented in sequence: the city of Jerusalem, the Temple as redesigned by Herod, and the synagogue of Alexandria.[11] The intention of the Talmud seems to be to highlight the ability of the

4. Hyginus, *Stories* 223, Cassiodorus, *Letters* 7.15 (which has a list of eight), and Gregory Tours, *On the Course of Stars* preface. Hyginus describes "the house of King Cyrus in Ecbatana, built by Memnon out of white and variegated marbles covered with gold."

5. Bede, *Of the Seven Wonders of the World*. Pliny the Elder also mentions Rome in his broader list of notable sites.

6. Gregory Tours, *On the Course of Stars* 1–35.

7. Strabo, *Geography* 14.2.5, 14.2.16, 16.1.5, 16.1.15, 17.1.33. Pliny the Elder, *Natural History* 36.16–24, Aulus Gellius, *Attic Nights* 10.18, Ammianus Marcellinus, *Res Gestae* 22.15.28.

8. Vitruvius, *Ten Books on Architecture*, II.8.11 (Halicarnassus) and VII.Preface.13 (Mausoleum).

9. Lionel Casson, *Travel in the Ancient World* (Johns Hopkins University Press, 1994) 230.

10. Ibid, 232–4.

11. bSuk 51b. They are presented as an exemplary city, building, and representation of the honor of Israel. For more on the Alexandrian synagogue, see my commentary on Bamidbar 11:16.

Jewish nation to produce monumental and first-rate architecture, rather than to encourage pilgrimages to visit the sites.[12]

Several other lists of significant sites are recorded in the Talmud. One contains sites connected to Babylon: the city of Babylon, the palace of Nebuchadnezzar,[13] the lion's den where Daniel was saved, and the furnace where Chananiya, Mishael, and Azariya were saved.[14] A *beraita* contains eight notable places where miracles happened to the Jewish people and a blessing is to be recited: where the sea was crossed during the Exodus, where the Jordan was crossed in the time of Yehoshua, the ford of Arnon, the stones of Elgavish near the slopes of Beit Choron, the boulder that the giant Og wished to throw on Bnei Yisrael, the stone Moshe sat on during the battle against Amalek, the pillar of salt that was formerly Lot's wife,[15] and the ruined walls of Yericho.[16] The counterpart of this collection can perhaps be found in a list of sites that require the tearing of one's clothing out of mourning: ruined Judean cities, the ruined Temple, and the ruined city of Jerusalem.[17] The Talmud also records where to go to see the hidden location of Miriam's well.

These lists, mentioned in the context of ritual obligation, present the sites from the point of view of a pilgrim or sightseer. In an article about the list of miraculous sites, Meir Bar Ilan asserts that in ancient times, like today, there were tour guides who specialized in leading groups to these famous places.[18] He points out that most of these sites were on main routes, so they would be good places to take pilgrims or travelers. The significance of the *beraita*, according to Bar Ilan, is that it bestows a halachic standing on these site-seeing trips, providing a blessing to be said and thus lending greater significance to the visits.[19]

---

12. Many scholars likewise feel that, based on the geographic distribution of the Seven Wonders, these lists were intended to do the same for the Hellenic world and may have been driven by the Pan-Hellenic movement in the wake of Alexander the Great's conquests. See Peter Clayton, *The Seven Wonders of the Ancient World*, 9. It is also noteworthy that all three – Jerusalem, the Temple, and the Alexandrian synagogue – were destroyed by the Romans.

13. Note the existence of the Palace of Cyrus in some lists of the Seven Wonders.

14. yBer 9:1 (12d), bBer 57b.

15. See my commentary on Bereshit 19:26.

16. bBer 54a.

17. bMK 26a. See also Semachot 9:19.

18. Josephus claims to have seen Lot's wife himself. See *Antiquities*, 1.203. See also bBB 73b–74a, where Rabba bar bar Chana is shown several historic sites in the desert by a local, including where Korach and his men were entombed.

19. Meir Bar Ilan, "*Mekomot Pela Be'eretz Yisrael Ba'et Haatika*" in *Mechkarei Yehuda Veshomron* 5 (5765) 229–239. (Hebrew). Online at https://faculty.biu.ac.il/~barilm/articles/publications/publications0049.html.

The Seven Wonders of the World was a list of worthwhile and popular places to visit. The list also highlighted great cultural accomplishments in the ancient world. Jewish sources contain similar lists that seem to serve these same two purposes. One list notes exemplary Jewish buildings, promoting the achievements of Jewish culture, while the other highlights important historical sites worth visiting. The blessings and ritual obligations that are to be done at these sites take the ordinary concept of tourism and connect it to Jewish history, infusing these sites with religious significance. Similarly, the city of Chevron was an attractive destination, both because it was an impressive city and because of its connection with the forefathers.

# Structural Supports and Dividing Loads Between the Spies

וַיָּבֹאוּ עַד נַחַל אֶשְׁכֹּל וַיִּכְרְתוּ מִשָּׁם זְמוֹרָה וְאֶשְׁכּוֹל עֲנָבִים אֶחָד וַיִּשָּׂאֻהוּ בַמּוֹט בִּשְׁנָיִם וּמִן הָרִמֹּנִים וּמִן הַתְּאֵנִים. (במדבר יג:כג)

And they came to the valley of Eshkol and cut a branch with one cluster of grapes, and they carried it on a pole between two, they brought also some pomegranates and figs. (Bamidbar 13:23)

DURING their mission to Canaan, the twelve spies gathered fruit specimens to submit with their report. The Torah tells that they cut down pomegranates, figs, and a cluster of grapes.

The simple reading of the text states that two men, each holding the end of a pole, carried the cluster of grapes between them.[1] From a practical standpoint, this is a sensible way to carry a heavy object, allowing two people to split the weight. The load is placed at an equal distance between the two carriers, thus allowing each to shoulder half of the burden. In structural terms, this is a "simple beam."

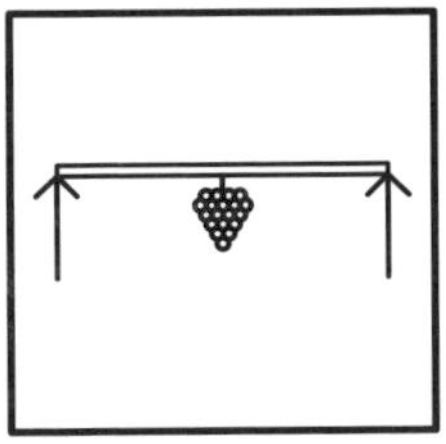

77. Structural diagram of grapes suspended on a pole.

Despite this straightforward reading of the text, the Talmud presents more elaborate explanations for how the grape cluster was carried.[2] Stating that the cluster was carried with a pole is enough to convey that two people

1. As in the commentary of Saadia Gaon and with elaborations in the Zohar (Shelach 160:2, quoted in Rabeinu Bachya) and HaEmek Davar.

2. bSot 34a. For additional cases of poles for carrying a load see bBM 83a.

were involved. When the Torah adds that it was carried "on a pole *between two*" the Talmud suggests that the Torah is hinting that there were two poles carried by *four* people. A second opinion, by R. Yitzchak, uses a Greek word for "scales" to describe the configuration, saying that the spies carried the cluster with "*trutina* and *trutina of trutina*."[3] This, according to the commentaries, means that *eight* spies carried the cluster. In the Yerushalmi, one opinion claims that the cluster was carried by *sixteen* spies.[4]

While dividing the weight between two people is straightforward, commentators must resort to more creative explanations for eight spies carrying the cluster. Rashi[5] and Meiri[6] describe an octothorpe (#) configuration – two poles running in one direction with two poles crossing beneath at ninety degrees(*fig. a*).[7] Both mention that the lower poles help support the upper poles. Tosafot, based on R. Chananel, describe two main poles with a litter hung between them, supported by four short poles (*fig. b*). Another possibility is that the two main poles were supported by four people each (*fig. c*), but many other creative solutions have been suggested.[8]

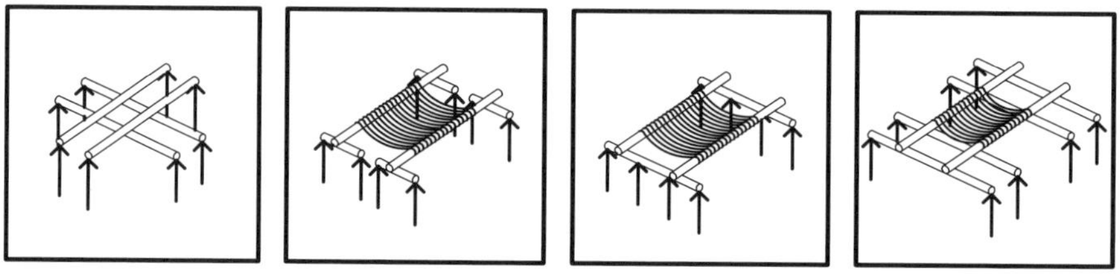

(a) (b) (c) (d)

78. Proposed configurations for carrying the load of grapes.

3. *Trutina* is the Latin term for the Greek "phalanx," which in addition to its military definition means a carrying pole used by porters to divide heavy loads equally. See Joyce van Leeuwen, "Image, Word and Translation in Niccolò Leonico Tomeo's Quaestiones Mechanicae" in *Translating Early Modern Science*, ed. Sietske Fransen, Niall Hodson and Karl A.E. Enenkel (Brill, 2017), 189.

4. ySot 7:5 (21d). This per the opinion of R. Akiva that there were twenty-four spies.

5. bSot 34a amar Rabbi Yitzchak.

6. On bSot 33b.

7. Some interpret Rashi's use of the word "diagonal" to mean that the lower two poles crossed in an X. The Schottenstein edition of the Talmud shows the lower poles crossed (bSot 34a note 30), while the Steinsaltz edition has the poles parallel (bSot page 148). In the Tosafot Rosh there are diagrams of both possibilities.

8. For a summary of the various opinions and configurations, see *Heichalei Torah* 24 Sivan 5768, https://daf-yomi.com/Data/UploadedFiles/DY_Item/343-sFile.pdf.

Commentators raise a number of concerns about the different configurations. Tosafot Rosh questions whether it is possible to march effectively in a diagonal formation. He also wonders why R. Chananel thought it necessary to have pairs of short poles as supports, instead of long poles.[9] The Maharal[10] correctly explains that any configuration in which one pole is underneath another results in an unequal sharing of the burden. He also rejects the possibility of having four parallel beams or a single beam with all eight holding it, as those closest to the load would end up providing most of the support. These are all legitimate structural concerns.

The arrangement of the poles contains many of the same principles needed to design the structural grid of a building. Most structural supports are arranged in a grid, evenly spaced to allow them to share loads efficiently. The loads must be carefully considered to ensure that no single column is carrying too much weight. The spies used poles to support the grape cluster, while a building employs a system of columns, beams, walls, and slabs to support the weight and content of the building.

While the complicated eight-person configuration may seem overly complex, this description reflects a common method of transporting heavy loads in the era before mechanization. Niccola Zabaglia, an Italian master mason, wrote a book detailing traditional construction practices in 18th-century Europe. In it, he included an image of porters carrying loads split between four, six, eight, sixteen, and thirty-two men.[11] Vitruvius describes a similar arrangement for splitting loads between four or six porters.[12] The images could just as well be included as illustrations of this passage in the Talmud. Assuming this was a normal way to carry large loads, the insistence on four or eight porters was likely to emphasize the great weight of the grapes.

Alternatively, perhaps the Talmud was considering a different

---

9. There is a logical reason to arrange the supports as per R. Chananel, with four short poles rather than two long ones. When two people each support a pole which is evenly loaded in the middle, they share the weight equally. Each pair of people holding the short poles also support an equal amount of weight, as the longer poles rest in the middle of the shorter poles. This is the configuration which best allows the eight people to share an *equal* portion of the load. If, as the Tosafot Rosh suggests, four people were to all hold the same post, it would be impossible to ensure that they were sharing the burden equally.

10. In his Gur Aryeh commentary on this verse.

11. Niccola Zabaglia, *Castelli e Ponti di Maestro Niccola Zabaglia Con Alcune Ingegnose Pratiche* (1743), plate XVII. A similar set of images appears in Giuseppe Valadier's *L'architettura Pratica*, plate CXCVI. See also John Fitchen, *Building Construction Before Mechanization* (MIT Press, 1992), 172–3.

12. Vitruvius, *Ten Books on Architecture*, X.3.7.

contemporary device that was occasionally used in a similar manner. Wealthy Romans were sometimes transported using litters, or beds supported by poles and carried by servants. Most of the time these were serviced by two burly workers, who each lifted one or two poles from either side of the litter. Sometimes, four servants were tasked with carrying the litter. However, we occasionally hear of a litter carried by eight servants, known as an *octaphoros*.[13] Latin texts that mention this device commonly do so in a mocking or derisive tone as if poking fun at the self-important aristocrats. As one modern scholar describes it, "the portrait of the wealthy freedman, lounging in his deluxe *octaphoros* ... is one which appears repeatedly, taking shape in the late Republic and reaching a climax of frequency in the satires of Juvenal and the epigrams of Martial, in the first century CE."[14] Perhaps the Talmud is doing the same with the spies, showing them as self-aggrandizing and pompous, with eight of them carrying the single grape cluster.

13. Phoros or phoron comes from the same word as the Hebrew word for litter, *apiryon*, found in Shir Hashirim 3:9 and other locations in Rabbinic Literature. Virtuvius uses the same terminology for his porters, dubbing them *hexaphoris* and *tetraphoris*.

14. Jared McCabe Hudson *On the Way: A Poetics of Roman Transportation* (University of California, 2013). See Cicero, *Against Verres* 2.5.27, used as a way to denounce Verres; Suetonius Tranquillus, *Caligula* 43, where *Caligula* marches his soldiers at an exhaustive pace but himself travels in an exaggerated, leisurely manner; and Martial, *Epigrams*, 6.84, as a way of mocking someone. See also Juvenal, *Satires* 1.63–68 which mentions a six-servant litter.

79. Porters Carrying Construction Materials. (Niccola Zabaglia, *Castelli, e ponti di Maestro Niccola Zabaglia*, 1743, plate XVII. The Theater that was Rome. Brown Digital Repository. Brown University Library. https://repository.library.brown.edu/studio/item/bdr:253243/)

# Light Quality and Visual Tasks

וְהָיָה לָכֶם לְצִיצִת וּרְאִיתֶם אֹתוֹ וּזְכַרְתֶּם אֶת כָּל מִצְוֹת ה׳ וַעֲשִׂיתֶם אֹתָם וְלֹא
תָתֻרוּ אַחֲרֵי לְבַבְכֶם וְאַחֲרֵי עֵינֵיכֶם אֲשֶׁר אַתֶּם זֹנִים אַחֲרֵיהֶם. (במדבר טו:לט)

And it shall be to you for a fringe that you may look upon it and remember all the commandments of the Lord and do them, and that you go not after your own heart and after your own eyes after which you use to go astray. (Bamidbar 15:39)

THE Torah describes the commandment of fringes, or *tzitzit*, and stipulates "that you may look upon it." This section of the Torah is one of the three sections of the *shema* prayer, and the Talmud explains that when you look upon the fringes you should remember to recite *shema*.[1] The Mishna also suggests that the sight of the *tzitzit* is integral to the timing of this prayer – one can only recite *shema* in the morning when one can gaze upon the *tzitzit* and distinguish between the two colors of the strings – white and azure.[2] This test – a relatively simple visual task – is given as a way of determining that there is enough daylight for it to be considered morning.

Several factors affect how well we see. Some of these are personal – the age and visual ability of the individual. Others are empirical – how light is oriented and reflected toward the viewer and the amount of light present. The difficulty of the task also plays a role – a hotel hallway might have enough light to locate the correct room, yet an inadequate amount of light for reading a book. While the Mishna does not adjust for individual ability, it does try to set a specific task – distinguishing the colors of the strings[3]

1. bMen 43b.
2. mBer 1:2. See also bBer 9b and yBer 1:2 (3a).
3. Halacha ultimately rejects the appointed task of distinguishing between blue and white strings – and the second suggestion in this mishna, by R. Eliezer, of distinguishing between blue and green strings, for a different visual task – recognizing an

– to arrive at some sort of empirical time for saying *shema*. The logic here is clear: the prescribed time for saying *shema* is morning, and morning is defined in some manner by the onset of daylight and sunrise. Since performing visual tasks is dependent on the amount of light available, it makes sense to determine the onset of daylight through a visual task.

While the task of distinguishing colors helps us determine when it is morning, we have the opposite situation when it comes to the laws of *tzaraat*. The Torah uses the word "day" in several verses, from which the halacha is derived that all inspections of *tzaraat* must take place during the day,[4] specifically when the sun is neither directly overhead nor low in the sky.[5] The inspections cannot take place on cloudy days and must all occur out of doors.[6] This helps ensure that there is balanced lighting that will neither wash out nor intensify the color of the affliction.

These rules were established before the invention of electric lighting, and aim to establish lighting standards for the inspection. Nowadays, artificial lights can have a high degree of variability, depending on the type of bulb and fixture, which can change how colors appear in a particular room. Architects know that when choosing finish materials for a room, it is important to have a light source similar to the light of the room in question. Otherwise, you may end up with something that looks red in the store but seems brown or grey in a living room. To ensure an even and unchanging baseline for the *tzaraat* examination, the Rabbis did their best to eliminate any variables in terms of the light quality.

When designing lighting in a room, the designer must take into account the type of activities taking place in that space. Trade organizations, such as IESNA,[7] publish guidelines for how much lighting is required for different activities. Corridors and dining halls are low on the scale of required lighting, while hospitals and inspection rooms are on the high

---

acquaintance at a distance of four cubits. It should be noted that the task of distinguishing between blue and white strings has additional factors that change the difficulty of the task, including the cleanliness of the white strings, the color of the field (i.e. the pants) against which the strings hang, the distance of the strings from the eye, the thickness of the strings, the amount of time one is given to glimpse the strings, and the glossiness of the material.

4. Rambam Hilchot Tumat Tzaraat 9:6, Sifra Tazriya Nega'im, parsha 2 perek 2:3.

5. R. Meir rules that the third–fifth and seventh–ninth hours are acceptable, while R. Yehuda limits inspections to the fourth, fifth, eighth and ninth hours. See mNeg 2:2.

6. Ibid. See also Sifra above.

7. Illuminating Engineering Society of North America. Illumination required is determined by the task, the age of the inhabitants, and the surface reflectance of the room.

end. The amount and quality of light alters how well tasks can accurately be performed and is, therefore, a crucial component of designing the space.

In both determining the time for *shema* and in inspections for *tzaraat,* the Rabbis tried to establish a lighting baseline. In the former, the amount of light helps define when morning begins. In the latter, the lighting ensures a similar baseline condition for the inspection.

# Figure/Ground Theory in Urban Design

וַיִּקָּהֲלוּ עַל מֹשֶׁה וְעַל אַהֲרֹן וַיֹּאמְרוּ אֲלֵהֶם רַב לָכֶם כִּי כָל הָעֵדָה כֻּלָּם קְדֹשִׁים
וּבְתוֹכָם ה׳ וּמַדּוּעַ תִּתְנַשְּׂאוּ עַל קְהַל ה׳. (במדבר טז:ג)

> And they assembled against Moshe and against Aharon and said to them: "You take too much upon you, seeing all the congregation are holy, every one of them, and the Lord is among them. Why then do you raise yourselves up above the assembly of the Lord?" (Bamidbar 16:3)

KORACH and his followers complained that Moshe and Aharon created a hierarchical order and placed themselves in positions of importance when really all members of Bnei Yisrael were holy. The members of Korach's group also felt, somewhat contradictorily, that they deserved leadership roles, either because they were Leviim, first-borns, or from the tribe of Reuven.[1] Still, they contended that *all* members of Bnei Yisrael ought to be able to interact directly with God. In their view, no preferential roles were required.[2]

Although Korach's complaint is primarily about the role of leadership, some commentators see it as a criticism of the physical setup of the camp and its concentric levels of holiness.[3] The *Mishkan*, located in the center, could be accessed only by a select few; no others could enter the Temple and offer sacrifices. Korach argued that no such hierarchy of space should exist and that everyone should be able to offer sacrifices as they pleased.[4]

To appreciate this disagreement, we can look at the changing makeup of

---

1. Ibn Ezra mentions the complaints of all three on Bamidbar 16:1. Chizkuni emphasizes the complaints of the first-borns.
2. Daat Mikre, note 16, Malbim, and the Targumim on this verse.
3. See my commentary on Bamidbar 1:53.
4. See Ohr Hachayim and R. Hirsch. In the same manner, BamR 18:2 writes that Korach argued no special azure string should be required in the *tzitzit*.

urban areas in the twentieth century. Traditional cities were mostly comprised of "background" buildings, from which public spaces and edifices emerged as lively forces in the urban fabric. Modern architecture upended this order. Le Corbusier reimagined cities as huge towers separated by open spaces. This influential idea caused a drastic shift in how buildings related to one another. Modern architecture promoted the freedom for each to be a free-standing sculpture rather than to serve the urban fabric. The figure/ground relationship flipped so that instead of buildings acting as the background and shaping public spaces, the buildings became figures upon a background of open space.[5] The result was that most cities ceased to function as a unit and failed to create welcoming and functional public spaces. As one book put it, "the city of modern architecture become [sic] a congeries of conspicuously disparate objects."[6]

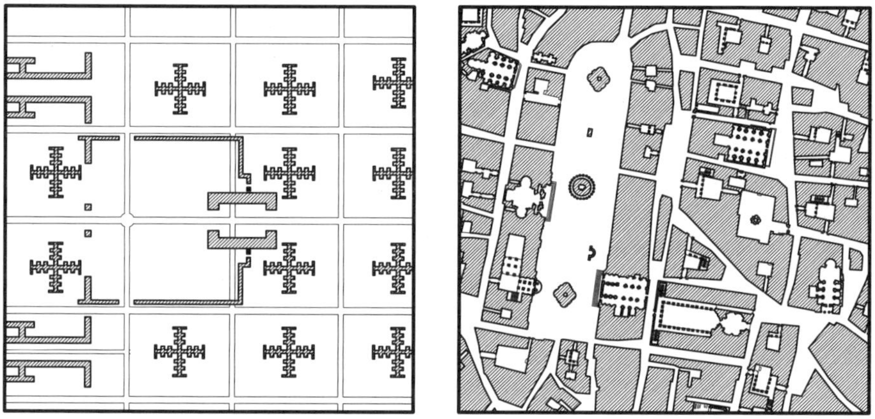

80. Contrast between Modern city (left) and Medieval city (right), with hatch showing the built structures. On the left (Plan Voisin, Le Corbusier's 1925 plan for Paris), buildings sit on a background of open space. On the right (after the 1748 map of Rome by Giambattista Nolli), open spaces are shaped by the built environment.

Many architectural theorists sought to combat this problem in the second half of the century. They lauded the importance of hierarchy in cities and the need to create buildings that were part of the city fabric. Without this hierarchy, they claimed, cities would continue to be unwelcoming and lose their dynamic energy. Buildings themselves were more valuable when they were harnessed together to serve a greater purpose, like the shaping of public space. Douglas Kelbaugh, an advocate of designing more traditional

5. Colin Rowe and Fred Koetter, *Collage City* (MIT Press, 1984), 62–63.
6. Ibid, *Collage City*, 58.

cities, wrote that "Background or collateral buildings gain their strength from the public space they define."[7] Whereas the typical Modern building is "a freestanding, abstract, minimalist object in unbounded universal space," forming a figure upon the background of open space, traditional architecture works together as part of a larger collective. Even Modern architecture works best within a traditional urban fabric that serves as a foil to the building.

Much like the early Modern architects who failed to grasp the ramifications of their theories, Korach and his followers did not understand the important role of the priests and the Temple in the nascent Israelite society. The singular and central place of the Temple gave Bnei Yisrael a focus and served as a way of uniting the disparate tribes, rather than allowing each tribe, or each individual, to develop his own independent Judaism. The leadership and the Temple gave Bnei Yisrael a focus. In turn, the collective mass of Bnei Yisrael was what gave the Temple meaning as a holy location where God could be sought. Appointed leaders and an ordered camp with the Temple at the center, were vital, uniting forces for Bnei Yisrael.

7. Douglas Kelbaugh, "Typology: An Architecture of Limits" in *Repairing the American Metropolis* (University of Washington Press, 2002), 99.

KORACH

# Cladding for the Altar

אֵת מַחְתּוֹת הַחַטָּאִים הָאֵלֶּה בְּנַפְשֹׁתָם וְעָשׂוּ אֹתָם רִקֻּעֵי פַחִים צִפּוּי לַמִּזְבֵּחַ כִּי הִקְרִיבֻם לִפְנֵי ה׳ וַיִּקְדָּשׁוּ וְיִהְיוּ לְאוֹת לִבְנֵי יִשְׂרָאֵל. (במדבר יז:ג)

Even the fire-pans of these men who have sinned at the cost of their lives, and let them be made into beaten plates for a covering of the altar, for they have become holy because they were offered before the Lord, that they may be a sign to Bnei Yisrael. (Bamidbar 17:3)

ELAZAR was instructed to repurpose the censers used by Korach and his followers in their showdown with Aharon. The metal censers were to be beaten into thin foil and used as cladding for the bronze altar in the *Mishkan*.[1]

Two reasons are given in the Torah for reusing the censers in this way. First, the censers had become sanctified ("they have become holy") and could therefore not be discarded. The commentators debate the mechanism by which the censers, used to challenge the established order in the *Mishkan*, could be considered holy, but no matter the process, the Torah clearly says they *were* holy and thus could not be discarded.

Second, the Torah writes that the new cladding on the altar "may be a sign to Bnei Yisrael." R. S.R. Hirsch explains that the cladding served as proof that Aharon's descendants were the rightful priests. Malbim adds that it reminded any non-priests who might try to bring offerings that such an action is punishable by death. Rashi sees the cladding as a marker of the historical event. In any case, the reuse of the metal from the censers for the altar met both needs, keeping the sanctified objects in use in the Temple while also serving as a sign for Bnei Yisrael.

This is not the only time when inanimate objects are used as a sign or

1. yChag 3:8 (79d) discusses the halachic ramifications of the extreme thinness of the cladding. mShek 4:4 states that leftover *teruma* coins were used to make cladding for the Holy of Holies.

even called upon to testify. Moshe twice calls upon the heavens and earth to serve as witnesses.[2] Yehoshua does the same with an altar[3] as does Lavan with a heap of stones.[4] In each of these cases, the object bearing witness lasts longer than living memory and therefore could serve as a reminder or guarantor long after all living witnesses are gone.[5]

81. Burnside Bridge Sycamore, witness tree to the Battle of Antietam. (James W. Rosenthal, Library of Congress HALS MD-8-2)

Memorials often make use of inanimate objects to recall past events. On American battlefields like Gettysburg, "witness trees" that were alive at the time of the Civil War help create a link between the present and the past.[6] In a study of the National Memorial Arboretum in England, Howard Williams reviewed several monuments that make use of stones,

2. Devarim 4:26 and 30:19.
3. Yehoshua 2:27–28.
4. Bereshit 31:48.
5. bChag 16a states that the stones and beams of your house will be called to testify about your sins. This is to emphasize that it is impossible to hide sins from God.
6. In Israel, a similar phenomenon involves the tree outside of Alon Shvut.

shards, bullet casings, etc., taken from historical sites. Williams wrote that Holocaust memorials were ground-breaking and influential in this practice, using artifacts to strengthen the connection between visitors and the historical events. The British German Friendship Garden uses repurposed stones taken from the rubble of Dresden.[7] Around the world, there are memorials to the destruction of the World Trade Center on September 11, 2001, which make use of remnants of the towers. In one case, reclaimed steel from the buildings was used to build a military ship, the USS New York. Bricks, stones, or metal from an old building might be purposefully used in a new one to draw a link between the two. Williams wrote that "monument reuse offers direct 'time travel', prompting different experiential empathies through an emotive and mnemonic touchstone between past and present." Interacting with a tangible object transports you to different times and places. It is a powerful way of conveying a message or telling a story. This is why memorials so often try to anchor themselves with a relic or authentic piece of the story.

In the case of the altar, the metal from the censers filled a similar role. The cladding connected people with the ancient events that took place during the confrontation with Korach and served to recall these events and bolster the faith of later devotees.

7. Howard Williams, "Monument and Material Reuse at the National Memorial Arboretum" in *Archaeological Dialogues* 21(1), 2014.

# Architecture of the Red Heifer

וְאָסַף אִישׁ טָהוֹר אֵת אֵפֶר הַפָּרָה וְהִנִּיחַ מִחוּץ לַמַּחֲנֶה בְּמָקוֹם טָהוֹר וְהָיְתָה לַעֲדַת בְּנֵי יִשְׂרָאֵל לְמִשְׁמֶרֶת לְמֵי נִדָּה חַטָּאת הִוא. (במדבר יט:ט)

And a man that is *tahor* shall gather up the ashes of the heifer and lay them up outside the camp in a *tahor* place and it shall be kept for the congregation of Bnei Yisrael for a water of sprinkling, it is a purification offering. (Bamidbar 19:9)

THE Torah describes the procedure for producing the ashes of a red heifer. The high priest takes an unblemished red heifer outside the camp and slaughters it. The body of the heifer is burned along with cedarwood, hyssop, and scarlet. The ashes are then gathered and brought outside the camp, to be made into a mixture for sprinkling on people who are *tameh* (spiritually impure).

The Mishna fleshes out this process, adding details about the heifer and how the mixture was protected from becoming *tameh*. The description includes three architectural features that were designed to ensure the purity of the mixture. First, the Mishna states that seven days before the burning of the heifer, the kohen was cloistered in a room on the Temple Mount, specially designed to be impervious to *tumah*.[1] This was also done in the week leading up to Yom Kippur when the high priest was required to remain pure.[2] The room was equipped with only stone, coprolite, and earthen vessels, which according to Jewish law cannot become impure. The priest was sprinkled daily with the remnants of the mixture from previous red heifers to ensure his purity.

For the second phase of preparation, the Mishna describes how the

1. mPar 3:1.

2. mYom 1:1. In the case of the red heifer, there is less concern about purity, but nonetheless these measures were instituted to reinforce the gravity of the ritual. See bYom 2a.

person charged with retrieving the water for the mixture was protected from becoming *tameh.* Special enclosures were prepared in Jerusalem, designed so that children could be born and raised in isolation. These rooms were built over cavities so that even if graves existed in the earth below, the cavity would prevent the transmission of impurity from these theoretical graves. Women would give birth in these rooms and remain in them to raise their children until they were old enough to perform the duty of drawing water from the Shiloach spring for the red heifer's ashes.[3] According to the Mishna, the Temple Mount was similarly designed to prevent unmarked graves from contaminating the space above.[4]

In the third phase, the kohen would cross to the Mount of Olives via a special ramp prepared for the occasion.[5] The ramp is described as expensive, with each high priest privately funding the dismantling of the old ramp and the construction of a new one.[6] As with the other spaces mentioned, the ramp was designed to prevent the spread of impurity, with "arches upon arches."

Although this description relies upon the same concept of open cavities, there are several obscure points. First, the Talmud itself does not understand the purpose of demolishing and rebuilding the ramp. It suggests that this was done out of pride but then decides that it was done to honor the event.[7] Second, the description of "arches upon arches," while halachically sensible, makes little sense architecturally. To interrupt the transfer of *tumah* from unmarked graves, the arches needed to be staggering. However, we rarely find instances when the crown of a lower arch supports the pier of an upper arch. The crown, as the weakest part of the arch, is a bad place to support the full weight of the next tier of the structure. Rather, tiers are arranged so that each register of arches transfers its load to the pier below, allowing forces to be efficiently carried to the ground. There are many

---

3. mPar 3:2, tPar 3:2, quoted in bZev 113a. This seems like a drastic step to take, considering the alternative of using existing ref heifer mixture to purify someone, as was done with the high priest. Instead, it is more likely that this procedure was only used when no choice was available. This is indicated in tPar 3:5 by R. Yehuda, who says it only applied when the Jews returned from Babylon. The Temple Mount Institute has suggested that this was included in the Mishna to let future generations know what to do when the Temple is rebuilt.

4. mPar 3:3.

5. mYom 6:4 describes another ramp, built for the high priest on Yom Kippur. In yYom 6:4 (43d) there is a disagreement whether this was a real ramp.

6. mShek 4:2, mPar 3:6, tShek 2:6, tPar 3:7, yShek 4:2 (48a), and PdRK 4:7. The special clothes used by the high priest on Yom Kippur were also only used once, as per bYom 24a and parallel texts.

7. yShek 4:2 (48a).

(a) (b)

82. Tiers of arches: (a) typical alignment with stacked piers (b) arrangement needed to prevent the spread of *tumah*. Arches must bear the weight of the structure above at their weakest point.

examples of construction with tiers of arches, but such an arrangement does not block the transfer of *tumah*. Third, no mention is ever made of a passage crossing the Kidron Valley in any of the physical descriptions of Mishna-era Jerusalem, nor have archaeological remnants ever been found for such a structure.

Eyal Ben-Eliyahu raised some of these questions in an essay about the red heifer ramp. He noted that while many understand this to be talking about a large, masonry bridge, it makes more sense for it to have been a simpler ramp with two levels of short voids, stacked alternately as described in the Mishna.[8] Indeed, this is a design solution currently marketed by the Akerstein company for use in civil engineering over ancient burial sites. This creates a situation of "arches upon arches" despite the lack of literal arches and without any dramatic architecture.

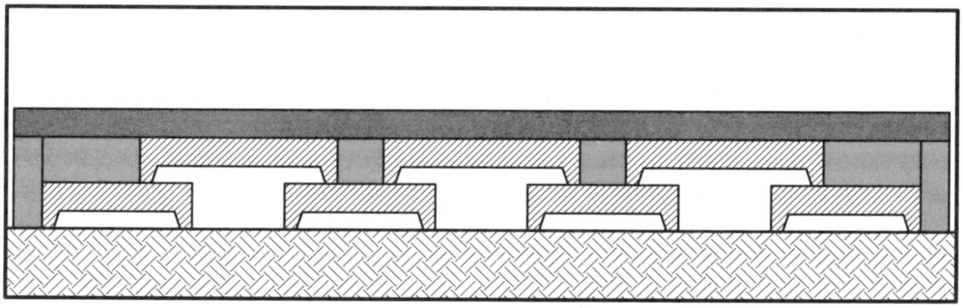

83. Akerstein "Kohen Element" for covering graves in civil engineering projects.

8. Eyal Ben-Eliyahu, "*Keves Para Aduma*" in *Cathedra* 107, 183–186. (Hebrew)

This solution answers some of the difficulties noted above. It resolves the structural problems, protects against *tumah,* and is a more plausible scenario for the high priest destroying and rebuilding the ramp. It explains why such a bridge does not appear in any descriptions and has left no archaeological remains. The only unresolved point is that it does not explain why it would cost so much, a description that appears in all the sources. This can be explained by assuming that high priests did not use precast concrete slabs that were mass-produced, but rather made an elaborately designed walkway befitting the important ceremony.

The Mishna describes three different architectural solutions employed to help ensure the purity of the red heifer mixture. The high priest was isolated in a special room, the people preparing the mixture were born and raised in a special chamber, and the ramp constructed by the high priest was specially made to allow passage over the Kidron Valley without fear of contamination. These demonstrate some ways in which architecture was used to address the laws of spiritual purity during the Second Temple period.[9]

9. See my commentary on Vayikra 21:1 for more on this topic.

# Separating Entrance and Exit

הַנֹּגֵעַ בְּמֵת לְכָל נֶפֶשׁ אָדָם וְטָמֵא שִׁבְעַת יָמִים. (במדבר יט:יא)

He that touches the dead, even any man's dead body, shall be *tameh* for seven days. (Bamidbar 19:11)

THE laws of ritual purity dictate that impurity is transmitted, in the most basic way, through touch. Touching a dead body, or even another person who has touched a dead body, renders one *tameh*. All cases of *tumah* ultimately require immersion in a *mikva* to complete the purification process.

One of the defining features of a *mikva* (as opposed to a cistern) is its stairs, which allow an able-bodied person to descend and immerse without difficulty. In many ancient *mikvaot*, archaeologists have noted a slight rise along the middle of the stairs, separating the steps into two aisles. This is especially common around Jerusalem. Ronny Reich has suggested that this was done to demarcate separate lanes for entering and exiting the *mikva*, to help prevent cross-contamination between people who are still *tameh* and people who have finished immersing in the *mikva* and are now *tahor*.[1]

This design is reflected in a mishna which rules that vessels found in Jerusalem on the downward direction toward a *mikva* are considered *tameh*, while those found on the upward direction are assumed to be pure.[2] This arrangement is also described in the Letter of Aristeas, which explains that on the steps "some people are always going up and others down, and they keep as far apart from each other as possible on the road because of those who are bound by the rules of purity, lest they should touch anything unlawful."[3]

1. Ronny Reich, *Miqvaot Tahara* (YBZP, 2013), 61–67 (Hebrew).
2. mShek 8:2. See also Rashi on bPes 19b, who explains that there were different paths for descending and ascending.
3. Letter of Aristeas 106.

84. *Mikva* in the Old City of Jerusalem, opposite Robinson's Arch.

Reich points out that *mikvaot* were places where *tahor* and *tameh* people were found in close proximity, so extra care would have been needed to prevent contamination. The divided stairs design, he explains, allows a far greater number of people to immerse at the same time, without increasing the likelihood of recontamination.[4] This architectural decision is very common for controlling the flow of large crowds. For example, in train stations, there are usually separate paths for passengers entering and exiting the train station. This helps keep the masses of people from obstructing one another. As in *mikvaot,* it also helps keep order and control. Not surprisingly, the Mishna describes a similar arrangement for the Temple Mount, with people entering on the right side and exiting on the left.[5] Traffic on the altar ramp was similarly divided.[6] Separate entrances and exits help establish a more efficient flow of people, improving access to the site.

4. Reich, *Mikvaot Tahara,* 63.

5. mMid 2:2.

6. mYom 4:5, bYom 45a. For traffic entering and exiting bathhouses and public toilets, see yBM 3:5 (3d).

# Impurity Transmitted by Tents

זאת הַתּוֹרָה אָדָם כִּי יָמוּת בְּאֹהֶל כָּל הַבָּא אֶל הָאֹהֶל וְכָל אֲשֶׁר בָּאֹהֶל יִטְמָא שִׁבְעַת יָמִים. (במדבר יט:יד)

This is the Torah: if a man dies in a tent, everyone that comes into the tent and everything that is in the tent shall be *tameh* seven days. (Bamidbar 19:14)

ONE of the ways that *tumah* (spiritual impurity) can be transmitted from one person or object to another is by "tent." Being under the same roof as a source of impurity, such as a dead body, makes one *tameh.*

(a) (b) (c)

85. Tents transmitting *tumah* (T = source of *tumah*).

To be more precise, the concept of a tent transmitting *tumah* can work in three ways. First, if a dead body is *under* a tent, the *tumah* is spread to the other objects or people that are also underneath the tent (*fig. 85a*). Second, if the dead body is *above* a person or object, they become impure (*fig. 85b*). Third, if a person or object is above the dead body, itself acting as a tent, it becomes *tameh* (*fig. 85c*). Although the Torah uses the word "tent" to explain this concept, it is not talking about a tent in the strict sense of the word. Any type of shelter or overhang qualifies – a taut canvas sheet, a wooden plank, an overhang, a bridge, a big straw basket, a roosting bird, a protruding cornice, or a column capital[1] – all can belong to the category if they provide cover and are at least the minimum size of one square handbreadth.[2]

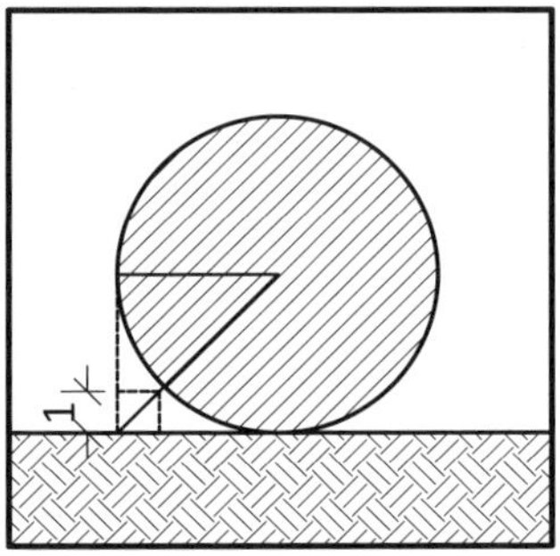


86. Column on side.

Another mishna, dealing with a column laying on its side, explains that a column must have a circumference of twenty-four handbreadths for there to be a gap of one square handbreadth.[3] However, when it comes to calculating the overhang of a capital above a standing column, the relationship of column size to capital overhang is not as straightforward. Though Doric columns do have square capitals, other orders have irregular-shaped capitals. Many classical columns had a circumference that swelled and tapered as the column rose. This curvature, called entasis, resulted in the column being noticeably thinner at the top than at the base.[4] Third, the base of the column was almost always wider than the column shaft and would have limited traffic under the protruding capital.[5]

1. mOhal 6:6–7. R. Yisrael Lifschitz, in his *Tiferet Yisrael – Yachin* commentary (note 55), translates the term in the Mishna as "capital," and explains that it protrudes at a slant around the circumference of the column, "like rose petals."

2. mOhal 3:7.

3. mOhal 12:7. Commentators argue about whether this is correct, adjusting for the biblical approximations of $\pi$ and $\sqrt{2}$ to try and make the math work. It was difficult to compute simple fractions – let alone irregular numbers – in a system that relies on cubits, palms, and digits for measurements. See J.J. Coulton, *Ancient Greek Architects at Work* (Cornell University Press, 1982), 67. As a reference, the columns of Herod's royal portico on the Temple Mount were one meter in diameter, and had acanthus leaves that projected approximately 12.5 cm, based on the fragments uncovered. See Orit Peleg-Barkat, *The Temple Mount Excavations in Jerusalem, Vol. V* (Institute of Archaeology, Hebrew University, 2017), 38 and 50.

4. Vitruvius, III.3.12–13. However, many classical columns in Israel lack entasis.

5. Vitruvius, III.5.1.

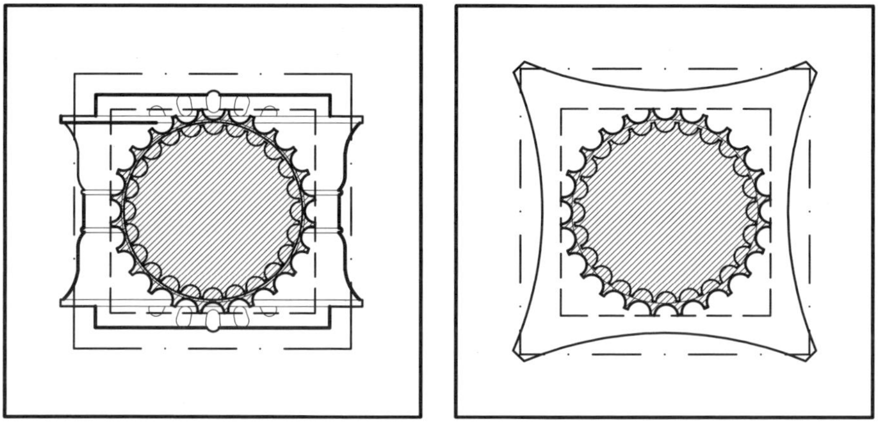

87. View looking up through typical Roman Ionic and Corinthian columns. Hatched area shows column size at the base, with the smaller contour showing the column size where it meets the capital. The dashed line shows the square circumscribing the column, while the solid line shows the underside of a classical capital. Note that the dash-dot line shows the size of the column's base, so almost no overhang exists where someone could pass. (Based on Cyclopedia of Architecture, Carpentry and Building, VIII, 1908)

Leaving aside the issue of capitals, not every overhang is considered a tent for the transmission of impurity. The Mishna lists several structures that cannot be counted as tents: an ice shelf, a dome of ice, a snow shelter, and a house made of salt.[6] These structures are not considered permanent enough to count as shelters, and therefore do not transfer impurity by this mechanism.[7] Just as birds in flight, flapping flags, or unanchored boats would not be sufficiently tent-like due to their movement and impermanence, so too a quickly-decaying shelter does not count for this purpose. Similarly, the Mishna differentiates between various types of living plants. It lists broad-leafed plants, such as lilies and ivy,[8] which would count as tents, but excludes other types of growth with skimpier leaves.[9]

There are two opinions for the reason why most plants are excluded. Rambam writes that only a plant that retains its leaves in all seasons can count as a tent.[10] Tosafot, on the other hand, explain that the problem is that other plants can be moved too easily by the wind.[11] Both explanations

6. mOhal 8:5. See also tOhal 14:6, where salt is not grouped with snow and ice.

7. In the case of a permanently inhabited igloo in a frigid climate, it seems that the dwelling would be considered a tent.

8. mOhal 8:1.

9. mOhal 8:5.

10. In his commentary to mOhal 8:5.

11. bSuk 13b *yirakot* toward the end.

relate to permanence, but there are practical differences between the two explanations. For example, it is often desirable to control the amount of sunlight that shines into a building. Too much sunlight can make the building uncomfortably warm and require additional mechanical cooling. To prevent this solar heat gain, architects will sometimes design sunshades that block sunlight entering the building at certain times of the day and year. One option is to use plants to shade the windows. During the summer the leaves grow and block the sunlight. In the colder winter months, the plants lose their leaves and allow more sunlight to reach the building. In this situation, the plant remains in place regardless of the wind, yet is specifically chosen because of its lack of leaves during the winter. In such a case, Tosafot might consider the plant a tent, while Rambam would presumably deny it this status.

When discussing *tumah* transmitted by tents, the Mishna draws examples from the surrounding environment. Columns, trees, bridges, and overhangs were all common features that illustrated the principles well. While the point of these examples is not to call out specific design practices, their presence in the Mishna can nonetheless afford opportunity for exploring how the nuances of design may have ramifications on the transmission of *tumah.*

# Passage Width

וַיַּעֲמֹד מַלְאַךְ ה׳ בְּמִשְׁעוֹל הַכְּרָמִים גָּדֵר מִזֶּה וְגָדֵר מִזֶּה. (במדבר כב:כד)

Then the angel of the Lord stood in a path between the vineyards, a fence being on this side and a fence on that side. (Bamidbar 22:24)

As Bilam traveled to confront Bnei Yisrael, the Torah describes his route along three different types of paths. He started on a road through a field. He continued on a narrow path through a vineyard with walls on either side. Finally, he traveled along a narrow place with no space on either side. The story hinges on the width of the roads, the amount of shoulder space on either side, and the ability to pass another traveler on the path.

Passage width affects both road design and hallway design. In buildings, hallways need to allow for adequate traffic flow. Service corridors, where only one workman enters, can be quite narrow, whereas most hallways must be able to accommodate two people passing one another. In some situations, such as high-rise apartment buildings, the halls must be wide enough to turn a stretcher, so that in an emergency someone can be carried out of the building. Hallways must be able to facilitate a timely evacuation in case of a fire or other emergency. Accessible corridors must be wide enough for wheelchairs and must have spaces that are wide enough for a wheelchair to fully rotate. The minimum width of each passage is determined by these factors.[1]

As with corridors inside buildings, a street's width is often dictated by law. The Mishna quantifies this, explaining that a private road must be four cubits wide, while a public road must be sixteen cubits wide.[2] In the United

1. bChul 91b discusses these issues with regard to the width of the ladder in Yaakov's dream, which needed to accommodate two pairs of angels passing one another as per Bereshit 28:12.

2. mBB 6:7. A *beraita* on bBB 99a–b adds that an intercity path is eight cubits, and

States, some roads are required to be wide enough for two firetrucks to pass each other, which usually means twenty feet wide.[3] Traffic speed and frequency also affect the recommended width of a street. Historically, wider streets have been associated with safer, healthier, and more progressive conditions. Napoleon III famously embarked on a campaign of widening the streets of Paris in the mid-nineteenth century. At the time, the city was primarily comprised of narrow and crowded passages. He appointed Georges Eugene Haussmann to beautify the city[4] and improve its overall design, granting him substantial authority. Haussmann created new boulevards throughout the city, carving through existing buildings as necessary, and widening streets. While this destroyed existing buildings and neighborhoods, the project did succeed in the goals of modernizing the city and making the streets safer, cleaner, and more ventilated.

On the other hand, excessively wide roads contribute to urban sprawl and make it harder for pedestrians to navigate cities. This has led some cities to rewrite their laws to allow for narrower streets, or to repurpose unneeded width for bike lanes and other amenities.

The fact that Bilam passed through several different paths seems unremarkable, serving mainly to build towards the climax of the confrontation with his donkey. However, we can also look for a deeper meaning behind these descriptions. On his way to confront the massive camp of Bnei Yisrael, one would expect Bilam to be able to make his way along main routes of travel. Wherever Bnei Yisrael were camped, their numbers dictate that they must have traveled along wide spaces. The image depicted in the Torah, though, shows Bilam traveling along increasingly narrow paths. The closer Bilam got to Bnei Yisrael, the smaller a path he took, despite our assumption that Bnei Yisrael must have cut a wide path. This makes it seem like Bilam wished to approach Bnei Yisrael secretly. Indeed, we find that Bilam was not looking to confront Bnei Yisrael directly, but rather to stand at a distance. Bilam's increasingly backwater route may reflect his fear or reluctance to directly attack Bnei Yisrael. This also reinforces the mixed emotions that Bilam showed in the earlier portion of this story. Instead of meeting Bnei Yisrael head-on, Bilam meandered along byroads and avoided main routes.

---

a path to a city of refuge is thirty-two cubits. For an analysis of the authenticity of these dimensions, see Daniel Sperber, *The City in Roman Palestine* (Oxford Press, 1998) 103–4.

3. yBB 5:1 (15a) gives a similar criterion (with wagons) for determining street width.

4. A major impetus of this redesign was to make the city riot-proof, allowing troops to quickly reach different parts of the city.

# Windows, Privacy, and Light

מַה טֹּבוּ אֹהָלֶיךָ יַעֲקֹב מִשְׁכְּנֹתֶיךָ יִשְׂרָאֵל. (במדבר כד:ה)

How goodly are your tents, oh Yaakov, and your dwellings, oh Yisrael. (Bamidbar 24:5)

While blessing Bnei Yisrael, Bilam called the tents and tabernacles of Israel "goodly." Some interpret this as a comment about the *batei midrash* and synagogues that are prevalent in Jewish communities or the Temple that served as the center of Jewish life.[1] Others explain this as a blessing about Bnei Yisrael's future settlements in Canaan[2] or referring to separate tents for men and women.[3] The Talmud, however, states that Bilam saw how the openings of Bnei Yisrael's tents did not face one another, allowing each tent to maintain privacy.[4] This respect for privacy, Bilam thought, made Bnei Yisrael worthy of hosting the Divine Presence.[5]

The Talmud makes this point during a discussion about property law. If several houses share a courtyard, it is forbidden to create a new window

1. See Sforno, Ohr Hachayim, and TPsY.
2. Rabeinu Bachya.
3. HaEmek Davar.
4. bBB 60a, referenced by Rashi on our verse and in Bamidbar 24:2. This midrash may have reflected building concerns at the time – most houses needed to leave their doors open to admit daylight. Therefore, courtyard openings were deliberately positioned in a different alignment, so no direct sightlines would compromise modesty. See Yizhar Hirschfeld, *The Palestinian Dwelling*, 250. In Islamic architecture, houses were often separated from the street with a bent corridor, which functioned both as a defensive mechanism and to ensure privacy. See Stephen Kite, *Shadow Makers* (Bloomsbury, 2017), 192–3. For another example of using design to preserve privacy, see ySot 8:9 (23a), which states that burnt offerings and sin offerings were slaughtered in the same place so as to prevent people from being singled out as sinners.
5. This point can be contrasted with the end of this Torah portion, when Zimri and Kozbi sinned "in the sight of all the congregation of Bnei Yisrael." See Bamidbar 25:6.

or door opposite an existing opening.[6] Likewise, one window cannot be divided into two, and a small window cannot be enlarged. Frosted or tinted glass cannot be replaced with clear glass.[7] If neighbors give permission to make a new window, it still must be kept at a certain distance from existing ones.[8] These laws, codified in the Shulchan Aruch,[9] protect the privacy of the various inhabitants. The Talmud derives the importance of privacy, and specifically the staggering of windows, from Bilam's words.

While this law places limits on windows, another halacha is predicated on the importance of windows. The Mishna and Tosefta rule that one may not build a wall near a window.[10] The Tosefta gives two reasons for this prohibition: to prevent people from standing upon the walls and peeking in, and so as not to block the sunlight.[11] R. Yoel Sirkis codified this halacha and explained that existing apartments have an established right to the sunlight they receive.[12] R. Ammi rules that small windows four cubits above ground can always be created, as their only function is to provide air.[13] Especially before the invention of air conditioning and electric lighting, windows were necessary for a building to be livable.

Many early building codes were also concerned with access to sunlight. In England, the Law of Ancient Lights made it illegal to block an existing window's light.[14] Howard Davis argued that this law led to greater consideration between neighbors: "People were making decisions about buildings in light of the rule, acting with a respect toward neighbors' ancient lights, perhaps even a respect toward windows that were not ancient lights."[15] In the United States, some building codes mandated deeper setbacks the higher a building rose, ensuring that light would reach the street and the windows of adjacent structures. The New York City zoning code of 1916

---

6. mBB 3:7.

7. *Kesef Hakedoshim* commentary on the CM.

8. In tBB 1:5, in a slightly different scenario, a window must be offset by four cubits to prevent people from peeping. Opinions range as to what is acceptable, and whether there needs to be no visibility at all, or if limited visibility is sufficient.

9. CM 154:3.

10. mBB 2:4, tBB 1:5. See also yBB 2:4 (13b), bBB 2b, and bBB 22b.

11. Ulpian, a Roman legal authority, records a similar law regarding trees and shade, in his *Digest* 8.2.17.

12. *Bayit Chadash* on the Tur Shulchan Aruch CM 154.

13. yYev 12:3 (12d).

14. As per the Prescription Act of 1832, the window must have received light for at least twenty years, without interruption. See Robert Kerr, *On Ancient Lights* (John Murray, 1865), 10.

15. Howard Davis, "The Future of Ancient Lights" in *Journal of Architectural and Planning Research* 6.2 (Summer, 1989), 137.

was particularly groundbreaking in this regard and influenced some of the city's most iconic buildings. Though these codes limited freedom in a sense, as they prevented people from building freely on their own property, they were deemed to be enough of a public good that these concerns were overruled.

The halachot about privacy and window obstruction represent two values that are potentially in conflict. Windows provide sunlight and ventilation, yet they can also facilitate invasions of privacy. Despite the importance of windows, one cannot simply install them with disregard of the neighbors. The two factors need to be balanced.

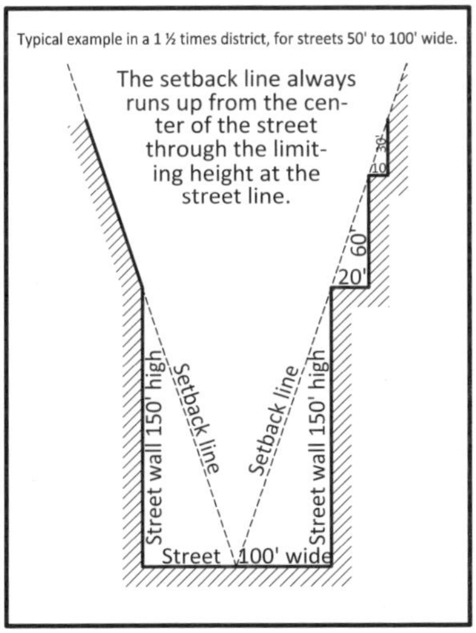


88. Diagram based on 1916 New York City Zoning Resolution, 259, showing setback requirements for upper levels, to allow sunlight to reach the streets.

The same give and take exists in the very concept of a window. A window allows light and air to enter a room and can serve as an emergency exit. However, creating an opening in a wall causes a whole host of problems. It allows heat and cold to enter, as well as thieves, animals, and insects. Equally perilous, one can fall or be thrown out of a window. A window can create a view, or it can compromise privacy.[16] People have continuously sought technology to accentuate the positive aspects while mitigating the negative ones. Installing glass in an opening keeps the window translucent while closing it to the elements.[17] Allowing the window to open and shut provides more control. Shutters, bars, and shading devices help people

16. This occurs when Avimelech spies on Yitzchak and Rivka in Bereshit 26:8.

17. Until the early eighteenth century, there were several alternatives to glass used in windows, such as thin parchment and linen coated with wax or egg water. See James

determine their privacy and protect themselves from thieves and accidents.[18] There is a constant conflict between trying to create openings in the building, while also trying to control and seal the openings.

This same tension is present in halacha. Halacha values the beneficial qualities of windows, while at the same time placing limits on where they can be installed, preserving the quality which Bilam found so meritorious.

---

Steven Curl, *Oxford Dictionary of Architecture and Landscape Architecture* (Oxford University Press, 2007), "window."

18. All these are referenced in Rabbinic literature. See mOhal 8:4 and 13:1, mShab 24:5, tOhal 14:1, tEruv 11:17, yShab 4:1 (7b), and bNid 17a.

# Lateral Loads

כִּנְחָלִים נִטָּיוּ כְּגַנֹּת עֲלֵי נָהָר כַּאֲהָלִים נָטַע ה' כַּאֲרָזִים עֲלֵי מָיִם. (במדבר כד:ו)

As rivers stretched out, as gardens by the river-side, as aloes planted of the Lord, as cedars beside the waters. (Bamidbar 24:6)

Bilam's third attempt to curse Bnei Yisrael ended, as the previous two, with him blessing them instead. After complimenting Bnei Yisrael's camp, he compared them to a garden planted by God, with aloes and "cedars beside the waters." The simile of cedar trees is interpreted in several ways, but it is generally considered to be a positive comparison. Cedar trees are lofty and strong, so the comparison with Bnei Yisrael blesses the Israelites with strength and longevity.[1]

Despite these positive connotations, the Talmud reports that Bilam was trying to sneak in a curse.[2] It cheekily explains that Bilam's "blessing" was actually worse than a curse that was uttered by Achiya the Shiloni, when he compared the Kingdom of Israel to a "reed in water."[3] While a cedar tree is strong and unbending, this can be viewed detrimentally, as a strong gale can uproot the tree. A reed, on the other hand, is flexible and can bend with the wind. Once the storm passes, it returns to its upright position. A reed can also regenerate much more quickly than a cedar tree.

Like a tall cedar tree, buildings must be able to withstand lateral loads. When we think of forces acting on a building, the first and most obvious consideration is gravity – any building must be able to support its own weight and the weight of everything within. However, other forces act on buildings as well – air pressure from the side and earthquakes that shake

1. As per Ibn Ezra, referencing Tehilim 92:13, and Malbim. R. S.R. Hirsch refers to the "firm strength of cedars." HaEmek Davar compares cedars specifically to Torah scholars.
2. bTaan 20a and bSan 105b.
3. Melachim I 14:15.

the foundations.[4] This is especially a concern when dealing with tall structures. The taller a building, the more of a problem it has with wind loads.

Besides ensuring that a building will not topple over, lateral loads must also be calculated to ensure that a building will not sway excessively. All buildings move laterally, but at a certain threshold, buildings become uncomfortable to inhabit if they are moving too much. This can be prevented somewhat by increasing the rigidity of the building's frame or having a rigid central core of elevators and stairs, but as the buildings grow taller this becomes less practical. As per the Talmud's analysis, an overly rigid building also has drawbacks. Instead, some tall buildings use a tuned mass damper[5] to help reduce the building's movement back and forth. Other buildings isolate themselves slightly from the ground, to limit the impact of tremors.

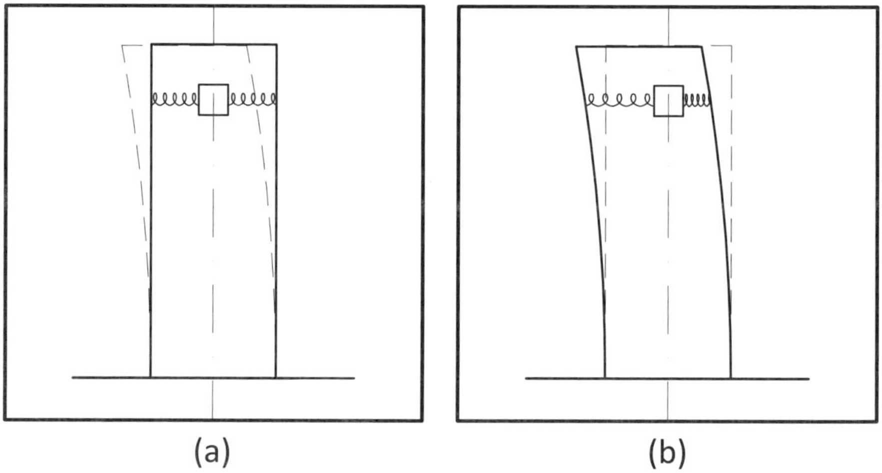

89. Tuned mass damper: (a) building at rest (b) building sways, mass initially remains in place and helps damp the swaying.

According to this analysis, the superiority of the reed is far from certain. While too much rigidity and too much exposure to wind puts the cedar at risk, excessive flexibility is also dangerous for a building and can make it uninhabitable. Although too much rigidity can be problematic, in this case, the comparison to cedar trees was likely meant to be positive.

4. Although the Rabbis quote a number of "causes" of earthquakes, one in particular relates the force of earthquakes specifically to the destruction of buildings. yBer 9:2 (13c) states that "When God sees theaters and circuses standing safely, but study halls are destroyed, he unleashes destruction on the world."

5. A heavy mass mounted on rollers and installed in the upper portion of a building. Inertia keeps this mass at rest, and it counteracts lateral building movement.

# Dividing the Land

לָאֵלֶּה תֵּחָלֵק הָאָרֶץ בְּנַחֲלָה בְּמִסְפַּר שֵׁמוֹת. לָרַב תַּרְבֶּה נַחֲלָתוֹ וְלַמְעַט תַּמְעִיט
נַחֲלָתוֹ אִישׁ לְפִי פְקֻדָיו יֻתַּן נַחֲלָתוֹ. אַךְ בְּגוֹרָל יֵחָלֵק אֶת הָאָרֶץ לִשְׁמוֹת מַטּוֹת
אֲבֹתָם יִנְחָלוּ. עַל פִּי הַגּוֹרָל תֵּחָלֵק נַחֲלָתוֹ בֵּין רַב לִמְעָט. (במדבר כו:נג-נו)

To these, the land shall be divided for an inheritance according to the number of names. To the more numerous you shall give the more inheritance and to the fewer, you shall give the less inheritance. To each one according to those that were numbered of it shall its inheritance be given. Nevertheless, the land shall be divided by lot, according to the names of the tribes of their fathers they shall inherit. According to the lot shall their inheritance be divided between more and fewer. (Bamidbar 26:53–56)

FOLLOWING a national census, Moshe was told how to divide up the land of Canaan. The division was to be done by tribe, by population, and by lottery.[1]

The Talmud records an argument over which census controlled the division of land: the census taken leaving Egypt (as claimed by R. Yoshiya), or the one taken before entering Canaan (as explained by R. Yonatan). R. Shimon ben Elazar felt that both censuses were taken into account so that every person who left Egypt *or* entered the land was given a portion, and those present in both counts received two portions.[2]

There are a number of opinions about the meaning of the verse "To the more numerous you shall give the more inheritance and to the fewer you shall give the less inheritance." According to Rashi and Sforno, the land was divided into twelve portions (for twelve tribes) that were monetarily equal but not of equal size. A tribe with a large population was given a

1. In Roman colonies, land was also distributed by lottery once surveyors finished laying out the plots of land. See Joseph Rykwert, *The Idea of a Town* (MIT Press, 1995), 60.

2. bBB 117a–b and yBB 8:2 (16a).

large portion of low-quality land, while a tribe with a small population was given a smaller portion of high-quality land. In this way, the tribes were given an area depending on their population, yet in the end, they each received a monetarily equal inheritance. Even though each portion was seemingly tailor-made for a specific tribe, a lottery was still used to prove the authenticity of the division.

Abarbanel and Malbim had similar views. However, they felt that the lottery only dictated the geographic region in which each tribe would settle, not the exact boundaries. Once the tribes were divided up into general geographic areas, the exact boundaries were set based on population, to ensure that large tribes received more land.

Ramban writes that every tribe was given territory of equal area. Each tribe then divided its land among the families based on their size, with large families receiving a bigger portion and small families getting a smaller one.

The various commentators focus on how to divide the land fairly. They consider two factors: the population of each tribe, and the best way to create twelve equitable parcels of land. Some explain that each *individual* got an equal portion, while others write that each *tribe* got an equal portion, resulting in different allotments for the individuals. At the same time, the Talmud discusses what determines the value of each parcel, based on area, value, natural resources, beauty, or location.[3] The focus is on the division of the land as a necessary way of divvying up something of value.

Despite this focus by the commentators, the division of land into tribes and families does more than just split the land equitably between the various inheritors. Dividing land into smaller, more manageable units, or parcelization, is one technique for transforming wilderness into private property. By dividing territory into smaller sections, the land is made into a consumable good. For example, as the United States expanded, this was one of the main ways it applied sovereignty to its new land. Thomas Jefferson ordered all new U.S. territory to be surveyed, and a grid applied across the land. This grid enabled the property to be divided into increasingly smaller units and sold, making way for the population to spread across the continent. Major gridlines were placed every six miles, which formed the boundaries of future townships. These were in turn divided into thirty-six squares, each a square mile, and considered an appropriate size for a homestead. Eventually, these square mile grids were

3. bBB 122a. In terms of location, proximity to Yehuda is the desirable quality, either due to the location of the Temple or its distance from the border. HaEmek Davar writes that value was determined by the land's fertility. In a discussion in bMeg 6a, we see that Zevulun's land was valuable due to its fishing, dye, and glassmaking resources.

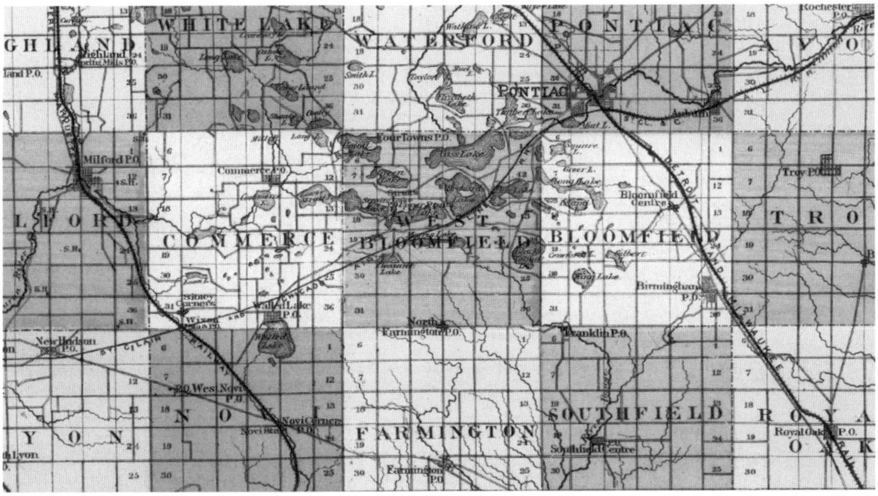


90. Partial map of Oakland County, MI, showing 6 × 6 mile townships divided into 1 × 1 mile sections. (Ogel & Col, 1908)

further quartered and then quartered again, creating smaller parcels of one-sixteenth of a mile, equal to forty acres. This pattern of division is still very visible in aerial maps of the United States, especially in farmland. The division of the land helped the United States assert its control over all its territory.

Similarly, dividing Canaan into parcels helped Bnei Yisrael assert their control and truly take possession of it. The division of the land was therefore not just a byproduct of the need to demarcate the boundaries of each tribe; it was a vital component of controlling the land.

# Natural vs. Manmade

וּשְׂעִיר עִזִּים אֶחָד חַטָּאת מִלְּבַד עֹלַת הַתָּמִיד וּמִנְחָתָהּ וְנִסְכֵּיהֶם. (במדבר כט:יט)

And one he-goat for a sin offering, besides the continual burnt offering and its meal offering and their drink offerings. (Bamidbar 29:19)

THE Torah describes, in a repetitive fashion, the offerings that are brought on each day of Sukkot. While the wording for each day is almost identical, R. Yehuda ben Batera points out that three extra letters appear: *Mem, Yud,* and *Mem,* spelling out the word *mayim,* water. This, he explains, hints at the mitzva of water libations on Sukkot. R Akiva learns from the wording that there are two types of libations in the Temple: water and wine.[1]

The libation ceremony is described in the Mishna and Tosefta, which include descriptions of the physical infrastructure in the Temple. The altar had two drains: one for water and one for wine, each with different-sized holes to account for the unequal viscosity of wine and water.[2] There is also a dispute about the terminus of these drains. R. Yosi taught that the liquid seeped into the depths of the earth, while R. Elazar ben R. Tzadok claimed that the liquid would gather in a cistern that was cleaned out every seventy years.[3]

One of the main points of discussion involves the *shitin,* fissures in the

1. bTaan 2b and yRH 1:3 (57b)/ySuk 4:1 (54b), where it is quoted in the name of R. Akiva. See also R. Natan's opinion in Sifri Bamidbar 143, concerning Bamidbar 28:7.

2. mSuk 4:9 and tSuk 3:14. tMen 12:10 states that oil was poured out along with the wine. There was also a drain for blood – see my commentary on Vayikra 4:7. An altar in Alalakh was found with a similar stone for libations at its base. See Leonard Woolley, *Tell Atchana* (The Society of Antiquaries, 1955), 63.

3. tSuk 3:14–15, ySuk 4:6 (54d), bSuk 48b–49a. Use of a cistern or pit is fairly normal. For example, typical fireplace details call for an ash pit, which can be emptied from below as needed.

bedrock beneath the altar which served as part of the drainage system. While the Tosefta specifically mentions that the two drains emptied in a channel that "was built by the builder of the Temple,"[4] the Tosefta and both Talmuds highlight that the fissures were natural phenomena. Each source uses a different phrase as proof: in the Talmud Bavli, R. Yohanan states that "the fissures were created during the six days of creation." The Talmud uses wordplay to make this point, breaking up the word *bereshit* into *bara/shit*, "He created the fissure."[5] The Tosefta uses slightly more ambiguous terminology, explaining that the liquid drained into the "fissure which God made."[6] Another mystical discussion about the origin of the fissures is found in a legend about King David's preparations for the eventual building of the Temple. When he meddles with the fissures, the result is nearly catastrophic.[7]

The most clear-cut treatment of this question, however, appears in the Talmud Yerushalmi, where R. Shimon says that the fissures were "the work of heaven," and goes on to explain that these fissures were natural, yet they were more beautiful than the work of an artist. The assumption, which is clearly stated in the Talmud, is that natural features are not as pleasant or fine as man-made ones.[8]

Humans have a long history of revering natural phenomena, for their beauty and because they are "natural."[9] There is an idea that raw nature, even in a place as designed as the Temple, gives a direct connection to Creation and to God. With the fissures, there is a desire to see God as involved in the construction and infrastructure of the Temple. Something as mundane as plumbing becomes a sign that this is the location and design that was intended from the dawn of time. The fissures help connect the structure of the Temple with God's will.

At the same time, there is a tension between the desire to use natural features and the impulse to build and sculpt with our own hands. This is the same tension that is highlighted in the midrash about R. Akiva

4. tSuk 3:14.

5. bSuk 49a.

6. tSuk 3:15. The word *hamakom* used in this expression could mean "the place" or can be a euphemism for God.

7. bSuk 53a.

8. ySuk 4:6 (54d).

9. Some architects have tried to achieve "organic" architecture, which they felt was more harmonious with nature, and therefore more beautiful. One common method is to try and build without using right angles. The lack of right angles in nature was noted by Rabbi Shimon ben Gamliel in tMaas 3:15, who states that "there are no squares from the six days of creation."

and Turnus Rufus, who argue over circumcision and making wheat into bread.[10] Traditional Judaism does not believe in worshiping nature or using it alone to commune with God. Perhaps this is why there is an emphasis in the Tosefta on the man-made pipes that lead to the fissures. One might even argue that this is the underlying disagreement about whether the fissures lead to the depths of the earth or feed into a cistern that needs to be cleaned from time to time. The former opinion takes humans out of the process, while the latter keeps humankind in the design. With the fissures, the clear impulse is to highlight God's involvement in the design of the Temple, but also to see man as a partner, necessary to create the Temple.

10. Tanchuma Tazria 5.

# Circulation in Synagogues

וּבַיּוֹם הַשְּׁבִיעִי פָּרִים שִׁבְעָה אֵילִם שְׁנָיִם כְּבָשִׂים בְּנֵי שָׁנָה אַרְבָּעָה עָשָׂר תְּמִימִם.
(במדבר כט:לב)

And on the seventh day seven bullocks, two rams, and fourteen he-lambs of the first year without blemish. (Bamidbar 29:32)

THE Torah details, day by day, all the sacrifices brought on the seven days of Sukkot. While each day has a different number of sacrifices, the components remain similar, with the offerings comprised of bulls, rams, lambs, and a goat. However, as rabbinic Judaism developed, additional elements were added to the service. In the Temple, the worshipers would walk a circuit around the altar holding willow branches. On the seventh day, they walked seven circuits.[1] When the Temple was destroyed, this was adapted for synagogue prayer services: during morning prayers, worshipers walk in a loop around the *bima* in the synagogue, a ceremony called *hoshanot*.[2] On the seventh day, rather than circling once, the *bima* is circled seven times.[3]

In the *hakafot* performed on Sukkot, the *bima* acts as the center of the revolutions. This is fitting as the *bima* is traditionally located in the center of the synagogue. It is also one of the two poles of synagogue design, serving along with the ark that holds the Torah scrolls as the spine of

---

1. mSuk 4:5 and VayR 30:5. ySuk 4:3 (54c) connects the number of circuits with the story of the conquest of Yericho.

2. Originally, the four species were used for the seven days only in the Temple; elsewhere their use was limited to the first day. However, to memorialize the Temple, they are now used every day of Sukkot except for Shabbat. Midrash Tehilim 17:5 records an alternative tradition, in which the congregants circle around the cantor, "who would stand like an angel of God with a Torah scroll in his arm."

3. Shulchan Aruch OC 760:1.

the synagogue.[4] While the *bima* corresponds to the altar in the Temple,[5] the ark is akin to the Temple's Ark of the Covenant.[6] However, not all traditions located the *bima* in the center of the synagogue. In her history of European synagogues, Carol Herselle Krinsky explains that while Ashkenazi tradition generally prefers this location,[7] Sefardi synagogues often put the *bima* on the side of the room opposite the ark.[8]

The location of the *bima* became a point of contention between the Orthodox and Reform movements. R. Yechiel Michel Epstein noted that in Reform synagogues the *bima* was moved away from the center, something that he felt would result in "great punishment."[9] R. Moshe Feinstein wrote in a responsa that he feared synagogues would start using a microphone on Shabbat and holidays if the *bima* was not centrally located.[10]

Clarifying why Reform synagogues changed the location of the *bima*, Krinsky explains that before the nineteenth century, synagogue seats were usually moveable. During prayers, people would face forward, toward the ark, while during the reading of the Torah they would shift their seats to face the *bima*. It was only with the rise of Reform Judaism that synagogues began to adopt the trappings of church architecture and use fixed pews. It became more practical to locate the *bima* toward the front of the synagogue, as it was no longer possible for people to reorient their seats toward the *bima* during times of Torah reading.[11] Moving the *bima* forward also solved the difficulty of having people seated between the *bima* and the ark, with their backs toward the *bima*, which was outlawed by many rabbinic

4. Carol Herselle Krinsky, *Synagogues of Europe* (MIT Press, 1985), 21–22. See also tSuk 4:6, which discusses the synagogue of Alexandria and mentions the wooden *bima* in the middle. See also Lee Levine, *The Ancient Synagogue* (Yale Press, 2005), 93–94 and 343–347, for the archaeological record of *bimot* in synagogues in the Roman world.

5. bMeg 31b, as quoted in Mishna Berura O.C. 660:1.

6. For example, the synagogue liturgy recited when opening the ark is a verse about taking out the ark of the covenant. See Bamidbar 10:35.

7. See R. Moshe Isserles on OC 150:5. See also Rambam, Hilchot Tefila, 11:3. Magen Avraham, quoting Zohar Vayakhel 369, adds that the *bima* should not be more than six steps above floor level.

8. The earliest synagogues did not have a special Torah shrine. Rather, the Torah was brought in from a separate room as necessary. See Levine, *The Ancient Synagogue*, 75 and 351–356. As the building type developed, it became accepted for a special niche or platform to exist in the front, Jerusalem-oriented wall, in the direction in which prayers were directed. See tMeg 3:21–22 and Shulchan Aruch OC 150:5.

9. Aruch Hashulchan OC 150:9.

10. Igrot Moshe, OC II:41. In the following *teshuva*, he specifically calls out Reform as a driving force behind the changing norms for *bima* placement.

11. Krinsky, 23.

authorities.[12] However, architecturally this location deemphasized the importance of the *bima* and made it subordinate to the ark.[13]

This change in synagogue furniture, and the subsequent realignment of the *bima,* helps explain one of the most poorly functioning aspects of synagogue architecture, the *hoshanot* circuits performed on Sukkot. In many synagogues, the existing aisles in the sanctuary simply do not permit the worshipers to perform the circuits effectively. That is, in the time it takes to recite the liturgy associated with *hoshanot,* even a crowd that is only a fraction of the synagogue's capacity will not successfully be able to complete a circuit. It seems unlikely that such a situation would have persisted for a thousand years[14] without a correction. Rather, based on the above analysis of the *bima* position, the problem is modern in nature. Previously, when furniture was not fixed, it was easy enough for the congregants to wend their way around chairs, or else quickly move the seats aside before the circuits. However, with the advent of fixed furniture, this was no longer possible. Congregations continue to attempt the circuits as best as possible, and some choose to relocate to a more open space, such as a courtyard or social hall, but predominantly the fixed furniture results in poor traffic flow and failed *hakafot.* This can be contrasted with the *hakafot* on Simchat Torah, which last far longer and are treated as more significant. As a result, a greater effort is made to rearrange the synagogue furniture to create a more functional space. On the days of Sukkot – even with the lengthy liturgy of the seventh day – the same effort is not seen as practical.

While safety codes in synagogues do require wide aisles for egress in the case of an emergency, this space requirement differs from what is needed for *hakafot.* In an emergency, the synagogue begins to empty. The people in front clear the area, leaving space for the ones further in to progress toward the exit. With *hakafot,* no one is leaving the premises, so no additional space opens up for forward progress. It seems impractical for synagogues

12. See Magen Avraham, Levush, and Turei Zahav.

13. It should be noted that a similar conflict existed in church design, manifested in the two major styles of churches – basilica-plan churches, facing one direction, and central-plan churches, which were multi-directional and focused on the central space below the rotunda. See Marilyn Stokstad, *Art History,* Vol. I (Prentice Hall Inc., 1999), 297.

14. Since the time of Saadia Gaon, as per his siddur, 238. The only halachic reference to the *hoshanot* traffic problem that I have been able to find is by R. Simchah Ben Zion Isaac Rabinowicz in *Piskei Teshuvot* on O.C. 660. He mentions people who cut corners in their attempt to circle the *bima,* cutting across the *bima* itself. He finds this practice problematic. *Piskei Teshuvot* was written between 1991–2011.

to be designed with aisles wide enough to accommodate *hakafot.* At the same time, it is important to recognize that the situation today is not identical to how *hakafot* functioned two hundred years ago and to consider alternative solutions such as performing the circuits outside the sanctuary or taking the time to move furniture.

# *Nedarim* and Communal Space

אִישׁ כִּי יִדֹּר נֶדֶר לַה' אוֹ הִשָּׁבַע שְׁבֻעָה לֶאְסֹר אִסָּר עַל נַפְשׁוֹ לֹא יַחֵל דְּבָרוֹ
כְּכָל הַיֹּצֵא מִפִּיו יַעֲשֶׂה. (במדבר ל:ג)

When a man vows a vow to the Lord or swears an oath to bind his soul with a bond, he shall not break his word, he shall do according to all that proceeds out of his mouth. (Bamidbar 30:3)

THE laws of vows, mentioned in simple terms in this verse, are fleshed out in two tractates of the Talmud. One of these tractates, Nedarim, discusses what happens if someone vows not to get any benefit from a specific person, or vows not to give any benefit to that person. The Talmud questions what such a blanket statement entails: if you find a lost object belonging to him can you return it?[1] Can you teach his son Torah?[2] Can you sleep in the same bed with him?[3] What happens if he has no food to eat?[4]

Among the many issues that arise in this discussion is the question of communal property. The Mishna states that if two people are mutually forbidden to benefit from one another, they are still allowed to use things that belong to all of Israel[5] but are forbidden from using items belonging to their city.[6] The Mishna then gives examples for these two categories: the first group includes the Temple Mount, Temple courtyards, and public cisterns along the highways. The second category includes the town square, bathhouse, synagogue, ark, and public library books.[7]

1. mNed 4:2.
2. mNed 4:3.
3. mNed 4:4.
4. mNed 4:7, bNed 47b–48a.
5. Literally, "items belonging to the immigrants from Babylon."
6. mNed 5:4–5.
7. As edifices like theaters are often grouped with synagogues and *batei midrash*, it seems that they count as items belonging to the city. See yBer 4:2 (7d), yBer 9:2 (13c),

Why is there a difference between these two categories? It may be related to funding and ownership. R. Nissim of Gerona[8] explains that city aldermen have the right to sell things belonging to the city, while presumably no one is entrusted to sell the Temple Mount or public cisterns. They belong to the nation. For this reason, the Talmud Yerushalmi and the Tosefta[9] also distinguish between the town square, which is property of the city, and squares that are along the main highways, which are not.[10]

Another possibility is that there is a difference in the immediacy of the connection. Rambam writes that when something is jointly owned by all of Israel, there is only a minuscule and insignificant percentage of ownership for each individual.[11] Therefore, one individual's oath is not enough to make it prohibited. However, there is a greater sense of ownership over things that belong to just your city.

While the first two explanations relate to ownership, we can also think of the distinction as corresponding to the national or local significance of a building. National institutions and municipal institutions provided two different kinds of benefits. Nationally significant spaces are important for shaping the collective ethos of the nation, making a diverse populace feel like they belong to a single nation. Local spaces have a different kind of importance, creating communal cohesion. When communities share spaces and facilities, they are more willing to help one another. This can positively impact the safety and prevalence of lovingkindness in the communities. These local benefits are a real boon for the city residents. In times of disaster, they can be the difference between life and death. In one example, neighborhoods in Chicago with strong social infrastructure, like libraries and civic centers, fared better during a deadly heatwave, as the neighbors were familiar with each other and checked to make sure others were okay.[12] Shared spaces in a neighborhood tend to be of *immediate benefit* to the individuals in the community and lead directly to mutual assistance. Therefore, the utility of local amenities is significant enough to be outlawed by two people swearing not to provide benefit to one another.

One of the examples in the Mishna, the town square, demonstrates this

---

bMeg 6a, and PdRK 28:2.

8. In his R"an commentary, printed on bNed 48a, *ve'asurin bedavar shel ota ha'ir.*

9. tNed 2:9, yNed 5:5 (39b).

10. See Saul Lieberman's long commentary on tNed 2:9, p.436.

11. Hilchot Nedarim 7:2 and especially his commentary on the Mishna.

12. Eric Klinenberg, *Heat Wave: A Social Autopsy of Disaster in Chicago* (University of Chicago Press, 2003.

nicely. The town square was a gathering spot for commerce,[13] prayer,[14] and mourning.[15] It was typically surrounded by other public buildings, such as basilicas, the treasury, the jail, and the local government.[16] In short, access to this space provided real benefit to an inhabitant of the town. It was of great civic (though not national) importance and considered to be jointly owned by all members of the city. It thus makes sense that if two citizens are forbidden to benefit from one another, they would both be prohibited from using the town square.

---

13. See both Korban HaEida and Pnei Moshe on yNed 5:5 (39b), *harechava*.
14. bMeg 25a, tMeg 2:12, and bTaan 16a.
15. bKet 8b.
16. Vitruvius, V.2.

MATOT

# Siege Warfare

וַיִּצְבְּאוּ עַל מִדְיָן כַּאֲשֶׁר צִוָּה ה׳ אֶת מֹשֶׁה וַיַּהַרְגוּ כָּל זָכָר. (במדבר לא:ז)

And they warred against Midian as the Lord commanded Moshe, and they slew every male. (Bamidbar 31:7)

THE Torah relates that Bnei Yisrael fought with and killed all the Midianite males. The Sifri nonetheless uses this verse to teach a halacha of ethical warfare. It records a debate about sieges, with R. Natan ruling that an army may not circumvallate a city, but must instead leave an opening for the enemy army to flee.[1] While this is a minority opinion in the Sifri, Rambam codifies the prohibition as the law.[2] This is somewhat surprising because a siege in which the defenders can come and go has little hope of succeeding.

There are two main theories as to why a complete siege of a city is prohibited. Rambam writes that this gives the besieged the option of fleeing from the conflict and Meir Simcha of Dvinsk explains that allowing escape is a military tactic – if the enemy has no choice but to fight to the death, they will do so desperately and with all their might.[3] However, leaving an escape route allows the enemy to flee rather than fight, making the conquest easier.[4] Ramban gives a different reason, writing that it is a moral

1. Sifri Bamidbar 157. Devarim 20:10 also demands that before initiating a siege, one must offer the city terms to surrender. See also Sifri Devarim 199. For a view of these laws in the context of the ancient Near East, see Israel Eph'al, *The City Besieged: Siege and its Manifestations in the Ancient Near East* (Magnes Press, 2013) 14–15 and 46–48.

2. Rambam Hilchot Melachim 6:7. According to R. Baruch Epstein's Torah Temima commentary, Rambam rules like R. Natan due to Yehoshua's example of letting nations flee rather than fight, as per ySheviit 6:1 (36c).

3. This exact reaction is described by Josephus at the siege of Yodfat. See Josephus, *The Jewish War* 3.149. In the same section, Josephus describes the measures and countermeasures of the siege.

4. Meshech Chochma on this verse. According to Roman law, defenders inside a city could surrender until the moment a battering ram first made contact with the city walls.

imperative to show compassion even during battle.[5] These approaches are not mutually exclusive, and both sages may acknowledge the validity of the other's opinion.

Vitruvius addresses the tactics of siege warfare from both the offensive[6] and defensive[7] positions. Preparing for sieges was one of the many fields of expertise that an architect was expected to master. Another ancient architect, Apollodorus of Damascus, wrote a second-century treatise on siege warfare.[8] Architects were expected to be familiar with the various siege machines, including scorpions, catapults, *ballistae*, battering rams, equipment for filling in moats, and various ladders and towers for assaulting fortifications.[9] The construction of these apparatus often required the cutting of all the nearby trees, a practice also constrained by the Torah.[10]

Jewish sources were also familiar with siege warfare. Sieges of Yodfat, Gamla, Jerusalem, and Masada are described by Josephus and in rabbinic literature. Stories of earlier sieges by the Assyrians are found in the Bible.[11] The Romans were particularly skilled at sieges and the defenders were often treated appallingly by the conquering armies. Dirges about the horrible conditions in Jerusalem during various sieges are recited on the Ninth of Av, keeping them in the Jewish collective memory. Siege weapons are also mentioned in descriptions of sieges found in rabbinic literature.[12] There is, for example, a recurring passage in rabbinic literature in which

---

Once this occurs, all those inside were liable to be massacred or raped. See Adrian Goldsworthy, *Roman Warfare* (Cassell PLC, 2000), 145. Not all sieges were designed with attrition in mind. Some were extended campaigns to assault the city.

5. Ramban *Sefer Hamitzvot* positive commandment addendum 5. See also the Yakar Tiferet commentary of R. David ben Shlomo ibn Abi Zimra (Radbaz) on Rambam's Hilchot Melachim 6:7.

6. Vitruvius, *Ten Books on Architecture* X.10–15.

7. Vitruvius, *Ten Books on Architecture* I.5, X.16.

8. He designed many buildings in Rome, including Trajan's Column.

9. For a possible, very early, reference to defensive siege weapons, see Divrei Hayamim II 26:15.

10. Devarim 20:19–20 prohibits the cutting of fruit trees. This could be a very pressing need, especially in areas largely devoid of forests. For example, when the Crusaders reached Jerusalem in June 1099, they established a siege around the city but were unable to obtain enough wood for the simple task of building siege ladders. Eventually they resorted to disassembling ships in the Jaffa port. See also my commentary on those verses as well as bEruv 17a and yEruv 1:10 (19c) for laws concerning stealing wood during war.

11. Remains of the circumvallation that occurred during the siege of Gat, described in Melachim II 12:18, are the earliest examples that have been uncovered by archaeologists.

12. Pesikta Rabati 29–30, EichaR 2:2, PdRK 7:11.

*ballistae* are compared to divine artillery, particularly in the context of the plagues in Egypt.[13]

While one might be inclined to assume that R. Natan's prohibition of circumvallation demonstrates a lack of understanding of how sieges work, the many references to these technologies that appear in rabbinic literature and the recollections of sieges in Jewish liturgy make it clear that the Rabbis were familiar with siege tactics. Their knowledge of the horrors of sieges may have provided the motivation to allow an escape for the besieged, or perhaps even to ban sieges altogether, as some scholars have claimed.[14] In either case, it is safe to assume that the prohibition against all-out sieges comes from a deep familiarity with siege, not from ignorance.

91. Reconstructed small Roma *ballista* at Hecht Museum, Haifa. (Photo by Oren Rozen, Wikimedia)

13. MdRY Beshalach (vayehi) 2, MdRS Beshalach 14:13, ySot 8:3. For additional sources, see Mireille Hadas–Lebel, *Jerusalem Against Rome* (Peeters Publishers, 2006), 239–242. Whereas the Sifri seems to frown on sieges, this comparison to the Egyptian plagues makes siege warfare seem acceptable.

14. Michael Walzer, "The Ethics of Warfare in the Jewish Tradition" in *Philosophia* 40:4 (Dec 2012) 633–641.

MATOT

# Tents and Palaces

וְאֵת כָּל עָרֵיהֶם בְּמוֹשְׁבֹתָם וְאֵת כָּל טִירֹתָם שָׂרְפוּ בָּאֵשׁ. (במדבר לא:י)

And all their cities in the places where they dwelled, and all their *tirot*, they burned with fire. (Bamidbar 31:10)

BNEI Yisrael were ordered to exact vengeance from the Midianites for their aggression. Each tribe selected one thousand soldiers. This army succeeded in killing all the men and the kings of Midian, taking the women captive and burning the cities and *tirot* to the ground.

Most commentators believe that the word *tirot* refers to temples or palaces.[1] Malbim elaborates on these two possibilities. He explains that the places of worship were essentially astrological observatories used for communing with the stars. The palaces, on the other hand, were the places where the leaders would congregate.

These two options each represent a locus of authority in ancient society. In the story of Bilam, we see two main actors: Balak, the king of Midian, and Bilam, a priest. They share the responsibility of leading the Midianites against Bnei Yisrael. Therefore, it is sensible that the homes of the priests and kings would each be a target for retribution. As centers of power in Midianite society, their destruction would be both logical and symbolic. In addition, the temples and palaces were probably among the most notable buildings in terms of their grandeur and importance. Therefore, they would be natural targets and their sacking would also deserve special mention.[2]

1. Onkelos translates the word as "temples." Yonatan ben Uziel, Ibn Ezra, the Sifri, and Rashi all offer both suggestions.

2. For a discussion of Roman treatment of sacred sites, see Steven H. Rutledge, "The Roman Destruction of Sacred Sites" in *Historia: Zeitschfit für Alte Geschichte* Bd. 56, H. 2 (2007), 179–195. Rutledge notes that sacred sites were especially targeted when they also served as a center of rebellion (181). He also discusses the destruction of the Temple in Jerusalem (189–90).

In stark contrast to these two interpretations is the explanation found in Daat Mikre. There the meaning of *tirot* is given as a simple encampment of tents surrounded by a stone wall. As proof, Daat Mikre points to a verse in Tehilim[3] which reads "Let their *tirot* be desolate, let none dwell in their tents." Linguistically, the commentary explains that only in a later period did the word *tirot* take on the meaning of a palace, but that the original meaning was a much simpler arrangement of tents.

Following the same logic as above, this interpretation would seem to indicate that the Midianites were all held responsible for their actions against Bnei Yisrael. Not just the leaders were killed, but so were all the men. Not only the temples and palaces were destroyed, but so were all the cities, and even the simple encampments were razed. This interpretation, in which the regular settlements were attacked, fits well with the Torah's description of the total destruction of Midian.

The term *tirot* can be interpreted in two ways. It can either refer to temples and palaces, or it can imply simple dwellings. Depending on the interpretation, we can understand who was ultimately held responsible for the Midianite crimes against Bnei Yisrael. If *tirot* means palaces, this implies that the leadership was guilty. If *tirot* means simple dwellings, then we can assume that all the Midianites were held equally responsible.

3. Tehilim 69:26.

# Naming Cities

וְאֶת נְבוֹ וְאֶת בַּעַל מְעוֹן מוּסַבֹּת שֵׁם וְאֶת שִׂבְמָה וַיִּקְרְאוּ בְשֵׁמֹת אֶת שְׁמוֹת הֶעָרִים אֲשֶׁר בָּנוּ. (במדבר לב:לח)

And Nevo and Baal Meon, their names being changed, and Sivma, and gave other names to the cities which they built. (Bamidbar 32:38)

THE Torah describes the cities which the tribes of Reuven, Gad, and Menashe constructed east of the Jordan River. Some of the cities already existed and had preestablished names, which Bnei Yisrael opted to change. At the same time, however, the Torah also says that Bnei Yisrael built these cities.

Rashi explains that the cities were originally named after foreign gods and Bnei Yisrael wished to purge these references. Chizkuni writes that the names had been fluid, changing with each successive conquest – first named by Ammon and Moab, then renamed by the Emorites, and finally rebranded by the Israelites. Ramban understood that Bnei Yisrael revived the original Moabite names.[1] Later in the Torah, we find a similar record of renaming Chermon. There, Rashi comments that the Land of Israel was very desirable, and every nation wanted to leave an imprint on it.[2]

The origin of a city's name is often lost to history. Cities are most commonly named for individuals, geographic features, or functions. One midrash highlights the role of important figures in city names, pointing to Tiberias, Constantinople, Antioch, Rome, and Alexandria, among others.[3] City names do tend to change over time to ease difficult pronunciations, adjust to the shifting spoken language, adaptation, misinterpretation, and new cultural meanings. Another midrash explains that some locations

1. Ramban suggests that this was either for convenience or to embarrass Moab.
2. Devarim 3:9 and bChul 60b.
3. BerR 23:1 and Midrash Tehilim 9:8. See also Bereshit 4:17.

mentioned in the Torah had multiple names because multiple kingdoms renamed them.[4]

As per Rashi's explanation, pagan religions are thought to have been the source of some ancient place-names. This phenomenon has been studied extensively in England,[5] though less so in ancient Israel. Israel has some prominent examples of names linked to ancient religion, such as Banias (Pan), Beit Shemesh (Shapash), and Beit Horon (Horus). Similarly, Ramallah contains the name of Allah.

Although our verse states that the cities were renamed, it also says that they were built by the Israelites.[6] Perhaps this is best explained by noting that a deliberate name change to a place can, as the midrashim indicate, be used to imprint a new personality upon the city.[7] When this happens, the name change is usually accompanied by a change in the fabric of the city, with building programs that remake the built environment. For example, during the Hellenistic period, many of the major settlements in Israel were given new names and were also recast as Greek or Roman cities. Herod did this on several occasions as well, renaming two existing towns – Tiberias[8] and Caesarea – to go along with his massive construction projects. It seems likely that the Israelites both changed the names of the cities and initiated new building projects to remake them, to more firmly take control of the sites, and imprint their own image upon them. This is why the cities are described as both built and renamed by Bnei Yisrael.

4. SZ Bamidbar 27:12, with regard to Hor Hahar. While the particular etymology may be questionable, the phenomenon it describes – of renaming locations according to different cultures – very much exists.

5. Margaret Gelling, "Place-Names and Anglo-Saxon Paganism" in *University of Birmingham Historical Journal* VIII:1, 1961.

6. R. Saadia Gaon.

7. bAZ 46a states that switching a geographic name from one celebrating idol worship to one that is derogatory or mocking may fulfill the commandment to rid Israel of pagan sites.

8. bMeg 5b.

# *Tabula Rasa* and Complexity in Architecture

וְאִם לֹא תוֹרִישׁוּ אֶת יֹשְׁבֵי הָאָרֶץ מִפְּנֵיכֶם וְהָיָה אֲשֶׁר תּוֹתִירוּ מֵהֶם לְשִׂכִּים בְּעֵינֵיכֶם וְלִצְנִינִם בְּצִדֵּיכֶם וְצָרְרוּ אֶתְכֶם עַל הָאָרֶץ אֲשֶׁר אַתֶּם יֹשְׁבִים בָּהּ.
(במדבר לג:נה)

But if you will not drive out the inhabitants of the land from before you then shall those that you let remain of them be as thorns in your eyes, and as pricks in your sides, and they shall harass you in the land wherein you dwell. (Bamidbar 33:55)

THE Torah warns Bnei Yisrael that upon entering Israel they must drive out the previous inhabitants. This verse appears in the context of removing all idol worship from the land, so most commentators explain that the earlier polytheistic inhabitants would corrupt Bnei Yisrael and lead them to forsake monotheism.[1] Yehoshua repeats this warning at the time of the conquest.[2]

The fear of foreign influences was powerful and shows up in many situations in which one culture interacts and subsumes another. Designers often prefer to demolish an existing structure and start new with a *tabula rasa,* rather than deal with existing conditions. In architecture, the Modern movement sought to rethink architecture from scratch and eliminate historical influences, which were believed to corrupt design. This led to a deep concern with purity of thought. To achieve this purity, many Modern buildings were set on detached sites, uninfluenced by surrounding conditions. External factors could be ignored, and a pure vision realized.

By the second half of the twentieth century, this growing quest for pure design generated backlash as the architecture became increasingly bland. In his book *Complexity and Contradiction,* Robert Venturi argued that architecture that deals with external pressures, addresses multiple issues,

1. See, for example, Ramban and R. S.R. Hirsch.
2. Yehoshua 23:13.

and considers different vantage points is richer and preferable. Design theory is needed, but its rules can be broken as necessary, and in doing so, more complex and interesting forms are created. Venturi wrote that "when circumstances defy order, order should bend or break: anomalies and uncertainties give validity to architecture." He specifically called out site conditions and existing buildings as examples of things that challenge the purity of design and force architects to adapt, creating more carefully considered buildings.[3] The original order of the building must be strong, but given such a design, it should be robust enough to accommodate deviations.

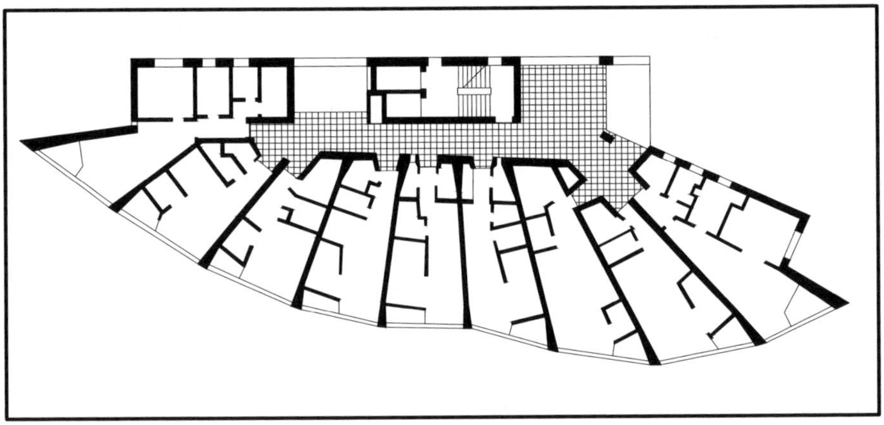

92. Plan of Apartment Building in Bremen, designed by Alvar Aalto. Venturi contrasts the "pure" rectangular form of Modernist apartment buildings with Aalto's design, which adjusts the façade to orient each apartment toward the south for the light and the view.

When Bnei Yisrael were first conquering the Land, it was important that the embryonic nation organize itself solidly, without foreign influence. Perhaps this is the reason why the Torah stressed the importance of removing all the inhabitants from the land. However, this may have only been necessary for this original period. Once the nation was firmly established, such a homogeny was no longer needed. The civilization could even be strengthened by encountering foreign ideas and applying those ideas to Torah thought. Like Venturi's Postmodernism, one can argue that a strong theory is capable, and even enriched, by interacting with complex issues and outside challenges.

3. Robert Venturi, *Complexity and Contradiction in Architecture* (Museum of Modern Art, 1977), 41–42.

# Levite Cities: Size, Beauty, and Zoning

וְהָיוּ הֶעָרִים לָהֶם לָשָׁבֶת וּמִגְרְשֵׁיהֶם יִהְיוּ לִבְהֶמְתָּם וְלִרְכֻשָׁם וּלְכֹל חַיָּתָם. וּמִגְרְשֵׁי הֶעָרִים אֲשֶׁר תִּתְּנוּ לַלְוִיִּם מִקִּיר הָעִיר וָחוּצָה אֶלֶף אַמָּה סָבִיב. וּמַדֹּתֶם מִחוּץ לָעִיר אֶת פְּאַת קֵדְמָה אַלְפַּיִם בָּאַמָּה וְאֶת פְּאַת נֶגֶב אַלְפַּיִם בָּאַמָּה וְאֶת פְּאַת יָם אַלְפַּיִם בָּאַמָּה וְאֵת פְּאַת צָפוֹן אַלְפַּיִם בָּאַמָּה וְהָעִיר בַּתָּוֶךְ זֶה יִהְיֶה לָהֶם מִגְרְשֵׁי הֶעָרִים. (במדבר לה:ג-ה)

And the cities shall they have to dwell in, and their open lands shall be for their cattle and for their goods and for all their beasts. And the open land of the cities that you shall give to the Leviim shall be from the wall of the city outward a thousand cubits round about. And you shall measure from outside the city on the east side two thousand cubits, and on the south side two thousand cubits, and on the west side two thousand cubits, and on the north side two thousand cubits, the city being in the midst. This shall be to them the open land about the cities. (Bamidbar 35:3–5)

THE tribe of Levi was not given its own territory. Instead, Bnei Yisrael were commanded to set aside cities for the Leviim. Each city came with surrounding territory, "for their cattle and for their goods and for their beasts."

The Torah gives two different dimensions for the space around the cities, once saying "a thousand cubits round about" and then stating "two thousand cubits." The Mishna notes this contradiction and suggests two explanations: either the two thousand cubits relates to the separate law of Shabbat boundaries,[1] or that there are to be two separate rings of open space: one thousand cubits for open space, and then another two thousand cubits set aside for agricultural activity.[2] Rashi understands this similarly,

1. One may only walk 2,000 cubits beyond the occupied area of a city on Shabbat. See also my commentary on Bereshit 19:30.

2. mSot 5:3. The former opinion is in the name of R. Akiva. The latter is attributed

explaining that a *total* of 2,000 cubits encircles the city, divided into two rings of 1,000 cubits each. Ramban gives a different interpretation: the overall distance covered by the city *and* its fields was 2,000 cubits: the city itself was 1,000 cubits square, surrounded by protrusions in each direction, to give a square shape that was 2,000 cubits in each direction.[3]

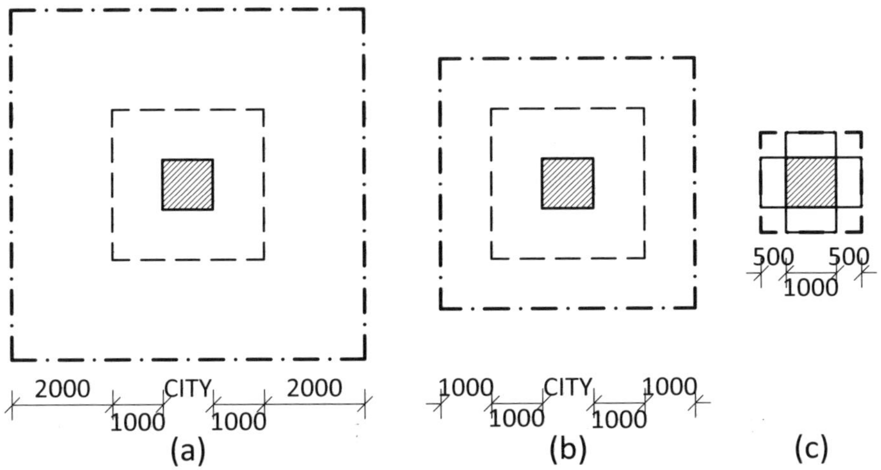


93. Levite cities as per: (a) Mishna (b) Rashi (c) Ramban.

Most commentators explain that there are two types of lands outside each city: an inner ring of open space and an outer ring used for city needs. This outer ring is associated with crops and vineyards, but Sforno includes beehives, dovecotes, and grazing land as other acceptable uses. Another source explains that this territory can be used for laundry.[4] These functions are necessary for a city, so it is logical that there is space set aside for them.[5]

Two aspects of the Levite cities may be done for aesthetic reasons.

---

to R. Eliezer ben R. Yosi Haglili and is quoted by Rambam in Hilchot Shemita Veyovel 13:2. The existence of two types of open spaces is hinted at in the verse by the word *migrashehem* (their open spaces), which is plural.

3. As demonstrated by Yosef Ofer, almost half of the manuscripts of Ramban contain a diagram to explain Ramban's words. The diagram did not make it into most of the printed editions, and later editors added their own diagrams that are different from the one in the manuscripts. See Yosef Ofer, "A Diagram of the Open Lands of the Levite Cities in Nahmanides' Commentary on the Torah" in *Jewish Quarterly Review* 99:2 (Spring 2009), 271–283.

4. bNed 81a.

5. Larger cities are supported by surrounding villages, but most towns make use of the surrounding lands to support their settlements. bMak 10a states that all cities of refuge – associated with Levite cities – should be medium-sized settlements.

Ramban mandates that Levite cities be exactly 1,000 cubits squared and, together with the surrounding territory, cover 2,000 square cubits. In explanation, he writes that "it is pleasant for cities to have a square territory."[6] Cities are occasionally planned according to geometric shapes for functional or symbolic reasons. For example, Roman army camps were usually square, presumably to project an image of order and organization. Still, this requirement is very limiting and requires a highly planned society. In contrast, rabbinic literature acknowledges that most cities are irregularly shaped, listing many different configurations in the context of Shabbat boundaries.[7] In Ramban's view, however, the cities must be square for aesthetic reasons.

A second aesthetic motivation may be related to the two separate rings. While the Torah explains that one ring is for cattle and beasts, it does not list a second function for the other ring. Rashi resolves this problem by explaining that the inner ring was left open to beautify the city. This echoes a statement in the Talmud that there shall be no trees within twenty-five cubits of a city to beautify the city.[8] The assumption is that having a wide, open space in front of a city gives it a certain grandeur and beauty.

Another way of looking at the inner ring is as a type of zoning. The Talmud Yerushalmi suggests that trees must be distanced from cities to ensure the city will have ample sunlight and because trees make the city unhealthy.[9] Today we think of trees as a way of beautifying a city, rather than something that detracts from its beauty. While it is true that trees can block sunlight, they also provide shade from the hot sun. They help create a healthy environment, produce oxygen, reduce erosion, block harsh winds, and provide fruit and fuel. However, this is a relatively new way of thinking about trees. In earlier centuries trees were seen as potentially harmful. Forests were associated with crime, outlaws, danger, and magic.[10] Without

---

6. See bKid 39a–39b for another example of orthogonal patterns viewed as aesthetically pleasing, in reference to Rav's garden.

7. tEruv 4:4, quoted in bEruv 55a. However, Gil P. Klein suggests that this tosefta was influenced by the *Corpus Agrimensorum Romanorum*, a text that records Roman surveying practice, which contains as a teaching tool cases of cities shaped like various Greek letters, including two of the cases that appear in the Tosefta. See Gil P. Klein, "Squaring the City: Between Roman and Rabbinic Urban Geometry" in *Phenomenologies of the City* ed. Henriette Steiner and Maximilian Sternberg (Ashbate, 2015), 41–42.

8. bBB 24b.

9. yBB 2:7 (13c).

10. For the contradiction between useful trees and the desire to cut down trees, see JB Jackson, "Beyond Wilderness" in *A Sense of Place, a Sense of Time* (Yale University Press, 1996), 85, and his essay "In Favor of Trees," 95–102 in the same collection. Jackson closes the latter essay by quoting John Evelyn's introduction to *Sylva*, from the

electric light, sunlight was much more important and shade deleterious. Pre-industrial cities did not feel the need to be surrounded by trees to feel connected with nature.

While Levite cities are instructed to have these surrounding areas, there are additional zoning rules which apply to all cities. The second chapter of Baba Batra lists things that must be distanced from the city. One example listed is a granary because the waste produced by the threshing causes damages to the city[11] and crops. R. Yosi mandates that beekeeping be done outside the city so that people are not stung.[12] Other examples from the Mishna include cemeteries[13] and ponds for retting flax.[14] Tanneries, which create a horrible smell and would be detrimental to the city, must be built downwind from the city.[15] Spiro Kostof described this phenomenon in European cities, mentioning streets on the outskirts of cities named Skinners Lane or Tanners Street.[16] This is similar to modern zoning that tends to separate industrial areas from residential ones.[17]

---

mid-seventeenth century, which echoed the story of Choni (bTaan 23a): "Men seldom plant trees until they begin to be wise; that is, till they grow old and find by experience the prudence and necessity of it." See also Henry W. Lawrence, *City Trees* (University of Virginia Press, 2008), 3–4, which lists some reasons why trees were not welcome in cities for thousands of years, including obstruction of traffic, damage caused by roots and branches, and their status as fire hazards. He mentions that in some cities one could not get fire insurance if a tree was growing on one's property.

11. mBB 2:8. Chazal apparently viewed chaff as an element that undermined construction. In ySan 10:1 (50a), the Talmud discusses the effects of a heretic. In a conversation between R. Elazar and R. Shmuel b. Nachman, one compares it to a stone dome: if but one stone is unstable, the whole dome becomes unstable. The other compares it to a house full of grain, which even if you clear out all the grain, some chaff will still be left, and this will make the walls unstable. In both parables, a single heretic is viewed as a powerful corrupting influence. See also similar imagery in BerR 101:10.

12. tBB 1:7.

13. Roman law also forbade burial or cremation with the city, which led to the proliferation of family tombs along the main roads leading into the city. See James C. Anderson, Jr., *Roman Architecture and Society* (Johns Hopkins University Press, 1997), 321.

14. mBB 2:10.

15. mBB 2:9. For ancient restrictions on tanneries, see Artemidorus, *Interpretation of Dreams,* 1.51 and 2.20.

16. Spiro Kostof, *The City Assembled,* 34. See also the sixth-century design rules of Julian of Askelon, who wrote extensively about building workshops for undesirable industries like glassmaking, pottery, baking, rope making and lime kilns, as well as taverns, in his time. See Harmenopoulos, *Hexabiblos* 19, as well as Saul Lieberman, "A Few Words on the Book by Julian the Architect of Ascalon *The Laws of Palestine and its Customs*" in *Tarbiz* 40 (Tamuz–Elul 5731), 416. (Hebrew)

17. Today in the United States, it is more common to find industrial zones in the city center and residential areas in the periphery.

Within cities, additional limitations were placed on commercial and industrial uses. Ovens could not be located within houses except under special circumstances.[18] Stores could not be opened in courtyards and additional restrictions were placed on bakeries, dyeries, and barns for cattle.[19]

The arrangement of the cities of the Leviim is mandated by the Torah to include an open area around the city. This was done to meet the needs of the Leviim, while at the same time preserving the quality of life in the city proper. Similarly, there are halachic rules about industry in regular cities, akin to modern-day zoning laws, mandating that destructive industries be placed outside the city. Distances are dictated to ensure the visual, material, and olfactory nature of the city are not harmed. Together, these rules can be viewed as early prototypes of zoning codes, making cities more livable.

---

18. mBB 2:2. For ancient requirement to place smelting ovens in a way that the smoke will not cause damage, see Strabo, *Geography,* 3.2.8.

19. mBB 2:2.

# Signage, Wayfinding, and Cities of Refuge

וְהִקְרִיתֶם לָכֶם עָרִים עָרֵי מִקְלָט תִּהְיֶינָה לָכֶם וְנָס שָׁמָּה רֹצֵחַ מַכֵּה נֶפֶשׁ בִּשְׁגָגָה.
(במדבר לה:יא)

> Then you shall appoint yourselves cities to be cities of refuge for you, that the slayer who kills any person through error may flee there. (Bamidbar 35:11)

AMONG the forty-eight cities that Bnei Yisrael are commanded to set aside for the Leviim are six cities of refuge. Anyone who kills by accident must flee to one of these cities, where they will be protected from retribution but confined to the city, living in exile.

For these cities to serve their role, it is necessary to provide easy access to them. The Torah highlights three ways to do so.[1] First, the cities must be spread out, so that there is always one nearby. Second, there must be roads leading to each city. Third, proper signage must be installed to allow people to navigate to the nearest city of refuge.[2]

The Torah writes that the Land of Israel should be divided "into three parts."[3] The Talmud explains that there should be the same distance between the northern border and the northernmost city of refuge, between each subsequent pair of cities, and between the southernmost city and the southern border.[4] Rashi points out that this actually divides the country into four portions rather than three. The Talmud also explains that this scheme means someone who must flee from the northern or southern border has twice as far to go as anyone else. For this reason, R. Eliyahu Mizrachi instead explains that the distance from the northern and southern

1. Devarim 19:3.
2. Rashi on Devarim 19:3, and bMak 10b.
3. Devarim 19:3.
4. bMak 9b.

borders to the nearest cities of refuge were half as far as the distance between each pair of cities.[5]

There must also be well-kept roads leading to the cities of refuge.[6] Rambam elaborates, saying the roads must be wide, free of obstacles, and level. If a road crosses a river, a bridge must be built. The roads must run directly toward the city.[7] These guidelines help the accidental murderer reach a city without delay but are also standard concerns for road builders.

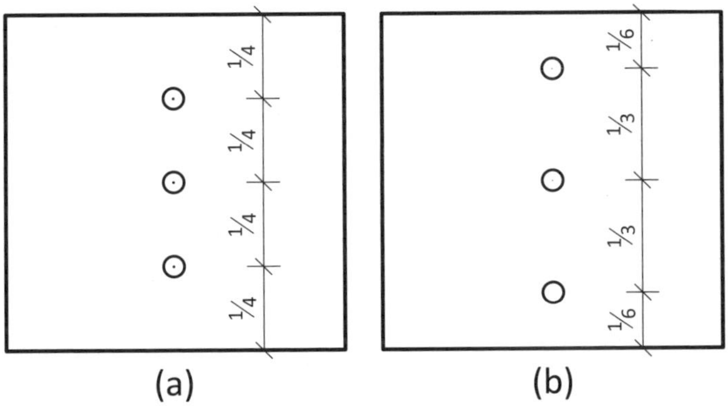


94. Dispersion of Cities of Refuge according to: (a) bMak 9b (b) R. Mizrachi.

While access to cities of refuge may seem like an unlikely reason for building a network of roads, road systems are sometimes justified through convoluted means. Roads are paved to reach natural resources, like mines or places where hydroelectricity can be generated. The United States interstate highway system was justified as a way to transport military equipment across the country in the case of invasion.[8] In addition to cities of refuge, the Mishna hints that pilgrimage to Jerusalem was a second justification for maintaining a network of roads.[9]

Perhaps the most interesting component is the requirement to post signs with directions to the nearest city of refuge. Rashi writes in his commentary on the Torah that the word "refuge" was marked at every intersection, while in the Talmud he explains that a wooden post was installed at each intersection with a sign toward the refuge.[10] R. Avon states that the

5. See his commentary on Devarim 19:3.
6. mMak 2:5, Sifri Devarim 180.
7. Rambam Hilchot Rotzeach 8:5.
8. The bill created a "national system of interstate and defense highways" and was justified as a way to prepare for evacuations in the event of nuclear attacks.
9. mShek 1:1.
10. Rashi on Devarim 19:3, as per bMak 10b.

marker also had the image of a hand pointing in the correct directions.[11] A midrash relates that stone pillars were set at crossroads with directions.[12]

This is not the only case in which markers are mandated by Halacha. The Mishna discusses various markings that are installed, with the symbol corresponding to the level of permanence required.[13] Turf cuts were sufficient to mark grapes grown during a vine's fourth year, as these symbols only need to last part of a year. Potsherds were used to indicate *orla* trees less than four years old, as these markers must remain for up to three years. Graves require the longest-lasting markers since graves continue to transmit impurity indefinitely. These were marked with lime and were refreshed yearly.[14] The treatment of graves was especially important when they occurred near roads, as pilgrims heading to Jerusalem had to be careful to remain spiritually pure. Shabbat boundaries may also have been marked.[15]

Besides these religious markers, the Romans used mile markers along their roads, with directions, distances, and the name of the reigning Caesar. These highlighted the role of the central authority responsible for the road system[16] but made the highway system easier to navigate. Hundreds of ancient mile markers have been discovered in Israel.[17] Joshua Levinson has identified these milestones as "the material basis" for the rabbinic descriptions of signs directing people to cities of refuge.[18]

---

11. yMak 2:6 (31d). See also Midrash Tehilim 25:10.

12. BamR 23:13.

13. mMS 5:1. tShek 1:4–5 explains that the central court is responsible for marking graves before Pesach, and gives guidelines for doing so, including that the marks should be on fixed stones, and how close the marks should be to the actual places of impurity. See also bMK 5a. The Talmud specifies a bright white hue to make sure it is visible. In another case, the invasion of Yericho, Rachav is instructed to hang a scarlet red string as a sign. See Yehoshua 2:18. Joseph Rykwert relates this story to the red string given by Ariadne to Theseus to escape the labyrinth. See Joseph Rykwert, *The Idea of a Town* (MIT Pres, 1988), 151–2.

14. yMS 5:1 (55c) and mShek 1:1.

15. See my commentary on Shemot 19:12 for more on this subject.

16. Israel Roll, "The Roman Road System in Judaea" in *The Jerusalem Cathedra* 3 (YBZP, 1983) 153. mAZ 4:6 mentions these markers and rules that they do not constitute idol worship. A similar reinforcing takes place with cities of refuge: the roads are maintained by the central court, and accidental murderers must remain there until the high priest dies.

17. Yoram Tsafrir, *Eretz Israel from the Destruction of the Second Temple to the Muslim Conquest* II, (YBZP, 1984), 51–53 (Hebrew).

18. Joshua Levinson, "The Language of Stones: Roman Milestones on Rabbinic Roads" in *Journal for the Study of Judaism in the Persian, Hellenistic and Roman Period* 47/2 2016), 274.

95. Roman milestone mentioning Vespasian and the 10th Legion, on display in the Davidson Center, Jerusalem.

Signs play an important role in navigation, both within a building and on roads. They must be legible and visible, but ideally a good system of signage helps a traveler to intuit the correct direction. In a building, a visual connection with the destination can be helpful, but subtle cues like tile patterns can also help lead people in the right direction. The Talmud requires that a random person on the road be able to ascertain the way to a city of refuge, but presumably, if this can be accomplished by other means, like special paving patterns or different visual cues, this would also be acceptable.[19] As we saw, R. Avon ruled that a pictogram be used, so that even the illiterate can follow the instructions and find their way to a city of refuge.

The Torah requires that cities of refuge be accessible to all. This is done in three ways: The cities must be spacing evenly throughout the country. Roads must be available to each city, according to the accepted standards. Signage must be provided, to make locating the cities efficient and easy. These ensure that an accidental murderer can safely reach a city of refuge.

19. In mMak 2:3 R. Yehuda and R. Meir debate whether blind people are subject to exile to a city of refuge. Presumably according to R. Meir, signage would have to be accessible by the visually impaired as well.

# DEVARIM

# The Ninth of Av And the Prohibition of Joyous Building

וַתֵּרָגְנוּ בְאָהֳלֵיכֶם וַתֹּאמְרוּ בְּשִׂנְאַת ה׳ אֹתָנוּ הוֹצִיאָנוּ מֵאֶרֶץ מִצְרָיִם לָתֵת אֹתָנוּ בְּיַד הָאֱמֹרִי לְהַשְׁמִידֵנוּ. אָנָה אֲנַחְנוּ עֹלִים אַחֵינוּ הֵמַסּוּ אֶת לְבָבֵנוּ לֵאמֹר עַם גָּדוֹל וָרָם מִמֶּנּוּ עָרִים גְּדֹלֹת וּבְצוּרֹת בַּשָּׁמָיִם וְגַם בְּנֵי עֲנָקִים רָאִינוּ שָׁם.
(דברים א:כז-כח)

And you murmured in your tents and said, Because the Lord hated us, he has brought us forth out of the land of Egypt to deliver us into the hand of the Emori, to destroy us. Whither are we going up? Our brethren have made our heart to melt, saying: "The people is greater and taller than we; the cities are great and fortified up to heaven; and moreover, we have seen the sons of the Anakim there." (Devarim 1:27–28)

MOSHE recalled how the spies he sent to Canaan returned from their mission and demoralized Bnei Yisrael with stories of the powerful natives. According to Moshe, Bnei Yisrael came to believe that God brought them to Canaan because He *hated* them. This statement shows the extent to which the spies had poisoned the mood of the nation. However, in the original telling of this story in Bamidbar, a different reaction is emphasized: Bnei Yisrael "lifted up their voice and cried, and the people wept that night."[1] Rather than verbal expressions of fear and frustration, there was a visceral reaction of tears.

The Talmud explains that the date the spies returned was the ninth of Av.[2] According to Rabba and R. Yochanan, God responded to Bnei Yisrael's tears by saying: "You have cried for no reason,[3] so in the future I will give you a reason to cry on this day." The Mishna goes on to describe

1. Bamidbar 14:1.
2. mTaan 4:6, bTaan 29a.
3. In yTaan 4:5 (68d), the Talmud uses a slightly different language, saying "you have cried frivolously" (בכיה של תפלות).

several national tragedies that occurred on the ninth of Av. To mark these sad events, various customs of mourning are observed during the period leading up to the ninth of Av, culminating with a fast on that day.

One of the customs of mourning for this time period is a prohibition of "joyous building," mentioned in the Shulchan Aruch.[4] The source comes from a separate discussion in the Talmud, pertaining to days of mourning that are decreed during crises. The Mishna explains that at a certain stage of a crisis, people must halt their business activities, stop celebrating marriages, must not greet one another, and must *stop building and planting*.[5] The Talmud clarifies that this only applies to joyous building and joyous planting.[6]

The text records two examples of joyous building: constructing a house for a child's marriage and adding decorative touches to an existing building. The Mishna Berura also forbids expansions that are not done out of necessity. However, other forms of construction, like repairing a rickety wall, are allowed during this period. R. David Halevi Segal writes that this applies even when there is no mortal danger from the wall, as a simple loss of money is enough to permit the repairs.[7]

Since the reason for fasting and mourning is to "awaken the hearts and to open the ways to repentance,"[8] it makes sense to ban joyous construction for two reasons. One, it is common for the completion of a building to be marked with a ceremony or celebration. This is both due to the excitement of having a new structure to use and due to the considerable amount of time and resources that a building requires. As a cause of joy, building is not a fitting activity for a fast day. Two, construction detracts from the solemnity of the day by keeping people busy, giving less incentive and opportunity to reflect and to repent.

In Devarim, although Moshe does not mention Bnei Yisrael crying over the spies' report, he does recall that Bnei Yisrael repented and "wept

---

4. OC 551:2.

5. mTaan 1:7.

6. bTaan 14b. The Talmud's example of joyous planting is planting a royal *avarnaki*. Rashi gives a few explanations of this term: a) It was the custom of kings to plant a tree when a son was born, and when that son ascended to the throne, the tree was cut down and made into a throne. b) A large shade tree. c) A royal garden. Jastrow, on the other hand, traced this word to the Persian *khorengah*, meaning a dining hall in the garden. He writes that this is listed to serve as an example of a temporary structure, which would also be forbidden to construct, besides the permanent structures that the Talmud refers to as "joyous building." He thus sees the word "planting" as referring to the act of temporarily erecting a structure.

7. See his Turei Zahav commentary.

8. Rambam, Hilchot Taaniyot 5:1.

before the Lord."[9] Ramban explains that their tears demonstrated genuine remorse. Nonetheless, God had sworn that their generation would not inherit the land, so this contrition was not enough to annul the decree. Ohr Hachayim adds that even though Bnei Yisrael were moved to tears – as the penitent should be – they had been so sinful that they were not forgiven.

The point of commemorating the ninth of Av is to evoke the same kind of response as we see in Devarim. While the day originated with unnecessary crying over the spies' report, tears are also part of the correct response, out of regret and a desire for forgiveness. To reach this level of repentance, it is necessary to both avoid happy activities and create time to reflect on sins, both reasons for avoiding joyous building.

9. Devarim 1:45.

# Fortified up to Heaven

אָנָה אֲנַחְנוּ עֹלִים אַחֵינוּ הֵמַסּוּ אֶת לְבָבֵנוּ לֵאמֹר עַם גָּדוֹל וָרָם מִמֶּנּוּ עָרִים
גְּדֹלֹת וּבְצוּרֹת בַּשָּׁמָיִם וְגַם בְּנֵי עֲנָקִים רָאִינוּ שָׁם. (דברים א:כח)

Whither are we going up? Our brethren have made our heart faint, saying: The people are greater and taller than we; the cities are great and fortified up to heaven; and moreover, we have seen the sons of the Anakim there. (Devarim 1:28)

MOSHE recalled how the spies sent to Canaan reported that the "cities are great and fortified up to heaven." The Talmud notes this verse as an example of exaggerated and imprecise language in the Torah.[1]

There is no shortage of examples of mythical or fantastical descriptions of architecture, exaggerated or invented entirely. Cities of gold,[2] cities in the sky or underwater and invisible cities,[3] have captured the imagination. Greek and Roman writers described floating islands.[4] These legends develop when oral stories are embellished with every telling. Each time the fortifications in Canaan were recalled, they became stronger, higher, and more imposing, as the description passed from mouth to mouth.

Although the portrayal is said to be an exaggeration, it is also possible that the spies were simply repeating, hearsay, tales they had heard during their mission. Moshe instructed the spies to assess the Canaanite fortifications,[5] but the only city which the spies are said to have approached

1. bChul 90b and Rashi there, *divrei havai.* Another example of exaggeration given in this passage, this time in the Mishna, is regarding the weight of a decorative grape vine hung at the entrance to the Temple, as per mMid 3:8. See also Sifri Devarim 25. For a similar expression, see Devarim 9:1.
2. El Dorado.
3. Biringan City.
4. See Pliny the Elder, *Natural History* 2.96, and Homer, *The Odyssey,* 10.1.
5. Bamidbar 13:19.

was Chevron, which may have only been visited by one spy.[6] Tales about towering fortifications, together with glimpses of the Anakim and the large produce, may have led the spies to repeat stories about the height of the walls. This would be akin to repeating tales of legendary cities without having seen them and only compounds the sin of the spies, who did not do their due diligence.[7]

Archaeologists who have studied the remains of cities from the time period of the Israelite conquest of Canaan have puzzled over the limited remains of fortifications from that era, the Late Bronze Age.[8] Although many impressive city walls existed in the Middle Bronze Age – centuries earlier – the time in question is seen as a period of decline. Some have tried to solve this incongruence with the Biblical description of highly fortified cities by saying that the older walls were still in existence.[9] Others have argued that the dearth of Late Bronze Age fortifications is overstated, and that some cities did in fact have fortifications.[10] My suggestion hints at another possibility: the spies' report of cities "fortified up to heaven" was based on outdated and exaggerated information rather than first-hand accounts. While stories of impressive fortifications persisted, the existing physical setting may have been less impressive.

6. bSot 34b, Rashi, and Ibn Ezra on Bamidbar 13:22.

7. Eicha Rabba records that the spies were punished for reporting things they did not see. See EichaR 3:48.

8. Rivka Gonen, "Urban Canaan in the Late Bronze Period," *Bulletin of the American Schools of Oriental Research*, 253, 1984, 64.

9. Yigael Yadin, "Is the Biblical Account of the Israelite Conquest of Canaan Historically Reliable?" in *Biblical Archaeology Review* 8, 1982, 2.

10. Aaron A. Burke, *Walled Up To Heaven: The Evolution of Middle Bronze Age Fortification Strategies in the Levant* (Eisenbrauns, 2008), 83.

# Praying toward Jerusalem

עֲלֵה רֹאשׁ הַפִּסְגָּה וְשָׂא עֵינֶיךָ יָמָּה וְצָפֹנָה וְתֵימָנָה וּמִזְרָחָה וּרְאֵה בְעֵינֶיךָ כִּי
לֹא תַעֲבֹר אֶת הַיַּרְדֵּן הַזֶּה. (דברים ג:כז)

Go up to the top of the Pisga and lift up your eyes westward and northward and southward and eastward, and behold with your eyes, for you shall not go over this Yarden. (Devarim 3:27)

ALTHOUGH Moshe was prohibited from entering Israel with Bnei Yisrael, he was permitted to see the land from beyond its border. The Sifri uses this verse to teach that Jews should direct their prayers toward Israel, Jerusalem, the Temple, and the Holy of Holies.[1] This is a way of unifying the Jewish people: regardless of location, all prayers are directed to one place. It is also a way of expressing the importance of Jerusalem to the Jewish people even when there is no Temple standing.

The decision to orient toward a central location was not a foregone conclusion. The Talmud records a debate about the correct direction for prayer, with one opinion arguing that one should always face west, while another claims that any direction is acceptable, as God is everywhere.[2] However, despite these opinions, the accepted practice is to pray facing Israel, Jerusalem, and the Temple.[3]

The requirement to face Jerusalem during prayer has had ramifications on the architecture of synagogues. In keeping with this law, the archaeological record shows that synagogues[4] are almost always oriented toward

1. Sifri Devarim 29. See also tBer 3:15–16, yBer 4:5 (8b), and bBer 30a. Outside of Israel one should pray toward Israel; in Israel one orients toward Jerusalem; in Jerusalem one faces the Temple; and in the Temple itself one faces the Holy of Holies.

2. bBB 25a. Tosafot point out that this contradicts the edict to pray facing Israel, Jerusalem and the Temple. (Ibid, *lekol ruchta okman*).

3. Rambam, Hilchot Tefila 5:3, Shulchan Aruch OC 94:1–2.

4. Synagogues dating to the Second Temple Period lack this orientation. However, it is unclear to what extent synagogues were used for prayer rather than as places

Jerusalem. This is sometimes confused by the fact that the primary exterior façade is not always located in the "correct" direction. However, the interior design of the prayer hall, including its furniture, is nearly always designed to facilitate prayer in the direction of Jerusalem.[5]

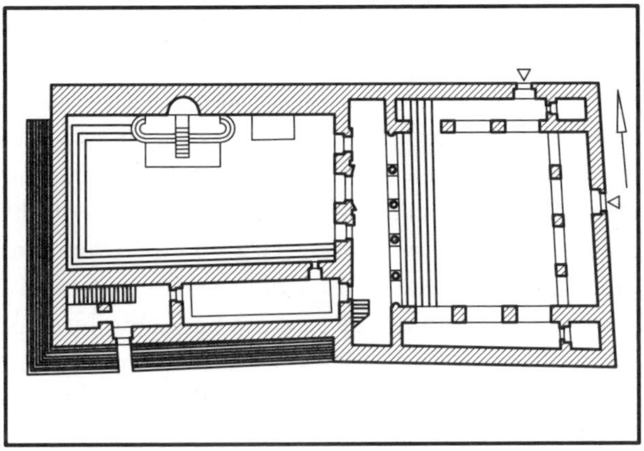

96. Plan of Synagogue in Susiya, with entrance and main façade to the east, but Torah niche and *bima* to the north, facing Jerusalem. (Based on Yevin and Gutman, "Excavations in the Synagogue at Horvat Susiya" in *Ancient Synagogues Revealed*)

The Tosefta states that the main entrance to a synagogue should be in the east.[6] This seems to have been obeyed, at least to some degree, as archaeological remains of synagogues in southern Judea almost all open to the east.[7] However, this demand has been recast to require an opening in the direction opposite Jerusalem, rather than specifically to the east,

of gathering for a variety of functions. See Lee Levine, *The Ancient Synagogue* (Yale University Press, 2005), 164.

5. Lee Levine, *The Ancient Synagogue*, 326–7. Levine also reviews the exceptions and suggests specific reasons why they may have been necessary. As part of the discussion in bBB 25a, there is instruction not to pray east, as that is the direction in which apostates pray. This was also true of pagan temples, as per Vitruvius, *Ten Books on Architecture*, IV.5.1–2. Compare this with yEruv 5:1 (22c), which states that the prophets worked to ensure that the eastern gate would have the sun rise within it during the equinox. R. Mordechai Jaffe, in the *Levush Techelet* 94, explains that since most communities in Europe are not due east of Jerusalem, this is not a difficulty, and recommends a way to ensure that synagogues are not built facing due east, by checking how the sun enters the building during the equinox and making sure the axis of the synagogue is not perfectly aligned with the east.

6. As per tMeg 3:22. See Rif (Meg 14a) and Rambam, Hilchot Tefila 11:1.

7. Lee Levine, *The Ancient Synagogue*, 335.

so that one enters a synagogue from the back.[8] This reinterpretation may be due to the influence of Jewish communities in Europe, located to the west of Israel. In Europe, where prayer must be directed to the east, it would be impractical and disruptive to have the entrance in the front of the synagogues.

Another discussion in the Talmud stipulates that places of prayer have windows.[9] This requirement is derived from a verse in Daniel which describes him opening a window "toward Jerusalem" before praying.[10] While Rashi[11] explains that a window allows one to look at the sky during prayer and have better concentration, Rambam[12] rules that the windows must be in the direction of Jerusalem to help worshipers focus on the holy city. A third opinion considers the windows as purely functional, necessary to bring light into the prayer space.[13] The Zohar states that twelve windows are preferable, though they do not all need to be facing Jerusalem.[14]

The orientation of synagogues toward Jerusalem may also have played a role in the design of the ark, where Torah scrolls are kept. In early synagogues, no special niche or podium was included in the synagogue. Rather, the Torah was brought into the synagogue as necessary, presumably once people had already taken their seats. Once synagogues were permanently oriented toward Jerusalem, it was possible to fix the Torah ark in place, reinforcing the importance of that direction.

The decision to orient the synagogue toward Jerusalem was one of the requirements that gave the synagogue its basic form, influencing its façade, layout, and furniture. As synagogues are the most significant structure in the Jewish community, this decision helps physically connect the far-flung Jewish communities of the world, a brick-and-mortar testament, visible in the archaeological record, to a shared heritage. This design decision has played a significant role in keeping Jerusalem in the forefront for Jews around the world.

---

8. Rashi on bBer 6b and Tosefot on bBer 6a *achorei beit hakneset,* accepted by Shulchan Aruch OC 150:5. For a discussion about the problems with the underlying assumption, see Chatam Sofer I OC 27. See also Rabeinu Manoach on Rambam, Hilchot Tefila 11:1, who requires only a secondary opening on the east side.

9. bBer 31a and 34b.

10. Daniel 6:11. See also Tuvia 3:11, which also describes prayer toward a window but without mention of Jerusalem.

11. bBer 34b *chalonot.*

12. Rambam, Hilchot Tefila 5:6.

13. See Rabeinu Manoch on Rambam.

14. Zohar Pekudei 251:1.

# Inheriting Canaanite Cities

וְהָיָה כִּי יְבִיאֲךָ ה׳ אֱלֹקֶיךָ אֶל הָאָרֶץ אֲשֶׁר נִשְׁבַּע לַאֲבֹתֶיךָ לְאַבְרָהָם לְיִצְחָק וּלְיַעֲקֹב לָתֶת לָךְ עָרִים גְּדֹלֹת וְטֹבֹת אֲשֶׁר לֹא בָנִיתָ. וּבָתִּים מְלֵאִים כָּל טוּב אֲשֶׁר לֹא מִלֵּאתָ וּבֹרֹת חֲצוּבִים אֲשֶׁר לֹא חָצַבְתָּ כְּרָמִים וְזֵיתִים אֲשֶׁר לֹא נָטָעְתָּ וְאָכַלְתָּ וְשָׂבָעְתָּ. הִשָּׁמֶר לְךָ פֶּן תִּשְׁכַּח אֶת ה׳ אֲשֶׁר הוֹצִיאֲךָ מֵאֶרֶץ מִצְרַיִם מִבֵּית עֲבָדִים. (דברים ו:י–יב)

And it shall be, when the Lord your God shall bring you into the land which he swore to your fathers, to Avraham, to Yitzchak, and to Yaakov, to give you great and goodly cities, which you did not build, and houses full of all good things, which you did not fill, and cisterns hewn out, which you did not hew, vineyards and olive trees, which you did not plant; when you shall eat and be full, then beware lest you forget the Lord, who brought you forth out of the land of Egypt, from the house of bondage. (Devarim 6:10–12)

Bnei Yisrael were told that they would find existing buildings and agricultural infrastructure in Canaan.[1] They were then warned not to forget God. The Torah does not explain why taking over existing cities could cause Bnei Yisrael to forget God, rather than to appreciate a land filled with goodness. What is the connection between existing cities and forgetting God?

The Talmud explains that when Bnei Yisrael began their conquest of Canaan, the soldiers were permitted to consume things that would normally be forbidden, like pig or consecrated wine.[2] According to the Netziv, they were warned not to forget God because eating forbidden foods can

1. MdRS Beshalach 13:17 and MdRY Beshalach Petichta relate that this was done deliberately, as God had promised the forefathers that he would give Bnei Yisrael a "land full of all good."

2. bChul 17a and Rambam Hilchot Shoftim 8:1.

have a powerful effect on the soul. Bnei Yisrael needed to be aware of this danger.

Sforno gives a second answer. He explains that the "houses full of all good things" represent wealth acquired without any effort. Obtaining wealth in this manner often leads to hubris and moral corruption, so an extra warning was appropriate.[3]

Another possible answer connects the inheritance of houses and cities to the abandonment of God. Bnei Yisrael were entering a foreign country filled with pagan culture. The architecture of these towns would have reflected this culture and could influence Bnei Yisrael's behavior.[4] If they repurposed pagan temples for Jewish functions, the underlying pagan structure could have a corrupting influence.[5] When Bnei Yisrael took over towns in which Paganism was the underlying culture, it would be possible to fall under the influence of these pagan trappings.[6] Therefore, taking over "cities which you did not build" is a difficult endeavor and warrants an additional warning.

The use of architecture to influence other peoples was a tactic that the Romans employed with their new colonies. Tactitus, a Roman senator and historian from the first-second centuries, described how when conquering Briton, the general Agricola promoted the construction of Roman-style temples, fora, and houses, to subversively get the locals to adopt Roman culture. 'Little by little, the Britons were seduced into alluring vices: to the lounge, the bath, the well-appointed dinner table. The simple natives gave the name of "culture" to this factor of their slavery.'[7] People living in

3. In Devarim 8:11–14, Bnei Yisrael are warned not to forget God after building their own "goodly houses." Here the problem is not getting wealth easily, but rather the opposite. R. S.R. Hirsch writes that buildings "give the self-satisfied feeling of one's own creative powers," which promote hubris and overlooking God's involvement in personal success. The Netziv has a similar commentary on that verse.

4. See also my commentary on Vayikra 18:3.

5. See yShek 2:5 (47a) for the corrupting influence of a synagogue built on the site of a pagan temple.

6. One example of architecture playing a key role in the spread of paganism occurred during the reign of Yoshiyahu, when idols were hidden in residential doorposts, as alluded to in Yishayahu 57:8. This example demonstrates how one of the commandments of Jewish architecture, putting a *mezuza* on the doorpost, can be corrupted by the foreign influence and result in having idols fixed on the doorpost. The act of hiding idols plays a role in a *kina* by Kalir that is read on Tisha B'Av: "Yirmiyahu's lament over Yoshiyahu."

7. Tacitus, *Agricola* 20–21. This may be the subtext in the debate with R. Shimon bar Yochai in bShab 33b.

spaces that were visually and physically Roman would absorb the Roman ways and become part of that culture.[8]

In later Jewish history Jews often tried to adapt the architecture of their host culture, sometimes with distinct results, such as the adaptation of Reform temples in Germany to reflect the architecture of contemporary Christian places of worship. We can also find other examples of architecture affecting religion. Christianity, an offspring of Judaism, took over the Roman styles of architecture and used it as the basis for their church architecture. It is impossible to quantify the effect of this Pagan architecture on the nascent Church, but it would be wrong to assume that there was no impact. The fear of the influence of foreign architecture may explain why a special warning was required for Bnei Yisrael before they entered the land and inherited the houses and cities of the Canaanites.

8. James C. Anderson, *Roman Architecture and Society* (Johns Hopkins University Press, 1997), 183–184.

# Slow Conquest And Urban Sprawl

וְנָשַׁל ה' אֱלֹקֶיךָ אֶת הַגּוֹיִם הָאֵל מִפָּנֶיךָ מְעַט מְעָט לֹא תוּכַל כַּלֹּתָם מַהֵר פֶּן תִּרְבֶּה עָלֶיךָ חַיַּת הַשָּׂדֶה. (דברים ז:כב)

And the Lord your God will cast out those nations before you little by little. You may not consume them quickly, lest the wild beasts of the field increase upon you. (Devarim 7:22)

ANTICIPATING the conquest of the Promised Land, Moshe reminded Bnei Yisrael that God promised to banish the land's existing inhabitants gradually, "lest the land become desolate."[1] Rashi explains that if the residents were driven out at once, Bnei Yisrael would not have enough people to inhabit all the land, which would then return to nature and be overrun by wild animals.

The emptiness of the land and the multiplication of wild beasts is presented as a negative phenomenon. However, it is unclear whether the land being desolate is itself a problem, or if it is only the condition that allows wild beasts to multiply.

The concern with wild beasts can be understood both literally and symbolically. Wild beasts pose a danger to personal safety, threatening people both within and beyond settled areas.[2] Symbolically, these beasts represent the collapse of civilization and the rolling back of progress. Prophecies about destruction describe wild animals invading ruined buildings.[3] Inhabited places returning to the wild is a sign of the collapse of civilization.

---

1. This is originally stated in Shemot 23:29–30.
2. See mSan 1:4, which prescribes the death penalty for wild animals. See also Melachim II, 2:23–24, in which bears attack locals, and mTaan 3:6, in which a fast is decreed because wolves are spotted.
3. Yishayahu 5:17, 13:19–22, 34:13–15, Yirmiyahu 50:14–16, 50:39–40, Yechezkel 13:4, 25:3–5, Tzephania 2:14, and many others.

In terms of desolation as an independent problem, this can also be considered in two ways. On the one hand, having a part of the country that is uninhabited implies a lack of production, as the land lies fallow. Animals are simply a way of indicating that the land has been abandoned. On the other hand, while the Torah describes wild animals moving in to fill the vacuum, it is equally plausible that foreign armies would take advantage of the lack of defense and try to seize the land.[4] In the scenario described in the Torah, God would clear the land of its previous inhabitants and leave the land uninhabited. However, if there is not a population of people ready to move in, the land could be claimed by others.

Strategic planning continues to dictate that the population be spread throughout a country. Before the establishment of the State of Israel, the Zionists tried to establish population centers throughout the country as a way of taking possession of the land. This was done with cooperative farming settlements, Tower and Stockade settlements, and the establishment of new cities. The areas that were settled formed the nucleus of Israel in 1948.

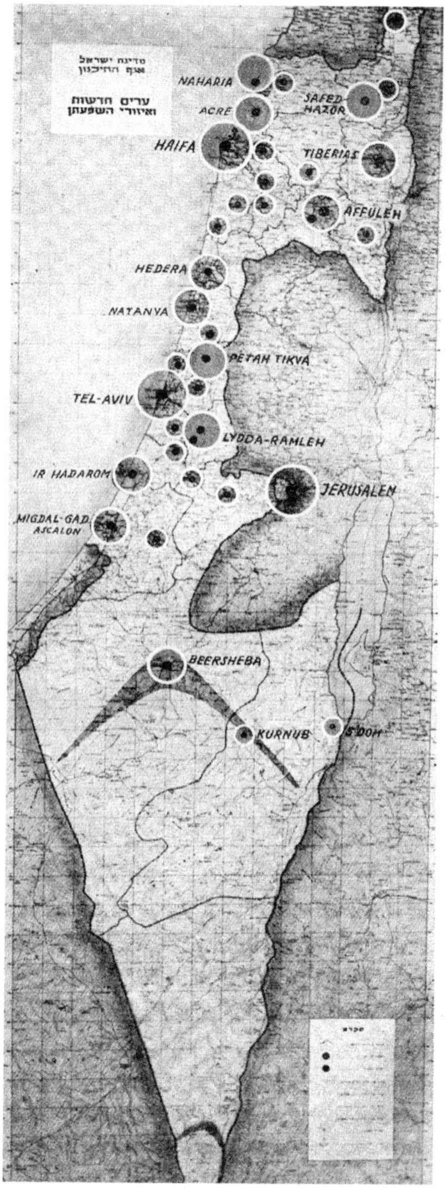


97. Sharon's plan for dispersion of population into the new towns and southward into the Negev desert, 1950.

In 1951, Israeli architect Arieh Sharon developed a plan for dispersing the population throughout the country, rather than keeping it

4. The Rabbis echo this concern with special laws for border cities. See mSan 1:5, tEruv 3:5, bYev 48b.

concentrated on the coastal plain.[5] The country was divided into twenty-four planning zones, each with its own major city. Twenty "development cities" were designed to fill out this number. Developing new parts of the country was part of the Zionist enterprise, a practical way of redeeming the land and reducing its desolation. A similar process took place after 1967 when communities were established strategically throughout the newly acquired lands.

However, there are also modern theories that view land use quite differently. Today many regional planning boards concentrate on *reducing* the extent of city growth as a means of preventing urban sprawl. Cities and regions that are spread out face challenges of transportation, pollution, access to amenities, and viability of communities. Some cities have implemented urban growth boundaries to limit the extent to which the city can expand, refusing to provide municipal services like sewage and electricity beyond a set border. This has the effect of increasing the population density of existing cities, making them more walkable and saving natural resources, though keeping cities compact also tends to increase property costs.[6] This allows regions to deliberately leave areas undeveloped and rural. From this perspective, "desolation of land" can be viewed as a desirable thing, a sign of successful land use management. Nature preserves ensure that areas remain undeveloped. In some situations, governments even try and reintroduce wild animals into places where they have been entirely exterminated to restore the earlier natural condition before the intervention of modern man.

One example can be found in Jerusalem, where in recent years there have been efforts to keep Jerusalem from expanding to the west, to leave that area undeveloped. Instead, activists have championed greater density within the existing residential areas of the city.

The difference between the two ways of seeing undeveloped, uninhabited land has to do with the political situation. The Torah verses relate specifically to the conquest of the land, and as such take a military perspective. However, in times of peace when there is the luxury of planning with other things in mind, it is possible to take a more progressive view of the matter. Peace allows planners to pursue ideals, rather than be preoccupied with defense above all other concerns. Perhaps this is part of the reason why it was fitting that the Temple be built by Shlomo during times of peace. David, who was involved in war, would not have had the flexibility to consider alternative policies.

---

5. The National Outline Plan, also sometimes known as the Sharon Plan.
6. Juergensmeyer & Roberts, *Land Use Planning Control Law*, 1998, 369.

# *Mezuzot*

וּכְתַבְתָּם עַל מְזוּזוֹת בֵּיתֶךָ וּבִשְׁעָרֶיךָ. (דברים יא:כ)

And you shall write them upon the doorposts of your house and on your gates. (Devarim 11:20)

In two nearly identical lines,[1] the Torah instructs Bnei Yisrael to write certain verses upon the doorposts of their house and on their gates. The words in question, two paragraphs of *shema*, tell Bnei Yisrael to love God, teach their children, and keep the commandments. In practice, rather than writing the verses upon the doorposts,[2] Jewish law dictates that they are written upon a scroll, which is fastened to the doorpost. Chizkuni explains that the verses act as a reminder to keep the mitzvot.[3]

Several architectural issues relate to the mitzva of affixing a *mezuza*. Only houses that are at least four cubits by four cubits require *mezuzot*.[4] Opinions differ as to whether this refers to minimum dimensions of the length and width of a single space in the dwelling[5] or a minimum area (roughly 3.7 $m^2$).[6] These dimensions are likely required because they approximate the length of a grown person;[7] a house lacking a room with these dimensions – at least in one direction – would not be suitable for sleeping. The same logic informs modern legal requirements for other

1. See also Devarim 6:9.
2. bMen 34a suggests this possibility.
3. PdRK 28 (intro) implies that affixing a *mezuza* also demonstrates gratitude to God for having given you a house.
4. bSuk 3a–3b. This passage also mentions other mitzvot that apply only to houses of this size: affixing guardrails (Devarim 22:8), *tumat nega'im* (Vayikra 14:37), and soldiers who return from battle (Devarim 20:5–7). mBB 6:4 lists other default measurements for buildings: four by six cubits for a barn, six by eight cubits for a small house, eight by ten cubits for a large house, and ten by ten cubits for a *triclinium*.
5. R. Asher ben Yechiel, Hilchot Ketanot, Hilchot Mezuza, 16.
6. Rambam, Hilchot Tefilin Vemezuza Vesefer Torah, 6:2.
7. See my commentary on Shemot 16:29.

minimum dimensions. For example, according to Israeli building code, a bedroom must legally be at least 8 $m^2$.[8] At the same time, the building code sets a minimum width: a bedroom cannot be narrower than 2.60 meters, while a "half-bedroom" must be at least two meters wide, approximately four cubits. These requirements ensure that the rooms can accommodate standard bedroom furniture and can thus be used as intended, accommodating at least one bed.[9]

The mitzva of *mezuza* applies to internal doorways as well. R. Yechiel Michel Epstein rules that a building requires a *mezuza* even if people do not eat, sleep, and live in it.[10] Still, it must be inhabitable, with a roof[11] and a minimum height of ten handbreadths.[12] The Talmud includes houses built into the earth.[13] Bathrooms, filthy barns, and synagogues without living quarters are exempt from *mezuzot*.

The basic doorway that requires a *mezuza* consists of two jambs and a lintel (*fig. 98a*). However, some doors have different arrangements, lacking one (*fig. 98b*) or both jambs, or having no lintel below the ceiling (*fig. 98c*). A *beraita* in the Talmud discusses archways:[14] R. Meir says an arch requires a *mezuza*, while the Rabbis state that it does not; but if the arch is on top of vertical supports that are ten handbreadths high, all agree that a *mezuza* is required (*fig. 98d*).[15] A flat lintel is not, therefore, a basic requirement, as long as there are two jambs of sufficient height and something bridging between them.

While arched doorways were relatively rare in Israel in Late Antiquity, it was more common to have arches span the width of the house, providing support for the ceiling as an alternative to central, wooden beams, which

8. If it is 6 $m^2$ it is termed a "half-bedroom," but anything less cannot legally be called a bedroom. A two-bedroom dwelling must also have a space that is at least 12 $m^2$. See *Tekanot Hatichnun Vehabeniya*, addendum 2, Part 2, 2.04.

9. Parts of a room which are narrower than this dimension are not counted toward the overall area requirement mentioned earlier.

10. Aruch Hashulchan, YD 286:4.

11. Shulchan Aruch YD 286:14.

12. bBK 51a.

13. yYom 1:1 (38c).

14. Ritva, in his commentary on bEruv 11b, uses the transliterated foreign term "arch" to explain the passage. Ritva explains that the solid wall above the arch counts as a lintel, even if the curved arch does not.

15. bYom 11b and bEruv 11b. The former also mentions a type of doorway called a "Medi gate," which Rashi explains is an arch. However, R. Shmuel Strashun suggests that this is a typo and that the opening should be the "Tedi gate," switching the graphically similar מ and ט letters. The Tedi gate is mentioned in mMid 3:1 as being composed of two diagonal jambs that meet at a point with no lintel at all.

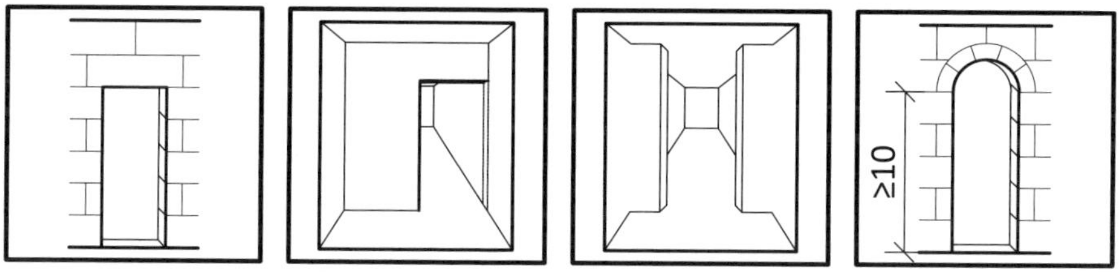


(a) (b) (c) (d)

98. Doorway configurations.

were hard to attain. These arches often sat on short abutments that stuck out into the room slightly (*fig. 99e+f*).[16] While the Talmud's discussion of *mezuzot* typically deals with doorways, comments by Abaye about an archway with lintels that are only three handbreadths high seem to pertain to this situation.

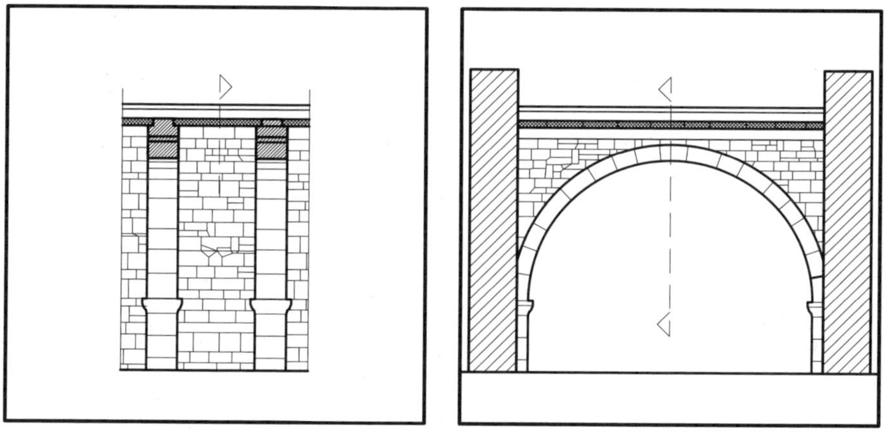

(e) (f)

99. Cross-section of arches supporting a stone roof in the Negev, typical of third century CE and onward. (Based on drawing in Hirschfeld, *Palestinian Dwelling*, 241)

Another architectural discussion related to *mezuzot* involves wall thickness. In the past, walls were almost always thicker than doors. Thick walls were necessary to support roofs, prevent forced entry, and provide thermal insulation. Doors, on the other hand, had to be easy to open and therefore needed to be thinner and lighter. This meant that the door jambs were

16. Yizhar Hirschfeld, *The Palestinian Dwelling in The Roman-Byzantine Period* (Israel Exploration Society, 1995), 239–243. Chocha, located outside Maale Gamla, has buildings with similar arched supports.

thicker than the door leaf, and there was almost always ample space to install a *mezuza* on the inner face of the jamb. However, in modern times, there are at least two situations in which walls are no wider than the door leaf. The first is common in gates when the door frame and leaf are made from metal profiles of the same size. The second situation is with glass curtainwalls, in which the glass door is the same thickness as the rest of the glass surface. In both situations, no space exists to affix the *mezuza* on the inner face of the "jamb." In this situation, R. Yechiel Michel Epstein rules that it is acceptable to attach the *mezuza* to the outside face on the right side at the appropriate height.[17]

The mitzva of *mezuza* is one of the few commandments named after an architectural feature. It makes sense that its halachot contain rich architectural discussions about the houses and the construction of doorways.

17. Aruch Hashulchan YD 289:11, though some authorities rule that one must manufacture a niche in the curtainwall to hold the *mezuza*.

# Locating Foreign Altars

אַבֵּד תְּאַבְּדוּן אֶת כָּל הַמְּקֹמוֹת אֲשֶׁר עָבְדוּ שָׁם הַגּוֹיִם אֲשֶׁר אַתֶּם יֹרְשִׁים אֹתָם אֶת אֱלֹהֵיהֶם עַל הֶהָרִים הָרָמִים וְעַל הַגְּבָעוֹת וְתַחַת כָּל עֵץ רַעֲנָן. וְנִתַּצְתֶּם אֶת מִזְבְּחֹתָם וְשִׁבַּרְתֶּם אֶת מַצֵּבֹתָם וַאֲשֵׁרֵיהֶם תִּשְׂרְפוּן בָּאֵשׁ וּפְסִילֵי אֱלֹהֵיהֶם תְּגַדֵּעוּן וְאִבַּדְתֶּם אֶת שְׁמָם מִן הַמָּקוֹם הַהוּא. לֹא תַעֲשׂוּן כֵּן לַה׳ אֱלֹקֵיכֶם כִּי אִם אֶל הַמָּקוֹם אֲשֶׁר יִבְחַר ה׳ אֱלֹקֵיכֶם מִכָּל שִׁבְטֵיכֶם לָשׂוּם אֶת שְׁמוֹ שָׁם לְשִׁכְנוֹ תִדְרְשׁוּ וּבָאתָ שָּׁמָּה. (דברים יב:ב-ה)

You shall surely destroy all the places in which the nations whom you are to dispossess served their gods, upon the high mountains and upon the hills and under every leafy tree. And you shall break down their altars and dash in pieces their pillars and burn their *asherim* with fire, and you shall hew down the graven images of their gods and destroy their name out of that place. This you shall not do to the Lord your God. But to the place which the Lord your God shall choose out of all your tribes to put His name there, there shall you seek him, at his dwelling and there shall you come. (Devarim 12:2–5)

BNEI Yisrael are told several times in Devarim that when they reach the Promised Land they should destroy all traces of idol worship that they find, including altars, trees, and idols.[1] The verses mention that sites of worship are found on mountains, on hills, and under trees. A mishna adds that buildings that are themselves worshiped are included in this prohibition.[2] There is even a blessing to say in a place where idol worship has been removed.[3]

While the Torah seems to be outlining a very broad commandment,

1. Devarim 7:5 and 7:25, as well as Shemot 23:24, Shemot 34:13, and Bamidbar 33:52.
2. mAZ 3:7 and Sifri Devarim 61. See Rashi on bAZ 47b *bayit* and Rambam, Hilchot Avoda Zara, 8:4. Buildings that are themselves objects of worship are quite uncommon.
3. bBer 57b.

there are some limitations on what must be destroyed. The Mishna learns that even if a mountain were to be the object of devotion, the mountain would not be forbidden, nor would one be obligated to destroy it.[4] However, this exemption does not apply to all natural phenomena, as evident by the mention in the verse of *ashera* trees. In that case, the trees, though natural and attached to the ground, are forbidden because "man has had a hand in them." This may either refer to the role of people in planting trees, or their ability to uproot trees if desired.[5] The Mishna does not address whether cave dwellings or earth-sheltered houses would count as man-made or as part of nature.[6]

In the Mishna, R. Akiva states that the reason the Torah mentions high mountains, hills, and trees is to inform us that these are the locations where idol worship was sure to have taken place. This makes it easier to locate former sites of iniquity and thus facilitates the destruction of foreign altars. The Mechilta also implies that the Torah provides this list to make it easier to locate sites of idolatry.[7]

Natural phenomena, topography, and flora can be indicative of past uses of a site. Archaeologists who are searching for promising excavation sites often look for abnormalities, such as changes in topography or soil composition, which can show up in aerial reconnaissance or heat radiation maps.[8] These abnormalities might be traces of ancient walls or roads. Vegetation can also serve as a hint. For example, in Israel, it is common to see almond trees or sabra cacti planted in seemingly random locations. These groves are common indications of past villages that have been destroyed but whose agricultural footprint persists. R. Akiva's understanding of this verse works similarly. Existing physical features like mountain tops or vegetation could indeed be a useful way to find ancient pagan cultural sites.

4. mAZ 3:5. See also Sifri Devarim 60. As per mBer 9:2, there is also a special blessing to say on seeing mountains.

5. As per Gur Aryeh on Devarim 12:2.

6. Ohr Hachayim writes that a *built* house that is attached can become forbidden but does not comment on a house that is excavated. See also bAZ 47b.

7. MdRY Mishpatim (Nezikin) 17.

8. One Israeli example is an administrative center detected by aerial photography in Churvat Amuda.

100. Aerial photo revealing previously undetected temple of Novioregum, an ancient Gallo-Roman city, beneath the modern French city of Barzan. (Photo by Jacques Dassié, 1975, Wikimedia)

# Building in Israel

כִּי יַכְרִית ה' אֱלֹקֶיךָ אֶת הַגּוֹיִם אֲשֶׁר אַתָּה בָא שָׁמָּה לָרֶשֶׁת אוֹתָם מִפָּנֶיךָ
וְיָרַשְׁתָּ אֹתָם וְיָשַׁבְתָּ בְּאַרְצָם. (דברים יב:כט)

When the Lord your God shall cut off the nations from before you, whither you go in to dispossess them, and you dispossess them and dwell in their land. (Devarim 12:29)

BEFORE entering the Promised Land, Bnei Yisrael were warned not to worship the native gods. Later, when recounting the need to set up cities of refuge, Moshe explained that Bnei Yisrael would "dwell in their cities and their houses."[1] This phrasing makes it seem that Bnei Yisrael *could only* live in the existing cities and houses, without making any changes. However, the Sifri teaches that Moshe's statement had the opposite purpose: it assured Bnei Yisrael that they could build as they pleased.[2]

While there is disagreement as to whether living in the Land of Israel counts as one of the 613 commandments,[3] there is consensus about the importance of the Land of Israel to the Jewish people. The Tosefta even claims that living in Israel is as important as all other commandments combined.[4] However, while living in Israel is clearly significant, is there any special value to *building* in Israel? Is the Sifri saying that it is *allowed* to build in Israel, or is there actually a mitzva to do so?

Several rabbinic statements imply a special value of building in Israel, especially as a remedy for the ruinous landscape that persisted for hundreds of years. R. Yochanan states that Omri merited to become king because

1. Devarim 19:1.
2. Sifri Devarim 80 and 179.
3. Rambam leaves it off his list, while Ramban includes it. See Ramban's list of positive commandments omitted by Rambam, 4.
4. tAZ 4:3. A similar statement appears in Sifri Devarim 80.

he constructed a new city in Israel.[5] Based partially on this statement, R. Yissachar Tamar explains that building cities in Israel is an independent mitzva and that settling in new or rebuilt cities fulfills this commandment.[6] A special blessing is said upon seeing Jewish houses in Israel, demonstrating that houses are signs of the Redemption.[7] One cannot demolish houses to create open space or gardens, "so as not to destroy the cities of Israel."[8] The Talmud implies that building one wall in Israel is enough to merit reviving the dead.[9] One who builds in a ruin without the owner's permission must pay damages, but the newly-built structure cannot be demolished, due to the importance of settling the Land of Israel.[10] All these statements indicate that building in Israel is a positive act.

Beyond the simple act of building, there is also some evidence that it is important to build in a way that beautifies Israel. Discussing the open space mandated around Levite cities, Ula explains that it beautifies the cities,[11] and may only be required in Israel.[12] R. Yitzchok Zilberstein uses this as a proof that it is important to beautify houses in Israel.[13] Elsewhere, he suggests that hiring an architect is the best way to achieve positive results.[14]

Despite the high value placed on building houses in Israel, this is clearly not the only consideration. Israel could maximize the quantity of its housing stock by churning out cheap and shoddy buildings, turning a blind eye to the necessary infrastructure, and ignoring the aesthetic appeal of the buildings. As a safeguard against this happening, the State of Israel, and most countries, require that an architect be part of the design team for all large projects.[15] While hiring an architect increases the cost of a building,

---

5. bSan 102b, based on Melachim I 16:24. For a similar sentiment, see Ben Sira 40:19, which states "Children and the building of a city establish a man's name."

6. Alei Tamar on yMK, 2:4, *keitzad hu oseh.* See also a discussion in bMeg 10a and bAra 32b about rebuilding cities from the time of Yehoshua bin Nun.

7. bBer 58b.

8. tAra 5:18–19. This tosefta led the Ben Ish Chai (Shu"t Torah Lishma 287) to rules that one looking to buy property in Israel should purchase a house rather than agricultural land. See also Chemed I, bBM 101b. Similarly, a court cannot condemn more than one *ir hanidachat,* lest the land become desolate (tSan 14:1).

9. yBer 4:4 (8b) and ySan 10:2 (28c).

10. yBK 9:1 (6d), along with Pnei Moshe there. See also bBM 101a–b.

11. See my commentary on Bamidbar 35:3–5.

12. Ramban on bBB 24b.

13. Chashukei Chemed, bBB 22b 2.

14. Chashukei Chemed, bNed 48a, with regard to renovating an old synagogue so that it is beautiful but retains its historic essence.

15. A "simple building" has a simple structural arrangement, with less than a six-meter span between supports, and a top floor no more than 11.5 meters above the ground. All other buildings require an architect on the design team.

the architect helps ensure that the building will be thoughtfully designed, livable, and enhance the fabric of the city. Municipalities are also encouraged to create master plans, which help cities develop thoughtfully and deliberately. For a country that values its built environment and wants it to be both appealing and well-designed, the involvement of an architect in all building projects is a worthwhile requirement to impose on all projects. This helps balance the desire to build in Israel with the wish to enhance the beauty of the country.

101. Housing development in Katamon, Jerusalem, 1955. Cheap, quick construction projects boosted the housing supply but had little architectural aspiration. (Israel State Archive Yehuda Eisenstark Photo collection)

# Excavating an *Ir Hanidachat*

הַכֵּה תַכֶּה אֶת יֹשְׁבֵי הָעִיר הַהִוא לְפִי חָרֶב הַחֲרֵם אֹתָהּ וְאֶת כָּל אֲשֶׁר בָּהּ
וְאֶת בְּהֶמְתָּהּ לְפִי חָרֶב. וְאֶת כָּל שְׁלָלָהּ תִּקְבֹּץ אֶל תּוֹךְ רְחֹבָהּ וְשָׂרַפְתָּ בָאֵשׁ
אֶת הָעִיר וְאֶת כָּל שְׁלָלָהּ כָּלִיל לַה׳ אֱלֹקֶיךָ וְהָיְתָה תֵּל עוֹלָם לֹא תִבָּנֶה עוֹד.
(דברים יג:טז–יז)

You shall surely smite the inhabitants of that city with the edge of the sword, destroying it utterly and all that is in it, and its cattle with the edge of the sword. And you shall gather all the spoil of it into the midst of the broad place thereof, and shall burn with fire both the city and all the plunder taken in it, for the Lord your God; And it shall be an eternal heap, it shall not be built again. (Devarim 13:16–17)

THE Torah rules that if a city is enticed by its leaders to worship idols, the entire city, known as an *ir hanidachat,* must be demolished. Men, women, cattle, property, and, according to some opinions, children, are all to be destroyed. The Torah declares that such a city "shall be an eternal heap" and "it shall not be rebuilt again."

The Talmud lists the precise circumstances by which a city is declared an *ir hanidachat* and is subject to harsh punishment. There must be at least two leaders from the same city and tribe.[1] The majority – and a minimum of one hundred – of the townspeople must follow their leadership.[2] However, if over fifty percent of the *tribe* is participating, the city does not qualify. The settlement itself must be neither large nor small and cannot be on the border.[3] Extensive requirements for witnesses are also expounded,

1. bSan 111b.
2. bSan 15b. R. Yoshiah rules there must be between 10–100 followers.
3. mSan 1:5.

all but making the circumstances of such a city impossible. The Tosefta even states that no *ir hanidachat* has ever existed.[4]

The expression "eternal heap" found in these verses brings to mind archaeological remains of settlements, which are also found in "heaps" built up over centuries of towns being destroyed and rebuilt. Archaeology as a field of study did not exist in the time of the Talmud, so we cannot expect to find reference to it. Nonetheless, in the hypothetical case of an *ir hanidachat*, in which the city was utterly destroyed, would excavation of the site be permitted, or would doing so violate the precept for it to be "an eternal heap?"

While the Talmud does not deal with excavation, the Mishna does discuss whether an *ir hanidachat* can be made into a garden.[5] R. Yosi Haglili writes that even gardens may not be built on the site. No redevelopment of the city can occur. On the other hand, R. Akiva argues that the prohibition to rebuild only includes settlements. A garden, in his opinion, would be permitted. Rambam rules like R. Akiva.[6]

At first glance, R. Akiva's position seems to allow for archaeological redevelopment of a site, as it does not constitute a re-habitation. However, the parallel between garden and archaeological site is not exact. While a garden could be built to cover up the former site, with no references to the nefarious deeds that occurred in its dark past, an archaeological excavation would certainly bring attention to the site as a former location of an *ir hanidachat*. The author of Sefer Hachinuch writes that part of the commandment to annihilate the city is to erase any remembrance of the city.[7] If so, then the difference between garden and excavation is indeed significant, and excavation would not be permitted. It is not, however, clear if this is a factor, because several *rishonim*, including Rashi, specifically explain R. Akiva's opinion as meaning that you cannot have habitation on the site, but say nothing about *damnatio memoriae*, the idea of erasing something from history.[8] As most archaeological digs tend to celebrate the

4. tSan 14:1. However, in bSan 71a R. Yonatan claims to have sat in the ruins of an *ir hanidachat*.

5. mSan 10:5 and tSan 14:6. Sifri Devarim 96 adds that you cannot use it for columbaria either. SZ Bamidbar 35:11 teaches that cities of refuge also cannot be turned into gardens. According to ARN A 35 and bBK 82b, it is forbidden to plant gardens in Jerusalem.

6. Rambam Hilchot Avoda Zara 4:8.

7. Sefer Hachinuch 443.

8. ShmR 15:21 records a midrash that in future times all destroyed cities will be rebuilt, including Sedom. Elsewhere, the Talmud records a case of *damnatio memoriae* for Torah scholars who eat too much: his house will be destroyed, his wife widowed, his children orphaned, his Torah forgotten, and his words not spoken. See bPes 49a.

site they uncover, it seems to me that excavating an *ir hanidachat* would not be appropriate.

One final point comes out of this discussion. If it is true that we are not supposed to leave any trace of an *ir hanidachat,* then it raises a serious question as to the veracity of the claim that there has never been an *ir hanidachat.* Had there been one, we would not expect the Rabbis to keep its memory alive.

# A Soldier with a New House

וְדִבְּרוּ הַשֹּׁטְרִים אֶל הָעָם לֵאמֹר מִי הָאִישׁ אֲשֶׁר בָּנָה בַיִת חָדָשׁ וְלֹא חֲנָכוֹ יֵלֵךְ וְיָשֹׁב לְבֵיתוֹ פֶּן יָמוּת בַּמִּלְחָמָה וְאִישׁ אַחֵר יַחְנְכֶנּוּ. (דברים כ:ה)

And the officers shall speak to the people saying: What man is there that has built a new house and has not dedicated it? Let him go and return to his house, lest he die in the battle and another man dedicate it. (Devarim 20:5)

BEFORE going to war, the nation's officers must address Bnei Yisrael and order some of the soldiers to return home rather than fight. Men with a new house, vineyard,[1] or wife are told not to enlist, for fear that they will die in battle and leave their house, vineyard, or wife to someone else.[2] The death of such a soldier is seen as an especially tragic occurrence. Still, why should these people, and particularly someone who built a new house, be exempted from going to war?

Some commentators understand that the three groups would not make good soldiers. The soldier might be preoccupied with his new house, causing him to be distracted.[3] Therefore, from a strategic point of view, such a soldier would not make a good recruit. Rashbam suggests that the soldier would be demoralized from the onset, lamenting his bad luck. His lack of self-confidence would make him ill-suited to be a soldier. Sforno points out

1. MdRY Mishpatim (Kesafa) 20 explains that "vineyard" is only an example and that other types of orchards are also included.

2. Soldiers who are afraid are also told to return but constitute a separate category. This occurred at least twice: in Shoftim 7:3, Gidon instructs soldiers who are afraid to depart, and in Maccabim I 3:56, Yehuda tells soldiers who have just built houses, married women, planted vineyards, and who are afraid to leave. Uriel Rappaport points out that since it was for a defensive battle, this was not actually required. See Rappaport, Maccabim I (YBZP, 2004), 152.

3. Ibn Ezra, Ramban, and Chizkuni.

that this turn of events appears in a list of things that will happen to Bnei Yisrael if they sin, known as the *tochacha*.[4] He explains that it indicates that the man is a sinner, which, again, makes him undesirable as a soldier, since he would not receive any divine assistance in battle.

Rashi, however, follows a different line of thought. He explains that when a person builds a house and someone else dedicates it, this causes *agmat nefesh*, or the remorse of the soul.[5] The act of building a house creates a deep connection between the person and the structure, akin to the connection between husband and wife. The Talmud explains that God is involved in pairing people up with spouses, houses, and plots of land,[6] bolstering this understanding of a metaphysical connection between spouses similar to a house or a field. On this metaphysical level, it would be a great tragedy for him not to be the one to dedicate his house. Therefore, he receives a special exemption from war. It is not a practical, strategic commandment, but rather one that recognizes the bond between a person and house, and which tries to prevent the rift that would occur if this person were not given the opportunity to dedicate the house.[7]

R. Meir Benyamin Menachem Danon explains Rashi's words, writing that this pain would even affect the soul of the dead soldier.[8] The connection between person and house is such that even after death, the soul would still be pained by another person moving in when he was unable to do so himself. It should be noted that this applies not only when a man builds a house, but also when he buys or inherits one, as these cases are also included in this commandment.[9]

In summary, there are two main ways of viewing the nature of this

---

4. Devarim 28:30.

5. *Agmat nefesh* is the same reason given in mMeg 3:3 for letting ruined synagogues be overgrown with plants. There seems to be some connection between this emotion and architectural disappointment.

6. bSot 2a, which states "Every day a heavenly voice declares 'this woman for that man, this house for that man, this field for that man.'" See also bMK 18b, which omits houses from the statement. One might further suggest that, just as a matchmaker plays a role in God's work of pairing up a couple, so too a real estate broker and an architect play a role in pairing up people with a house.

7. Yishayahu 65:22 understands that in the time of the Messiah these specific tragedies will no longer occur.

8. See his Be'er Basadeh supercommentary on Rashi.

9. mSot 8:2, bSot 43a, and Sifri Devarim 229. Another interesting aspect of this commandment is that it applies only to one who builds a house *in Israel* (as per ySot 8:4 (22d). R. Avraham Gombiner uses this as a proof that a house dedication feast is only considered a *seudat mitzva* when the house is in Israel. See Magen Avraham, OC 568:5.

commandment. The first, taken by most commentators, views it as a practical concern for the battle. This person will not make a good soldier, and therefore should not be in the fight. The second view sees the joy and pleasure that a man gets from his new home as a deep, spiritual connection that should not be broken.

# Cutting Fruit Trees

כִּי תָצוּר אֶל עִיר יָמִים רַבִּים לְהִלָּחֵם עָלֶיהָ לְתָפְשָׂהּ לֹא תַשְׁחִית אֶת עֵצָהּ לִנְדֹּחַ עָלָיו גַּרְזֶן כִּי מִמֶּנּוּ תֹאכֵל וְאֹתוֹ לֹא תִכְרֹת כִּי הָאָדָם עֵץ הַשָּׂדֶה לָבֹא מִפָּנֶיךָ בַּמָּצוֹר. רַק עֵץ אֲשֶׁר תֵּדַע כִּי לֹא עֵץ מַאֲכָל הוּא אֹתוֹ תַשְׁחִית וְכָרָתָּ וּבָנִיתָ מָצוֹר עַל הָעִיר אֲשֶׁר הִוא עֹשָׂה עִמְּךָ מִלְחָמָה עַד רִדְתָּהּ. (דברים כ:יט–כ)

When you shall besiege a city a long time, in making war against it to take it, you shall not destroy its trees by wielding an axe against them, for you may eat of them, but you shall not cut them down, for is the tree of the field a man, that it should be besieged by you? Only the trees which you know that they are not trees for food, them you may destroy and cut down and you may build bulwarks against the city that makes war with you until it falls.
(Devarim 20:19–20)

THE Torah outlaws the destruction of fruit trees around a city during a siege. An invading army might wish to cut down the fruit trees for several reasons. Sieges aim to cut off the city's food supply, and fruit trees represent a source of food for the besieged, who may be able to forage at night.[1] Trees can provide cover for defenders wishing to sabotage equipment or infiltrate the enemy camp. Trees might interfere with artillery, guarding cities against bombardment.[2] Invaders may choose to raze trees and ravage the countryside as a psychological tactic.[3] The

1. Chizkuni rejects the possibility that it is the defenders who might wish to cut down the fruit trees, to keep the fruit from the invading army.

2. Ramban gives these reasons, as does Rashbam, who learns from the word *ki* that trees which are being used for staging attacks may be cut down.

3. Sforno explains that only armies that are unsure about the outcome of their war cut down trees just to inflict damage. Bnei Yisrael, who should be confident of their conquest, do not need to resort to such actions. Sefer Hachinuch 530 says that the reason for cutting down the trees is "to pain their hearts."

invaders may also need the trees for wood to build siege instruments.[4] Despite the many tactical reasons for wishing to do so, the Torah prohibits cutting down fruit trees.[5]

The explanation given in the Torah for this prohibition is enigmatic. It asks, "For is the tree of the field a man, that it should be besieged by you?" The Sifri clarifies that this question highlights the tree's value as a source of food, which should not be wasted.[6] This reading is reinforced by the next verse in the Torah, which states that non-fruit-bearing trees may be cut down for use in the siege.

Despite the emphasis of the Torah on fruit trees, the Talmud rules that both fruit trees and shade trees alike can be harvested, provided that they are being cut down for productive use.[7] The Sifri teaches that trees can be cut down to make *tormenta* and *ballista*, two types of Roman siege weapons.[8] Furthermore, if trees are harming the war effort they may be cut down.[9] The reason fruit trees and shade trees are contrasted in our verses is to point out that because fruit trees have an extra commodity, it is preferable to harvest shade trees first.[10]

While this seems to limit the scope of the commandment, it is also broadened in a different way. Rambam writes that the wasteful destruction of fruit trees in any situation, even outside of war, is also forbidden. Even more significantly, he rules that any type of purposeless destruction is

---

4. Rashbam also gives this explanation.

5. For Near Eastern examples of cutting trees as part of a siege, see Israel Eph'al, *The City Besieged: Siege and its Manifestations in the Ancient Near East* (Magness Press, 2013), 52–54.

6. Sifri Devarim 203. See also ShmR 35:2, which states that the *Mishkan* was built from non-fruit-bearing trees to serve as an example for others.

7. Rashi specifically mentions the value of ceiling beams. See bBK 92a *yachol afilu meula bedamim.* For more on this, see my commentary on Vayikra 5:23.

8. *Tormenta* is a general word describing engines used for hurling missiles of various types, including javelins, arrows, rocks, etc. The word comes from the Latin word meaning "to twist," as the mechanism involves winding to generate tension. *Ballista* is a specific type of catapult used by the Romans. Vitruvius describes how to make and use *ballista*e in *Ten Books on Architecture* X.10–11, in addition to a variety of other siege machines used by the Greeks and Romans. *Ballista* stones were found in Masada. Josephus, *Jewish War* 5.258 describes spear-throwers, catapults and stone-throwers used in the siege of Jerusalem. Maccabim I 6:20 describes how the Jewish army under Yehuda Hamaccabi built siege machines when attacking the Akra fortress in Jerusalem, and 6:50 describes how the Seleucid army did the same when attacking Beit Tzur. For additional discussion of siege warfare, see my commentary on Bamidbar 31:7.

9. bBK 92a tells how Shmuel cut down a tree because it was damaging nearby vineyards.

10. bBK 91b.

forbidden, such as breaking plates, tearing clothes, razing buildings, and blocking water sources.[11] This is the source of the widely known prohibition against wasting, *bal tashchit*.

It seems clear from this discussion that the Rabbis consider the primary uses of trees to be the production of food and as a source of wood. Trees should be preserved because they provide fruit. A tree that produces fruit is normally considered more valuable than a tree that does not. However, if the wood is particularly valuable, its value may outweigh the utility provided by fruit. When wood is needed for any reason, it is permissible to harvest the trees, regardless of their fruit production. This halachic discussion implies that trees were only valued as a source of wood or fruit, but not for beauty[12] or shade, and certainly not in terms of increasing air quality or providing a natural habitat for animals. Nonetheless, there is a willingness to evaluate the trees from multiple perspectives in order to assess their value.

The law against cutting down fruit trees can also have an impact on architectural design. Building plans which call for fruit trees to be cut down can be halachically problematic, though many halachic authorities are lenient on this matter. R. Asher ben Yechiel rules that if space is needed, one may cut down a fruit tree.[13] Based on this ruling, R. David Halevi Segal writes that one may clear fruit trees for the purpose of building houses.[14] Others are more strict, based on R. Yehuda Hachasid's warning on the subject.[15] R. Ovadia Yosef rules that one can cut a tree to expand a house if the extra space is needed, but not if it is simply to make the house more beautiful.[16] In 2012, the New York Times ran an article about how some communities of Jews in New York are very scrupulous about not cutting down trees and brought some examples of architectural solutions to avoid harming fruit trees.[17]

---

11. Hilchot Melachim 6:8–10 The Kesef Mishna quotes bShab 105b, in which R. Eliezer rules that this behavior is akin to idol worship.

12. Though in the context of Devarim 16:21, which forbids the planting of *ashera* trees by the altar, beauty does seem to be the primary use of the tree. See, for example, Sforno and Ramban's commentaries on that verse. See also my commentary on Bamidbar 35:3–5 for trees planted near cities.

13. Rosh BK 8:15.

14. Taz on YD 116:6.

15. Tzivaat Rebbe Yehuda Hachasid 45.

16. Yabiya Omer V, YD 12. mMeg 3:2 contains a tangential law about selling synagogues and their subsequent redevelopment, which also deals with the value of one land use versus another.

17. Elizabeth A. Harris, "Instead of Taking Down a Fruit Tree, Building Around It" in the New York Times, 30 July 2012, retrieved online on 15 Nov 2019. https://www.ny

Many cities have strict laws about cutting down trees of value during construction. In the planning stages, architects are often required to order an agronomic survey of the construction site to see which trees may be harmed by the design plans. The agronomist classifies each tree and can demand that certain ones be left untouched or replanted elsewhere. In such a case, the architect must then alter the design accordingly. In some situations, the client or architect can choose to make a point of celebrating existing trees on-site by designing the building around them.[18] In either situation, the desire or demand to preserve trees impacts the design of a building. As with the Torah's commandment, there is a desire to avoid cutting down trees out of a recognition of their value.

102. Model of United States Federal Courthouse, Springfield, MA, with curved colonnade surrounding the historic trees on the site. (Image courtesy of Safdie Architects, photo by John Horner)

times.com/2012/07/31/nyregion/for-some-orthodox-jews-a-rule-against-chopping-down-fruit-trees.html.

18. Such was the case with the United States Federal Courthouse in Springfield, MA, designed by Moshe Safdie and Associates.

# Measuring Between Cities

וְיָצְאוּ זְקֵנֶיךָ וְשֹׁפְטֶיךָ וּמָדְדוּ אֶל הֶעָרִים אֲשֶׁר סְבִיבֹת הֶחָלָל. (דברים כא:ב)

Then your elders and your judges shall come forth and they shall go out and measure the distances from the corpse to the nearby cities. (Devarim 21:2)

WHEN a dead body is found in a field and the circumstances of death are unknown, the Torah mandates that the elders and judges of the nearest city[1] take responsibility. A ceremony is held in which they break the neck of a cow as a form of atonement, which is known as *egla arufa*.

To ascertain the location of the closest city, the elders must measure the distance between the body and the various nearby cities. While there is a disagreement in the Mishna about where on the dead body to begin the measurement,[2] no guideline is given for the endpoint of the measurement. It is unclear if the measurement is to the city wall, the furthest dwelling on the outskirts of the city, or to some other point.[3] In a similar law about measuring the 2000 cubit Shabbat perimeter around a city, the Mishna rules that individual houses set the outer limits of a city.[4] In a discussion about young children going on a pilgrimage to Jerusalem, there is some debate as to whether we measure from walls, houses, or a topographical

1. There are some limitations: the city cannot be a on the border, must have a majority of Jews, and must have a Jewish court. In addition, Jerusalem is ineligible. See mSot 9:2 and tSot 9:1.

2. R. Eliezer: the navel. R. Akiva: the nose. R. Eliezer ben Yaakov: the neck. See mSot 9:4.

3. bEruv 57a and yEruv 5:2 (22c) learn from Bamidbar 35:4 that for an *eruv* we measure from the city wall. However, yEruv 5:7 says this is only true for old cities, whereas new cities are measured from the farthest house.

4. mEruv 5:1.

feature.[5] Roman milestones, marking the distance to major cities, tended to reference landmarks near the center of the city and measure from that point. Israel Roll, an archaeologist who studied the Roman road system in Judea, suggested that measurements to Caesarea were taken from the city's tetrapylon and measurements to Jerusalem may have referred to the column located near what we today call the Damascus Gate, which appears on the Madaba map.[6] For the mitzva of *egla arufa*, it might make sense to measure to the location of the court. In short, there is no explicit ruling about the part of the city to which the measurement is taken.

Although the discussion about *egla arufa* does not explain the method and tools for measuring the distance to surrounding cities, there is a detailed description given for how to measure the Shabbat boundary. The Talmud implies that similar surveying techniques were used for *egla arufa* as well.[7] The Mishna explains that measurements were taken with a cord of fifty cubits[8] and had to be done by professionals,[9] who in Roman times were called *agrimensores* (land surveyors). In the Talmud, R. Assi specifies that the cord is to be made of palm fibers. R. Yehoshua ben Chananiya states that iron chains would give a more accurate measurement.[10] With Shabbat boundaries, measurements were taken as the crow flies, with obstacles and topography largely ignored and circumvented. The assumption is that similar principles applied to *egla arufa*, though one could argue that, if we are concerned with jurisdiction of cities over surrounding land, topography should be more important for *egla arufa*; a spot on the main road from a city is more closely connected to that city than to another city that is technically closer but less accessible.[11] Still, this does not seem to be the accepted protocol.

---

5. yChag 1:1 (76a).

6. Israel Roll, "The Roman Road System in Judaea" in *The Jerusalem Cathedra 3* (YBZP, 1983), 152.

7. bEruv 58b, which explains that the method for estimating distance around obstacles cannot be used for *egla arufa*, implying that the general method of measuring with cords *was* used for that purpose.

8. mEruv 5:4.

9. mEruv 5:5. Gil P. Klein argues that the Rabbis were familiar with standard Roman survey practices and Roman literature on surveying. This is based on some of the techniques for surveying found in rabbinic literature, as well as the practice of "squaring the city" for Shabbat boundaries. See Gil P. Klein, "Squaring the City: Between Roman and Rabbinic Urban Geometry" in *Phenomenologies of the City* ed. Henriette Steiner and Maximillian Sternberg (Ashgate, 2015), 38–44.

10. bEruv 58a.

11. A similar distinction is proposed in yBB 2:6 (13c) for determining the ownership of stray birds.

In the Greek world, measurements like these were most commonly taken with one-hundred-cubit cords called *schoinion*, made of twisted rushes.[12] In a treatise on measuring, Hero was concerned with making sure that the cord would give an accurate reading, insisting that it remain well-tensioned.[13] However, like R. Yehoshua, Hero suggested chains as an alternative.[14] Measurements were also sometimes taken with a rod, or *decempeda*, which was ten feet long. The rod gave a more uniform measurement but was impractical for measuring long distances.[15] There were potentially other ways to carry out these measurements, that may have saved labor. Both Vitruvius and Hero describe the hodometer, a device for measuring distance mounted on a carriage,[16] though it is questionable whether these devices were practical. R. Gamliel had a tube that he used for estimating distances.[17] Still, by far the most common tools and methods are those described in the Mishna.

Another difficulty with taking such a measurement is determining the direction in which to measure. If a body is found within view of one or more cities, it is relatively straightforward to measure directly to the city. However, if a body is recovered and no city is visible from that point, how would the officials determine in which direction to begin measuring? Modern maps would make this simple, but such cartography was not available in Late Antiquity.[18] Locals would need to suggest one or more candidates in the area based on their own geographic knowledge. The surveyors would then need to ascertain the angle at which to begin their measurements to each of these cities so that the distances could be determined and compared. The angles were presumably calculated using the same methods used by Roman road builders to determine the correct direction of intercity roads.[19]

Surveying the area to determine the correct direction in which to

12. M.J.T. Lewis, *Surveying Instruments of Greece and Rome* (Cambridge, 2003), 19.

13. Hero, *Dioptra*, 20.

14. Ibid, 34.

15. Lewis, *Surveying*, 21.

16. Vitruvius, *Ten Books on Architecture*, X.9.1–4 and Hero, *Dioptra*, 34.

17. bEruv 43b, yEruv 5:3 (22d), and Daniel Sperber, *Nautica Talmudica* (Bar Ilan University Press, 1986), 107–109. See also Lewis, *Surveying*, 46–7.

18. The use of maps in determining the Shabbat boundary is discussed by R. Yisrael Rosen and R. Uri Desberg. They determine that 4% of the distance should be subtracted due to possible topographical changes of elevation. See their article "*Techumei Shabbat Bemaarach Yeshuvim Gushi*" in *Tehumim* 5, 24–27. (Hebrew)

19. For one explanation, see Adrian Kerton, "Roman Roads, A Simple Surveying Technique" at https://adriankerton.wordpress.com/roman-roads-a-simple-surveying-technique/, retrieved 22 Nov 2019.

measure would have simultaneously yielded all the necessary geometric information to determine the distance between those cities without additional measurements.[20] Furthermore, even if the identity of the closest city is obvious, it is still necessary to carry out the measurements. Both these facts suggest that instead of simply determining the closest city, the act of measuring was presumably a way to publicize the death, aid in the investigation, and possibly help foster repentance. This is why taking measurements constituted an integral part of the commandment.

For the ceremony of *egla arufa*, it was necessary to measure to the closest city. This was done using standard surveying techniques. However, the main reason for taking measurements was to help publicize the murder, and not just to establish the location of the nearest city.

20. Even if something like the fourth century original of the Peutinger Table, showing distances between cities, had been available, measurements would still be needed. See also Rambam Hilchot Rotzeach 9:1 and R. Eliyahu Mizrachi on our verse, who states that if it is obvious which city is the closest, it is enough to measure only to that one city, and Mishna Lamelech on Rambam above, which explains this opinion.

# Guardrails

כִּי תִבְנֶה בַּיִת חָדָשׁ וְעָשִׂיתָ מַעֲקֶה לְגַגֶּךָ וְלֹא תָשִׂים דָּמִים בְּבֵיתֶךָ כִּי יִפֹּל הַנֹּפֵל מִמֶּנּוּ. (דברים כב:ח)

When you build a new house, then you shall make a guardrail for your roof, that you bring not blood upon your house, if any man falls from it. (Devarim 22:8)

THE Torah commands that guardrails be installed on roofs to prevent accidents. Although the Torah phrases this commandment narrowly – railings on the roof of a new house – most commentators agree that this commandment is broadly applicable. Saadia Gaon learns from the word "blood" that this commandment applies to all potential domestic hazards. As examples, the Talmud lists violent dogs and rickety ladders.[1]

Though the Talmud seemingly puts these hazards in a single category, R. Shmuel Eidels explains that there is a fundamental difference between a guardrail and a violent dog or rickety ladder. A guardrail protects the main occupant of the house, the owner, as well as any guests. On the other hand, a violent dog and a rickety ladder do not pose great dangers to the owner, who knows the ladder is shaky and with whom the dog is familiar. Nonetheless, these items are not to be kept in the house, specifically because they might injure *others*. Owners must protect others as well as themselves.[2]

Rabeinu Bachya writes that the simple meaning of the text is that a man "should be careful to guard himself from danger." In other words, this precept is not only about your house – it is also about *all things you do*. A guardrail is only an example of a broader idea. The Minchat Chinuch agrees, listing it as a mitzva "to remove all stumbling blocks and hazards

1. bKet 41b, bBK 15a, and 46a.
2. Marasha on bBK 16b, *minayin*.

from your dwelling places" and that one "needs to guard himself from all the occurrences of the world, because God created the world with the foundations of nature and decreed that fire will burn and water will extinguish." The Shulchan Aruch includes guardrails under a more general law demanding "the removal of all obstacles that pose a mortal danger."[3] In sum, this commandment is interpreted very broadly, demanding that people ensure the safety of their houses and themselves as well.

Other sources, however, limit the application of this commandment. The Talmud states that only structures that are at least four square cubits and have a living quarter require a guardrail.[4] One need not erect a guardrail on the roof of a public building, such as a synagogue or a *beit midrash*.[5] R. Yechiel Michel Epstein suggests that railings are only mandated on flat roofs. If the roofs are not part of the living space, there is no requirement for a guardrail.[6]

It is puzzling that no guardrail is required on a public building. Rashi[7] gives two reasons widely quoted in halacha. First, since a public building does not have an owner, no one is responsible for erecting a guardrail. Second, a public building has no dwelling, so it is exempt. Although these provide technical explanations for the exemption, they go against our understanding of how public space is used, which should demand an even higher level of safety. Furthermore, it seems to contradict the broad application of this commandment, to protect yourself and others in all situations.

One way to understand this odd exemption is to look at modern safety codes. As in Jewish law, which specifies the height, location, and strength of a railing,[8] building codes mandate railing height, strength, and how high a ledge must be to necessitate a railing. Different scenarios have different requirements. For example, Israeli building code distinguishes between roofs in normal use and roofs which are entered only by technicians for repairs. Such spaces still require railings, but the requirements are not as strict.[9]

It is possible that when the Talmud exempts public buildings from railings, it is referring to spaces that are like these technical spaces. R. Baruch Epstein and the Chazon Ish suggest this interpretation, writing

3. Shulchan Aruch CM 427.
4. bSuk 3a.
5. bChul 136a.
6. Aruch Hashulchan CM 427:5.
7. bChul 136a *batei kenesiyot.*
8. Shulchan Aruch CM 427:7.
9. Teken Yisraeli 1142 6.1.4.2.

that "public" is a code word meaning "rarely used." The roof of a synagogue is not open to the public, and therefore does not require a guardrail.[10] There is no concern that someone will wander into this space and fall. Presumably, if the roof of a public building *were* in use, it *would* require a guardrail.[11] This fits with the wide application of this mitzva given by the Rabbis.

The commandment to erect a guardrail has a broad scope. It is extended to all inhabited structures and even to non-architectural circumstances of danger. Although the Talmud excludes public spaces, this is likely because roofs in public buildings were not widely used.

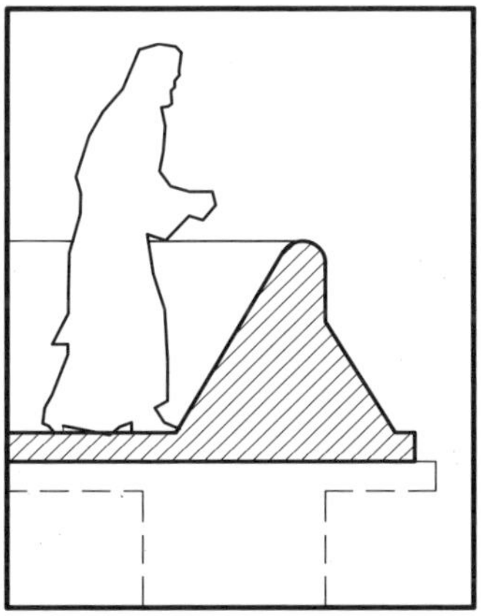

103. Section of parapet around the Temple Mount retaining wall.

10. See Torah Temima commentary on our verse, regarding bChul 136a and Chazon Ish, CM, likutim 18.

11. This is supported by a ruling in yMK 1:10 (81a) that while a balcony requires a railing of ten handbreadths, a railing on a roof only needs to be three handbreadths. Korban HaEida explains that this is because of its usage – the balcony is in regular use, so it needs a more secure railing. For an analysis of this issue, see Menachem Slae, *Safety Regulations in Building in the Halachah* (Harry Fischel Institute, 1984), 51. (Hebrew)

# Fences

לֹא תִזְרַע כַּרְמְךָ כִּלְאָיִם פֶּן תִּקְדַּשׁ הַמְלֵאָה הַזֶּרַע אֲשֶׁר תִּזְרָע וּתְבוּאַת הַכָּרֶם.
(דברים כב:ט)

> You shall not sow your vineyard with two kinds of seed, lest the fruit of the seed which you have sown and fruit of the vineyard be forfeited together with the increase of the vineyard. (Devarim 22:9)

THE Torah prohibits planting grapevines alongside other grains and vegetables. This is one of several types of "mixtures" outlawed by the Torah, such as clothes made of wool and linen and interbreeding animal species.[1] A distance of at least four cubits must be maintained between the trunk of the vine and other species.[2] However, if there is a wall next to the vineyard, one can plant other crops immediately on the other side of the wall, without any minimum distance from the vines.[3]

To clarify this ruling, the Mishna and Tosefta set out the minimum requirements for a fence. It must be ten handbreadths tall[4] and can be made of stones, reed mats, straw, sticks, or ropes.[5] The fence need not be solid; if made of sticks or ropes, for example, the elements can be separated by up to three handbreadths.[6] The fence as a whole can have gaps that are up to ten cubits, or even more, so long as the majority of the fence is standing.[7] Both the Mishna and the Tosefta explain that the three-handbreadth maximum is to ensure that the fence will prevent a goat from passing through.

1. See my commentary on Vayikra 19:19 for more on this topic.
2. Rambam Hilchot Kilayim 7:1. Measurements are taken from the tree trunk at a specified height. In architecture, hallways sometimes have a required width, and the building code also specifies at what height the width must be measured.
3. Rambam, Hilchot Kilayim 7:15, Shulchan Aruch YD 296:45.
4. mKil 4:3. For a similar ruling relating to *eruvin*, see tEruv 6:17.
5. tKil 4:3. For a similar ruling relating to the Sabbatical Year, see tSheviit 2:19.
6. tKil 4:3.
7. mKil 4:4.

Fences are used for two distinct but related purposes. On the one hand, a fence can be a physical barrier, designed to separate and prevent passage. This is emphasized by the ruling about the goat – the elements of the fence must be spaced closely enough to prevent the animal's free passage. However, fences can also serve to visually distinguish between two parcels of land. Though not preventing people from passing, the fence still demarcates where one field ends and another begins.[8] A partially-ruined fence cannot serve as a real barrier – things can pass freely through the gaps – however, if enough of the wall exists it still *reads* as a border, marking a line between two different areas.[9] R. S.R. Hirsch remarks that only a visible separation is necessary "which would not effect a real separation of the species." To create this type of separation, one may either leave a wide distance of four cubits between the vines and other crops, which marks a break between the crops, or one can construct a wall. Both fulfill the requirement.

R. Hirsch supports this understanding when he writes that "the mere sight of this land cultivated under the regime of the *kilayim* laws must have called out to every passer-by" to let them know that the ground was holy and that respect must be paid to Divine law. While the law demands separation, it is the visual component which he emphasizes.

8. This, I believe, is the function of the fence mentioned in mGit 8:3, in which a divorce document is thrown to a woman standing on a roof which, according to bGit 79a, is surrounded by a fence.

9. mPea 2:1, tPea 1:8, and Sifra Kedoshim 2:1 list various topographical features that separate fields for the purpose of *pe'ah*. These include rivers, cisterns, and paths of various sizes. Here too the borders need not be physical barriers, but rather visible edges. Compare this with mBK 6:4, which deals with acceptable barriers for protecting against the spread of fire.

KI TEITZEI

# Stair Design

וְשָׂם לָהּ עֲלִילֹת דְּבָרִים וְהוֹצִא עָלֶיהָ שֵׁם רָע וְאָמַר אֶת הָאִשָּׁה הַזֹּאת לָקַחְתִּי וָאֶקְרַב אֵלֶיהָ וְלֹא מָצָאתִי לָהּ בְּתוּלִים. (דברים כב:יד)

And lay wanton charges against her, and bring out an evil name upon her, saying: "I took this woman and when I came to her, I found her not to be a virgin." (Devarim 22:14)

A WOMAN betrothed as a virgin who does not show signs of virginity on her wedding night can, under certain conditions, be sentenced to death. This law leads to several discussions in rabbinic literature about circumstances under which such signs might be absent for halachically permissible reasons.

The Talmud relates one such case brought before R. Chanina, in which a woman claimed her situation was caused by the stairs in her father's house, which were excessively high. R. Chanina accepted this argument, and the woman was given the full value of her *ketuba*.[1] R. David Herschel Fränkel explains that the long, high strides she took on the steps were the cause.[2]

In the seventeenth century, French architect François Blondel developed a formula for designing stairs with tread depths and riser heights that would be comfortable for climbing. Blondel observed that the average person, walking on a level surface, took strides measuring twenty-four inches, or about sixty-five cm.[3] However, when climbing, he postulated that the average step was half this distance or only twelve inches. Blondel concluded that the correct formula for ergonomic stairs was for two times the height of the step plus the depth of the tread to equal approximately

1. yKet 1:1 (25a).
2. In his Korban HaEida commentary on the passage in the Yerushalmi. See also bShab 63b, which discusses a family that forced its daughters to take short steps, to prevent this from happening.
3. Blondel's inch was the French royal inch, slightly larger than today's measure.

twenty-four inches.[4] In the subsequent centuries, this formula has been widely adopted in many countries, though with varying numbers for the acceptable range. Israeli code requires an output of 61–63 cm.[5]

One famous example of contrasting proportions of stairs can be found in the approach to the Campidoglio in Rome, where Michelangelo designed a massive, gradual staircase at the entrance. The stairs were intended to accommodate not just pedestrians but also horses. Next to Michelangelo's stairs is a separate, steeper, and more imposing flight of stairs that leads up to an adjacent basilica.[6] The juxtaposition of these two staircases demonstrates how dramatic a difference stair proportions can make.

Acknowledging that certain dimensions make stairs suitable for human use, one can also see situations in which stairs were deliberately designed *not* to be comfortable for people to climb. Greek temples were usually situated on stone bases with steps around all four sides.[7] However, these steps were almost always too high and too deep to be comfortable for human use.[8] The same was true of the stairs in the Jerusalem Temple, which the Mishna reports had risers and treads that were each a half-cubit,[9] a

---

4. François Blondel, *Cours D'Architecture* Book III Ch. VI (Roulland, 1683), 684. See Vitruvius, *Ten Books on Architecture* IX.Preface.8 for an earlier attempt at a rule for correct stair proportions. For a history of rules for stair proportions, see John Templer, *The Staircase: Studies of Hazards, Falls and Safer Design* (MIT Press, 1994), 25–29. bEruv 58b considers the rise and run of a sloped terrain when surveying distances for an *eruv*.

5. *Takanon Hatichnun Vehabeniya*, second addendum, 3.2.2.5 stipulates that 2 rises + 1 tread = 61–63 cm. It also sets the acceptable height of risers as 10–17.5 cm, and the minimum depth of treads as 26 cm. *Architectural Graphic Standards* includes a chart for calculating acceptable dimensions and lists two rules of thumb: rise × run = 75 inches, or rise + run = 17 ½ inches.

6. The Basilica of St. Mary of the Altar of Heaven, also known as the Aracoeli. These stairs were designed in 1348 by Simone Andreozzi, to commemorate the end of the Black Death. These are known as the Stairway to Heaven. Climbing them is thought to be a type of penitence.

7. Vitruvius writes that there should always be an odd number of steps, so that both the first and last step can be taken with the right foot. This was seen as respectful. See Vitruvius, V.4.4 and Petronius, *Satyricon*, 30.5. A similar sentiment exists in Jewish law, as per bYom 53b.

8. Joseph Rykwert, *The Dancing Column* (MIT Press, 1996), 173.

9. mMid 2:3. A half cubit, according to Rambam, is approximately 23.5 cm. The surviving steps in front of the Double Gate are an average height of 22.7 cm as per David M. Jacobson, "The Plan of Herod's Temple" in *Bulletin of the Anglo-Israel Archaeological Society* (1990–1, Vol. 10), 48. Note also mMid 3:6, which has the more appropriate *proportion* for stairs of a half cubit riser and cubit tread, though this also results in stairs that are too large to walk with normal strides. (2 × 23.5 + 47 = 94 cm!) See also Rambam Hilchot Beit Habechira 6:4, which in some versions records that those steps also had

104. Giovanni Battista Piranesi, *Campidoglio*, 1751. (Wikimedia)

dimension that is quite tall for the risers and very narrow for the treads. In both cases, this may have been done to make the architecture more imposing and to accentuate its monumental nature. Having excessively tall steps helps demarcate the Temple as a special and privileged space that should not be entered frivolously.

In spaces intended for everyday usage, building codes demand stairs that fall within an ergonomic range. Like many areas of building code, this helps ensure that the steps will be comfortable and safe to use. While deviating from the code might not cause physical harm as described in the Talmud, it would certainly result in stairs that are difficult to climb and cumbersome to use.

treads of a half-cubit. This is called an "obvious mistake" in the textual variants of the Shabsai Frankel edition, VIIa, 890.

# City Gates

וְהוֹצֵאתֶם אֶת שְׁנֵיהֶם אֶל שַׁעַר הָעִיר הַהִוא וּסְקַלְתֶּם אֹתָם בָּאֲבָנִים וָמֵתוּ אֶת הַנַּעֲרָ עַל דְּבַר אֲשֶׁר לֹא צָעֲקָה בָעִיר וְאֶת הָאִישׁ עַל דְּבַר אֲשֶׁר עִנָּה אֶת אֵשֶׁת רֵעֵהוּ וּבִעַרְתָּ הָרָע מִקִּרְבֶּךָ. (דברים כב:כד)

Then you shall bring them both out to the gate of that city and you shall stone them with stones that they die. The maiden, because she cried not, being in the city, and the man, because he has humbled his neighbor's wife, so you shall put away evil from your midst. (Devarim 22:24)

WHILE describing the punishment for an engaged woman who has relations with another man, the Torah states that the pair must be brought "out to the gate of that city," where they will be stoned. This is one of several laws in which justice is carried out at the gates of the city. In the laws of a stubborn and rebellious son, one who falsely claims his wife was not a virgin, and levirate marriage,[1] the Torah explicitly says that the elders of the city were to be found at the city gate. Onkelos even translates "gate" as "the court."[2]

In addition to a court, the city gate was a place of gathering. This may have been due to the unplanned nature of ancient cities: the plaza before the city gate was often the only open space available in the city. The gate thus took the role that would later be filled by a central square. The threshold between the city and the wilderness was also treated as a place of importance in many cultures.[3]

There are several other uses of the city gate highlighted in Tanach. We

1. Devarim 21:19, 22:15 and 25:7 respectively. See also Devarim 16:18 and 17:8. In the fourth chapter of Ruth, Boaz also goes to the city gate to perform levirate marriage on Ruth.

2. See his translation of Devarim 25:7.

3. Frank Frick, *The City in Ancient Israel* (Scholars Press, 1997), 125–6.

find examples of the gate serving as a place of business: Avraham and Efron haggled over the Cave of Machpela there,[4] Elisha mentioned that grain was traded in the gate of Shomron,[5] and Nechemia acted to shut down market trade by the gate of Jerusalem on Shabbat.[6] The gate was sometimes used as a place for the king to hold court, as Achav and Yehoshafat did during their campaign for Ramot Gilad,[7] as David did following his mourning period for Avshalom,[8] and as Tzidkiyahu did when Yirmiyahu was thrown into a pit.[9] Similarly, it was also a place where people gathered to hear prophets speak, as Amos referred to a prophet as "him who reproves in the gate."[10] The city gate was used as a gathering point, as done before Sennacherib's attack.[11] Finally, we have several examples of the gate being used for religious practices: Yoshiyahu commanded that the idols which were worshiped in the city gate be destroyed, and most strikingly, Nechemia described how all of Bnei Yisrael gathered together in the month of Tishrei "into the open place that was before the water gate and they spoke to Ezra the scribe to bring the book of the Torah of Moshe," which Ezra read before them.[12]

All these examples demonstrate that the city gate served as a dynamic public space, widely used for civic, governmental, and religious practices. These new functions represented a shift in how the gate complex was used in the Iron Age. This is reflected in the archaeological remains. During the earlier Bronze Age, any rooms that were part of the gate were not connected with the main passage. Iron Age gates had separate cells, sometimes had benches, and were not completely defensive in nature, allowing them to serve civilian needs as well.[13]

Lee Levine has argued that the gate was also the forerunner of the synagogue.[14] He suggests that the synagogue developed as a replacement for the city-gate space, which in the Iron Age was the site of all the activities described in Tanach and consisted of several separate rooms and plazas that comprised the gate "complex." However, as the design of city

4. Bereshit 23:10.
5. Melachim II 7:1.
6. Nechemia 13:19–21.
7. Melachim I 22:10.
8. Shmuel II 19:9.
9. Yirmiyahu 38:7.
10. Amos 5:10.
11. Divrei Hayamim II 32:6.
12. Nechemia 8.
13. Zeev Herzog, "Settlement and Fortification Planning in the Iron Age" in *The Architecture of Ancient Israel* (Israel Exploration Society, 1992), 271–2.
14. Lee Levine, *The Ancient Synagogue* (Yale University Press, 2005), 26–31.

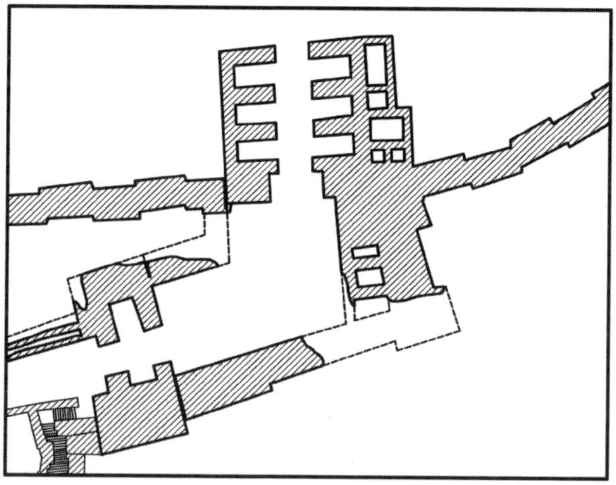

105. Six cell gate of Megiddo, Stratum IVB, mid-tenth century BCE. (Based on Zeev Herzog, *Das Stadttor in Israel und in den Nachbarländern*)

gates became primarily defensive during the Hellenistic period, the gate complexes were reduced to a simple passageway and were no longer suitable for public functions. A new public space was sought, and thus the synagogue was born.

Early synagogues served many different roles. Sources refer to the reading and studying of the Torah and other texts. For example, the Tosefta lists which passages are to be read at various times of the year.[15] Philo describes Essene[16] and mainstream worship,[17] and the Theodotus inscription refers to the synagogue as a place for reading and studying the law.[18] Luke[19] describes Jesus as reading from Yishayahu in a Nazareth synagogue and Josephus writes that:

> He [Moshe] appointed the Law to be the most excellent and necessary form of instruction, ordaining, not that it should be once for all or twice or on several occasions, but that every week men

15. tMeg 3:1–13.

16. Philo, *Every Good Man is Free*, 81–82.

17. Philo, *Embassy*, 156.

18. An archaeological artifact found in an excavation of the City of David, which reads (in Hebrew) "Theodotus, the son of Vettenos, priest and archisynagogos, son of an archisynagogos, grandson of an archisynagogos, built this synagogue for the reading of the Law and the study of the commandments, and a guesthouse and rooms and water installations for hosting those in need from abroad, it having been founded by his fathers, the presbyters, and Simonides."

19. Luke 4:16–17.

> should desert their other occupations and assemble to listen to the Law and to obtain a thorough and accurate knowledge of it, a practice which all other legislators seem to have neglected.[20]

Books of the New Testament illustrate that synagogues were a place for preaching. There was also a tradition of communal prayer.

However, in addition to these sources that show the synagogue as a place of religious activity, many sources show that the synagogue was used for community activities. Synagogues could be used as schools: the Talmud[21] states that there were 394 courts in Jerusalem, each with a synagogue, school, and house of study attached. Synagogues could be related to business and the marketplace: the Tosefta describes how seating in the Alexandrian synagogue was done by guild, to afford newcomers with an opportunity to make business connections.[22] There is a debate between Beit Shamai and Beit Hillel about whether, in the synagogue on Shabbat, it is permissible to collect charity for orphans, act as a matchmaker, and pray for someone to be healed.[23] This implies that all these would be normal synagogue activities. The Theodotus inscription mentions that the synagogue was a place for the visitors to lodge. Burial societies met in an Egyptian synagogue.[24] There is some evidence from Roman decrees quoted by Josephus that synagogues were recognized as places for communal gathering. This is supported by the architecture of the early synagogues that have been uncovered. Synagogues in Gamla, Masada, Herodium, and Kiryat Sefer are constructed with a rectangular plan, surrounded on all sides by benches. When in use, the congregants would all face the center, rather than forward as is the case in today's synagogues. Furthermore, the synagogues did not have a Torah ark in the front to serve as a focus of attention.

Finally, we see that synagogues were also used as places of justice. In the Book of Shoshana, an apocryphal story that tells of the trial of Shoshana, the Septuagint relates that the court case took place in a synagogue.[25] The Mishna[26] writes that in the case of a false witness, an official from the synagogue was involved in the administration of punishment. Similarly,

20. Josephus, *Against Apion* 2:175.
21. bKet 105a.
22. tSuk 4:4. See also bSuk 52b and ySuk 5:1.
23. tShab 17:14.
24. Levine, *The Ancient Synagogue*, 129, references Egyptian papyri.
25. Other versions of the story omit reference to the location as a synagogue.
26. mMak 3:12.

Matthew writes “But beware of men; for they will deliver you up to the councils and they will scourge you in their synagogues.”[27]

Returning to Levine’s thesis, that city gates served as the prototype for early synagogues, we can see that there are many parallel uses. Both the city gate and the synagogue were used for religious functions, but also for many community uses. Market activities, preaching, town meetings, and court trials all occurred in the space of the early synagogue, just as it had in the city gate. A corollary of this argument is that nowadays when the synagogue has supplanted the city gate as the location of these various functions, the various halachot discussed above, might now be adjudicated in the synagogue, rather than in the gate of a non-existent city wall.

27. Matthew 10:17.

# Plumbing and Sewage

וְיָתֵד תִּהְיֶה לְךָ עַל אֲזֵנֶךָ וְהָיָה בְּשִׁבְתְּךָ חוּץ וְחָפַרְתָּה בָהּ וְשַׁבְתָּ וְכִסִּיתָ אֶת צֵאָתֶךָ. (דברים כג:יד)

And you shall have a spade among your weapons and it shall be, when you will ease yourself outside, you shall dig with it and shall cover up that which comes from you. (Devarim 23:14)

In describing the proper decorum during a military campaign, the Torah dictates that a site be established outside the camp to be used for defecation. The Torah mandates that all soldiers carry a spade with them for burying excrement. These are two of the ways in which the military camp is kept holy.

There are two important points to make about the nature of these commandments. First, they are framed from the perspective of holiness, rather than hygiene. The Torah explains them as stemming from God's presence in the camp, which must therefore be kept holy.[1] Ramban understands them similarly, writing that just as one cannot pray near fecal matter,[2] so too one should keep it outside of the military camp. At most, some commentators see hygiene as a secondary motivation. The author of Sefer Hachinuch, for example, writes that this *also* promotes cleanliness, adding that this level of cleanliness would be lauded by other nations.[3]

Second, the mitzvot are clearly related to military encampments.[4] This may be because military campaigns are considered a time when God accompanies Bnei Yisrael, necessitating a higher level of holiness.[5] It might

1. Devarim 23:15.
2. As per bBer 25a.
3. Sefer Hachinuch 543. See also tMeg 3:25 and bBer 61b for additional bathroom rules, particularly regarding the direction in which one should urinate and defecate.
4. Devarim 23:10.
5. As per Ibn Ezra and Rabeinu Bachya on Devarim 23:10.

also be due to the heightened level of danger inherent in military conflicts, requiring a higher level of care to avoid peril.[6] Ramban,[7] however, emphasizes the transient nature of a military camp. While in a domestic setting, one expects that people will utilize the normative sanitary technology. It is specifically during wartime that special commandments must be put in place to make sure that holiness is maintained.

These two points indicate that no special commandment demands an elevated level of sanitation during normal life. Washing for ritual reasons – immersions in *mikvaot* or washing hands before meals – is sometimes credited with limiting the impact of epidemics on Jewish households.[8] However, as in our verses, these requirements stem from ritual purity rather than hygiene, and no clear halachic requirements exist regarding domestic toilet facilities.[9]

As with most architecture, in which Jewish structures largely reflect the local customs, Jewish houses tend to deal with household waste disposal similar to the norms of the time and place.[10] In Roman times, the richest households could construct a private latrine on the ground level of their house, but people who rented or lived on upper floors had no access to such facilities. Instead, they had to either go to one of the public latrines, which were common but charged entrance fees, or utilize chamber pots, which needed to be emptied into a local dung heap.[11] This reality is reflected in many rabbinic sources. Having a toilet nearby was considered a great blessing[12] or a reason to consider oneself rich.[13] A similar statement was made concerning bathing facilities – those lacking them were

---

6. As per Rashi on Devarim 23:10.

7. On Devarim 23:10–15. See also R. S.R. Hirsch.

8. This is most commonly mentioned when discussing the impact of the Black Plague on Europe. However, recent research has shown that this is driven by anti-Semitic claims that Jews did not die during the Black Plague. I would like to thank Joshua Teplitsky for sharing a copy of his forthcoming paper on the subject, "Imagined Immunities: Medieval Myths and Modern Histories of Jews and the Black Death."

9. See yPes 7:12 (35b), which stresses that sewage should not be equated with impurity but is rather a question of sanitation.

10. Under Herod, Jerusalem may have had some form of organized garbage disposal, but this represented a very rare exception to the general situation which existed in other cities in Judaea and across the Roman Empire. See Catherine Hezser, "Dirt and Garbage in the Ancient Jewish Religious Imagination and in Daily Life" in *Envisioning Judaism* (Mohr Siebeck, 2013), 109.

11. Jerome Carcopino, *Daily Life in Ancient Rome*, second ed. (Yale University Press, 2003), 40–42.

12. bBM 107a in the name of R. Yochanan, commenting on Devarim 28:3.

13. bShab 25b in the name of R. Yosi.

considered cursed.[14] Many passages mention public bathrooms, *batei kiseh,* or *corsvan,* some discussing proper decorum within[15] and others simply mentioning them as a part of everyday life.[16] One passage in the Tosefta discusses drainage from houses into public spaces.[17] A midrash about Haman's daughter mentions that she mistakenly emptied a chamber pot on the head of her father.[18] In the archaeological record, Ehud Netzer suggests that the latrine in Herod's Second Palace had baskets beneath the toilet seats, which servants would remove to bury the excrement.[19] In sum, the toilet facilities in Jewish houses were similar to those of the surrounding culture.

Modern Israeli plumbing code is also comparable to requirements in other Western countries. *Hora'ot Lemitkanei Tavrua* (Halat) specifies the required number of toilets, sinks, and showers based on the building's occupancy. It states what size pipes are needed and the necessary water pressure, giving the various details to ensure sanitary conditions. Having a modern plumbing code is not considered to be some great innovation, but rather a basic requirement of modern life.

The fact that there are no special, halachic demands on plumbing reinforces our understanding of the commandments to set aside latrines and carry a spade during times of war. This is not a commandment that addresses civilian life when we expect Jewish households to abide by the standards of society at large. Rather, these are commandments that specifically address wartime, when lax sanitation standards might become the norm, and when there is hope that God's presence will accompany the soldiers.

---

14. bEruv 55b.

15. For example, bBer 62a.

16. Daniel Sperber, *The City in Roman Palestine* (Oxford University Press, 1998), 137. One notable passage in bNed 49b has R. Yehuda stating that there were twenty-four toilets en route from his house to the *beit midrash,* and he had to frequent each one on every trip. See also Shmuel Krauss, *Kadmoniyot Hatalmud* I.2, 408.

17. tBK 2:6 and bBK 6a.

18. bMeg 16a, Midrash Lekach Tov Ester 6:11. See a similar scene in Juvenal, *Satires* 3, describing the perils and chaos of a typical Roman street.

19. Ehud Netzer, *The Architecture of Herod* (Baker Academic, 2006), 53–4.

# Baskets and Architectural Orders

וְלָקַחְתָּ מֵרֵאשִׁית כָּל פְּרִי הָאֲדָמָה אֲשֶׁר תָּבִיא מֵאַרְצְךָ אֲשֶׁר ה׳ אֱלֹקֶיךָ נֹתֵן לָךְ וְשַׂמְתָּ בַטֶּנֶא וְהָלַכְתָּ אֶל הַמָּקוֹם אֲשֶׁר יִבְחַר ה׳ אֱלֹקֶיךָ לְשַׁכֵּן שְׁמוֹ שָׁם.
(דברים כו:ב)

And you shall take of the first of all the fruit of the earth which you shall bring in from your land that the Lord your God gives you, and shall put it in a basket and shall go to the place which the Lord your God shall choose to cause His name to dwell there. (Devarim 26:2)

THE Torah states that first fruits should be placed in a basket, taken to Jerusalem, and given to kohanim. Chizkuni explains that the purpose of the basket is to make the offering more presentable. The Mishna records that it was customary to adorn the baskets, with fruits from the Seven Species as the preferred choice for décor.[1] The rich would make golden or silver baskets for their first fruit offerings. The Mishna[2] uses the Greek loanword *kalathos* in its description of these baskets. *Kalathos* baskets were used for wool, fruits, flowers, and even small animals, and were often carried in ritual processions.[3]

The word *kalathos* also appears in Vitruvius' description of the origins of the Corinthian architectural order.[4] He tells the story of a young Corinthian girl who died from illness. Her prized possessions were gathered in a basket and placed on her grave, where an acanthus plant grew around the basket. The architect Callimachus passed by, noticed the arrangement, and was impressed enough by the aesthetic effect that he

1. mBik 3:9, and Bartenura's commentary. See also tBik 2:12 and 2:14.
2. mBik 3:8. For another example of the *kalathos* in rabbinic literature, see mGit 8:1.
3. Elisabeth Trinkl, "The Wool Basket: Function, Depiction and Meaning of the *Kalathos*" in *Greek and Roman Textiles and Dress* (Oxbow Books, 2014), 191, 194.
4. Corinthian capitals (קרונתון) are mentioned in Targum Yonatan on Melachim I 7:20. See Jastrow's entry קרונתא p.1414.

adapted it as the basis for a new architectural order.[5] Joseph Rykwert writes that the anecdote told by Vitruvius reflects the ritual usage of the basket for small religious gifts.[6] As such, the use of a *kalathos* in classical temple architecture makes sense for those who view temple décor as reflecting materials used in sacrifices.[7]

106. Origin of the Corinthian order. (Claude Perrault's edition of Vitruvius)

107. Corinthian capital from Tholos of Epidaurus. (Wikimedia)

108. James Adam, British Order (detail), 1762. (Accession 1000.104, Dept. of Drawings & Archives, Avery Architectural & Fine Arts Library, Columbia University)

109. Latrobe's American Order. (Architect of the Capitol)

In the seventeenth and eighteenth centuries, several architects created new orders of architecture by adapting the Corinthian design, adding imagery specific to national identity. In 1672, Jean-Baptiste Colbert designed a French order for the Louvre.[8] Leonhard Christoph Sturm proposed a German order in 1699 and Luis de Lorenzana created a Spanish order in 1769. Robert and James Adams proposed a Britannic order with lions and unicorns in 1778. Benjamin Henry Latrobe designed an American order in

5. Vitruvius, *Ten Books on Architecture*, IV.1.9–10.
6. Joseph Rykwert, *The Dancing Column* (MIT Press, 1996), 320–1.
7. George Hersey, *The Lost Meaning of Classical Architecture* (MIT Press, 1998), 2, 64.
8. Joseph Rykwert, *On Adams's House in Paradise* (MIT Press, 1987), 77–80.

1803 for the U.S. Capitol Building, complete with tobacco leaves and corn.[9] The use of a national capital was considered patriotic and architecturally appropriate.

In the spirit of these national orders, it would make sense to use the imagery of first fruit baskets for columns in a classical design of the Temple. Josephus records that Corinthian columns were used by Herod in the Royal Stoa.[10] However, one could keep the shape of the *kalathos* basket in the Corinthian capital and replace the Corinthian acanthus leaves with fruits of the seven species.[11] This would create a capital that reflects ritual offerings, as was the norm, but utilize Jewish symbolism to create an order specific to the Temple and Jerusalem.

9. M. Wilson Jones, et al. *Architectural Orders* (Oxford University Press, 2016).

10. Josephus, *Antiquities*, 15.410–420.

11. bMen 28b suggests adorning capitals with the flowers of the *menora*. See Rashi, *prachei haamudim*. The Umm el Qanatir synagogue had a capital shaped like a basket.

# Jordan Monument

וְהָיָה בַּיּוֹם אֲשֶׁר תַּעַבְרוּ אֶת הַיַּרְדֵּן אֶל הָאָרֶץ אֲשֶׁר ה׳ אֱלֹקֶיךָ נֹתֵן לָךְ וַהֲקֵמֹתָ לְךָ אֲבָנִים גְּדֹלוֹת וְשַׂדְתָּ אֹתָם בַּשִּׂיד. וְכָתַבְתָּ עֲלֵיהֶן אֶת כָּל דִּבְרֵי הַתּוֹרָה הַזֹּאת בְּעָבְרֶךָ לְמַעַן אֲשֶׁר תָּבֹא אֶל הָאָרֶץ אֲשֶׁר ה׳ אֱלֹקֶיךָ נֹתֵן לְךָ אֶרֶץ זָבַת חָלָב וּדְבַשׁ כַּאֲשֶׁר דִּבֶּר ה׳ אֱלֹקֵי אֲבֹתֶיךָ לָךְ. (דברים כז:ב-ג)

And it shall be on the day when you shall pass over the Yarden to the land which the Lord your God gives you, that you shall set up great stones and plaster them with plaster. And you shall write upon them all the words of this Torah, when you are passed over, that you may go into the land which the Lord your God gives you, a land flowing with milk and honey, as the Lord God of your fathers has promised you. (Devarim 27:2–3)

BNEI Yisrael were commanded to create a stone monument on the day they would cross the Jordan River. The monument was to be made from "great stones" covered with plaster and to have "all the words of this Torah" written on them. The Torah specifies that this monument should be built on the day they cross the Jordan and then again on Mount Eival, where the stones were to be assembled as an altar, plastered, and again inscribed with "all the words of this Torah."[1] Sefer Yehoshua describes how this played out, first with a monument in the Jordan,[2] then again in Gilgal,[3] and finally on Mount Eival.[4]

1. Devarim 27:4–8.
2. Yehoshua 4:1–9.
3. Yehoshua 4:20.
4. Yehoshua 8:30–32. Commentators debate how many times this commandment was fulfilled. tSot 8:6 and bSot 35b state that the monument was built three times, as do Rashi and Maharam, though they disagree as to where these three took place. (The fourth possible location is in Arvot Moav, as per Devarim 1:5.) Chizkuni and Tosafot (bSot 35b *shelosha*) write that it was built four times. Both numbers are quoted in ySot 7:5 (21d). The three altars may echo the three that Avraham built upon arriving in Israel,

The commentators debate two related questions regarding this monument: what was meant to be written on the stones, and what was the purpose of the various monuments? Leaving aside any logistical and scribal challenges, the answers to these questions go in two directions. On the one hand, some argue that the monuments were directed at the nations of the world. Most commentators who advocate this position point to the clause in the Torah that the words be written *be'er heitev* – very plainly – which is understood to mean that the Torah was inscribed on the stones in seventy languages.[5] This enabled the other nations to access the Torah's wisdom.[6]

On the other hand, there is a school of thought that argues these monuments were directed at Bnei Yisrael. This could be for several reasons: as a reminder of the miraculous crossing of the Jordan River,[7] as encouragement to keep the mitzvot,[8] or as a master copy of the Torah.[9] In this case, there was no need to write the Torah in seventy languages, and the commentators suggest alternative interpretations of the Torah's instructions to "write upon them all the words of this Torah." Instead of the complete text of the Torah, perhaps only the number of mitzvot,[10] the blessings and curses recited on Mount Eival,[11] the Ten Commandments, or a thorough explanation of the "seventy faces" of the Torah[12] were inscribed on the stones.

The Netziv argues that both the nations of the world and Bnei Yisrael

---

as per BerR 39:12 (8).

5. Devarim 27:8, interpreted in mSot 7:5 and tSot 8:6–7. This is the assumption behind the argument of R. Yehuda and R. Shimon in bSot 35b.

6. R. Yehuda's opinion on bSot 35b records that the nations of the world would send copyists to remove the plaster covering the incised letters of the Torah and make for themselves a copy. Carefully removing the plaster would have rendered a mirror copy of the Torah which could then be used to "print" the Torah. If this was indeed R. Yehuda's intention, as Rashi may have felt, then this represents a *very* early theoretical suggestion of the printing press. Indeed, shortly after the introduction of the printing press in Europe, Matthäus Richter wondered why it had taken millennia for the Judeo-Christian world to develop this idea and concluded that printing was a divine gift. See Matthaeus Iudex, *De Typographiae Inventione,* 5.

7. tSot 8:6 and Gur Aryeh on Devarim 27:2.

8. Ibn Ezra and Ramban on Devarim 27:3.

9. Ramban on Devarim 27:3, quoting Sefer Tagi. See also Josephus, *Antiquities* 1.70, which states that Adam predicted that the world would be destroyed by fire and water, so he "made two pillars; the one of brick, the other of stone: they inscribed their discoveries on them both, that in case the pillar of brick should be destroyed by the flood, the pillar of stone might remain and exhibit those discoveries to mankind."

10. Ibn Ezra on Devarim 27:2.

11. Ralbag on Yehoshua 8:31.

12. Torah Temima.

were the audiences of the monuments. He points out that our verses repeat themselves twice, implying a double audience.[13]

Whomever the audience, the monuments mandated in our verses and described in Sefer Yehoshua attempt to communicate their message in two distinct ways. On the one hand, words are inscribed on the stones. While words are perhaps the most straightforward way of communicating a message, they do have some drawbacks. The most significant is highlighted by the commentators when they explain about different languages – not everyone will be able to understand the written word. Even if a story is translated into multiple languages, there will still be illiterate people and others who will not take the time to read the text. Inscriptions, although they can contain a greater depth of information, are not always the best way to create a meaningful monument. Victor Hugo described this reality in *The Hunchback of Notre-Dame* when he compared regular books with "books of stone," referring to how cathedral architecture tells a story to even the illiterate.

In addition to the inscriptions, the monuments have several symbolic qualities that can perhaps be understood instinctively. First and foremost, the monuments were comprised of stones that were taken out of the Jordan River when the water split. The smooth stones would presumably be noticeable, distinct, and offer physical evidence of a great miracle performed on behalf of Bnei Yisrael.[14] Secondly, the stones, at least in one location, were to be arranged like the altar, without the use of iron. This too might have been a symbolic gesture meant to reinforce the connection between Bnei Yisrael and God. Finally, the number of stones – twelve – represented the different tribes of Israel. Here as well, the number gives a non-verbal symbolic meaning to the monument.[15] In this way, the monument could communicate a message visually and symbolically, even to those who could not decipher the writing.

---

13. In his HaEmek Davar commentary on Devarim 27:2.

14. This is similar to the description in Devarim 29:21 of the ravaging of Israel that will result from Bnei Yisrael failing to keep this covenant. In this scenario, foreigners will question why God destroyed the land, and recall the sins of Israel. The Netziv states that it is the Jews who return to Israel from exile who will see the destruction and ponder its meaning.

15. See also Shemot 24:4 and Melachim I 18:31 for additional examples of using twelve stones to construct a monument. Shulchan Aruch OC 90:4 specifies that a synagogue ought to have twelve windows. This requirement originally appears in the Zohar, Pekudei 251a.

# Moving Boundary Markers

אָרוּר מַסִּיג גְּבוּל רֵעֵהוּ וְאָמַר כָּל הָעָם אָמֵן. (דברים כז:יז)

Cursed be he that removes his neighbor's landmark, and all the people shall say, Amen. (Devarim 27:17)

UPON crossing into Israel, Bnei Yisrael were commanded to array themselves on two mountains, Mount Gerizim and Mount Eival. Once assembled, the Leviim were to recite a list of curses for anyone who violates a number of transgressions. All the tribes would then affirm their commitment to keeping these laws by answering "Amen." Among this list was a curse against moving boundary markers, an action that was explicitly forbidden earlier in Devarim.[1] Commentators on both this verse and the earlier one point out that this crime is especially problematic because it happens secretly and is difficult to prove.[2]

The Sifri notes that this commandment is redundant, as there is already a prohibition against stealing,[3] and moving a boundary marker is simply a form of stealing.[4] Instead, the Sifri learns that there is a special, additional prohibition against moving a boundary in Israel. The boundaries in Israel were set up by Yehoshua and Elazar the high priest and as such were divinely sanctioned. Moving them is akin to discrediting these boundaries and is, therefore, worse than a simple act of thievery. In addition, since property in Israel is inherited in perpetuity due to the laws of *Yovel*, this theft has a longer-lasting impact than moving boundaries outside of Israel.[5]

Boundary markers are a basic part of any building code. Land is divided and marked, documenting the size and contour of a given lot. One of the

1. Devarim 19:14 states "You shall not remove your neighbor's landmark . . . ."
2. See, for example, Ibn Ezra and Malbim.
3. In Vayikra 19:13.
4. Sifri Devarim 188.
5. Torah Temima on Devarim 19:14.

first stages of requesting a building permit is having a surveyor map the property and clearly mark the property lines. Building code often prohibits construction up to the edge of a property; buildings are restricted by setbacks, which dictate how much space must be left between the property line and the edge of the building.[6] Even so, there are still cases where an owner will illegally build beyond the property's edge, essentially stealing from a neighbor or the public. In this case, though people are not physically moving the boundary markers, they are nonetheless violating the essence of this commandment. One mishna even forbids planting a certain plant that was historically used to mark boundaries, as this is considered a land grab.[7]

In many cultures, boundary markers were held to be sacred. In Rome, there was a shrine to Terminus, the god of boundaries, who was worshiped at boundary stones.[8] A curse was invoked by Numa Pompilius, the second king of Rome, against people who move boundary stones.[9] Many boundary stones from Babylonia have been uncovered, often inscribed with a curse. Joseph Rykwert writes that violating boundary stones was seen as a breach of the cosmic order, made all the more poignant because of the vulnerability of boundary stones. He goes on to explain that these types of curses "get more severe as the general political and social guarantees decline."[10] In places with strong government enforcement, metaphysical curses become less important in encouraging compliance.

The curses that were invoked on Mount Eival constituted something of a national pact to abide by certain laws. Taking oaths to obey these rules was seen as a way of bolstering trust in the nascent legal system. Today, though we have many social pacts, we also try to enact laws that will similarly safeguard our rights, including property rights. Whether this takes the form of property law or zoning code, building permits, or municipal inspectors, these things stand in the same tradition as the curse on Mount Eival.

6. For a required setback of four cubits when a property borders a place of idol worship, see mAZ 3:6.

7. mKil 1:8 and bBB 56a.

8. Siculus Flaccus, *On the Legal Status of Landholdings*, 11 and Joseph Rykwert, *The Idea of a Town* (MIT Press, 1995), 107.

9. Plutarch, *The Parallel Lives*, "Numa Pompilius," 16.

10. Rykwart, *The Idea of a Town*, 112–3.

110. Michaux Stone, an example of a Babylonian *kudurru* or boundary stone from the 11th century BCE, inscribed in Akkadian. (E. Leroux, Bibliothèque Nationale, 1900, Wikimedia)

KI TAVO

# City and Country

בָּרוּךְ אַתָּה בָּעִיר וּבָרוּךְ אַתָּה בַּשָּׂדֶה. (דברים כח:ג)

Blessed shall you be in the city and blessed shall you be in the field. (Devarim 28:3)

If Bnei Yisrael keep the commandments they will be blessed in both the city and the field. Ibn Ezra explains that this dichotomy refers to success in both trade and in agriculture, which typify life in the city and field, respectively. Likewise, a midrash uses this verse to distinguish between commandments that are done domestically, such as putting up a *mezuza* and a guardrail, and those done in the field, such as leaving portions of your crops for the poor.[1]

Urban and rural areas have been treated as foils since the rise of the first cities. The two are often contrasted, or even cast as stark opposites: the city's culture, technology, and social climbing versus the country's tradition, nature, and simplicity.[2] The dichotomy of city and country seems to cut across all cultures and eras. While the contrast in our verse between city and field is not precisely this archetypical pairing, the contrast of city and country appears in several halachot and numerous aggadot throughout rabbinic literature.[3]

1. DevR 7:5.

2. This is most famously presented in Aesop's fable, The City Mouse and Country Mouse.

3. There are a variety of terms used to describe city and country, and not all scholars agree what each term connotes. See Samuel Krauss, "*Hakrakh, Ha'ir Vehakfar Batalmud*" in *Haatid 3* (1923): 1–50 (Hebrew) and Shmuel Safrai, "*Ha'ir Hayehudit Be'Eretz Yisrael Betekufat Hamishna Vehatalmud*" in *Ha'ir Vehakehila* (Jerusalem: 1968), 227–236 (Hebrew) for two examples. The most common terms are *kerachim, kefarim*, and *ayarot*, though Krauss lists thirty separate terms. The context of most of the rabbinic sources I will quote is sufficient to understand that they are contrasting a large settlement with a small one.

The most widely known halacha that distinguishes between city and country involves the prescribed time for reading Megilat Esther. The *megila* is read in walled cities on the fifteenth of Adar, while in unwalled cities it is read on the fourteenth of Adar. In villages Megilat Esther is read even earlier, on the preceding market day.[4] In the Talmud, R. Chanina and Shmuel each explained that this is because villages provide water and food for the city and reading earlier frees the villagers to carry out this work.[5] As such, there is a halachic *distinction* between city and country that is based on a *relationship* between the two, with the countryside seen as the breadbasket of the city.

While the laws of reading Megilat Esther render a division between city and country based on an asymmetrical relationship, other halachic statements demonstrate an assumed *cultural* distinction between the high refinement of city-folk and the lesser standards of their country neighbors. Several rabbinic statements claim that food in cities was cleaner and of higher quality than country food.[6] Clothes in cities like Mechoza were finer and more delicate than country clothes.[7] R. Zeira ruled that if a countryman takes an oath that his wife cannot wear shoes, she can be expected to abide for three months before a divorce is required. However, city women cannot be expected to go even one day without shoes and must be divorced immediately.[8] Similarly, a countrywoman can tolerate two weeks without bathing while a city woman can only last only a single week. These halachot assume that city people are more refined, as opposed to the hardier and rougher country folk.

The rabbis presumed a difference in amenities between city and country. In cities, it was easy to find moneychangers, while such financial services were often unavailable in the country.[9] Villages had smaller markets for food[10] but also less housing pressure.[11] The sculptures in cities were categorized as part of the urban décor, while those in the country were assumed to be used for pagan worship.[12] R. Shimon ben Gamliel typified cities by their bathhouses and villages by their manual labor and claimed

---

4. mMeg 1:1.
5. bMeg 4a and yMeg 1:1.
6. City flour is cleaner (bPes 40a), city onions are superior (mTer 2:5), and poultry is not widely consumed in the country (bBech 10a).
7. bShab 12a.
8. yKet 7:4 (31b).
9. mBM 4:6 and tBM 3:20.
10. tPes 2:1 and bKet 4a.
11. mBM 8:6.
12. bAZ 41a. See also MdRY Bo 1.

that these significant differences altered the physiological development of the female populations in each.[13]

In marriage law, critical importance is ascribed to the distinction between city and country. The Mishna teaches that if a woman gets engaged to a man on the condition that he is from a big city but finds out that he is really from a smaller town, or vice versa, the engagement is nullified.[14] Likewise, a husband cannot force his wife to move from city to country or vice versa.[15] The Talmud explains that a large city has many more amenities and would therefore – presumably – be preferable. However, it also recognizes that not everyone is cut out for life in a large city, which is hard and less modest.[16] These halachot are predicated upon the understanding that cities contain a variety of benefits, but also have negative points.

While the halachic cases tend to address specific ways in which city and country were considered distinct from one another, several aggadic contrasts exist as well, which give a broad and stereotypical view of city and country. When stating that Yishayahu was a greater prophet than Yechezkel, Rava explains the vividness of the opening prophecy in Yechezkel by comparing him to "a country man who sees the king" while Yishayahu is a "city dweller who sees the king." While the vision is commonplace to Yishayahu, it seems wondrous and unique to the "country" prophet.[17] One parable tells of a country person and city person who are both arrested for the same crime. The king frees the country person but punishes the man from the city. He explains that the country person cannot be expected to know how to behave civilly, while the city person has no excuse.[18] Another parable tells of the wedding of a princess, in which the country folk praise the king and play their musical instruments, while the city people remain stoic. While the country folk display an unbridled exuberance, it is the city people who are criticized for not behaving appropriately, as they should know how to properly praise the king on such an occasion.[19]

While the country is sometimes portrayed as a place of ignorance, it

13. tNid 6:9 and bNid 48b. See also bShab 40b for an additional difference in bathhouses between city and country.

14. mKid 2:3. This clause in this mishna is followed by one about a man who conditions his engagement upon his living near the bathhouse, indicating that we are contrasting a settlement with amenities and one lacking them.

15. mKet 13:10.

16. bKet 110b and yKid 2:2 (62c).

17. bChag 13b.

18. Tanchuma Vayikra 6.

19. Pesikta Rabati 20.

is also seen as a place of morality and innocence. Rava explains a verse in Shir Hashirim by saying that Israel asks God to refrain from judging them like city dwellers, among whom there is theft, sexual immorality, and false oaths, but rather like scholars who learn Torah despite poverty.[20] While this does not explicitly state that the scholars are rural dwellers, their juxtaposition with "city dwellers" makes this a reasonable assumption. The city is thus depicted as a place of moral corruption, while the country – though poor – is a place where scholars can thrive. Rashi explains a statement in the Talmud by distinguishing between city and country; country girls require less personal modesty as they come from a simpler, more modest locale.[21] Finally, we also find an idealized view of the country: R. Eleazer ben Pedat claims that in the future (i.e. Messianic times) artisans will leave cities and take up agriculture. Still, he balances this by adding that there is no livelihood lowlier than farming.[22] These examples show that cities were occasionally demonized for immorality and thus compared unfavorably with the country, though at the same time it was impossible to ignore the negatives of rural life.[23]

The distinction between urban and rural was viewed as broad and highly significant. City folk were presumed to have access to more amenities, were more sophisticated, better dressed, more sensitive, cleaner, and less easily cowed. However, cities were considered crowded and difficult places to live, and could also be places of moral turpitude. The country, on the other hand, was associated primarily with agriculture and simple goods, while the people were less sophisticated and made do with less. Still, at times the country was idealized as a place of morality, tranquility, and stability. It is impossible to tell if this perception was caused by the influence of another culture, or if the nature of city and country naturally lends itself to this kind of contrast. What we can ascertain without question is that the Rabbis distinguished between the urban and rural parts of civilization and accepted that town and country each had separate, distinct features.

20. bEruv 21b.

21. Rashi, bShab 80a.

22. bYev 63a. See also Daniel Sperber, *Roman Palestine 200–400 – The Land: Crisis and Change in Agrarian Society as Reflected in Rabbinic Sources* (Ramat Gan, 1978), 56 and 208.

23. R. Liebman Adler, father of famed architect Dankmar Adler, wrote a sermon lamenting the fact that Jewish immigrants to the United States largely settled in cities. He believed that the world benefits from having both populations, and specifically felt that city dwelling caused Jews to be skeptical of religion and less faithful to Judaism. See Leibman Adler, "The Tower of Babel" in *Sabbath Hours* (Jewish Publication Society of America, 1893), 60–68.

# Woodcutters And Water Drawers

טַפְּכֶם נְשֵׁיכֶם וְגֵרְךָ אֲשֶׁר בְּקֶרֶב מַחֲנֶיךָ מֵחֹטֵב עֵצֶיךָ עַד שֹׁאֵב מֵימֶיךָ.
(דברים כט:י)

> Your little ones, your wives, and your stranger that is in your camp, from the hewer of your wood to the drawer of your water. (Devarim 29:10)

MOSHE assembled all the members of Bnei Yisrael: the young, the old, the weak, the strong, the rich, and the poor. He first mentioned the leaders, officers, and elders, and then contrasted them with "the hewers of your wood" and "the drawers of your water." These occupations were included to emphasize that even the lowliest of workers were also part of this assembly. The Talmud draws a connection with the Gibeonites, who performed these tasks during the days of Yehoshua. There too, these tasks were mentioned as lowly ones, usually consigned to slaves.[1]

In Roman times, woodcutters and water drawers occupied menial positions. The poet Juvenal mentions water carriers (*aquaria*) as the lowliest segment of the slave population.[2] Woodcutters were also part of the lower strata of Roman society.[3] Roman armies had people who were responsible for foraging for both wood and water, though it is unclear if they were slaves or soldiers.[4] Still, the supply of water and wood was crucial for the army. Cassius Dio specifically describes the Roman army's lack of water

1. bYev 79a, considering Yehoshua 9:21. See the Daat Mikre commentary on Yehoshua 9:21, which quotes a Sumerian poem illustrating this point.
2. Juvenal, *Satires* 6, 332.
3. James C. Anderson, Jr. *Roman Architecture and Society* (Johns Hopkins University Press, 1997), 138.
4. Jonathan Roth, *The Logistics of the Roman Army at War: 264 B.C. – A.D. 235* (Brill, 1999), 119–125.

during the siege of Jerusalem in 70 CE, and the consequent need to bring water from afar.[5]

Woodcutters, much like stone workers, played an important role in supplying raw materials for the construction industry. However, when studying the Roman building industry, James C. Anderson points out that, while in the stone and brick industries there were specialists and skilled workers, with woodcutters there was no similar hierarchy.[6] This is one reason why woodcutters were so low on the social ladder, as there was little room for any improved social standing with experience. Water carriers had a similar problem. While other professions allowed for the potential of greater success, these professions were dead ends. This may be why they are presented here in contrast with the leaders and powerbrokers of Bnei Yisrael.

The character of the woodcutters appears in many stories, often as a byword for a simple person. To mention a few examples, Aesop tells a parable of "the honest woodcutter." However, in his "The Woodcutter and the Trees" the woodcutter is depicted less favorably.[7] In the Talmud, R. Yishmael meets a woodcutter who takes advantage of his charity in a shrewd manner.[8] In the Torah, a woodcutter is used as the primary example of one who kills by accident.[9] I.L. Peretz's *If Not Higher* depicts a Chassidic rabbi who dresses as a woodcutter. In each case, the woodcutter's moral character may reflect how society views simple people. The Torah's mention of woodcutters and water carriers is meant to show that each person constitutes an important part of the nation.

---

5. Cassius Dio, *Roman History* 65.4.5. See also mSot 8:2 for support staff during wartime.

6. Anderson, *Roman Architecture and Society,* 138–139. He explains that skilled carpenters and woodworkers held a distinct status.

7. *Aesop's Fables,* 173 and 302. In the latter, the woodcutter uses a wooden handle, gifted to him by the trees, to cut down the trees.

8. bBM 30b.

9. Devarim 19:5.

# Pagan Parks and Baths

וַתִּרְאוּ אֶת שִׁקּוּצֵיהֶם וְאֵת גִּלֻּלֵיהֶם עֵץ וָאֶבֶן כֶּסֶף וְזָהָב אֲשֶׁר עִמָּהֶם. פֶּן יֵשׁ בָּכֶם אִישׁ אוֹ אִשָּׁה אוֹ מִשְׁפָּחָה אוֹ שֵׁבֶט אֲשֶׁר לְבָבוֹ פֹנֶה הַיּוֹם מֵעִם ה׳ אֱלֹקֵינוּ לָלֶכֶת לַעֲבֹד אֶת אֱלֹהֵי הַגּוֹיִם הָהֵם פֶּן יֵשׁ בָּכֶם שֹׁרֶשׁ פֹּרֶה רֹאשׁ וְלַעֲנָה.
(דברים כט:טז–יז)

And you have seen their detestable things and their idols, wood, and stone, silver and gold, which were with them. Lest there should be among you man or woman of family or tribe whose heart turns away this day from the Lord our God, to go to serve the gods of those nations, lest there should be among you a root that bears gall and wormwood. (Devarim 29:16–17)

As part of the general prohibition against idol worship, the Mishna discusses items that, if found on pagan altars, are forbidden.[1] With the above verses in mind, the Talmud rules that only objects which were made to beautify the altar are forbidden.[2] Despite the pagan connection, the Mishna rules that Jews may use a garden or bathhouse attached to a pagan temple, as long as the priest is not paid for entry.[3]

The case in this mishna reflects the reality of the sages in Late Antiquity. The urban fabric was filled with idols. Elaborate sculptures decorated city amenities, including theaters,[4] streets,[5] bathhouses, gardens, fountains,[6]

1. mAZ 4:2.
2. bAZ 51b, contrasting these verses with Devarim 7:25: "The carvings of their gods shall you burn with fire, you shall not desire the silver or gold that is on them, or take it to you, lest you be snared with it, for it is an abomination to the Lord your God."
3. As per Abaye on bAZ 51b and discussing mAZ 4:3.
4. mAZ 1:7 implies the presence of idols in many public buildings.
5. Both with statues along the roads, and in one incident recorded in bAZ 51a, with a street paved with stones from idols. See Saul Lieberman, "Palestine in the Third and Fourth Centuries" in *Jewish Quarterly Review* 36 (Apr. 1946), 366–370.
6. tAZ 5:6.

and markets.[7] A previous mishna delves into this balance, relating that R. Gamliel would bathe in a bathhouse decorated with a statue of the goddess Aphrodite. When questioned about this practice, he explained that the statute of Aphrodite was placed in the bathhouse to serve as decoration, rather than the bathhouse being constructed to venerate Aphrodite.[8] Furthermore, bathhouses were places of nudity and impurity, hardly venerating behavior. This proved that, despite the idol, the bathhouse was not a place of idol worship and could be used by the Jewish populace.[9]

These cases discuss two different scenarios: public spaces decorated with idols, and pagan temples which had adjacent amenities. The case of the sculpture in a bathhouse is indicative of the former. Sculptures were indeed an important part of the décor of Roman thermae. A survey of surviving fragments from Roman bathhouses revealed that Aphrodite was "by far the most popular deity represented."[10] Also popular were Asclepius and Hygieia, two health-associated deities, who helped reinforce the connection between attending the bathhouse and good health. Other common figures included Apollo, Athena, Herakles, Hermes, and Dionysus.[11]

Likewise, statues were commonly used to decorate Roman gardens. This followed the Greek custom of "displaying statuary in temple gardens, sacred groves, hero-shrines ... and family shrines.[12] As with bathhouses, figures in gardens usually had some connection to garden life, with the pagan gods being viewed as the givers of life, just as vegetation was a sign of life and fertility.[13] Aphrodite was the most popular figure. Herakles, Pan, Ares, and Dionysus were also commonly found in gardens. They were mainly used to set the mood in the garden as places of wonder, love, or hedonism. With pagan statues found in bathhouses, and one would presume, in private gardens, the Rabbis ruled that the sculptures were only decorative and did not imply pagan devotion.

The second scenario under discussion involves religious sites that had

---

7. Yaron Eliav, "Viewing the Sculptural Environment" in *The Talmud Yerushalmi and Graeco-Roman Culture,* ed. Peter Schafer (Mohr Siebeck, 2002), 413–414.

8. See VayR 34:3 for a similar story involving Hillel.

9. mAZ 3:4, bAZ 44b.

10. Miranda Marvin, "Freestanding Sculptures from the Baths of Caracalla" in *American Journal of Archaeology* 87 (Jul 1983), 379.

11. Garrett G. Fagan, *Bathing in Public in the Roman World* (University of Michigan Press, 2002), 89–90.

12. Katharine T. von Stackelberg, *The Roman Garden: Space, Sense and Society* (Routledge, 2009), 26–7. Yishayahu 60:13 seems to describe a similar tendency in ancient Israel.

13. Maureen Carroll, "Temple Gardens and Sacred Groves" in *Gardens of the Roman Empire,* ed. Wilhelmina F. Jashemski, et al (Cambridge University Press, 2017), 152.

associated amenities that the public could use. In these cases, the pagan trappings were not merely decorative. Some temples made use of water channels, pools, or springs as part of a sacred precinct. While baths could be useful for pilgrims after a long journey, they could also be a part of the religious experience. Bathing near the temple could be a way of communing with the deity.[14] Such a situation would constitute the "baths belonging to foreign worship" mentioned in the Mishna.

When it comes to gardens that are connected to pagan deities, Greek distinguishes between sacred groves[15] (*alsos*) and regular gardens (*kepos*). Latin, too, makes a distinction between sacred garden crafted by man (*nemus*), natural grove inhabited by divine spirits (*lucus*), and secular garden (*hortus*).[16] Archaeological remains show the existence of sacred groves outside temples, as in the Temple of Hephaistos in Athens. More specifically, many temples had large estates, which were worked by tenants for the profit of the temple.[17] This was a way of generating revenue. In the Jewish tradition, the Talmud relates that Shlomo planted fruit trees outside the Temple.[18] While the Romans may have seen the sacred groves as extensions of the temples, "revered as places belonging to and inhabited by the gods," the Mishna seems to instead focus on the gardens through this latter function, as potential money-makers that could be safely used without fear of worshiping foreign gods, provided that no direct economic benefit is given to the temple. This perspective allowed the Rabbis to permit groves or waters, so long as the funds did not go directly to idolatrous priests.

The mishnayot relate to two different situations: an edifice or garden with idols, and a pagan temple with gardens or waterways. In the former, the Mishna rules that the idols do not indicate that the institution is religious in nature. Instead, the idols are viewed as decorative. In the latter, the gardens and baths are not viewed as connected to worship, but rather as a secondary source of income for the temple. Both these perspectives allowed Jews to make use of these edifices, despite their pagan association.

14. Eleanor Ghey, "Immersed in the Gods: Water in Gallo-Roman Sanctuaries" (Academia, 2005), 1.

15. Sacred groves are described in BerR 94:4 and yTaan 1:6 (64c), regarding trees planted for use in the construction of the *Mishkan*.

16. Carroll, "Temple Gardens," 153–4.

17. Carroll, "Temple Gardens," 163.

18. yYom 4:4 (41d). These corresponded to golden fruit trees inside the Temple.

VAYELECH

# The Acoustics of *Hakhel*

הַקְהֵל אֶת הָעָם הָאֲנָשִׁים וְהַנָּשִׁים וְהַטַּף וְגֵרְךָ אֲשֶׁר בִּשְׁעָרֶיךָ לְמַעַן יִשְׁמְעוּ
וּלְמַעַן יִלְמְדוּ וְיָרְאוּ אֶת ה׳ אֱלֹקֵיכֶם וְשָׁמְרוּ לַעֲשׂוֹת אֶת כָּל דִּבְרֵי הַתּוֹרָה
הַזֹּאת. (דברים לא:יב)

Assemble the people, the men and the women, and the children, and your stranger that is within your gates, that they may hear and that they may learn and fear the Lord your God, and observe to do all the words of this Torah. (Devarim 31:12)

EVERY seven years, Bnei Yisrael are instructed to congregate in Jerusalem for a public reading of the Torah by the king, known as *Hakhel*.[1] This gathering is intended to unify the nation by promoting shared heritage and initiating Torah study.[2] The event also serves as a reenactment of the reception of the Torah on Mount Sinai.[3]

The verses stress the importance of hearing the king read the Torah, saying that it should be "in their hearing," "that they may hear," and that "the children may hear."[4] The Talmud reinforces this notion, commenting that the point is for all of Israel to hear.[5] People who are deaf and ones who are not in hearing range cannot fulfill the commandment. The Mishna also teaches that a wooden platform was built in the courtyard of the Temple for the king to stand on while reading, presumably to allow him to be heard.[6]

1. Josephus writes that it was the high priest. See *Antiquities* 4.209–211.
2. Malbim, for example, explains that the ceremony will help demonstrate the importance of Torah study. Sforno writes that it will give the unlearned an opportunity to ask questions from those who are more knowledgeable. Ramban says it will help children be inspired to learn.
3. Sefer Hachinuch, 612 and Rambam, Hilchot Chagiga 3:6.
4. Devarim 31:11–13.
5. bChag 3a.
6. mSot 7:8. This stage is also mentioned in tSot 7:13, which connects this ceremony

Despite the effort to improve the acoustical setup, it would have still been difficult to hear the king. In ancient times, orators relied upon specially designed spaces with good acoustics, such as theaters with steep slopes, where the seating was designed to maximize the proximity of the audience to the speaker and allow the sound to reach the audience. Even with good acoustics, the speaker generally needed to possess a quality known as *megalophonia* – the ability to speak very loudly.[7] This is why in oratory competitions held in ancient times, volume was the most important factor,[8] and why in Persian schools, students practiced speaking loudly.[9] The Jewish king would need *megalophonia* to be heard. The Talmud even states that for certain public ceremonies, God helped the speaker declaim in a loud voice.[10] And still, without good acoustics, even a loud king would have difficulty making himself heard.

Nonetheless, the architects of the Temple seem to have ignored acoustics when they designed the Women's Courtyard, where *Hakhel* took place. According to most opinions, the courtyard was a flat, unroofed, cruciform space. The lack of a roof would have limited the distance voices would carry. The cross shape has nooks that trap sound and cause undesirable reverberation. The flat layout, in contrast to theaters, would have further limited the projection of sound. When running an acoustics simulation, in which the king is located in the center of the courtyard,[11] facing one direction, and listeners surround him on all sides, only those in front of the king have a reasonable chance to hear the Torah. There is a drop in decibels on either side, but those in the back have the lowest decibel level and a significant delay in sound, which must reflect off the far wall before

---

with a similar one in the time of Ezra, described in Nechemia 8:3–5. See also bSot 41a. Rambam describes the setup and specifically mentions that the stage is to help the king be heard. See Hilchot Chagiga 3:4.

7. For megalophonia, see Dio Chrysostum, *Discourses* 19.4–5, Diodorus Siculus *Historical Library* 16.92. Other factors included *euphonia* – goodness of voice – and *lamprotes* – clearness. See Eleonora Rocconi, "Theatres and Theatre Design in the Graeco-Roman World" in *Archaeoacoustics*, ed. Chriss Scarre and Graeme Lawson (McDonald Institute for Archaeological Research, 2006), 72.

8. Julius Pollux, *Onomasticon*, 4.91.

9. Strabo, *Geography* 15:3.

10. ySot 7:2 (21c) and MdRY Yitro (Bachodesh) 4. yPes 5:5 (32c) attributes the same divine assistance to Pharaoh. See also Tosafot *bekolo* on bBer 45a, which discusses how Moshe had to yell "with all his strength" to make his voice heard at Mount Sinai, and bYom 20b and yShek 5:1 (48d) for the powerful voice of Gabini, who was rewarded by King Agrippas for this quality. God's voice is also described as powerful and far-reaching in Shemot 19:16 and Tehilim 29:4–5.

11. As per Rambam Hilchot Chagiga 3:4.

it will reach their ears.[12] If the king were to have stood at one side of the courtyard, his performance would have been slightly better. However, the sound of his voice would have had difficulty penetrating the transept of the courtyard, and those at the far end of the courtyard, 135 cubits away, would be too distant to have heard his voice even in quiet conditions.[13]

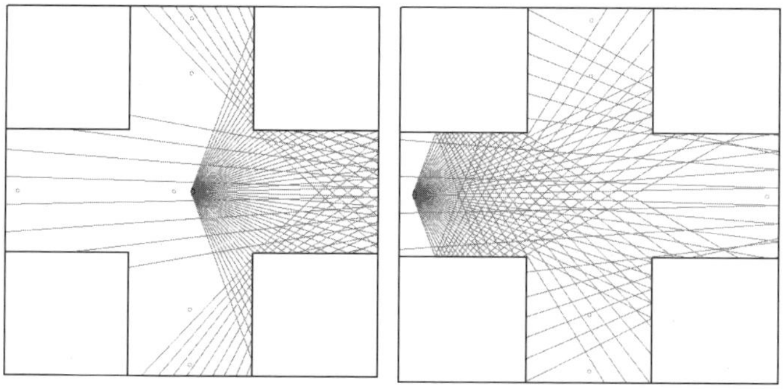

111. Acoustic study of the courtyard of the Temple with the speaker in the center and at the entrance.

If the acoustics of the space were insufficient to allow everyone to hear, how could the gathered crowd fulfill the commandment? One possibility is that additional interventions allowed the king to project his voice with

12. In the simulation, those in front hear at a decibel level of 46.5, while those on the side have 36 dB and in the rear only 23 dB. Note that for some mitzvot, such as hearing the *shofar*, too much echo is problematic, as per mRH 3:7.

13. Michael Barron, *Auditorium Acoustics and Architectural Design* (Spon Press, 1993), 228. Acoustics also play a role in the laws of hearing the *shofar* on Rosh Hashana. Excessive reverberation can prevent one from fulfilling this commandment, though bRH 27b rules that this is only true if one is standing outside the space where the *shofar* is being blown. There is some disagreement as to whether this only applies in a subterranean space or also in an above-ground building, as per R. David Halevi Segal in his Turei Zahav commentary on OC 587:1, as well as R. Eliyahu Shapira's Eliya Raba. R. Asher ben Yechiel notes the average person's limited level of acoustical understanding and questions whether an individual can correctly assess if they are hearing the *shofar* itself or an echo.

In an essay about the acoustics of various places of worship, David Lubman and Brenda Kiser note that synagogues have traditionally valued acoustics that enhance the clarity of the spoken word, due to a liturgy focused on recital of verses and prayers. They note that while Christian places of worship originally were similar, cathedral acoustics forced the liturgy to change to a more musical variety. With the Reformation, and a refocus on the spoken word, this trend in church acoustics was reversed. See D. Lubman and B. Kiser, "The History of Western Civilization Told Through the Acoustics of its Worship Spaces" in *Acoustics of Worship Buildings*, 2001.

greater success. Vitruvius mentions that wooden floors in theaters help sound to carry.[14] Perhaps the wooden stage served a similar function.

A second option, one which is supported by some commentators, is that the importance of hearing the king is overstated and that the ceremonial act of congregating around the leaders of Israel in the Temple is the primal reason for *Hakhel*. This is partially borne out by the name of the commandment – *Hakhel* – meaning "congregate," and by the pomp and ceremony described in the Mishna, with all the leaders of that nation on stage, passing the Torah from one to another. Watching the ceremony, more so than hearing the text read aloud, would have made a positive impression on the children. Ramban focuses on *Hakhel* as a catalyst for having parents learn together with their children. From this point of view, the goal was not to *hear* the king, but rather to increase the level of Torah scholarship and to see the Torah as a uniting factor.

These two possibilities may be at the base of an argument in the Talmud over why we do not do *Hakhel* on Shabbat. R. Chiya bar Aba argues that *Hakhel* is not done on Shabbat because trumpets cannot be blown to call people together. R. Yitzchak bar R. Chiya states that it is because the wooden stage cannot be built on Shabbat.[15] The trumpets symbolize the importance of *Hakhel* as an act of gathering Bnei Yisrael together, while the stage represents the importance of hearing the king read the Torah. If the main purpose of *Hakhel* is to gather the people together as part of an impressive ceremony, then the trumpets have primary importance. However, if the goal was truly to hear the king read from the Torah, then the building of the stage would have been the greater concern.

14. Vitruvius, *Ten Books on Architecture,* V.5.1–7.
15. yMeg 1:4 (70c).

VAYELECH

# Decorating with Verses

וְעַתָּה כִּתְבוּ לָכֶם אֶת הַשִּׁירָה הַזֹּאת וְלַמְּדָהּ אֶת בְּנֵי יִשְׂרָאֵל שִׂימָהּ בְּפִיהֶם לְמַעַן תִּהְיֶה לִּי הַשִּׁירָה הַזֹּאת לְעֵד בִּבְנֵי יִשְׂרָאֵל. (דברים לא:יט)

Now, therefore, write this poem for yourselves and teach you it to Bnei Yisrael, put it in their mouths that this poem may be a witness for me against Bnei Yisrael. (Devarim 31:19)

THE final commandment in the Torah, found in this verse, is to write a copy of the Torah.[1] Rambam, in quoting our verse to teach this commandment, rules that one may not write separate sections of the Torah to stand alone.[2] One may not even write a section of the Torah to teach children.[3] Elsewhere, Rambam takes this further, ruling that one cannot embroider a Torah verse onto a *talit*. He gives two reasons: first, he explains that writing individual Torah verses is not allowed, and second, he worries that proper decorum will not be maintained in the presence of this verse, and thus the Torah will be debased.[4]

Rambam's various rulings led subsequent arbiters of halacha to consider whether it is forbidden to decorate using Torah verses. R. David Halevi Segal wrote that it is not proper to write verses on walls "to promote good luck."[5] R. Yechiel Michel Epstein similarly ruled that it is improper to write verses on the walls of synagogues and study halls,[6] and R. Yisrael Meir Kagan ruled that one cannot write Torah verses on the walls of a *sukka*.[7]

Although ancient synagogues were decorated with many inscriptions,

1. Sefer Hachinuch, 613.
2. Rambam, Hilchot Tefilin Vemezuza Vesefer Torah, 7:1.
3. Rambam, Hilchot Tefilin Vemezuza Vesefer Torah, 7:14, based on bGit 60a.
4. *Shu"t Harambam*, 268. See also Shulchan Aruch YD 283:4.
5. Turei Zahav, YD 383:1.
6. Aruch Hashulchan, YD 283:13.
7. Mishna Berura, 638:24.

especially dedications, it was rare to find biblical verses used in the décor.[8] A seventh-century synagogue in Yericho contains a mosaic with a quote from Tehilim.[9] This same quote appears in synagogues in Husifa, Ein Gedi, and Susiya.[10] In a seventh-century synagogue and beit midrash in Merot, the lintel over the entrance is inscribed with a verse from Devarim, "Blessed shall you be when you come in and blessed shall you be when you go out."[11] The same building contains a mosaic with a verse about the Messianic age.[12] A synagogue in Tzippori contains a floor mosaic depicting the dedication of the *Mishkan*, including a verse about the daily sacrifices.[13] Another verse is graffitied onto a stone of the Western Wall, under Robinson's Arch, possibly dating from the fourth century.[14] It was also rare to find biblical verses on objects. In 1979, two silver scrolls were discovered in Jerusalem, dating to the seventh century BCE, with one scroll containing the priestly blessing.[15] Two excavated oil lamps from between the second and seventh century, were inscribed with verses.[16] It is impossible to say if the dearth of biblical verses is due to a rabbinic prohibition. Nonetheless, the rarity of these finds, along with the lack of halachic rulings decrying this phenomenon before the sixteenth century, seem to indicate that it was once quite uncommon to use Torah verses in this manner.

This ambivalence toward decorating with verses stands in stark contrast to the Islamic world. Even more so than Jewish aniconism, Islam has a very strict interpretation of the prohibition against images. Instead of figures, buildings were often decorated with calligraphy. The Dome of the Rock and Hagia Sophia have extensive verses from the Quran along their walls and ceilings. In Islamic architecture, calligraphy is seen as a solution to the limits against images, rather than a disrespectful use of holy verses.

Despite the concerns by some Jewish authorities with using verses in architecture, others pointed to the widespread practice of using verses on synagogue walls and were inclined to allow the practice to continue. R.

8. For inscriptions, see Joseph Naveh, *On Stone and Mosaic* (Carta, 1978) (Hebrew) and for mosaics, Rachel Hachlili, *Ancient Mosaic Pavements* (Brill, 2009).

9. Tehilim 125:5.

10. Naveh, *On Stone*, 65, 103, 107, and 115.

11. Devarim 28:6. Midrash Tanchuma (Ki Tavo 4) interprets this verse as referring to entering and exiting synagogues and houses of study.

12. Yishayahu 65:25.

13. Shemot 29:39.

14. Yishayahu 66:14. Binyamin Mazar suggested that the inscription dated from the reign of Emperor Julian, 361–363.

15. Bamidbar 6:24–26. This is the earliest known evidence of a biblical verse.

16. One from Bet She'an, quoting Devarim 7:26 and 29:22, and the other from Caesaria, quoting Devarim 33:26.

112. Northeast façade of the Dome of the Rock. (Photo by Andrew Shiva, Wikimedia)

Yosef Trani, asked about displaying slips of paper or plaques with timely verses in synagogues, considered this to be a good thing, especially as it did not debase the Torah, but rather promoted heightened devotion.[17]

R. Yaakov Ariel, in analyzing this law, suggests that a distinction exists between decorating with verses for holy purposes, and for simple aesthetic reasons. In a synagogue, the verses are not in danger of being debased and serve to improve concentration during prayer.[18] He also suggests that those rabbis who prohibited verses in synagogues or *sukkot* may have had in mind verses *outside*, which would be exposed to weather and therefore at risk of degradation.[19] Verses used for holy purposes and safe from decay would be acceptable.

113. Emerson Hall, Harvard.

17. *Shu"t Hamaharit,* 2, OC 3, based in part on a ruling by the Rif in bGit on 28a.

18. R. Yaakov Ariel, *Beohela Shel Torah* I, 42 (Hebrew), available online at https://www.toraland.org.il.

19. It was, for example, common practice to write the text of the *kidush levana* prayer on an outside wall of the synagogue, so that congregants could recite the prayer outside without the need of a prayer book. This has given rise to the Hebrew expression "*kidush levana* letters," which refers to letters in a very large font.

At times, the distinction between aesthetics and holy purposes is difficult to parse. Using biblical verses does not automatically imbue a building with religious meaning. For example, Harvard's Emerson Hall is inscribed with a verse from Tehilim[20] that can certainly cause one to reflect on his or her relationship with God, yet the building hosts the philosophy department, not a religious function. The Bible, after all, is one of the foundational works of Western civilization. Still, when it comes to Jewish institutions, the decorative use of verses is usually intended to promote heightened devotion and does not debase the words of the Torah. As such, decorative verses in the synagogue meet both criteria set out by R. Ariel.

20. Tehilim 8:4 "What is man that thou art mindful of him?" Different rules may apply when the characters are not in the square Hebrew font.

# Brick Patterns

הַאֲזִינוּ הַשָּׁמַיִם וַאֲדַבֵּרָה וְתִשְׁמַע הָאָרֶץ אִמְרֵי פִי. (דברים לב:א)

Give ear, O heavens, and I will speak / And hear, O earth, the words of my mouth. (Devarim 32:1)

MOSHE'S farewell speech to Bnei Yisrael is recorded in the Torah as a song or poem. This is denoted by the special justification of the text, in two vertical columns. Moshe's speech is the second-most famous song in the Torah, following the Song of the Sea that marked the nation's salvation from the Egyptian army after the splitting of the sea.[1] In contrast to the justification of the text found here, the Song of the Sea is written in a staggered pattern. There are a number of other songs in the Bible: the Song of Devora[2] and the Song of David[3] are laid out similarly to the Song of the Sea, while a list of Canaanite kings,[4] the Song of Times,[5] a list of Haman's sons,[6] and the Levite families[7] are arranged similarly to Moshe's speech.[8]

The Talmud compares the two forms of textual justification to brickwork. R. Chanina bar Papa teaches that all songs are written "half-brick on top of full brick" (in a staggered pattern) except for the list of Canaanite kings and the sons of Haman, which are written "half-brick on top of

1. Shemot 15:1–19. According to yMeg 3:7 (74b), Moshe's speech was known as the Song of the Levites.

2. Shoftim 5.

3. Shmuel II 22.

4. Yehoshua 12:9–24.

5. Kohelet 3:1–8.

6. Ester 9:7–10.

7. Divrei Hayamim I 25:10–31.

8. R. Yaakov Moshe Shurkin lists 25 songs in the Bible. For some of these he provides examples of manuscripts in which they were written in columns like Moshe speech or even staggered, like the Song of the Sea. See R. Yaakov Moshe Shurkin, *"Ariach Al Gabei Ariach"* (Hebrew), accessed online at www.academia.edu/39350166.

half-brick and full brick on top of full brick" (in a stacked pattern.)[9] R. Yirmiya phrases this slightly differently, stating that the Song of the Sea and the Song of Devora are written staggered, while the sons of Haman and Canaanite kings are written stacked, as "buildings constructed this way do not last."[10] This layout, he explains, represents an unstable pattern, out of hope that the sons of Haman and Canaanite kings will have a fleeting impact. Accordingly, the two styles of writing for songs are not interchangeable.[11]

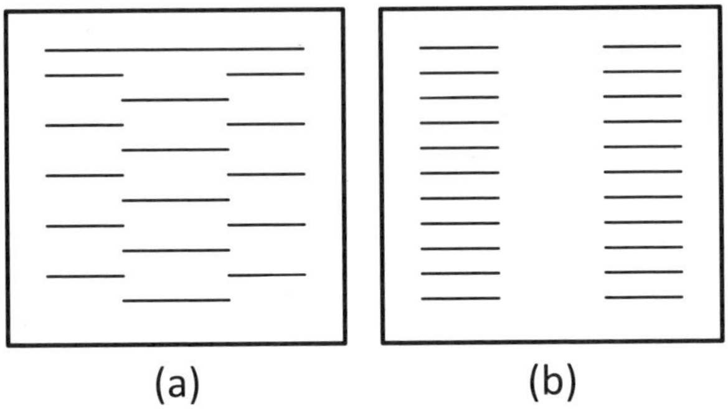


114. Song patterns: (a) staggered (b) stacked.

One of the main benefits of working with bricks is that their small size allows a bricklayer to hold a brick with one hand while holding a trowel with mortar in the other.[12] Brick walls are almost always constructed by staggering the rows of bricks. When bonded with mortar, this allows the bricks to act as a single unit rather than individual stacks which would be far less stable.[13] When used as solid walls, rather than as cladding, bricks are almost always placed in two or more wythes, which must also be bonded together by laying bricks as headers across the two wythes.[14]

9. bMeg 16b.

10. yMeg 3:7 (74b). See also Sofrim 12:9 and Rashi *deshavu nafshei* on bKid 60a.

11. Sofrim 1:11, Rambam, Hilchot Tefilin Vemezuza Vesefer Torah, 7:11.

12. The standard size of a brick is nominally 8 × 4 × 2⅔ inches. Concrete masonry units (cinderblocks) by contrast, are usually 16 × 8 × 8 inches, so that a stack of three bricks is the same height, and two bricks are the same length. CMUs, however, generally require two hands to lift and place. The other major advantage of brick is that it can be mass produced in consistent sizes using a mold. For measurements of Roman bricks, see Pliny the Elder, *Natural History,* 35:49 and Vitruvius, *Ten Books on Architecture,* II.3.3. For an additional discussion of brick size see yShev 3:4 (34d).

13. For the ineffectiveness of bricks without mortar, see bBeit 31b, describing how such bricks could be removed with ease.

14. For various methods of building masonry walls in ancient Israel, see Yizhar

These two requirements – staggering courses and overlapping wythes – led to the development of many patterns of brickwork. The simplest, running bond, consists of rows of overlapping bricks (*fig. 115b*). A pattern of running bond with the addition of a course of headers every five or six courses is known as common bond (*fig. 115c*). Many other patterns exist, with books detailing the variations. Stack bond, which has no overlapping bricks, similar to the text of Moshe's speech, cannot be used unless extra reinforcement in the form of concealed metal ties connects the different courses and wythes (*fig. 115f*). As the Talmud correctly pointed out, it is unsuitable for load-bearing walls, and therefore a fitting metaphor for the Canaanite kings and sons of Haman.

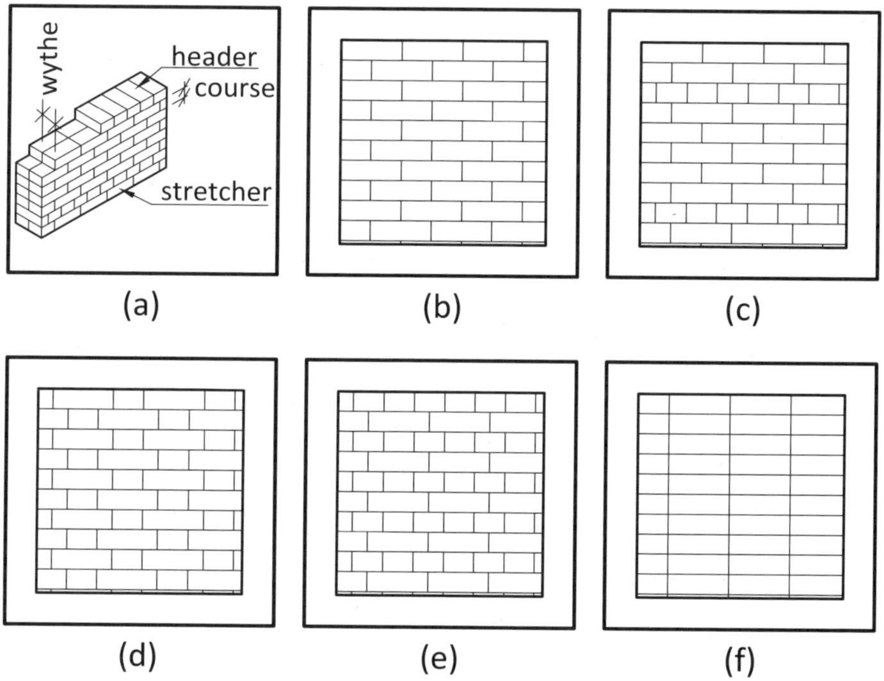


115. Brick patterns: (a) axonometric diagram of common bond (b) running Bond (c) common bond (d) Flemish bond (e) English Bond (f) stack bond.

Why would Moshe's speech be grouped with the Canaanite kings and the sons of Haman? Some commentators explain that Moshe's speech contains curses, so it is written with the weak stacked pattern in hope

Hirschfeld, *The Palestinian Dwelling* (Israel Exploration Society, 1995), 232–5.

that the curses will not come true.[15] Another possibility is that only songs that involve miraculous salvation and the reciting of Hallel are written staggered, and Moshe's speech contains neither.[16] Alternatively, Moshe's speech may not be a song at all. This is hinted at in Masechet Sofrim twice: first, it rules that "[A Torah in which] Haazinu is written as a song, or a song is written as Haazinu . . . one should not read from that Torah."[17] Later, it mentions that certain texts in the Bible are not given rigid regulations about how they are to be written, but that scribes nonetheless write them as per their received traditions.[18] Moshe's speech was not a song but was simply written this way out of custom. This approach was advanced by R. Mordechai Breuer.[19]

It may be that Haazinu really does have a form of staggered text. There are two competing versions of Rambam's description of Moshe's speech. One says that there are sixty-seven lines, while the other says that there are seventy.[20] Today almost all Torah scrolls are written with the speech covering seventy lines, but in Yemenite Torah scrolls it is sometimes written with sixty-seven, with four lines[21] having extra bridges in between the two stacked columns, forming overlapping "bricks." It could be that the Talmud considered this style of writing akin to staggered verses.

The Talmud uses bricks as a metaphor, but brickwork was relatively uncommon in Israel.[22] Stone masonry was much more prevalent but would not have made as good a metaphor. While ashlar stone walls are also built up using staggered units, it is normal for the stones to be of different lengths, and thus they do not create well-defined patterns in the same

15. Rabbi Nissim of Gerona on the Rif, bMeg 4a–b *kol*, quoting Rabeinu Tam. He calls out Devarim 32:42–43 as containing curses.

16. Ritva on bMeg 16b, *darash R. Shila*, and Meiri there.

17. Sofrim 1:11.

18. Sofrim 12:12.

19. R. Mordechai Breuer, *Keter Aram Tzuba Vehanusach Hamekubal shel Hamikre* (Mossad Harav Kook, 1976), 180.

20. Rambam, Hilchot Tefilin Vemezuza Vesefer Torah, 8. See alternate versions listed in Frankel edition, 189. See also in that edition, Yalkut Shinuyei Nusachot, 45.

21. The tenth, sixteenth, thirty-eighth and thirty-ninth lines.

22. Shmuel Krauss notes that the Bavli quotes a Babylonian sage regarding the brickwork, and rightfully points out that bricks were much more common in Mesopotamia than in Israel. Krauss also has the novel suggestion that the various texts are meant to represent walls in section, where the staggered pattern is a solid brick wall, but the stacked pattern is a wall with brick façade and a cavity for rubble filling. This was indeed a common way to build, but unlike what Krauss suggests, such walls were not any weaker than the former and the rubble was not liable to "spill out." See Shmuel Krauss, *Kadmoniot Hatalmud* (Harz, 1923), I Vol. 2, 292–3.

way as with brickwork.[23] Therefore, the Talmud speaks in terms of bricks, rather than stone rows.

The Talmud compares the two types of poems in the Bible to different brick patterns. The staggered pattern represents a wall with overlapping bricks, which can act as a solid unit and can serve as a structural wall. The stacked pattern, however, does not have overlapping bricks to connect the individual units and is therefore not structurally sound.

---

23. When building stone walls, the general rule concerning joints is that they should not be directly one upon the other. However, Ilan Sharon discusses stone patterns formed using stones of a uniform size in Tel Dor. See his "Phoenician and Greek Ashlar Construction Techniques at Tel Dor, Israel" in *Bulletin of the American Schools of Oriental Research,* No. 267 (Aug. 1987), 24–25. See also Rafael Frankel, "The Measure of Hewn Stone" in *Tel Aviv* (III, 1976), 74–78, for possibility of standardized stone sizes and patterns, based in part on Melachim I 7:9–11. Note, however, that in Frankel's footnote about Radak's commentary, Radak is basing this measurement on mBB 1:1 and it refers to the *thickness* of the wall, not the length of the stone.

# Foundations

הַצּוּר תָּמִים פָּעֳלוֹ כִּי כָל דְּרָכָיו מִשְׁפָּט קֵל אֱמוּנָה וְאֵין עָוֶל צַדִּיק וְיָשָׁר הוּא.
(דברים לב:ד)

The Rock, his work is perfect/for all His ways are justice/a God of truth and without iniquity/just and right is He. (Devarim 32:4)

At the beginning of his final address to Bnei Yisrael, Moshe declared, "He is *hatzur*, his work is perfect, for all his ways are justice." Most translations render *hatzur* as "the Rock." This is the first of several instances in scriptures in which the imagery of a rock is applied to God.[1]

The metaphor of a rock can be explained in two ways. The first is found in Onkelos, who understands the primary trait of a rock to be its strength.[2] The second group, including Sforno, write that God is like a rock in that He is unchanging.[3]

To understand the distinction between Onkelos and Sforno, we can think of this in terms of building construction. On the one hand, a building has a foundation – something designed to support the whole structure, primarily focusing on strength.[4] On the other hand, we can think of the bedrock: unbroken solid rock usually found under layers of less-solid dirt and rock fragments. The bedrock is always there, unchanged and

1. Other examples outside of this speech include Shmuel I 2:2, Yishayahu 17:10, Chabakuk 1:12, Tehilim 73:26, 78:35, and 92:16. Shmuel II 22:3 uses a different word, *sela,* for the same imagery.

2. See also Rashi and Ibn Ezra.

3. Prior to the modern study of geology, pioneered by James Hutton, rocks were largely understood to be unchanging and the byproduct of the Flood.

4. yBM 10:1 (12c) discusses who is responsible to lay foundations – the owner of the ground floor or the second story. The Talmud reports that the foundations serve both floors, and therefore both must pay for them. Here the Rabbis seem to rely on the opinion of the construction workers for their halachic ruling.

primordial.[5] Ultimately, it is usually what supports the building, as most foundation systems prefer to rest on bedrock. Both foundations and bedrock support the building, though the focus is slightly different. The bedrock is universal, while the foundation is designed with a specific building in mind.

However, there is also another group of commenters who explain *hatzur* to mean *hatzayar,* "the Creator."[6] Similar usage of the word *hatzur* can be found elsewhere in the Torah, supporting this interpretation.[7] Here too, *hatzur* is a metaphor for God.

R. S.R. Hirsch is poetic in explaining that the term *hatzur* was deliberately chosen to convey both interpretations.[8] On the one hand, it "presents that natural picture of strength, firmness, unalterable and unconquerable and so expresses the strongest and most dependable mainstay and protection." However, at the same time, the term denotes creation, "that is, to alter existing materials." Combined, we understand that God is both able to create permanent realities, but also able to alter those same creations. *Hatzur* is used to express "the unchangeable and the absolute power of overcoming everything." In this way, the strong *tzur* combines with the creator *tzayar*.

5. For the similar concept of "virgin soil," see bNid 8b, as well as bedrock itself in tOhal 16:4–5 and bNid 61a, with regard to checking for tumah.

6. bMeg 14a, Saadia Gaon, Sifri Devarim 307, Midrash Lekach Tov on Haazinu, Chizkuni, and HaEmek Davar. The Sifri gives the previous explanation as well, writing the *hatzur* can also mean "the strong."

7. For example, see Bereshit 2:7.

8. This same idea can also be found in Rabeinu Bachya.

# Topography, Property Lines, and the Site of the Temple

לְבִנְיָמִן אָמַר יְדִיד ה' יִשְׁכֹּן לָבֶטַח עָלָיו חֹפֵף עָלָיו כָּל הַיּוֹם וּבֵין כְּתֵפָיו שָׁכֵן.
(דברים לג:יב)

Of Binyamin he said: "The beloved of the Lord, shall dwell in safety by him, he covers him all the day and he dwells between his shoulders." (Devarim 33:12)

In his blessing to the tribe of Binyamin, Moshe called them "the beloved of the Lord" and stated that "he dwells between his shoulders." This is seen as an allusion to the location of the Temple in Binyamin's territory.[1]

The Talmud uses this verse to highlight two important features of the Temple's location. First, the Talmud notes that although the Temple was built at a high elevation, Mount Moriah is not the highest spot in the territory of Binyamin. The spot was chosen, according to Rava, specifically to match our verse, which references shoulders rather than the head.[2] This seems counterintuitive, as one would expect the Temple to be built at the highest spot, both for symbolic and strategic reasons. Even synagogues are supposed to be built at the highest spot in town.[3] A pilgrimage to the Temple is called "going up." Why would the Temple be deliberately built at a lower point?

The simplest answer is that Mount Moriah was always the intended location of the Temple, for reasons that have little to do with topography.

1. Rashi, Ibn Ezra, and Chizkuni. Alternate explanations include that it refers to the *urim* and *tumim*, which were worn between the shoulders of the high priest (Kli Yakar) or that it hints at Binyamin's location between two more powerful tribes (R. S.R. Hirsch).

2. bZev 54b and Rashi *nitati bei klil.*

3. tMeg 3:23 and Shulchan Aruch OC 150:2, based on Mishlei 1:21, as well as bShab 11a based on Ezra 9:9. ySan 11:3 (30a) states that the Temple should be built at "the height of the world."

The mention of shoulders in our verse may be a hint at this intended location. Alternatively, Mount Moriah's lower height may highlight that its importance is intrinsic and historic rather than topographic.[4] Finally, though synagogues were required to be built at the highest point in town, there is an inherent tension between this rule and the idea that the worshipers should be situated low down, to appear modest.[5] The lower topography may symbolize the need to remain modest before God. These are all potential reasons why a lower peak may have been chosen deliberately.

It is also possible that we are looking at too large a picture, and that local geography is more significant than regional topography. While Mount Moriah is not the highest point in all of Binyamin's tribal territory, it is the highest point in the portion of land that comprised the city of Jerusalem at the time of King Shlomo.[6] This is consistent with what we find in urban planning, especially in antiquity, where local features mattered far more than regional ones. For example, the Acropolis of Athens is not the highest peak in Greece, or even near Athens, yet it served as an elevated location in the city, towering over the surrounding lands.[7] Similarly, Mount Moriah is the highest point in the City of David, even if it is not the highest point in the expanded region.

In addition to the topography of Mount Moriah, the Talmud also discusses the property lines that ran through the Temple. One *beraita* explains that while most of the Temple sat on Binyamin's tribal land, the chambers, courtyards, and parts of the Temple Mount were in the territory of Yehuda.[8] A second midrash[9] describes the territorial border, stating that although the altar was in the area allotted to Binyamin, a spit of Yehuda's territory protruded into the site, reaching the edge of the altar.[10] This

4. Spiro Kostof points out that we tend to focus on the impact of topography on a city's shape and evolution "because it is visually the easiest to grasp." See Kostof, *The City Shaped* (Bulfinch Press, 1991), 53.

5. bBer 10b, Midrash Tehilim 130. See also Tosafot *lefi* on bBer 16a, which assumes that the floor level of a building is more significant than its objective height above sea level.

6. It was common for cities to begin on hilltops, where a stronghold or religious center would be constructed, and have the city spread out around it. See Spiro Kostof, *The City Assembled* (Bulfinch Press, 1992), 15, 71.

7. The Acropolis is about 150 meters above sea level. Within Athens, Lycabettus Hill is twice the height, and surrounding the city are four mountains, three of which are over 1,000 meters above sea level.

8. bYom 12a and bMeg 26a.

9. The identification of this as a separate midrash is based on it appearing alone in bZev 53b–54a and is attributed to R. Chama bar R. Chanina.

10. bYom 12a, bMeg 26a, and bZev 53b–54a.

condition was not unique to Jerusalem: in Shilo, the territory adjacent to the altar was split between the tribes of Binyamin and Yosef.[11] R. Yehuda believed that the Temple did not sit on the territory of *any* tribe, and one midrash supports this theory by explaining that King David purchased the Temple Mount with money collected from all the tribes.[12]

When beginning a new architectural project, one of the first requirements is a survey of the land, which is necessary both to understand the spatial conditions of the site and to receive a building permit. Surveys typically contain the natural features of the land, including topography, and show any existing structures, utilities, and flora. However, equally important are the property and setback lines, which show where one can build and the boundaries between parcels. If construction needs to be approved by multiple owners, or if the project straddles multiple parcels, this drastically increases the difficulty in getting approval for a project. Multiple groups must sign off on the construction and special procedures are necessary to allow such a building to be constructed. While the situation is not identical, having two tribes sharing the territory of the Temple would have only complicated the building process. Yet despite this added complication, the decision was made to locate the Temple between two tribes.

Instead of a simple scenario with one tribe hosting the Temple, there was a deliberate decision to split jurisdiction. For a nation split between twelve tribes, this makes sense. Splitting jurisdiction would help foster unity and demonstrate that the Temple belongs to all the tribes, not just the one hosting the Temple. This clearly outweighed any difficulty in coordinating between two tribes that hosted the Temple.

11. bZev 118b and yMeg 1:12 (72c–d).
12. Sifri Bamidbar 42, and Rashi on bYom 12a *ela makom mikdash bilvad*.

# Jerusalem and Tel Aviv

וְלִזְבוּלֻן אָמַר שְׂמַח זְבוּלֻן בְּצֵאתֶךָ וְיִשָּׂשכָר בְּאֹהָלֶיךָ. עַמִּים הַר יִקְרָאוּ שָׁם
יִזְבְּחוּ זִבְחֵי צֶדֶק כִּי שֶׁפַע יַמִּים יִינָקוּ וּשְׂפֻנֵי טְמוּנֵי חוֹל. (דברים לג:יח–יט)

And of Zevulun, he said, "Rejoice, Zevulun, in your going out, and Yissachar in your tents. They shall call the peoples to the mountain, there they shall offer sacrifices of righteousness, for they shall be nourished by the abundance of the seas and the hidden treasures of the sand." (Devarim 33:18–19)

MOSHE's blessing of Zevulun and Yissachar sets up a dichotomy between the two tribes. Both rejoice, but Zevulun will do so in their "going out" while Yissachar will remain in their tents.

According to a well-known midrash, Zevulun and Yissachar had an agreement, in which the people of Zevulun were merchants and would earn money, ("in your going out") while the tribe of Yissachar would sit at home and learn ("in your tents") while receiving support from Zevulun.[1] The idea is that "your tents" refers to the *beit midrash*, where people sit and learn.

This interpretation, however, stands in contrast to the explanations given by most other commentators, who do not understand "in your tents" to imply a lifestyle of only learning. Ibn Ezra explains the verse's dichotomy as being between war and peace. "In your going out" refers to going out to war, while "in your tents" is talking about times of peace. Chizkuni says that while the people of Zevulun were fated to be sailors, Yissachar would stay "in their tents" by remaining in Israel and farming the land. Malbim also understands that both tribes participate in the workforce, with Zevulun trading abroad while Yissachar would stay at home and meet merchants who came to Israel.

The Sifri elaborates on the important role that Yissachar and Zevulun's

1. BerR 100:13 and quoted by Rashi on this verse.

commerce will play in bringing other nations closer to God. Foreign merchants would arrive in the ports of Israel to do trade. They would grow curious about the Jewish people and their way of life. Eager to explore, they would journey inland to Jerusalem and view the city.[2] The monotheistic worldview would be a strong draw and the merchants would convert to Judaism.

The existence of two major cities in a single polity, each with its own strengths, is not uncommon and can lead to regional differences in each part of the country. The Sifri describes a reality in which the coastal plains are focused on commerce, while the hill country serves as a cultural and religious center.[3] Ideally, openness to the world works hand in hand with the spiritual center in Jerusalem. A similar dichotomy can be found today, with Tel Aviv and Jerusalem sharing influence over the country. Tel Aviv acts as Israel's gateway to the world with its air and seaports, as well as its international culture. It is Israel's most European city. It is even a UNESCO-protected site for its Modern architecture. Jerusalem, on the other hand, continues to be the spiritual center, where people come for a taste of traditional Judaism. The idea of landing in Tel Aviv and journeying inland to Jerusalem is today being encouraged by the development of a high-speed railway. Rather than stop the railway at the entrance to the city, the government hopes to bring the line right to the Old City. Even in modern times, visitors continue to arrive on the coast and journey inward to Jerusalem for spiritual reasons.

2. Sifri Devarim 354, also quoted by Rashi on our verses. A separate midrash states that Jerusalem was not given any special natural features, like hot springs or orchards, so that pilgrims would visit out of spiritual reasons, rather than for recreation. See bPes 8b, Sifri Bamidbar 89, and SZ Bamidbar 11:9.

3. In the time of the Talmud, a different dichotomy existed between Jerusalem and Caesarea, which was the center of Roman culture in Judea. However, they did not work in conjunction, but were rather said to be in conflict. See bMeg 6a. In the time of the Maccabim, Yafo was strategically important as it served as Jerusalem's port. (see Maccabim I 10:75 and Maccabim II 12 for the conquest of Yafo and Maccabim I 12:33–34 for the desire to hold it.) Its importance flagged after it was replaced by Caesarea during the reign of Herod.

VEZOT HABERACHA

# Sand and Glass

עַמִּים הַר יִקְרָאוּ שָׁם יִזְבְּחוּ זִבְחֵי צֶדֶק כִּי שֶׁפַע יַמִּים יִינָקוּ וּשְׂפֻנֵי טְמוּנֵי חוֹל.
(דברים לג:יט)

They shall call the people to the mountain, there they shall offer sacrifices of righteousness, for they shall be nourished by the abundance of the seas and the hidden treasures of the sand. (Devarim 33:19)

MOSHE's blessing of Zevulun mentions that the tribe will benefit from "treasures hid in the sand." The Talmud explains that the treasures in question are glass products made from the sand on the coast of Zevulun's territory.[1] The Talmud refers to this as "white glass," which is understood to be a superior type of glazing.[2]

This midrash reflects the reality of glass production at that time, as the region of Zevulun played an important role in the Roman glass industry. Pliny the Elder records a version of the invention of glass which mentions the Belus River, also known as the Naaman River near Akko. Pliny explains that the tide there purifies the white sand, so that "for many ages this was the only spot that afforded the material for making glass." He tells how sailors, heating their meals on the shore, surreptitiously discovered glass.[3]

1. bMeg 6a. See also TPsY on this verse. For creation of glassware from sand, and consequential status regarding ritual impurity, see also bShab 15b.

2. bSot 48b and ySuk 4:6 (54d) teach that white glass ceased to exist after the destruction of the First Temple. Tosafot on bChul 84b *bezugita chiyurta* explain that it did not completely disappear, but rather became less common. In the first century, glass was first produced using antimony, yielding a very clear form of glass, which was sometimes known as Alexandrian glass. A 2020 study demonstrated that this glass was indeed produced in Egypt. See Gry Barfod, et al, "'Alexandrian' Glass Confirmed by Hafnium Isotopes" in *Nature, Scientific Reports* 10, 11322 (2020).

3. Pliny the Elder, *Natural Histories,* 36:65. See also Strabo, *Geographies,* 16.758 and Josephus, *Jewish War,* 2.189–191, which mentions the "crystalline sand."

Some sources even list this area as the location where glassblowing was invented in the first century and introduced to the Roman world.[4]

Most Roman glass contained traces of iron, which causes the glass to have a greenish tinge. The sand from near Akko had a high calcium carbonate content, due to the large number of shell fragments it contained, which provided all the lime needed in the glass manufacturing process. Of all the beaches on the Israeli coast, the sand near the Bay of Haifa was the palest, from low iron oxide content, yielding pale-colored glass.[5] Most of the Roman glassware uncovered in Israel can be chemically shown to have been produced locally on the coast[6] and then shipped to smaller glass workshops that were found in most cities in the region. The discovery of shipwrecks along the coast also proves that glass was exported from Judea,[7] in keeping with the Talmud's understanding of Zevulun's blessing.

While the Talmud acknowledged the value of sand as the raw material of glass, today sand continues to be a vital resource in the construction industry. Sand is used for infill to reclaim land from the water. Sand is a vital component of concrete, asphalt, and as always, glass. Floor tiles are set on a layer of sand. Sand is even used in the production of fiberglass and silicone. Sand is an increasingly sought-after commodity that is one of the vital building blocks of the modern world. Just as once the coast of Israel was known for its glass production, today it is known for its towers of concrete and glass.

4. Dan Barag, *Glass Vessels of the Roman and Byzantine Periods in Palestine* (Ph.D. Thesis, Hebrew University, 1970), 273–7.

5. Ian C. Freestone, "Pliny on Roman Glassmaking" in *Archaeology, History and Science*, ed. Marcos Martinon-Torres and Thilo Rehren (Left Coast Press, 2009), 85–87.

6. Uzi Leibner, "Arts and Crafts, Manufacture and Production" in *The Oxford Handbook of Jewish Daily Life in Roman Palestine* (Oxford University Press, 2010), 275–6.

7. Yael Gorin-Rosen, "The Ancient Glass Industry in Israel" in *La Route du Verre* (MOM Editions, 2000), 54.

# Glossary

Aharon – Aaron

Aggada (pl. aggadot) – legend

Agmat Nefesh – Suffering, remorse of the soul

Anakim – Inhabitants of Canaan during the Israelite conquest who may have been giants

Ashlar – squared stones

Avraham – Abraham

Azara – Inner courtyard of the Temple complex

Bal Tashchit – Prohibition against waste

Bamidbar – *Numbers*

Bavli – Babylonian Talmud

Beit Midrash (pl. batei midrash) – House of study

Beraita – Rabbinic saying from the tannaitic period that was not included in the Mishna or Tosefta

Bereshit – *Genesis*

Bima (pl. bimot) – elevated stage in a synagogue used for reading the Torah

Bnei Yisrael – Children of Israel

Carmelit – a space that is closed to the public, but not fenced in; one of the four categories of space on Shabbat

Chava – Eve

Chazaka – Legal concept of effective ownership, where ownership is demonstrated by possession

Cheil – A thin ring of territory in the Temple complex, between the *soreg* and the walls of the *Azara*

Chizkiyahu – Hezekiah

Darkei Shalom – Practice done to maintaining the peace

Devarim – *Deuteronomy*

Divrei Hayamim – *Chronicles*

Dvar Torah (pl. Divrei Torah) – Words of Torah

Eicha – *Lamentations*

Erva – Forbidden due to sexual nature

Eruv (pl. eruvin) – device used to extend different Shabbat boundaries

Eruv Techumim (pl. Eruvei Techumim) – A device for extending the Shabbat boundary by establishing residence at a distance of up to 2000 cubits from your dwelling

Esav – Esau

Ester – *Esther*

Etrog (pl. etrogim) – Citron

Even Hashetiya – Foundation Stone, found on the Temple Mount

Ezrat Kohanim – Area inside the Temple sanctuary in which only priests were permitted

Ezrat Yisrael – Area inside the Temple sanctuary in which only Jewish men were permitted

Gematriya – Mathematical system in which every letter of the alphabet is assigned a numeric value, with the א = 1, ב = 2, etc.

Get (pl. gitin) – Jewish writ of divorce

Halacha (pl. halachot) – Jewish law

Hallel – Set of Tehilim read on holidays to praise God

Heichal – The enclosed section of the Temple

Hekdesh – Consecrated object

Hidur Mitzva – Enhancing the performance of a commandment by using beautiful ritual objects, usually at a premium cost

Hoshanot – Prayers said on the Sukkot festival while circling the *bima*

Ir Hanidachat – Rebellious city, which is halachically obligated to be razed

Iyov – *Job*

Karet – "Cutting off," a type of spiritual excommunication

Keruvim – Cherubs

Kina (pl. kinot) – Elegy, commonly recited on the ninth of Av

Kohelet – *Ecclesiastes*

Kohen (pl. kohanim) – Priest

Ktav Ashuri – Hebrew square script, which was adopted for use in Hebrew during the Jewish exile to Babylon

Ktav Ivri – Paleo-Hebrew script

Levi (pl. Leviim) – Levites

Maccabim – Maccabees

Matzeva – Sacred pillar

Me'ila – Sin in which one gets benefit from consecrated goods.

Melachim – *Kings*

Midrash (pl. midrashim) – Biblical interpretation

Mikdash – Temple

Mikva (pl. mikvaot) – Ritual baths

Mishkan – Tabernacle

Mishlei – *Proverbs*

Mishna – Rabbinic saying from the tannaitic period that was codified by R. Yehuda Hanasi at the beginning of the third century

Mitzva (pl. Mitzvot) – Commandment

Moshe – Moses

Muchni – A machine connected to the laver in the Second Temple.

Nechemia – *Nehemia*

Ner Tamid – Eternal light

Noach – Noah

Omer – Measurement equal to one-tenth of an *eifa*, around 2.5 liters

Parsha – One of 54 divisions of the Torah, read weekly to complete the Torah in one year

Pe'ah – Commandment to leave a corner of a field for the poor (lit. "corner")

Pesach – Passover

Rachav – Rahab

Revi'it – A measurement, lit. one-quarter

Rivka – Rebecca

Rut – *Ruth*

Sanhedrin – Jewish high court, consisting of seventy-one members (the Great Sanhedrin)

Se'ah – Unit of measurement, most commonly used to express the amount of water needed in a *mikva*

Segula – Purveyance of good luck

Seudat Mitzva – A festive meal celebrating a mitzva

Shabbat – Sabbath

Shamir – Creature or substance used to cut through stone

Shechita – (n.) Butchering according to Jewish law

Shema – A prayer recited twice daily, consisting of three parts of the Torah

Shemita – The seventh, sabbatical year when agricultural activity is prohibited.

Sheretz (pl. Sheratzim) – A halachic category of creatures, including some rodents, that transfer spiritual impurity (*tumah*).

Shir Hashirim – *Song of Songs*

Shoftim – *Judges*

Shlomo – Solomon

Shemot – *Exodus*

Shmuel – *Samuel*

Soreg – Boundary wall in the Temple courtyard

Sota – A woman suspected of adultery, who must undergo trial whereby she drinks a water-based potion

Sukka (pl. Sukkot) – Temporary hut, usually roofed with branches, which must be inhabited during the seven days of the Sukkot festival

Sukkot – Feast of Tabernacles

Tahor – Ritually purity

Talmud – Central text of rabbinic Judaism, recording explanations of the

Mishna and including halachic and aggadic portions

Tameh – Ritually unpure

Tameh Met – Ritual impurity caused by contact with a corpse

Tanach – The Old Testament

Targum (pl. Targumim) – Translation of part of the Bible into Aramaic

Techum Shabbat – Shabbat boundary of 2000 cubits, beyond which one may not walk on Shabbat

Tosefta – Rabbinic saying from the tannaitic period that was not included in the Mishna but was included in a separate authoritative collection

Tumah – ritual impurity

Trei Asar – *Twelve*

Tzaraat – Punishment consisting of a skin affliction

Tzimtzum – precise accuracy

Tzitz – high priest's headplate

Tzitzit – Fringes worn on a four-cornered garment, with strings of white and blue

Ulam – Entranceway to the enclosed Temple

Urim Vetumim – Elements on the high priest's breastplate, which according to legend was used to communicate with God

Vayikra – *Leviticus*

Yechezkel – *Ezekiel*

Yehoshua – *Joshua*

Yerushalmi – Jerusalem Talmud

Yirmiyahu – *Jeremiah*

Yishayahu – *Isaiah*

Yitzchak – Isaac

Yosef – Joseph

Yovel – fiftieth year, during which the land must be left fallow and property reverts to its original owner

# Bibliography

Abdalla, Aly. "The Cenotaph of the Sekwaskhet Family from Saqqara," *The Journal of Egyptian Arachaeology* 78 (1992) 93–111.

Al-Tabari. *The Early 'Abbasi Empire: The Reign of Abu Jafar al-Mansur, A.D. 754–775,* tr. John Alden Williams. Cambridge University Press, 1988.

Alberti, Leon Battista. *De Re Aedificatoria.*

Alexander, Philip S. "Jerusalem as the *Omphalos* of the World: On the History of a Geographical Concept," *Jerusalem: Its Sanctity and Centrality to Judaism, Christianity and Islam,* ed. Lee Levine. Continuum, 1998, 104–119.

Allen, Edward. *Fundamentals of Building Construction, 3rd ed.* Wiley, 2000.

Anderson Jr., James C. Jr. *Roman Architecture and Society.* Johns Hopkins University Press, 2002.

Aviam, Mordechai. "The Shabbat Boundary at Timrat" in *Eretz Magazine.* Aug.–Sep. 2011, 53–55.

Balasubramaniam, R. *Story of the Delhi Pillar.* Foundation Books, 2005.

Ball, Warwick. *Rome in the East: The Transformation of an Empire.* Routledge, 2001.

Ballantyne, Andrew. "The Nest and the Pillar of Fire" in *What is Architecture?* Routledge, 2002.

Banham, Reyner. *The Architecture of the Well-Tempered Environment.* Architectural Press, 1969.

Bar-Asher Siegal, Michal. *Early Christian Monastic Literature and the Babylonian Talmud.* Cambridge University Press, 2013.

Bar Ilan, Meir. "Mekomot Pela Be'eretz Yisrael Ba'et Haatika" in *Mechkarei Yehuda ve-Shomron* 4 (5765) 229–239 (Hebrew).

Barag, Dan. *Glass Vessels of the Roman and Byzantine Periods in Palestine.* Ph.D. Thesis, Hebrew University, 1970.

Barfod, Gry, Freestone, Ian, Lesher, Charles, Lichtenberger, Achim and Raja, Rubina. "'Alexandrian' Glass Confirmed by Hafnium Isotope" in *Scientific Reports* 10, 11322 (2020).

Barkay, Gavriel. "Burial Caves and Burial Practices in Judah in the Iron Age" in *Graves and Burial Practices in Israel in the Ancient Period,* ed. Itamar Singer Yad Ben Zvi Press, 1994 (Hebrew).

Barron, Michael. *Auditorium Acoustics and Architectural Design.* Spon Press, 1993.

Beall, Christine. "Water Penetration in Building Envelopes" in *Interface,* Oct. 2000.

Ben-Eliyahu, Eyal, "Keves Para Aduma" in *Cathedra* 107, 183–186.

Ben Shahar, Meir. "The Prediction to Vespasian" in *Josephus and the Rabbis* Vol. 2 (Yad Ben Zvi Press, 201), 604–664 (Hebrew).

Biale, David; Assaf, David; Brown, Benjamin; Gellman, Uriel; Rosman, Moshe; Sagiv, Gadi, and Wodzinski, Marcin. *Hasidism: A New History.* Princeton University Press, 2017.

Bianca, Stefano. *Urban Form in the Arab World: Past and Present.* (Thames & Hudson, 2000).

Birren, Faber. "Color and Human Appetite" in *Food Technology,* 17 (May 1963).

Blidstein, Gerald J. "Talmudic Prostration and Mosaics" in *Bulletin of the Institute of Jewish Studies* II (1974).

Bloom, Jonathan M. *Architecture of the Islamic West: North Africa and the Iberian Peninsula, 700–1800.* Yale University Press, 2020.

Bradshaw, Vaughn. *Building Control Systems* 2nd Edition. John Wiley & Sons, 1993.

Blondel, François. *Cours D'Architecture* III. Roulland, 1683.

Bohak, Gideon. "Ethnic Continuity in the Jewish Diaspora in Antiquity" in *Jews in the Hellenistic and Roman Cities,* ed. John R. Bartlett. Routledge, 2002, 175–192.

Branham, Joan R. "The Temple That Won't Quit: Construction Sacred Space in Orlando's Holy Land Experience Theme Park" in *Harvard Divinity Bulletin,* 36:3 (Autumn, 2008), 20–31.

Breuer, Mordechai. *Keter Aram Tzuba Vehanusach Hamekubal Shel Hamikre.* Mossad Harav Kook, 1976 (Hebrew).

Brooker, Donald. *Drying and Storage of Grains and Oilseeds.* Springer Science and Business Media, 1992.

Brookes, John. *Gardens of Paradise: The History and Design of the Great Islamic Gardens.* Meredith Press, 1987.

Broshi, Magen. "Daily Life at Qumran" in *The Qumran Scrolls and their World,* I ed. Menahem Kister. Yad Ben Zvi Press, 2009 (Hebrew).

Banham, Reyner. *The Architecture of the Well-Tempered Environment.* Architectural Press, 1969.

Burke, Aaron A. *Walled up to Heaven: The Evolution of Middle Bronze Age Fortification Strategies in the Levant.* Eisenbrauns, 2008.

Canaan, Tawfiq. *The Palestinian Arab House: Its Architecture and Folklore.* Syrian Orphanage Press, 1933.

Canales, Jimena and Herscher, Andrew, "Criminal Skins: Tattoos and Modern Architecture in the Work of Adolf Loos" in *Architectural History,* 48, 235–256.

Cantor, Norman. *After We Die.* Georgetown University Press, 2010.

Carcopino, Jerome. *Daily Life in Ancient Rome,* 2nd edition. Yale University Press, 2003.

Carpo, Mario. *Architecture in the Age of Printing: Orality, Writing, Typography, and Printed Images in the History of Architectural Theory,* tr. Sarah Benson. MIT Press, 2001.

Carroll, Maureen. "Temple Gardens and Sacred Groves" in *Gardens of the Roman Empire, ed. Wilhemlmina F. Jashemski.* Cambridge University Press, 2017.

Casson, Lionel. *Travel in the Ancient World.* The Johns Hopkins University Press, 1994.

Chadwick, Jeffrey. "Discovering Hebron" in Biblical Archaeology Review, Sep/Oct 2005.

Ching, Francis D.K., *A Visual Dictionary of Architecture.* Wiley, 2011.

Clayton, Peter. *The Seven Wonders of the Ancient World.* Routledge, 1990.

Coulton, J.J. *Ancient Greek Architects at Work.* Cornell University Press, 1982.

Cuomo, Serafina. *Technology and Culture in Greek and Roman Antiquity.* Cambridge University Press, 2007.

Curl, James Steven. *Oxford Dictionary of Architecture and Landscape Architecture.* Oxford University Press, 2007.

Darwin, Charles. *The Descent of Man.*

Davis, Howard. "The Future of Ancient Lights" in *Journal of Architectural and Planning Research* 6.2 (Summer, 1989), 132–153.

Dell'Acqua, Antonio. "The Use of the Heart-Shaped Pillar in Ancient Architecture: Examples and Circulation. 1139–1150 in *SOMA 2012: Identity and Connectivity, Proceedings of the 16th Symposium on Mediterranean Archaeology, II* (B.A.R. International Series 2581 II).

Delumeau, Jean. *History of Paradise: The Garden of Eden in Myth & Tradition.* University of Illinois Press, 1995.

Didron, Adolphe Napoleon. *Bulletin Archéologique,* 1.

Dinsmoor, William Bell, "Iron in Greek Architecture" in *American Journal of Archaeology,* Vol. 26 No. 2 (Apr.–Jun. 1922).

Ditchey, Mallory, "Body Language: Tattooing and Branding in Ancient Mesopotamia," in *Journal of Ancient Near Eastern History,* II.1 (2017) 1–24.

Doering, Lutz, "New Aspects of Qumran Sabbath Law from Cave 3 Fragments" in *Legal Texts and Legal Issues: Proceedings of the Second Meeting of the International Organization for Qumran Studies.* Brill, 1997.

Donaldson, T.L. *Architectura Numismatica.* Day & Son, 1859.

Drexler, Arthur. *Architecture of Japan.* Museum of Modern Art, 1955.

Dvorjetski, Esti. "Hatiatron Besafrut Chazal" in Arthur Segal, *The History and Architecture of The Theaters in Roman Palestine.* Bialik Institute, 1999 (Hebrew).

Eliav, Yaron, "Viewing the Sculptural Environment: Shaping the Second Commandment" in *The Talmud Yerushalmi and Graeco-Roman Culture* Vol. III, ed. Peter Shäfer. Mohr Siebeck, 1998.

Elior, Rachel, *The Three Temples.* Littman Library of Jewish Civilization, 2004.

Elior, Rachel. "From Priestly (and Early Christian) Mount Zion to Rabbinic Temple Mount" in *Where Heaven and Earth Meet: Jerusalem's Sacred Esplanade* ed. Oleg Grabar and Benjamin Kedar. University of Texas Press, 2010.

Elitzur, Yehuda and Kiel, Yehuda. *Atlas Daat Mikra.* Mossad Harav Kook, 1998.

Eph'al, Israel. *The City Besieged: Siege and its Manifestations in the Ancient Near East.* Magnes Press, 2013.

Eshel, Hanan. "The History of the Discoveries at Qumran" in *The Qumran Scrolls and their World* Vol. I, ed. Menahem Kister. Yad Ben Zvi Press, 2009 (Hebrew).

Fagan, Garrett G. *Bathing in Public in the Roman World.* University of Michigan Press, 2002.

Fernández-Galiano, Luis. *Fire and Memory: On Architecture and Energy,* tr. Gina Cariño. MIT Press, 2000.

Filarete (Antonio di Piero Averlino), *Treatise on Architecture,* tr. John R. Spencer. Yale University Press, 1965.

Fine, Steven, *Art & Judaism in the Greco-Roman World.* Cambridge University Press, 2005.

Fitchen, John. *Building Construction Before Mechanization.* MIT Press, 1992.

Fonrobert, Charlotte E. "From Separatism to Urbanism: The Dead Sea Scrolls and the Origins of Rabbinic 'Eruv" in *Dead Sea Discoveries* 11,1 (2004).

Frampton, Kenneth. *Modern Architecture.* Thames and Hudson, 1992.

Frampton, Kenneth. *Studies in Tectonic Culture: The Poetics of Construction in Nineteens and Twentith Century Architecture.* MIT Press, 1995.

Frankel, Rafael. "The Measure of Hewn Stone" in *Tel Aviv* III, 1976.

Freedman, Samuel G. "Frank Gehry's Mideast Peace Plan" in *New York Times,* 1 Aug. 2004.

Freestone, Ian C. "Pliny on Roman Glassmaking" in *Archaeology, History and Science,* ed. Marcos Matinon-Torres and Thilo Rehren. Left Coast Press, 2009, 77–100.

Frick, Frank. *The City in Ancient Israel.* Scholars Press, 1977.

Gafni, Isaiah, "Yerushalayim Besafrut Chazal" in *Sefer Yerushalayim – Hatekufa Haromit Vehabizantit* ed. Yoram Tzafrir and Shmuel Safrai. Yad Ben Zvi Press, 1999 (Hebrew).

Garstang, John. "Askalon" in *Palestine Exploration Fund Quarterly Statement* 56:24–35 (1924).

Gelling, Margaret. "Place-Names and Anglo-Saxon Paganism" in *University of Birmingham Historical Journal* VIII:1, 1961.

Ghey, Eleanor. "Immersed in the Gods: Water in Gallo-Roman Sanctuaries." Academia, 2005.

Gibbon, Edward. *The History of the Decline and Fall of the Roman Empire.* Strahan & Cadell, 1776.

Gibson, Shimon. "The Pilaster Enclosure Wall of the Temple Mount in Jerusalem" in *New Studies on Jerusalem* 20 (2014) 17–40.

Goldsworthy, Adrian. *Roman Warfare.* Cassell PLC, 2000.

Gonen, Rivka. "Urban Canaan in the Late Bronze Period" in *Bulletin of the American Schools of Oriental Research* 253 (Winter, 1984) 61–73.

Gorin-Rosen, Yael. "The Ancient Glass Industry in Industry in Israel" in *La Route du Verre.* MOM Editions, 2000.

Gray, Christopher. "Not Just a Perch for King Kong" in the New York Times Sept 23, 2010.

Gruber, Samuel D. "Lone Star (of David) Story: A 'Moving' Tale of a Synagogue Being Trucked Across Texas" in *Tablet,* 24 Dec. 2014, online at https://www.tabletmag.com/jewish-life-and-religion/187754/lone-star-of-david-story and retrieved on 29 Nov. 2019.

Guiley, Rosemary. *The Encyclopedia of Witches, Witchcraft and Wicca.* Checkmark Books, 2008.

Hachlili, Rachel. *Ancient Mosaic Pavements: Themes, Issues and Trends.* Brill, 2008.

Hadas-Lebel, Mireille. *Jerusalem Against Rome.* Peeters Publishers, 2006.

Hales, Shelley. *The Roman House and Social Identity.* Cambridge University Press, 2003.

Harris, Elizabeth. "Instead of Taking Down a Fruit Tree, Build Around It" in *The New York Times,* New York Edition, 30 July 2012, 19.

Hastings, James, Selbie, John Alexander, and Gray, Louis Herbert. *Encyclopaedia of Religion and Ethics* Vol. 4. Scribner, 1951.

Hersey, George. *The Lost Meaning of Classical Architecture.* MIT Press, 1988.

Hersey, George. *The Monumental Impulse: Architecture's Biological Roots.* MIT Press, 2001.

Herzog, Zeev. "Settlement and Fortification Planning in the Iron Age" in *The Architecture of Ancient Israel.* Israel Exploration Society, 1992.

Hezser, Catherine. "Dirt and Garbage in the Ancient Jewish Religious Imagination and Daily Life" in *Envisioning Judaism.* Mohr Siebeck, 2013.

Hirsch, Antoine Pierre. *Ancient Egyptian Cubits – Origins and Evolution.* Thesis, University of Toronto, 2013.

Hirschfeld, Yizhar. *The Palestinian Dwelling in the Roman-Byzantine Period.* Israel Exploration Society, 1995.

Howard, Ebenezer. *Garden Cities of Tomorrow.* Swan Sonnenschein & Co., 1898.

Huang, Lingjiang and Wu, Jiafen. "Effects of the Splayed Window Type of Daylighting and Solar Shading" in *Building and Environment* 81 (November 2014).

Hudson, Jared McCabe. *On the Way: A Poetics of Roman Transportation.* University of California, 2013.

Huehnergard, John and Liebowitz, Harold. "The Biblical Prohibition Against Tatooing" in *Vetus Testamentum* 63 (2013) 59–77.

Hurowitz, Victor. *I Have Built You an Exalted House: Temple Building in the Bible in Light of Mesopotamian and North-West Semitic Writings.* Sheffield Academic Press, 1992.

Ilan, Tal and Noam, Vered, ed. *Josephus and the Rabbis.* Yad Ben Zvi Press, 2017 (Hebrew).

Jackson, J.B. *Discovering the Vernacular Landscape.* Yale University Press, 1986.

Jackson, J.B. *A Sense of Place, A Sense of Time.* Yale University Press, 1996.

Jacobs, Jane. *The Death and Life of Great American Cities.* Random House, 1961.

Jacobson, David M. "The Plan of Herod's Temple" in *Bulletin of the Anglo-Israel Archaeological Society,* 1990–1, Vol. 10, 36–66.

Jastrow, Marcus. *A Dictionary of the Targumim, The Talmud Babli and Yerushalmi, and the Midrashic Literature.* Drugulin, 1903.

Johnston, George Barnett. *Drafting Culture: A Social History of Architectural Graphic Standards.* MIT Press, 2008.

Jones, M. Wilson; Dwyer, Eugene; Sanabria, Sergio L; Lyttleton, Margaret; Coldstream, Nicola; *Architectural Orders.* Oxford University Press, 2016.

Kalman, David Zvi. "Turning Clockwise: Jews and Timekeeping from Antiquity to Modernity" in *Ancient Jewish Review* (18 Dec 2019), https://www.ancientjewreview.com/articles/2019/12/13/dissertation-spotlight-becoming-clockwise-jews-and-timekeeping-from-antiquity-to-modernity.

Kant, Immanuel. *The Critique of Judgment,* tr. J.H. Bernhard, Macmillan and Co, 1914.

Kaplony, Andreas. "635/638–1099: The Mosque of Jerusalem" in *Where Heaven and Earth Meet: Jerusalem's Sacred Esplanade,* ed. Oleg Grabar and Benjamin Kedar. University of Texas Press, 2010.

Kelbaugh, Douglas, "Typology: An Architecture of Limits" in *Repairing the American Metropolis.* University of Washington Press, 2002.

Kerr, Robert. *On Ancient Lights and the Evidence of Surveyors Thereon.* John Murray, 1865.

Kerton, Adrian. "Roman Roads, A Simple Surveying Technique" at https://adriankerton.wordpress.com/roman-roads-a-simple-surveying-technique/

Kirshenbaum, Karen. *Furniture of the Home in the Mishnah.* Yad Ben Zvi Press, 2013 (Hebrew).

Kite, Stephen. *Shadow-Makers: A Cultural History of Shadows in Architecture.* Bloomsbury, 2017.

Klein, Gil P. "Squaring the City: Between Roman and Rabbinic Urban

Geometry" in *Phenomenologies of the City: Studies in the History and Philosophy of Architecture,* ed. Henriette Steiner and Maximilian Sternberg. Ashgate, 2015, 33–48.

Klinenberg, Eric. *Heat Wave: A Social Autopsy of Disaster in Chicago.* University of Chicago Press, 2003.

Kohut, Alexander. *Aruch HaShalem.* 1878 (Hebrew).

Kostof, Spiro. *A History of Architecture.* Oxford University Press, 1995.

Kostof, Spiro. *The City Assembled.* Thames & Hudson, 1999.

Kostof, Spiro. *The City Shaped: Urban Patterns and Meanings Through History.* Thames & Hudson, 1999.

Krauss, Samuel. "Hakrakh, Ha'ir Vehakfar Batalmud" in *Haatid 3* (1923).

Krauss, Samuel. *Kadmoniyot Hatalmud.* Moriah, 1913.

Krautheimer, Richard. "Introduction to an 'Iconography of Medieval Architecture.'" *Journal of the Warburg and Courtauld Institutes* V (1942): 1–33. Reprinted in *Studies in Early Christian, Medieval, and Renaissance Art.* New York University Press, 1969.

Kravtsov, Sergey R. "Juan Bautista Villalpando and Sacred Architecture in the Seventeenth Century" in *Journal of the Society of Architectural Historians,* 64:3.

Krinsky, Carol Herselle. *Synoagogues of Europe.* MIT Press, 1985.

Krueger, Derek. "The Old Testament in Monasticism" in *The Old Testament in Byzantium,* ed. Paul Magdalino and Robert Nelson. Dumbarton Oaks, 2010, 199–221.

Landels, J.G. *Engineering in the Ancient World.* University of California Press, 2000.

Lang Andrew. "Bronze and Iron in Homer" in *Revue Archéologique* Quatrième Série, T.7 (Janvier–Juin 1906), 280–296.

Lantis, Margaret. "The Alaskan Whale Cult and its Affinities" in *American Anthropologist New Series.* 40:3, Jul–Sep 1938, 438–464.

Larson, Kent. *Louis I Kahn, Unbuilt Masterworks.* Monacelli Press, 2000.

Lawrence, Henry W. *City Trees: A Historical Geography from the Renaissance through the Nineteenth Century.* University of Virginia Press, 2008.

Layard, John. *Stone Men of Malekua Vao.* Chatto & Windus, 1942.

Lehrman, Jonas. *Earthly Paradise: Garden and Courtyard in Islam.* University of California Press, 1981.

Leibner, Uzi. "Arts and Crafts, Manufacture and Production" in *The Oxford Handbook of Jewish Daily Life in Roman Palestine,* ed. Catherine Hezser. Oxford University Press, 2010.

van Leeuwen, Joyce. "Image, Word and Translation in Niccolò Leonico Tomeo's Quaestiones Mechanicae" in *Translating Early Modern Science,* ed. Sietske Fransen, Niall Hodson and Karl A.E. Enenkel (Brill, 2017), 182–206.

Levine, Lee I. *The Ancient Synagogue.* Yale Press, 2005.

Levinson, H.Z. "Storage and Insect Species of Stored Grain and Tombs in Ancient Egypt." In *Journal of Applied Entomology* 100:321–339, Jan 1985.

Levinson, Joshua. "The Language of Stones: Roman Milestones on Rabbinic Roads" in *Journal for the Study of Judaism in the Persian, Hellenistic, and Roman Period* 47/2 (2016), 257–276.

Lewis, M.J.T. *Surveying Instruments of Greece and Rome.* Cambridge University Press, 2003.

Lieberman, Saul. "A Few Words on the Book by Julian the Architect of Ascalon *The Laws of Palestine and its Customs*" in *Tarbiz* 40 (Tamuz–Elul 5731), 409–417.

Lieberman, Saul. "Palestine in the Third and Fourth Centuries" in *Jewish Quarterly Review* 36 (Apr. 1946).

Liddel, H.G. and R. Scott, *A Greek-English Lexicon.* Oxford University Press, 1843.

Loos, Adolf, "Ornament and Crime," (1908) reprinted in *Ornament and Crime: Selected Essays,* tr. Michael Mitchell. Ariadne Press, 1998, 167–176.

Loudon, J.C. *On the Laying Out, Planting and Managing of Cemeteries,* 1843.

Lubman, David and Kiser, Brenda. "The History of Western Civilization Told Through the Acoustics of its Worship Spaces" in *Acoustic of Worship Buildings,* 2001.

Marvin, Miranda. "Freestanding Sculptures from the Baths of Caracalla" in *American Journal of Archaeology* 87 (July 1983).

Mindrup, Matthew. *The Architectural Model: Histories of the Miniature and the Prototype, the Exemplar and the Muse.* MIT Press, 2019.

Moneo, Rafael. "On Typology" in *Oppositions: A Journal for Ideas and Criticism in Architecture,* Summer 1978 (13).

Mostafavi, Mohsen and Leatherbarrow, David, *On Weathering: The Life of Buildings in Time,* MIT Press, 1993.

Mumford, Lewis. *The City in History.* Mariner Books, 1968.

Naveh, Joseph. *On Stone and Mosaic: The Aramaic and Hebrew Inscriptions from Ancient Synagogues.* Carta, 1978 (Hebrew).

Netzer, Ehud. *The Architecture of Herod the Great Builder.* Baker Academic, 2008.

Netzer, Ehud. "Domestic Architecture in the Iron Age" in *The Architecture of Ancient Israel.* Israel Exploration Society, 1992.

Netzer, Ehud. "Massive Structures: Processes in Construction and Deterioration" in *The Architecture of Ancient Israel.* Israel Exploration Society, 1992.

Neufert *Architects' Data, 2nd edition.* Wiley & Blackwell, 1991.

Nicholson, Peter. *The New Practical Builder, and Workman's Companion.* Thomas Kelly, 1823.

Noam, Vered. "The Miracle of the Rainfall in Herod's Day" in *Josephus and the*

*Rabbis I*, ed. Tal Ilan and Vered Noam. Yad Ben Zvi Press, 2017, 411–416 (Hebrew).

O'Connor, Colin. *Roman Bridges.* Cambridge University Press, 1994.

Ofer, Yosef. "A Diagram of the Open Land of the Levite Cities in Nahmanides' Commentary on the Torah" in *Jewish Quarterly Review* 99:2 (Spring 2009) 271–283.

Oleson, John Peter. *Greek and Roman Mechanical Water-Lifting Devices.* University of Toronto Press, 1984.

Pagolu, Augustine. *The Religion of the Patriarchs.* A&C Black, 1998.

Panofsky, Erwin. *Abbot Suger on the Abbey Church of St-Denis and Its Treasures.* Princeton University Press, 1979.

Patrich, Joseph, "Graves and Burial Practices in Talmudic Sources" in *Graves and Burial Practices in Israel in the Ancient Period*, ed. Itamar Singer. Yad Ben Zvi Press, 1994.

Patrich, Joseph. *Studies in the Archaeology and History of Caesarea Maritima.* Brill, 2011.

Patton, Katherine and Savelle, James. "The Symbolic Dimensions of Whale Bone Use in Thule Winter Dwellings" in *Inuit Studies* (30:2), 137–161.

Peleg, Yitzchak. "What Do Jacob's Ladder, the Tower of Babel, and the Babylonian Ziggurat Have in Common?" in *Bethsaida in Archaeology, History and Ancient Culture*, ed. J. Harrold Ellens. Cambridge Scholars, 2014.

Peleg-Barkat, Orit. *The Temple Mount Excavations in Jerusalem, Vol. V 1968–1978 Directed by Benjamin Mazar,* Vol. V*: Herodian Architectural Decoration and King Herod's Royal Portico.* Institute of Archaeology, The Hebrew University of Jerusalem, 2017.

Peleg-Barkat, Orit. "Interpreting the Uninterpreted: Art as a Means of Expressing Identity in Early Roman Judaea" in *Jewish Art in its Late Antique Context,* ed. Uzi Leibner and Catherine Hezser. Mohr Siebeck, 2016, 27–48.

Peterson, Steven. "Space and Anti-Space" in *Harvard Architectural Review* Vol. I, Spring, 1980.

Pevsner, Nikolaus. *An Outline of European Architecture.* Harmondsworth, 1957.

Pierce, Jefferson Lawrence Daniel, *The Organization of Roman Building During the Late Republic and Early Empire.* Ph.D. thesis, Cambridge University, 1974.

Points, Guy. *An Introduction to Anglo-Saxon Church Architecture & Anglo-Scandinavian Stone Sculpture.* Guy Points, 2015.

Radner, Karen. "Death and Burial Practices in Ancient Mesopotamia." In Bogucki, Peter, ed. *Encyclopedia of Society and Culture in the Ancient World.* Facts on File, 2007.

Ramsey, Charles G. and Sleeper, Harold R. *Architectural Graphic Standards,* 3rd ed. John Wiley and Sons, 1947.

Reich, Ronny. "Building Materials and Architectural Elements in Ancient Israel" in *The Architecture of Ancient Israel.* Israel Exploration Society, 1992.

Reich, Ronny and Billig, Yaakov. "Excavations Near the Temple Mount and Robinson's Arch, 1994–1996" in *Qadmoniot* (117, 1999) 33–40 (Hebrew).

Reich, Ronny and Kempinski, Aharon. *The Architecture of Ancient Israel.* Israel Exploration Society, 1992.

Reich, Ronny. *Miqvaot Tahara BeTekufat HaBayit HaSheni UBeTekufot haMishna veHaTalmud.* Yad Ben Zvi Press, 2013 (Hebrew).

Regev, Eyal. "Emdat Hatzedukim Veha'isim Beyachas La'eruv Chazal," Ktav Et La'iyun Vemechkar 6, 2000, 185–203 (Hebrew).

Riba, Naama and Hasson, Nir, "Contentious Jerusalem Pyramid Skyscraper Gets Downsized" in *Haaretz,* Oct. 29, 2015.

Richter, Gisela M.A. *The Furniture of the Greeks, Etruscans and Romans.* Phaidon Press, 1966.

Rocconi, Eleonora. "Theatres and Theatre Design in the Graeco-Roman World" in *Archaeoacoustics,* ed. Chriss Scarre and Graeme Lawson. McDonald Institute for Archaeological Research, 2006.

Roll, Israel. "The Roman Road System in Judaea" in *The Jerusalem Cathedra* 3. Yad Ben Zvi Press, 1983.

Rosen, Yisrael. In *Shabbat B'Shabbato* 120, 16.02.2008.

Rosen, Yisrael and Desberg, Uri. *"Techumei Shabbat Bemaarach Yeshuvim Gushi"* in *Tehumim,* 5, 1985. 13–54 (Hebrew).

Roth, Jonathan. *The Logistics of the Roman Army at War: 264 B.C. – A.D. 235.* Brill, 1999.

Rowe, Colin and Koetter, Fred. *Collage City.* MIT Press, 1984.

Rutledge, Steven H. "The Roman Destruction of Sacred Sites" in *Historia: Zeitschrift für Alte Geschichte* Bd. 56, H. 2, 2007, 179–195.

Rybczynski, Witold. *The Look of Architecture.* Oxford University Press, 2001.

Rybczynski, Witold. *Home: A Short History of an Idea.* Penguin Books, 1987.

Rykwert, Joseph. *On Adam's House in Paradise.* MIT Press, 1981.

Rykwert, Joseph. *The Dancing Column.* MIT Press, 1988.

Rykwert, Joseph. *The Idea of a Town.* MIT Press, 1988.

Safrai, Shmuel, "Ha-'ir Hayehudit ba'Eretz Yisrael Betekufat haMishna vehaTalmud" in *Ha'ir Vehakehilla.* Magnes, 1968 (Hebrew).

Schuddeboom, Feyo L. "The Conversion of Temples in Rome." *Journal of Late Antiquity* 10, no. 1 (2017): 166–186.

Schwartz, Joshua. "Jubilees, Bethel and the Temple of Jacob." *Hebrew Union College Annual,* 56 (1985): 63–85.

Segal, Arthur. *The History and Architecture of the Theaters in Roman Palestine,* Bialik Institute, 1999 (Hebrew).

Semper, Gottfried, "The Four Elements of Architecture," in Harry Francis

Mallgrave and Wolfgang Herrmann, *The Four Elements of Architecture and Other Writings.* Cambridge University Press, 1989.

Semper, Gottfried, *Style in the Technical and Tectonic Arts,* tr. Harry Francis Mallgrave and Michael Robinson. Getty Publications, 2004.

Shafran, Menachem Mendel. "Hatzaa Latikun Baayat Tumat Kohanim Bebatei Cholim", *Techumin* 5, 5784 (Hebrew).

Shahar, Ilan. "Fear of Ritual Impurity at Terminal 3" in *Haaretz,* Nov 3, 2004.

Shama, Sehdev. *Five Great Civilizations of Ancient World.* Educreation Publications, 2017.

Sharon, Ilan. "Phoenician and Greek Ashlar Construction Techniques at Tel Dor, Israel" in *Bulletin of the American Schools of Oriental Research,* No. 267 (Aug. 1987), 21–42.

Shurkin, Yaakov Moshe. "*Ariach Al Gabei Ariach*" at www.academia.edu/3935 0166 (Hebrew).

Skarf, Joshua. "Ancient Water-Raising Devices and the Temple *Muchni*" in *Bekhol Derakhekha Daehu* 26 (Apr. 2012).

Slae, Menachem. *Safety Regulations in Building in the Halachah.* The Harry Fischel Institute for Research in Jewish Law, 1984. (Hebrew)

Smith, Robert Payne. *Thesaurus Syriacus.* Oxonii, 1879–1901.

Smith, W. Stevenson and Simpson, William Kelly. *The Art and Architecture of Ancient Egypt.* Yale University Press, 1999.

Snyder, Frankie and Avraham, Assaf. "The *Opus Sectile* Floor in a Caldarium of the Palatial Fortress at Cypros" in *Hasmonean and Herodian Palaces at Jericho: Final Reports of the 1973–1987 Excavations, Volume V: The Finds from Jericho and Cypros,* director Ehud Netzer. Israel Exploration Society, 2013, 178–204.

Snyder, Frankie, Barkay, Gabriel and Dvira, Zaachi. "Shichzur Harizpot Hatzivoniyot shel Chatzerot Beit Hamikdash Beshalhei Yemei Habayit Hasheni" 2016 (Hebrew), at www.mealim.org.il.

Sperber, Daniel. *The City in Roman Palestine.* Oxford University Press, 1998.

Sperber, Daniel. *Material Culture in Eretz-Israel during the Talmudic Period.* Yad Ben Zvi Press, 1993 (Hebrew).

Sperber, Daniel. *Nautica Talmudica.* Brill, 1986.

Sperber, Daniel. *Roman Palestine 200–400: The Land.* Bar Ilan University Press, 1978.

Von Stackelberg, Katharine T. *The Roman Garden: Space, Sense and Society.* Routledge, 2009.

Stevens, Susan. "A Legend of the Destruction of Carthage" in *Classic Philology* 83,1 (1988), 39–41.

Stiebel, Guy. "A Light Unto the Nations: Symbolic Architecture of Ritual Buildings" in *Eretz-Israel: Archaeological, Historical and Geographical Studies.* Teddy Kollek Volume (2007).

Stokstad, Marilyn. *Art History I Revised Edition.* Prentice Hall Inc., 1999.

Sturton, S.L., Bilanski, W.K., and Menzies, D.R. "Drying of Cereal Grains with the Desiccant Bentonite" in *Canadian Agricultural Engineerings.* 23:101–103, 1981.

Sullivan, Louis H. *The Autobiography of an Idea.* Press of the AIA, 1924.

Sullivan, Louis H. "Ornament in Architecture" in *The Engineering Magazine,* III.5 (1892).

Sullivan, Louis H. "The Tall Office Building Artistically Considered" in *Lippincott's Magazine,* March 1896.

Taylor, Lily Ross and Scott, Russell T. "Seating Space in the Roman Senate and the Senatores Pedarii" in *Transactions and Proceedings of the American Philological Association* 100 (1969) 529–582.

Templer, John. *The Staircase: History and Theories.* MIT Press, 1992.

Templer, John. *The Staircase: Studies of Hazards, Falls and Safer Design.* MIT Press, 1994.

Thompson, Homer. "Building on the West Side of the Agora" in *Hesperia* 6.1, 1937.

Trinkl, Elisabeth. "The Wool Basket: Function, Depiction and Meaning of the *Kalathos*" in *Greek and Roman Textiles and Dress.* Oxbow Books, 2014.

Tsafrir, Yoram. *Eretz Israel from the Destruction of the Second Temple to the Muslim Conquest, II.* Yad Ben Zvi Press, 1984 (Hebrew).

Tzonis, Alexander and Lefaivre, Liane, *Classical Architecture: The Poetics of Order.* MIT Press, 1986.

Venturi, Robert. *Complexity and Contradiction in Architecture.* Museum of Modern Art, 1977.

Venturi, Robert, Scott Brown, Denise, and Izenour, Steven. *Learning from Las Vegas.* MIT Press, 1977.

Wagner, Donald. *Iron and Steel in Ancient China.* Brill, 1993.

Walzer, Michael, "The Ethics of Warfare in the Jewish Tradition" in *Philosophia* 40:4, Dec 2012, 633–641.

White, K.D. *Greek and Roman Technology.* Cornell University Press, 1984.

Wigley, Mark. *White Walls, Designer Dresses.* MIT Press, 1996.

Williams, Howard, "Monument and Material Reuse at the National Memorial Arboretum" in *Archaeological Dialogues* 21(1), 2014.

Yadin, Yigal. "Is the Biblical Account of the Israelite Conquest of Canaan Historically Reliable?" in *Biblical Archaeology Review* 8 (Mar/Apr 1982), 16–23.

Zarfati, Gad Ben-Ami, "*Arba Rishuyot Hashabbat*" in *Sidra 16* Bar Ilan Press, 2000 (Hebrew).

Zohary, Daniel. And Hopf, Maria. *The Domestication of Plants in the Old World.* Oxford University Press, 2000.

Zoref, Ephraim. "*Mikdash Chonio*" in *Mahanayim* 105, 1966 (Hebrew).

Zucker, Paul. *Town and Square: From the Agora to the Village Green.* Columbia University Press, 1959.

# Primary Source Index

## TANACH

## SECOND TEMPLE JEWISH WRITINGS

## RABBINIC LITERATURE

## Talmud Yerushalmi



## Talmud Bavli

## CLASSICAL LITERATURE

# General Index

## In Memory of Our Grandparents and Great-Grandparents

**יוסף חיים בן ר׳ משה אליהו**
שקאראווסקי
נפטר י״ז תמוז תשמ״ה
Nathan Skarofsky
Born 1913, Pogrebishche
Died 1985, Montreal

ר׳ משה אליהו שקאראווסקי
בן פסח וסעסא

ברכה ממשפחת ספיוואק
בת יצחק הכהן וחיה

**שינדל בת יצחק**
ממשפחת וועקסעלמאן
נפטרה י״א כסלו תשל״ה
Jean (Wexelman) Skarofsky
Born 1914, Montreal
Died 1974, Montreal

יצחק וועקסעלמאן
בן אליהו

ליבע ממשפחת גערבער
בת לוי ושרה

**יוסף זעליג בן שלמה**
קירקאווסקי
נפטר כ״ט אדר ב תשי״ז
Joe Kerkofsky
Born 1920, Koniecpol
Died 1957, Toronto

שלמה קירקאווסקי
בן אלטער ושרה רייזל

רבקה רחל ממשפחת קירקאווסקי
בת מאיר ובלומע

**רוזע מרים בת משה מאיר**
ממשפחת ראקאווסקי
נפטרה כ״ט אב תשפ״א
Rose (Rakowsky) Kerkofsky
Born 1921, Bedzin
Died 2021, Toronto

משה מאיר ראקאווסקי
בן שלמה איזיק ושיינדל בלימע

שרה גיטל ממשפחת ווינדלינג
בת משה וחיה

## *In Memory of Our Grandparents and Great-Grandparents*

**חיים בן יוסף**
לויקה
נפטר ב׳ תשרי תשל״ז
Charles Loike
Born 1906, Grodno
Died 1976, Rochester

יוסף לויקה
בן יצחק

יצחק יוסף קלושינר
בן שמחה בינם ואיטה רבקה

**חיה פעסע בת יצחק יוסף**
ממשפחת קלושינר
נפטרה ה׳ אב תשס״ח
Paula (Kalushiner) Loike
Born 1917, Zdunska Wola
Died 2008, North Miami Beach

דבורה ממשפחת קלמפנר
בת נתן וחסיה

נעכא ציפורה ממשפחת אברמוביץ׳
בת מאיר שלמה ופייגע

**משה אברהם בן יוסף צבי**
שטאלץ
נפטר כ״ח אדר, תשנ״ו
Morris Stoltz
Born 1912, Brooklyn
Died 1996, Brooklyn

יוסף צבי שטאלץ
בן יחיאל הירש ושרה לאה

חיה בילה ממשפחת ווגל
בת חיים וועלף וטובה מינטשה

**סעסע פייגע בת דן**
ממשפחת וויסמן
נפטרה ח׳ אדר תשס״ט
Sylvia (Weissman) Stoltz
Born 1920, Queens
Died 2009, Queens

דן וויסמן
בן יהודה ולאה דינה

חיה פריידא ממשפחת פוקס
בת יעקב שמואל ודורה

# About the Author

Joshua Skarf is a licensed architect living and working in Jerusalem. He studied in Yeshivat Har Etzion and has degrees in architecture from the University of Michigan and Bezalel Academy. He has designed hospitals, train stations, shopping malls, Israeli consulates, army installations, elementary schools, museums, and research facilities in Israel. Skarf was born in Toronto, grew up in Michigan, and has been living in Israel since 2004.